BOOK of DOOMS

ARTESIA
ARTESIA AFIELD
ARTESIA AFIRE

forthcoming

ARTESIA BESIEGED

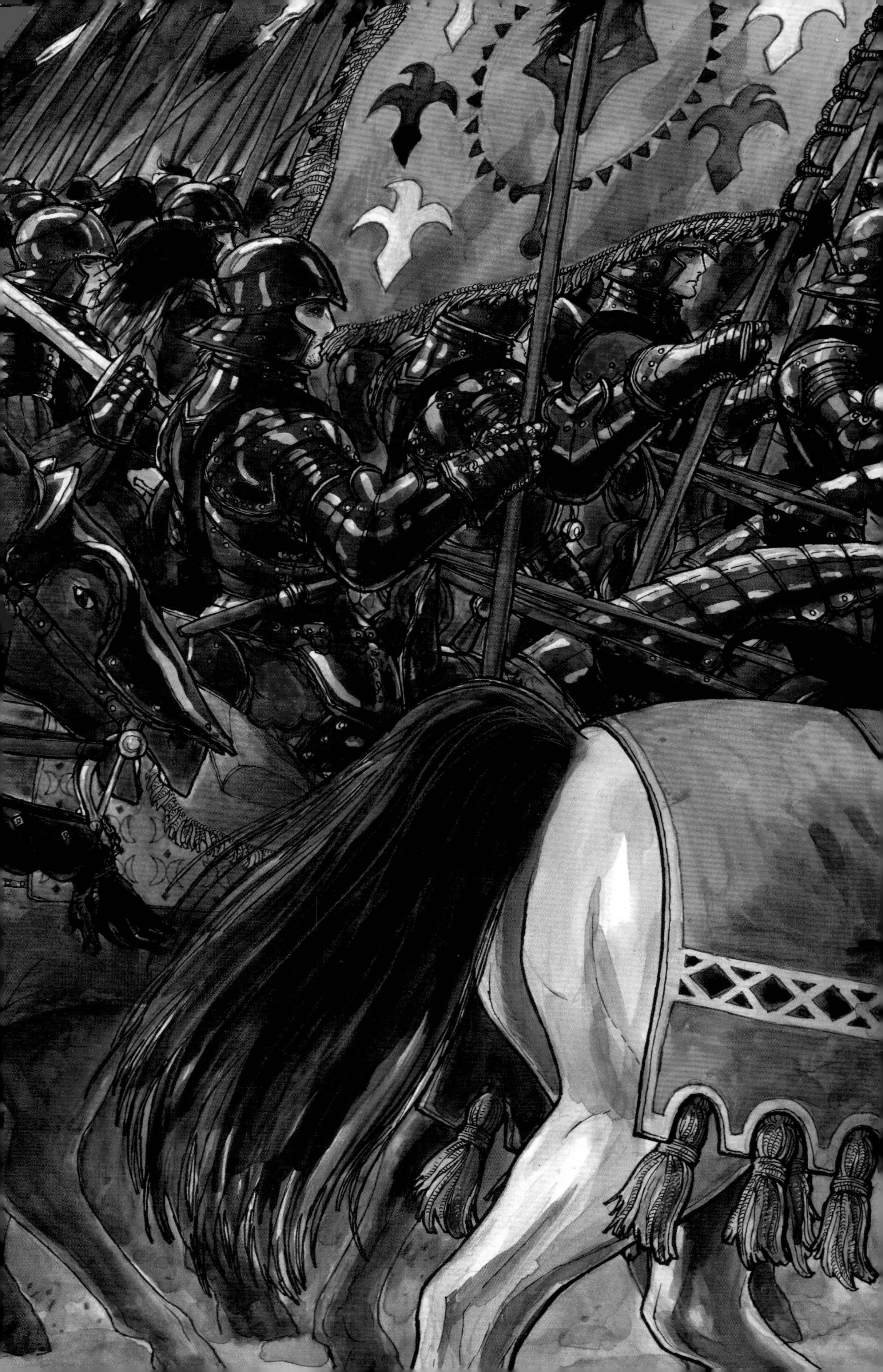

Artesia Afire

Written and Illustrated by
Mark Smylie

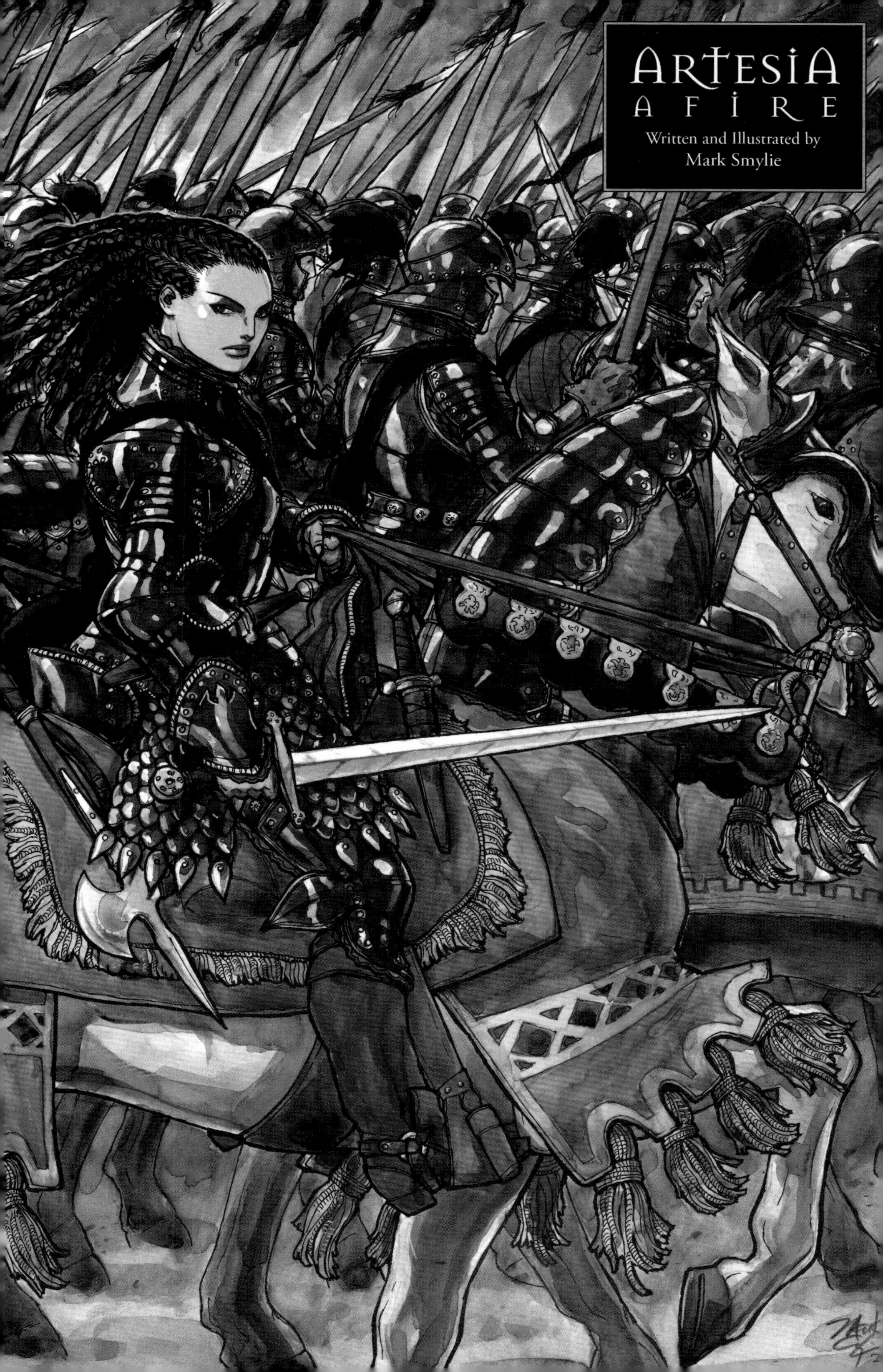

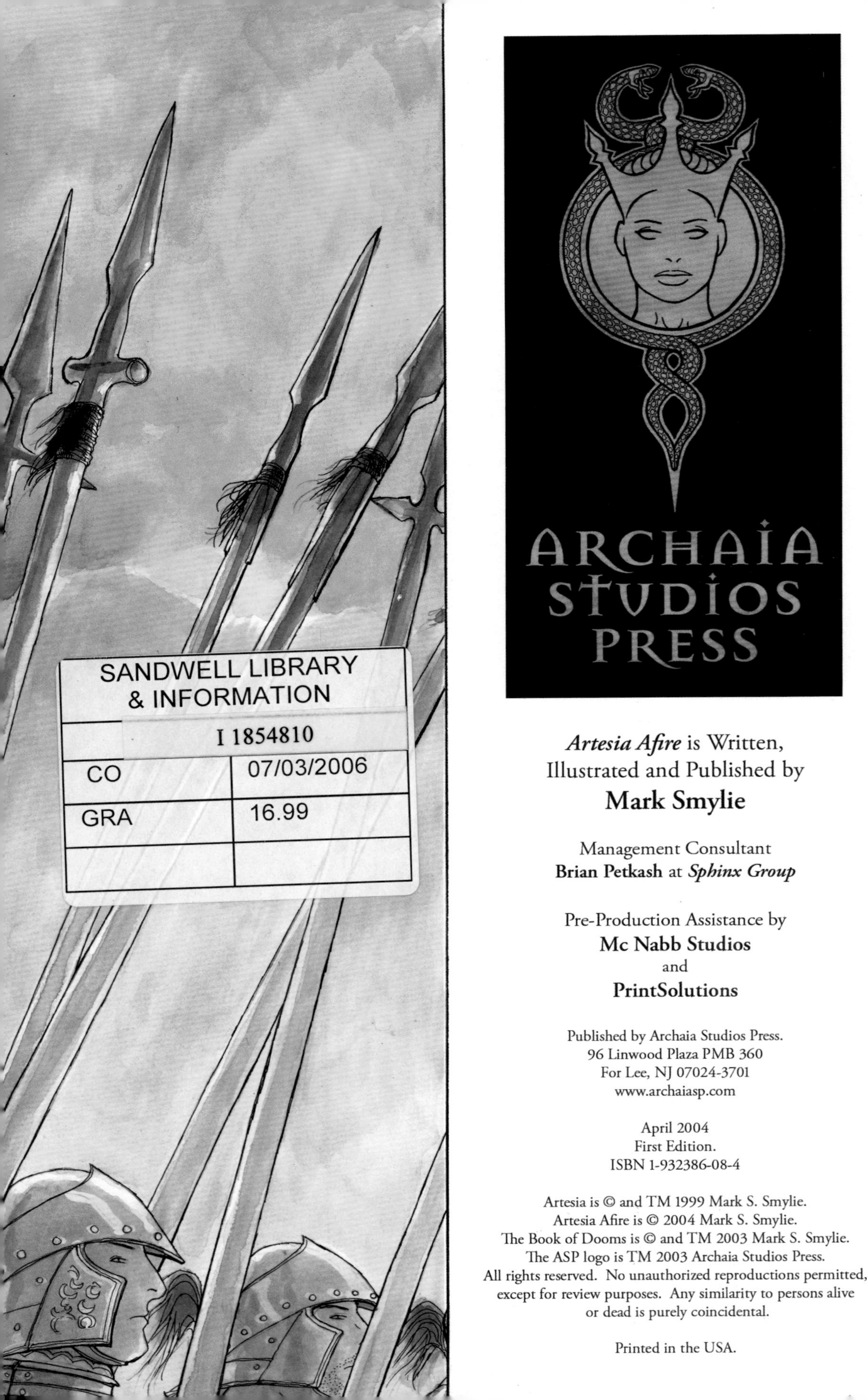

ARCHAIA
STUDIOS
PRESS

Artesia Afire is Written,
Illustrated and Published by
Mark Smylie

Management Consultant
Brian Petkash at ***Sphinx Group***

Pre-Production Assistance by
Mc Nabb Studios
and
PrintSolutions

Published by Archaia Studios Press.
96 Linwood Plaza PMB 360
For Lee, NJ 07024-3701
www.archaiasp.com

April 2004
First Edition.
ISBN 1-932386-08-4

Printed in the USA.

Table of Contents

Appendixes

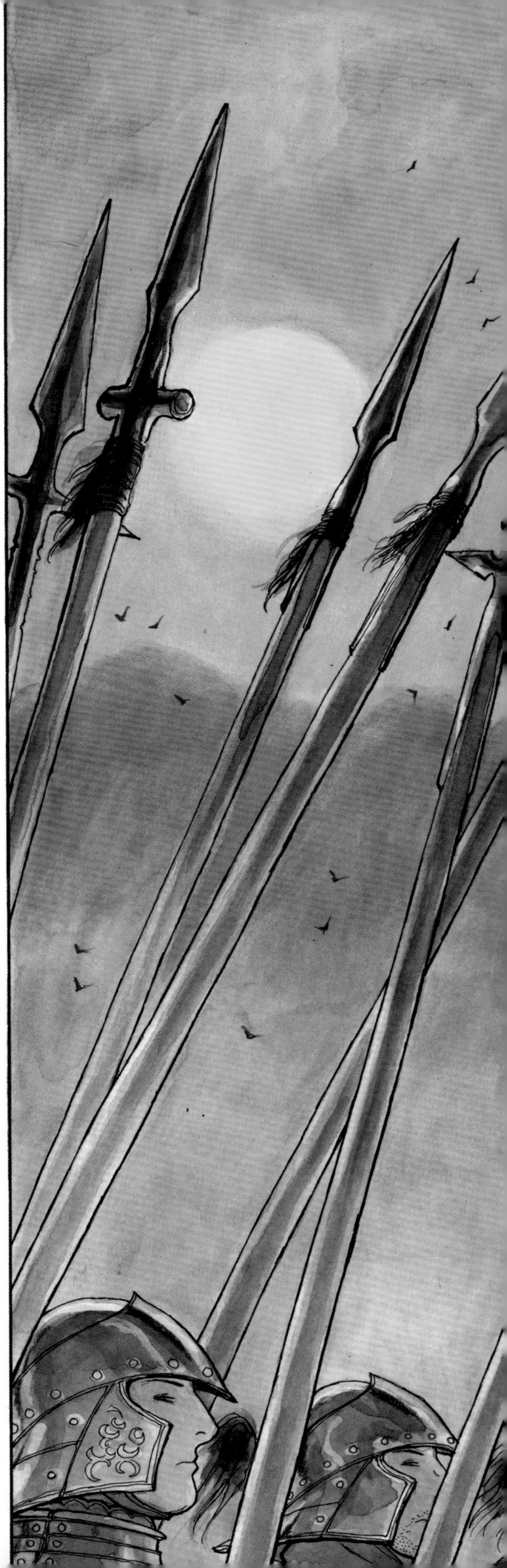

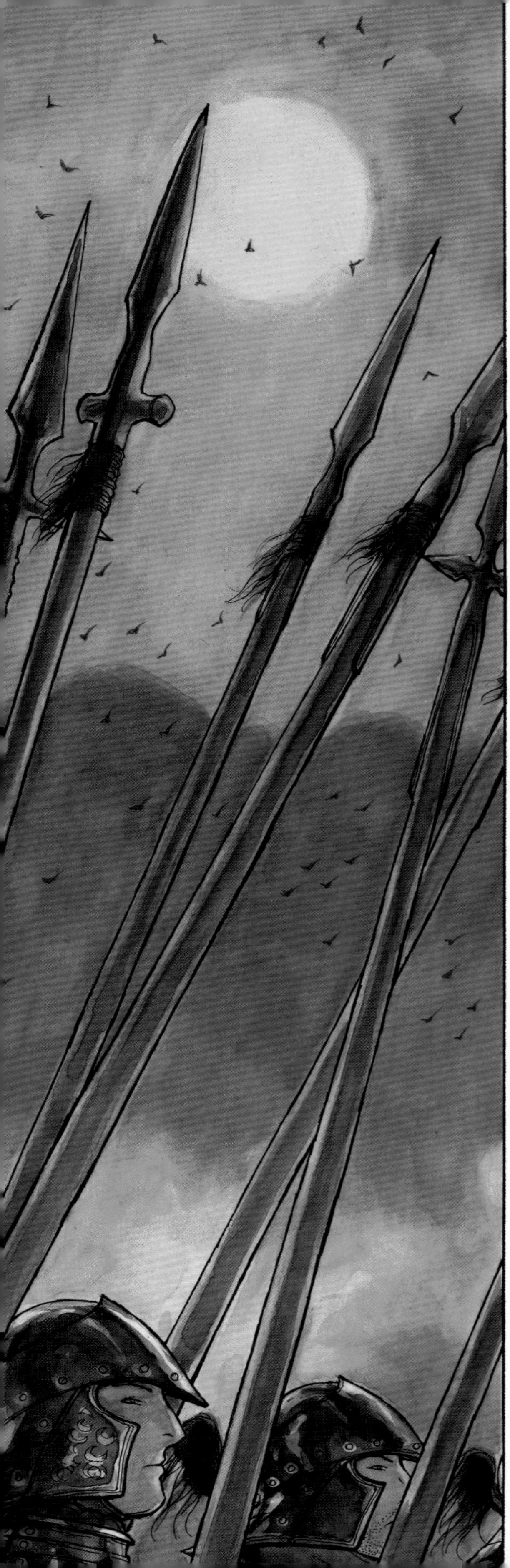

LIST OF RUNES AND SIGNS

AVA AND THE QUEEN'S GUARD IN

RIGHT HANDS, LEFT HANDS

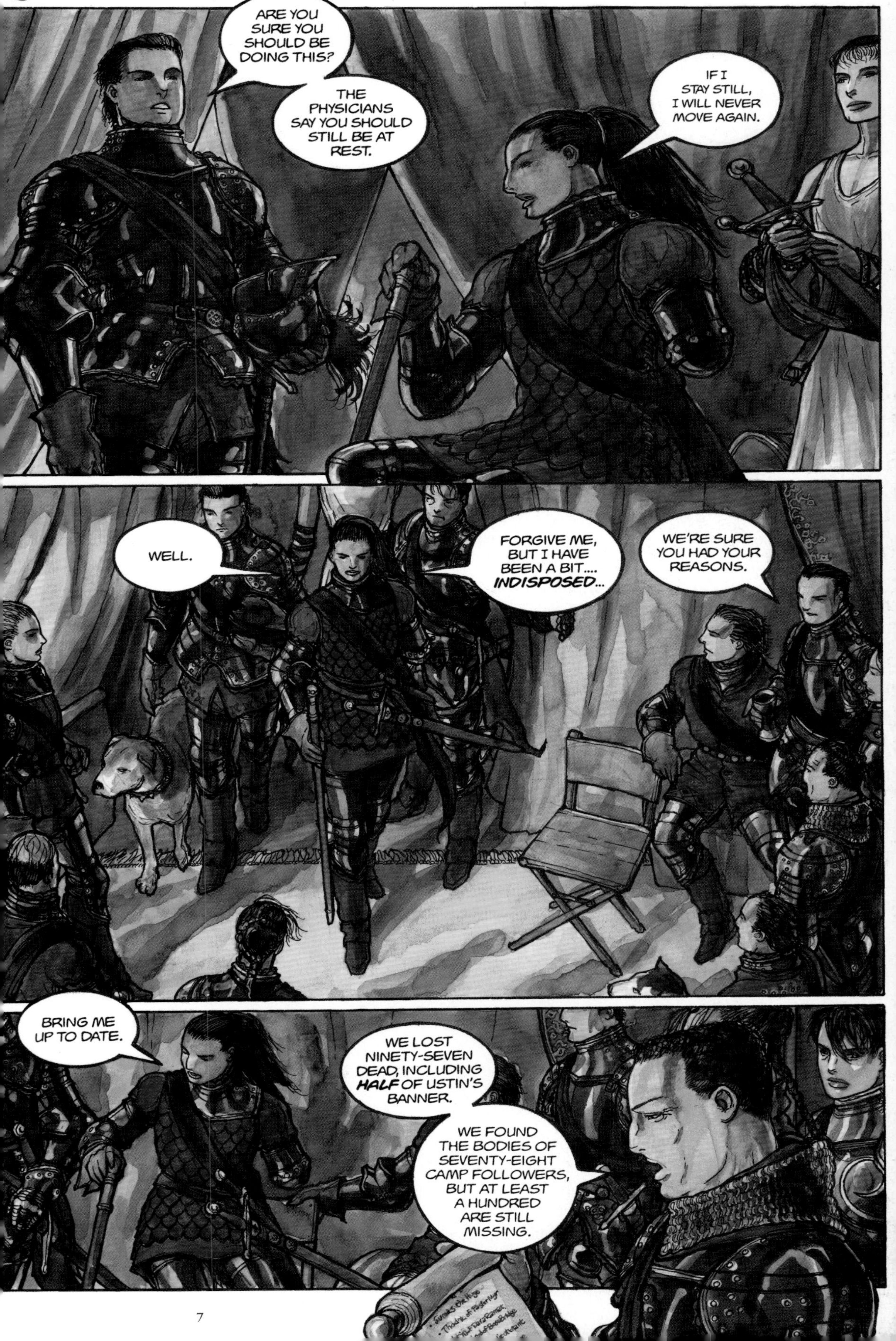
ARE YOU SURE YOU SHOULD BE DOING THIS?
THE PHYSICIANS SAY YOU SHOULD STILL BE AT REST.
IF I STAY STILL, I WILL NEVER MOVE AGAIN.
WELL.
FORGIVE ME, BUT I HAVE BEEN A BIT.... *INDISPOSED*...
WE'RE SURE YOU HAD YOUR REASONS.
BRING ME UP TO DATE.
WE LOST NINETY-SEVEN DEAD, INCLUDING *HALF* OF USTIN'S BANNER.
WE FOUND THE BODIES OF SEVENTY-EIGHT CAMP FOLLOWERS, BUT AT LEAST A HUNDRED ARE STILL MISSING.

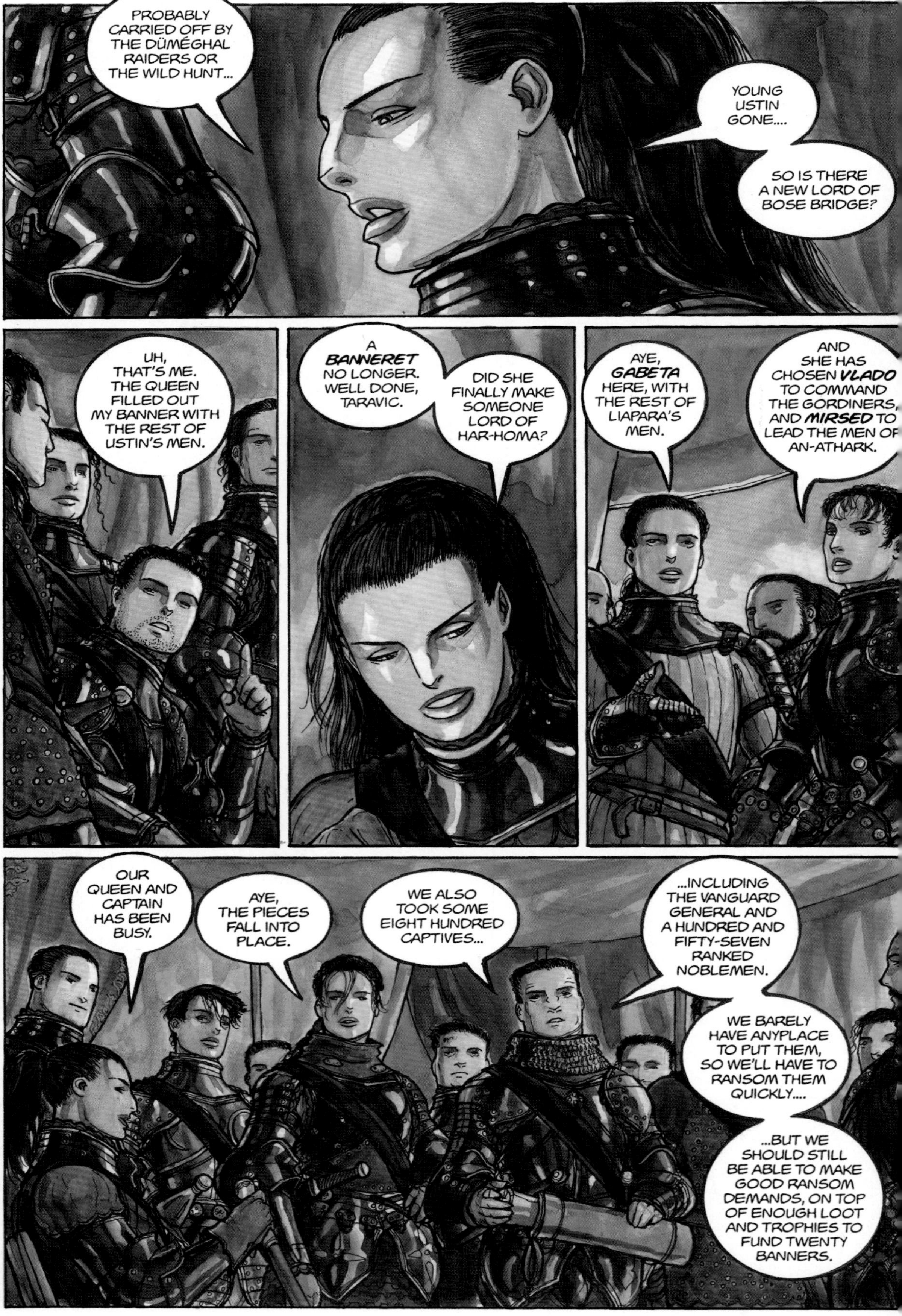
PROBABLY CARRIED OFF BY THE DÜMÉGHAL RAIDERS OR THE WILD HUNT...
YOUNG USTIN GONE....
SO IS THERE A NEW LORD OF BOSE BRIDGE?
UH, THAT'S ME. THE QUEEN FILLED OUT MY BANNER WITH THE REST OF USTIN'S MEN.
A **BANNERET** NO LONGER. WELL DONE, TARAVIC.
DID SHE FINALLY MAKE SOMEONE LORD OF HAR-HOMA?
AYE, **GABETA** HERE, WITH THE REST OF LIAPARA'S MEN.
AND SHE HAS CHOSEN **VLADO** TO COMMAND THE GORDINERS, AND **MIRSED** TO LEAD THE MEN OF AN-ATHARK.
OUR QUEEN AND CAPTAIN HAS BEEN BUSY.
AYE, THE PIECES FALL INTO PLACE.
WE ALSO TOOK SOME EIGHT HUNDRED CAPTIVES...
...INCLUDING THE VANGUARD GENERAL AND A HUNDRED AND FIFTY-SEVEN RANKED NOBLEMEN.
WE BARELY HAVE ANYPLACE TO PUT THEM, SO WE'LL HAVE TO RANSOM THEM QUICKLY....
...BUT WE SHOULD STILL BE ABLE TO MAKE GOOD RANSOM DEMANDS, ON TOP OF ENOUGH LOOT AND TROPHIES TO FUND TWENTY BANNERS.

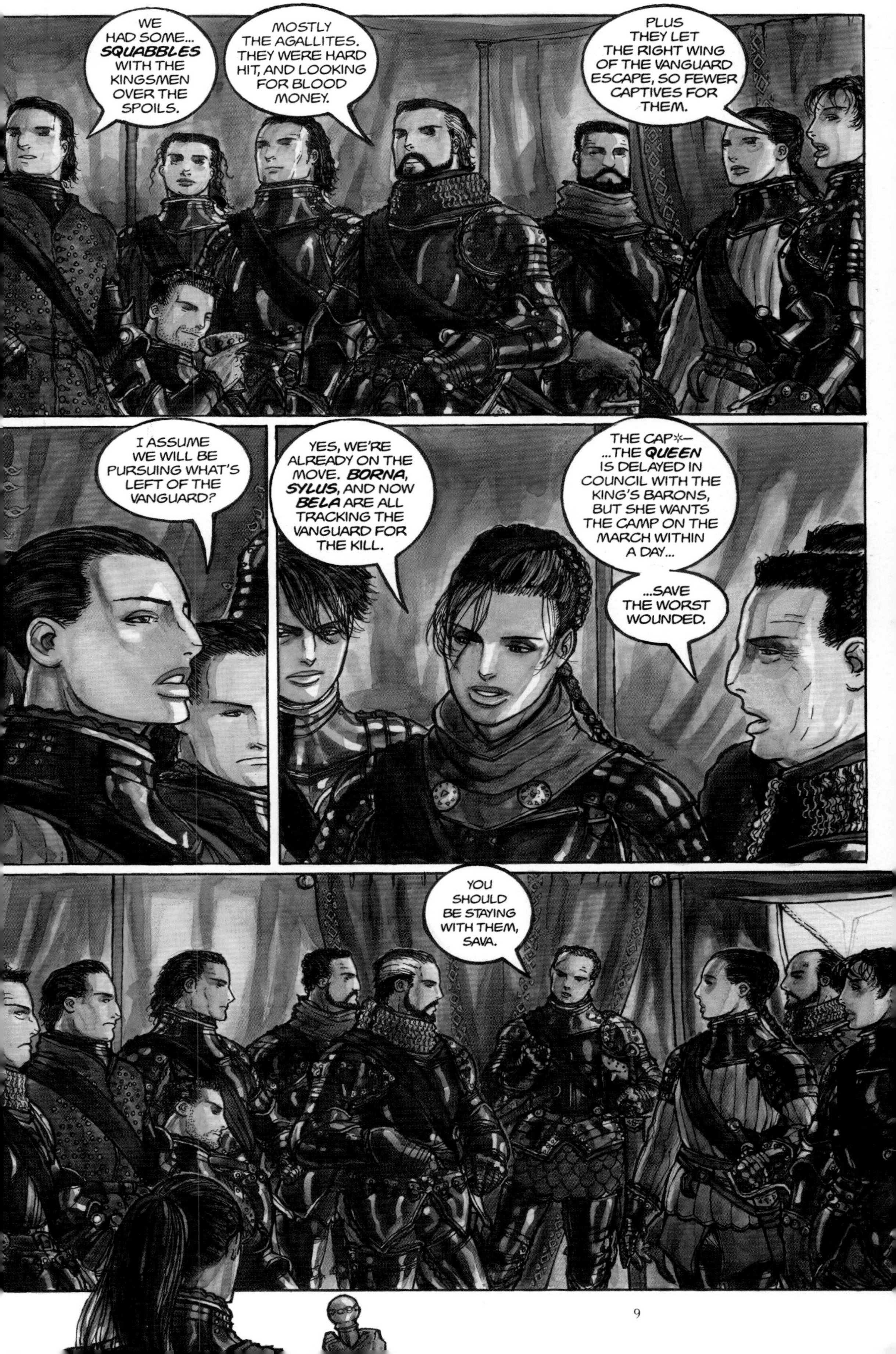
WE HAD SOME... SQUABBLES WITH THE KINGSMEN OVER THE SPOILS.
MOSTLY THE AGALLITES. THEY WERE HARD HIT, AND LOOKING FOR BLOOD MONEY.
PLUS THEY LET THE RIGHT WING OF THE VANGUARD ESCAPE, SO FEWER CAPTIVES FOR THEM.
I ASSUME WE WILL BE PURSUING WHAT'S LEFT OF THE VANGUARD?
YES, WE'RE ALREADY ON THE MOVE. BORNA, SYLUS, AND NOW BELA ARE ALL TRACKING THE VANGUARD FOR THE KILL.
THE CAP-- ...THE QUEEN IS DELAYED IN COUNCIL WITH THE KING'S BARONS, BUT SHE WANTS THE CAMP ON THE MARCH WITHIN A DAY...
...SAVE THE WORST WOUNDED.
YOU SHOULD BE STAYING WITH THEM, SAVA.

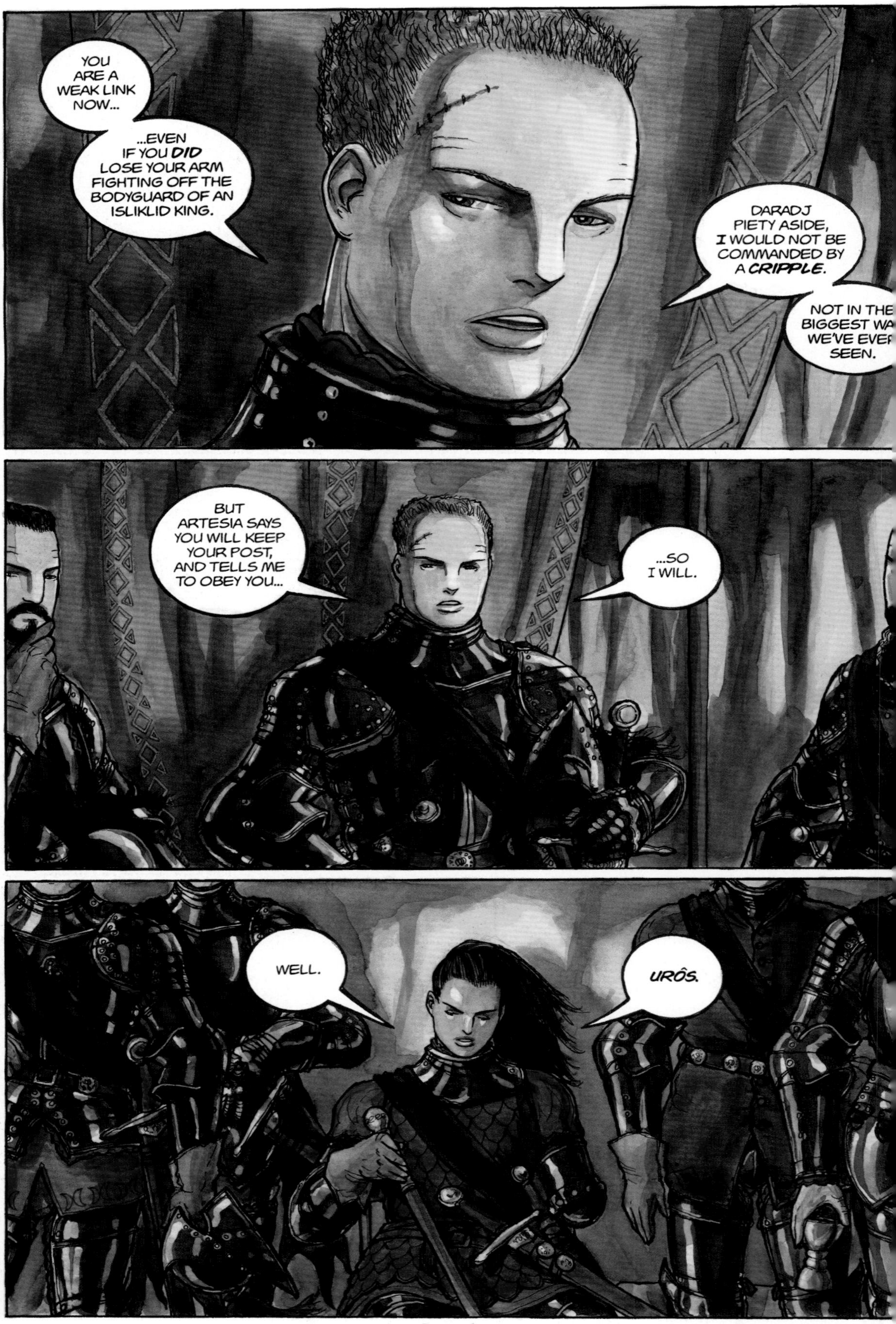
YOU ARE A WEAK LINK NOW...
...EVEN IF YOU DID LOSE YOUR ARM FIGHTING OFF THE BODYGUARD OF AN ISLIKLID KING.
DARADJ PIETY ASIDE, I WOULD NOT BE COMMANDED BY A CRIPPLE.
NOT IN THE BIGGEST WA WE'VE EVEF SEEN.
BUT ARTESIA SAYS YOU WILL KEEP YOUR POST, AND TELLS ME TO OBEY YOU...
...SO I WILL.
WELL.
URÔS.

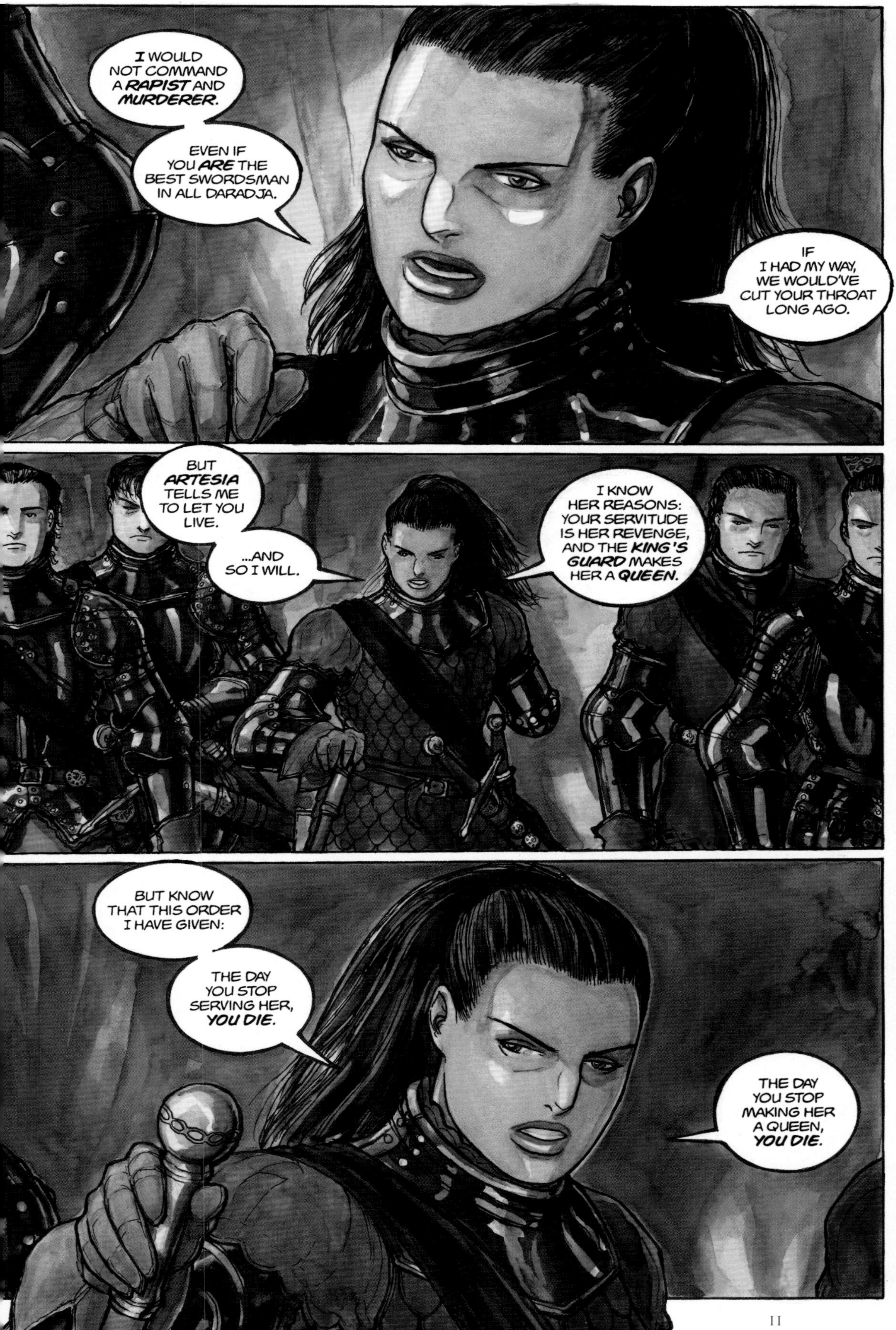

I WOULD NOT COMMAND A RAPIST AND MURDERER.
EVEN IF YOU ARE THE BEST SWORDSMAN IN ALL DARADJA.
IF I HAD MY WAY, WE WOULD'VE CUT YOUR THROAT LONG AGO.
BUT ARTESIA TELLS ME TO LET YOU LIVE.
...AND SO I WILL.
I KNOW HER REASONS: YOUR SERVITUDE IS HER REVENGE, AND THE KING'S GUARD MAKES HER A QUEEN.
BUT KNOW THAT THIS ORDER I HAVE GIVEN:
THE DAY YOU STOP SERVING HER, YOU DIE.
THE DAY YOU STOP MAKING HER A QUEEN, YOU DIE.

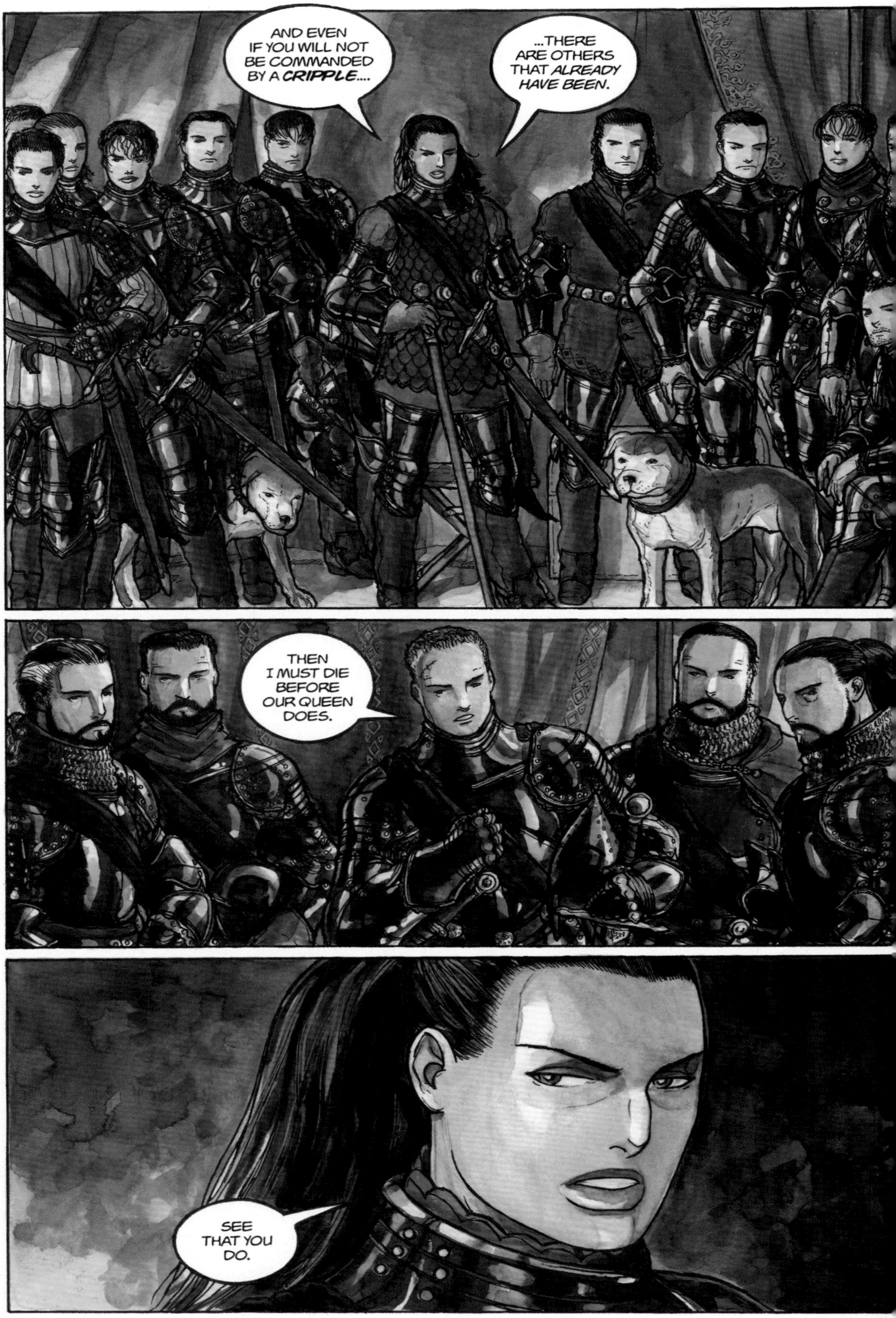
AND EVEN IF YOU WILL NOT BE COMMANDED BY A *CRIPPLE*....
...THERE ARE OTHERS THAT *ALREADY* HAVE BEEN.
THEN I MUST DIE BEFORE OUR QUEEN DOES.
SEE THAT YOU DO.

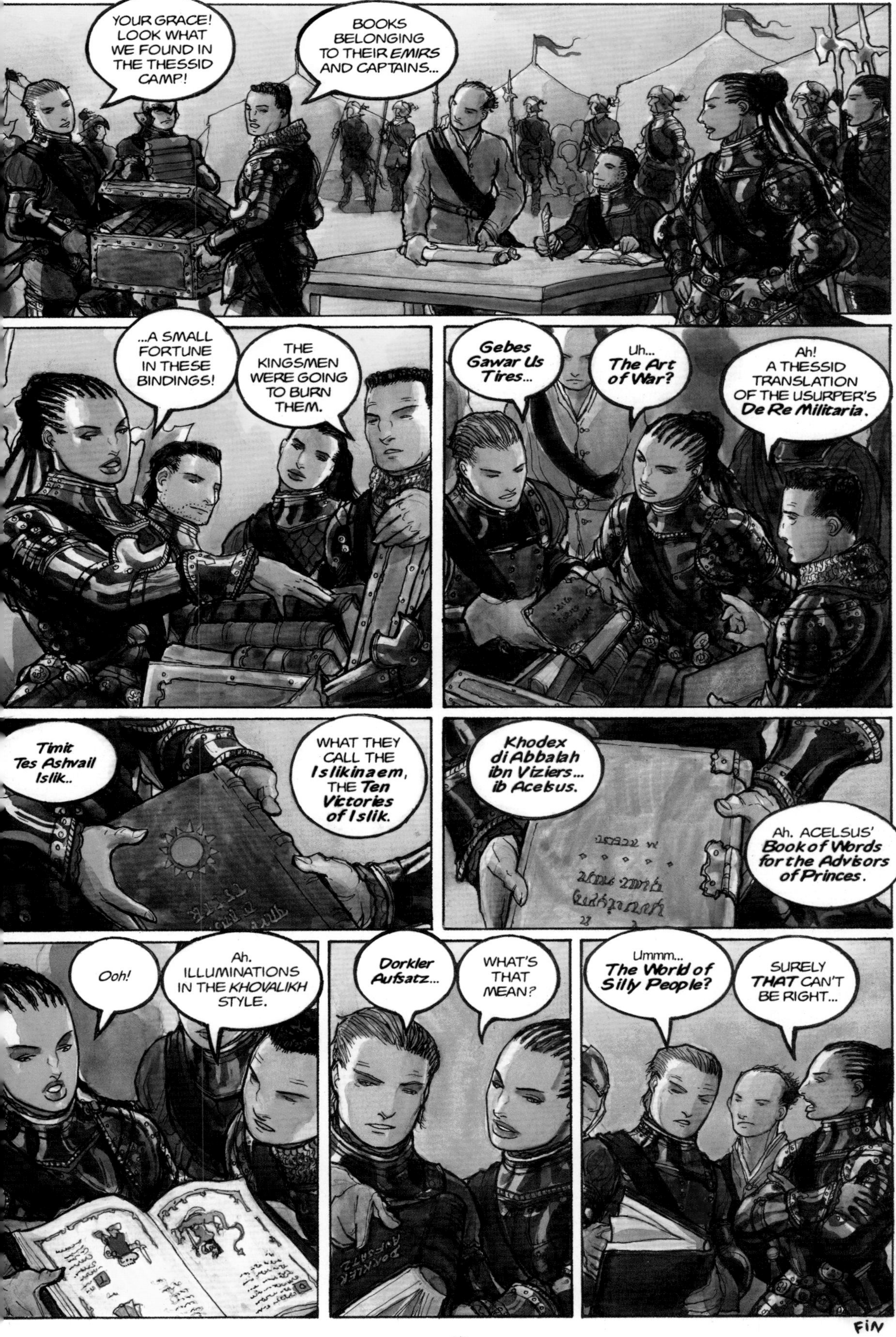
YOUR GRACE! LOOK WHAT WE FOUND IN THE THESSID CAMP!
BOOKS BELONGING TO THEIR EMIRS AND CAPTAINS...
...A SMALL FORTUNE IN THESE BINDINGS!
THE KINGSMEN WERE GOING TO BURN THEM.
Gebes Gawar Us Tires...
Uh... The Art of War?
Ah! A THESSID TRANSLATION OF THE USURPER'S De Re Militaria.
Timit Tes Ashvail Islik..
WHAT THEY CALL THE Islikinaem, THE Ten Victories of Islik.
Khodex di Abbalah ibn Viziers... ib Acelsus.
Ah. ACELSUS' Book of Words for the Advisors of Princes.
Ooh!
Ah. ILLUMINATIONS IN THE KHOVALIKH STYLE.
Dorkler Aufsatz...
WHAT'S THAT MEAN?
Ummm... The World of Silly People?
SURELY THAT CAN'T BE RIGHT...
FIN

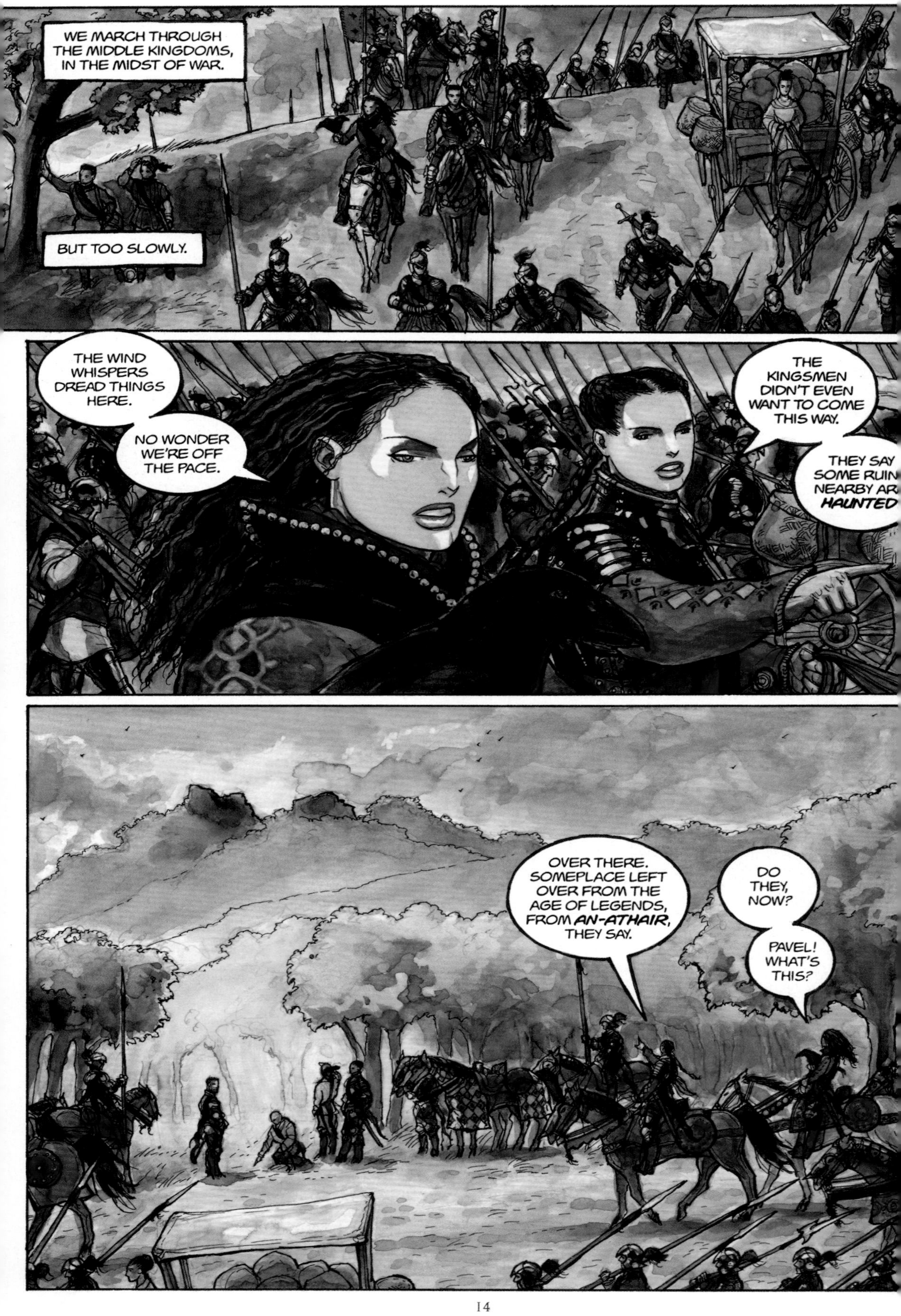
WE MARCH THROUGH THE MIDDLE KINGDOMS, IN THE MIDST OF WAR.
BUT TOO SLOWLY.
THE WIND WHISPERS DREAD THINGS HERE.
NO WONDER WE'RE OFF THE PACE.
THE KINGSMEN DIDN'T EVEN WANT TO COME THIS WAY.
THEY SAY SOME RUIN NEARBY AR *HAUNTED*
OVER THERE. SOMEPLACE LEFT OVER FROM THE AGE OF LEGENDS, FROM *AN-ATHAIR*, THEY SAY.
DO THEY, NOW?
PAVEL! WHAT'S THIS?

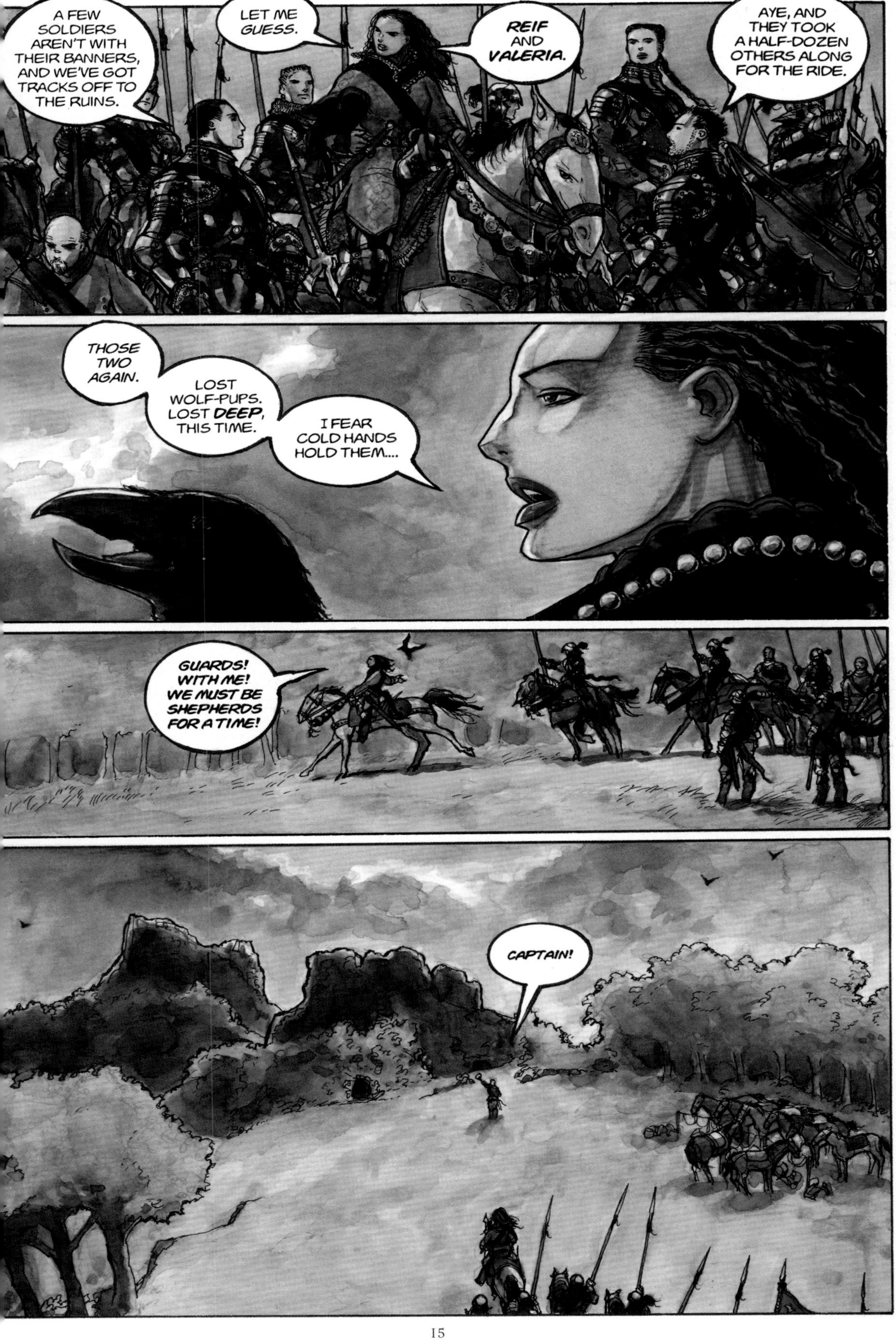
A FEW SOLDIERS AREN'T WITH THEIR BANNERS, AND WE'VE GOT TRACKS OFF TO THE RUINS.
LET ME GUESS.
REIF AND VALERIA.
AYE, AND THEY TOOK A HALF-DOZEN OTHERS ALONG FOR THE RIDE.
THOSE TWO AGAIN.
LOST WOLF-PUPS. LOST DEEP, THIS TIME.
I FEAR COLD HANDS HOLD THEM....
GUARDS! WITH ME! WE MUST BE SHEPHERDS FOR A TIME!
CAPTAIN!

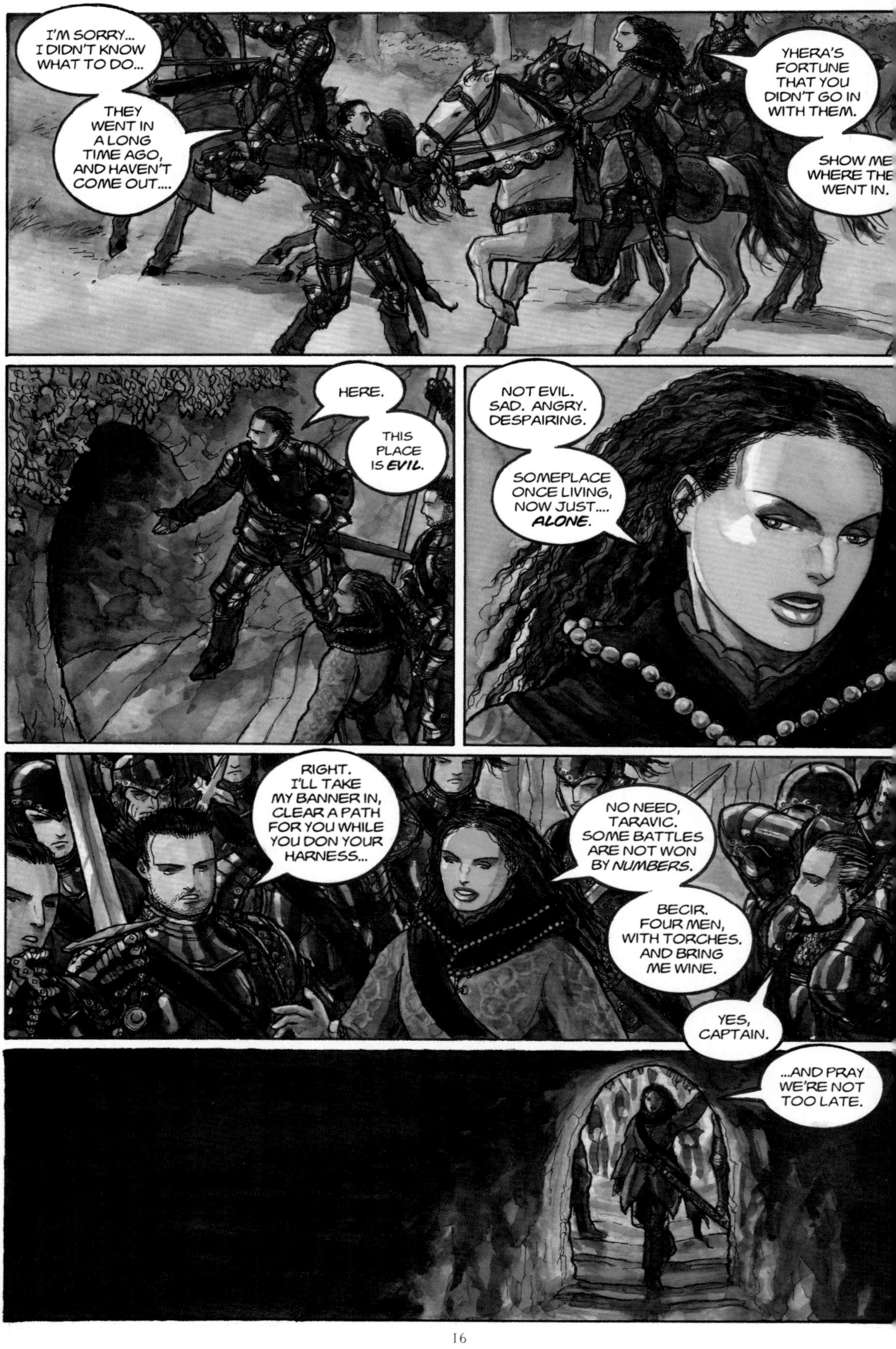
I'M SORRY... I DIDN'T KNOW WHAT TO DO...
THEY WENT IN A LONG TIME AGO, AND HAVEN'T COME OUT....
YHERA'S FORTUNE THAT YOU DIDN'T GO IN WITH THEM.
SHOW ME WHERE THE WENT IN.
HERE.
THIS PLACE IS EVIL.
NOT EVIL. SAD. ANGRY. DESPAIRING.
SOMEPLACE ONCE LIVING, NOW JUST.... ALONE.
RIGHT. I'LL TAKE MY BANNER IN, CLEAR A PATH FOR YOU WHILE YOU DON YOUR HARNESS...
NO NEED, TARAVIC. SOME BATTLES ARE NOT WON BY NUMBERS.
BECIR. FOUR MEN, WITH TORCHES. AND BRING ME WINE.
YES, CAPTAIN.
...AND PRAY WE'RE NOT TOO LATE.

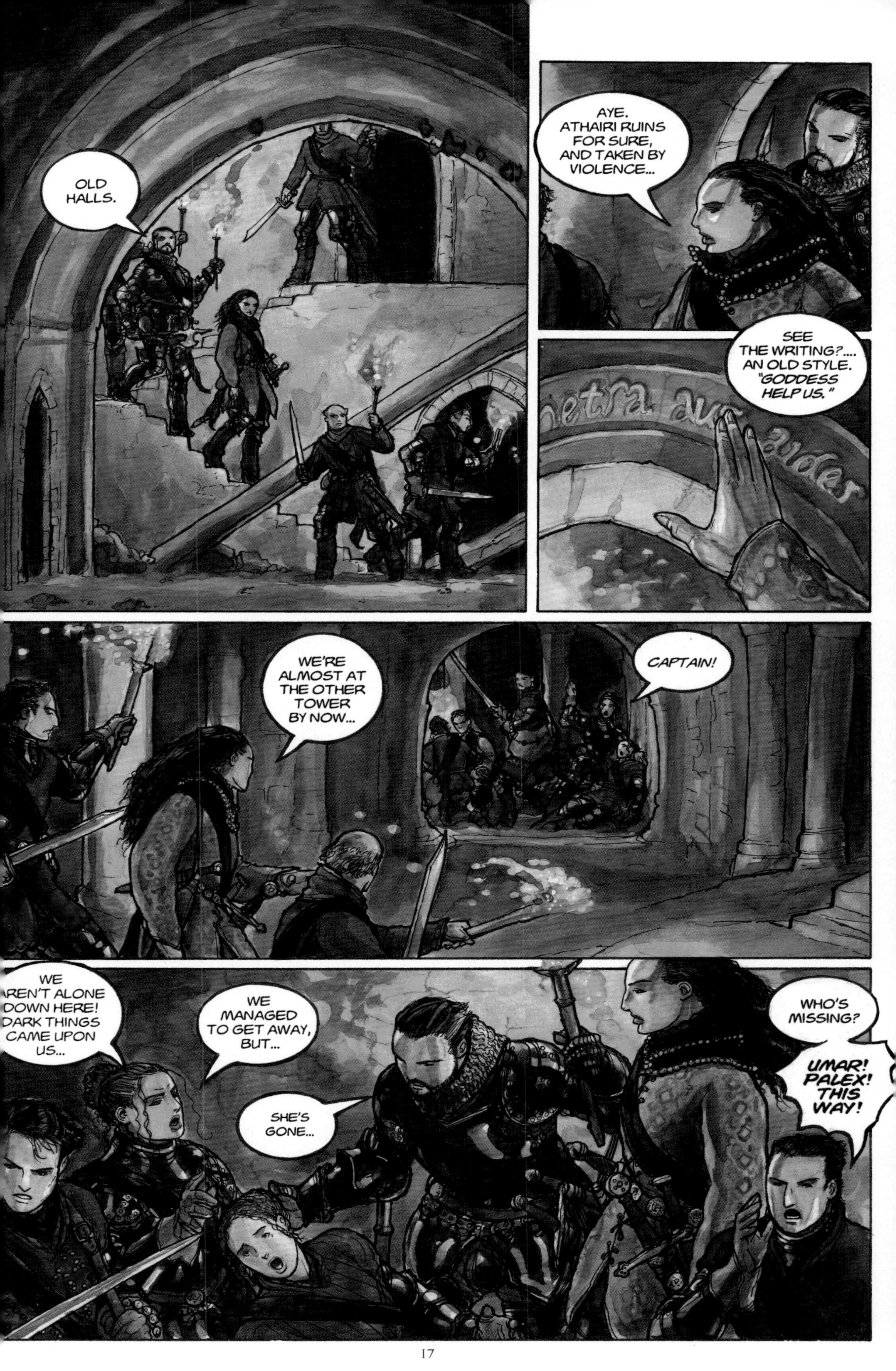
OLD HALLS.
AYE. ATHAIRI RUINS FOR SURE, AND TAKEN BY VIOLENCE...
SEE THE WRITING?.... AN OLD STYLE. "GODDESS HELP US."
WE'RE ALMOST AT THE OTHER TOWER BY NOW...
CAPTAIN!
WE AREN'T ALONE DOWN HERE! DARK THINGS CAME UPON US...
WE MANAGED TO GET AWAY, BUT...
SHE'S GONE...
WHO'S MISSING?
UMAR! PALEX! THIS WAY!

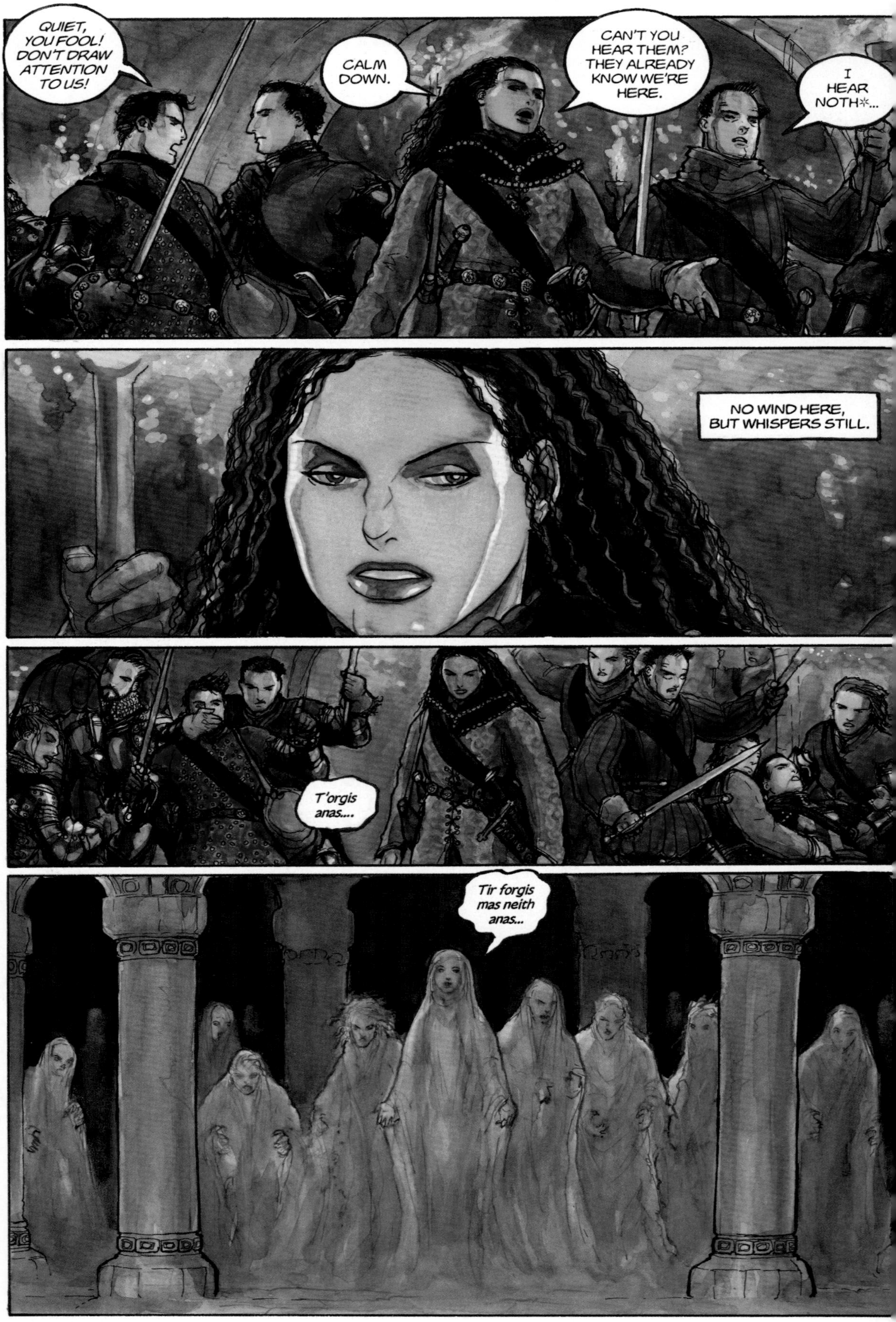
QUIET, YOU FOOL! DON'T DRAW ATTENTION TO US!
CALM DOWN.
CAN'T YOU HEAR THEM? THEY ALREADY KNOW WE'RE HERE.
I HEAR NOTH✳...
NO WIND HERE, BUT WHISPERS STILL.
T'orgis anas....
Tir forgis mas neith anas...

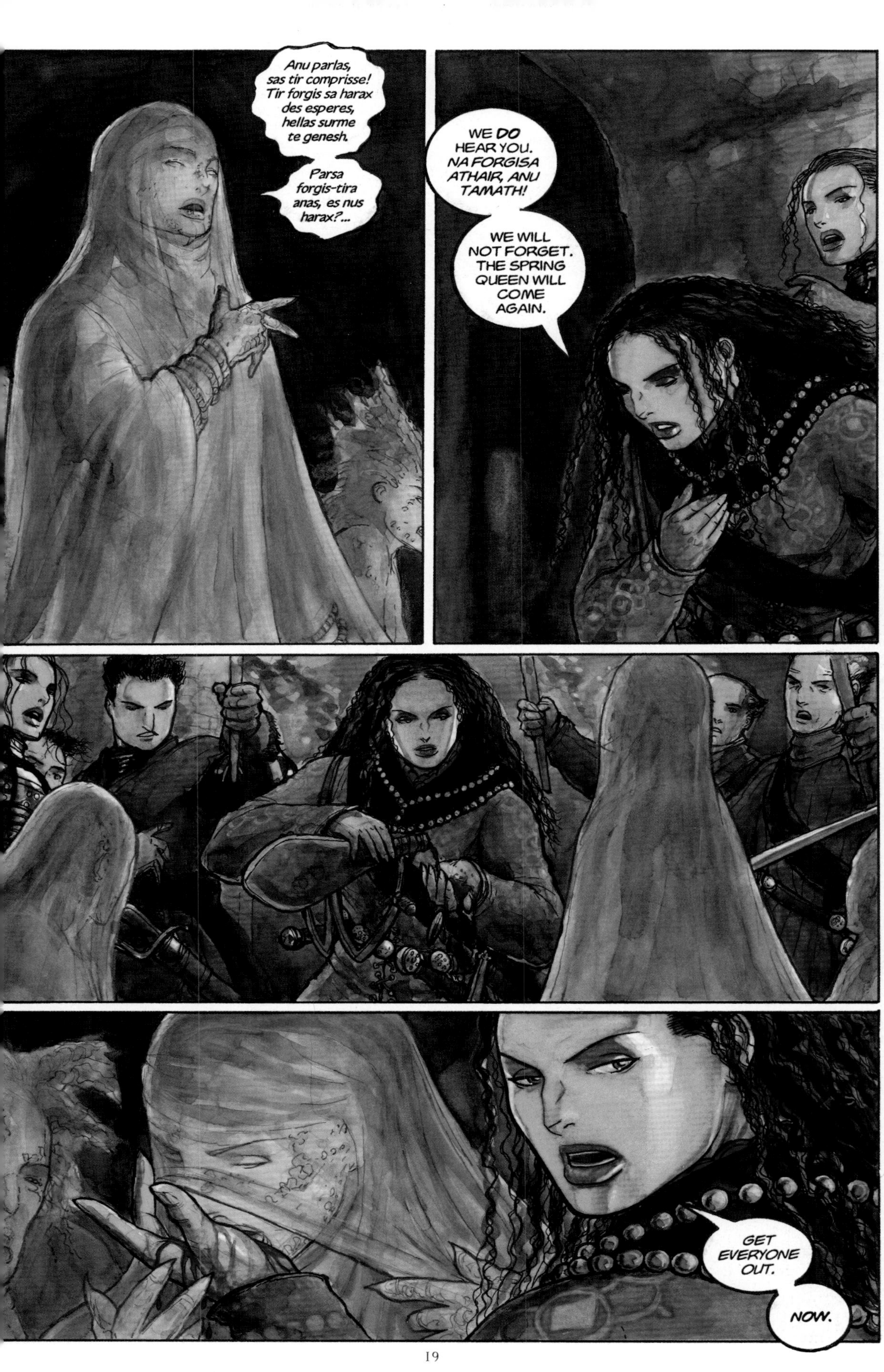
Anu parlas, sas tir comprisse! Tir forgis sa harax des esperes, hellas surme te genesh.
Parsa forgis-tira anas, es nus harax?...
WE DO HEAR YOU. NA FORGISA ATHAIR, ANU TAMATH!
WE WILL NOT FORGET. THE SPRING QUEEN WILL COME AGAIN.
GET EVERYONE OUT.
NOW.

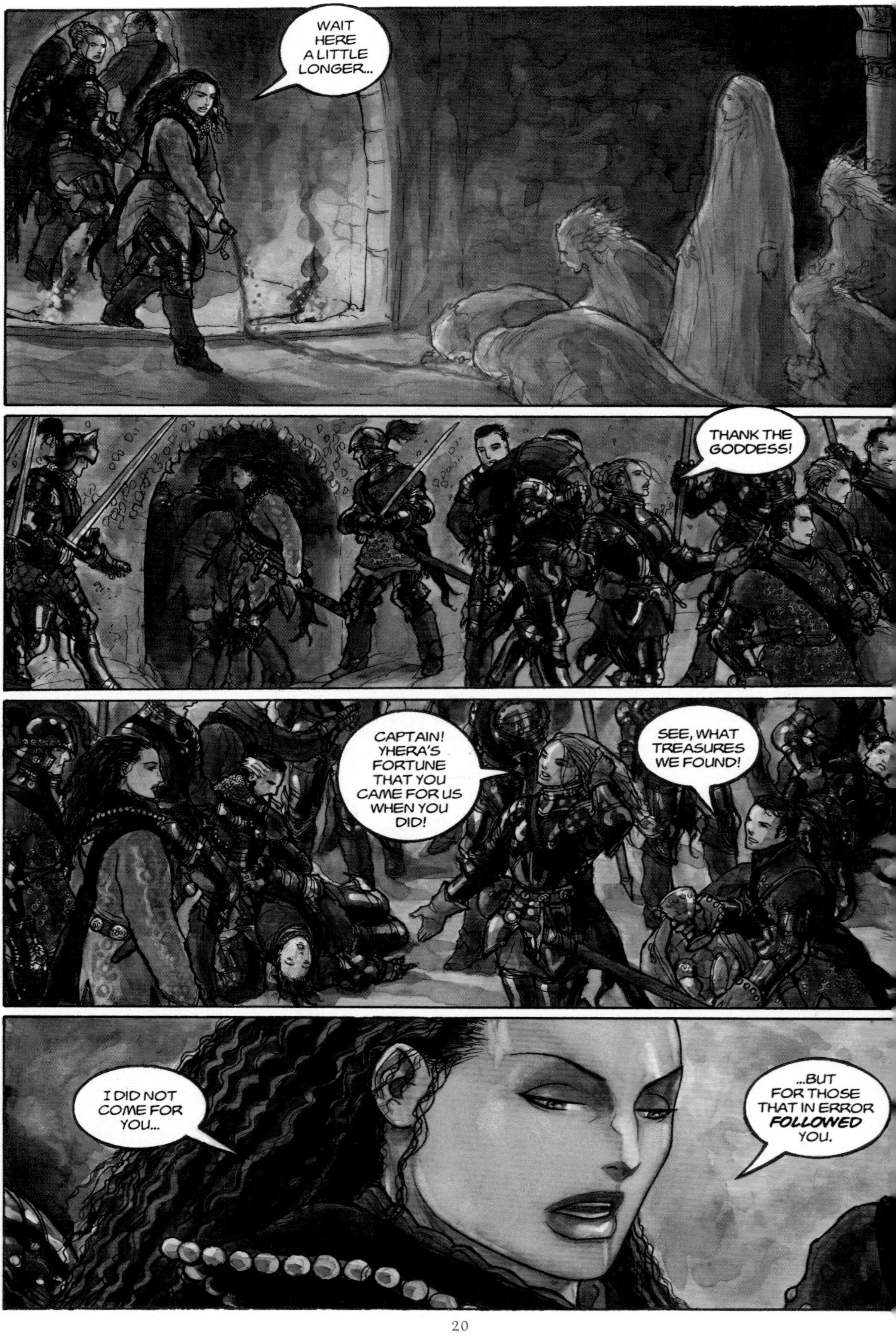
WAIT HERE A LITTLE LONGER...
THANK THE GODDESS!
CAPTAIN! YHERA'S FORTUNE THAT YOU CAME FOR US WHEN YOU DID!
SEE, WHAT TREASURES WE FOUND!
I DID NOT COME FOR YOU...
...BUT FOR THOSE THAT IN ERROR FOLLOWED YOU.

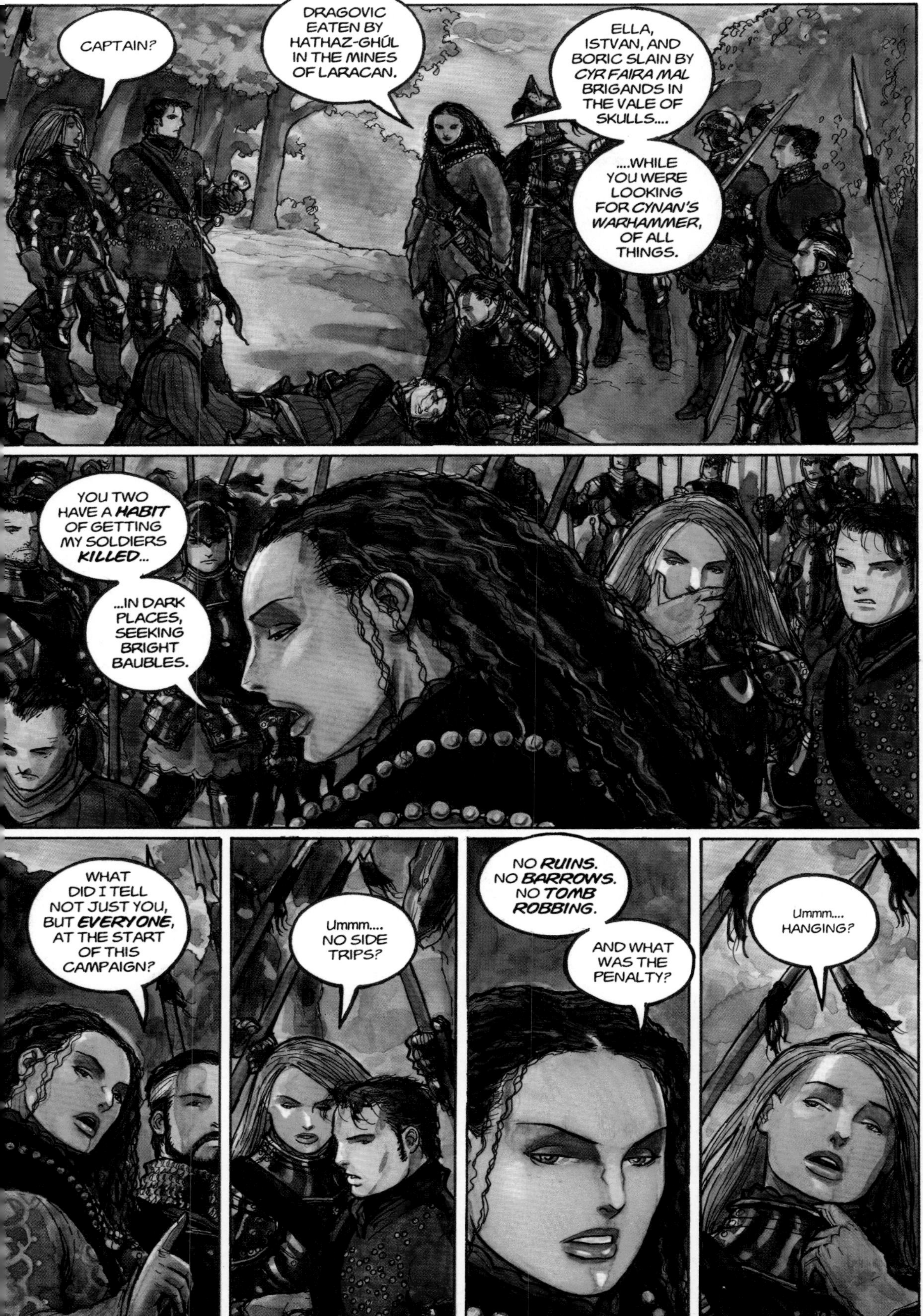
CAPTAIN?
DRAGOVIC EATEN BY HATHAZ-GHÚL IN THE MINES OF LARACAN.
ELLA, ISTVAN, AND BORIC SLAIN BY *CYR FAIRA MAL* BRIGANDS IN THE VALE OF SKULLS....
....WHILE YOU WERE LOOKING FOR *CYNAN'S WARHAMMER*, OF ALL THINGS.
YOU TWO HAVE A ***HABIT*** OF GETTING MY SOLDIERS ***KILLED***...
...IN DARK PLACES, SEEKING BRIGHT BAUBLES.
WHAT DID I TELL NOT JUST YOU, BUT ***EVERYONE***, AT THE START OF THIS CAMPAIGN?
Ummm.... NO SIDE TRIPS?
NO ***RUINS***. NO ***BARROWS***. NO ***TOMB ROBBING***.
AND WHAT WAS THE PENALTY?
Ummm.... HANGING?

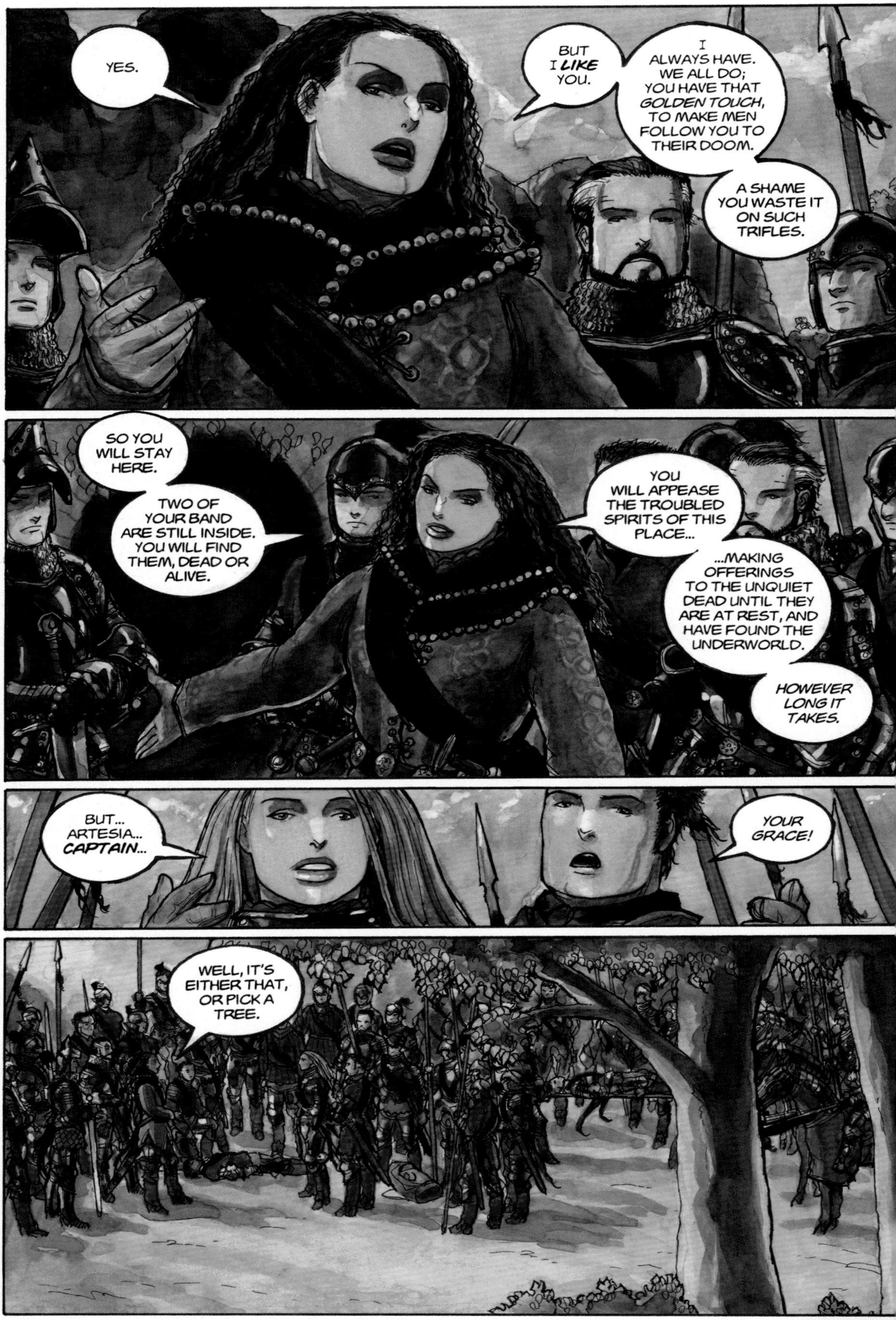
YES.
BUT I LIKE YOU.
I ALWAYS HAVE. WE ALL DO; YOU HAVE THAT GOLDEN TOUCH, TO MAKE MEN FOLLOW YOU TO THEIR DOOM.
A SHAME YOU WASTE IT ON SUCH TRIFLES.
SO YOU WILL STAY HERE.
TWO OF YOUR BAND ARE STILL INSIDE. YOU WILL FIND THEM, DEAD OR ALIVE.
YOU WILL APPEASE THE TROUBLED SPIRITS OF THIS PLACE...
...MAKING OFFERINGS TO THE UNQUIET DEAD UNTIL THEY ARE AT REST, AND HAVE FOUND THE UNDERWORLD.
HOWEVER LONG IT TAKES.
BUT... ARTESIA... CAPTAIN...
YOUR GRACE!
WELL, IT'S EITHER THAT, OR PICK A TREE.

FİП?

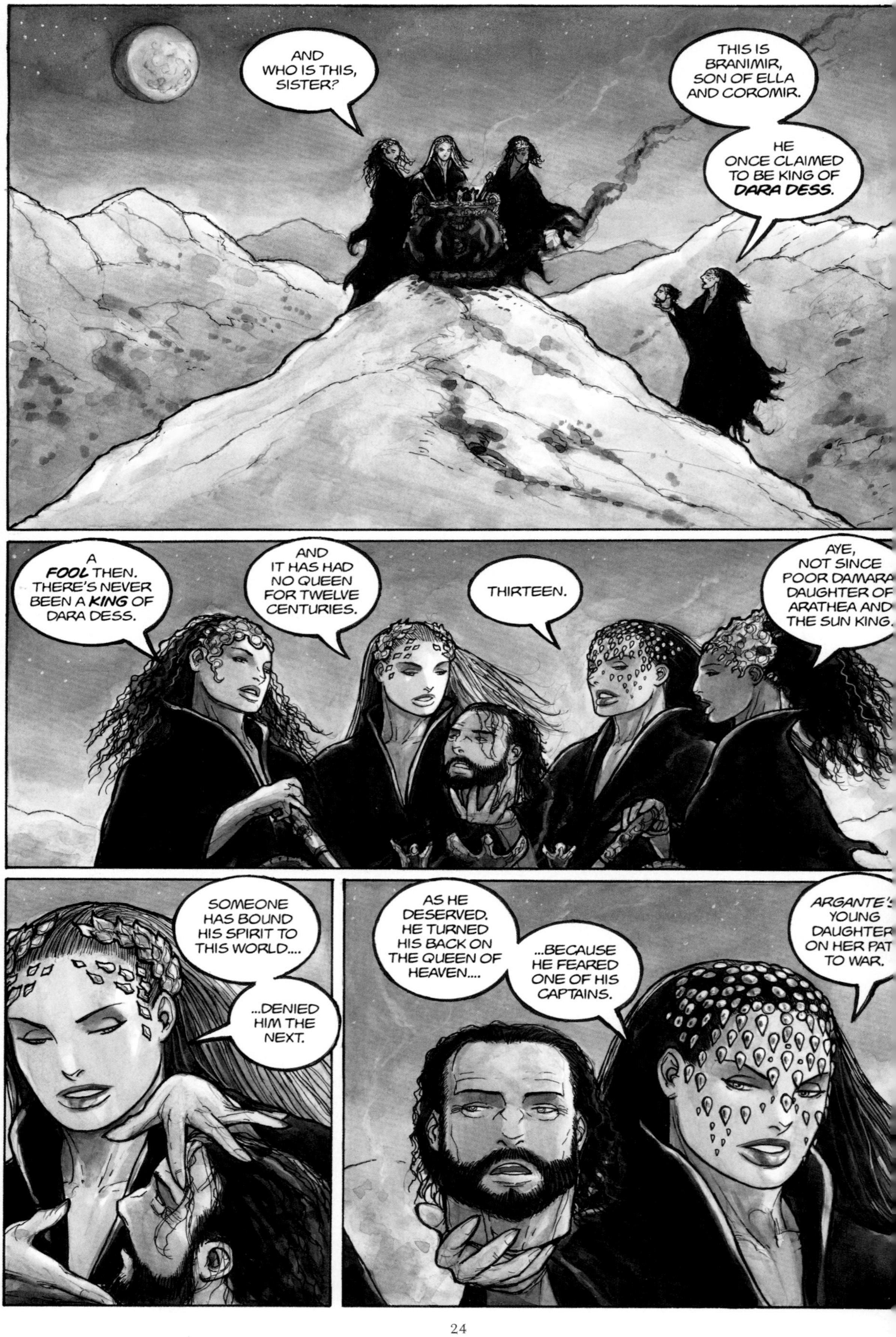
AND WHO IS THIS, SISTER?
THIS IS BRANIMIR, SON OF ELLA AND COROMIR.
HE ONCE CLAIMED TO BE KING OF DARA DESS.
A FOOL THEN. THERE'S NEVER BEEN A KING OF DARA DESS.
AND IT HAS HAD NO QUEEN FOR TWELVE CENTURIES.
THIRTEEN.
AYE, NOT SINCE POOR DAMARA DAUGHTER OF ARATHEA AND THE SUN KING.
SOMEONE HAS BOUND HIS SPIRIT TO THIS WORLD....
...DENIED HIM THE NEXT.
AS HE DESERVED. HE TURNED HIS BACK ON THE QUEEN OF HEAVEN....
...BECAUSE HE FEARED ONE OF HIS CAPTAINS.
ARGANTE'S YOUNG DAUGHTER ON HER PAT TO WAR.

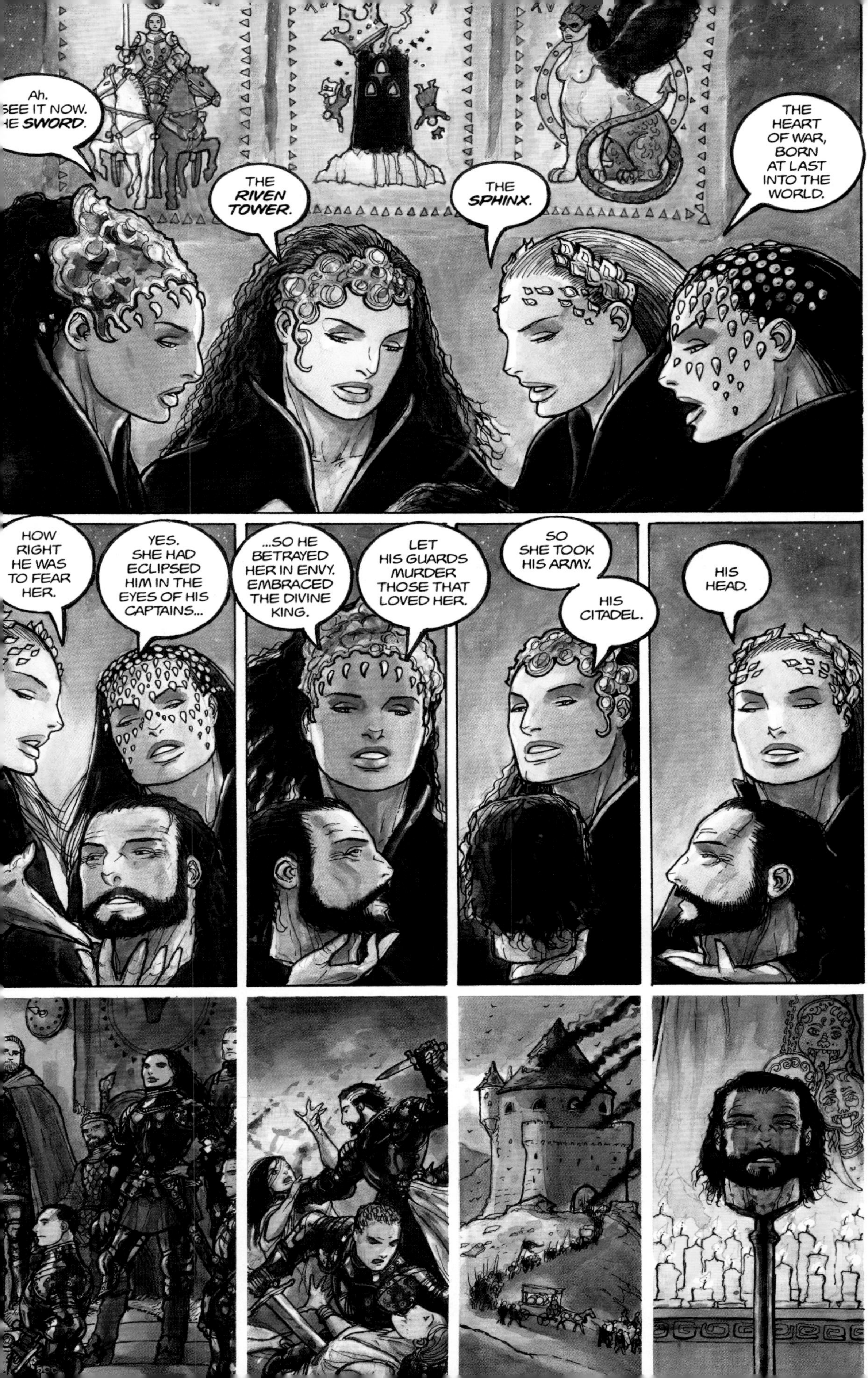
Ah.
SEE IT NOW.
HE SWORD.
THE RIVEN TOWER.
THE SPHINX.
THE HEART OF WAR, BORN AT LAST INTO THE WORLD.
HOW RIGHT HE WAS TO FEAR HER.
YES. SHE HAD ECLIPSED HIM IN THE EYES OF HIS CAPTAINS...
...SO HE BETRAYED HER IN ENVY. EMBRACED THE DIVINE KING.
LET HIS GUARDS MURDER THOSE THAT LOVED HER.
SO SHE TOOK HIS ARMY.
HIS CITADEL.
HIS HEAD.

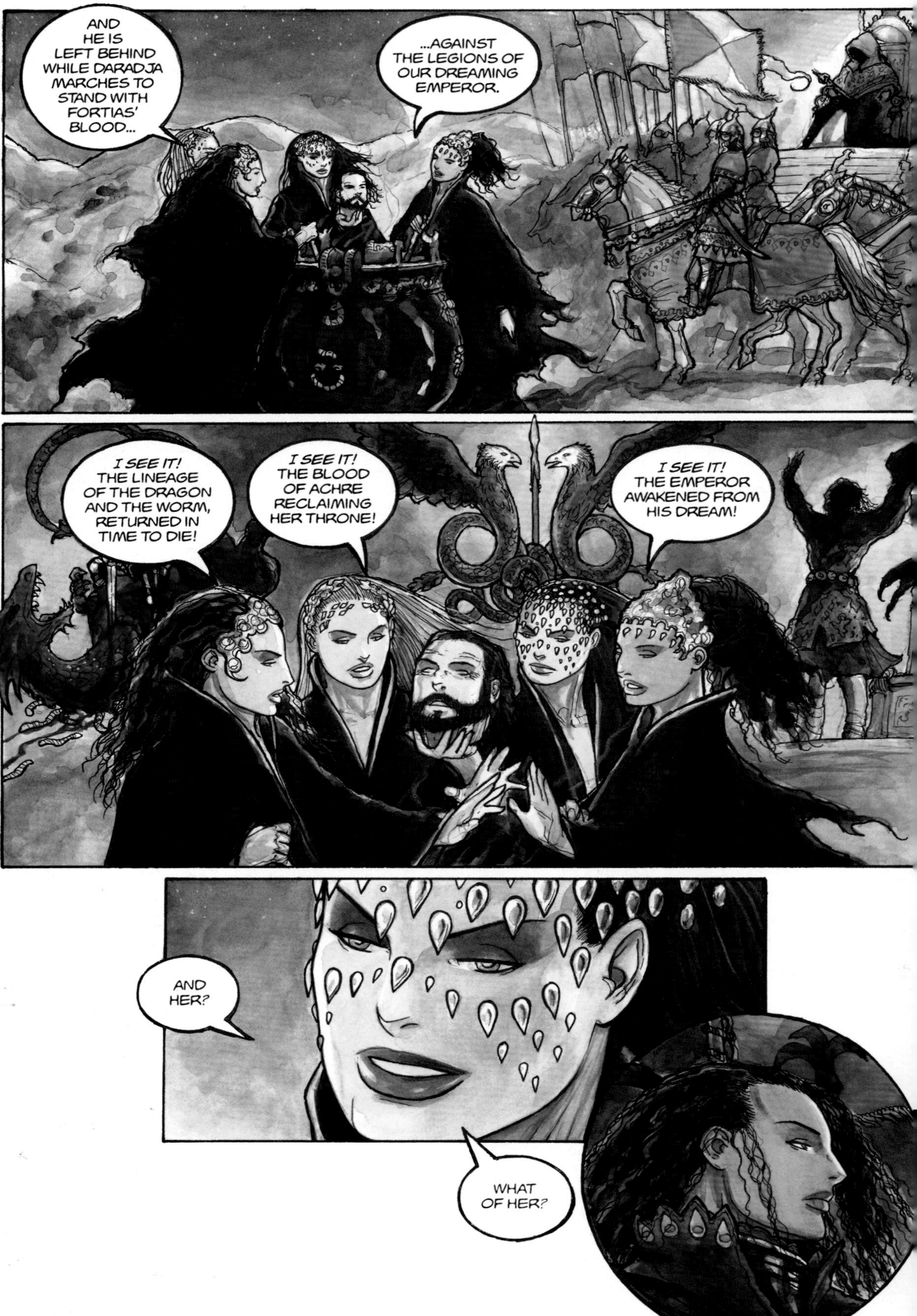

AND HE IS LEFT BEHIND WHILE DARADJA MARCHES TO STAND WITH FORTIAS' BLOOD...
...AGAINST THE LEGIONS OF OUR DREAMING EMPEROR.
I SEE IT! THE LINEAGE OF THE DRAGON AND THE WORM, RETURNED IN TIME TO DIE!
I SEE IT! THE BLOOD OF ACHRE RECLAIMING HER THRONE!
I SEE IT! THE EMPEROR AWAKENED FROM HIS DREAM!
AND HER?
WHAT OF HER?

THE THIRD
BOOK OF DOOMS

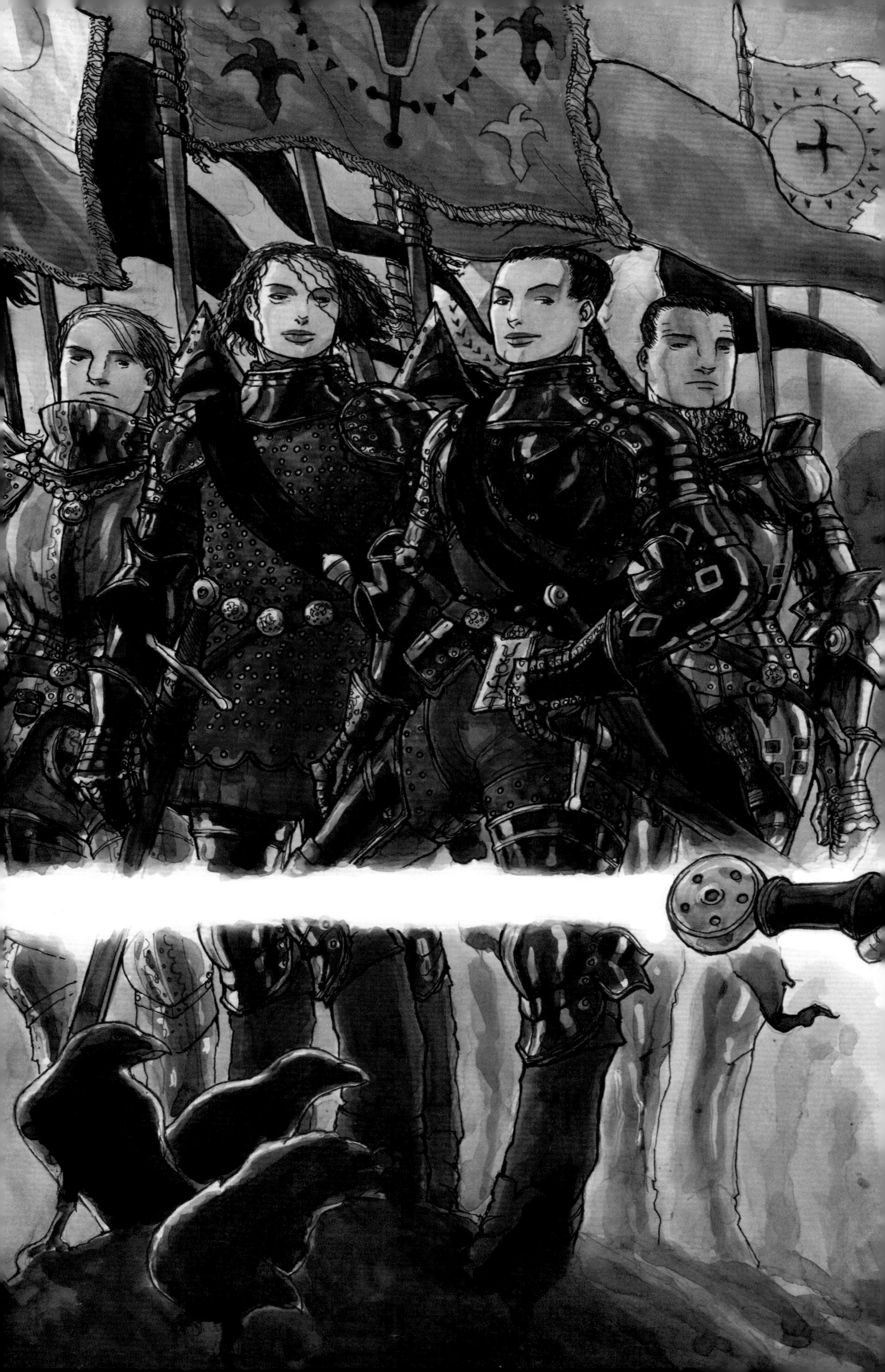

Chapter One

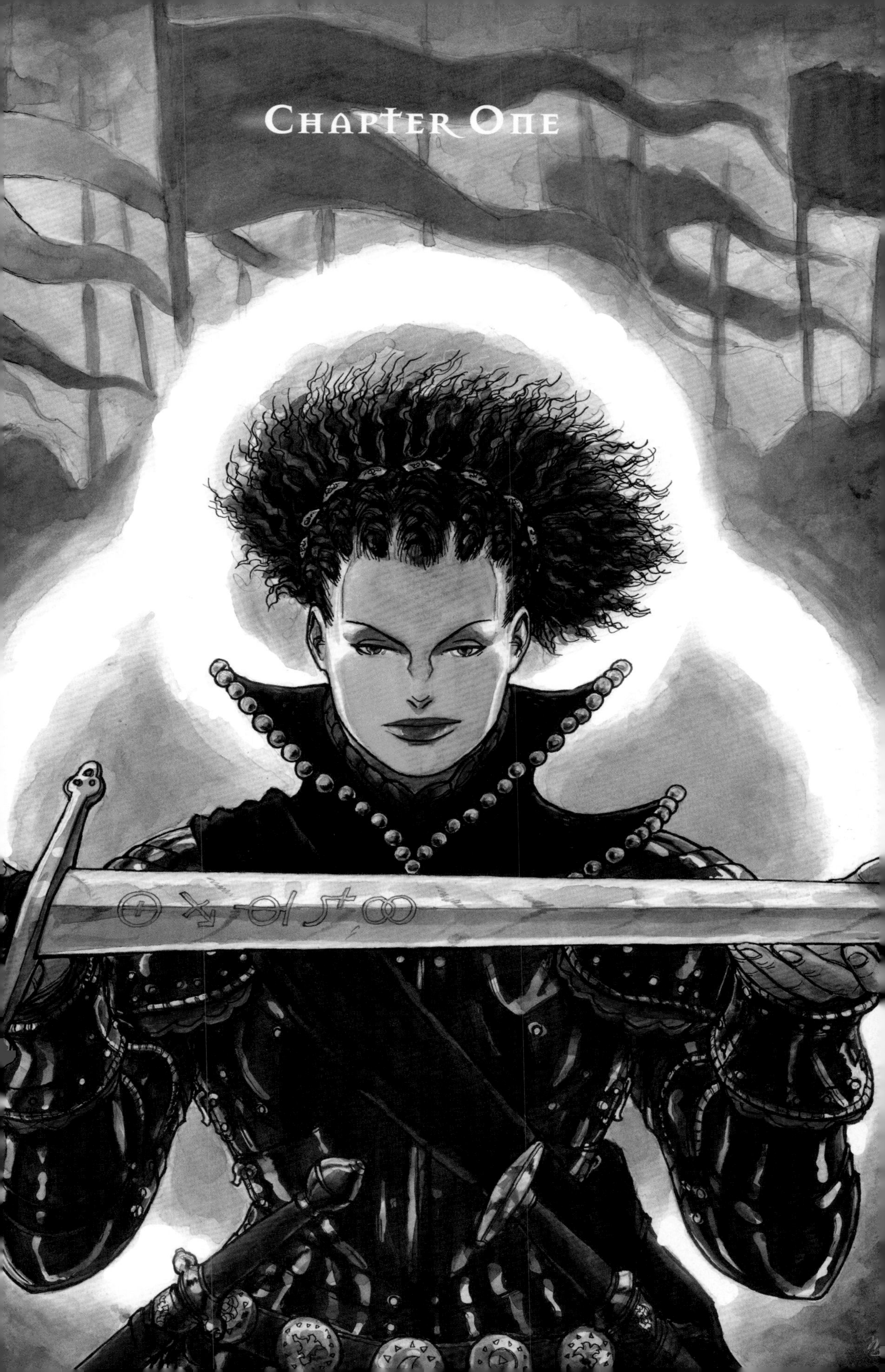

The Remains

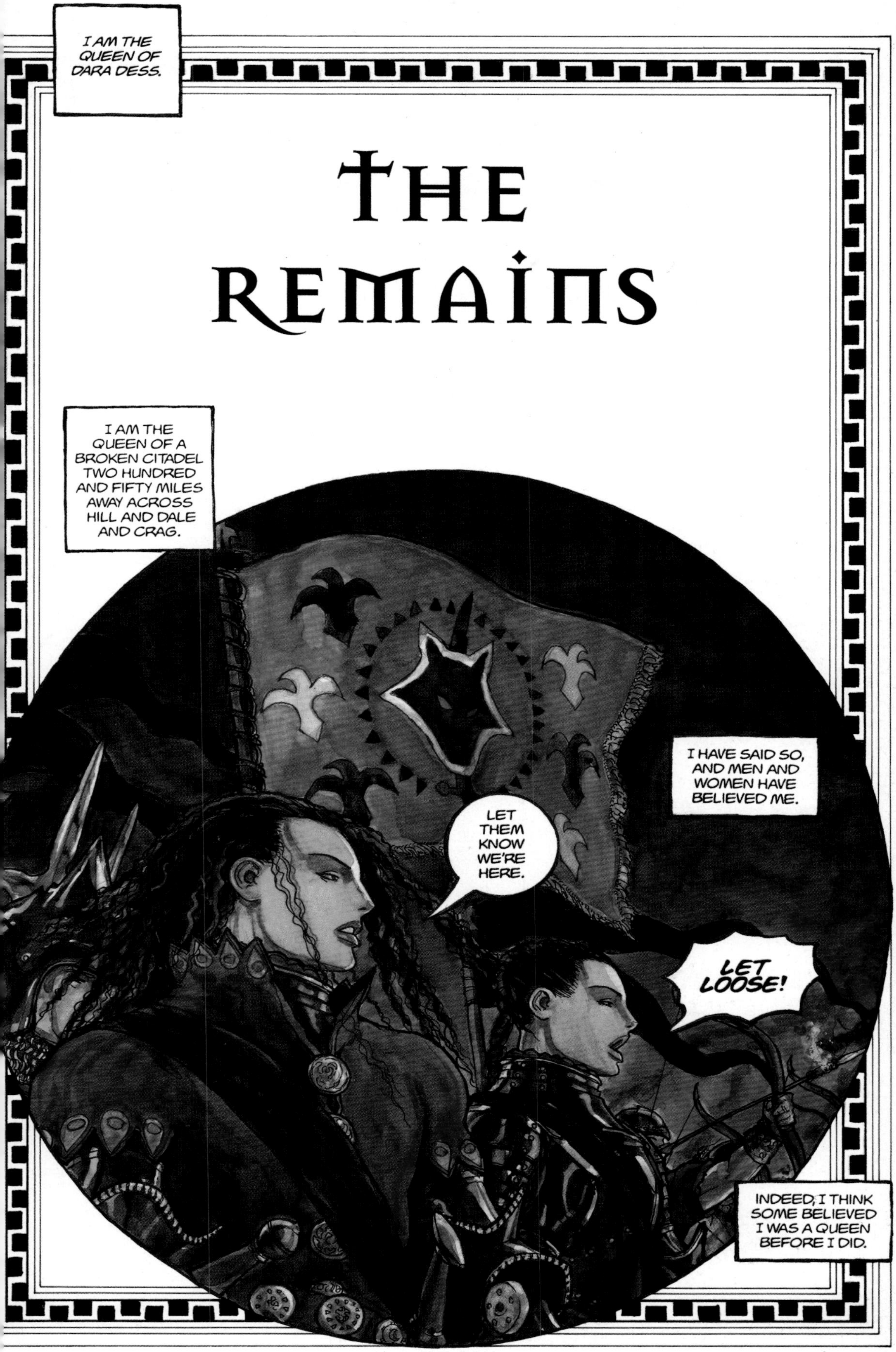
I AM THE QUEEN OF DARA DESS.
I AM THE QUEEN OF A BROKEN CITADEL TWO HUNDRED AND FIFTY MILES AWAY ACROSS HILL AND DALE AND CRAG.
I HAVE SAID SO, AND MEN AND WOMEN HAVE BELIEVED ME.
LET THEM KNOW WE'RE HERE.
LET LOOSE!
INDEED, I THINK SOME BELIEVED I WAS A QUEEN BEFORE I DID.

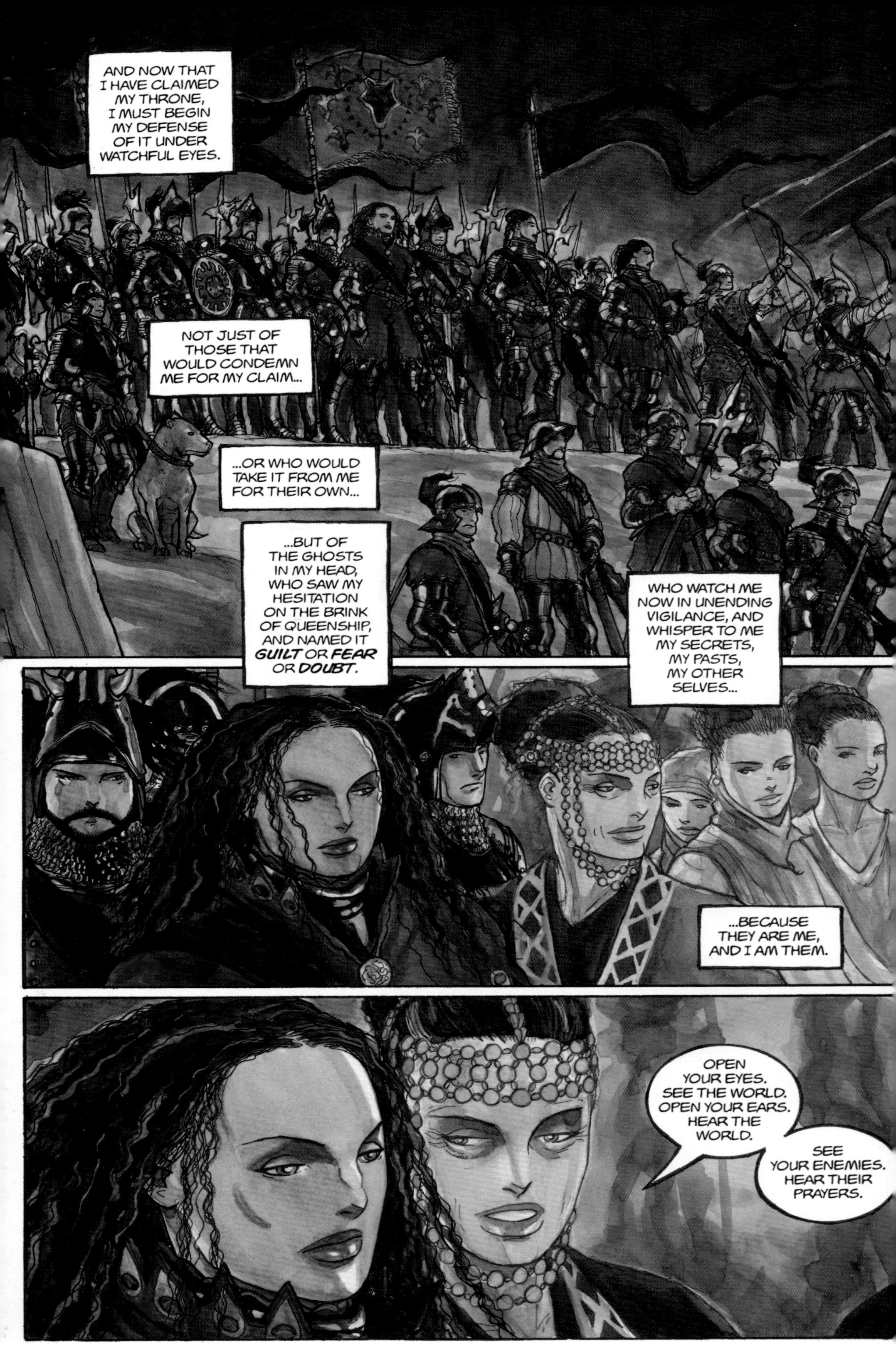
AND NOW THAT I HAVE CLAIMED MY THRONE, I MUST BEGIN MY DEFENSE OF IT UNDER WATCHFUL EYES.
NOT JUST OF THOSE THAT WOULD CONDEMN ME FOR MY CLAIM...
...OR WHO WOULD TAKE IT FROM ME FOR THEIR OWN...
...BUT OF THE GHOSTS IN MY HEAD, WHO SAW MY HESITATION ON THE BRINK OF QUEENSHIP, AND NAMED IT GUILT OR FEAR OR DOUBT.
WHO WATCH ME NOW IN UNENDING VIGILANCE, AND WHISPER TO ME MY SECRETS, MY PASTS, MY OTHER SELVES...
...BECAUSE THEY ARE ME, AND I AM THEM.
OPEN YOUR EYES. SEE THE WORLD. OPEN YOUR EARS. HEAR THE WORLD.
SEE YOUR ENEMIES. HEAR THEIR PRAYERS.

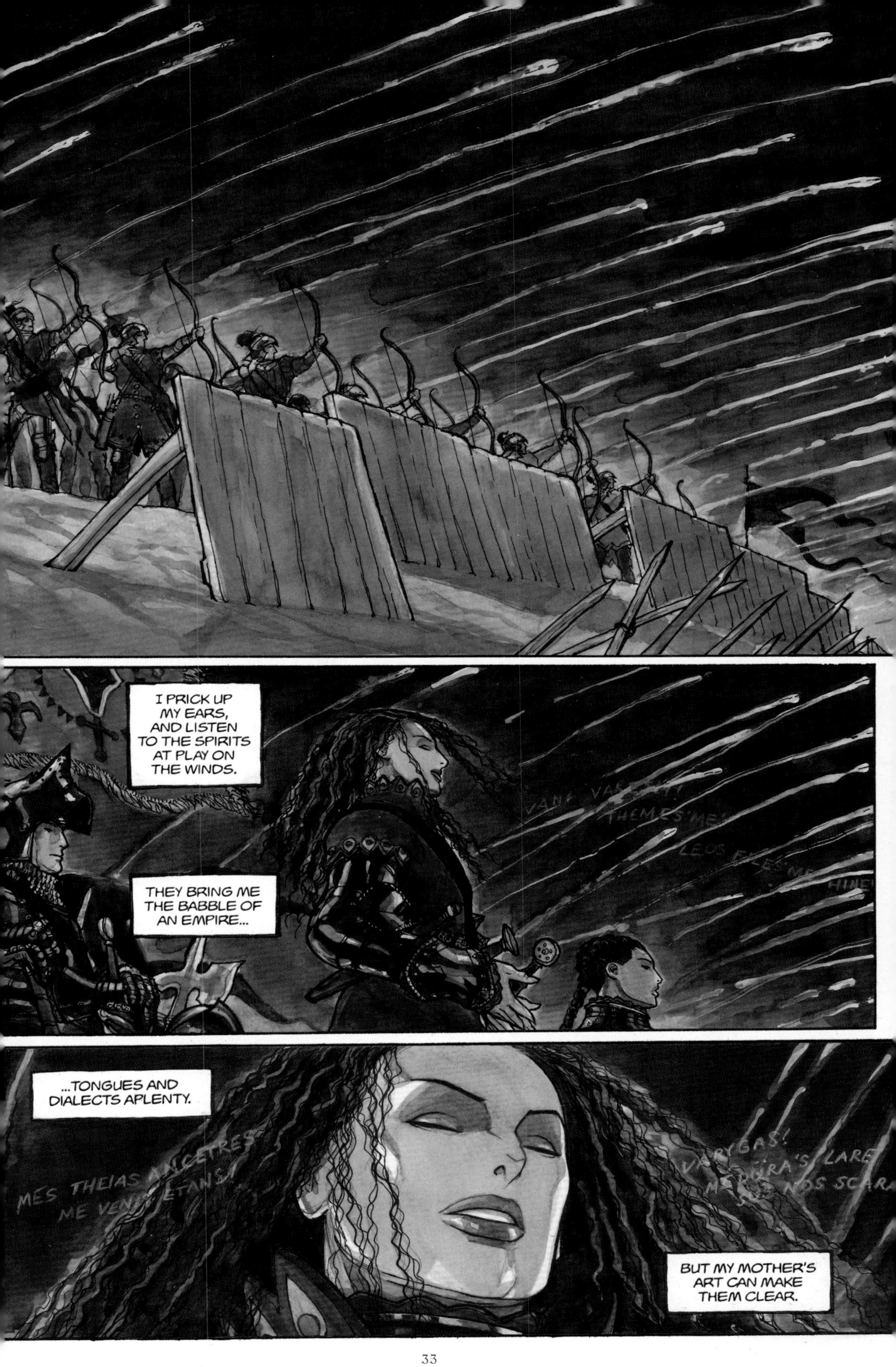
I PRICK UP MY EARS, AND LISTEN TO THE SPIRITS AT PLAY ON THE WINDS.
THEY BRING ME THE BABBLE OF AN EMPIRE...
...TONGUES AND DIALECTS APLENTY.
BUT MY MOTHER'S ART CAN MAKE THEM CLEAR.

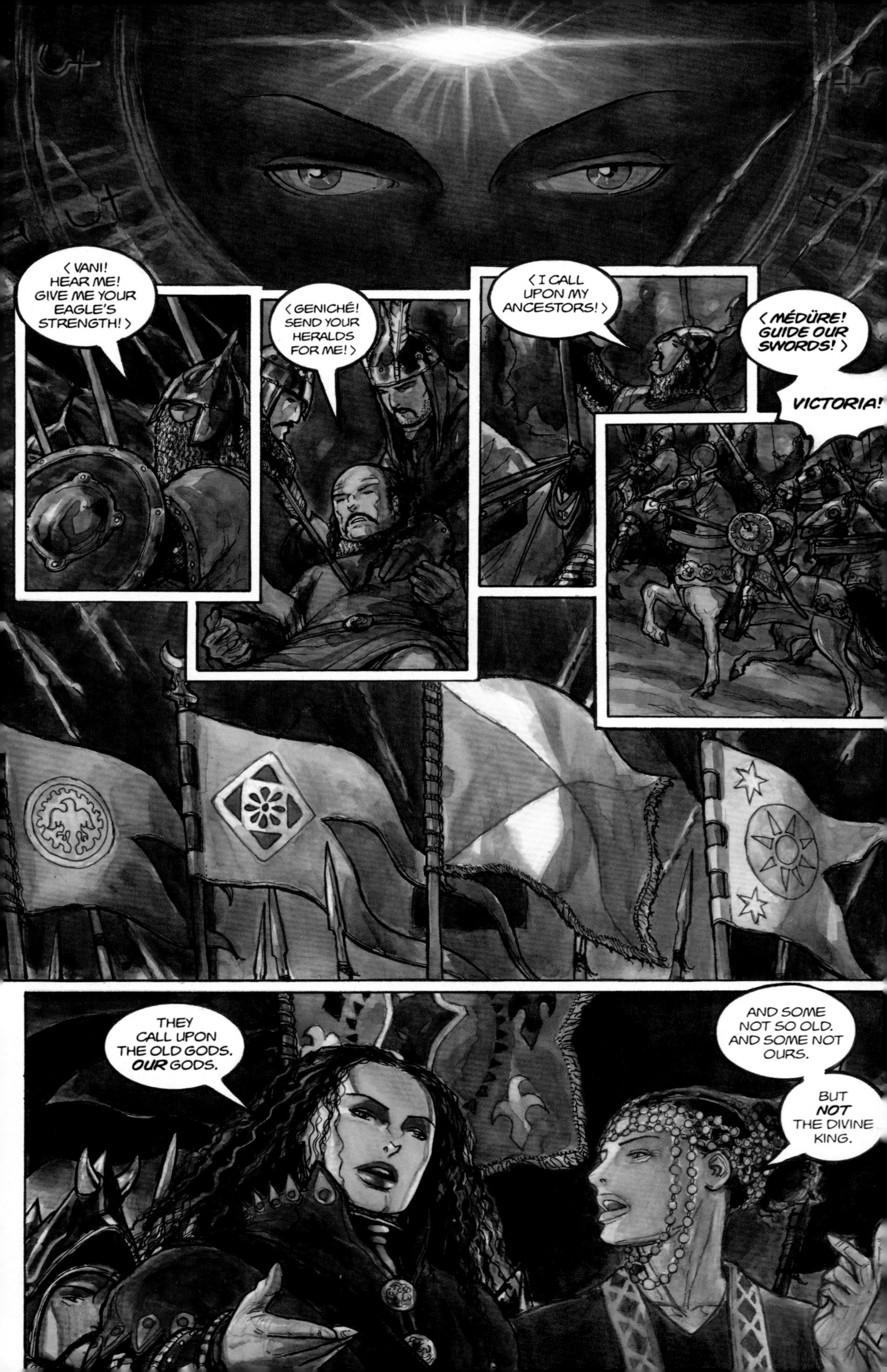

⟨ VANI! HEAR ME! GIVE ME YOUR EAGLE'S STRENGTH! ⟩
⟨ GENICHÉ! SEND YOUR HERALDS FOR ME! ⟩
⟨ I CALL UPON MY ANCESTORS! ⟩
⟨ MÉDÜRE! GUIDE OUR SWORDS! ⟩
VICTORIA!
THEY CALL UPON THE OLD GODS. OUR GODS.
AND SOME NOT SO OLD. AND SOME NOT OURS.
BUT NOT THE DIVINE KING.

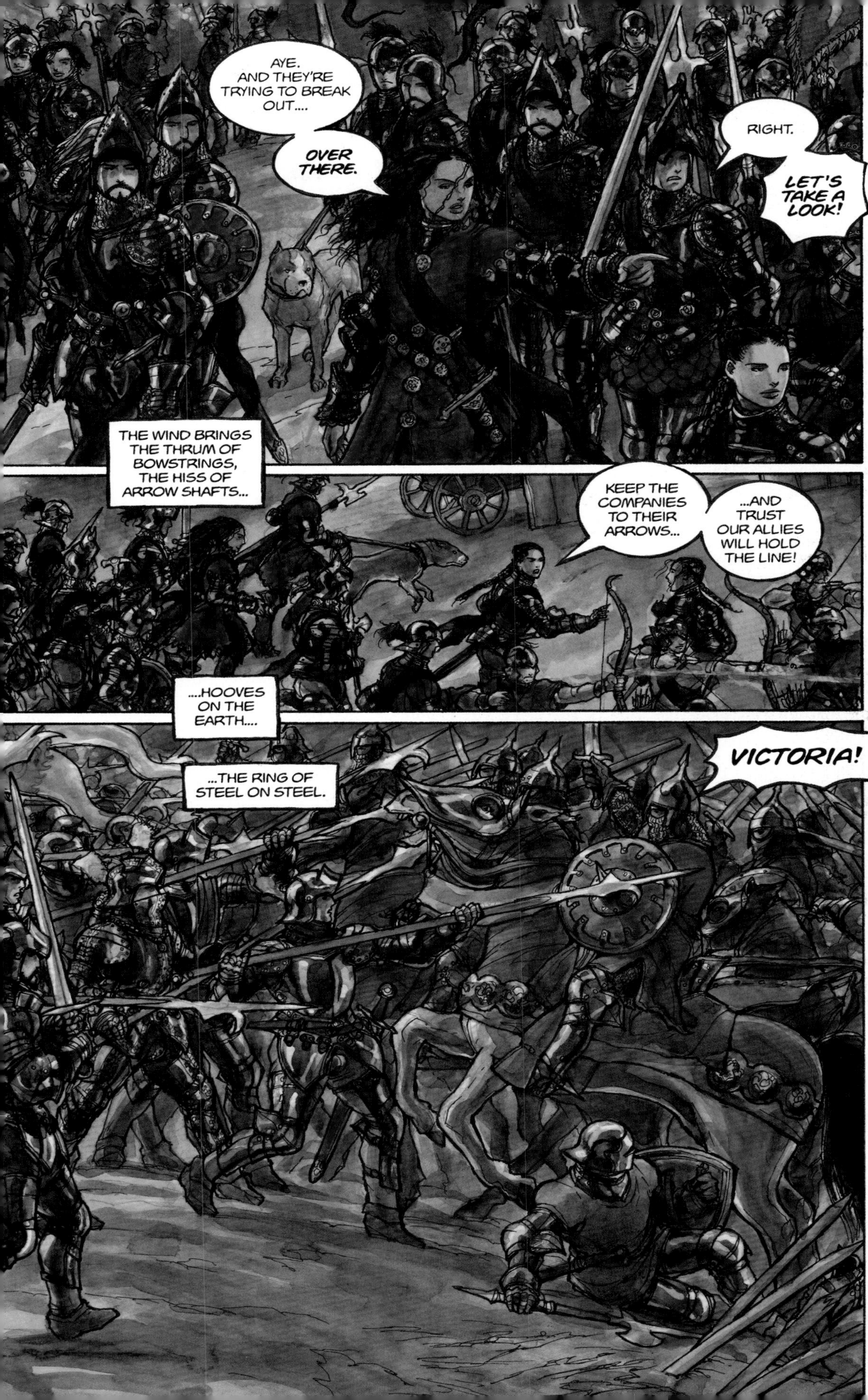
AYE. AND THEY'RE TRYING TO BREAK OUT....
OVER THERE.
RIGHT.
LET'S TAKE A LOOK!
THE WIND BRINGS THE THRUM OF BOWSTRINGS, THE HISS OF ARROW SHAFTS...
KEEP THE COMPANIES TO THEIR ARROWS...
...AND TRUST OUR ALLIES WILL HOLD THE LINE!
....HOOVES ON THE EARTH....
...THE RING OF STEEL ON STEEL.
VICTORIA!

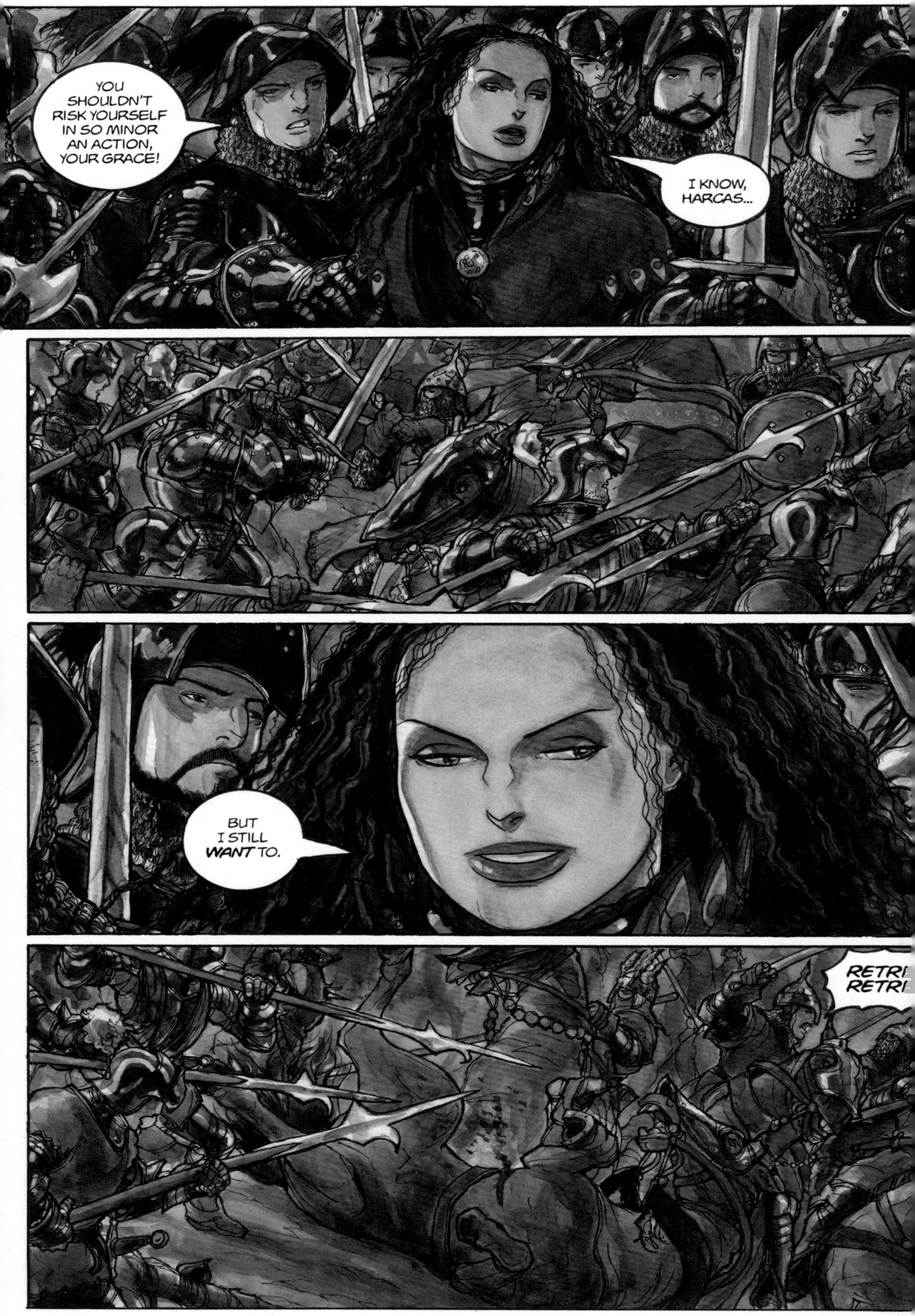
YOU SHOULDN'T RISK YOURSELF IN SO MINOR AN ACTION, YOUR GRACE!
I KNOW, HARCAS...
BUT I STILL WANT TO.
RETRI RETRI

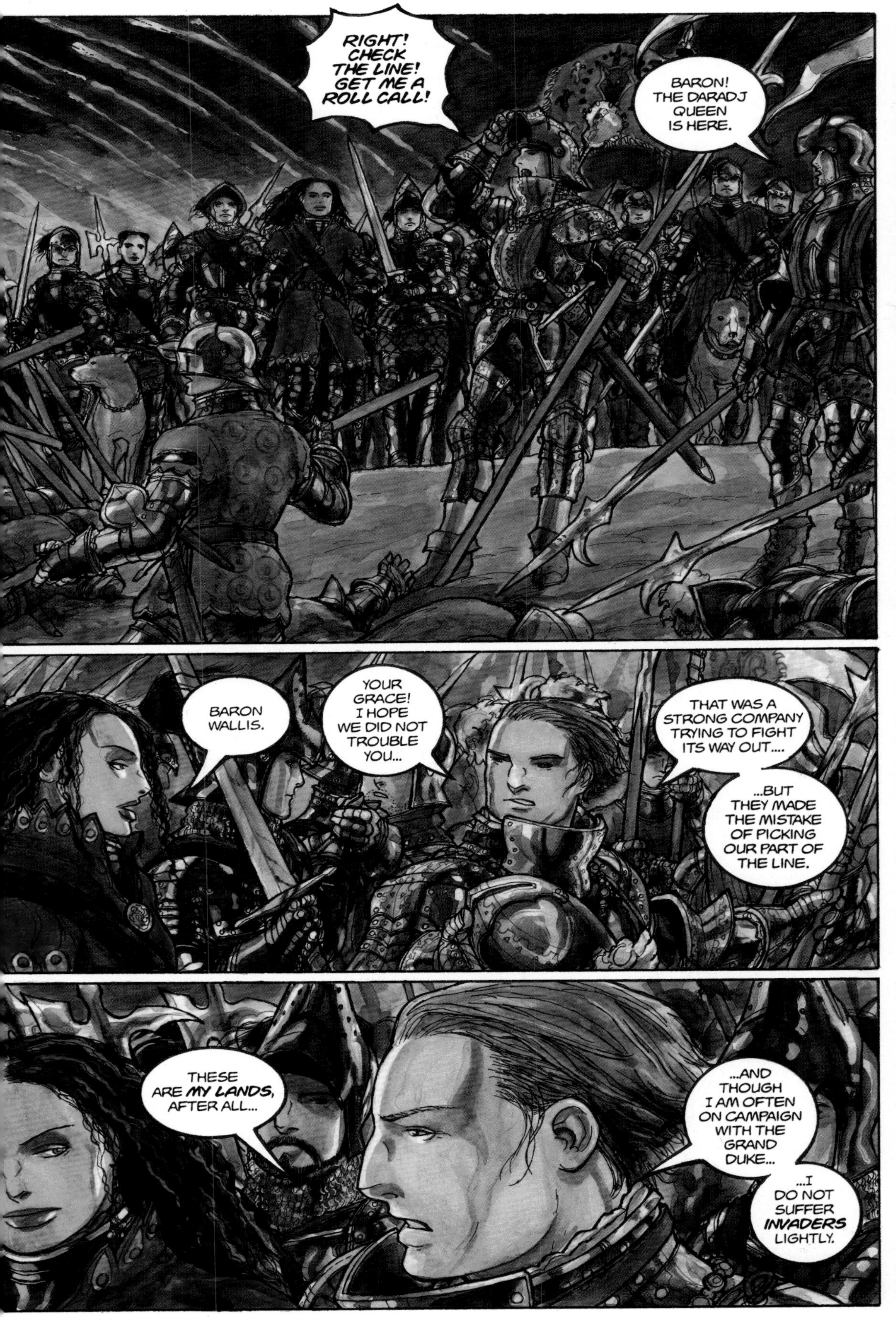
RIGHT! CHECK THE LINE! GET ME A ROLL CALL!
BARON! THE DARADJ QUEEN IS HERE.
BARON WALLIS.
YOUR GRACE! I HOPE WE DID NOT TROUBLE YOU...
THAT WAS A STRONG COMPANY TRYING TO FIGHT ITS WAY OUT....
...BUT THEY MADE THE MISTAKE OF PICKING OUR PART OF THE LINE.
THESE ARE MY LANDS, AFTER ALL...
...AND THOUGH I AM OFTEN ON CAMPAIGN WITH THE GRAND DUKE...
...I DO NOT SUFFER INVADERS LIGHTLY.

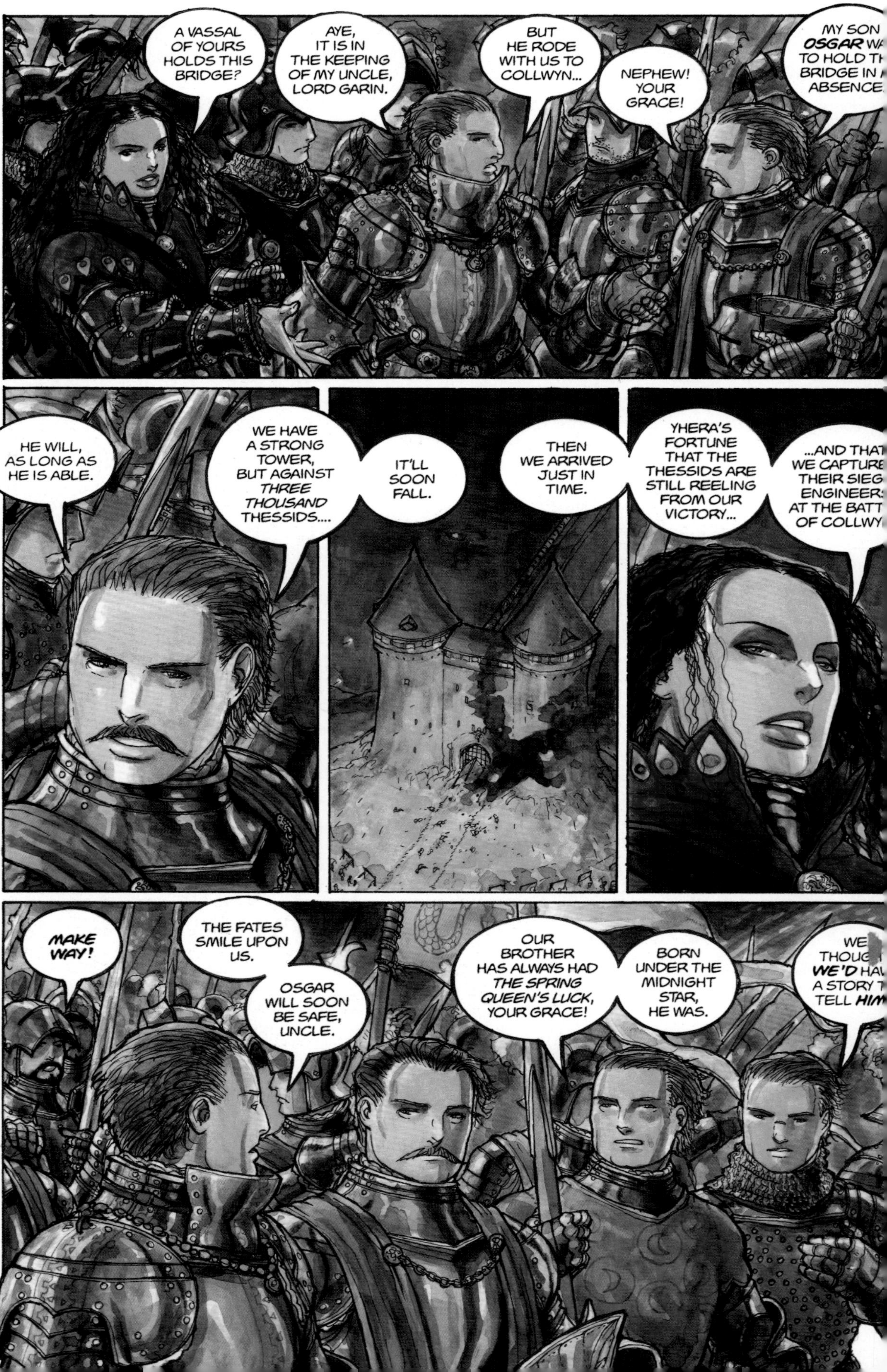
A VASSAL OF YOURS HOLDS THIS BRIDGE?
AYE, IT IS IN THE KEEPING OF MY UNCLE, LORD GARIN.
BUT HE RODE WITH US TO COLLWYN...
NEPHEW! YOUR GRACE!
MY SON *OSGAR* WA TO HOLD TH BRIDGE IN ABSENCE
HE WILL, AS LONG AS HE IS ABLE.
WE HAVE A STRONG TOWER, BUT AGAINST *THREE THOUSAND* THESSIDS....
IT'LL SOON FALL.
THEN WE ARRIVED JUST IN TIME.
YHERA'S FORTUNE THAT THE THESSIDS ARE STILL REELING FROM OUR VICTORY...
...AND THAT WE CAPTURE THEIR SIEG ENGINEER AT THE BATT OF COLLWY
MAKE WAY!
THE FATES SMILE UPON US.
OSGAR WILL SOON BE SAFE, UNCLE.
OUR BROTHER HAS ALWAYS HAD *THE SPRING QUEEN'S LUCK,* YOUR GRACE!
BORN UNDER THE MIDNIGHT STAR, HE WAS.
WE THOUG *WE'D* HA A STORY T TELL *HIM*

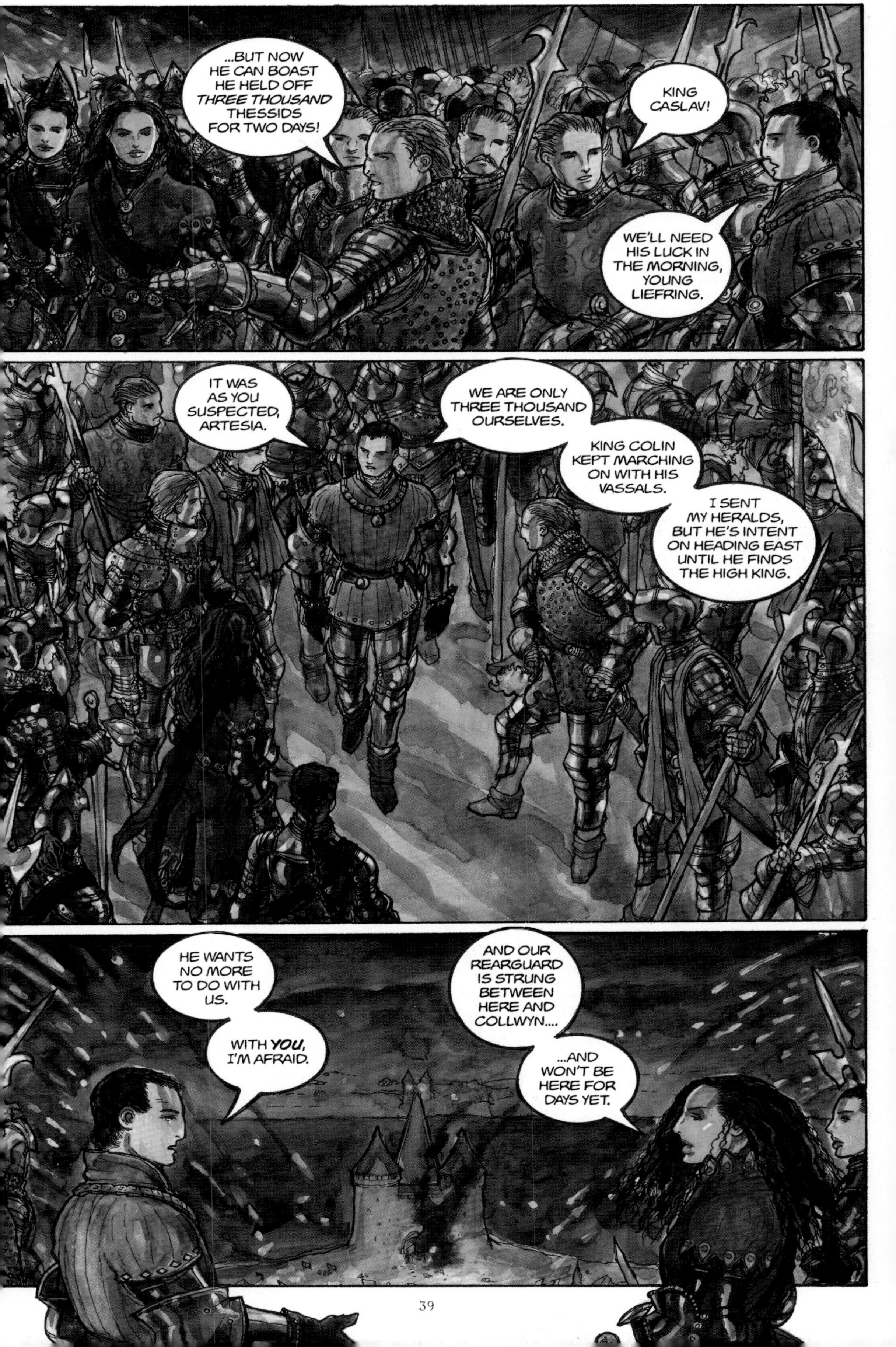
...BUT NOW HE CAN BOAST HE HELD OFF *THREE THOUSAND* THESSIDS FOR TWO DAYS!
KING CASLAV!
WE'LL NEED HIS LUCK IN THE MORNING, YOUNG LIEFRING.
IT WAS AS YOU SUSPECTED, ARTESIA.
WE ARE ONLY THREE THOUSAND OURSELVES.
KING COLIN KEPT MARCHING ON WITH HIS VASSALS.
I SENT MY HERALDS, BUT HE'S INTENT ON HEADING EAST UNTIL HE FINDS THE HIGH KING.
HE WANTS NO MORE TO DO WITH US.
WITH ***YOU***, I'M AFRAID.
AND OUR REARGUARD IS STRUNG BETWEEN HERE AND COLLWYN....
...AND WON'T BE HERE FOR DAYS YET.

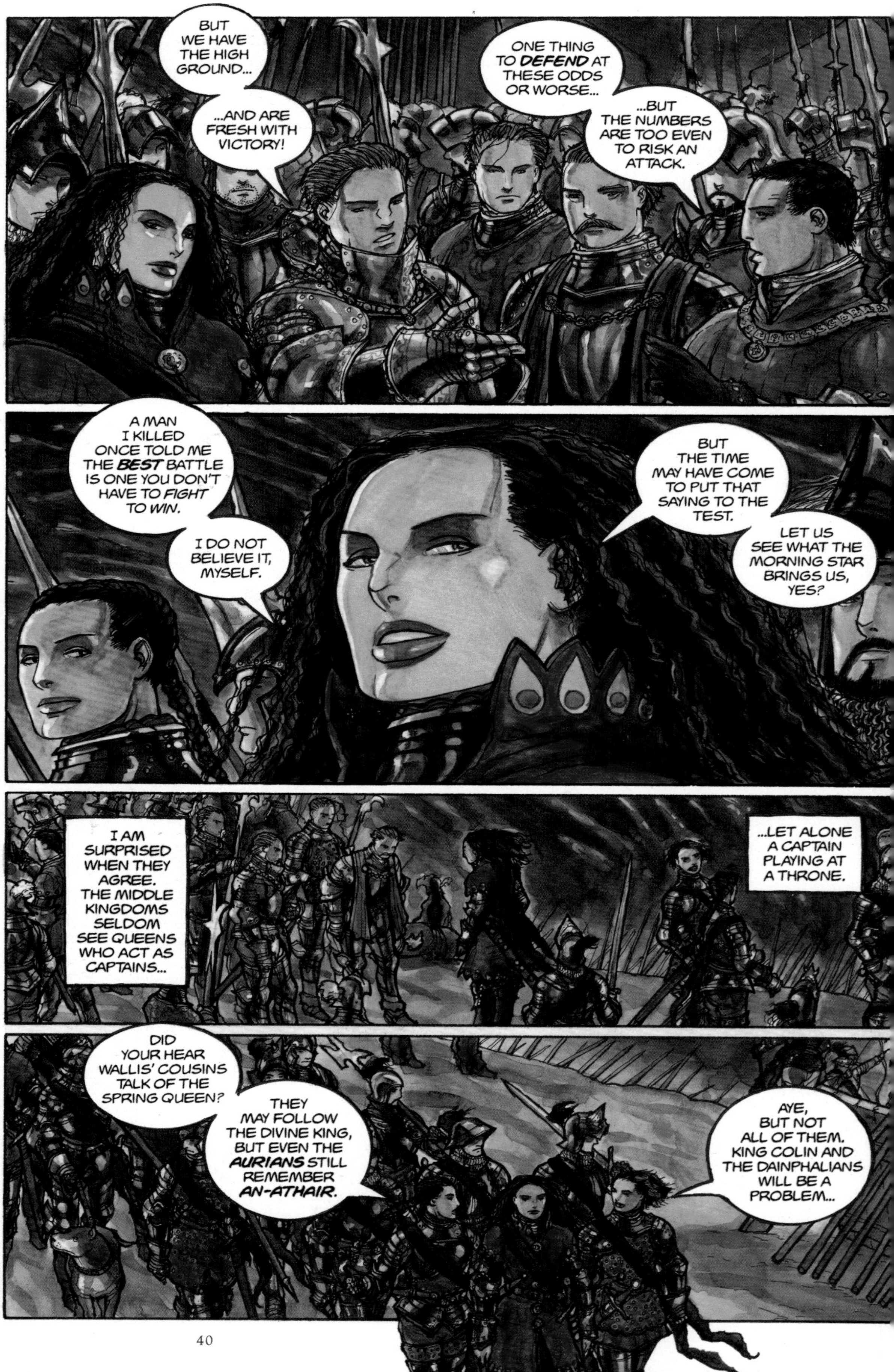
BUT WE HAVE THE HIGH GROUND...
...AND ARE FRESH WITH VICTORY!
ONE THING TO DEFEND AT THESE ODDS OR WORSE...
...BUT THE NUMBERS ARE TOO EVEN TO RISK AN ATTACK.
A MAN I KILLED ONCE TOLD ME THE BEST BATTLE IS ONE YOU DON'T HAVE TO FIGHT TO WIN.
I DO NOT BELIEVE IT, MYSELF.
BUT THE TIME MAY HAVE COME TO PUT THAT SAYING TO THE TEST.
LET US SEE WHAT THE MORNING STAR BRINGS US, YES?
I AM SURPRISED WHEN THEY AGREE. THE MIDDLE KINGDOMS SELDOM SEE QUEENS WHO ACT AS CAPTAINS...
...LET ALONE A CAPTAIN PLAYING AT A THRONE.
DID YOUR HEAR WALLIS' COUSINS TALK OF THE SPRING QUEEN?
THEY MAY FOLLOW THE DIVINE KING, BUT EVEN THE AURIANS STILL REMEMBER AN-ATHAIR.
AYE, BUT NOT ALL OF THEM. KING COLIN AND THE DAINPHALIANS WILL BE A PROBLEM...

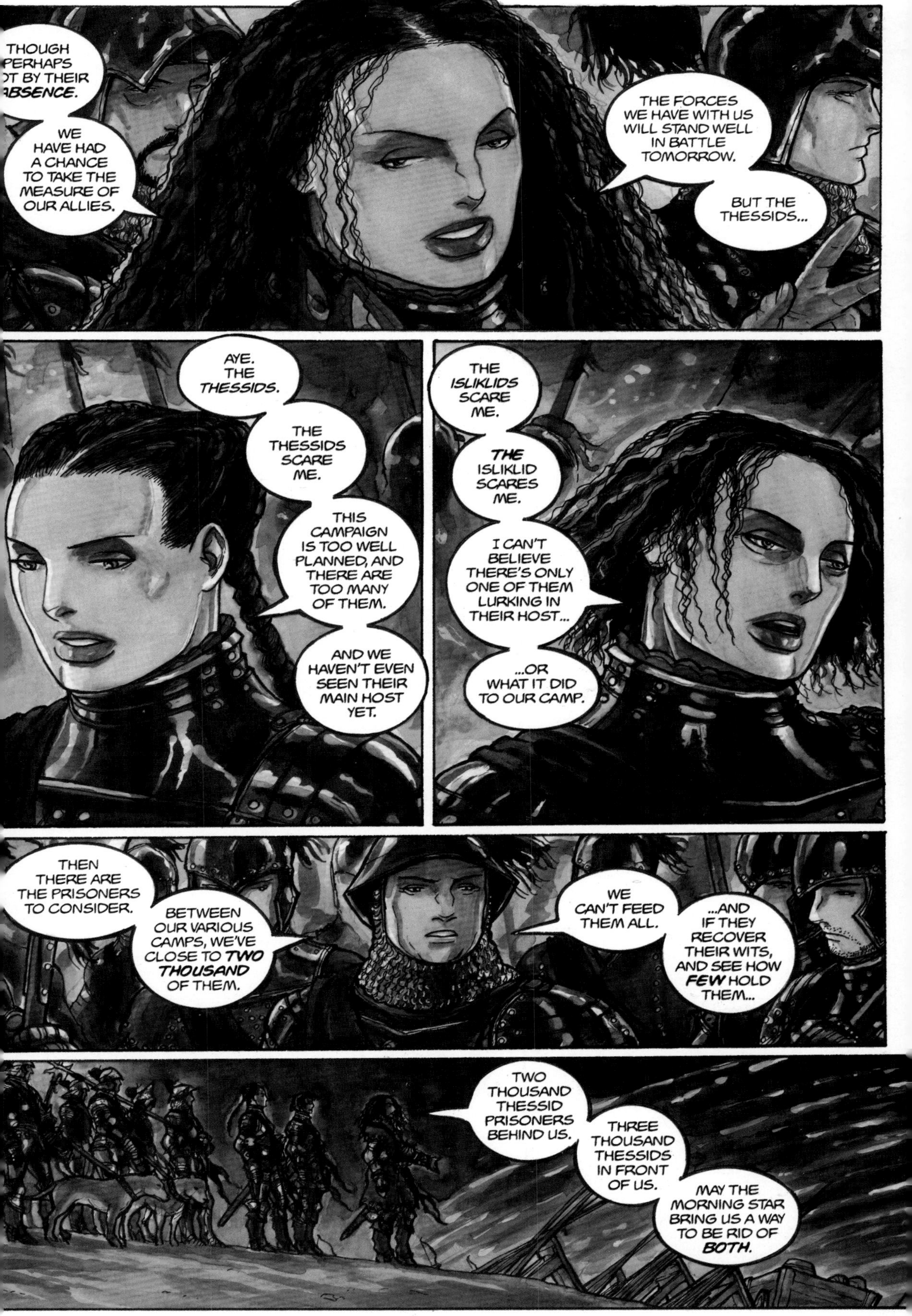
THOUGH PERHAPS OT BY THEIR ABSENCE.
WE HAVE HAD A CHANCE TO TAKE THE MEASURE OF OUR ALLIES.
THE FORCES WE HAVE WITH US WILL STAND WELL IN BATTLE TOMORROW.
BUT THE THESSIDS...
AYE. THE THESSIDS.
THE THESSIDS SCARE ME.
THIS CAMPAIGN IS TOO WELL PLANNED, AND THERE ARE TOO MANY OF THEM.
AND WE HAVEN'T EVEN SEEN THEIR MAIN HOST YET.
THE ISLIKLIDS SCARE ME.
THE ISLIKLID SCARES ME.
I CAN'T BELIEVE THERE'S ONLY ONE OF THEM LURKING IN THEIR HOST...
...OR WHAT IT DID TO OUR CAMP.
THEN THERE ARE THE PRISONERS TO CONSIDER.
BETWEEN OUR VARIOUS CAMPS, WE'VE CLOSE TO TWO THOUSAND OF THEM.
WE CAN'T FEED THEM ALL.
...AND IF THEY RECOVER THEIR WITS, AND SEE HOW FEW HOLD THEM...
TWO THOUSAND THESSID PRISONERS BEHIND US.
THREE THOUSAND THESSIDS IN FRONT OF US.
MAY THE MORNING STAR BRING US A WAY TO BE RID OF BOTH.

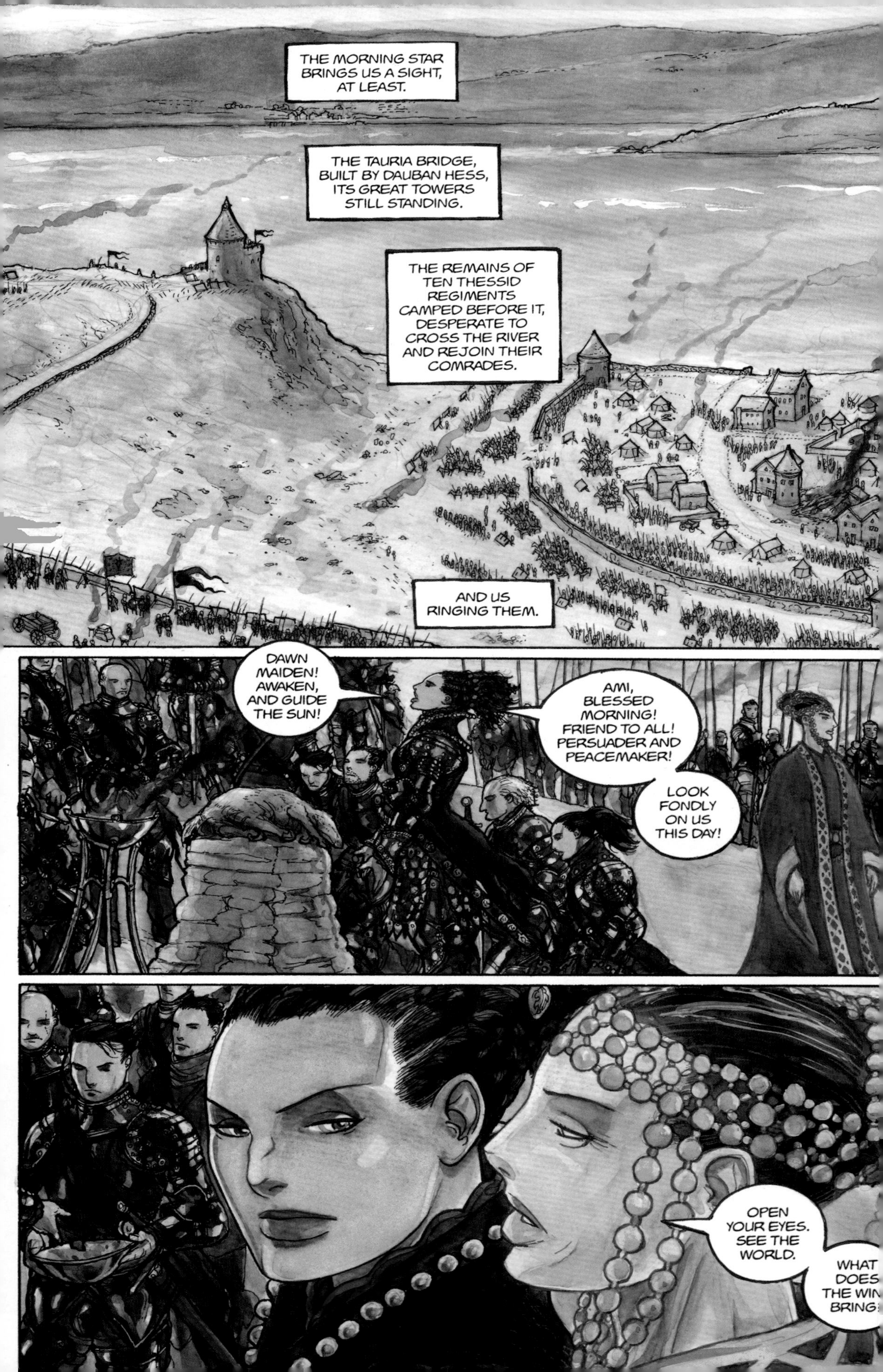
THE MORNING STAR BRINGS US A SIGHT, AT LEAST.
THE TAURIA BRIDGE, BUILT BY DAUBAN HESS, ITS GREAT TOWERS STILL STANDING.
THE REMAINS OF TEN THESSID REGIMENTS CAMPED BEFORE IT, DESPERATE TO CROSS THE RIVER AND REJOIN THEIR COMRADES.
AND US RINGING THEM.
DAWN MAIDEN! AWAKEN, AND GUIDE THE SUN!
AMI, BLESSED MORNING! FRIEND TO ALL! PERSUADER AND PEACEMAKER!
LOOK FONDLY ON US THIS DAY!
OPEN YOUR EYES. SEE THE WORLD.

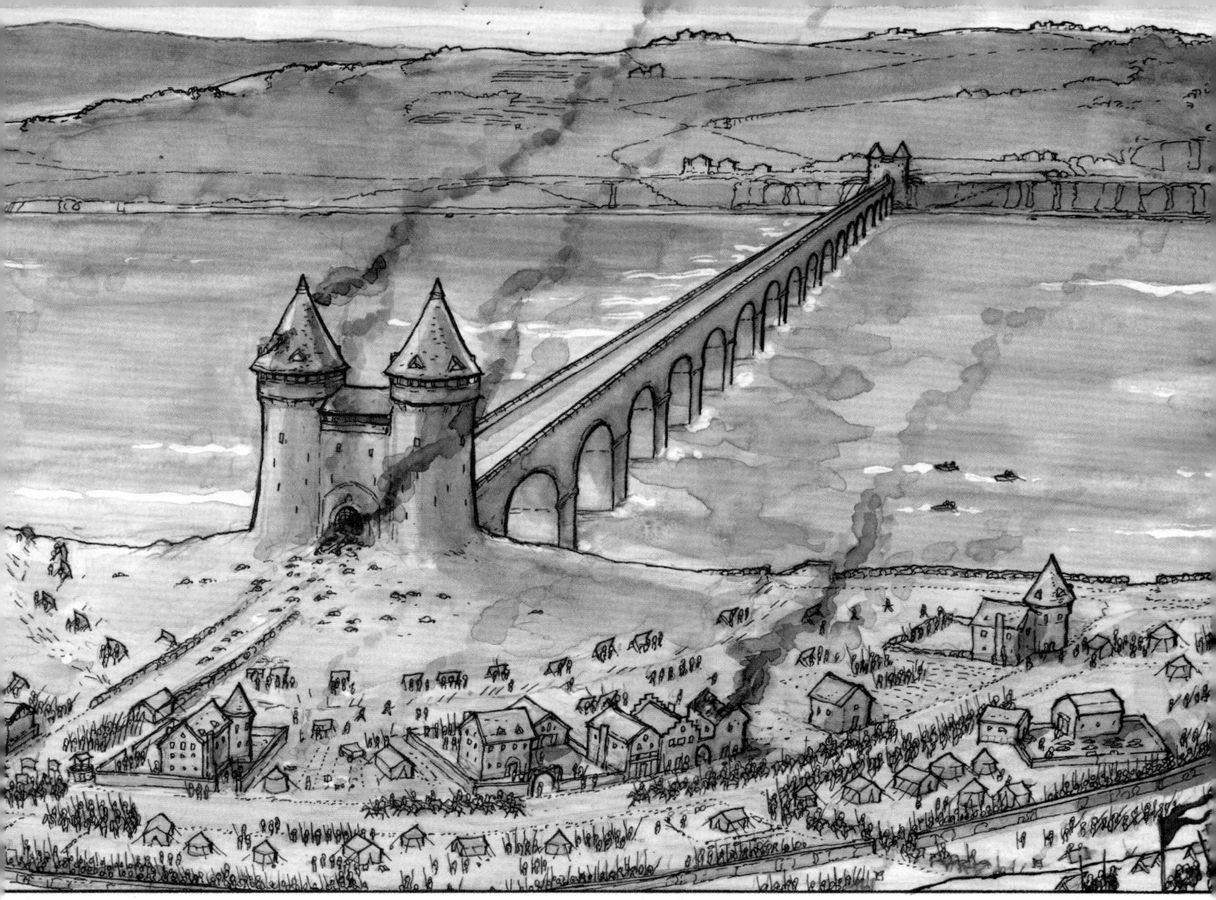

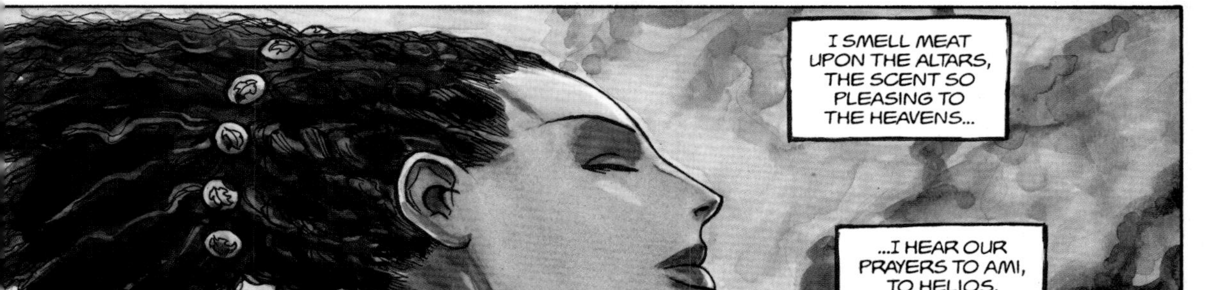
I SMELL MEAT UPON THE ALTARS, THE SCENT SO PLEASING TO THE HEAVENS...
...I HEAR OUR PRAYERS TO AMI, TO HELIOS, TO YHERA, TO THE GORGONAE – OUR GODS, OUR HEROES, OUR ANCESTORS...
AMIS! AMAT

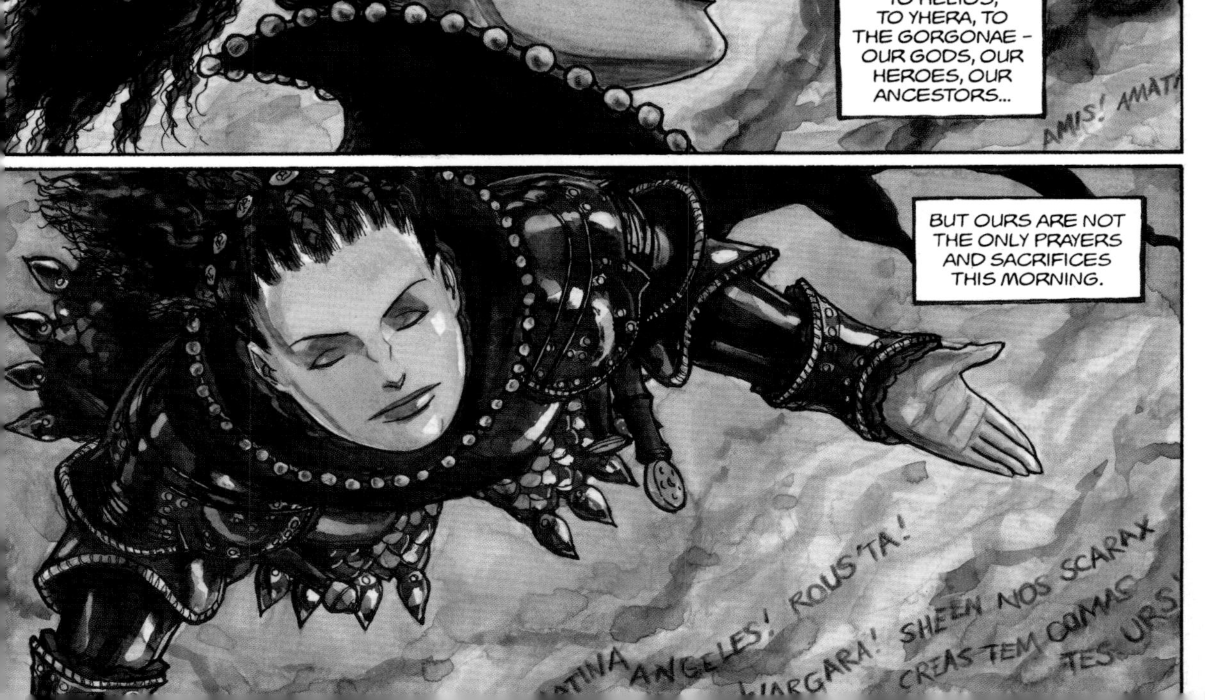
BUT OURS ARE NOT THE ONLY PRAYERS AND SACRIFICES THIS MORNING.
ATINA ANGELES! ROUS'TA!
WARGARA! SHEEN NOS SCARAX
CREAS TEM COMAS
TES URS

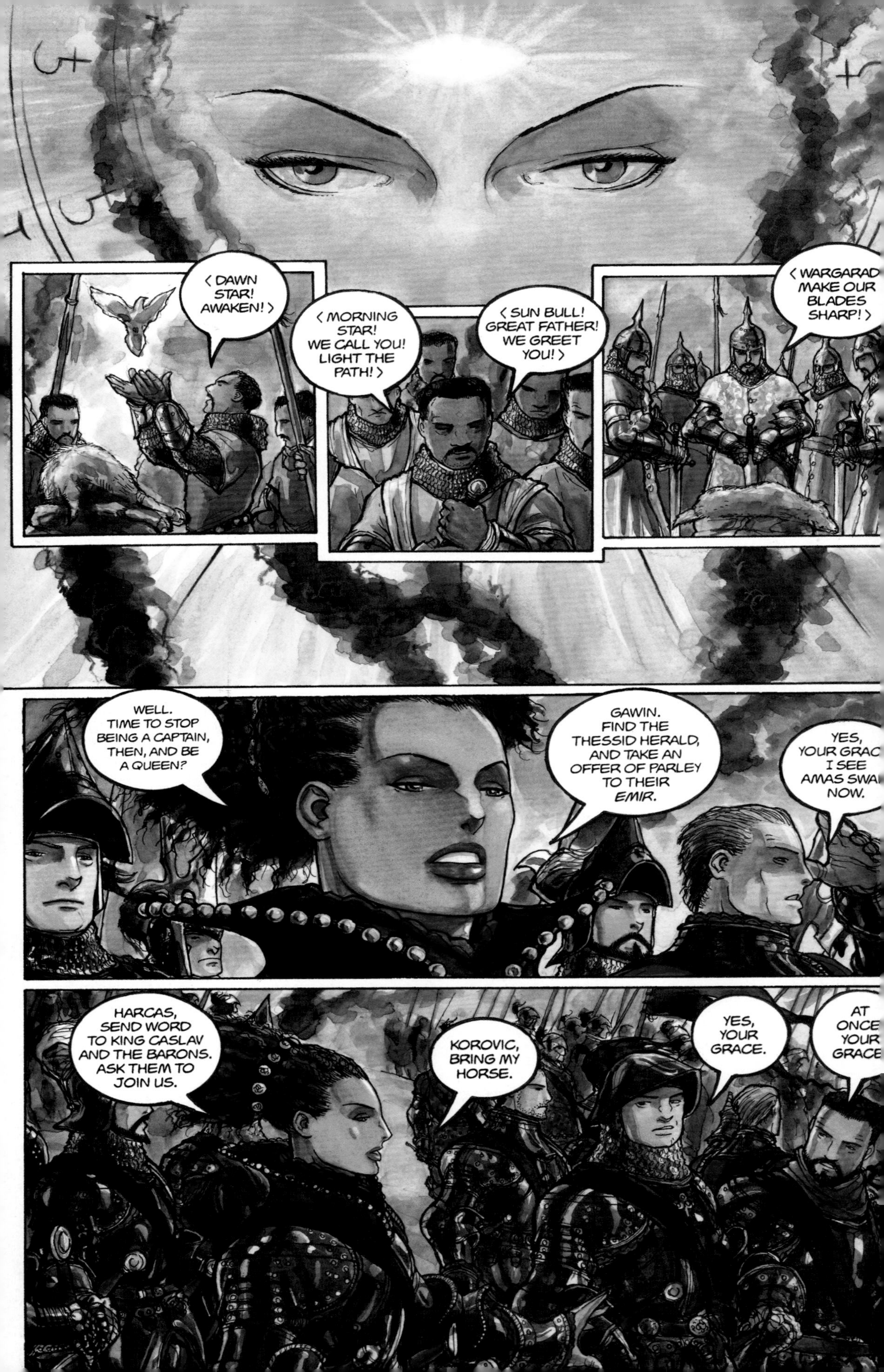
< DAWN STAR! AWAKEN! >
< MORNING STAR! WE CALL YOU! LIGHT THE PATH! >
< SUN BULL! GREAT FATHER! WE GREET YOU! >
< WARGARAD MAKE OUR BLADES SHARP! >
WELL. TIME TO STOP BEING A CAPTAIN, THEN, AND BE A QUEEN?
GAWIN. FIND THE THESSID HERALD, AND TAKE AN OFFER OF PARLEY TO THEIR *EMIR*.
YES, YOUR GRAC I SEE AMAS SWA NOW.
HARCAS, SEND WORD TO KING CASLAV AND THE BARONS. ASK THEM TO JOIN US.
KOROVIC, BRING MY HORSE.
YES, YOUR GRACE.
AT ONCE YOUR GRACE

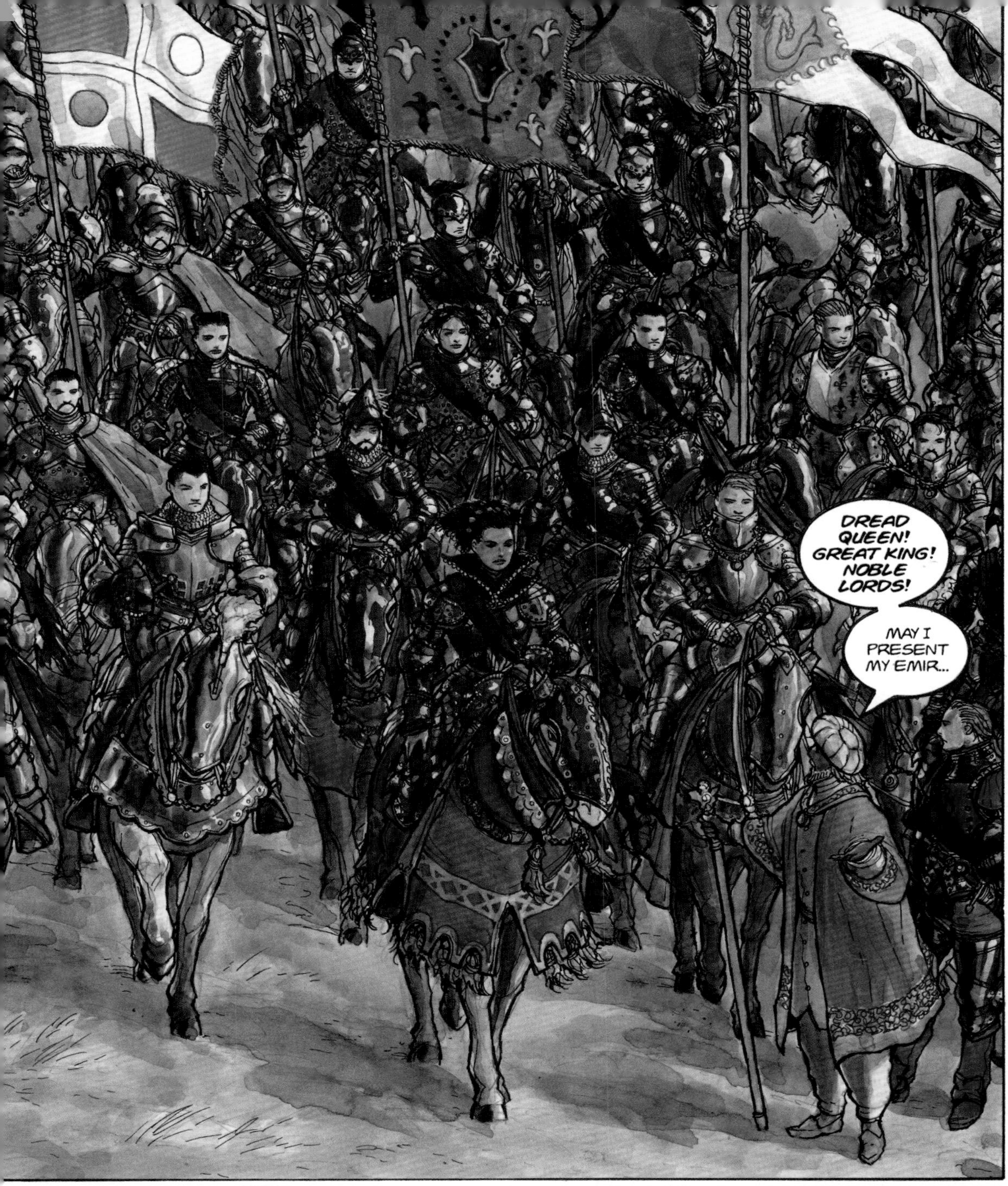
DREAD QUEEN! GREAT KING! NOBLE LORDS!
MAY I PRESENT MY EMIR...

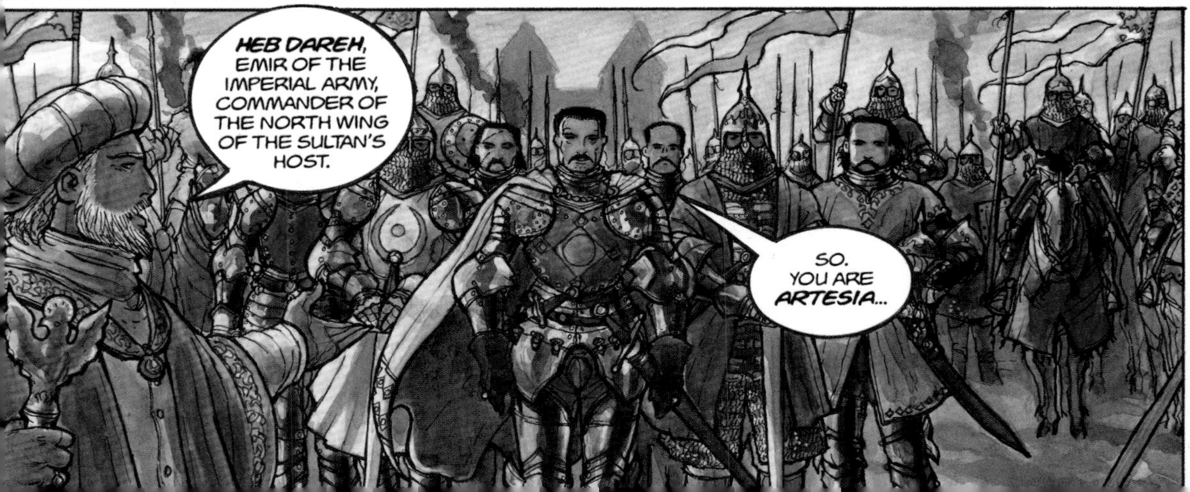
HEB DAREH, EMIR OF THE IMPERIAL ARMY, COMMANDER OF THE NORTH WING OF THE SULTAN'S HOST.
SO. YOU ARE ARTESIA...

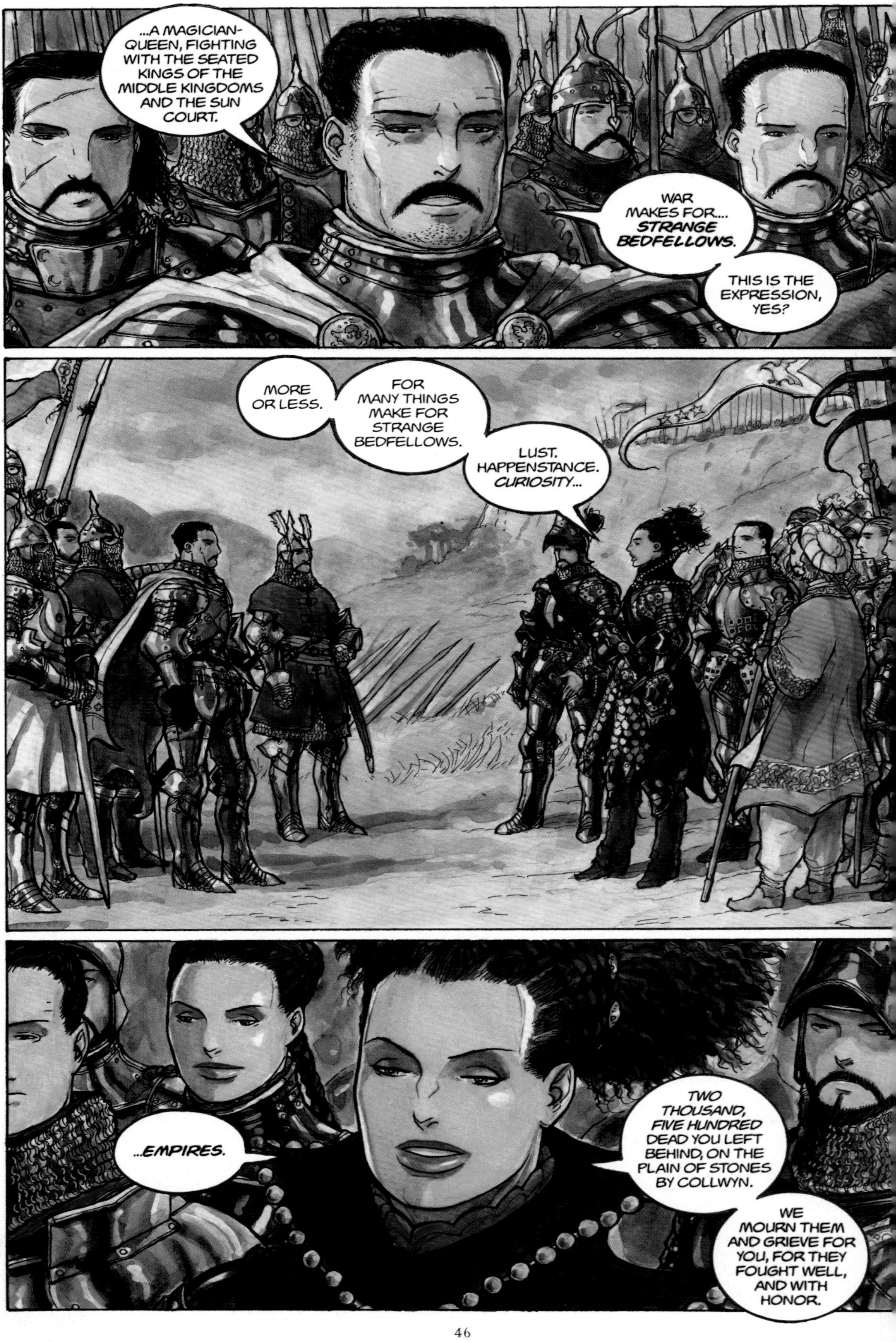
...A MAGICIAN-QUEEN, FIGHTING WITH THE SEATED KINGS OF THE MIDDLE KINGDOMS AND THE SUN COURT.
WAR MAKES FOR.... STRANGE BEDFELLOWS.
THIS IS THE EXPRESSION, YES?
MORE OR LESS.
FOR MANY THINGS MAKE FOR STRANGE BEDFELLOWS.
LUST. HAPPENSTANCE. CURIOSITY...
...EMPIRES.
TWO THOUSAND, FIVE HUNDRED DEAD YOU LEFT BEHIND, ON THE PLAIN OF STONES BY COLLWYN.
WE MOURN THEM AND GRIEVE FOR YOU, FOR THEY FOUGHT WELL, AND WITH HONOR.

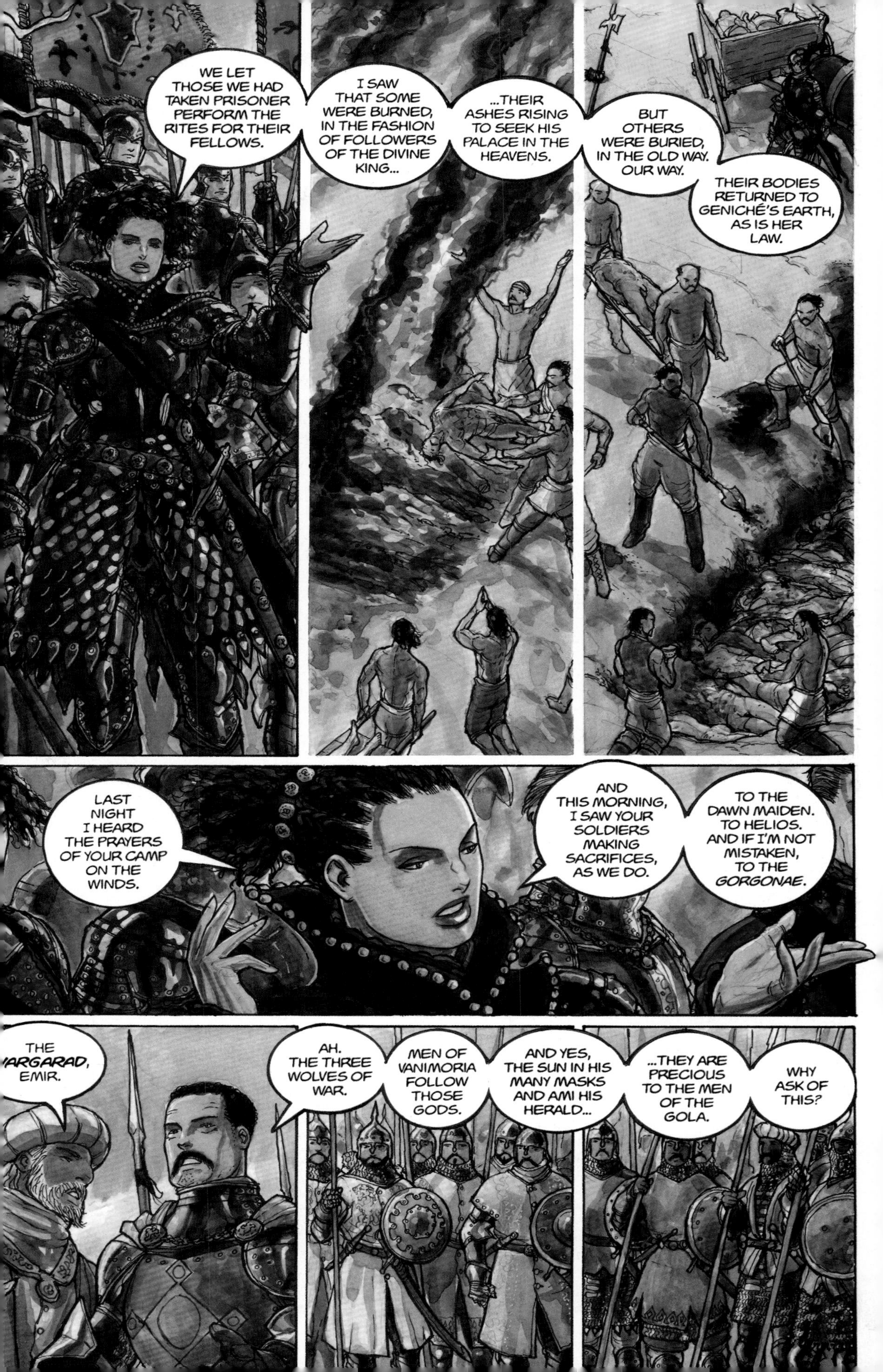
WE LET THOSE WE HAD TAKEN PRISONER PERFORM THE RITES FOR THEIR FELLOWS.
I SAW THAT SOME WERE BURNED, IN THE FASHION OF FOLLOWERS OF THE DIVINE KING...
...THEIR ASHES RISING TO SEEK HIS PALACE IN THE HEAVENS.
BUT OTHERS WERE BURIED, IN THE OLD WAY. OUR WAY.
THEIR BODIES RETURNED TO GENICHÉ'S EARTH, AS IS HER LAW.
LAST NIGHT I HEARD THE PRAYERS OF YOUR CAMP ON THE WINDS.
AND THIS MORNING, I SAW YOUR SOLDIERS MAKING SACRIFICES, AS WE DO.
TO THE DAWN MAIDEN. TO HELIOS. AND IF I'M NOT MISTAKEN, TO THE *GORGONAE*.
THE *VARGARAD*, EMIR.
AH. THE THREE WOLVES OF WAR.
MEN OF VANIMORIA FOLLOW THOSE GODS.
AND YES, THE SUN IN HIS MANY MASKS AND AMI HIS HERALD...
...THEY ARE PRECIOUS TO THE MEN OF THE GOLA.
WHY ASK OF THIS?

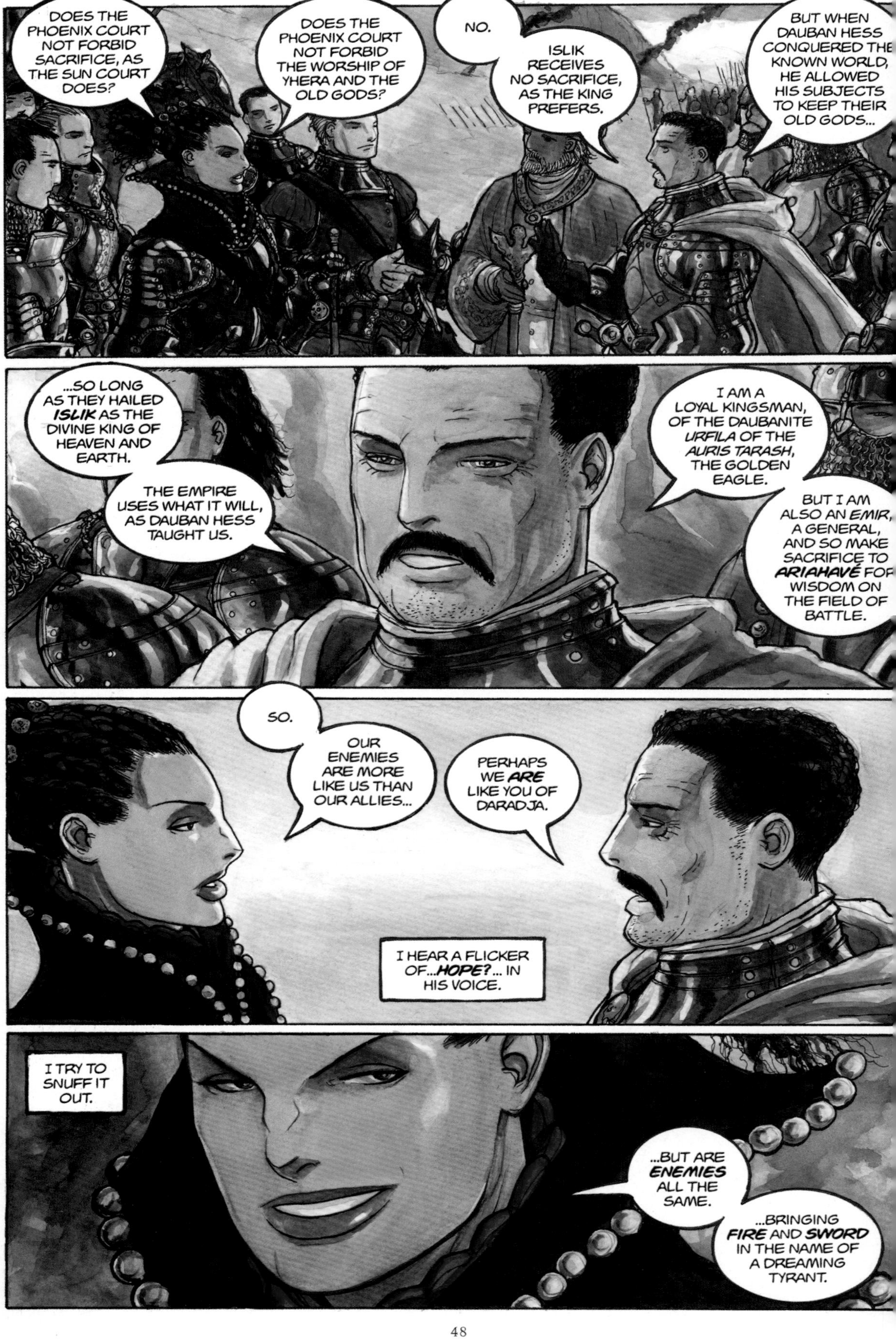

DOES THE PHOENIX COURT NOT FORBID SACRIFICE, AS THE SUN COURT DOES?
DOES THE PHOENIX COURT NOT FORBID THE WORSHIP OF YHERA AND THE OLD GODS?
NO.
ISLIK RECEIVES NO SACRIFICE, AS THE KING PREFERS.
BUT WHEN DAUBAN HESS CONQUERED THE KNOWN WORLD, HE ALLOWED HIS SUBJECTS TO KEEP THEIR OLD GODS...
...SO LONG AS THEY HAILED ISLIK AS THE DIVINE KING OF HEAVEN AND EARTH.
THE EMPIRE USES WHAT IT WILL, AS DAUBAN HESS TAUGHT US.
I AM A LOYAL KINGSMAN, OF THE DAUBANITE URFILA OF THE AURIS TARASH, THE GOLDEN EAGLE.
BUT I AM ALSO AN EMIR, A GENERAL, AND SO MAKE SACRIFICE TO ARIAHAVÉ FOR WISDOM ON THE FIELD OF BATTLE.
SO.
OUR ENEMIES ARE MORE LIKE US THAN OUR ALLIES...
PERHAPS WE ARE LIKE YOU OF DARADJA.
I HEAR A FLICKER OF...HOPE?... IN HIS VOICE.
I TRY TO SNUFF IT OUT.
...BUT ARE ENEMIES ALL THE SAME.
...BRINGING FIRE AND SWORD IN THE NAME OF A DREAMING TYRANT.

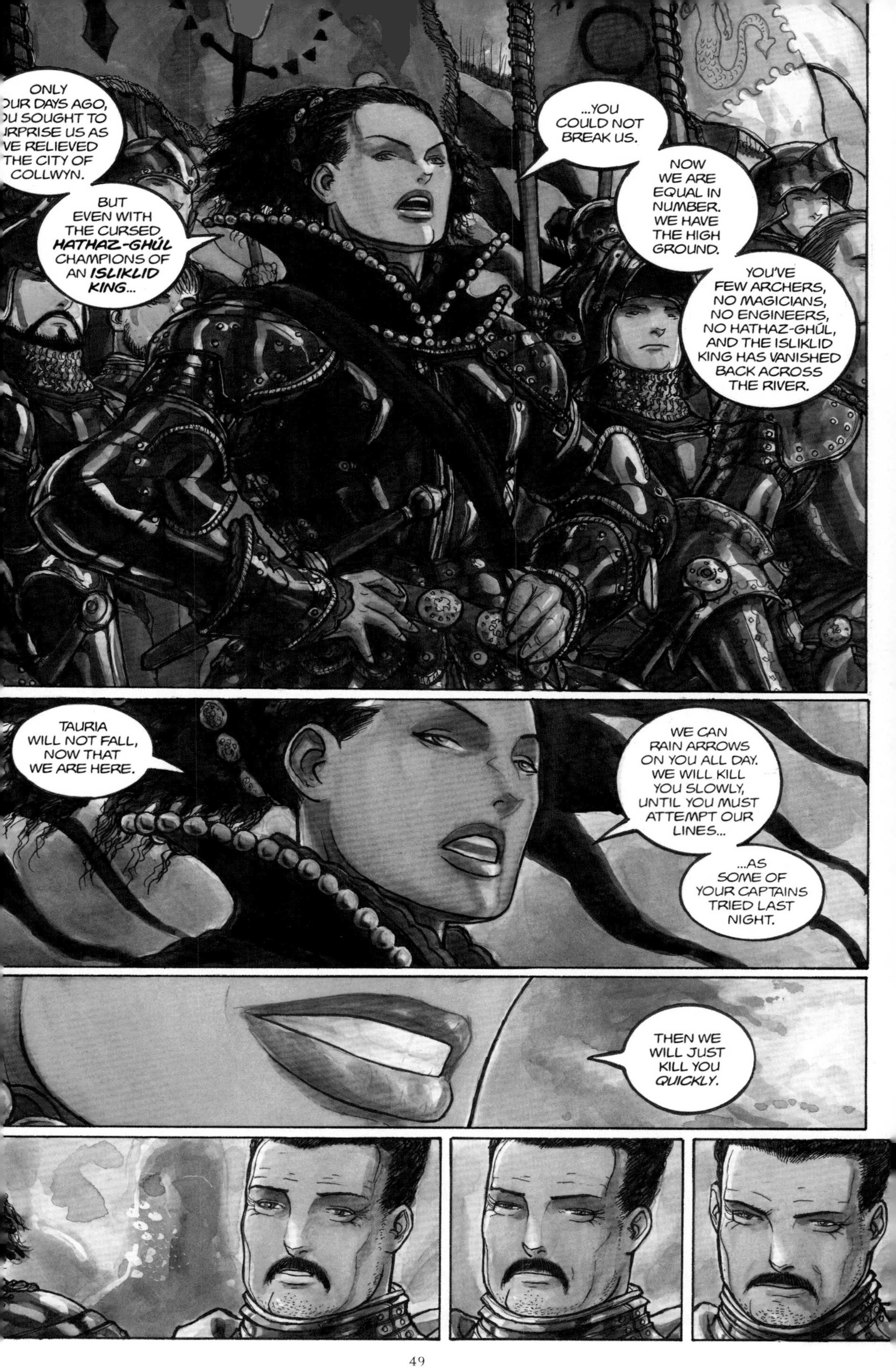
ONLY
OUR DAYS AGO,
OU SOUGHT TO
URPRISE US AS
VE RELIEVED
THE CITY OF
COLLWYN.
BUT EVEN WITH THE CURSED ***HATHAZ-GHÚL*** CHAMPIONS OF AN ***ISLIKLID KING***...
...YOU COULD NOT BREAK US.
NOW WE ARE EQUAL IN NUMBER. WE HAVE THE HIGH GROUND.
YOU'VE FEW ARCHERS, NO MAGICIANS, NO ENGINEERS, NO HATHAZ-GHÚL, AND THE ISLIKLID KING HAS VANISHED BACK ACROSS THE RIVER.
TAURIA WILL NOT FALL, NOW THAT WE ARE HERE.
WE CAN RAIN ARROWS ON YOU ALL DAY. WE WILL KILL YOU SLOWLY, UNTIL YOU MUST ATTEMPT OUR LINES...
...AS SOME OF YOUR CAPTAINS TRIED LAST NIGHT.
THEN WE WILL JUST KILL YOU *QUICKLY*.

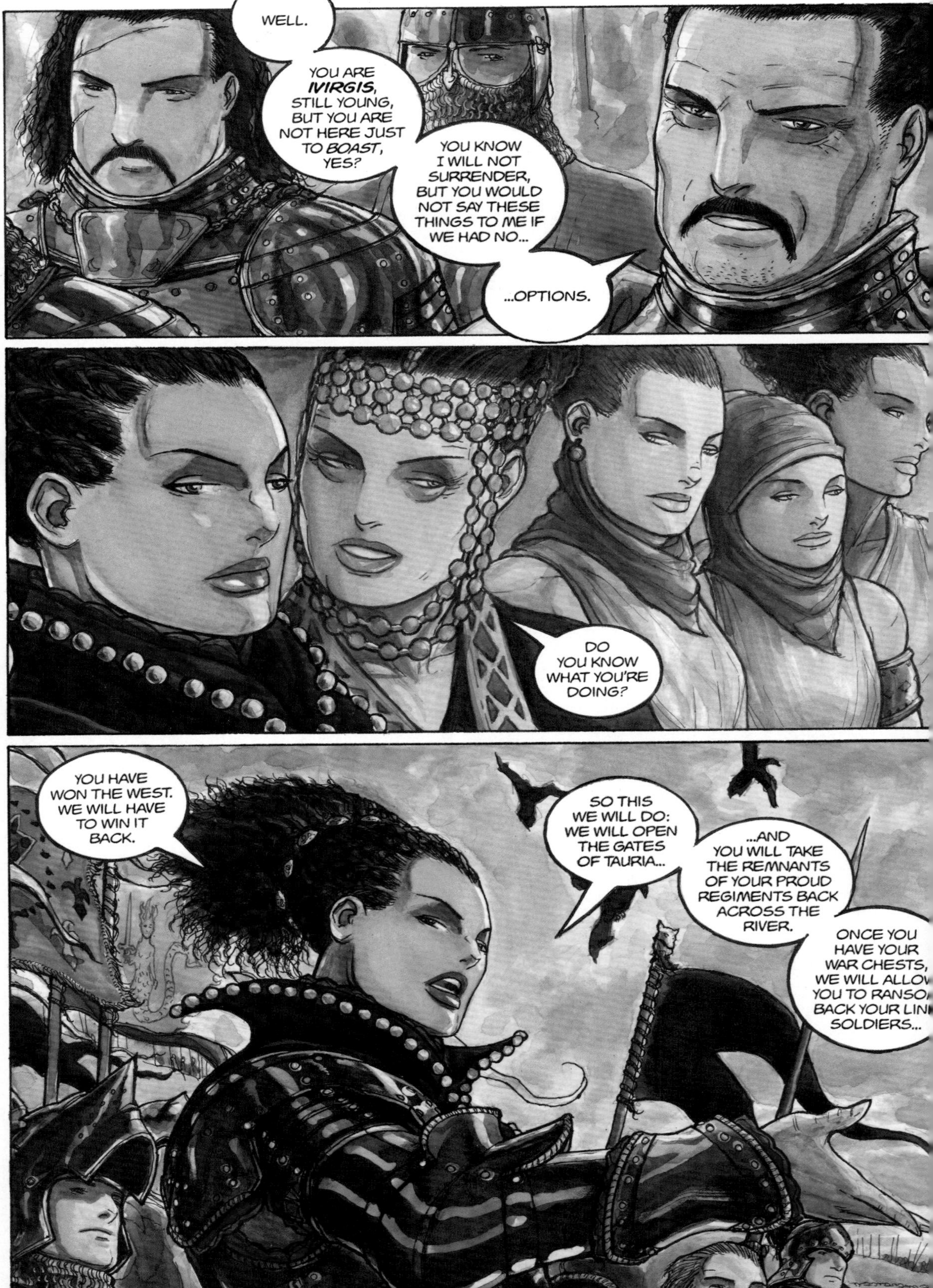
WELL.
YOU ARE ***IVIRGIS***, STILL YOUNG, BUT YOU ARE NOT HERE JUST TO *BOAST*, YES?
YOU KNOW I WILL NOT SURRENDER, BUT YOU WOULD NOT SAY THESE THINGS TO ME IF WE HAD NO...
...OPTIONS.
DO YOU KNOW WHAT YOU'RE DOING?
YOU HAVE WON THE WEST. WE WILL HAVE TO WIN IT BACK.
SO THIS WE WILL DO: WE WILL OPEN THE GATES OF TAURIA...
...AND YOU WILL TAKE THE REMNANTS OF YOUR PROUD REGIMENTS BACK ACROSS THE RIVER.
ONCE YOU HAVE YOUR WAR CHESTS, WE WILL ALLOW YOU TO RANSO BACK YOUR LIN SOLDIERS...

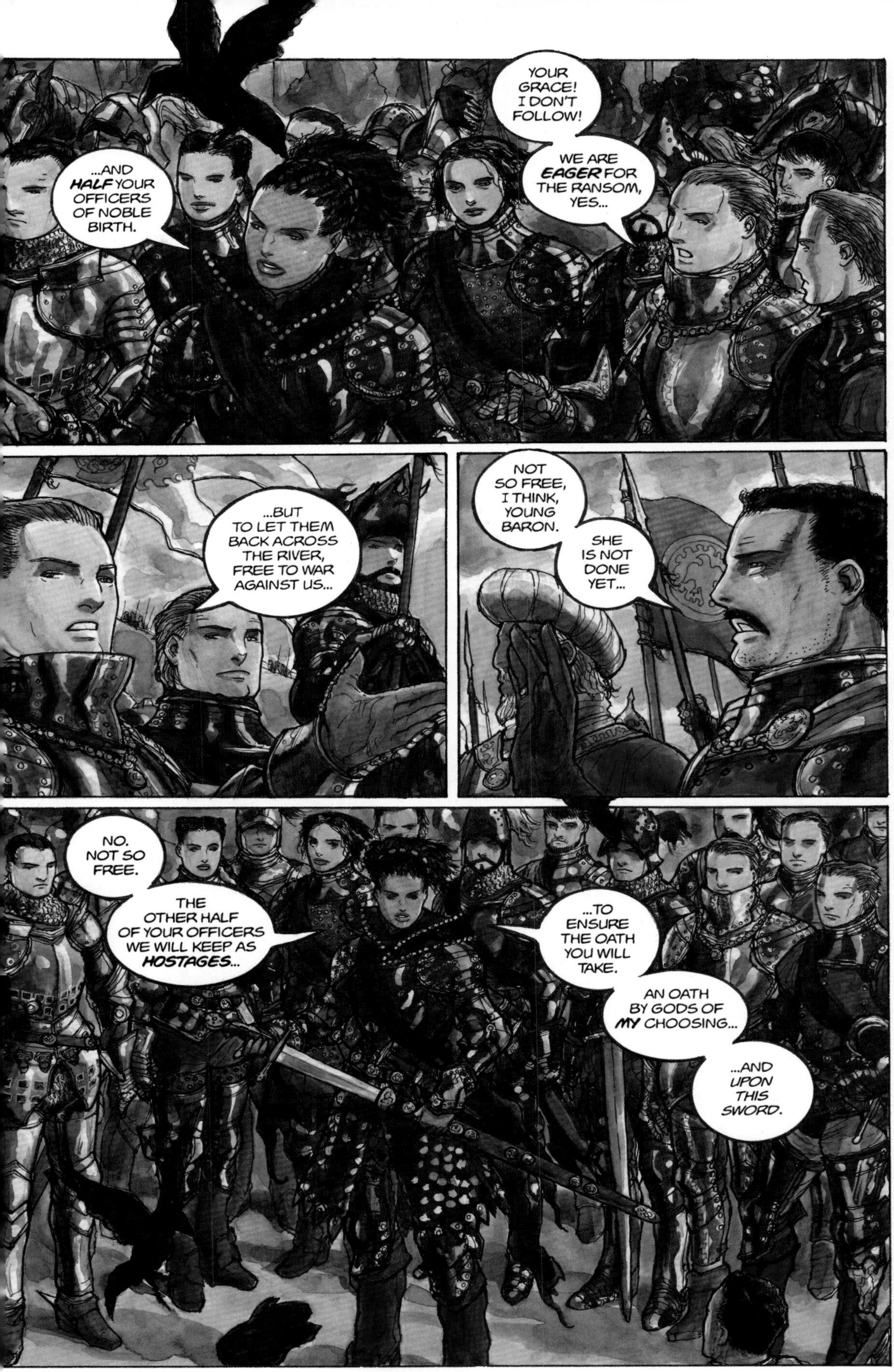
...AND HALF YOUR OFFICERS OF NOBLE BIRTH.
YOUR GRACE! I DON'T FOLLOW!
WE ARE EAGER FOR THE RANSOM, YES...
...BUT TO LET THEM BACK ACROSS THE RIVER, FREE TO WAR AGAINST US...
NOT SO FREE, I THINK, YOUNG BARON.
SHE IS NOT DONE YET...
NO. NOT SO FREE.
THE OTHER HALF OF YOUR OFFICERS WE WILL KEEP AS HOSTAGES...
...TO ENSURE THE OATH YOU WILL TAKE.
AN OATH BY GODS OF MY CHOOSING...
...AND UPON THIS SWORD.

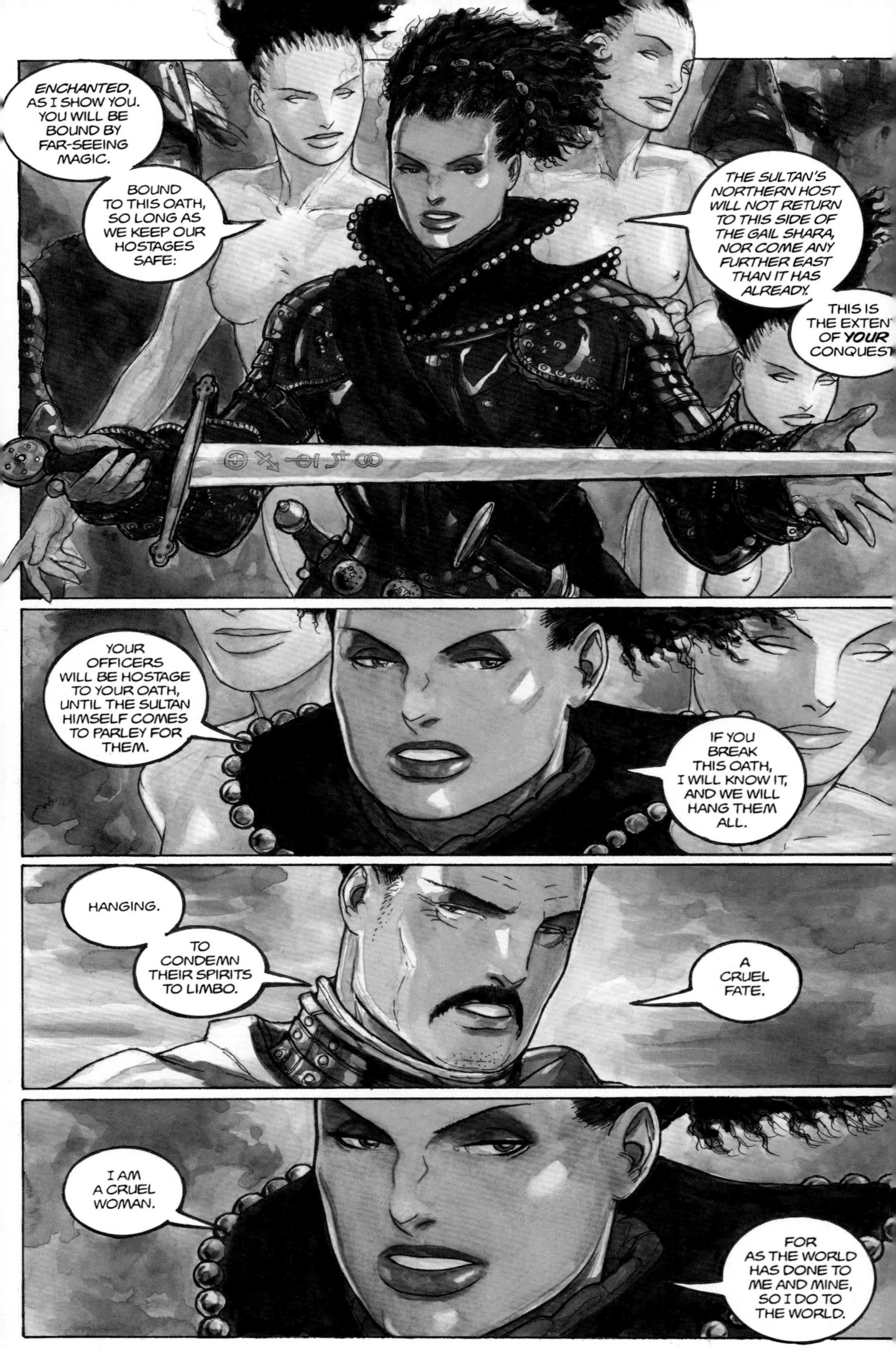
ENCHANTED, AS I SHOW YOU. YOU WILL BE BOUND BY FAR-SEEING MAGIC.
BOUND TO THIS OATH, SO LONG AS WE KEEP OUR HOSTAGES SAFE:
THE SULTAN'S NORTHERN HOST WILL NOT RETURN TO THIS SIDE OF THE GAIL SHARA, NOR COME ANY FURTHER EAST THAN IT HAS ALREADY.
THIS IS THE EXTEN OF YOUR CONQUES
YOUR OFFICERS WILL BE HOSTAGE TO YOUR OATH, UNTIL THE SULTAN HIMSELF COMES TO PARLEY FOR THEM.
IF YOU BREAK THIS OATH, I WILL KNOW IT, AND WE WILL HANG THEM ALL.
HANGING.
TO CONDEMN THEIR SPIRITS TO LIMBO.
A CRUEL FATE.
I AM A CRUEL WOMAN.
FOR AS THE WORLD HAS DONE TO ME AND MINE, SO I DO TO THE WORLD.

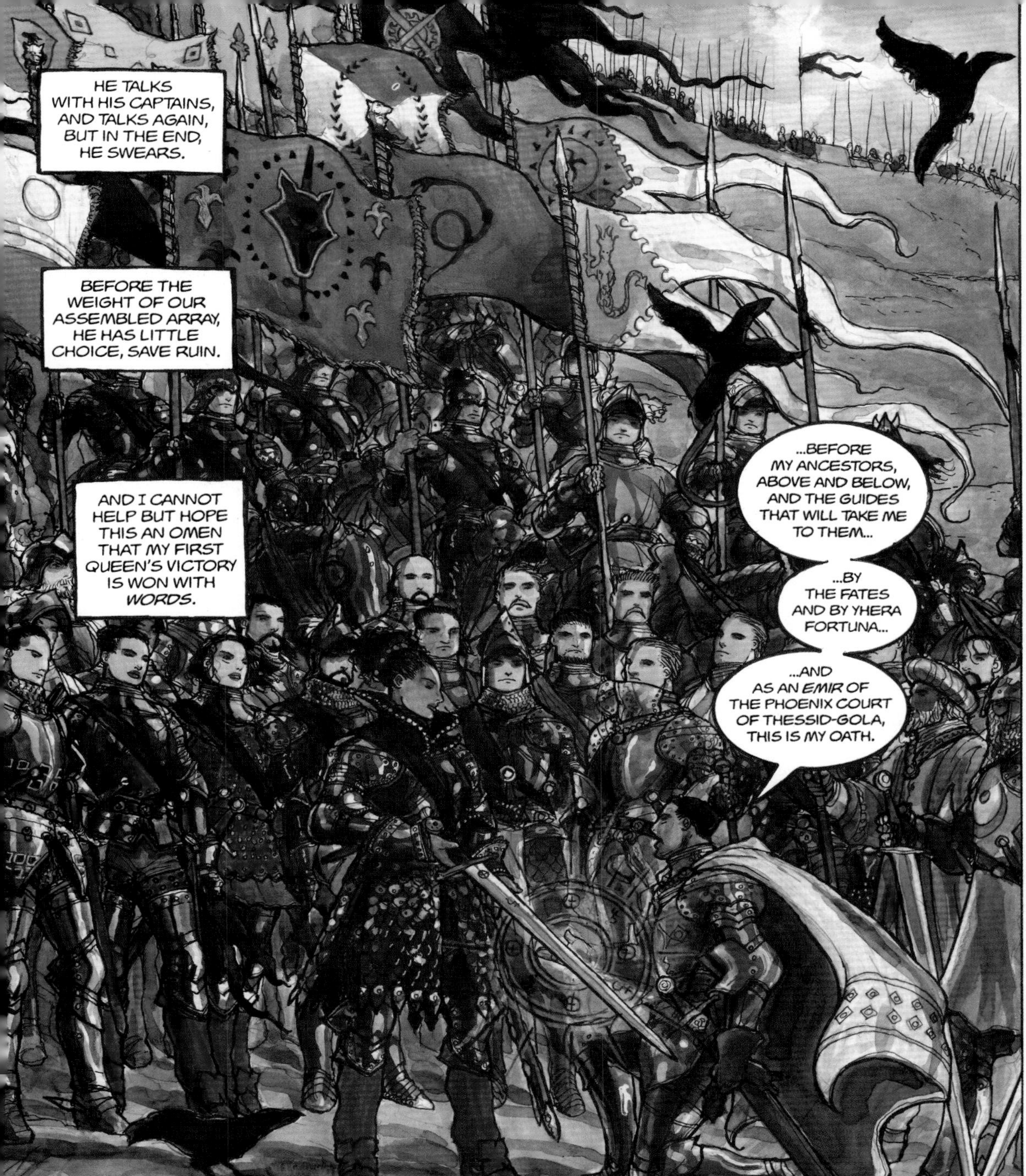
HE TALKS WITH HIS CAPTAINS, AND TALKS AGAIN, BUT IN THE END, HE SWEARS.
BEFORE THE WEIGHT OF OUR ASSEMBLED ARRAY, HE HAS LITTLE CHOICE, SAVE RUIN.
AND I CANNOT HELP BUT HOPE THIS AN OMEN THAT MY FIRST QUEEN'S VICTORY IS WON WITH *WORDS*.
...BEFORE MY ANCESTORS, ABOVE AND BELOW, AND THE GUIDES THAT WILL TAKE ME TO THEM...
...BY THE FATES AND BY YHERA FORTUNA...
...AND AS AN *EMIR* OF THE PHOENIX COURT OF THESSID-GOLA, THIS IS MY OATH.

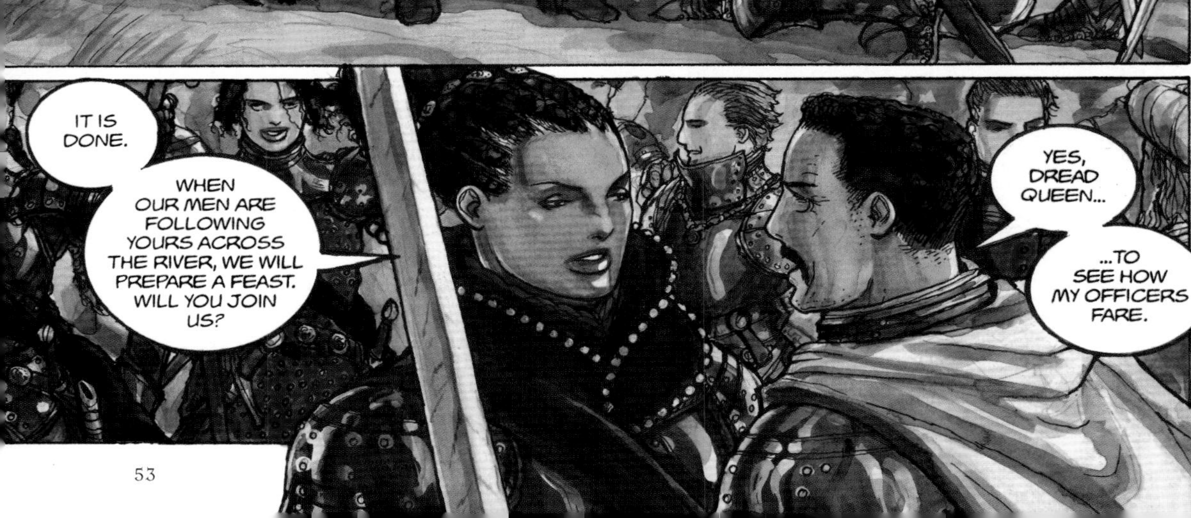
IT IS DONE.
WHEN OUR MEN ARE FOLLOWING YOURS ACROSS THE RIVER, WE WILL PREPARE A FEAST. WILL YOU JOIN US?
YES, DREAD QUEEN...
...TO SEE HOW MY OFFICERS FARE.

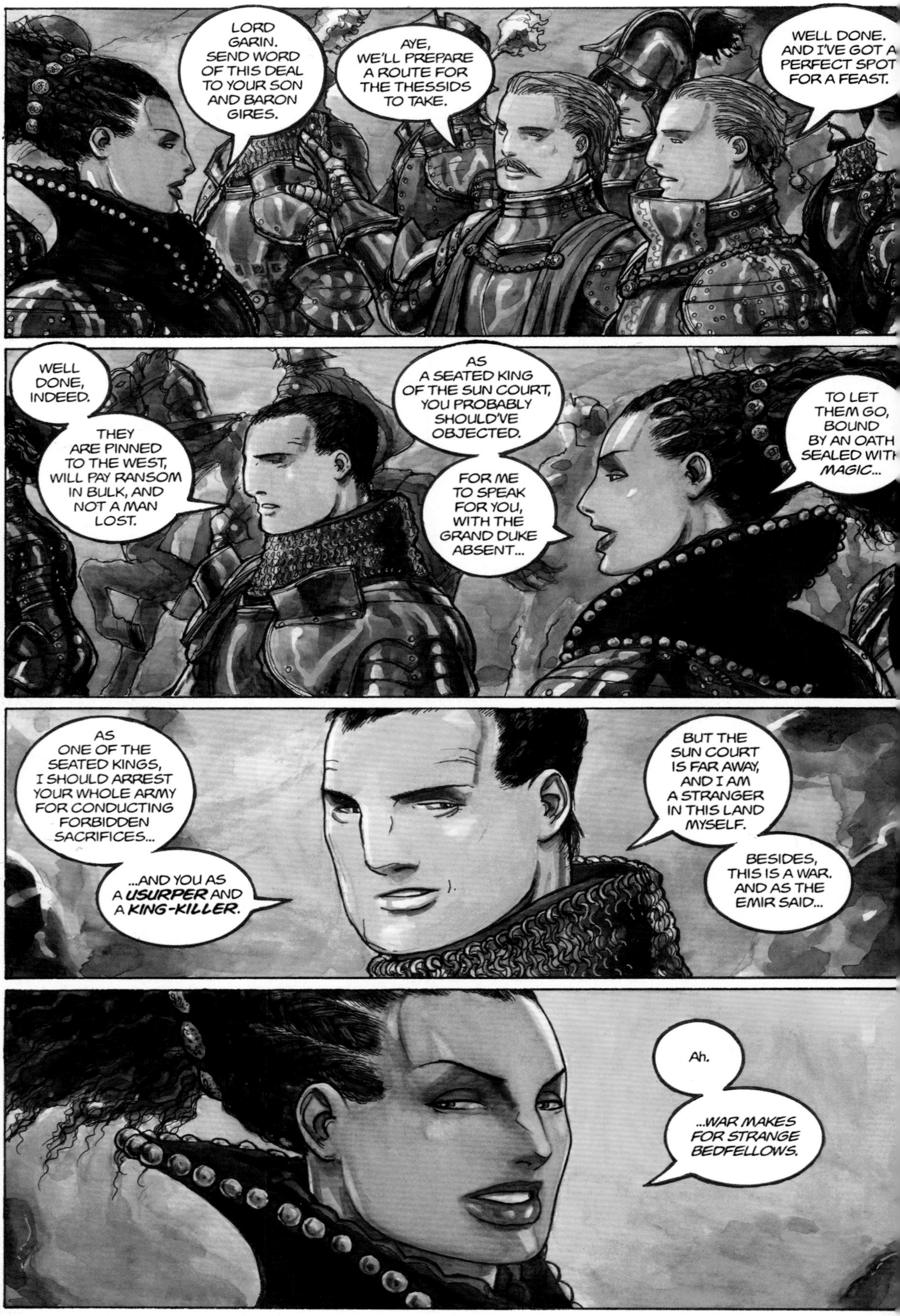
LORD GARIN. SEND WORD OF THIS DEAL TO YOUR SON AND BARON GIRES.
AYE, WE'LL PREPARE A ROUTE FOR THE THESSIDS TO TAKE.
WELL DONE. AND I'VE GOT A PERFECT SPOT FOR A FEAST.
WELL DONE, INDEED.
THEY ARE PINNED TO THE WEST, WILL PAY RANSOM IN BULK, AND NOT A MAN LOST.
AS A SEATED KING OF THE SUN COURT, YOU PROBABLY SHOULD'VE OBJECTED.
FOR ME TO SPEAK FOR YOU, WITH THE GRAND DUKE ABSENT...
TO LET THEM GO, BOUND BY AN OATH SEALED WITH MAGIC...
AS ONE OF THE SEATED KINGS, I SHOULD ARREST YOUR WHOLE ARMY FOR CONDUCTING FORBIDDEN SACRIFICES...
...AND YOU AS A USURPER AND A KING-KILLER.
BUT THE SUN COURT IS FAR AWAY, AND I AM A STRANGER IN THIS LAND MYSELF.
BESIDES, THIS IS A WAR. AND AS THE EMIR SAID...
Ah.
...WAR MAKES FOR STRANGE BEDFELLOWS.

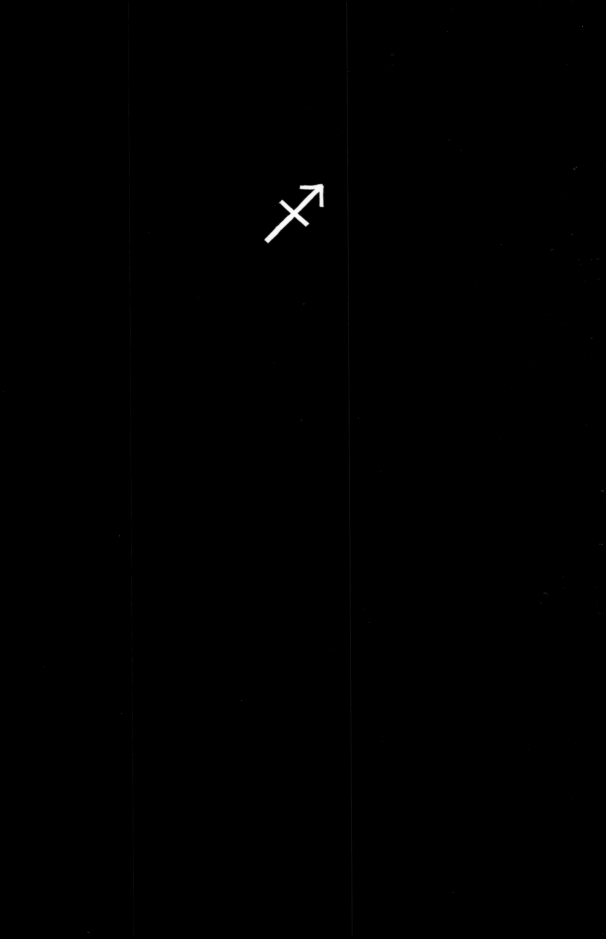

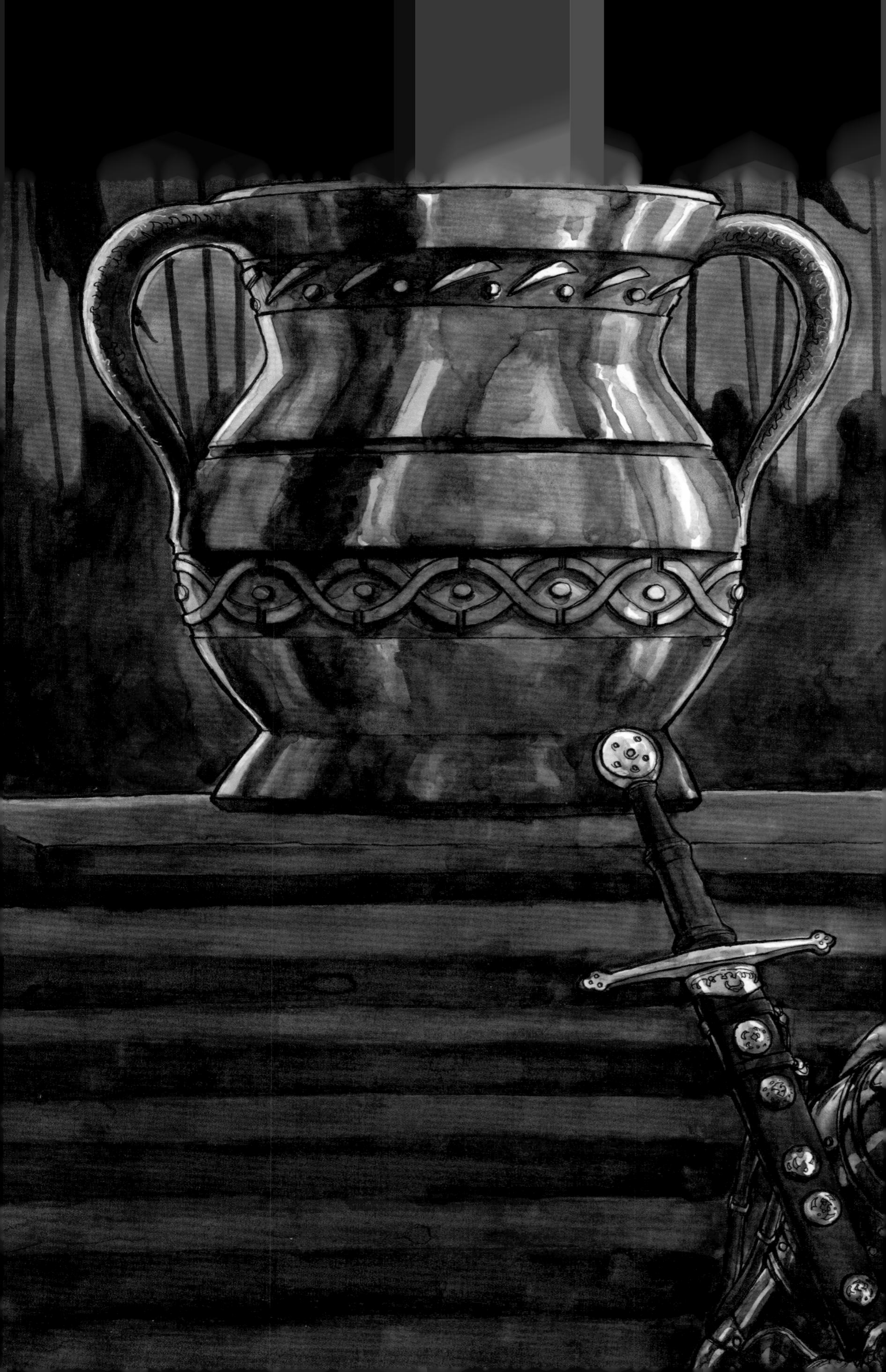

Chapter Two

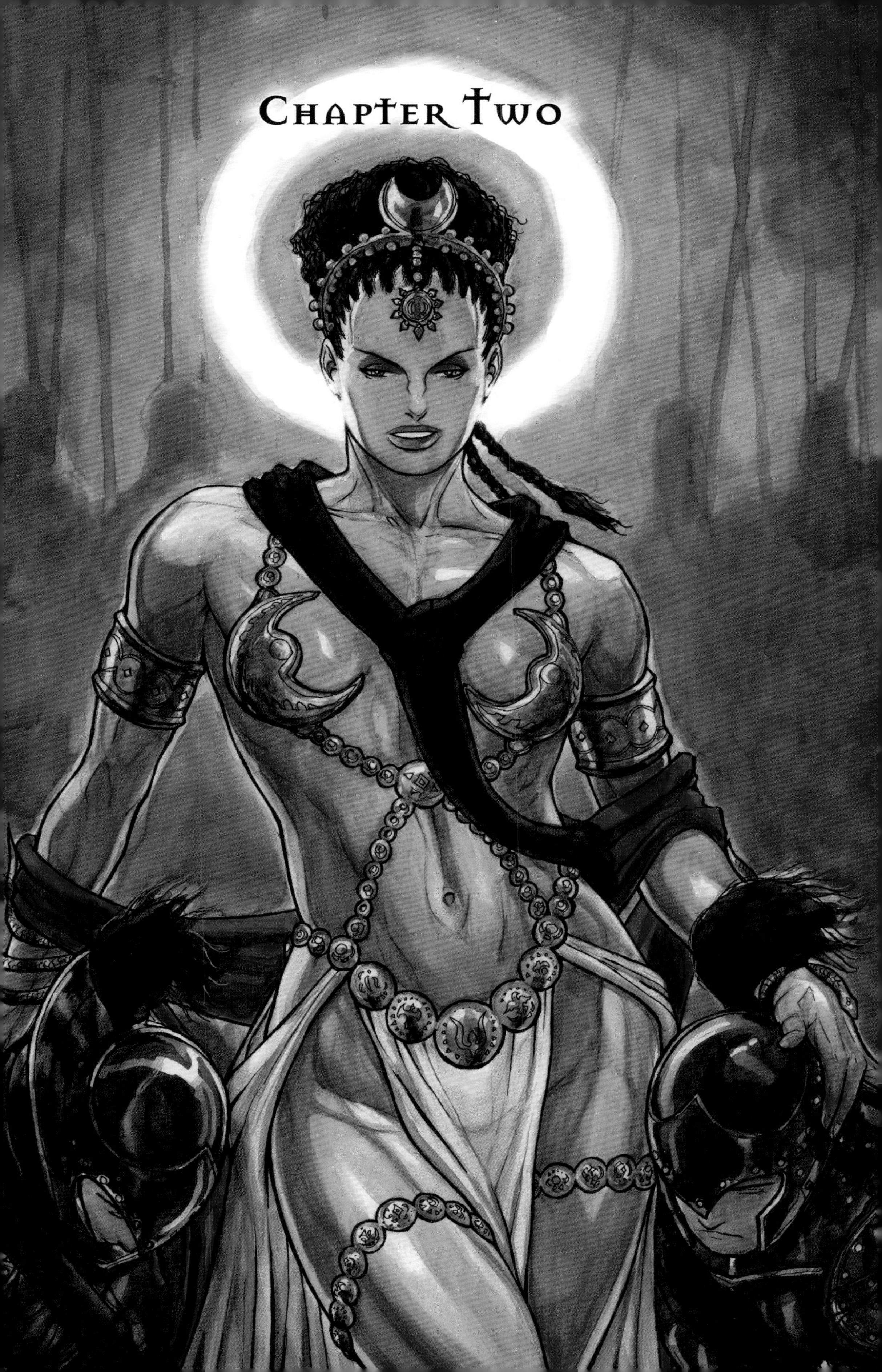

WE WAIT THREE DAYS WHILE THE REMAINS OF THE THESSID VANGUARD CROSS THE BRIDGE AT TAURIA AND WITHDRAW TO THE WEST, FOLLOWED BY OUR OWN FORCES, WHICH WILL MARSHAL IN THE EAST TO AWAIT THE HIGH KING'S SUMMONS.

THE FEAST

THREE DAYS, UNTIL THE SIXTEENTH DAY OF TWINS' MOON, WAITING FOR A VICTORY FEAST, A CELEBRATION OF A BATTLE WON AT COLLWYN AND A BATTLE AVOIDED HERE AT TAURIA.

THREE DAYS I MAKE HIM WAIT.

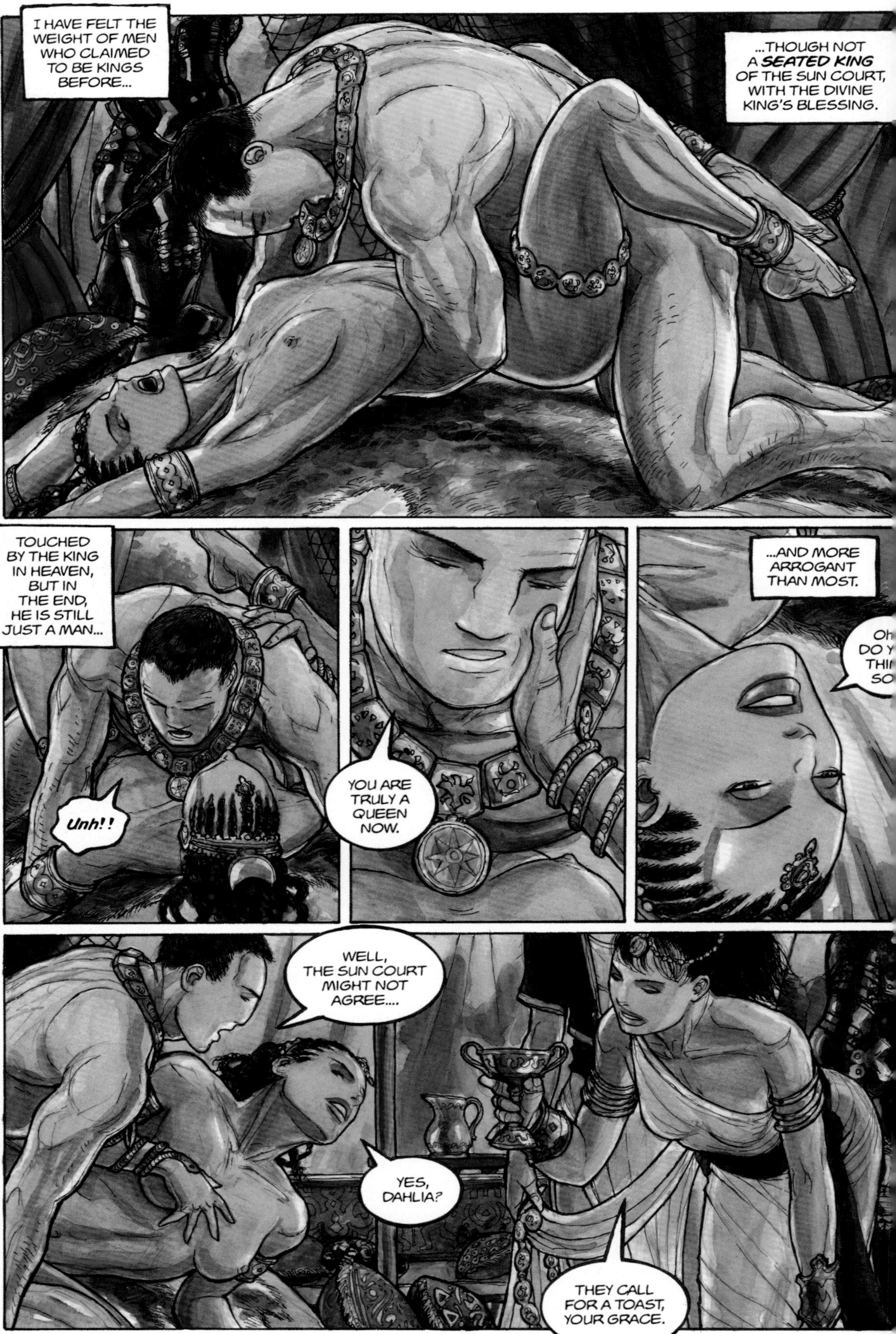
I HAVE FELT THE WEIGHT OF MEN WHO CLAIMED TO BE KINGS BEFORE...
...THOUGH NOT A **SEATED KING** OF THE SUN COURT, WITH THE DIVINE KING'S BLESSING.
TOUCHED BY THE KING IN HEAVEN, BUT IN THE END, HE IS STILL JUST A MAN...
Unh!!
YOU ARE TRULY A QUEEN NOW.
...AND MORE ARROGANT THAN MOST.
WELL, THE SUN COURT MIGHT NOT AGREE....
YES, DAHLIA?
THEY CALL FOR A TOAST, YOUR GRACE.

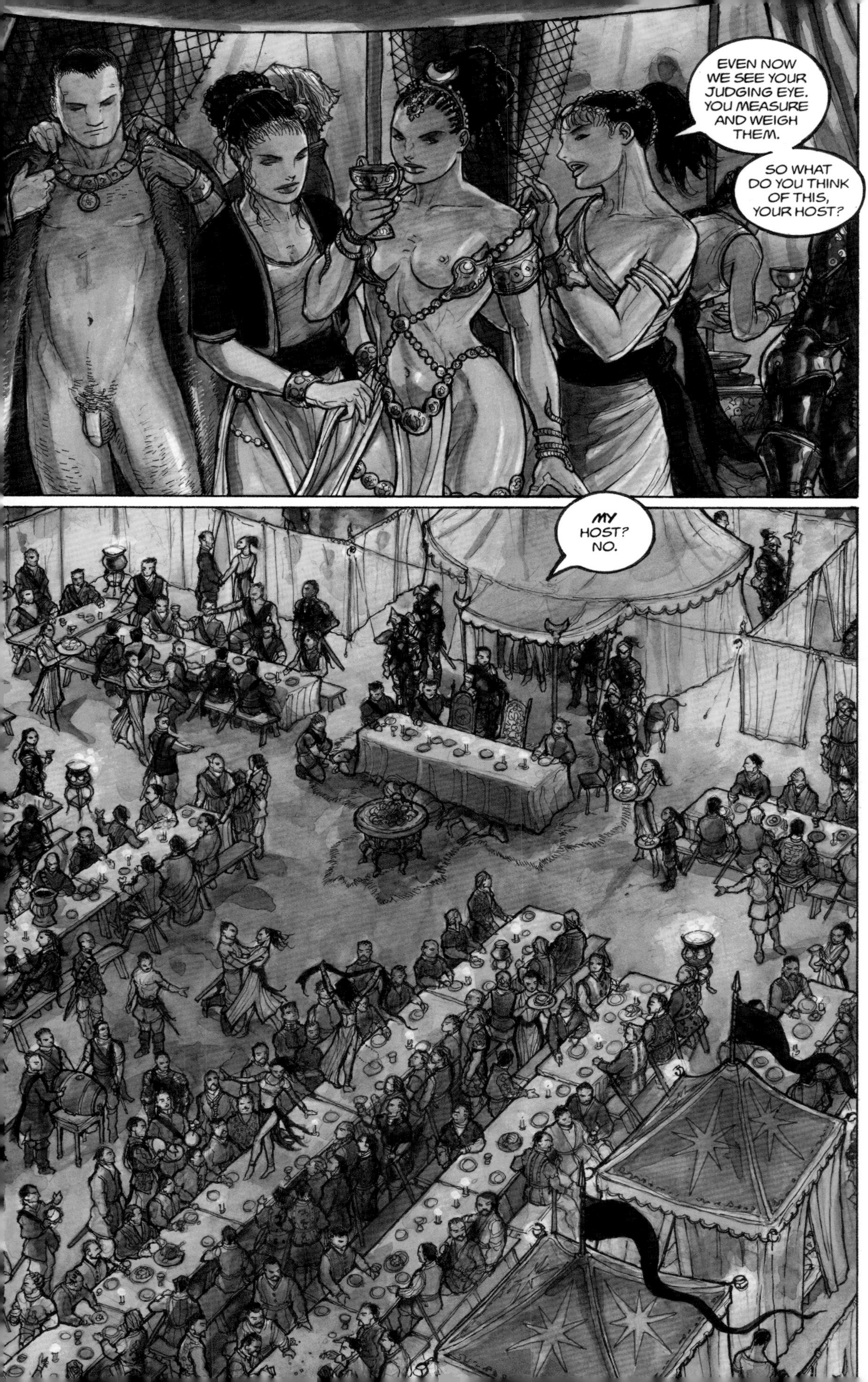
EVEN NOW WE SEE YOUR JUDGING EYE. YOU MEASURE AND WEIGH THEM.
SO WHAT DO YOU THINK OF THIS, YOUR HOST?
MY HOST? NO.

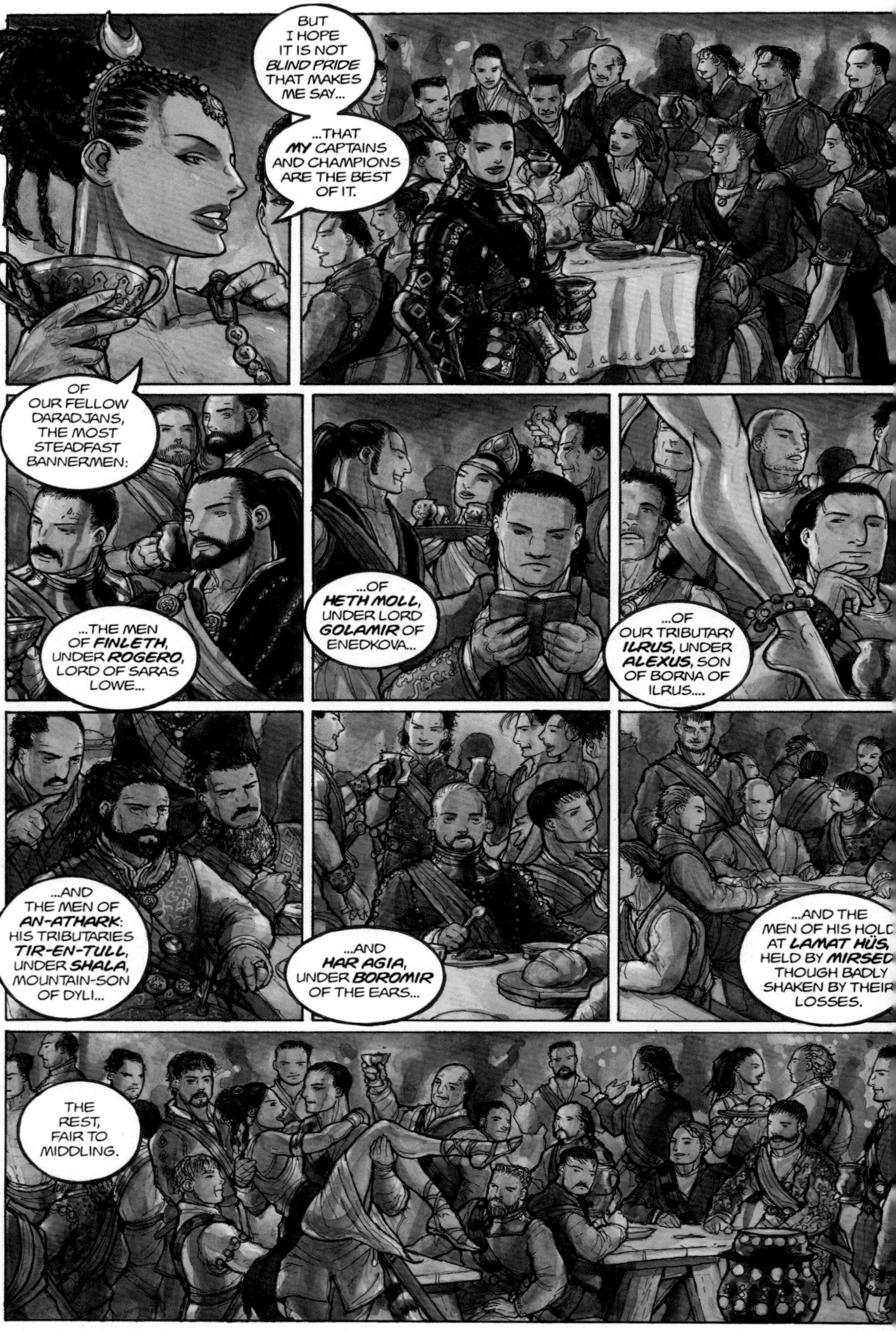
BUT I HOPE IT IS NOT BLIND PRIDE THAT MAKES ME SAY...
...THAT MY CAPTAINS AND CHAMPIONS ARE THE BEST OF IT.
OF OUR FELLOW DARADJANS, THE MOST STEADFAST BANNERMEN:
...THE MEN OF FINLETH, UNDER ROGERO, LORD OF SARAS LOWE...
...OF HETH MOLL, UNDER LORD GOLAMIR OF ENEDKOVA...
...OF OUR TRIBUTARY ILRUS, UNDER ALEXUS, SON OF BORNA OF ILRUS....
...AND THE MEN OF AN-ATHARK: HIS TRIBUTARIES TIR-EN-TULL, UNDER SHALA, MOUNTAIN-SON OF DYLI...
...AND HAR AGIA, UNDER BOROMIR OF THE EARS...
...AND THE MEN OF HIS HOLD AT LAMAT HÜS, HELD BY MIRSED THOUGH BADLY SHAKEN BY THEIR LOSSES.
THE REST, FAIR TO MIDDLING.

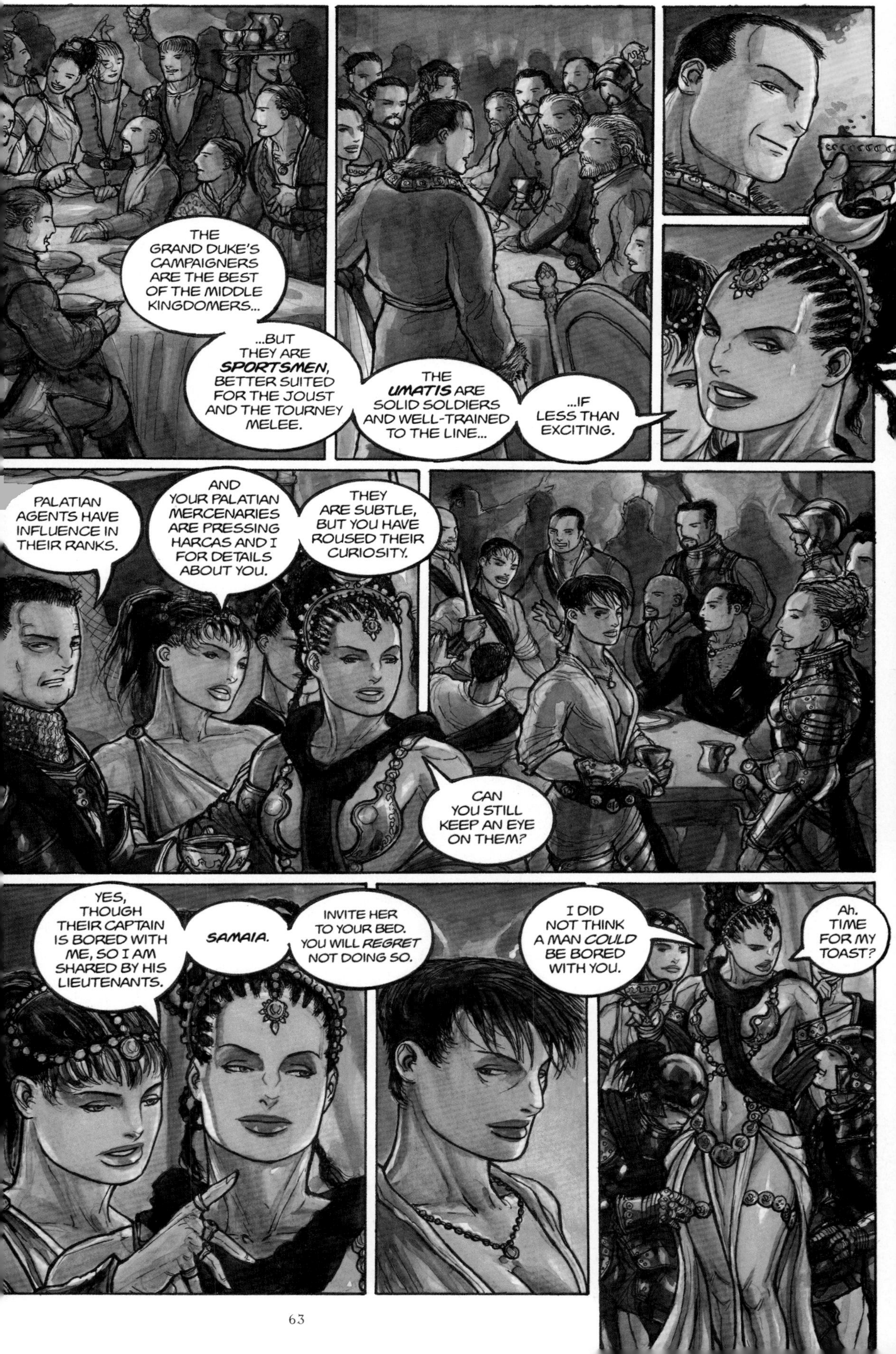
THE GRAND DUKE'S CAMPAIGNERS ARE THE BEST OF THE MIDDLE KINGDOMERS...
...BUT THEY ARE SPORTSMEN, BETTER SUITED FOR THE JOUST AND THE TOURNEY MELEE.
THE UMATIS ARE SOLID SOLDIERS AND WELL-TRAINED TO THE LINE...
...IF LESS THAN EXCITING.
PALATIAN AGENTS HAVE INFLUENCE IN THEIR RANKS.
AND YOUR PALATIAN MERCENARIES ARE PRESSING HARCAS AND I FOR DETAILS ABOUT YOU.
THEY ARE SUBTLE, BUT YOU HAVE ROUSED THEIR CURIOSITY.
CAN YOU STILL KEEP AN EYE ON THEM?
YES, THOUGH THEIR CAPTAIN IS BORED WITH ME, SO I AM SHARED BY HIS LIEUTENANTS.
SAMAIA.
INVITE HER TO YOUR BED. YOU WILL REGRET NOT DOING SO.
I DID NOT THINK A MAN COULD BE BORED WITH YOU.
Ah. TIME FOR MY TOAST?

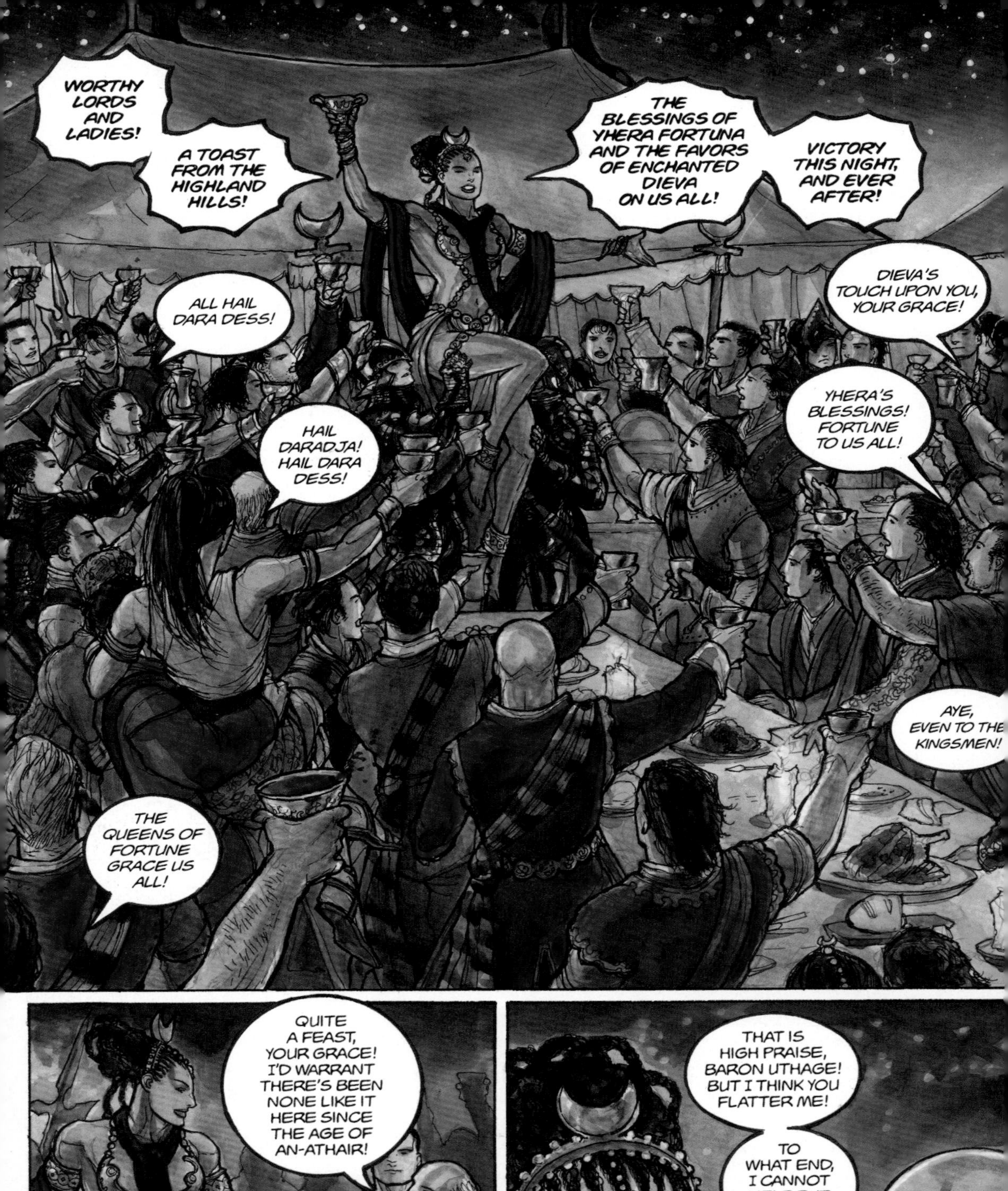
WORTHY LORDS AND LADIES!
A TOAST FROM THE HIGHLAND HILLS!
THE BLESSINGS OF YHERA FORTUNA AND THE FAVORS OF ENCHANTED DIEVA ON US ALL!
VICTORY THIS NIGHT, AND EVER AFTER!
ALL HAIL DARA DESS!
DIEVA'S TOUCH UPON YOU, YOUR GRACE!
HAIL DARADJA! HAIL DARA DESS!
YHERA'S BLESSINGS! FORTUNE TO US ALL!
AYE, EVEN TO THE KINGSMEN!
THE QUEENS OF FORTUNE GRACE US ALL!

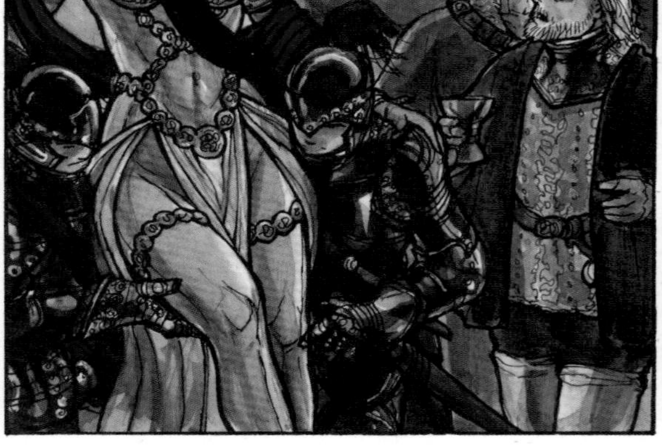
QUITE A FEAST, YOUR GRACE! I'D WARRANT THERE'S BEEN NONE LIKE IT HERE SINCE THE AGE OF AN-ATHAIR!

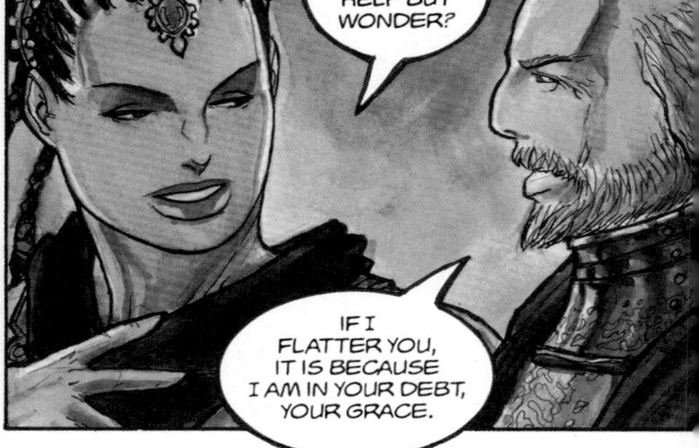
THAT IS HIGH PRAISE, BARON UTHAGE! BUT I THINK YOU FLATTER ME!
TO WHAT END, I CANNOT HELP BUT WONDER?
IF I FLATTER YOU, IT IS BECAUSE I AM IN YOUR DEBT, YOUR GRACE.

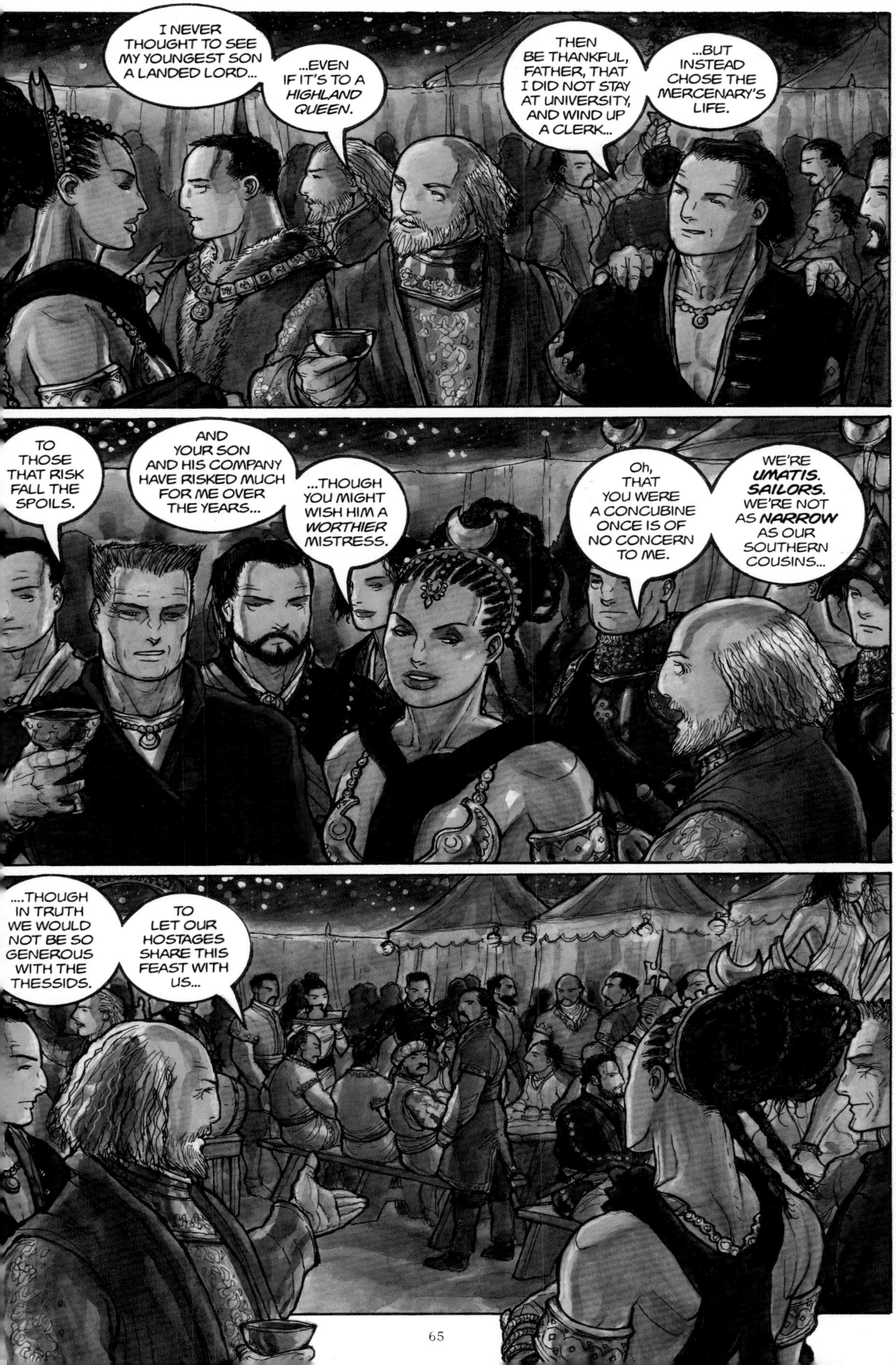
I NEVER THOUGHT TO SEE MY YOUNGEST SON A LANDED LORD...
...EVEN IF IT'S TO A *HIGHLAND QUEEN.*
THEN BE THANKFUL, FATHER, THAT I DID NOT STAY AT UNIVERSITY, AND WIND UP A CLERK...
...BUT INSTEAD CHOSE THE MERCENARY'S LIFE.
TO THOSE THAT RISK FALL THE SPOILS.
AND YOUR SON AND HIS COMPANY HAVE RISKED MUCH FOR ME OVER THE YEARS...
...THOUGH YOU MIGHT WISH HIM A *WORTHIER* MISTRESS.
Oh, THAT YOU WERE A CONCUBINE ONCE IS OF NO CONCERN TO ME.
WE'RE ***UMATIS. SAILORS.*** WE'RE NOT AS ***NARROW*** AS OUR SOUTHERN COUSINS...
....THOUGH IN TRUTH WE WOULD NOT BE SO GENEROUS WITH THE THESSIDS.
TO LET OUR HOSTAGES SHARE THIS FEAST WITH US...

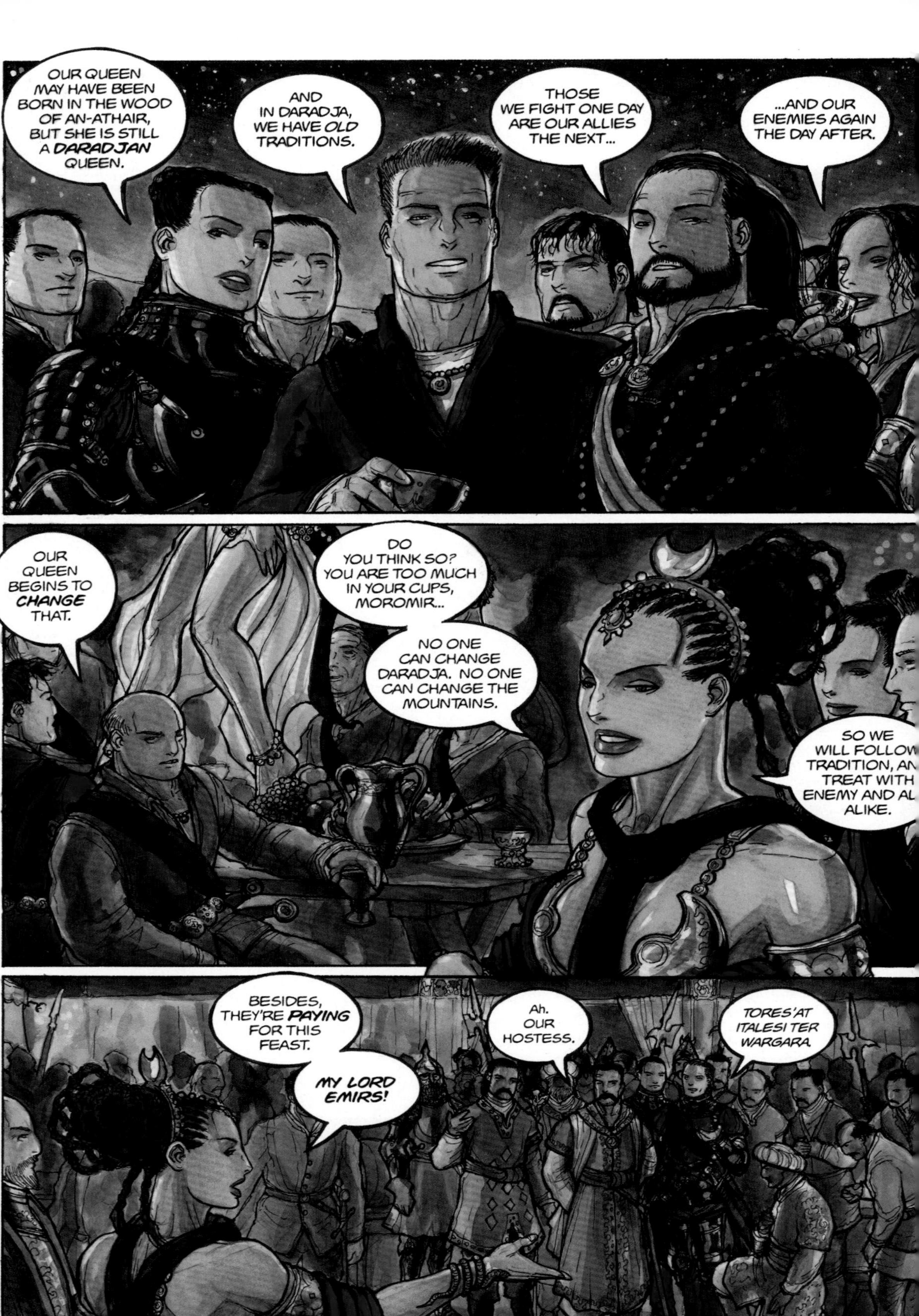
OUR QUEEN MAY HAVE BEEN BORN IN THE WOOD OF AN-ATHAIR, BUT SHE IS STILL A DARADJAN QUEEN.
AND IN DARADJA, WE HAVE OLD TRADITIONS.
THOSE WE FIGHT ONE DAY ARE OUR ALLIES THE NEXT...
...AND OUR ENEMIES AGAIN THE DAY AFTER.
OUR QUEEN BEGINS TO CHANGE THAT.
DO YOU THINK SO? YOU ARE TOO MUCH IN YOUR CUPS, MOROMIR...
NO ONE CAN CHANGE DARADJA. NO ONE CAN CHANGE THE MOUNTAINS.
SO WE WILL FOLLOW TRADITION, AN TREAT WITH ENEMY AND AL ALIKE.
BESIDES, THEY'RE PAYING FOR THIS FEAST.
MY LORD EMIRS!
Ah. OUR HOSTESS.
TORES'AT ITALESI TER WARGARA.

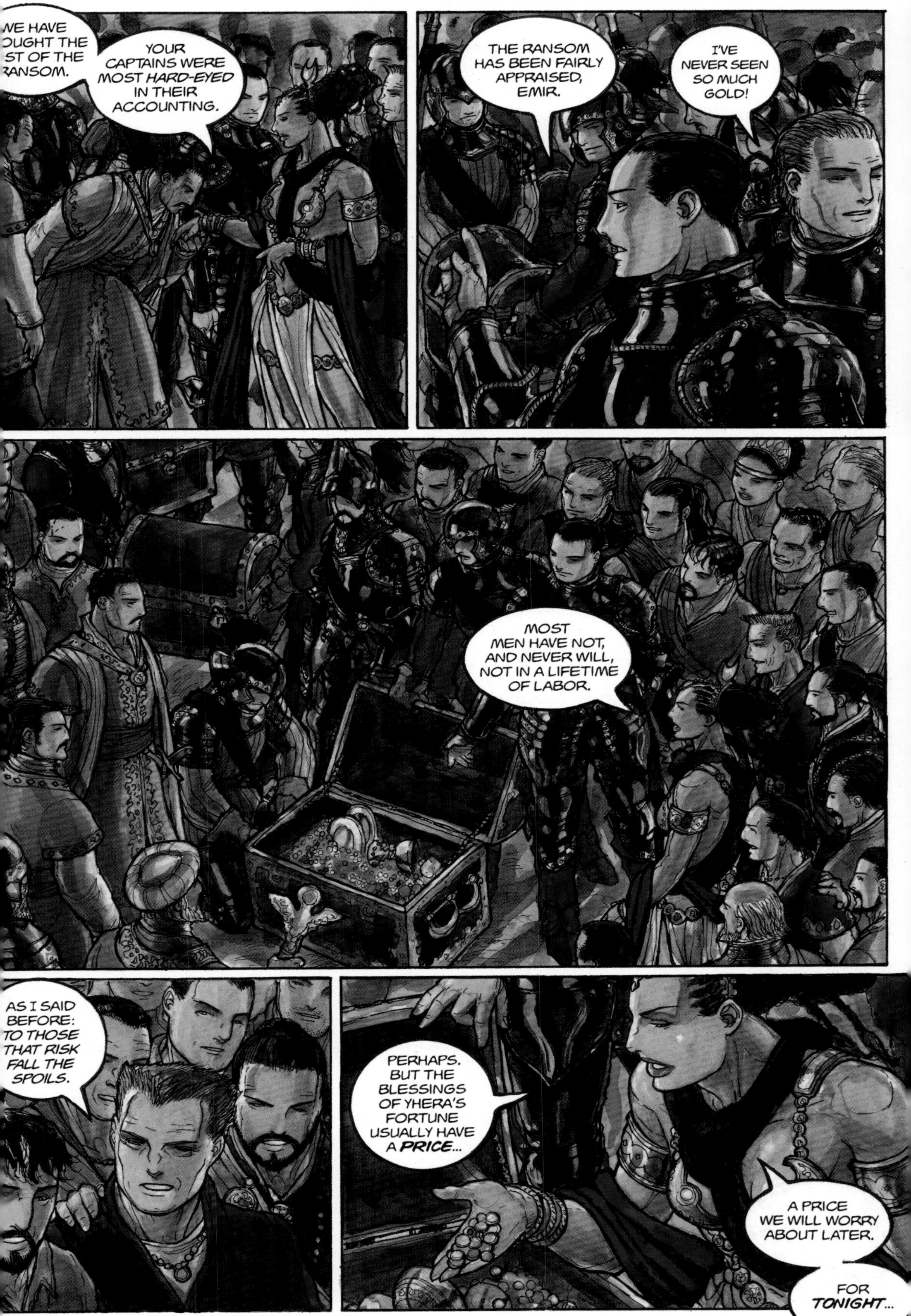
WE HAVE OUGHT THE ST OF THE RANSOM.
YOUR CAPTAINS WERE MOST *HARD-EYED* IN THEIR ACCOUNTING.
THE RANSOM HAS BEEN FAIRLY APPRAISED, EMIR.
I'VE NEVER SEEN SO MUCH GOLD!
MOST MEN HAVE NOT, AND NEVER WILL, NOT IN A LIFETIME OF LABOR.
AS I SAID BEFORE: *TO THOSE THAT RISK FALL THE SPOILS.*
PERHAPS. BUT THE BLESSINGS OF YHERA'S FORTUNE USUALLY HAVE A ***PRICE***...
A PRICE WE WILL WORRY ABOUT LATER.
FOR ***TONIGHT***...

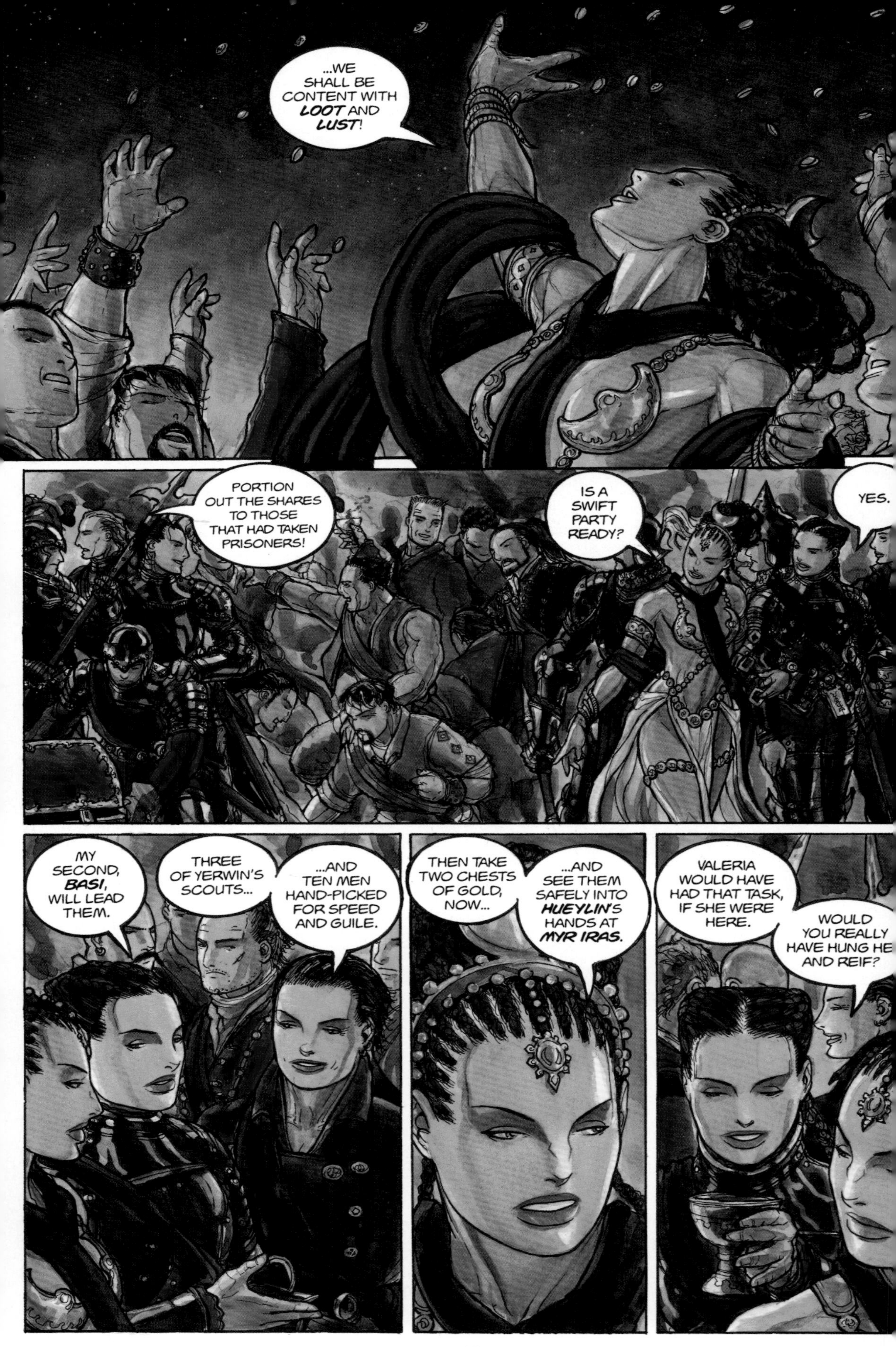
...WE SHALL BE CONTENT WITH LOOT AND LUST!
PORTION OUT THE SHARES TO THOSE THAT HAD TAKEN PRISONERS!
IS A SWIFT PARTY READY?
YES.
MY SECOND, BASI, WILL LEAD THEM.
THREE OF YERWIN'S SCOUTS...
...AND TEN MEN HAND-PICKED FOR SPEED AND GUILE.
THEN TAKE TWO CHESTS OF GOLD, NOW...
...AND SEE THEM SAFELY INTO HUEYLIN'S HANDS AT MYR IRAS.
VALERIA WOULD HAVE HAD THAT TASK, IF SHE WERE HERE.
WOULD YOU REALLY HAVE HUNG HE AND REIF?

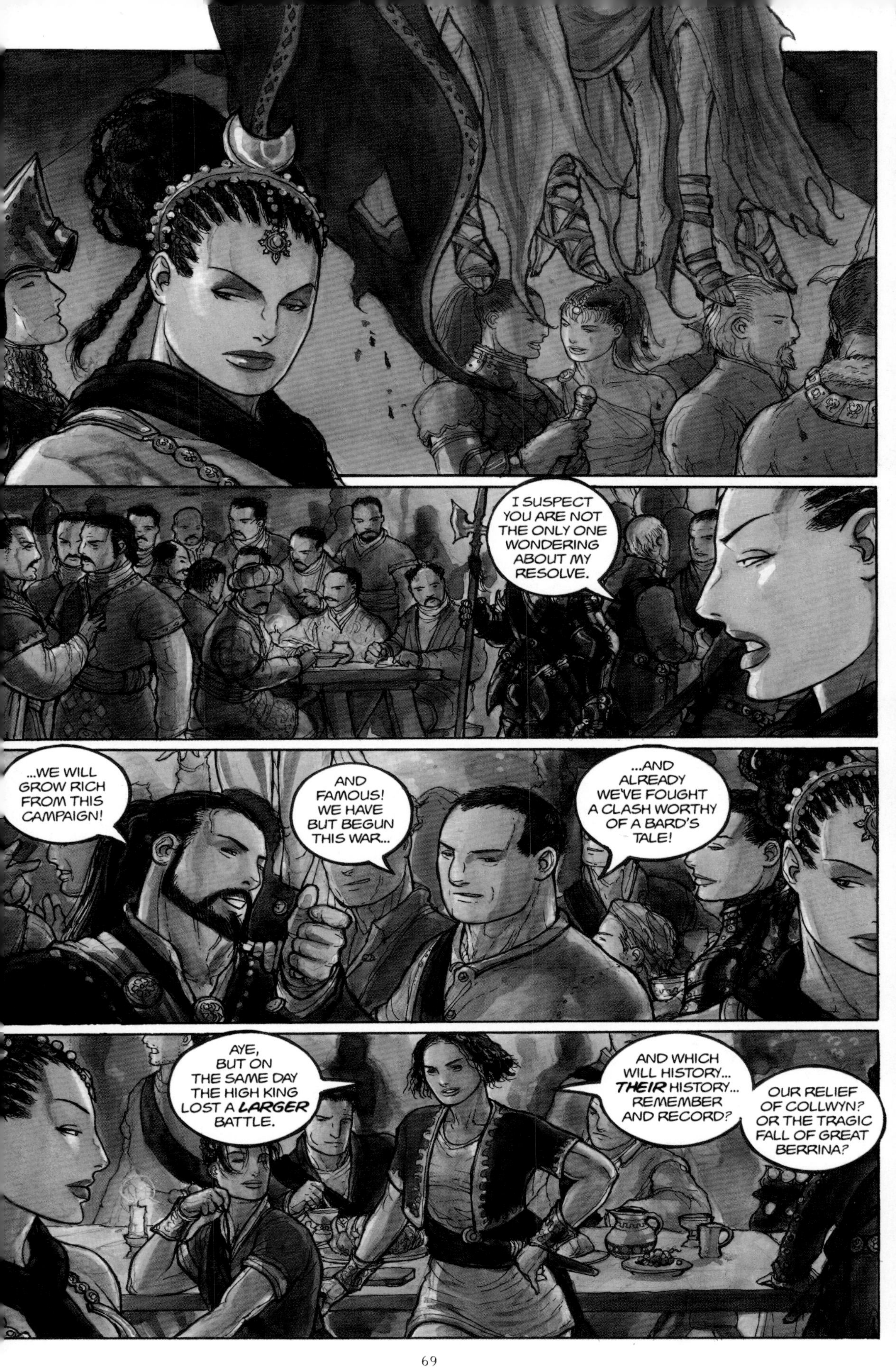
I SUSPECT YOU ARE NOT THE ONLY ONE WONDERING ABOUT MY RESOLVE.
...WE WILL GROW RICH FROM THIS CAMPAIGN!
AND FAMOUS! WE HAVE BUT BEGUN THIS WAR...
...AND ALREADY WE'VE FOUGHT A CLASH WORTHY OF A BARD'S TALE!
AYE, BUT ON THE SAME DAY THE HIGH KING LOST A LARGER BATTLE.
AND WHICH WILL HISTORY... THEIR HISTORY... REMEMBER AND RECORD?
OUR RELIEF OF COLLWYN? OR THE TRAGIC FALL OF GREAT BERRINA?

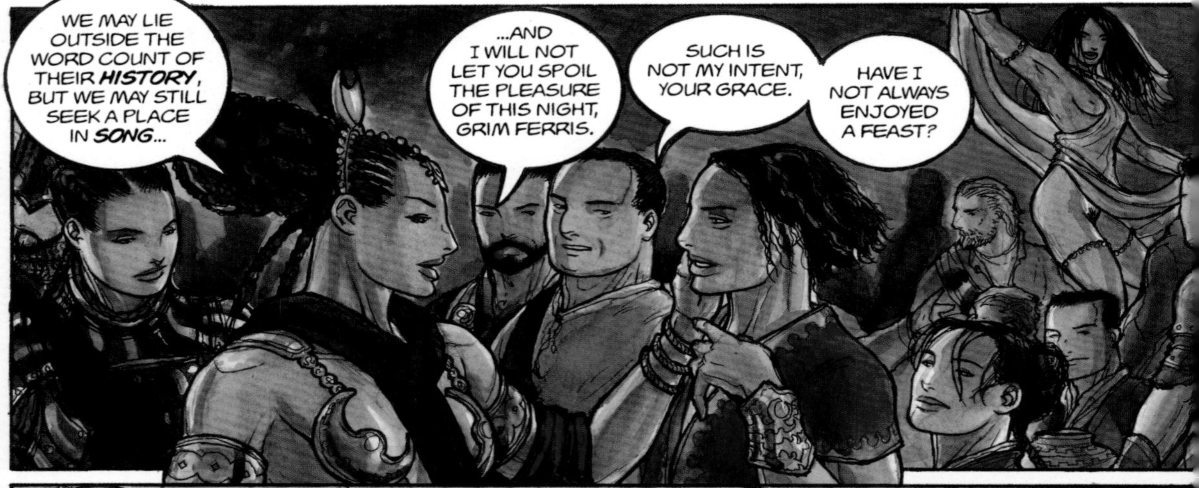
WE MAY LIE OUTSIDE THE WORD COUNT OF THEIR HISTORY, BUT WE MAY STILL SEEK A PLACE IN SONG...
...AND I WILL NOT LET YOU SPOIL THE PLEASURE OF THIS NIGHT, GRIM FERRIS.
SUCH IS NOT MY INTENT, YOUR GRACE.
HAVE I NOT ALWAYS ENJOYED A FEAST?

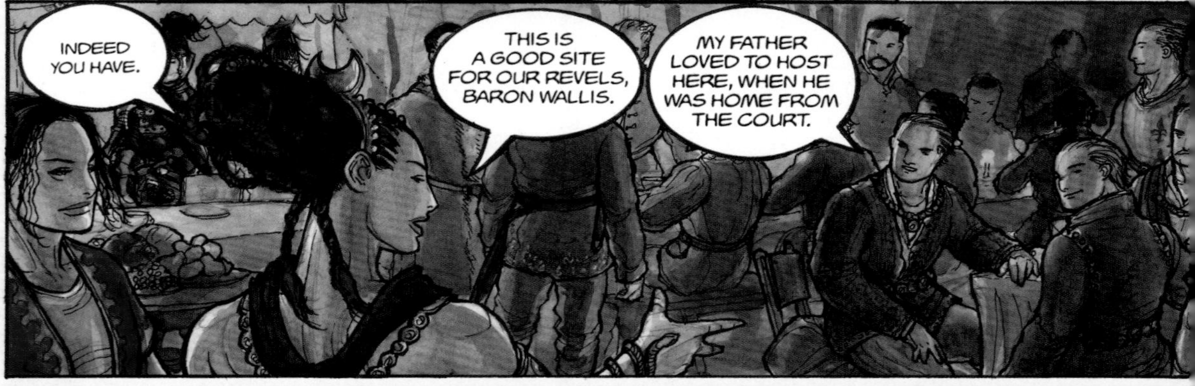
INDEED YOU HAVE.
THIS IS A GOOD SITE FOR OUR REVELS, BARON WALLIS.
MY FATHER LOVED TO HOST HERE, WHEN HE WAS HOME FROM THE COURT.

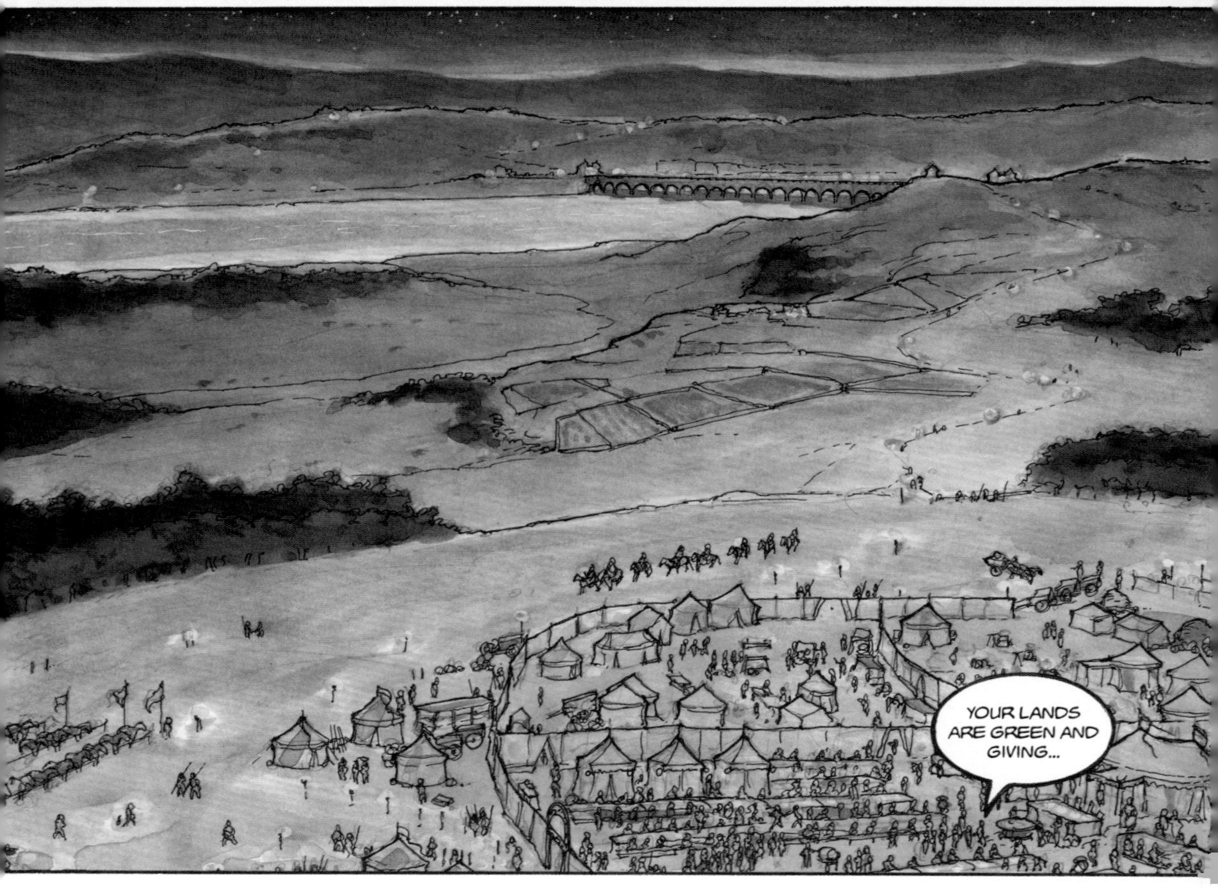
YOUR LANDS ARE GREEN AND GIVING...

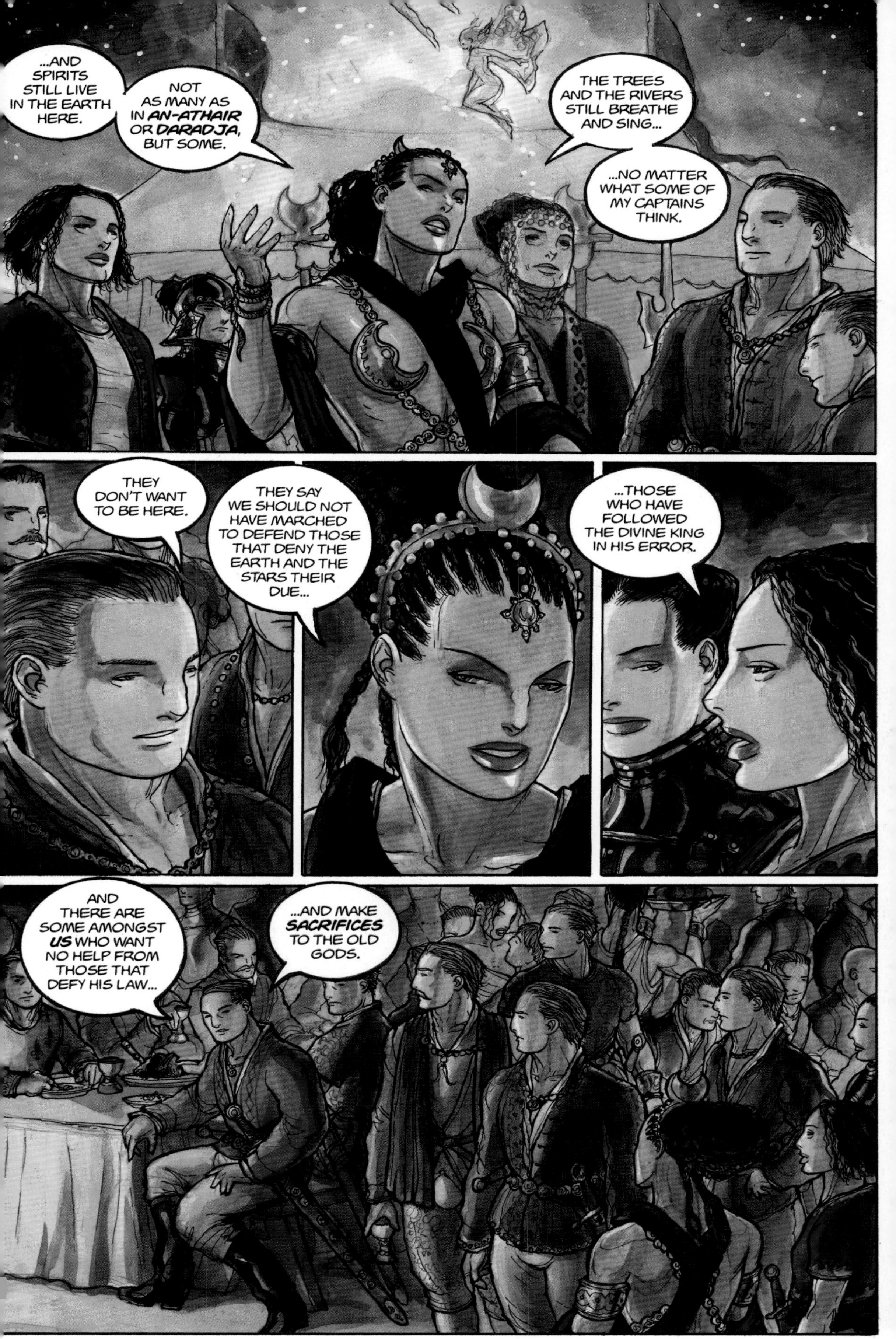
...AND SPIRITS STILL LIVE IN THE EARTH HERE.
NOT AS MANY AS IN AN-ATHAIR OR DARADJA, BUT SOME.
THE TREES AND THE RIVERS STILL BREATHE AND SING...
...NO MATTER WHAT SOME OF MY CAPTAINS THINK.
THEY DON'T WANT TO BE HERE.
THEY SAY WE SHOULD NOT HAVE MARCHED TO DEFEND THOSE THAT DENY THE EARTH AND THE STARS THEIR DUE...
...THOSE WHO HAVE FOLLOWED THE DIVINE KING IN HIS ERROR.
AND THERE ARE SOME AMONGST US WHO WANT NO HELP FROM THOSE THAT DEFY HIS LAW...
...AND MAKE SACRIFICES TO THE OLD GODS.

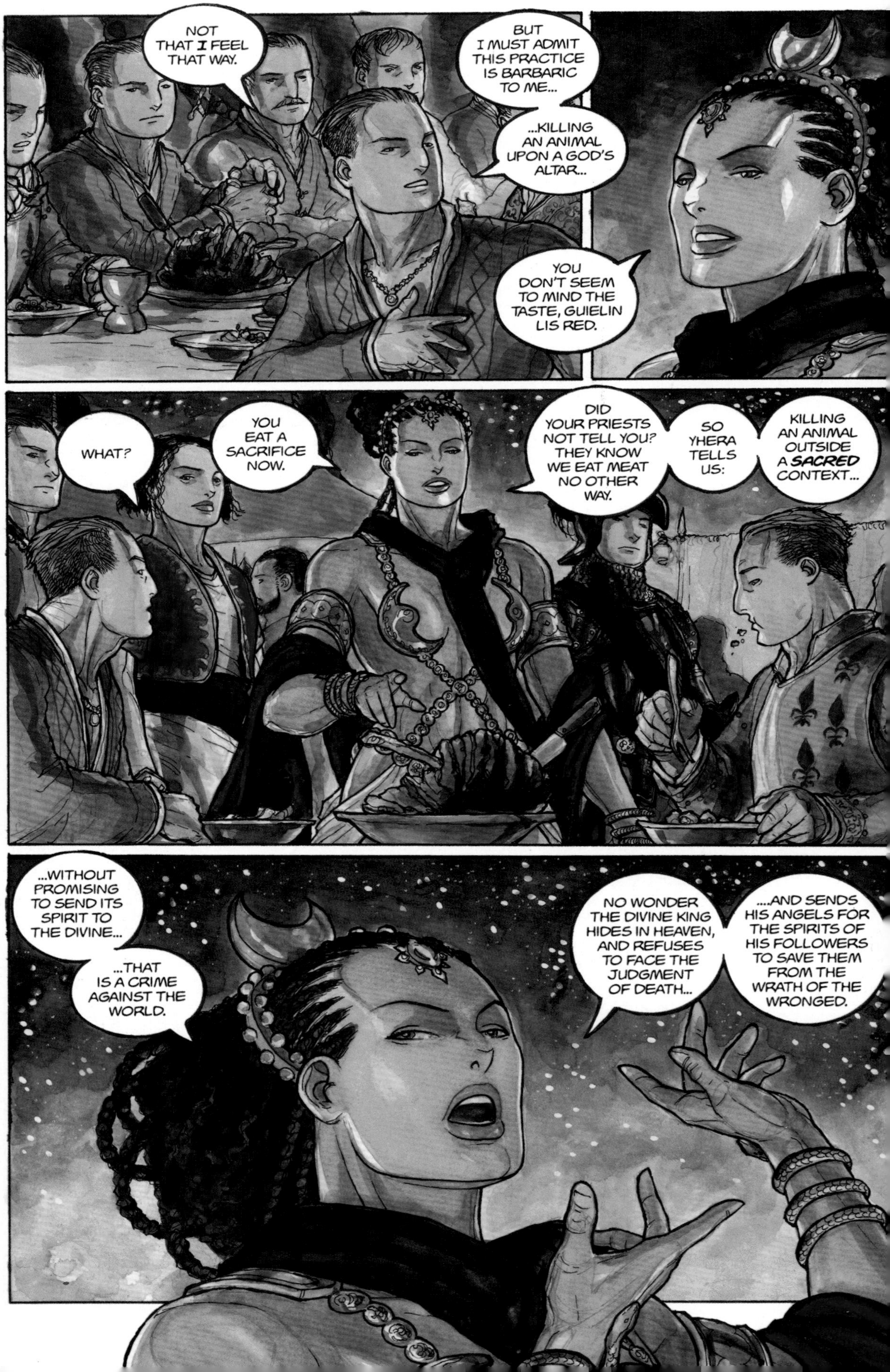
NOT THAT I FEEL THAT WAY.
BUT I MUST ADMIT THIS PRACTICE IS BARBARIC TO ME...
...KILLING AN ANIMAL UPON A GOD'S ALTAR...
YOU DON'T SEEM TO MIND THE TASTE, GUIELIN LIS RED.
WHAT?
YOU EAT A SACRIFICE NOW.
DID YOUR PRIESTS NOT TELL YOU? THEY KNOW WE EAT MEAT NO OTHER WAY.
SO YHERA TELLS US:
KILLING AN ANIMAL OUTSIDE A SACRED CONTEXT...
...WITHOUT PROMISING TO SEND ITS SPIRIT TO THE DIVINE...
...THAT IS A CRIME AGAINST THE WORLD.
NO WONDER THE DIVINE KING HIDES IN HEAVEN, AND REFUSES TO FACE THE JUDGMENT OF DEATH...
....AND SENDS HIS ANGELS FOR THE SPIRITS OF HIS FOLLOWERS TO SAVE THEM FROM THE WRATH OF THE WRONGED.

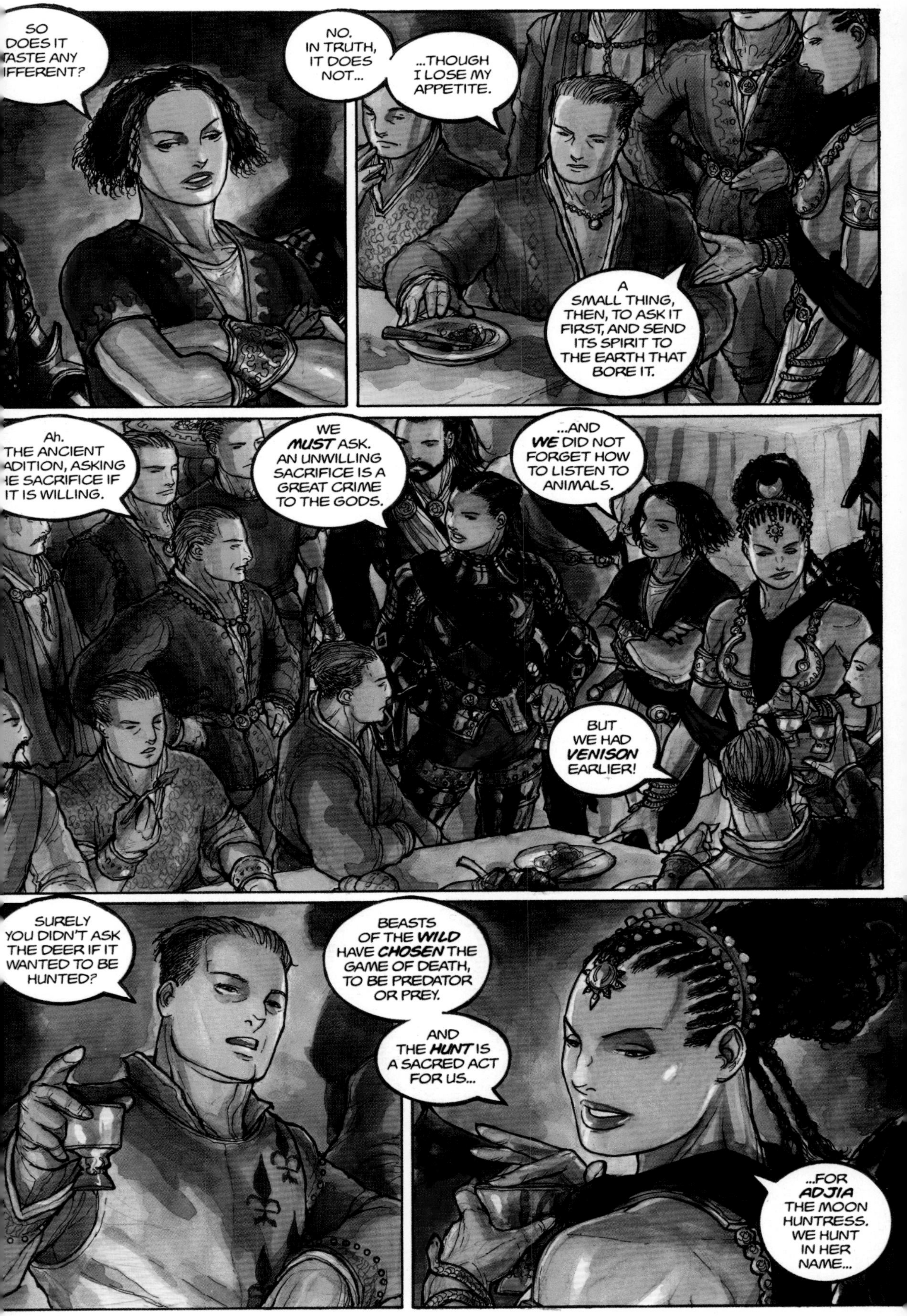
SO DOES IT TASTE ANY IFFERENT?
NO. IN TRUTH, IT DOES NOT...
...THOUGH I LOSE MY APPETITE.
A SMALL THING, THEN, TO ASK IT FIRST, AND SEND ITS SPIRIT TO THE EARTH THAT BORE IT.
Ah. THE ANCIENT ADITION, ASKING HE SACRIFICE IF IT IS WILLING.
WE MUST ASK. AN UNWILLING SACRIFICE IS A GREAT CRIME TO THE GODS.
...AND WE DID NOT FORGET HOW TO LISTEN TO ANIMALS.
BUT WE HAD VENISON EARLIER!
SURELY YOU DIDN'T ASK THE DEER IF IT WANTED TO BE HUNTED?
BEASTS OF THE WILD HAVE CHOSEN THE GAME OF DEATH, TO BE PREDATOR OR PREY.
AND THE HUNT IS A SACRED ACT FOR US...
...FOR ADJIA THE MOON HUNTRESS. WE HUNT IN HER NAME...

...AND THE OFFERINGS OF THE HUNT, LIKE THOSE OF THE TABLE, RECEIVE OUR PRAYERS...

...TO SPEED THEIR SPIRITS TO GENICHÉ'S BOSOM.

THIS SHOULD NOT BE STRANGE TO YOU.

THE HUNTER'S PRAYER IS STILL USED IN AN-ATHAIR, AT LEAST...

...WHERE WE STILL FELT THE SPRING QUEEN'S TOUCH, THOUGH SHE HAS BEEN GONE A THOUSAND YEARS.

THE LAND DOES NOT FORGET AS FAST AS MAN DOES...

...AND WE TOO STILL HOLD THE SPRING QUEEN IN OUR HEARTS.

I AM SURPRISED *AURIANS* WOULD SAY SO...

...SINCE THE SEA BULLS SPELLED THE *END* OF AN-ATHAIR.

BY *OUR* TRADITIONS, SOME AMONGST OUR ANCESTORS WERE ENSPELLED BY THE QUEEN'S BEAUTY.

'TWAS TH[E] *HORNED K[ING]* WHO STRO[VE] TO END TH[E] GOLDEN REALM.

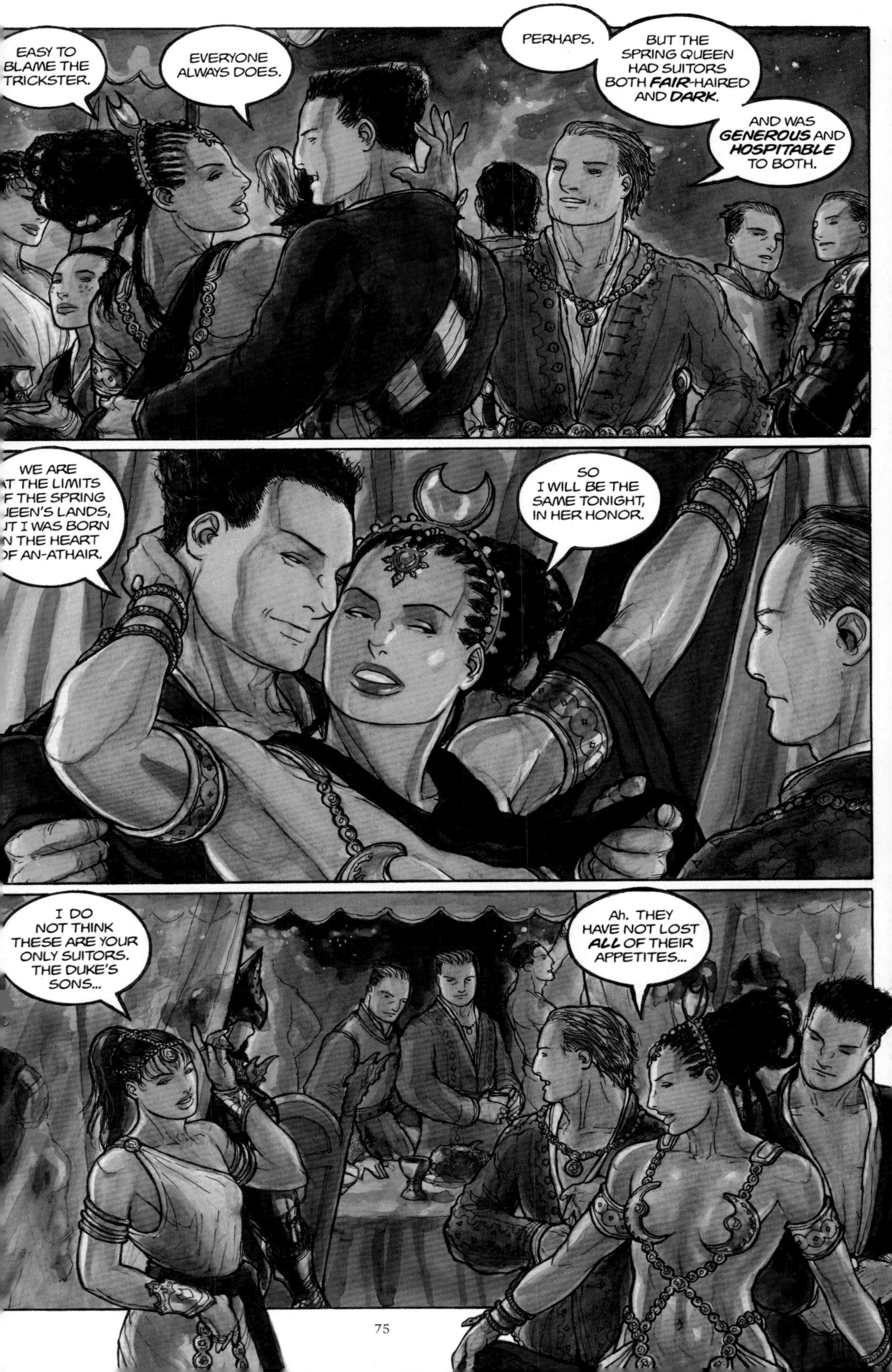
EASY TO BLAME THE TRICKSTER.
EVERYONE ALWAYS DOES.
PERHAPS.
BUT THE SPRING QUEEN HAD SUITORS BOTH **FAIR**-HAIRED AND **DARK**.
AND WAS **GENEROUS** AND **HOSPITABLE** TO BOTH.
WE ARE T THE LIMITS F THE SPRING UEEN'S LANDS, UT I WAS BORN N THE HEART OF AN-ATHAIR.
SO I WILL BE THE SAME TONIGHT, IN HER HONOR.
I DO NOT THINK THESE ARE YOUR ONLY SUITORS. THE DUKE'S SONS...
Ah. THEY HAVE NOT LOST **ALL** OF THEIR APPETITES...

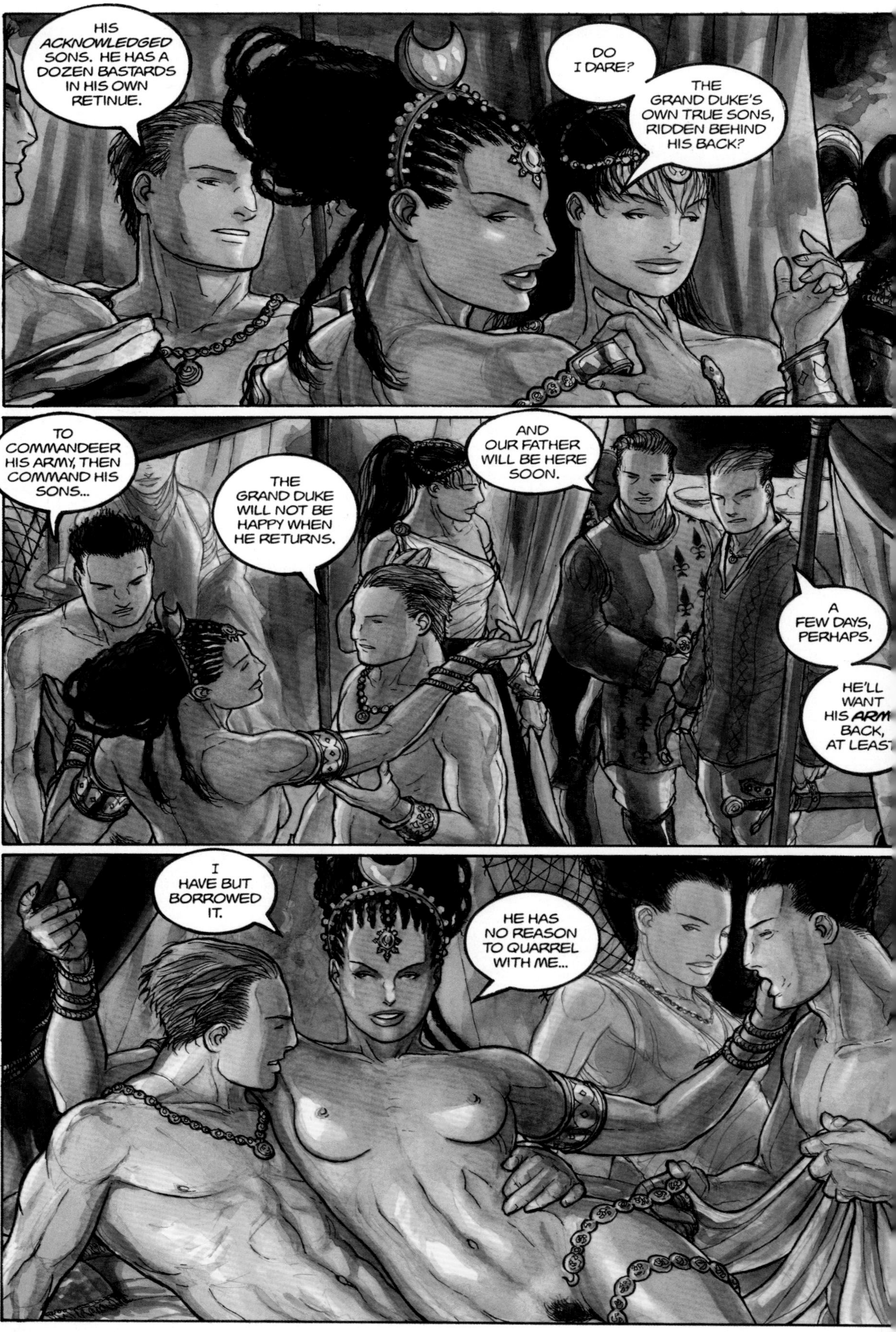
HIS *ACKNOWLEDGED* SONS. HE HAS A DOZEN BASTARDS IN HIS OWN RETINUE.
DO I DARE?
THE GRAND DUKE'S OWN TRUE SONS, RIDDEN BEHIND HIS BACK?
TO COMMANDEER HIS ARMY, THEN COMMAND HIS SONS...
THE GRAND DUKE WILL NOT BE HAPPY WHEN HE RETURNS.
AND OUR FATHER WILL BE HERE SOON.
A FEW DAYS, PERHAPS.
HE'LL WANT HIS *ARM* BACK, AT LEAS
I HAVE BUT BORROWED IT.
HE HAS NO REASON TO QUARREL WITH ME...

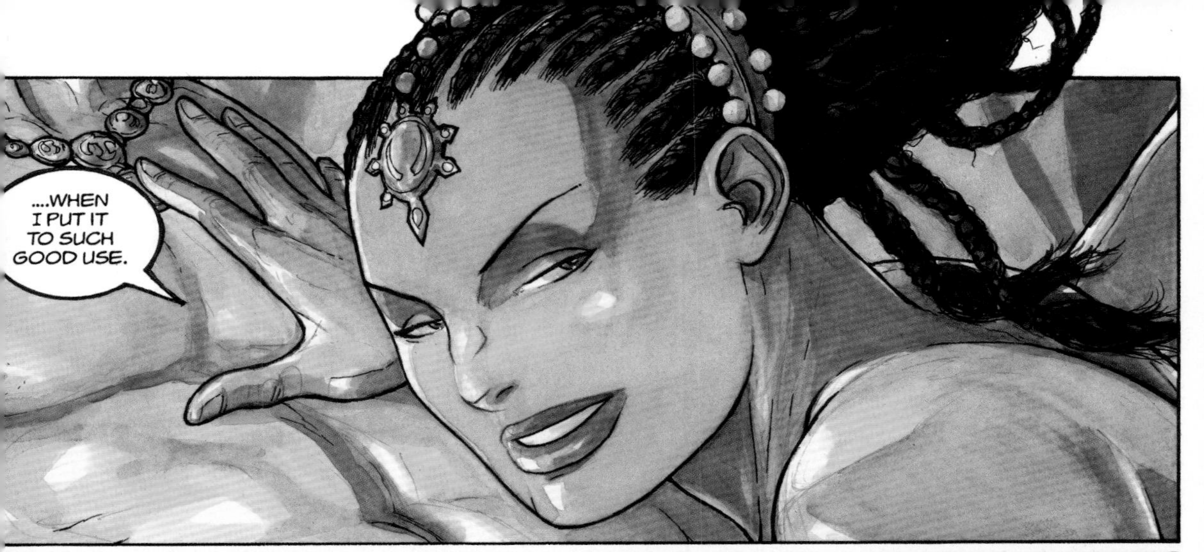
....WHEN I PUT IT TO SUCH GOOD USE.

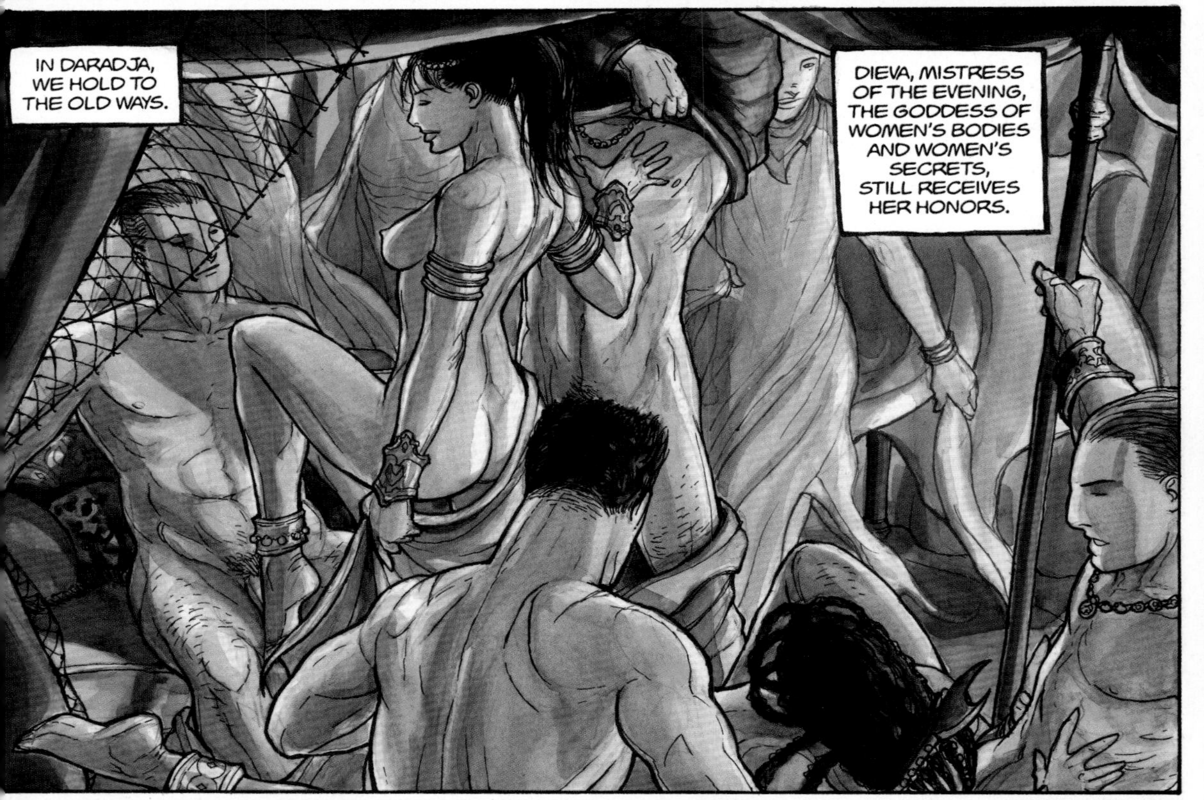
IN DARADJA, WE HOLD TO THE OLD WAYS.
DIEVA, MISTRESS OF THE EVENING, THE GODDESS OF WOMEN'S BODIES AND WOMEN'S SECRETS, STILL RECEIVES HER HONORS.

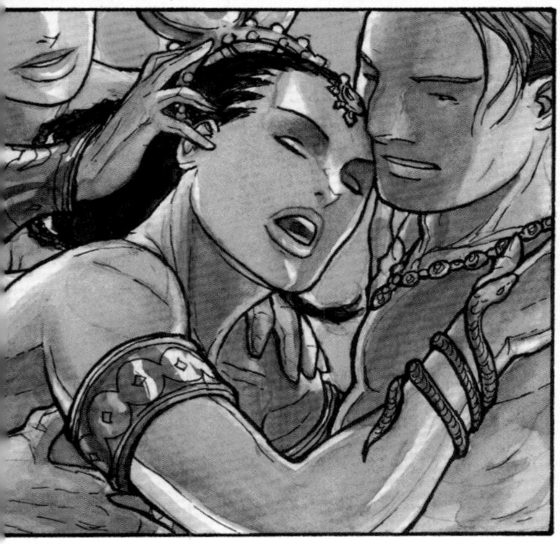

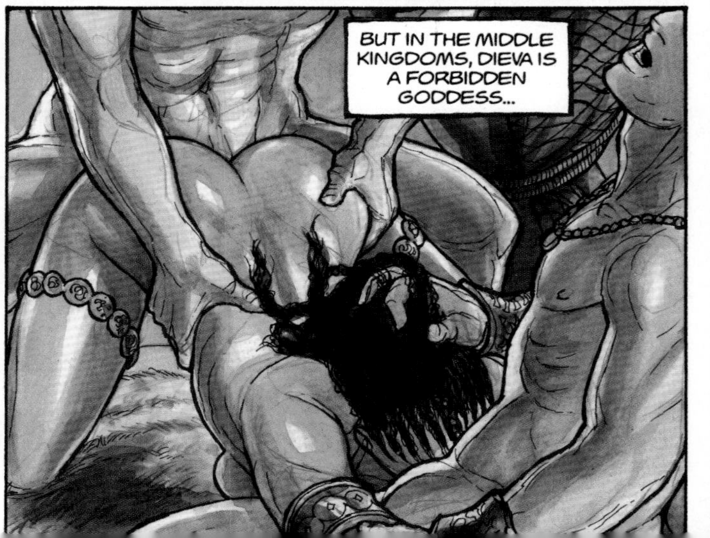
BUT IN THE MIDDLE KINGDOMS, DIEVA IS A FORBIDDEN GODDESS...

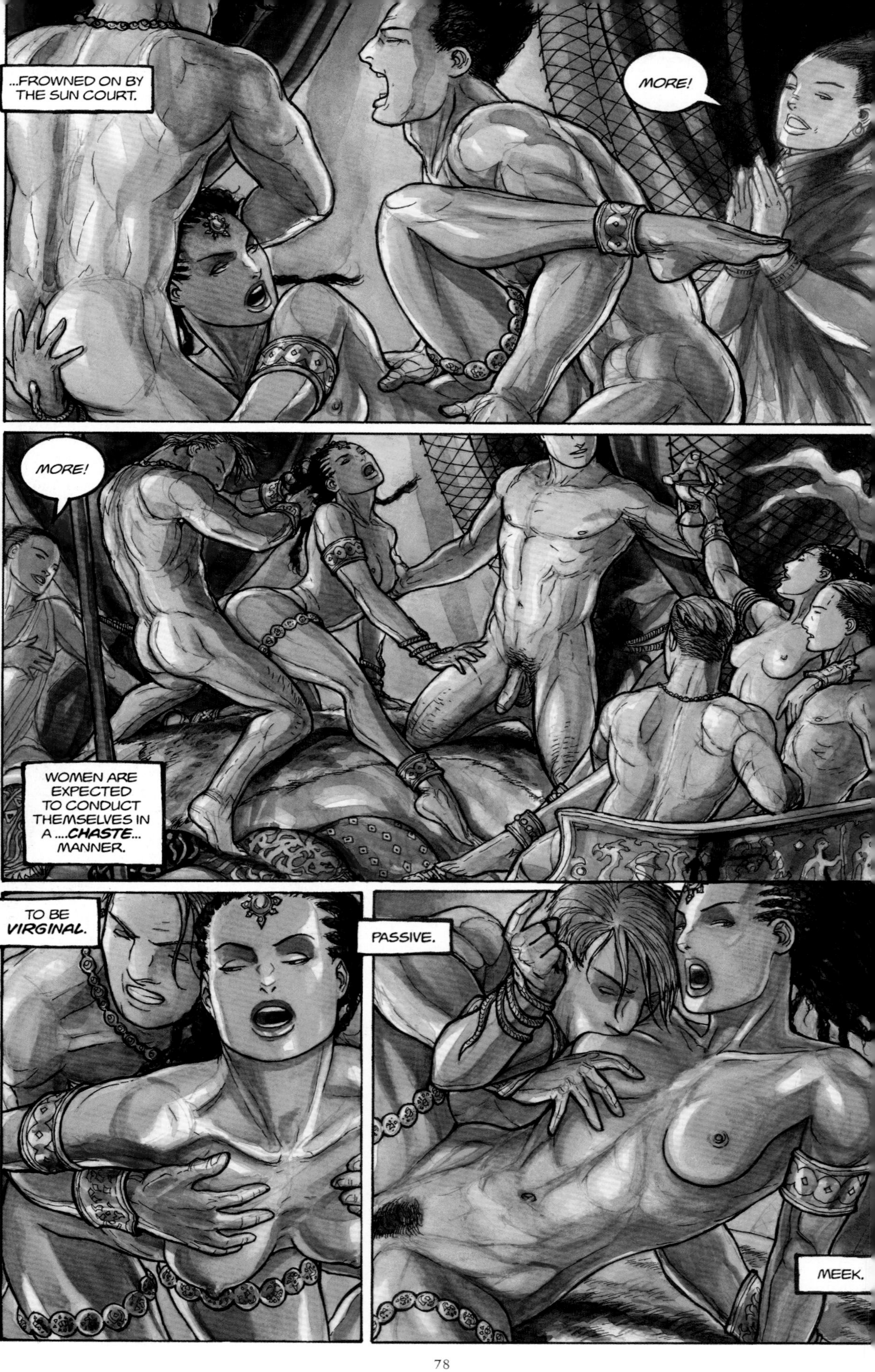
...FROWNED ON BY THE SUN COURT.
MORE!
MORE!
WOMEN ARE EXPECTED TO CONDUCT THEMSELVES IN A ....CHASTE... MANNER.
TO BE VIRGINAL.
PASSIVE.
MEEK.

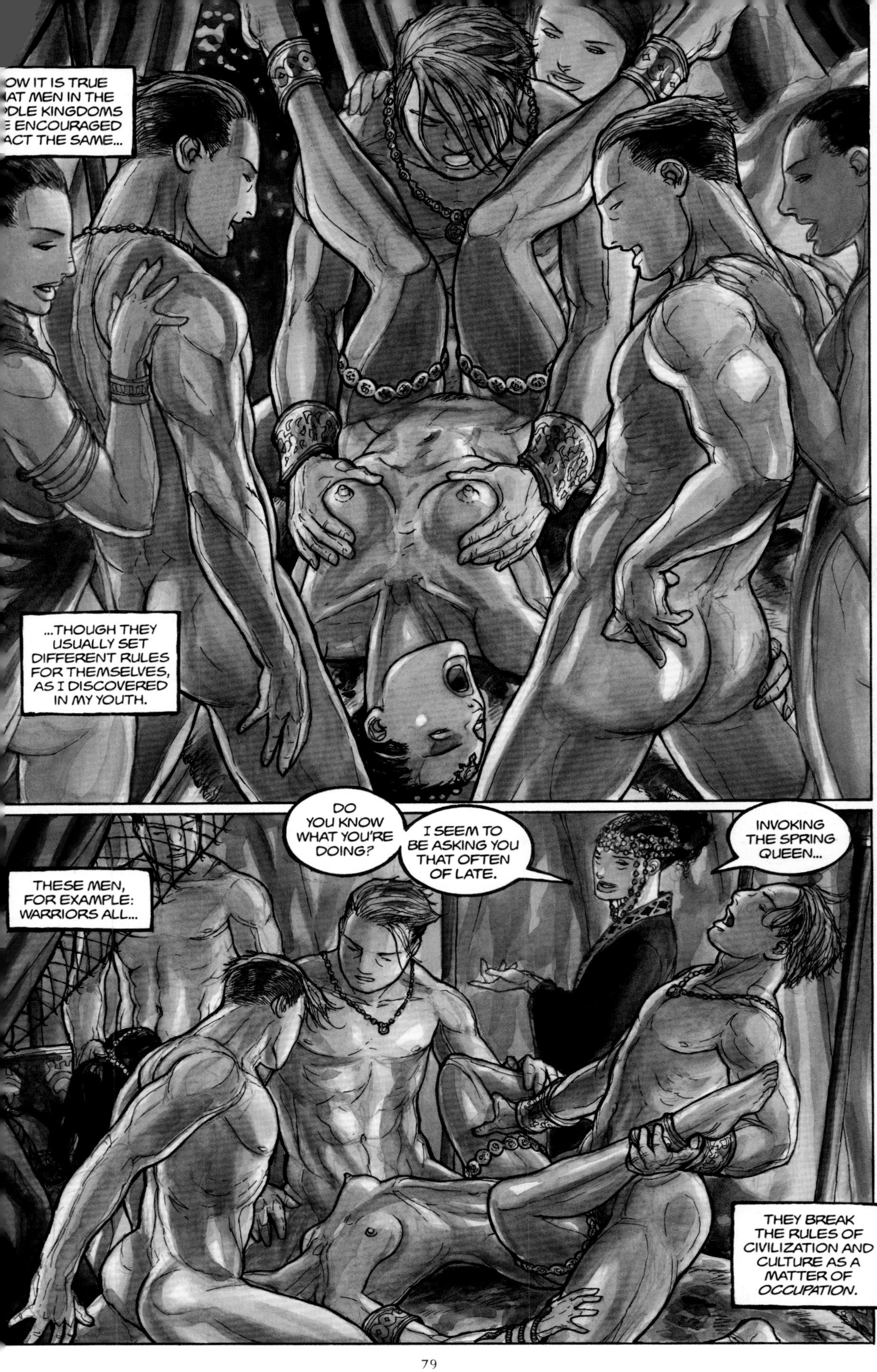
OW IT IS TRUE
AT MEN IN THE
DDLE KINGDOMS
E ENCOURAGED
ACT THE SAME...
...THOUGH THEY USUALLY SET DIFFERENT RULES FOR THEMSELVES, AS I DISCOVERED IN MY YOUTH.
THESE MEN, FOR EXAMPLE: WARRIORS ALL...
DO YOU KNOW WHAT YOU'RE DOING?
I SEEM TO BE ASKING YOU THAT OFTEN OF LATE.
INVOKING THE SPRING QUEEN...
THEY BREAK THE RULES OF CIVILIZATION AND CULTURE AS A MATTER OF OCCUPATION.

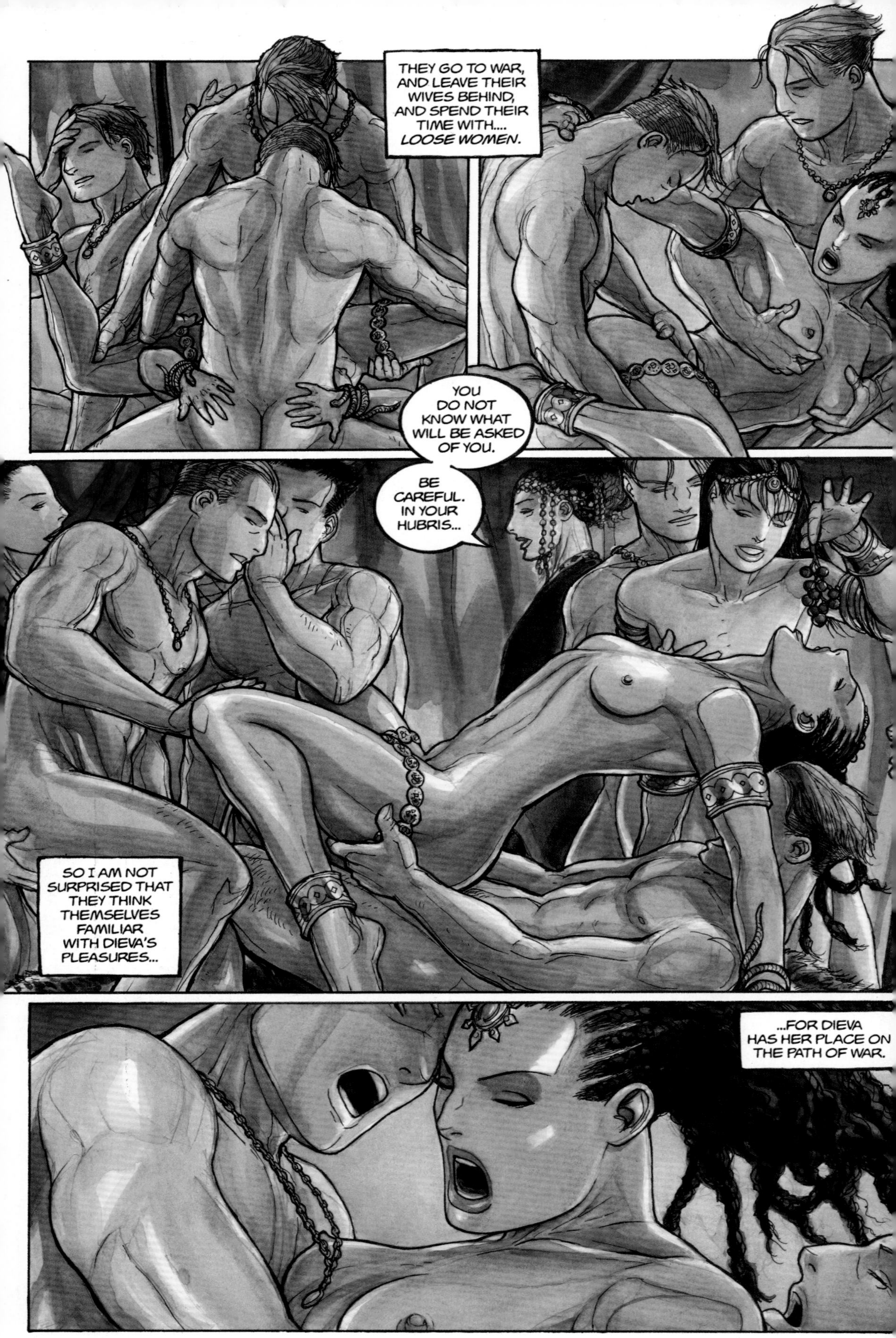
THEY GO TO WAR, AND LEAVE THEIR WIVES BEHIND, AND SPEND THEIR TIME WITH.... LOOSE WOMEN.
YOU DO NOT KNOW WHAT WILL BE ASKED OF YOU.
BE CAREFUL. IN YOUR HUBRIS...
SO I AM NOT SURPRISED THAT THEY THINK THEMSELVES FAMILIAR WITH DIEVA'S PLEASURES...
...FOR DIEVA HAS HER PLACE ON THE PATH OF WAR.

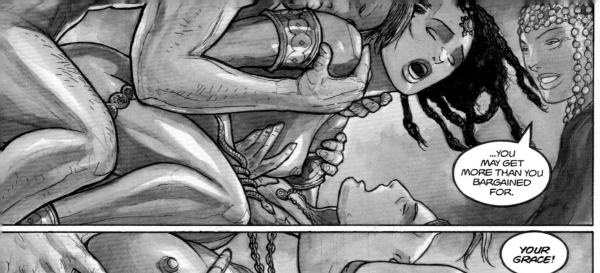

...YOU MAY GET MORE THAN YOU BARGAINED FOR.

YOUR GRACE!

Ahem. FORGIVE ME, BUT THEY WERE *MOST* INSISTENT...

MOTHER!

FATHER!

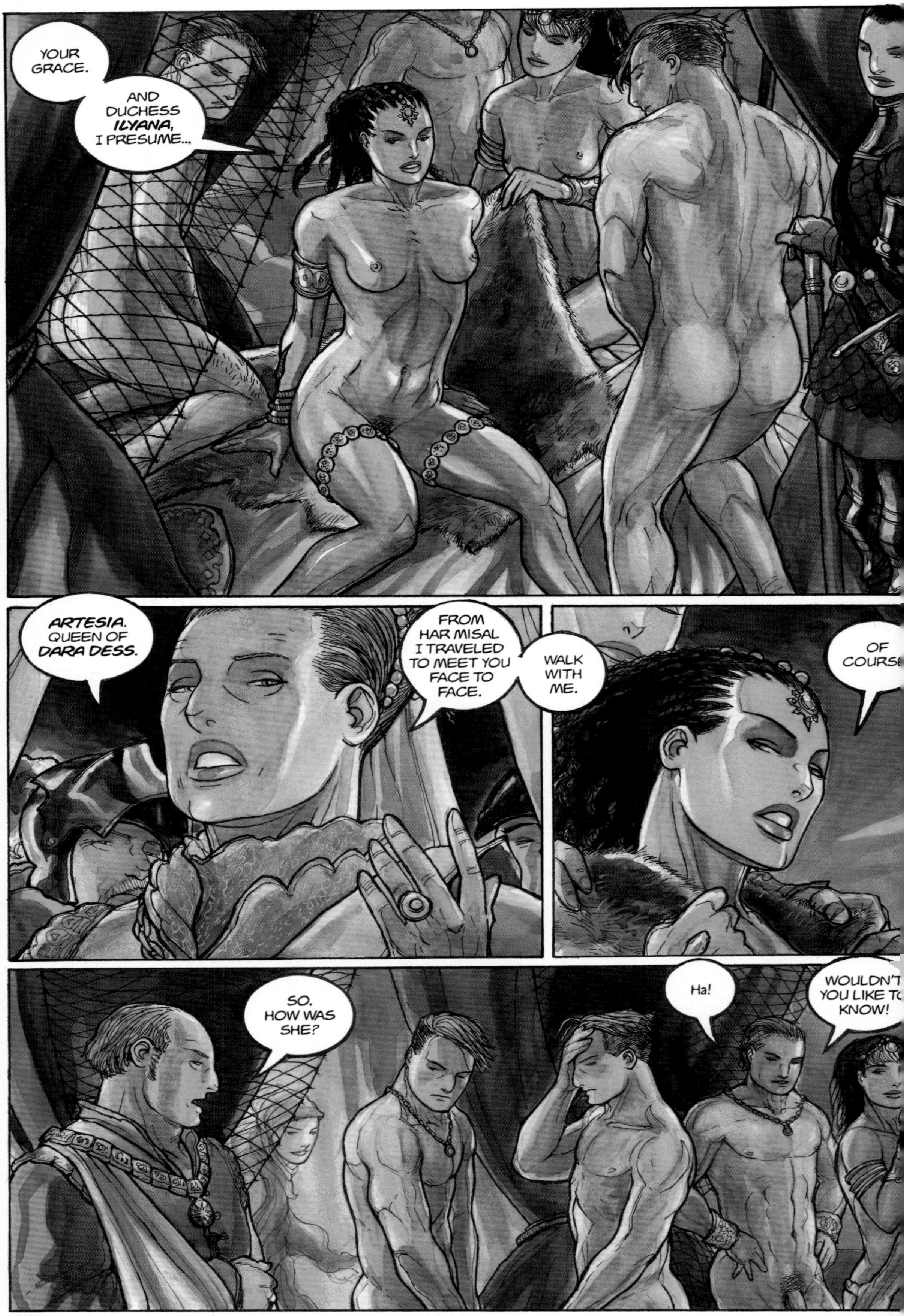
YOUR GRACE.
AND DUCHESS ILYANA, I PRESUME...
ARTESIA. QUEEN OF DARA DESS.
FROM HAR MISAL I TRAVELED TO MEET YOU FACE TO FACE.
WALK WITH ME.
OF COURS
SO. HOW WAS SHE?
Ha!
WOULDN'T YOU LIKE TO KNOW!

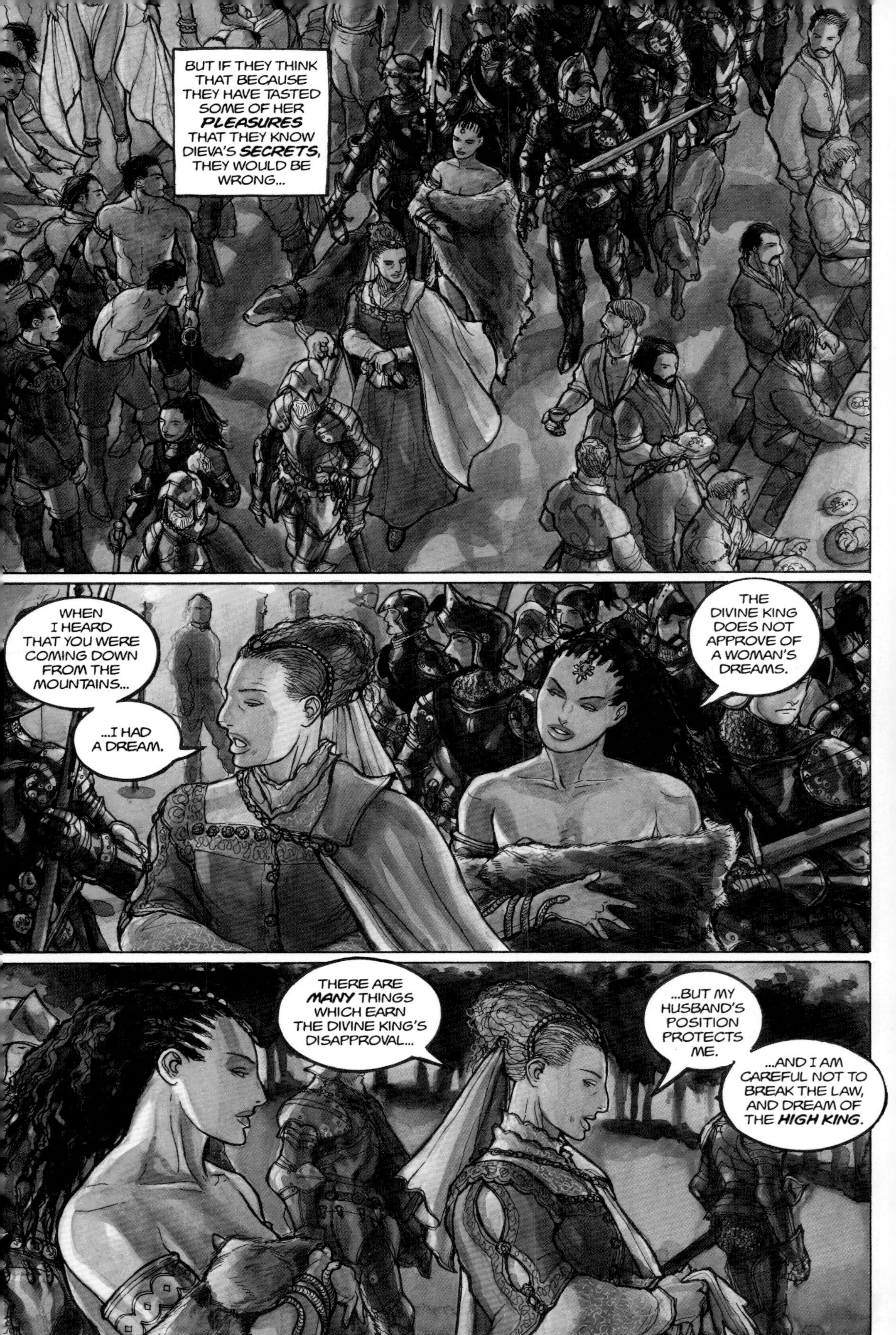

BUT IF THEY THINK THAT BECAUSE THEY HAVE TASTED SOME OF HER ***PLEASURES*** THAT THEY KNOW DIEVA'S ***SECRETS,*** THEY WOULD BE WRONG...
WHEN I HEARD THAT YOU WERE COMING DOWN FROM THE MOUNTAINS...
...I HAD A DREAM.
THE DIVINE KING DOES NOT APPROVE OF A WOMAN'S DREAMS.
THERE ARE ***MANY*** THINGS WHICH EARN THE DIVINE KING'S DISAPPROVAL...
...BUT MY HUSBAND'S POSITION PROTECTS ME.
...AND I AM CAREFUL NOT TO BREAK THE LAW, AND DREAM OF THE ***HIGH KING***.

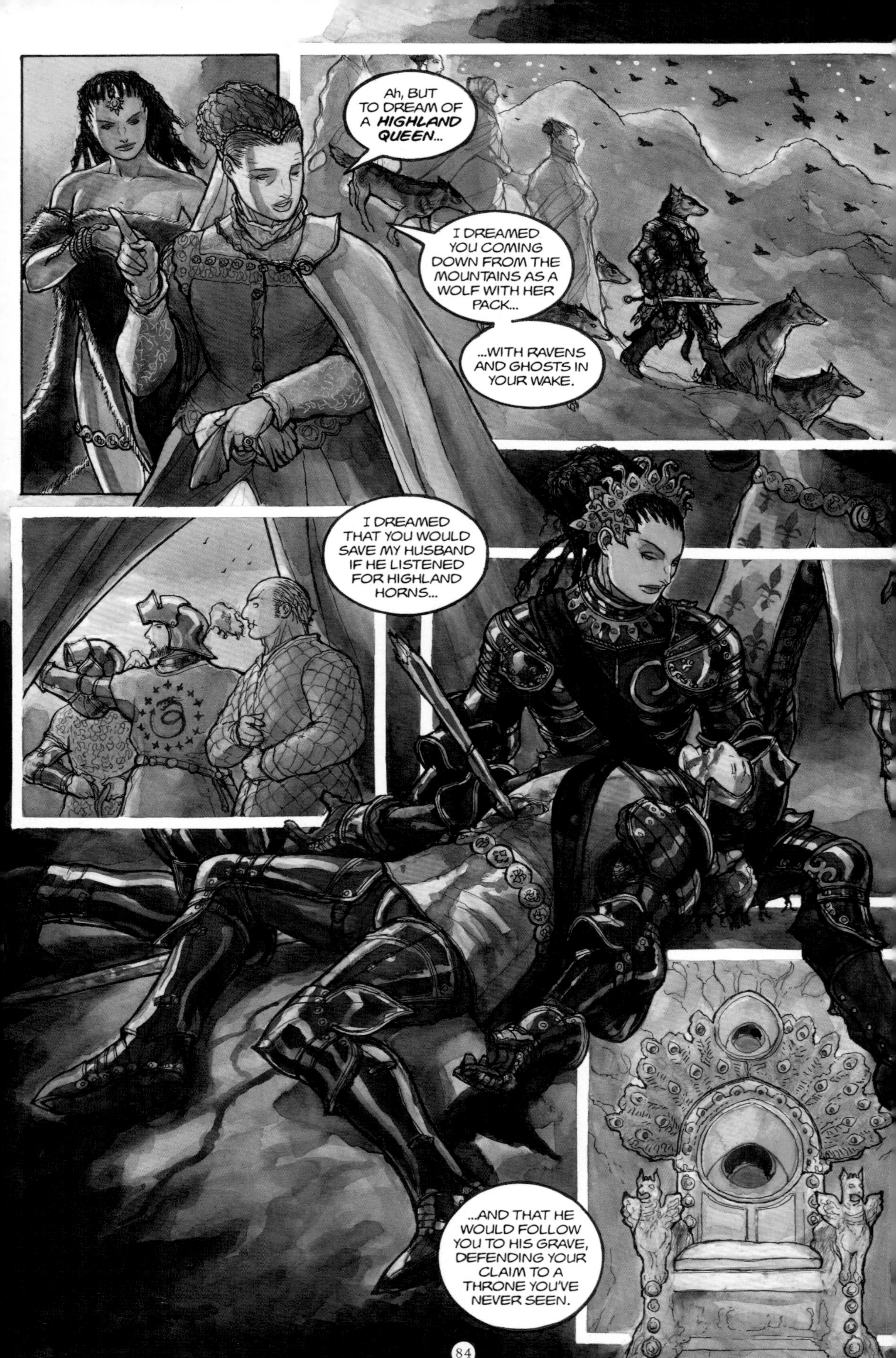
Ah, BUT TO DREAM OF A HIGHLAND QUEEN...
I DREAMED YOU COMING DOWN FROM THE MOUNTAINS AS A WOLF WITH HER PACK...
...WITH RAVENS AND GHOSTS IN YOUR WAKE.
I DREAMED THAT YOU WOULD SAVE MY HUSBAND IF HE LISTENED FOR HIGHLAND HORNS...
...AND THAT HE WOULD FOLLOW YOU TO HIS GRAVE, DEFENDING YOUR CLAIM TO A THRONE YOU'VE NEVER SEEN.

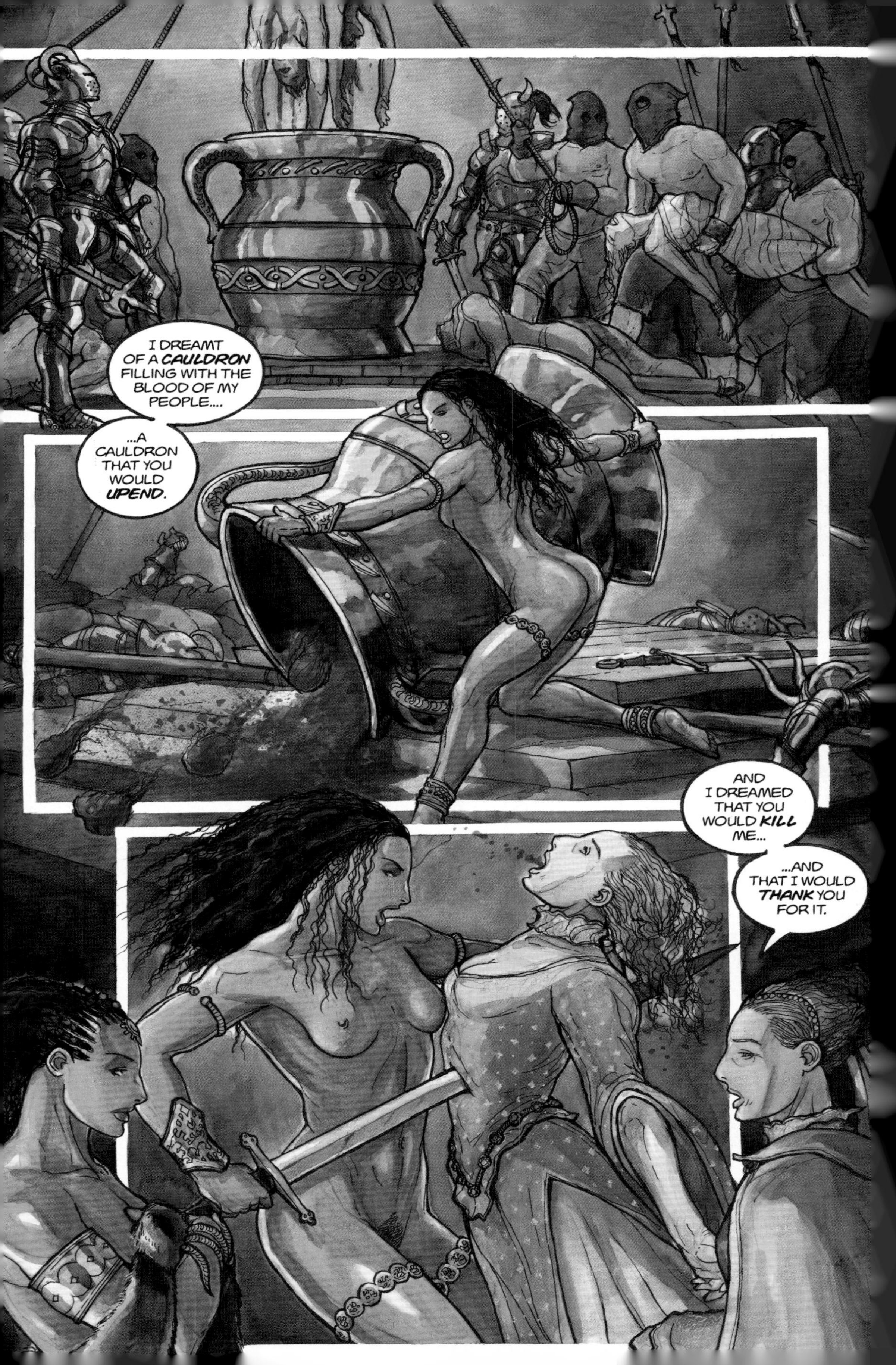
I DREAMT OF A CAULDRON FILLING WITH THE BLOOD OF MY PEOPLE....
...A CAULDRON THAT YOU WOULD UPEND.
AND I DREAMED THAT YOU WOULD KILL ME...
...AND THAT I WOULD THANK YOU FOR IT.

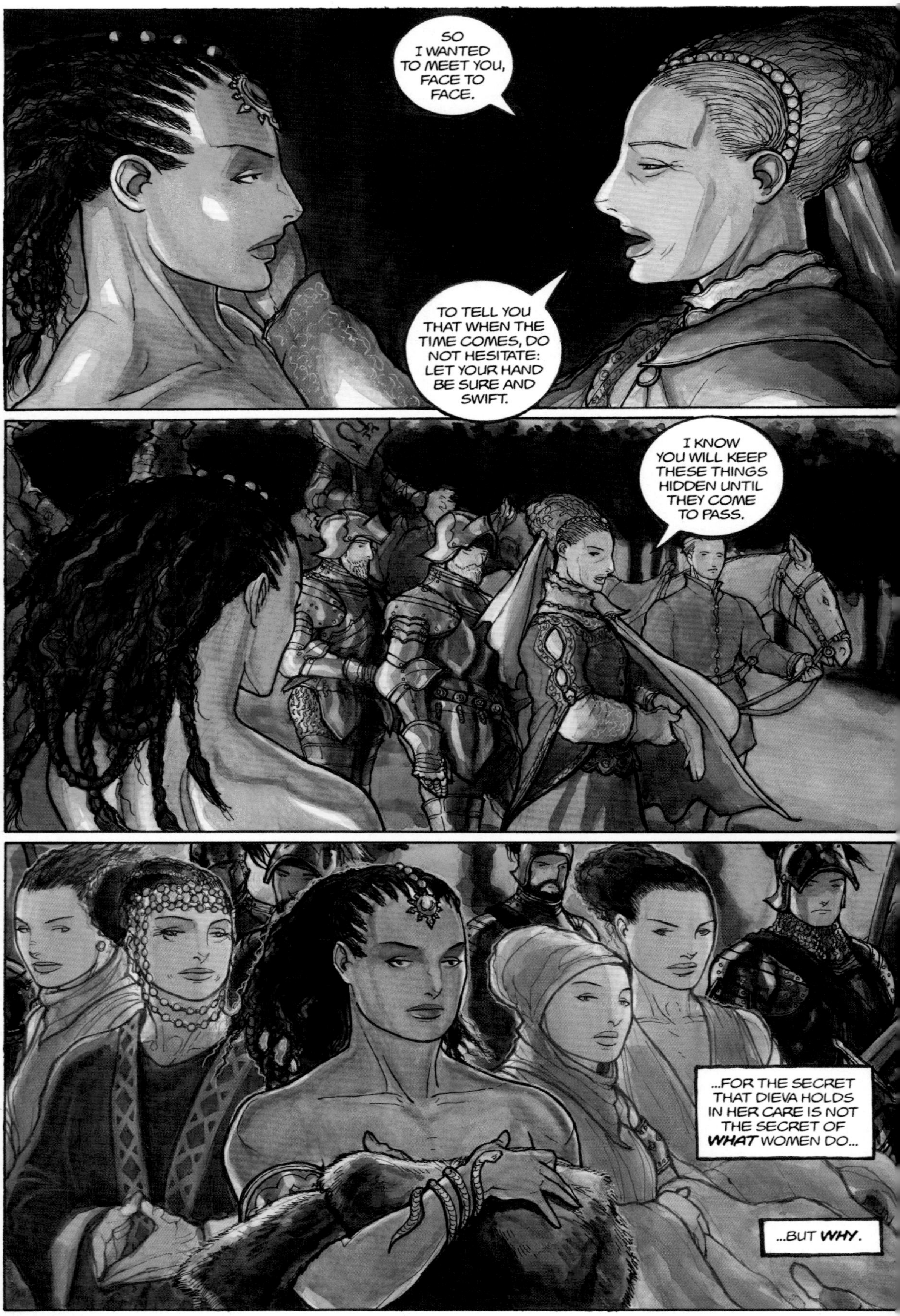
SO I WANTED TO MEET YOU, FACE TO FACE.
TO TELL YOU THAT WHEN THE TIME COMES, DO NOT HESITATE: LET YOUR HAND BE SURE AND SWIFT.
I KNOW YOU WILL KEEP THESE THINGS HIDDEN UNTIL THEY COME TO PASS.
...FOR THE SECRET THAT DIEVA HOLDS IN HER CARE IS NOT THE SECRET OF ***WHAT*** WOMEN DO...
...BUT ***WHY***.

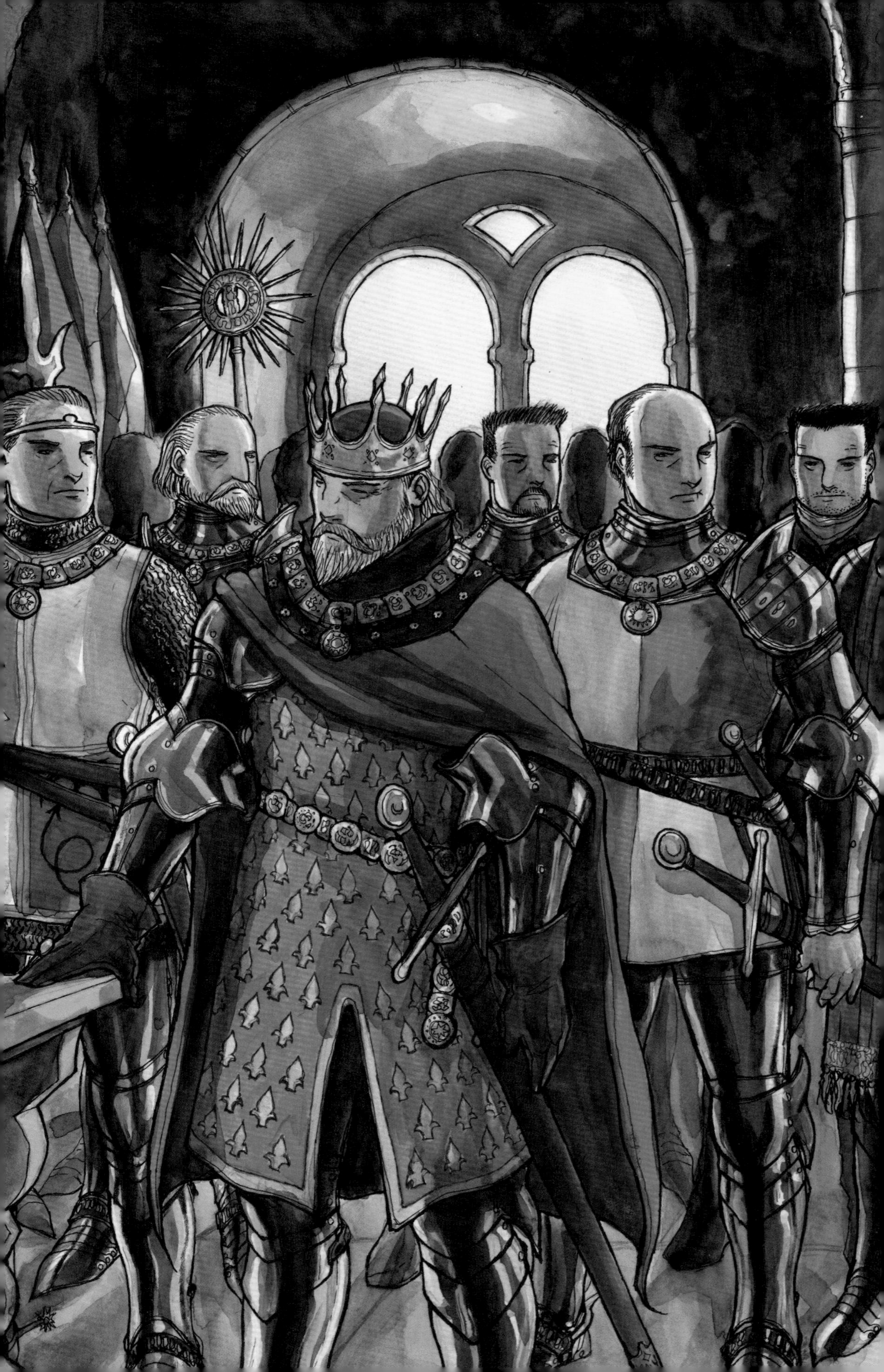

Chapter Three

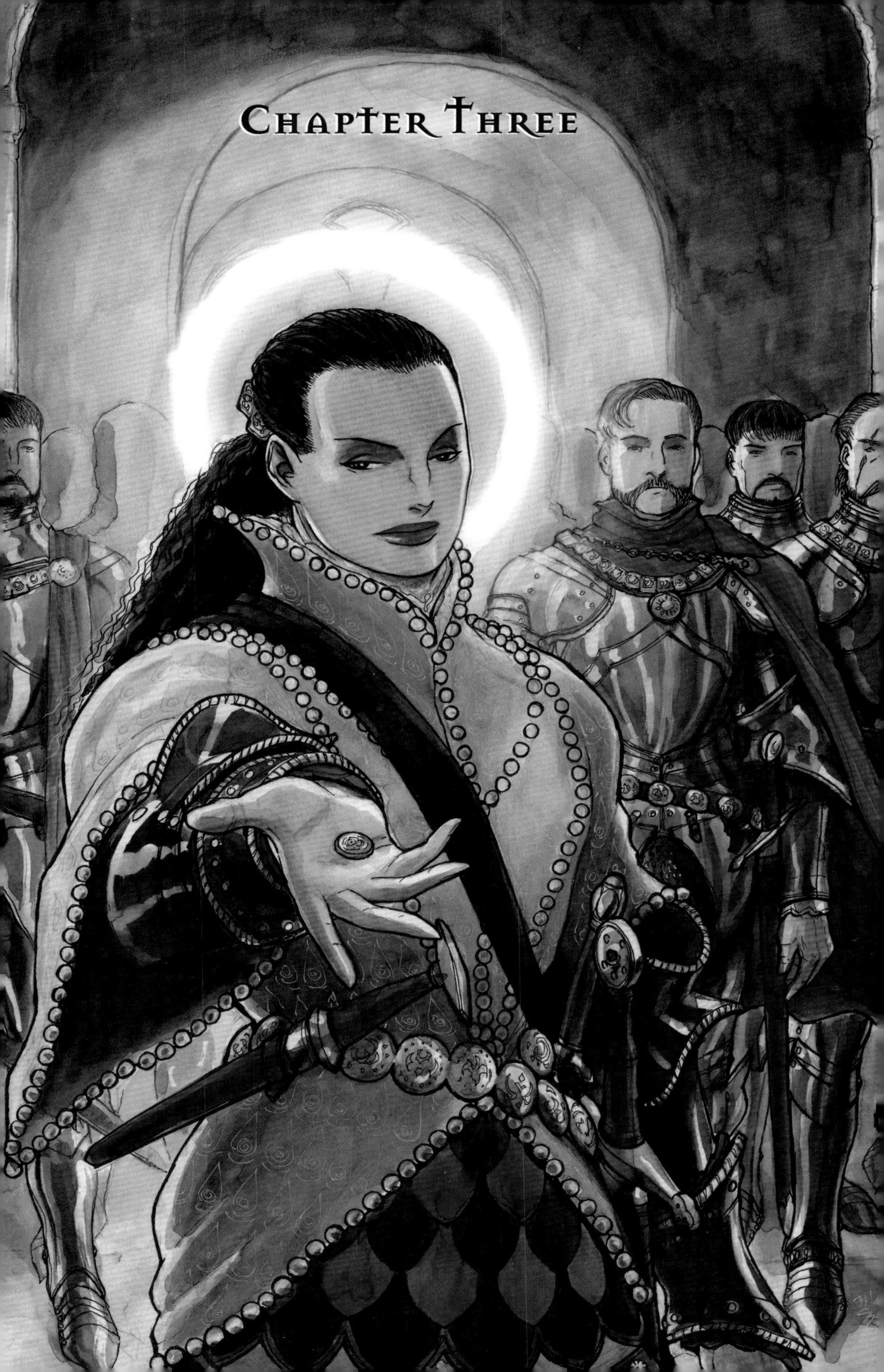

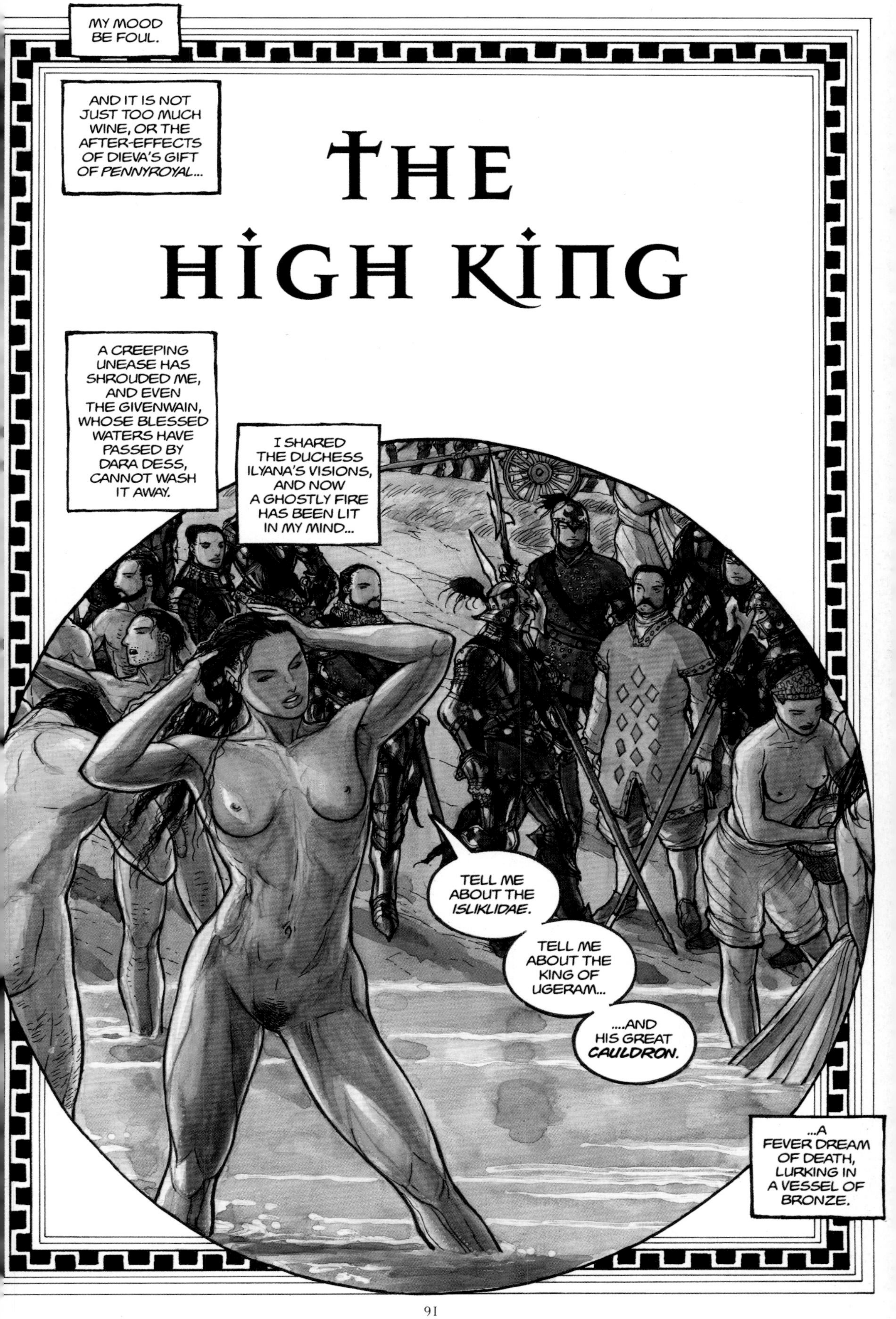
MY MOOD BE FOUL.
AND IT IS NOT JUST TOO MUCH WINE, OR THE AFTER-EFFECTS OF DIEVA'S GIFT OF *PENNYROYAL*...
THE HIGH KING
A CREEPING UNEASE HAS SHROUDED ME, AND EVEN THE GIVENWAIN, WHOSE BLESSED WATERS HAVE PASSED BY DARA DESS, CANNOT WASH IT AWAY.
I SHARED THE DUCHESS ILYANA'S VISIONS, AND NOW A GHOSTLY FIRE HAS BEEN LIT IN MY MIND...
TELL ME ABOUT THE *ISLIKIDAE*.
TELL ME ABOUT THE KING OF UGERAM...
....AND HIS GREAT ***CAULDRON***.
...A FEVER DREAM OF DEATH, LURKING IN A VESSEL OF BRONZE.

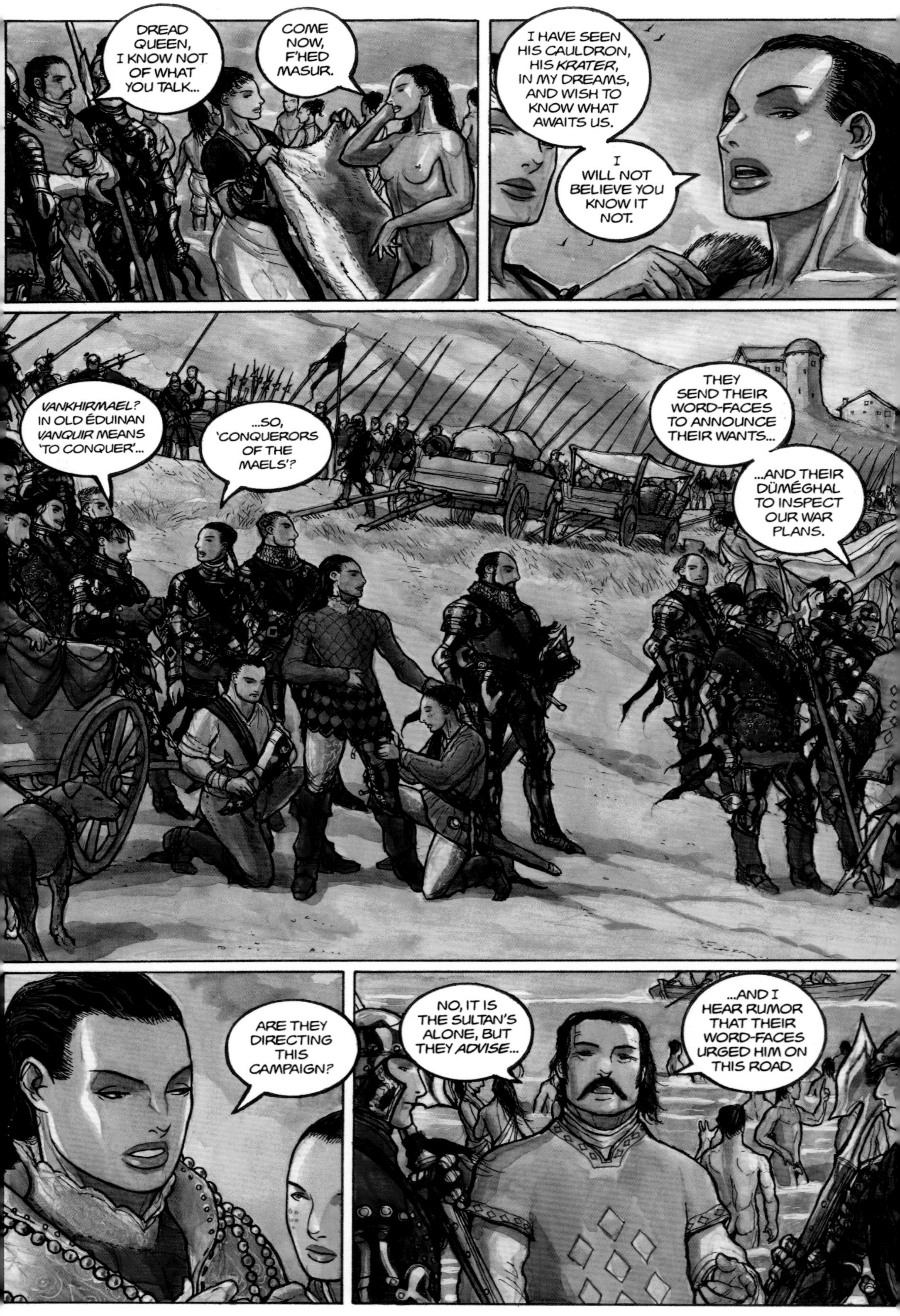
DREAD QUEEN, I KNOW NOT OF WHAT YOU TALK...
COME NOW, F'HED MASUR.
I HAVE SEEN HIS CAULDRON, HIS *KRATER*, IN MY DREAMS, AND WISH TO KNOW WHAT AWAITS US.
I WILL NOT BELIEVE YOU KNOW IT NOT.
VANKHIRMAEL? IN OLD ÉDUINAN *VANQUIR* MEANS 'TO CONQUER'...
...SO, 'CONQUERORS OF THE MAELS'?
THEY SEND THEIR WORD-FACES TO ANNOUNCE THEIR WANTS...
...AND THEIR DÜMÉGHAL TO INSPECT OUR WAR PLANS.
ARE THEY DIRECTING THIS CAMPAIGN?
NO, IT IS THE SULTAN'S ALONE, BUT THEY *ADVISE*...
...AND I HEAR RUMOR THAT THEIR WORD-FACES URGED HIM ON THIS ROAD.

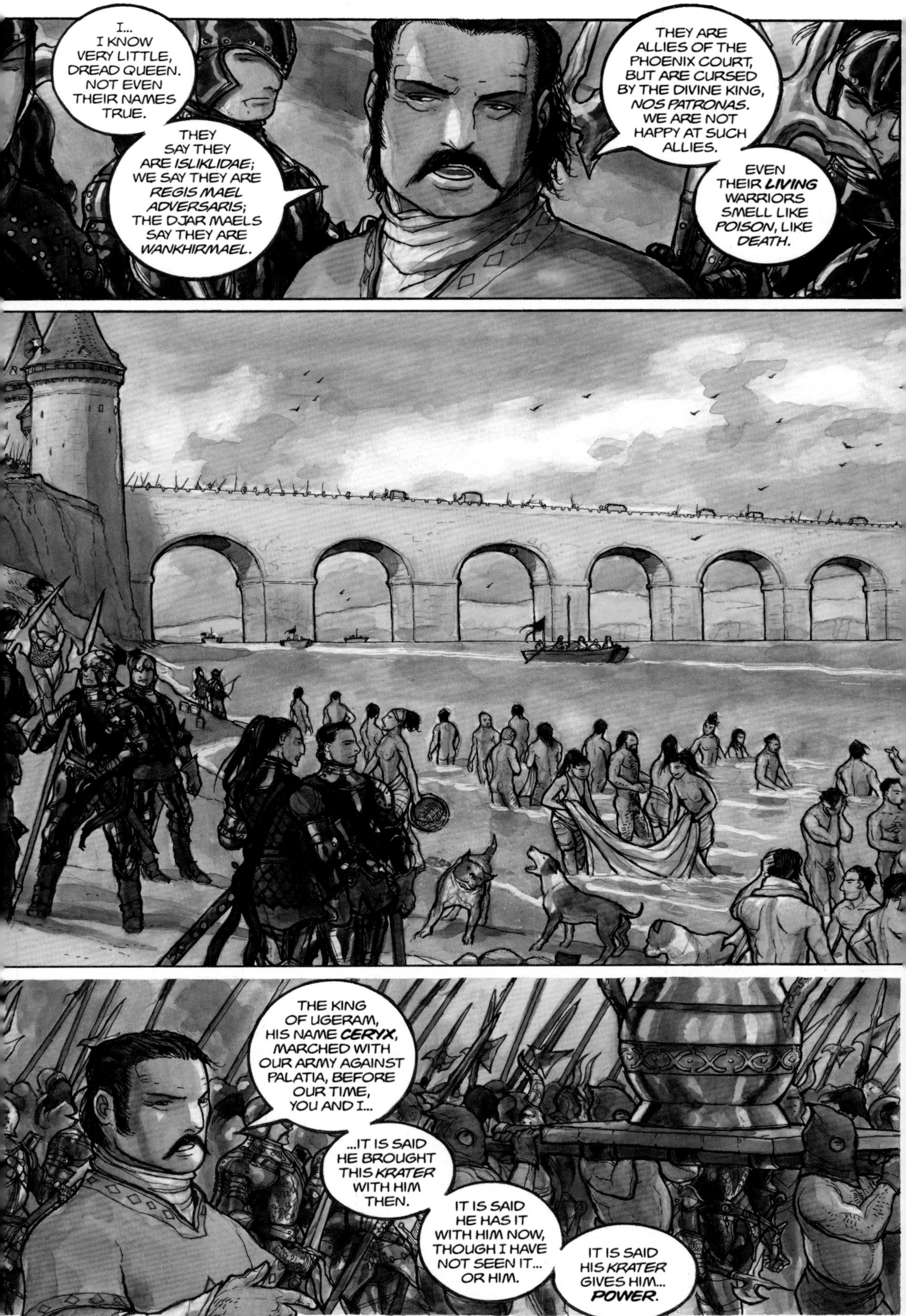
I... I KNOW VERY LITTLE, DREAD QUEEN. NOT EVEN THEIR NAMES TRUE.
THEY SAY THEY ARE *ISLIKLIDAE*; WE SAY THEY ARE *REGIS MAEL ADVERSARIS*; THE DJAR MAELS SAY THEY ARE *WANKHIRMAEL*.
THEY ARE ALLIES OF THE PHOENIX COURT, BUT ARE CURSED BY THE DIVINE KING, *NOS PATRONAS*. WE ARE NOT HAPPY AT SUCH ALLIES.
EVEN THEIR ***LIVING*** WARRIORS SMELL LIKE *POISON*, LIKE *DEATH*.
THE KING OF UGERAM, HIS NAME ***CERYX***, MARCHED WITH OUR ARMY AGAINST PALATIA, BEFORE OUR TIME, YOU AND I...
...IT IS SAID HE BROUGHT THIS *KRATER* WITH HIM THEN.
IT IS SAID HE HAS IT WITH HIM NOW, THOUGH I HAVE NOT SEEN IT... OR HIM.
IT IS SAID HIS *KRATER* GIVES HIM... ***POWER***.

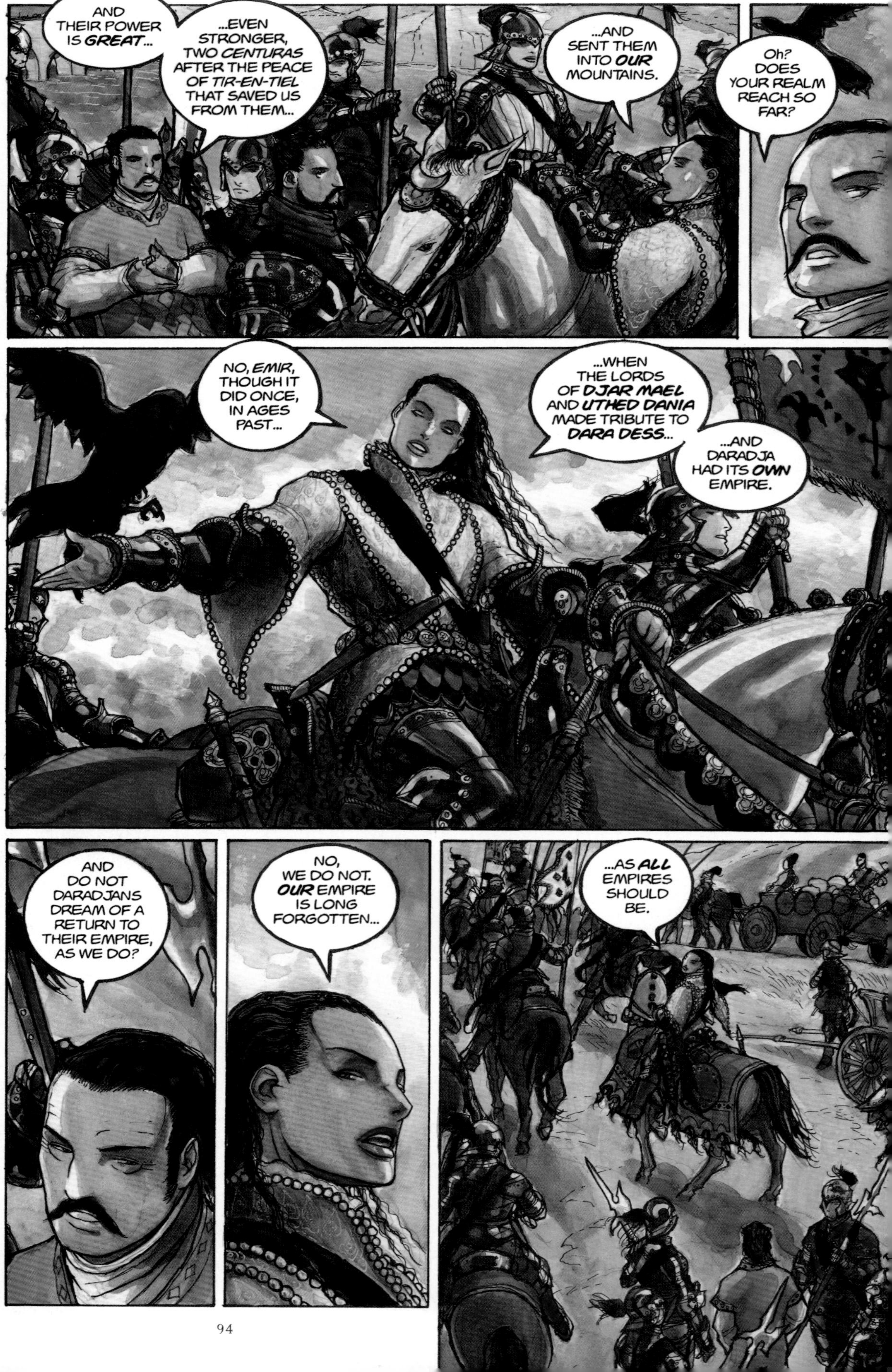
AND THEIR POWER IS GREAT...
...EVEN STRONGER, TWO CENTURAS AFTER THE PEACE OF TIR-EN-TIEL THAT SAVED US FROM THEM...
...AND SENT THEM INTO OUR MOUNTAINS.
Oh? DOES YOUR REALM REACH SO FAR?
NO, EMIR, THOUGH IT DID ONCE, IN AGES PAST...
...WHEN THE LORDS OF DJAR MAEL AND UTHED DANIA MADE TRIBUTE TO DARA DESS...
...AND DARADJA HAD ITS OWN EMPIRE.
AND DO NOT DARADJANS DREAM OF A RETURN TO THEIR EMPIRE, AS WE DO?
NO, WE DO NOT. OUR EMPIRE IS LONG FORGOTTEN...
...AS ALL EMPIRES SHOULD BE.

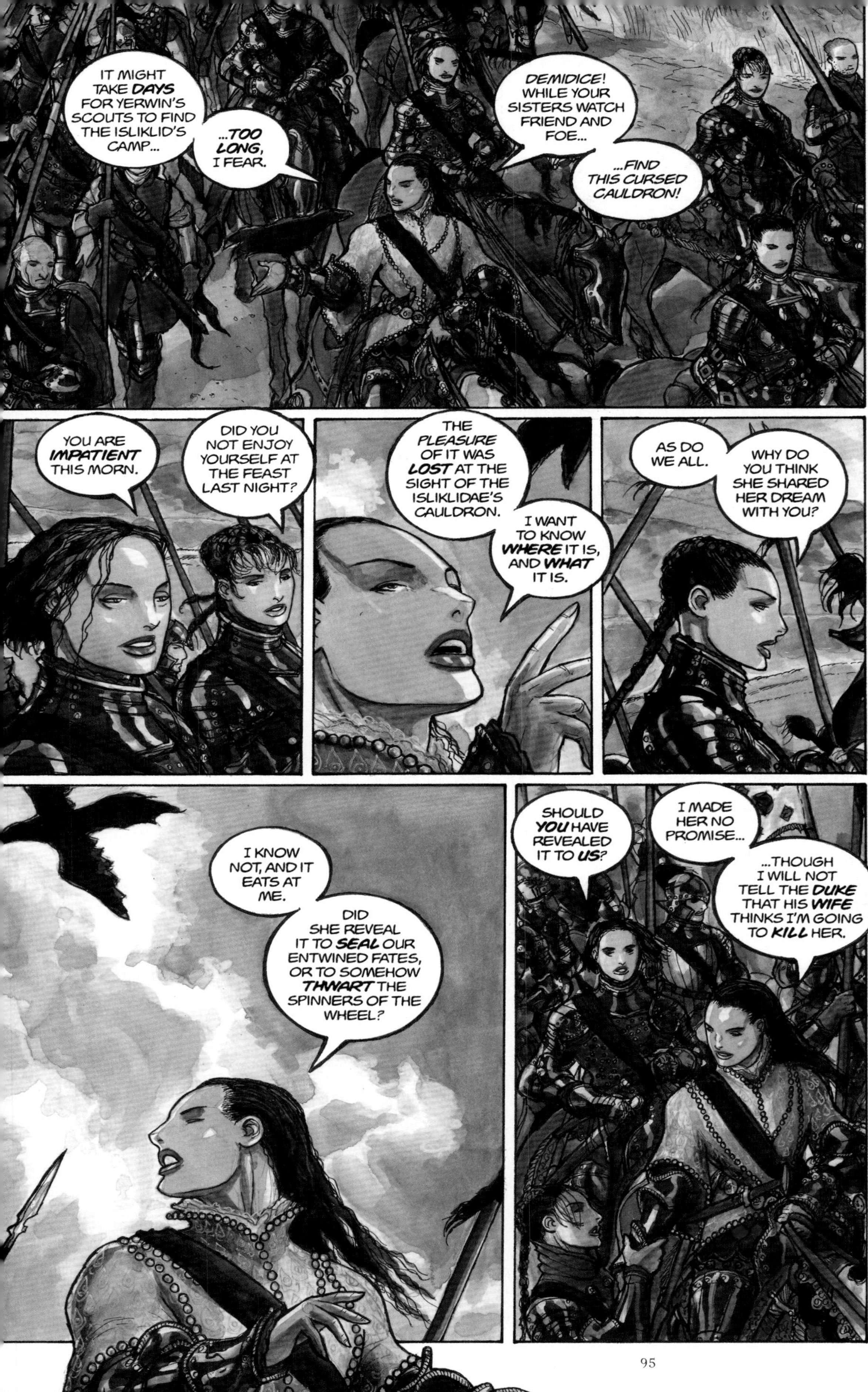
IT MIGHT TAKE DAYS FOR YERWIN'S SCOUTS TO FIND THE ISLIKLID'S CAMP...
...TOO LONG, I FEAR.
DEMIDICE! WHILE YOUR SISTERS WATCH FRIEND AND FOE...
...FIND THIS CURSED CAULDRON!
YOU ARE IMPATIENT THIS MORN.
DID YOU NOT ENJOY YOURSELF AT THE FEAST LAST NIGHT?
THE PLEASURE OF IT WAS LOST AT THE SIGHT OF THE ISLIKLIDAE'S CAULDRON.
I WANT TO KNOW WHERE IT IS, AND WHAT IT IS.
AS DO WE ALL.
WHY DO YOU THINK SHE SHARED HER DREAM WITH YOU?
I KNOW NOT, AND IT EATS AT ME.
DID SHE REVEAL IT TO SEAL OUR ENTWINED FATES, OR TO SOMEHOW THWART THE SPINNERS OF THE WHEEL?
SHOULD YOU HAVE REVEALED IT TO US?
I MADE HER NO PROMISE...
...THOUGH I WILL NOT TELL THE DUKE THAT HIS WIFE THINKS I'M GOING TO KILL HER.

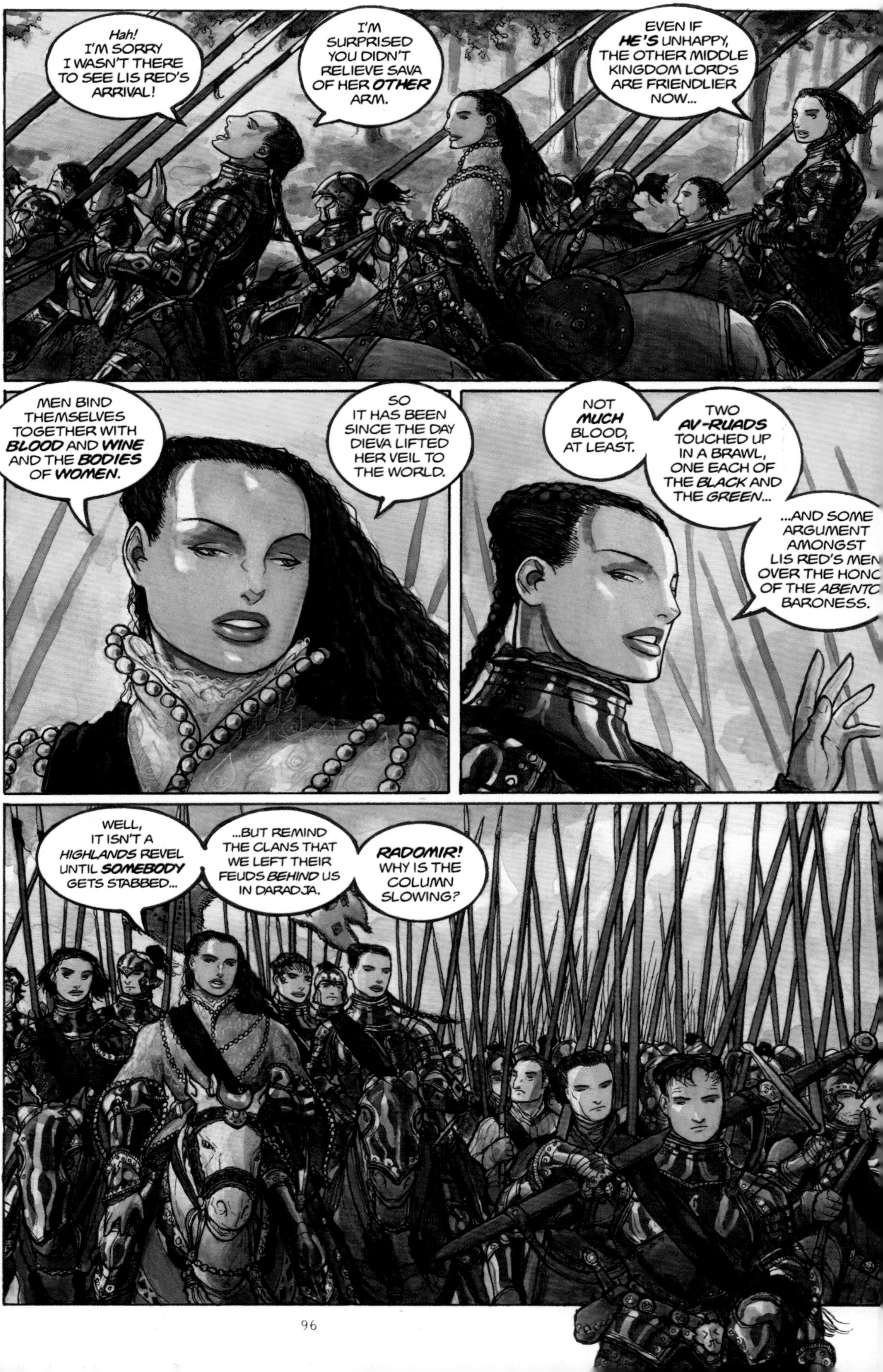
Hah! I'M SORRY I WASN'T THERE TO SEE LIS RED'S ARRIVAL!
I'M SURPRISED YOU DIDN'T RELIEVE SAVA OF HER OTHER ARM.
EVEN IF HE'S UNHAPPY, THE OTHER MIDDLE KINGDOM LORDS ARE FRIENDLIER NOW...
MEN BIND THEMSELVES TOGETHER WITH BLOOD AND WINE AND THE BODIES OF WOMEN.
SO IT HAS BEEN SINCE THE DAY DIEVA LIFTED HER VEIL TO THE WORLD.
NOT MUCH BLOOD, AT LEAST.
TWO AV-RUADS TOUCHED UP IN A BRAWL, ONE EACH OF THE BLACK AND THE GREEN...
...AND SOME ARGUMENT AMONGST LIS RED'S MEN OVER THE HONO OF THE ABENTO BARONESS.
WELL, IT ISN'T A HIGHLANDS REVEL UNTIL SOMEBODY GETS STABBED...
...BUT REMIND THE CLANS THAT WE LEFT THEIR FEUDS BEHIND US IN DARADJA.
RADOMIR! WHY IS THE COLUMN SLOWING?

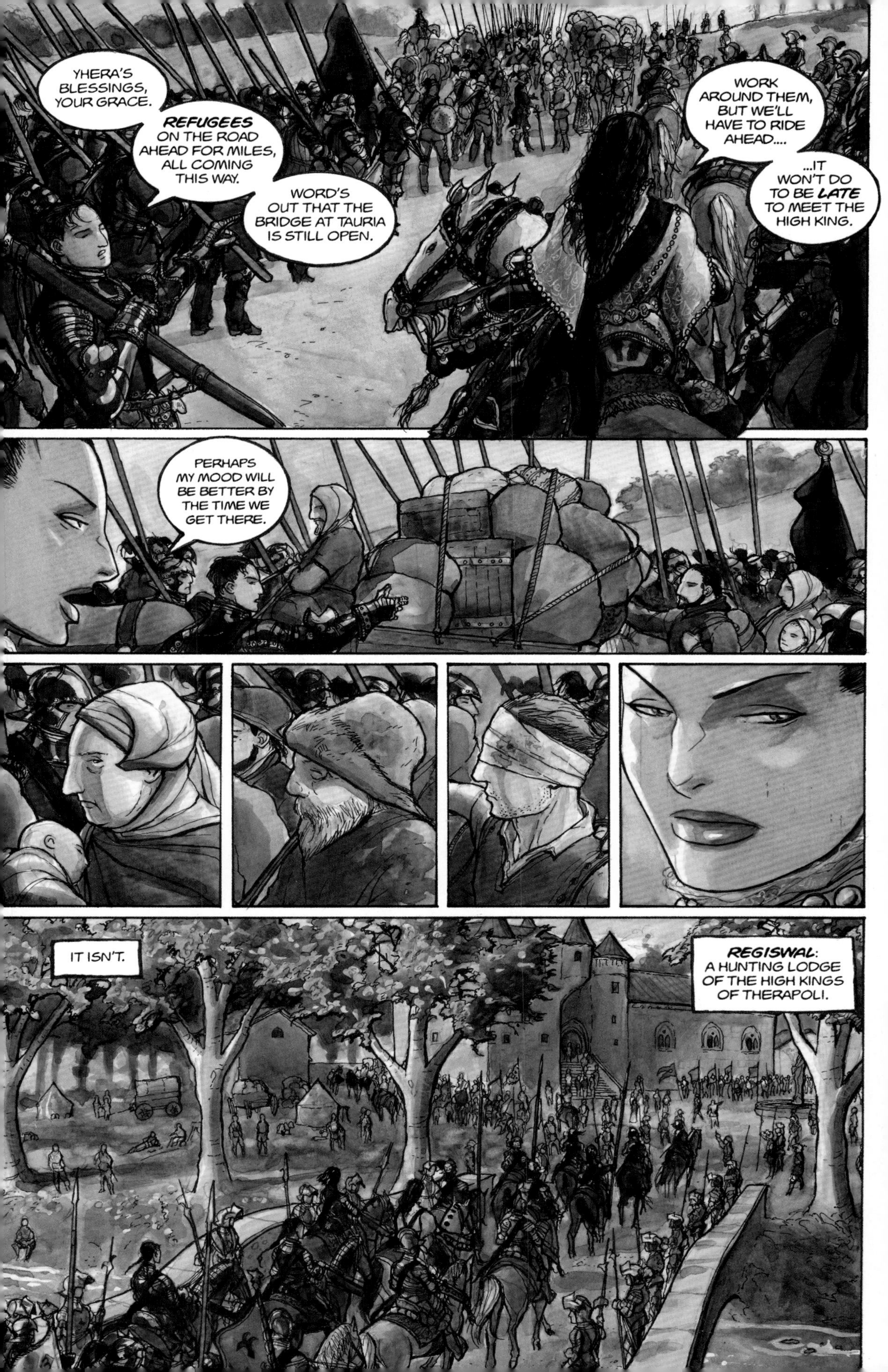
YHERA'S BLESSINGS, YOUR GRACE.
REFUGEES ON THE ROAD AHEAD FOR MILES, ALL COMING THIS WAY.
WORD'S OUT THAT THE BRIDGE AT TAURIA IS STILL OPEN.
WORK AROUND THEM, BUT WE'LL HAVE TO RIDE AHEAD....
...IT WON'T DO TO BE LATE TO MEET THE HIGH KING.
PERHAPS MY MOOD WILL BE BETTER BY THE TIME WE GET THERE.
IT ISN'T.
REGISWAL: A HUNTING LODGE OF THE HIGH KINGS OF THERAPOLI.

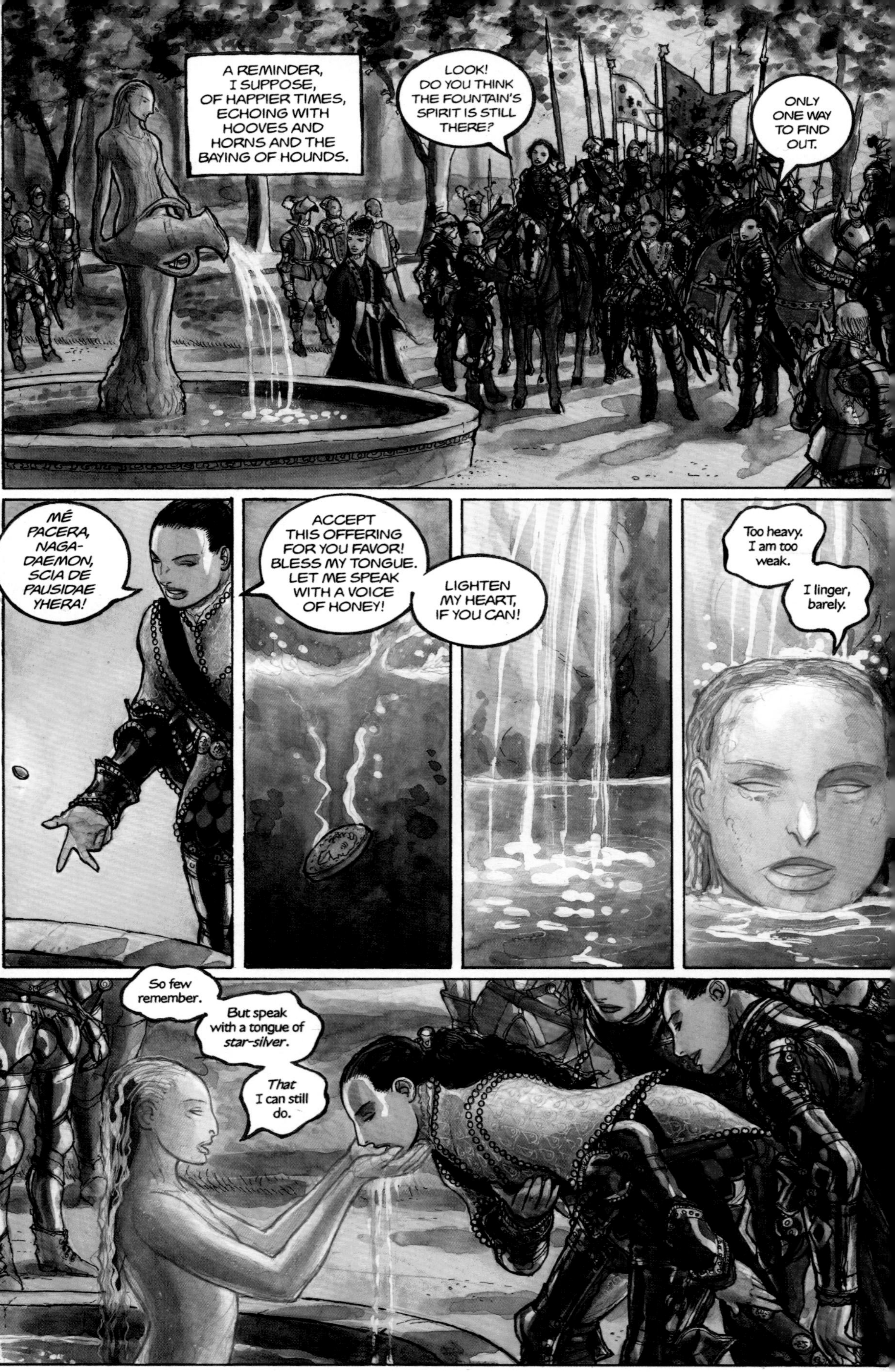
A REMINDER, I SUPPOSE, OF HAPPIER TIMES, ECHOING WITH HOOVES AND HORNS AND THE BAYING OF HOUNDS.
LOOK! DO YOU THINK THE FOUNTAIN'S SPIRIT IS STILL THERE?
ONLY ONE WAY TO FIND OUT.
MÊ PACERA, NAGA-DAEMON, SCIA DE PAUSIDAE YHERA!
ACCEPT THIS OFFERING FOR YOU FAVOR! BLESS MY TONGUE. LET ME SPEAK WITH A VOICE OF HONEY!
LIGHTEN MY HEART, IF YOU CAN!
Too heavy. I am too weak.
I linger, barely.
So few remember.
But speak with a tongue of *star-silver*.
That I can still do.

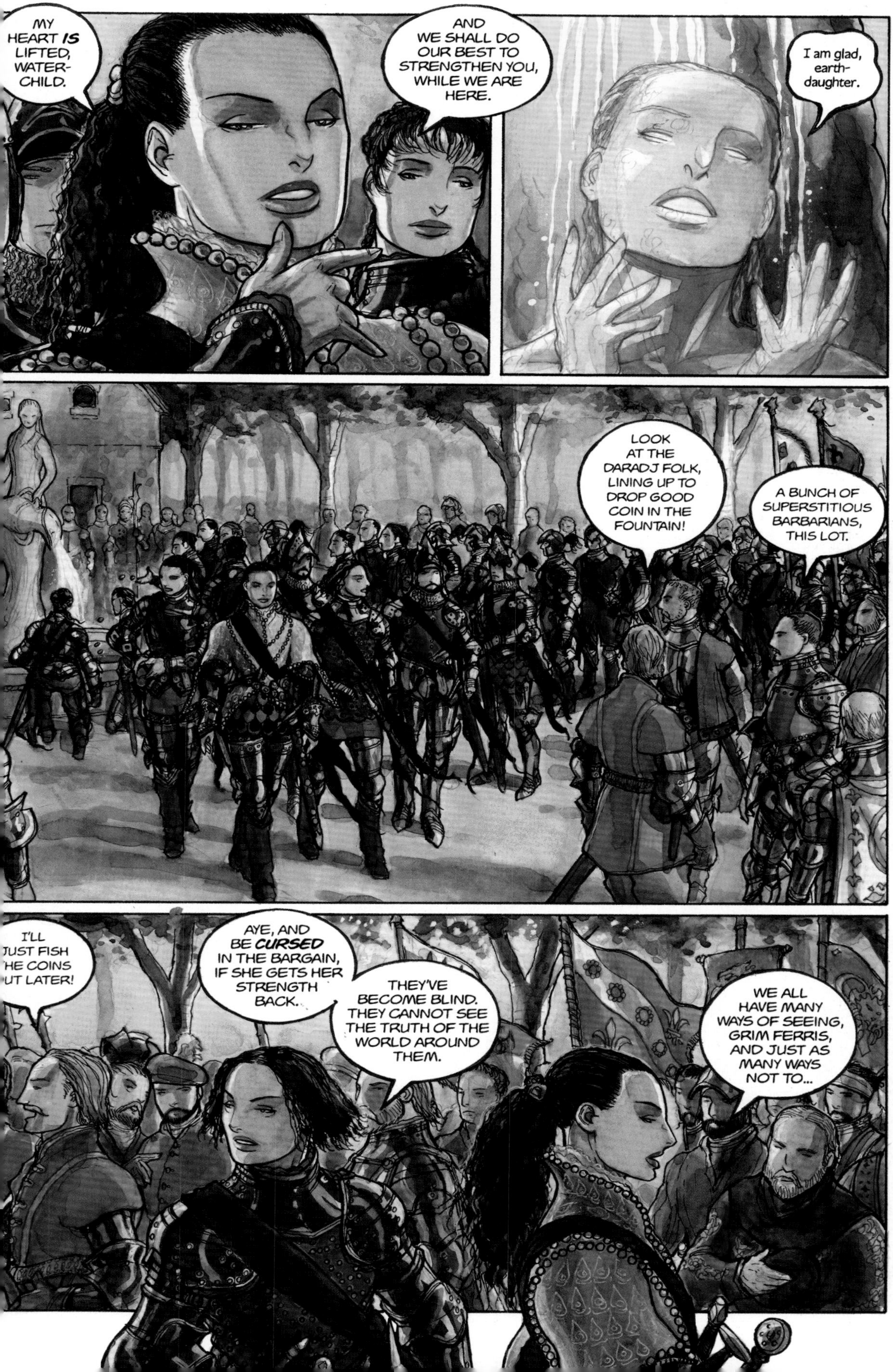
MY HEART *IS* LIFTED, WATER-CHILD.
AND WE SHALL DO OUR BEST TO STRENGTHEN YOU, WHILE WE ARE HERE.
I am glad, earth-daughter.
LOOK AT THE DARADJ FOLK, LINING UP TO DROP GOOD COIN IN THE FOUNTAIN!
A BUNCH OF SUPERSTITIOUS BARBARIANS, THIS LOT.
I'LL JUST FISH HE COINS UT LATER!
AYE, AND BE ***CURSED*** IN THE BARGAIN, IF SHE GETS HER STRENGTH BACK.
THEY'VE BECOME BLIND. THEY CANNOT SEE THE TRUTH OF THE WORLD AROUND THEM.
WE ALL HAVE MANY WAYS OF SEEING, GRIM FERRIS, AND JUST AS MANY WAYS NOT TO...

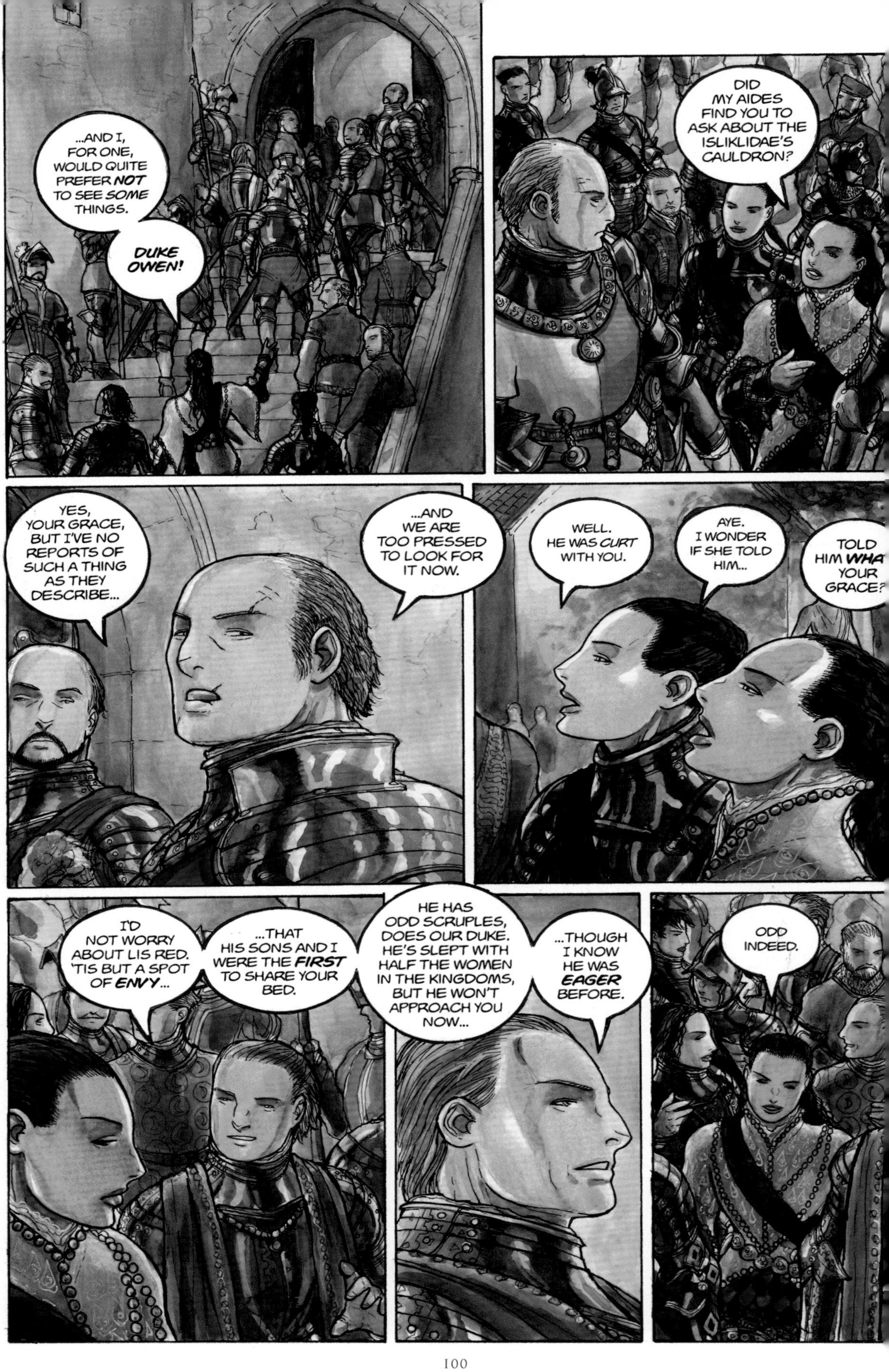
...AND I, FOR ONE, WOULD QUITE PREFER NOT TO SEE SOME THINGS.
DUKE OWEN!
DID MY AIDES FIND YOU TO ASK ABOUT THE ISLIKLIDAE'S CAULDRON?
YES, YOUR GRACE, BUT I'VE NO REPORTS OF SUCH A THING AS THEY DESCRIBE...
...AND WE ARE TOO PRESSED TO LOOK FOR IT NOW.
WELL. HE WAS CURT WITH YOU.
AYE. I WONDER IF SHE TOLD HIM...
TOLD HIM WHA YOUR GRACE?
I'D NOT WORRY ABOUT LIS RED. 'TIS BUT A SPOT OF ENVY...
...THAT HIS SONS AND I WERE THE FIRST TO SHARE YOUR BED.
HE HAS ODD SCRUPLES, DOES OUR DUKE. HE'S SLEPT WITH HALF THE WOMEN IN THE KINGDOMS, BUT HE WON'T APPROACH YOU NOW...
...THOUGH I KNOW HE WAS EAGER BEFORE.
ODD INDEED.

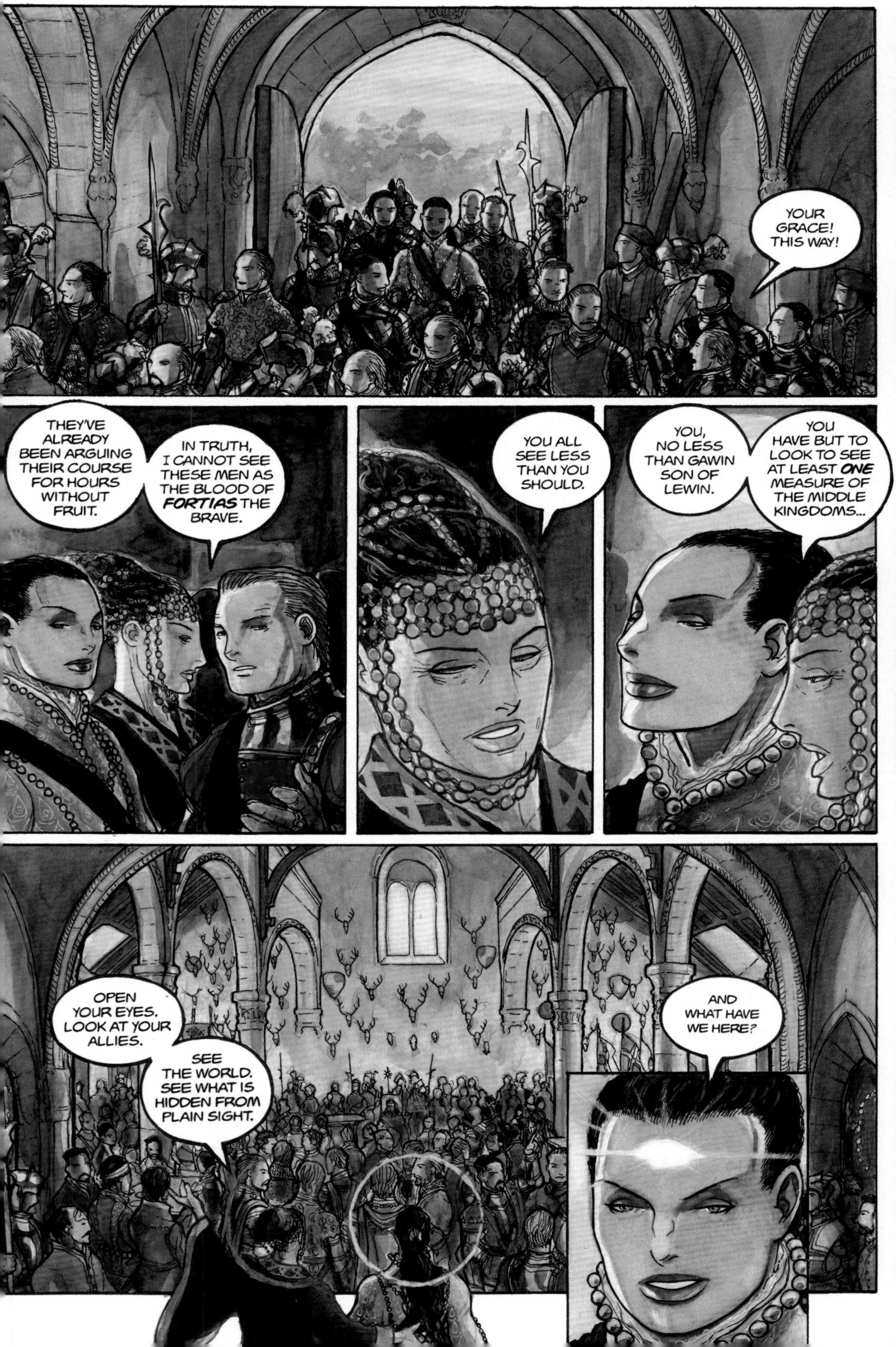
YOUR GRACE! THIS WAY!
THEY'VE ALREADY BEEN ARGUING THEIR COURSE FOR HOURS WITHOUT FRUIT.
IN TRUTH, I CANNOT SEE THESE MEN AS THE BLOOD OF FORTIAS THE BRAVE.
YOU ALL SEE LESS THAN YOU SHOULD.
YOU, NO LESS THAN GAWIN SON OF LEWIN.
YOU HAVE BUT TO LOOK TO SEE AT LEAST ONE MEASURE OF THE MIDDLE KINGDOMS...
OPEN YOUR EYES. LOOK AT YOUR ALLIES.
SEE THE WORLD. SEE WHAT IS HIDDEN FROM PLAIN SIGHT.
AND WHAT HAVE WE HERE?

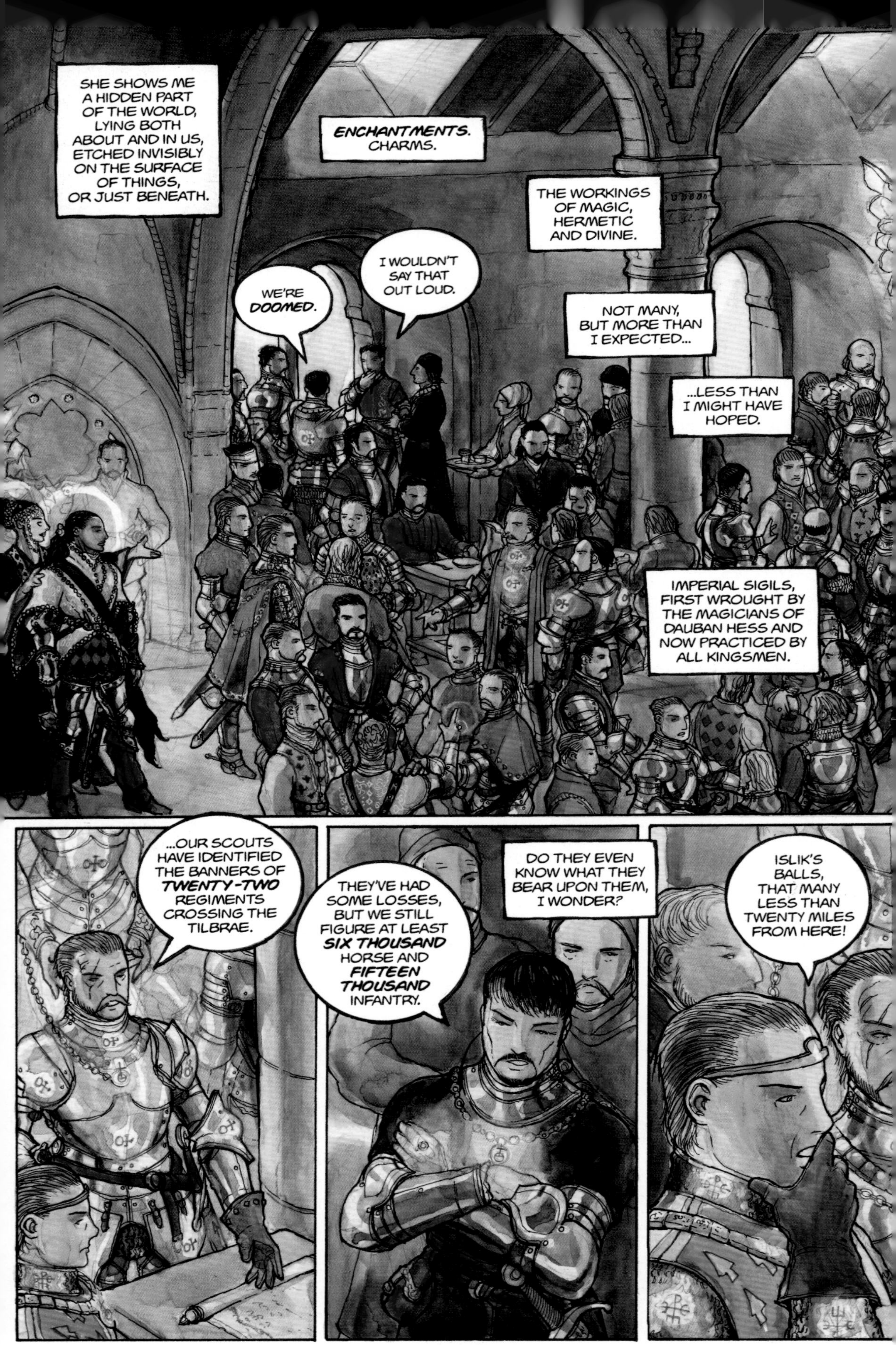
SHE SHOWS ME A HIDDEN PART OF THE WORLD, LYING BOTH ABOUT AND IN US, ETCHED INVISIBLY ON THE SURFACE OF THINGS, OR JUST BENEATH.
ENCHANTMENTS. CHARMS.
THE WORKINGS OF MAGIC, HERMETIC AND DIVINE.
WE'RE DOOMED.
I WOULDN'T SAY THAT OUT LOUD.
NOT MANY, BUT MORE THAN I EXPECTED...
...LESS THAN I MIGHT HAVE HOPED.
IMPERIAL SIGILS, FIRST WROUGHT BY THE MAGICIANS OF DAUBAN HESS AND NOW PRACTICED BY ALL KINGSMEN.
...OUR SCOUTS HAVE IDENTIFIED THE BANNERS OF TWENTY-TWO REGIMENTS CROSSING THE TILBRAE.
THEY'VE HAD SOME LOSSES, BUT WE STILL FIGURE AT LEAST SIX THOUSAND HORSE AND FIFTEEN THOUSAND INFANTRY.
DO THEY EVEN KNOW WHAT THEY BEAR UPON THEM, I WONDER?
ISLIK'S BALLS, THAT MANY LESS THAN TWENTY MILES FROM HERE!

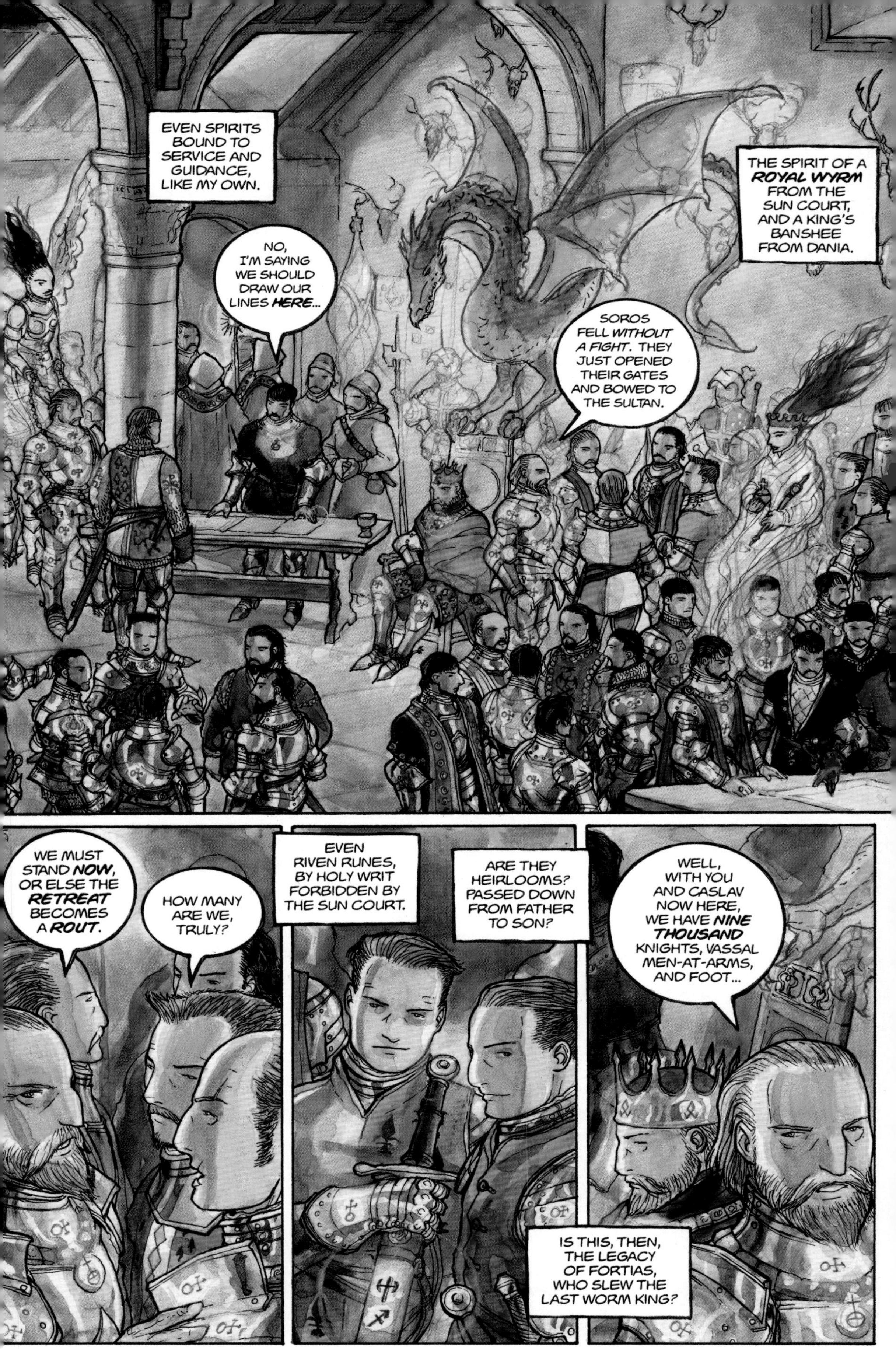
EVEN SPIRITS BOUND TO SERVICE AND GUIDANCE, LIKE MY OWN.
NO, I'M SAYING WE SHOULD DRAW OUR LINES HERE...
THE SPIRIT OF A ROYAL WYRM FROM THE SUN COURT, AND A KING'S BANSHEE FROM DANIA.
SOROS FELL WITHOUT A FIGHT. THEY JUST OPENED THEIR GATES AND BOWED TO THE SULTAN.
WE MUST STAND NOW, OR ELSE THE RETREAT BECOMES A ROUT.
HOW MANY ARE WE, TRULY?
EVEN RIVEN RUNES, BY HOLY WRIT FORBIDDEN BY THE SUN COURT.
ARE THEY HEIRLOOMS? PASSED DOWN FROM FATHER TO SON?
WELL, WITH YOU AND CASLAV NOW HERE, WE HAVE NINE THOUSAND KNIGHTS, VASSAL MEN-AT-ARMS, AND FOOT...
IS THIS, THEN, THE LEGACY OF FORTIAS, WHO SLEW THE LAST WORM KING?

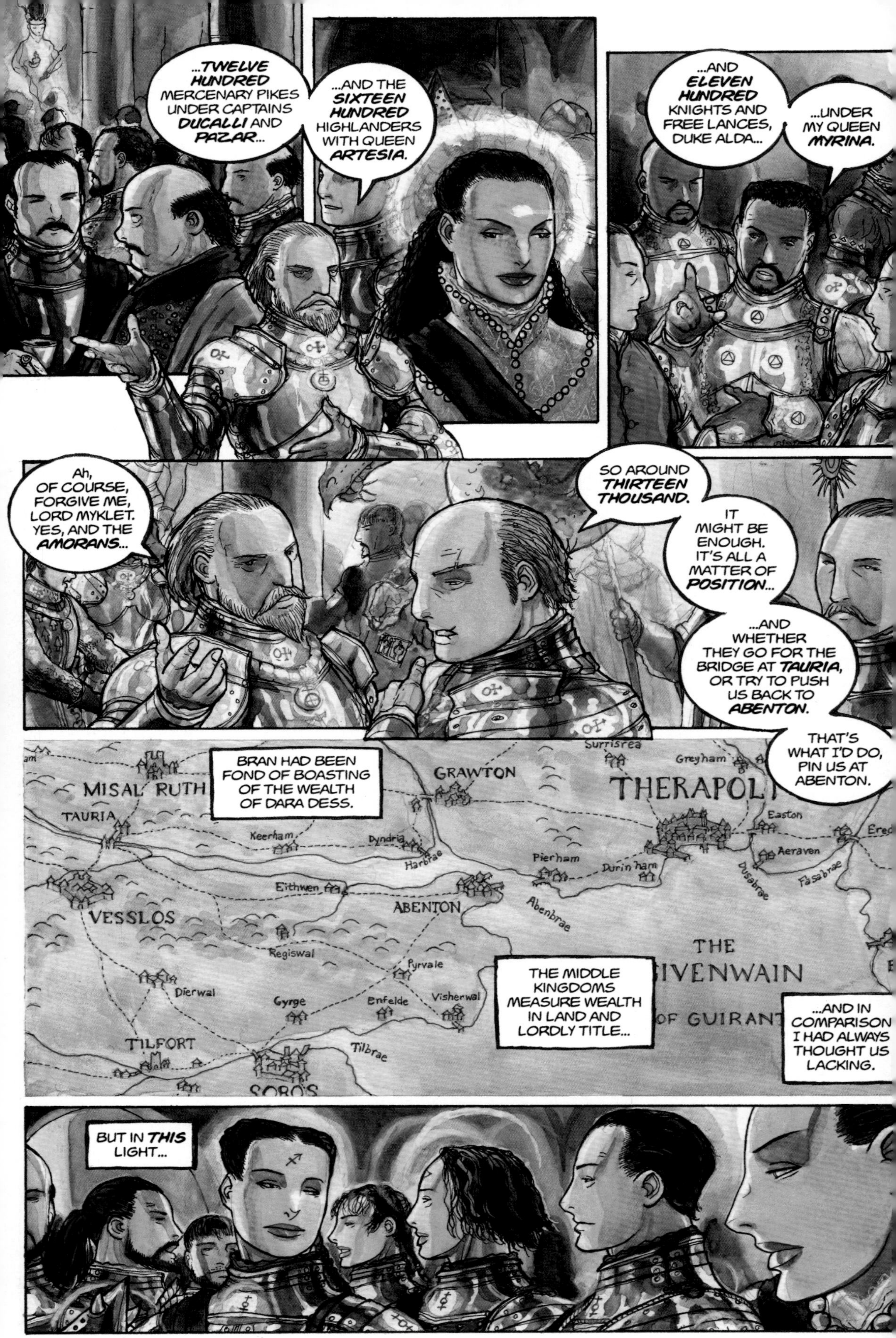
...TWELVE HUNDRED MERCENARY PIKES UNDER CAPTAINS DUCALLI AND PAZAR...
...AND THE SIXTEEN HUNDRED HIGHLANDERS WITH QUEEN ARTESIA.
...AND ELEVEN HUNDRED KNIGHTS AND FREE LANCES, DUKE ALDA...
...UNDER MY QUEEN MYRINA.
Ah, OF COURSE, FORGIVE ME, LORD MYKLET. YES, AND THE AMORANS...
SO AROUND THIRTEEN THOUSAND.
IT MIGHT BE ENOUGH. IT'S ALL A MATTER OF POSITION...
...AND WHETHER THEY GO FOR THE BRIDGE AT TAURIA, OR TRY TO PUSH US BACK TO ABENTON.
THAT'S WHAT I'D DO, PIN US AT ABENTON.
BRAN HAD BEEN FOND OF BOASTING OF THE WEALTH OF DARA DESS.
MISAL RUTH
TAURIA
GRAWTON
Surrisrea
Greyham
THERAPOL
Easton
Keerham
Dyndria
Harbrae
Pierham
Durin ham
Aeraven
Dusabrae
Fasabrae
Eithwen
ABENTON
Abenbrae
VESSLOS
Regiswal
Pyrvale
THE
GIVENWAIN
OF GUIRANT
Dierwal
Gyrge
Enfelde
Visherwal
TILFORT
Tilbrae
SOROS
THE MIDDLE KINGDOMS MEASURE WEALTH IN LAND AND LORDLY TITLE...
...AND IN COMPARISON I HAD ALWAYS THOUGHT US LACKING.
BUT IN THIS LIGHT...

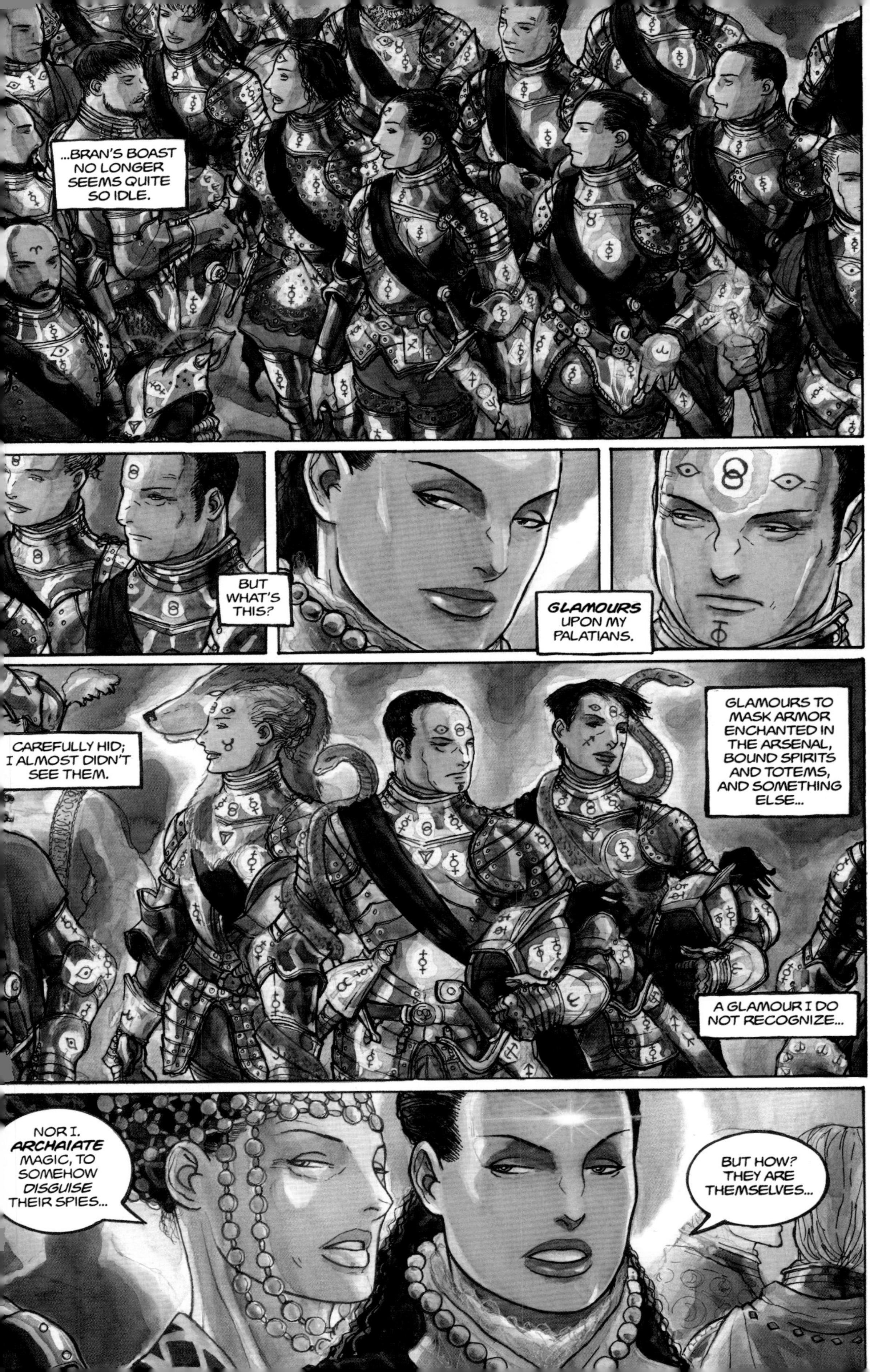
...BRAN'S BOAST NO LONGER SEEMS QUITE SO IDLE.
BUT WHAT'S THIS?
GLAMOURS UPON MY PALATIANS.
CAREFULLY HID; I ALMOST DIDN'T SEE THEM.
GLAMOURS TO MASK ARMOR ENCHANTED IN THE ARSENAL, BOUND SPIRITS AND TOTEMS, AND SOMETHING ELSE...
A GLAMOUR I DO NOT RECOGNIZE...
NOR I. ARCHAIATE MAGIC, TO SOMEHOW DISGUISE THEIR SPIES...
BUT HOW? THEY ARE THEMSELVES...

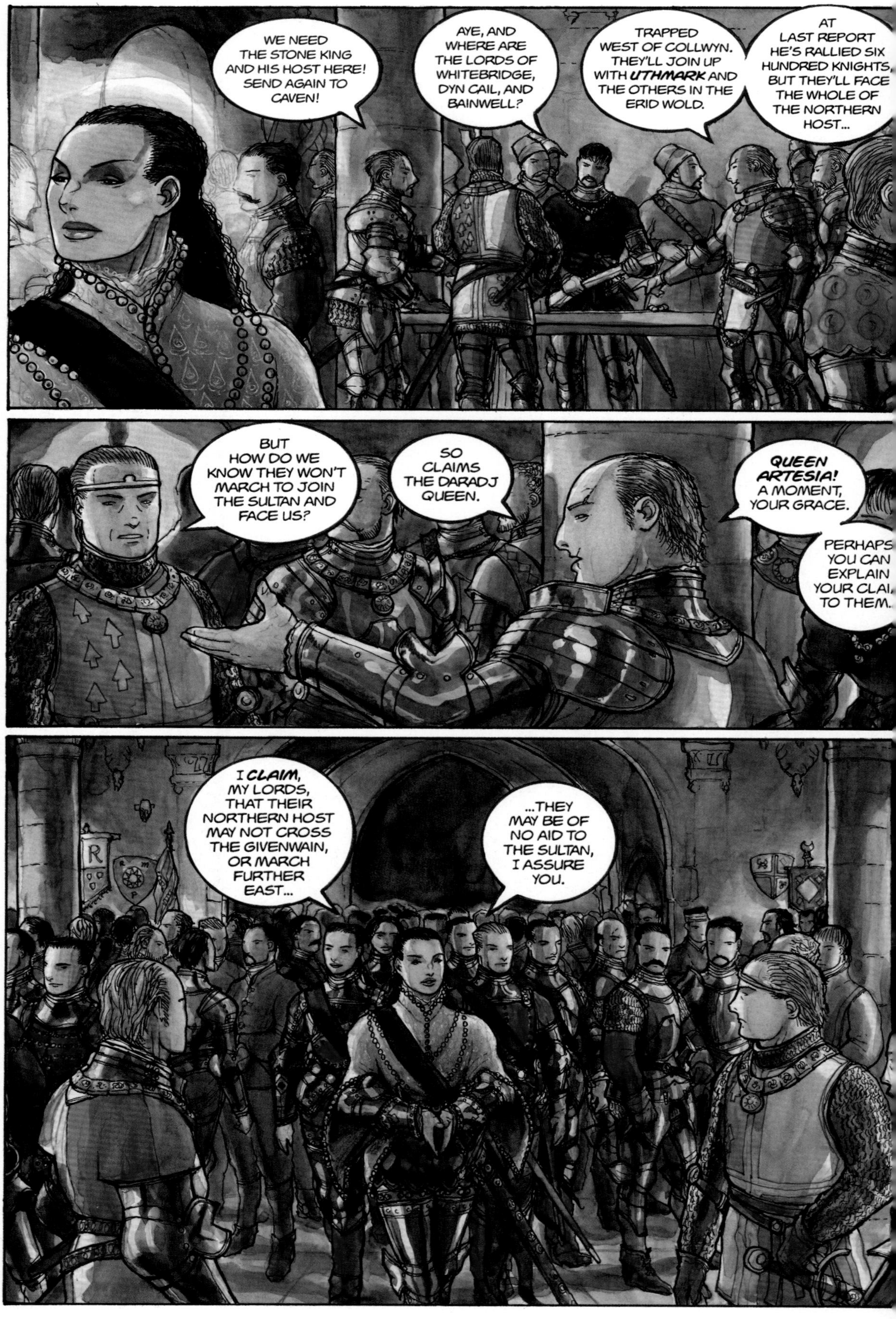
WE NEED THE STONE KING AND HIS HOST HERE! SEND AGAIN TO CAVEN!
AYE, AND WHERE ARE THE LORDS OF WHITEBRIDGE, DYN CAIL, AND BAINWELL?
TRAPPED WEST OF COLLWYN. THEY'LL JOIN UP WITH UTHMARK AND THE OTHERS IN THE ERID WOLD.
AT LAST REPORT HE'S RALLIED SIX HUNDRED KNIGHTS, BUT THEY'LL FACE THE WHOLE OF THE NORTHERN HOST...
BUT HOW DO WE KNOW THEY WON'T MARCH TO JOIN THE SULTAN AND FACE US?
SO CLAIMS THE DARADJ QUEEN.
QUEEN ARTESIA! A MOMENT, YOUR GRACE.
PERHAPS YOU CAN EXPLAIN YOUR CLAI TO THEM.
I CLAIM, MY LORDS, THAT THEIR NORTHERN HOST MAY NOT CROSS THE GIVENWAIN, OR MARCH FURTHER EAST...
...THEY MAY BE OF NO AID TO THE SULTAN, I ASSURE YOU.

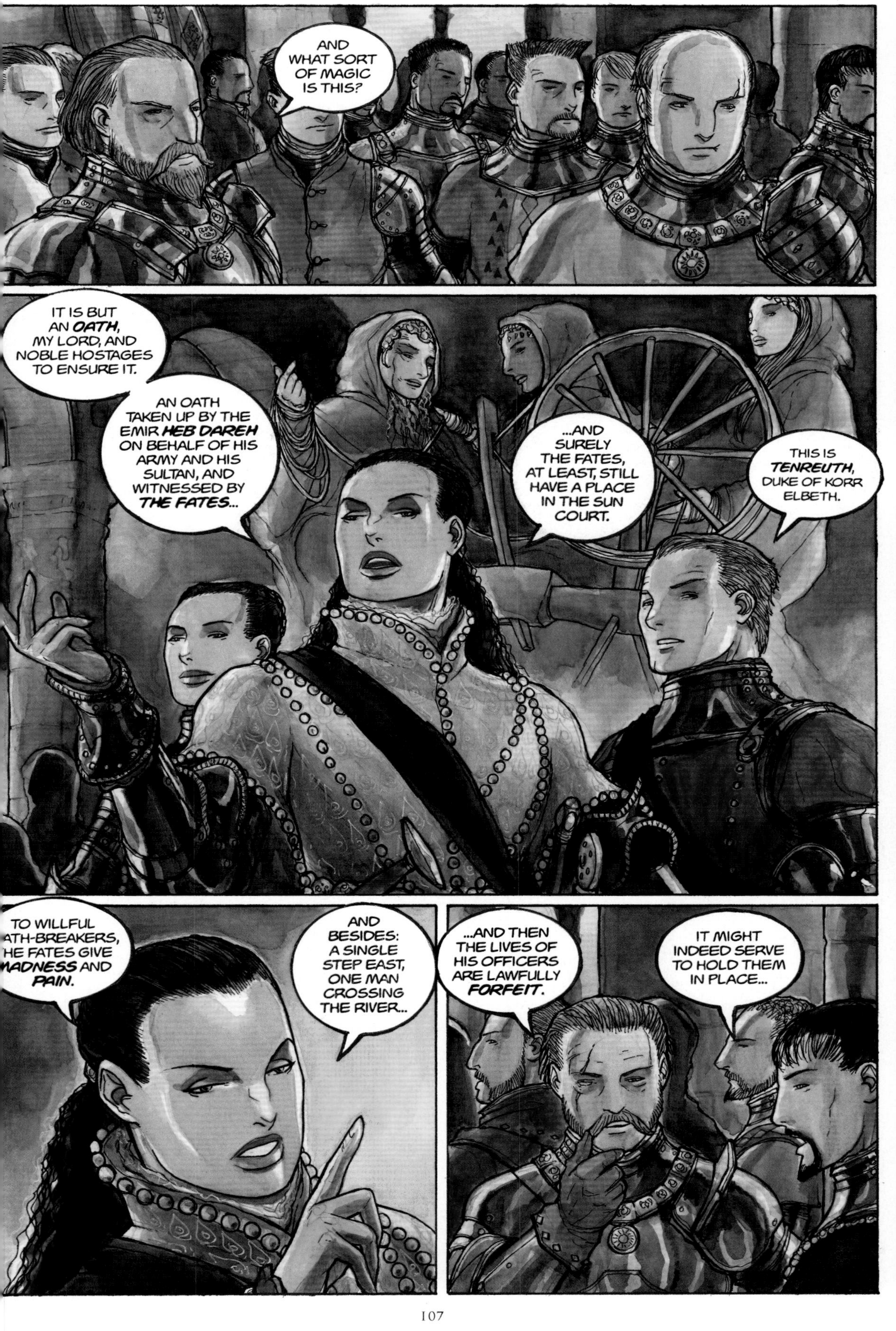
AND WHAT SORT OF MAGIC IS THIS?
IT IS BUT AN OATH, MY LORD, AND NOBLE HOSTAGES TO ENSURE IT.
AN OATH TAKEN UP BY THE EMIR HEB DAREH ON BEHALF OF HIS ARMY AND HIS SULTAN, AND WITNESSED BY THE FATES...
...AND SURELY THE FATES, AT LEAST, STILL HAVE A PLACE IN THE SUN COURT.
THIS IS TENREUTH, DUKE OF KORR ELBETH.
TO WILLFUL ATH-BREAKERS, THE FATES GIVE ADNESS AND PAIN.
AND BESIDES: A SINGLE STEP EAST, ONE MAN CROSSING THE RIVER...
...AND THEN THE LIVES OF HIS OFFICERS ARE LAWFULLY FORFEIT.
IT MIGHT INDEED SERVE TO HOLD THEM IN PLACE...

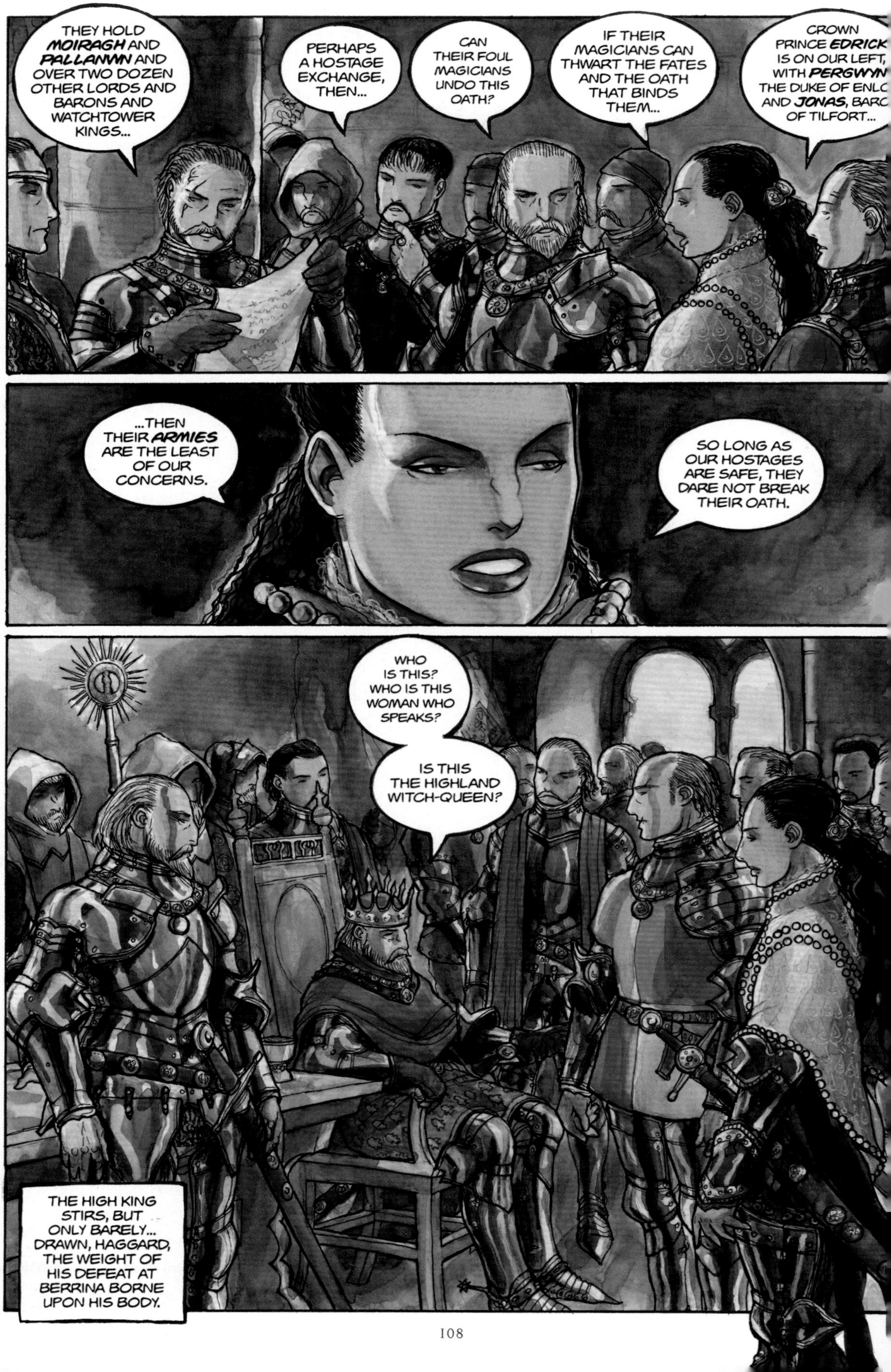
THEY HOLD MOIRAGH AND PALLANWN AND OVER TWO DOZEN OTHER LORDS AND BARONS AND WATCHTOWER KINGS...
PERHAPS A HOSTAGE EXCHANGE, THEN...
CAN THEIR FOUL MAGICIANS UNDO THIS OATH?
IF THEIR MAGICIANS CAN THWART THE FATES AND THE OATH THAT BINDS THEM...
CROWN PRINCE EDRICK IS ON OUR LEFT, WITH PERGWYN THE DUKE OF ENLO AND JONAS, BARC OF TILFORT...
...THEN THEIR ARMIES ARE THE LEAST OF OUR CONCERNS.
SO LONG AS OUR HOSTAGES ARE SAFE, THEY DARE NOT BREAK THEIR OATH.
WHO IS THIS? WHO IS THIS WOMAN WHO SPEAKS?
IS THIS THE HIGHLAND WITCH-QUEEN?
THE HIGH KING STIRS, BUT ONLY BARELY... DRAWN, HAGGARD, THE WEIGHT OF HIS DEFEAT AT BERRINA BORNE UPON HIS BODY.

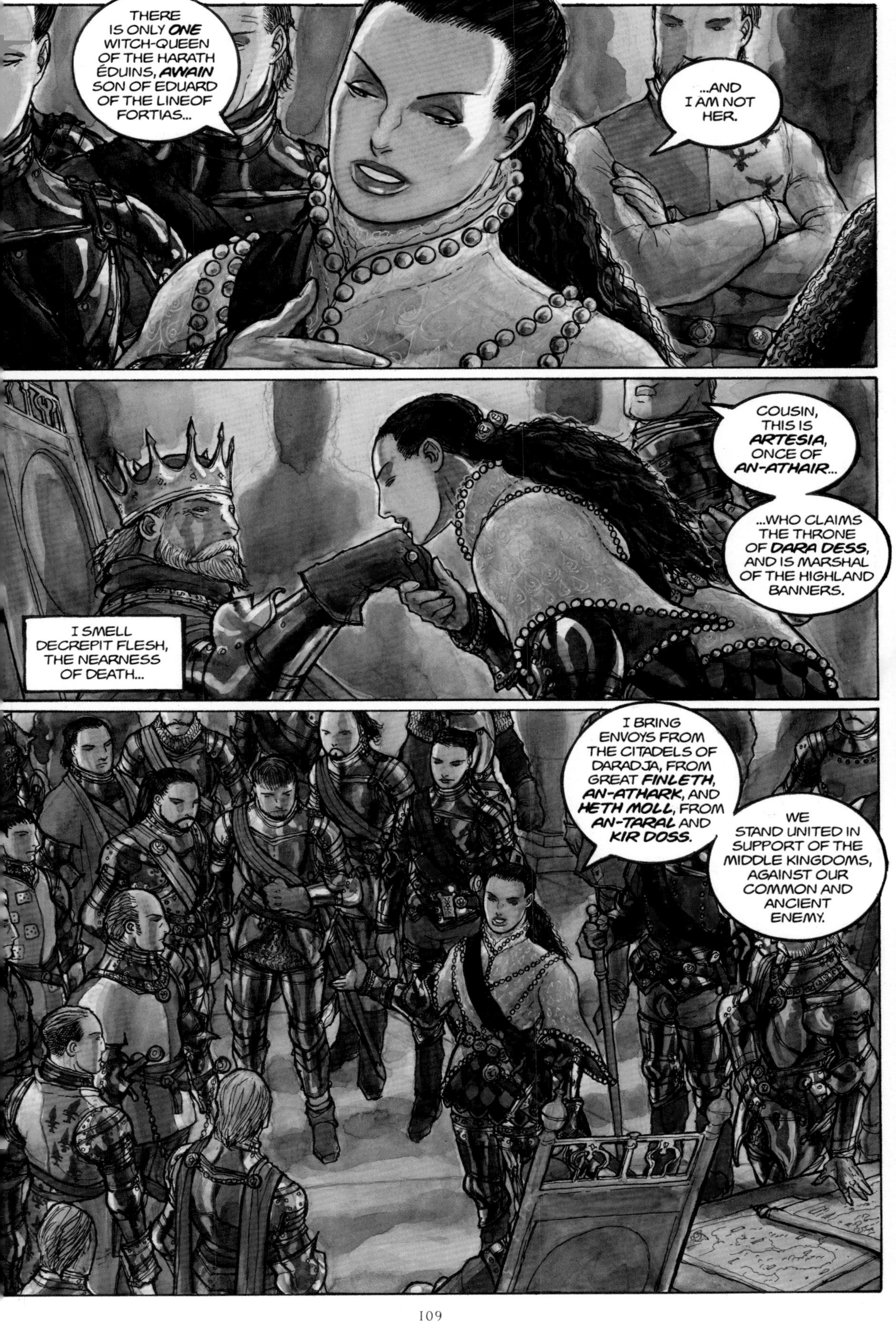
THERE IS ONLY ONE WITCH-QUEEN OF THE HARATH ÉDUINS, AWAIN SON OF EDUARD OF THE LINEOF FORTIAS...
...AND I AM NOT HER.
COUSIN, THIS IS ARTESIA, ONCE OF AN-ATHAIR...
...WHO CLAIMS THE THRONE OF DARA DESS, AND IS MARSHAL OF THE HIGHLAND BANNERS.
I SMELL DECREPIT FLESH, THE NEARNESS OF DEATH...
I BRING ENVOYS FROM THE CITADELS OF DARADJA, FROM GREAT FINLETH, AN-ATHARK, AND HETH MOLL, FROM AN-TARAL AND KIR DOSS.
WE STAND UNITED IN SUPPORT OF THE MIDDLE KINGDOMS, AGAINST OUR COMMON AND ANCIENT ENEMY.

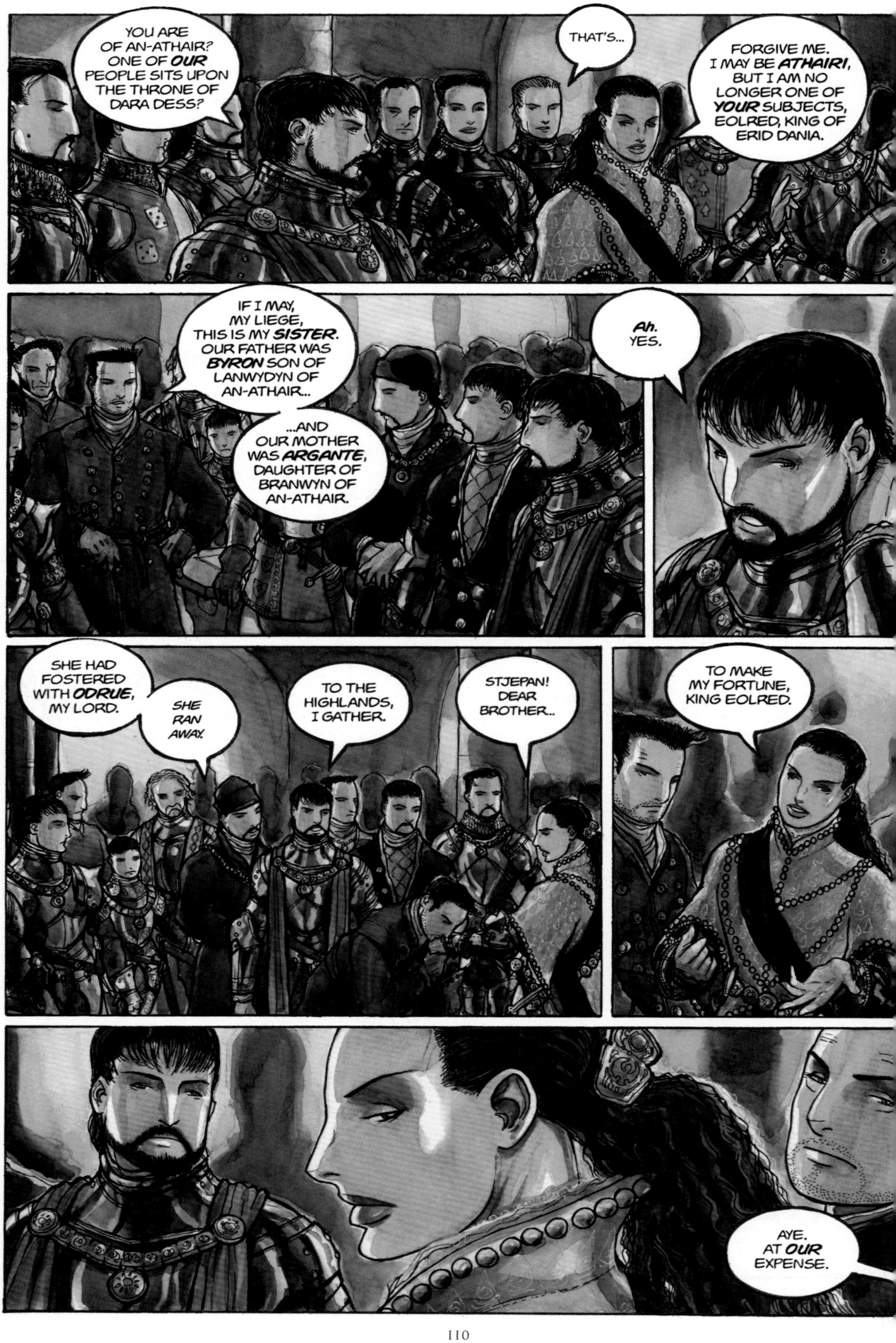
YOU ARE OF AN-ATHAIR? ONE OF OUR PEOPLE SITS UPON THE THRONE OF DARA DESS?
THAT'S...
FORGIVE ME. I MAY BE ATHAIRI, BUT I AM NO LONGER ONE OF YOUR SUBJECTS, EOLRED, KING OF ERID DANIA.
IF I MAY, MY LIEGE, THIS IS MY SISTER. OUR FATHER WAS BYRON SON OF LANWYDYN OF AN-ATHAIR...
...AND OUR MOTHER WAS ARGANTE, DAUGHTER OF BRANWYN OF AN-ATHAIR.
Ah. YES.
SHE HAD FOSTERED WITH ODRUE, MY LORD.
SHE RAN AWAY.
TO THE HIGHLANDS, I GATHER.
STJEPAN! DEAR BROTHER...
TO MAKE MY FORTUNE, KING EOLRED.
AYE. AT OUR EXPENSE.

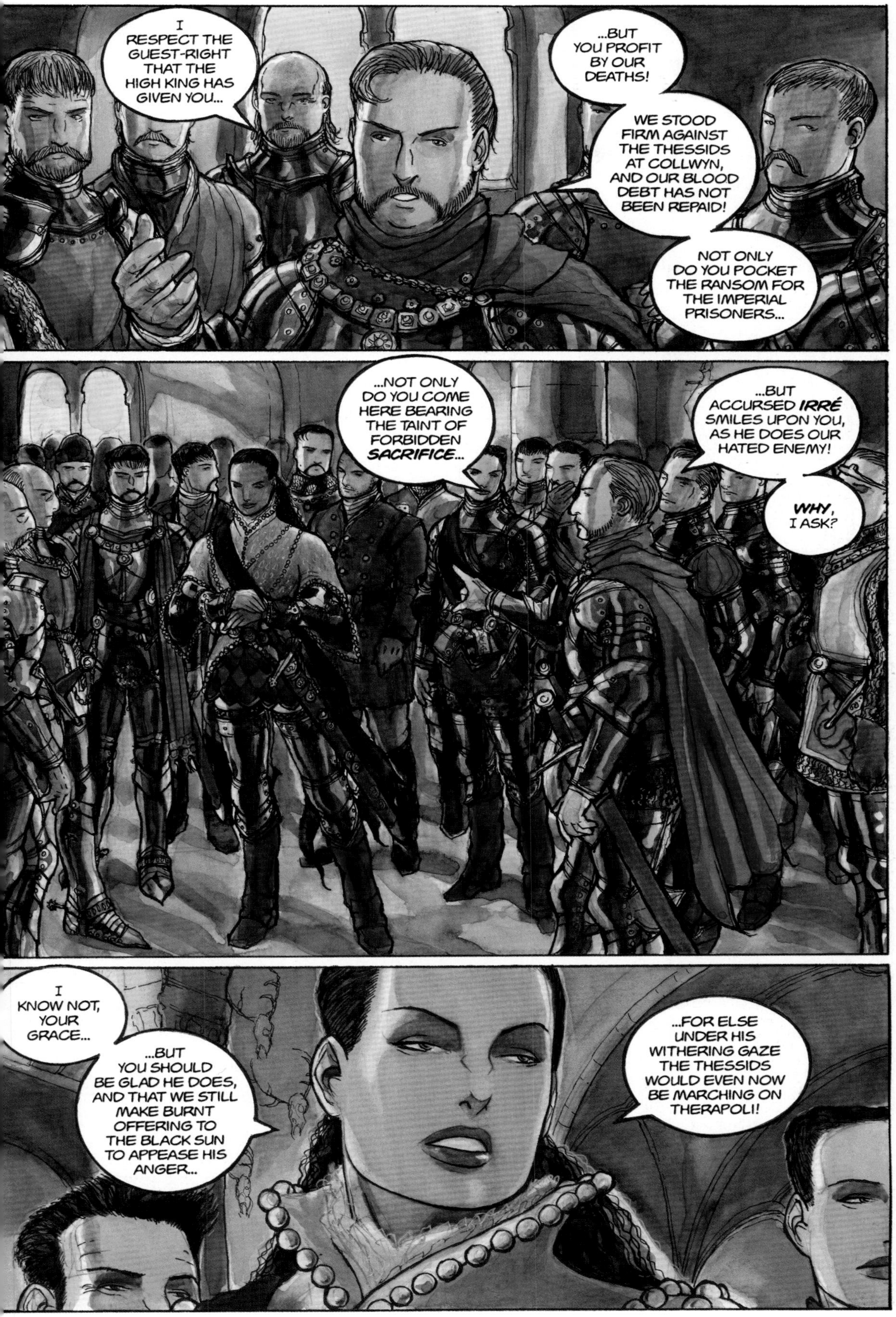
I RESPECT THE GUEST-RIGHT THAT THE HIGH KING HAS GIVEN YOU...
...BUT YOU PROFIT BY OUR DEATHS!
WE STOOD FIRM AGAINST THE THESSIDS AT COLLWYN, AND OUR BLOOD DEBT HAS NOT BEEN REPAID!
NOT ONLY DO YOU POCKET THE RANSOM FOR THE IMPERIAL PRISONERS...
...NOT ONLY DO YOU COME HERE BEARING THE TAINT OF FORBIDDEN **SACRIFICE**...
...BUT ACCURSED **IRRÉ** SMILES UPON YOU, AS HE DOES OUR HATED ENEMY!
WHY, I ASK?
I KNOW NOT, YOUR GRACE...
...BUT YOU SHOULD BE GLAD HE DOES, AND THAT WE STILL MAKE BURNT OFFERING TO THE BLACK SUN TO APPEASE HIS ANGER...
...FOR ELSE UNDER HIS WITHERING GAZE THE THESSIDS WOULD EVEN NOW BE MARCHING ON THERAPOLI!

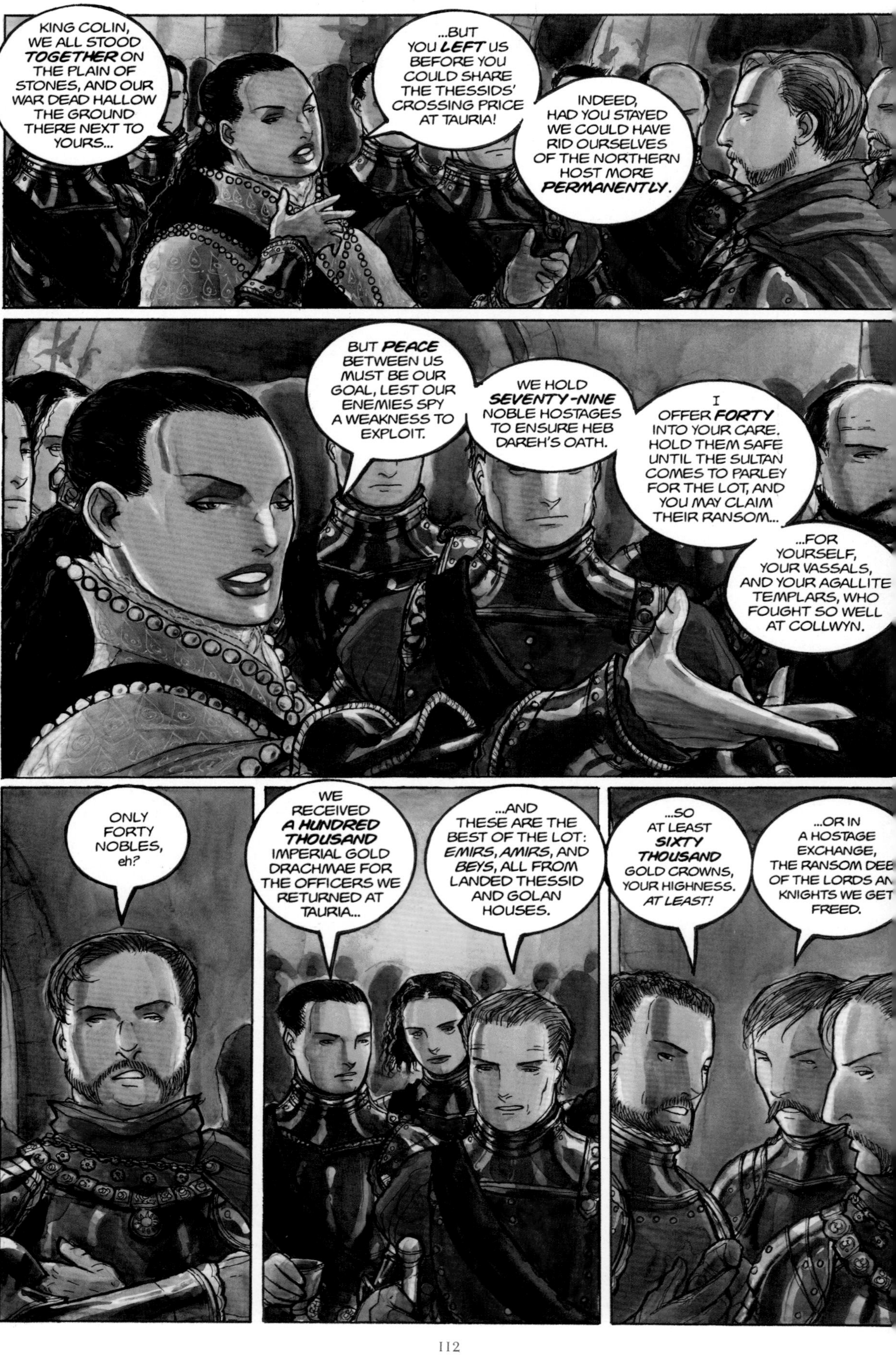
KING COLIN, WE ALL STOOD **TOGETHER** ON THE PLAIN OF STONES, AND OUR WAR DEAD HALLOW THE GROUND THERE NEXT TO YOURS...
...BUT YOU **LEFT** US BEFORE YOU COULD SHARE THE THESSIDS' CROSSING PRICE AT TAURIA!
INDEED, HAD YOU STAYED WE COULD HAVE RID OURSELVES OF THE NORTHERN HOST MORE **PERMANENTLY**.
BUT **PEACE** BETWEEN US MUST BE OUR GOAL, LEST OUR ENEMIES SPY A WEAKNESS TO EXPLOIT.
WE HOLD **SEVENTY-NINE** NOBLE HOSTAGES TO ENSURE HEB DAREH'S OATH.
I OFFER **FORTY** INTO YOUR CARE. HOLD THEM SAFE UNTIL THE SULTAN COMES TO PARLEY FOR THE LOT, AND YOU MAY CLAIM THEIR RANSOM...
...FOR YOURSELF, YOUR VASSALS, AND YOUR AGALLITE TEMPLARS, WHO FOUGHT SO WELL AT COLLWYN.
ONLY FORTY NOBLES, eh?
WE RECEIVED **A HUNDRED THOUSAND** IMPERIAL GOLD DRACHMAE FOR THE OFFICERS WE RETURNED AT TAURIA...
...AND THESE ARE THE BEST OF THE LOT: ***EMIRS, AMIRS***, AND ***BEYS***, ALL FROM LANDED THESSID AND GOLAN HOUSES.
...SO AT LEAST **SIXTY THOUSAND** GOLD CROWNS, YOUR HIGHNESS. *AT LEAST!*
...OR IN A HOSTAGE EXCHANGE, THE RANSOM DEB OF THE LORDS AN KNIGHTS WE GET FREED.

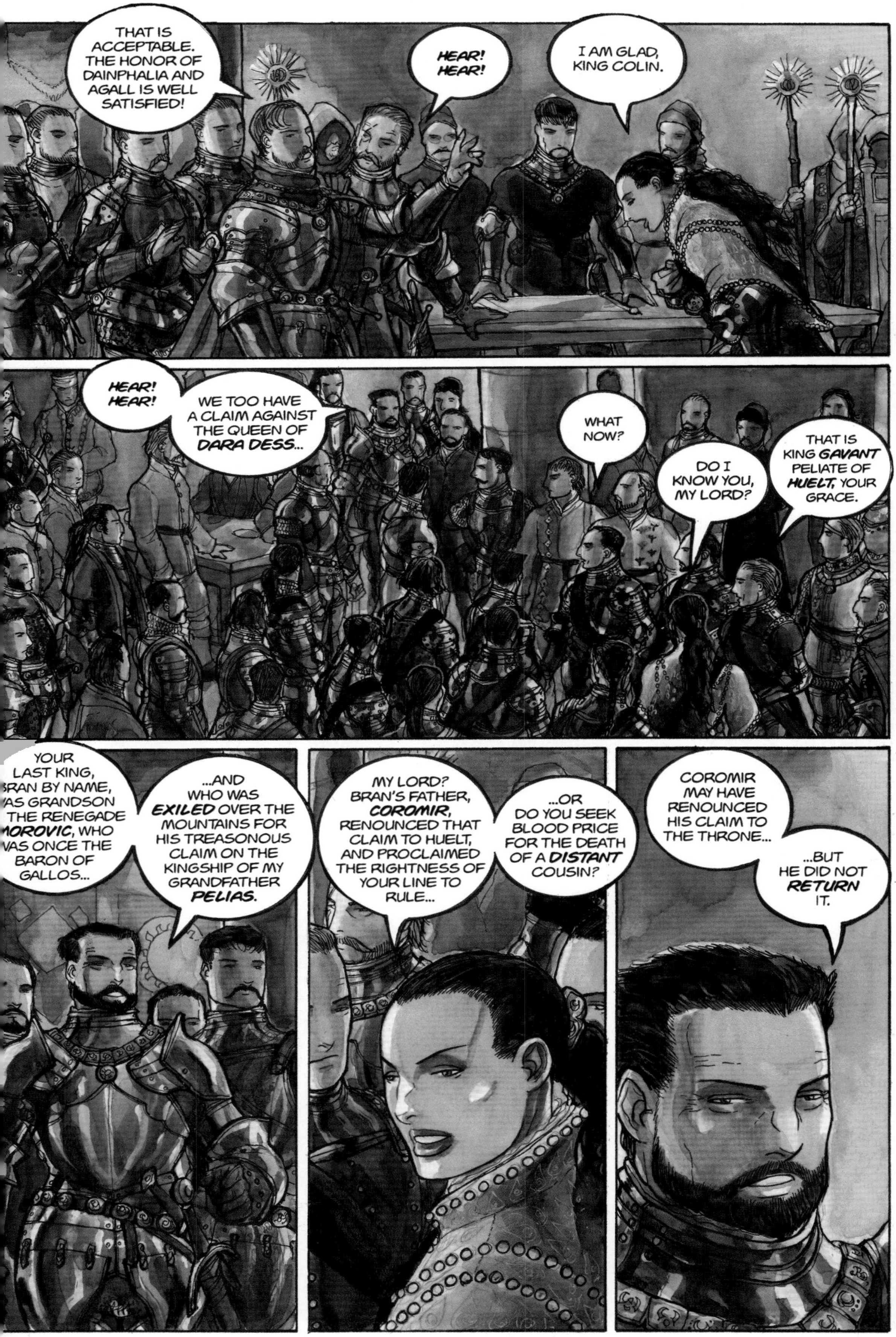

THAT IS ACCEPTABLE. THE HONOR OF DAINPHALIA AND AGALL IS WELL SATISFIED!
HEAR! HEAR!
I AM GLAD, KING COLIN.
HEAR! HEAR!
WE TOO HAVE A CLAIM AGAINST THE QUEEN OF DARA DESS...
WHAT NOW?
DO I KNOW YOU, MY LORD?
THAT IS KING GAVANT PELIATE OF HUELT, YOUR GRACE.
YOUR LAST KING, BRAN BY NAME, WAS GRANDSON THE RENEGADE MOROVIC, WHO WAS ONCE THE BARON OF GALLOS...
...AND WHO WAS EXILED OVER THE MOUNTAINS FOR HIS TREASONOUS CLAIM ON THE KINGSHIP OF MY GRANDFATHER PELIAS.
MY LORD? BRAN'S FATHER, COROMIR, RENOUNCED THAT CLAIM TO HUELT, AND PROCLAIMED THE RIGHTNESS OF YOUR LINE TO RULE...
...OR DO YOU SEEK BLOOD PRICE FOR THE DEATH OF A DISTANT COUSIN?
COROMIR MAY HAVE RENOUNCED HIS CLAIM TO THE THRONE...
...BUT HE DID NOT RETURN IT.

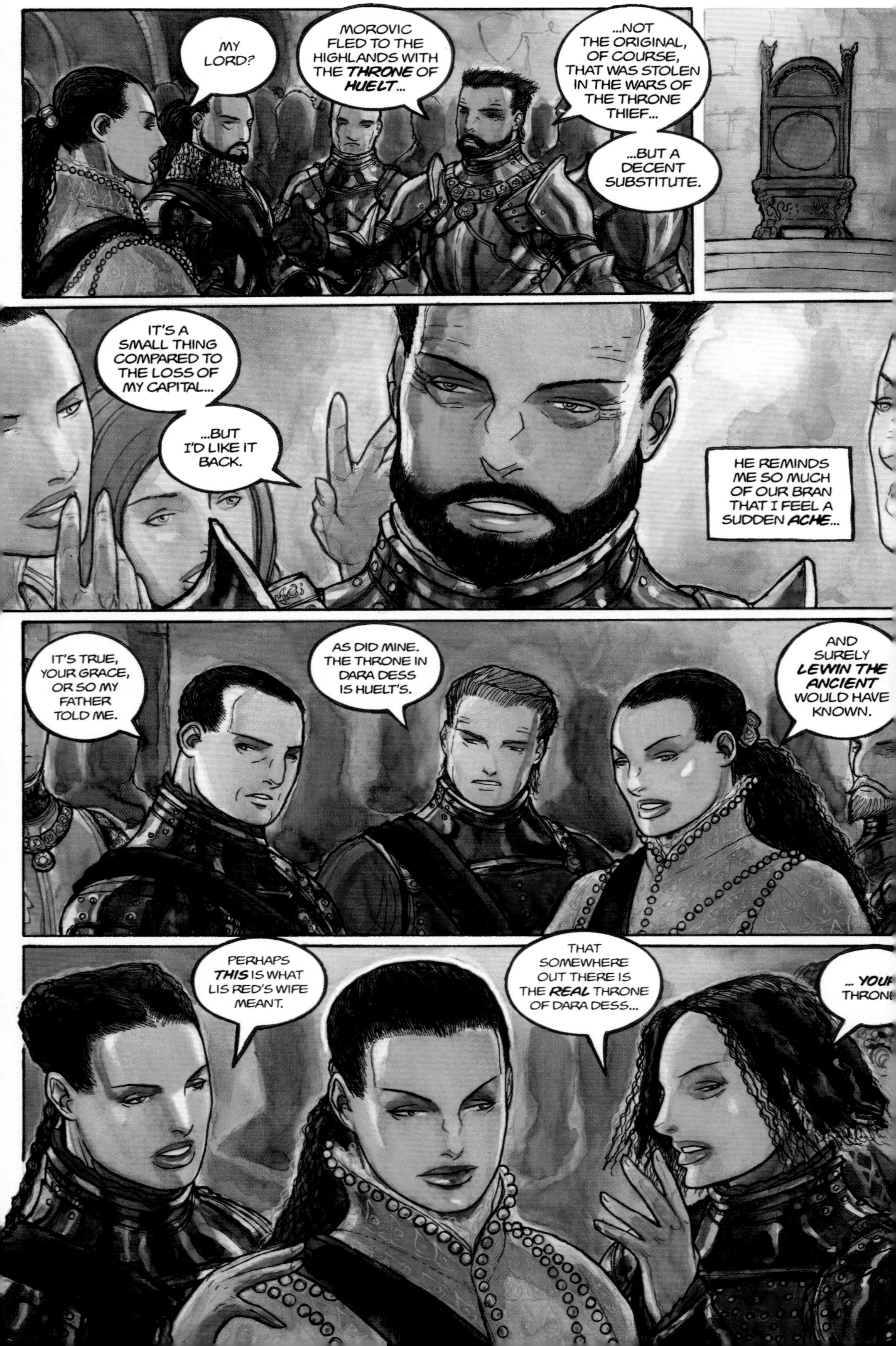
MY LORD?
MOROVIC FLED TO THE HIGHLANDS WITH THE ***THRONE*** OF ***HUELT***...
...NOT THE ORIGINAL, OF COURSE, THAT WAS STOLEN IN THE WARS OF THE THRONE THIEF...
...BUT A DECENT SUBSTITUTE.
IT'S A SMALL THING COMPARED TO THE LOSS OF MY CAPITAL...
...BUT I'D LIKE IT BACK.
HE REMINDS ME SO MUCH OF OUR BRAN THAT I FEEL A SUDDEN ***ACHE***...
IT'S TRUE, YOUR GRACE, OR SO MY FATHER TOLD ME.
AS DID MINE. THE THRONE IN DARA DESS IS HUELT'S.
AND SURELY ***LEWIN THE ANCIENT*** WOULD HAVE KNOWN.
PERHAPS ***THIS*** IS WHAT LIS RED'S WIFE MEANT.
THAT SOMEWHERE OUT THERE IS THE ***REAL*** THRONE OF DARA DESS...

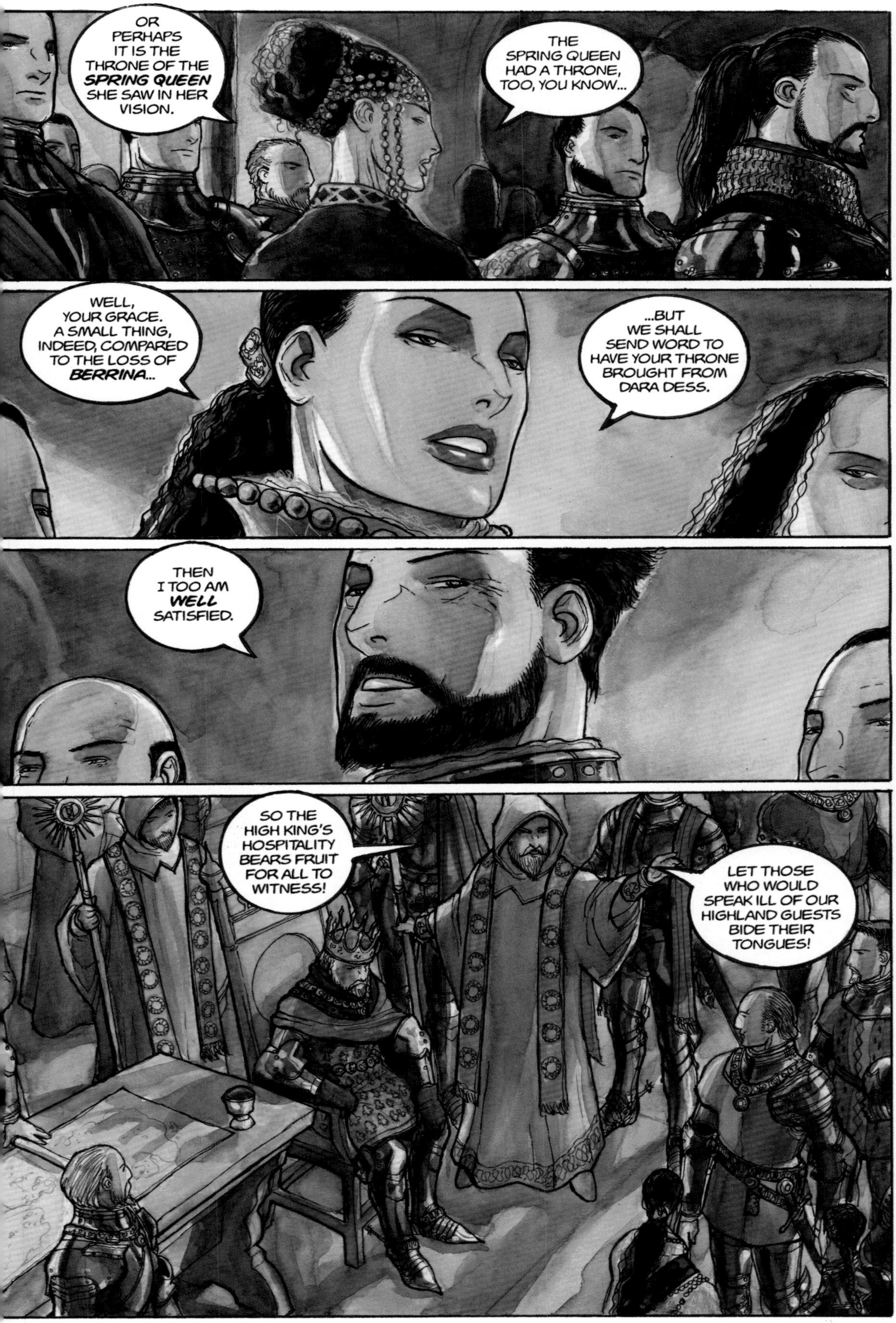
OR PERHAPS IT IS THE THRONE OF THE SPRING QUEEN SHE SAW IN HER VISION.
THE SPRING QUEEN HAD A THRONE, TOO, YOU KNOW...
WELL, YOUR GRACE. A SMALL THING, INDEED, COMPARED TO THE LOSS OF BERRINA...
...BUT WE SHALL SEND WORD TO HAVE YOUR THRONE BROUGHT FROM DARA DESS.
THEN I TOO AM WELL SATISFIED.
SO THE HIGH KING'S HOSPITALITY BEARS FRUIT FOR ALL TO WITNESS!
LET THOSE WHO WOULD SPEAK ILL OF OUR HIGHLAND GUESTS BIDE THEIR TONGUES!

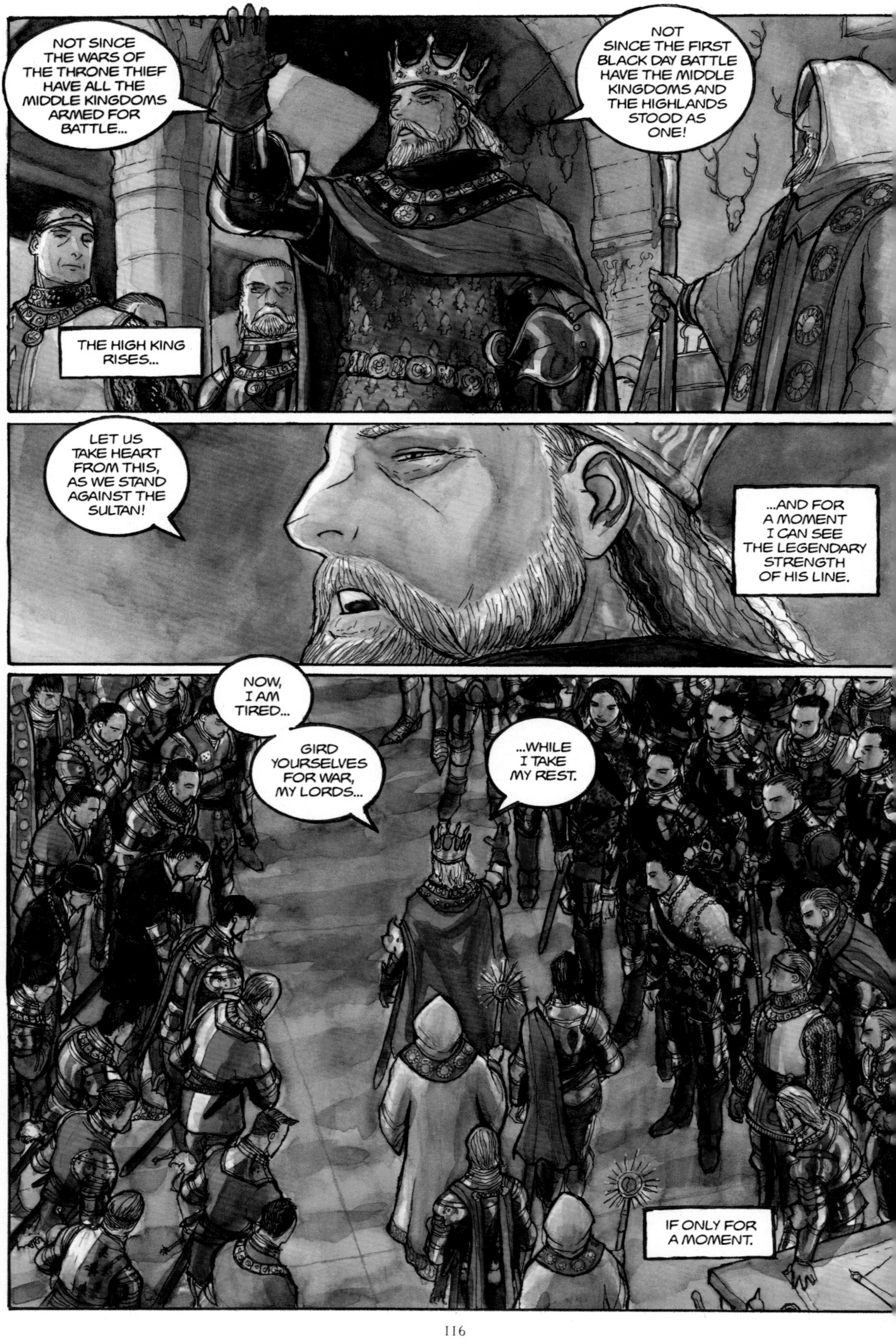
NOT SINCE THE WARS OF THE THRONE THIEF HAVE ALL THE MIDDLE KINGDOMS ARMED FOR BATTLE...
NOT SINCE THE FIRST BLACK DAY BATTLE HAVE THE MIDDLE KINGDOMS AND THE HIGHLANDS STOOD AS ONE!
THE HIGH KING RISES...
LET US TAKE HEART FROM THIS, AS WE STAND AGAINST THE SULTAN!
...AND FOR A MOMENT I CAN SEE THE LEGENDARY STRENGTH OF HIS LINE.
NOW, I AM TIRED...
GIRD YOURSELVES FOR WAR, MY LORDS...
...WHILE I TAKE MY REST.
IF ONLY FOR A MOMENT.

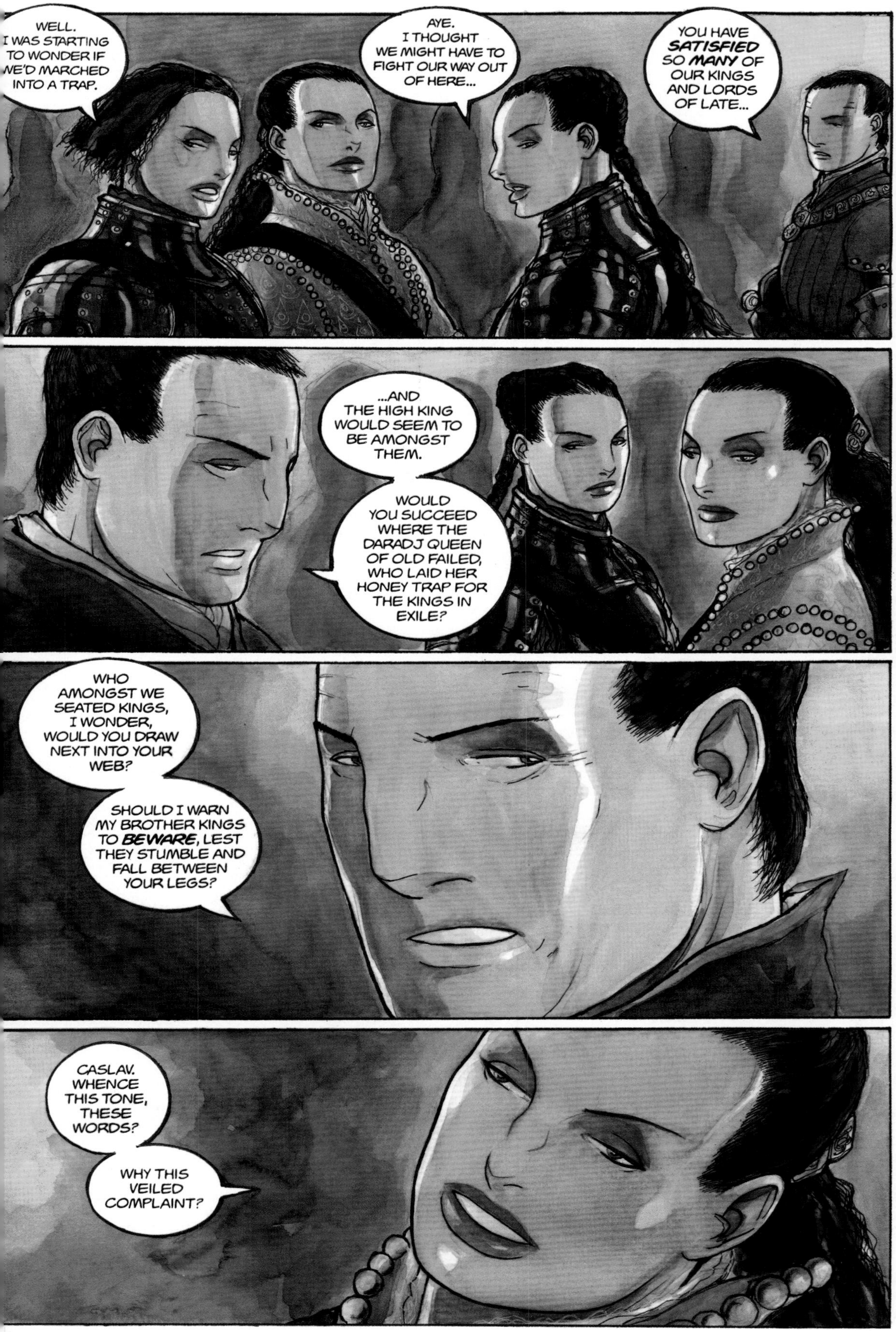

WELL. I WAS STARTING TO WONDER IF WE'D MARCHED INTO A TRAP.
AYE. I THOUGHT WE MIGHT HAVE TO FIGHT OUR WAY OUT OF HERE...
YOU HAVE SATISFIED SO MANY OF OUR KINGS AND LORDS OF LATE...
...AND THE HIGH KING WOULD SEEM TO BE AMONGST THEM.
WOULD YOU SUCCEED WHERE THE DARADJ QUEEN OF OLD FAILED, WHO LAID HER HONEY TRAP FOR THE KINGS IN EXILE?
WHO AMONGST WE SEATED KINGS, I WONDER, WOULD YOU DRAW NEXT INTO YOUR WEB?
SHOULD I WARN MY BROTHER KINGS TO BEWARE, LEST THEY STUMBLE AND FALL BETWEEN YOUR LEGS?
CASLAV. WHENCE THIS TONE, THESE WORDS?
WHY THIS VEILED COMPLAINT?

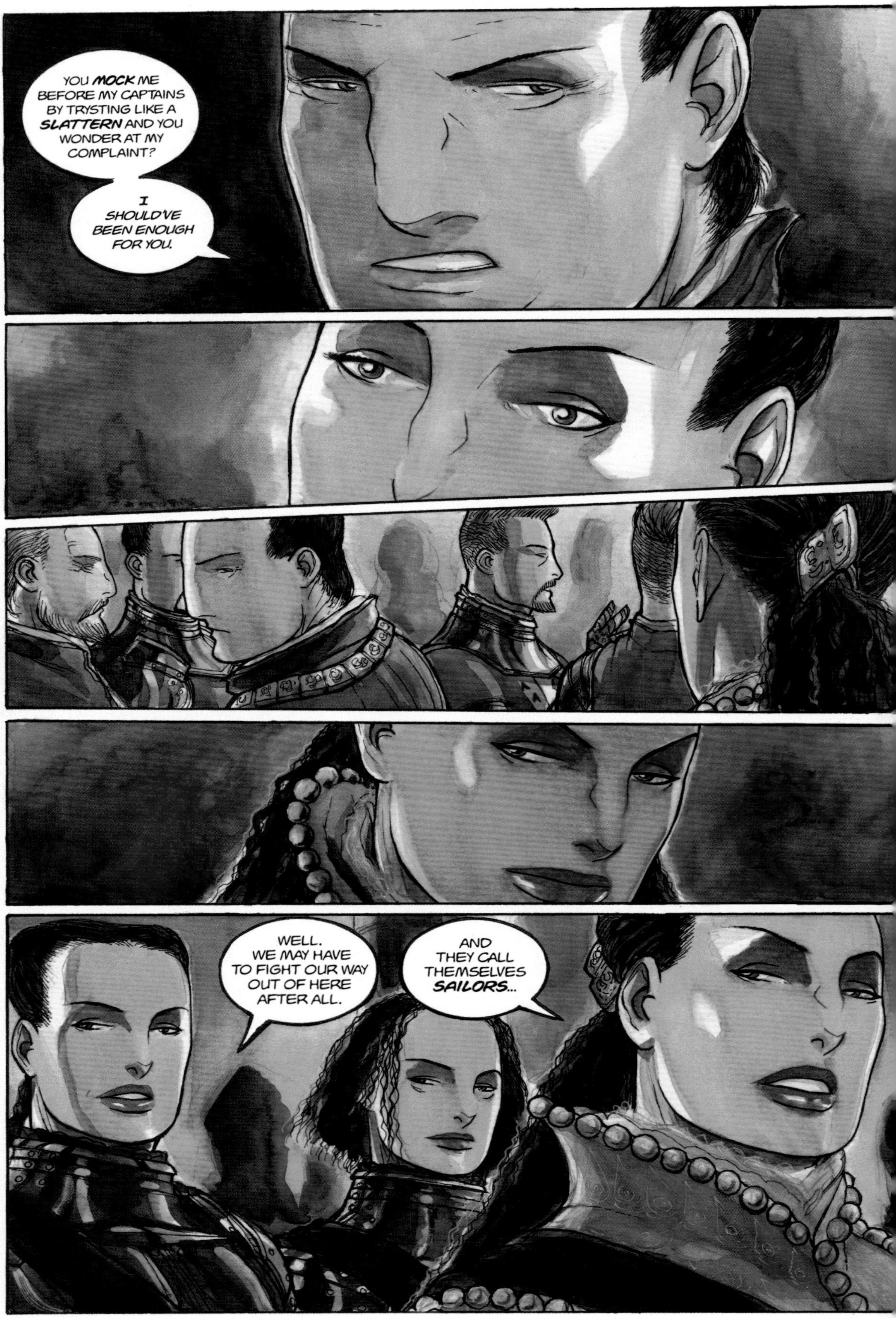
YOU MOCK ME BEFORE MY CAPTAINS BY TRYSTING LIKE A SLATTERN AND YOU WONDER AT MY COMPLAINT?
I SHOULD'VE BEEN ENOUGH FOR YOU.
WELL. WE MAY HAVE TO FIGHT OUR WAY OUT OF HERE AFTER ALL.
AND THEY CALL THEMSELVES SAILORS...

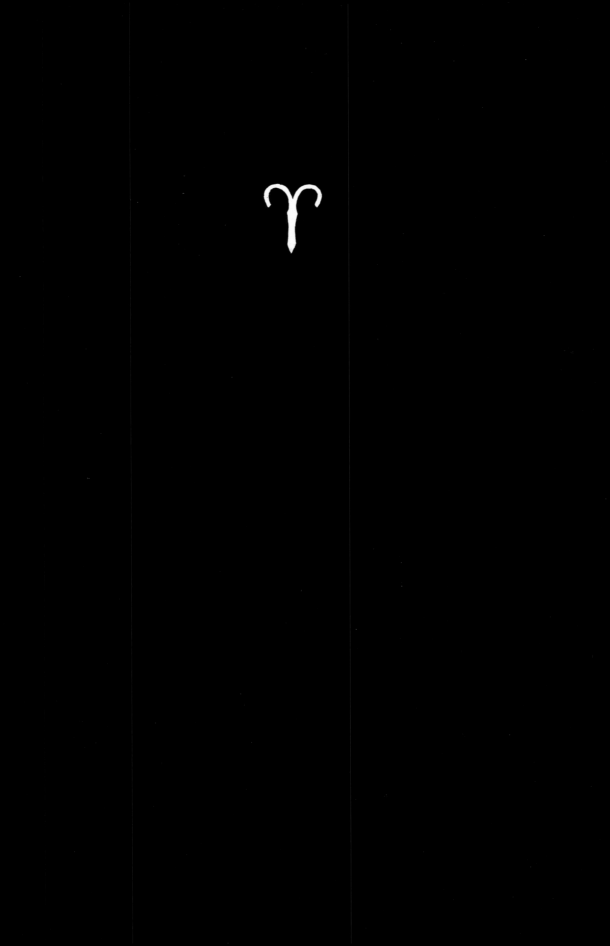

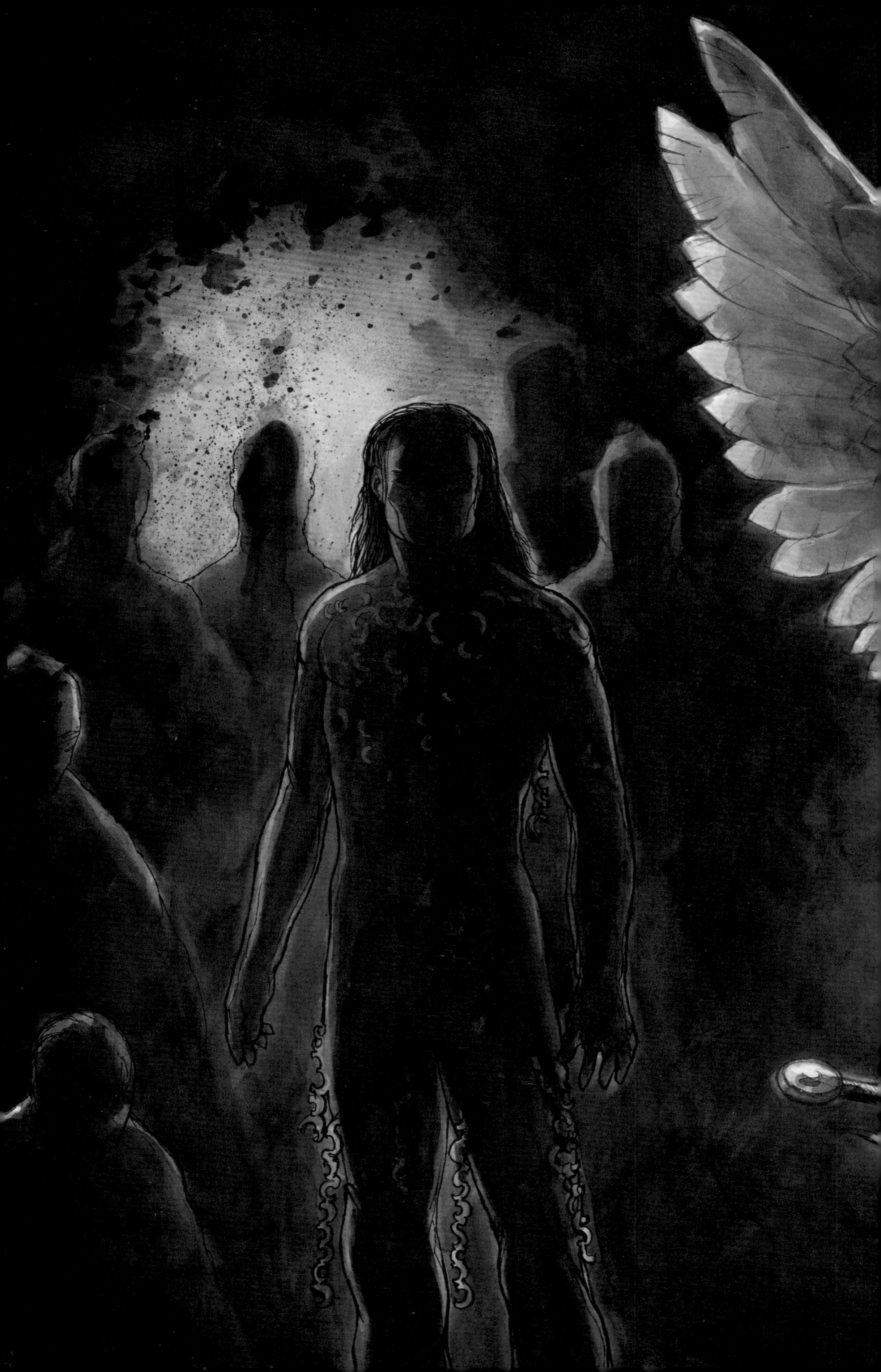

Chapter Four

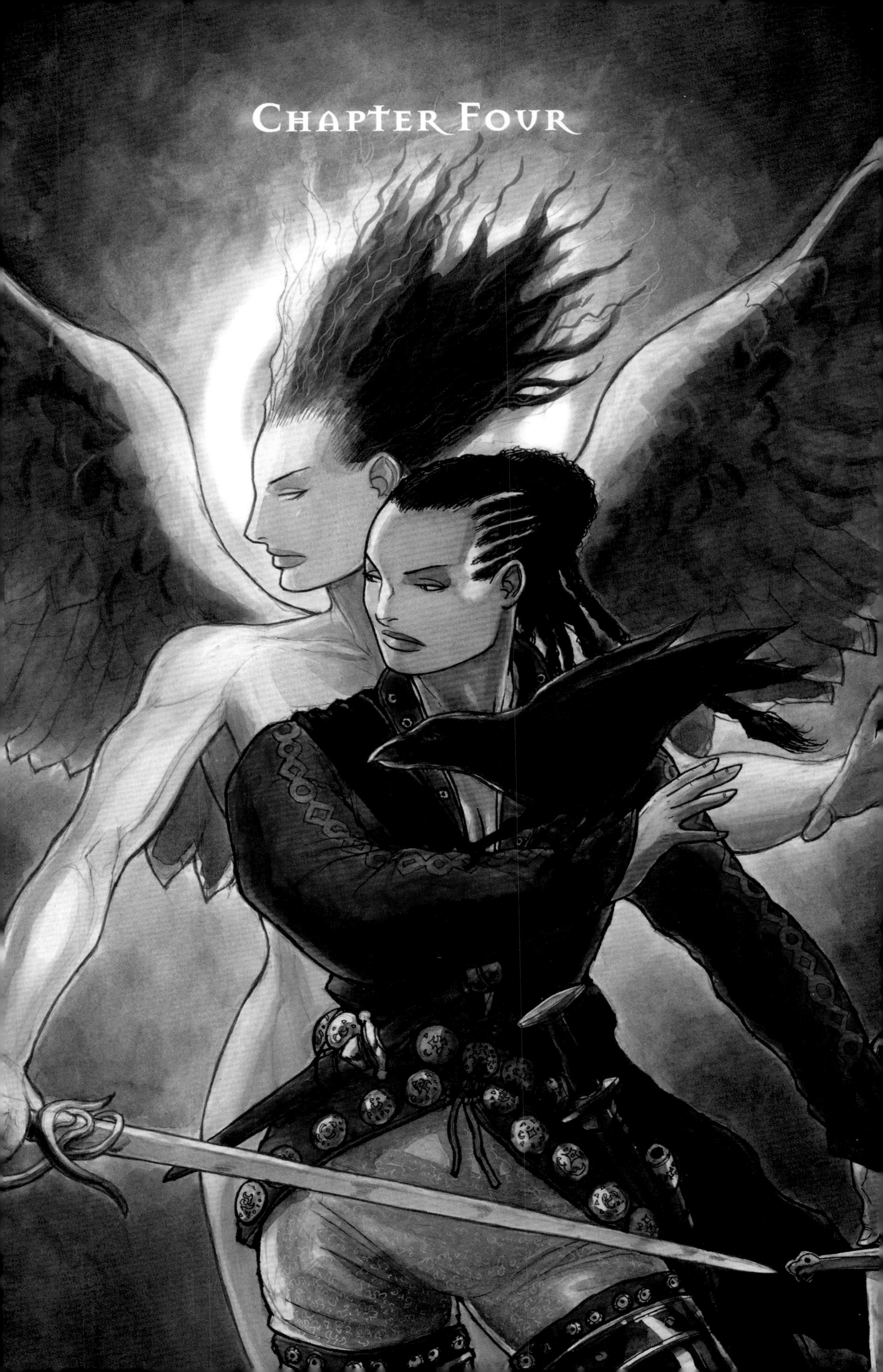

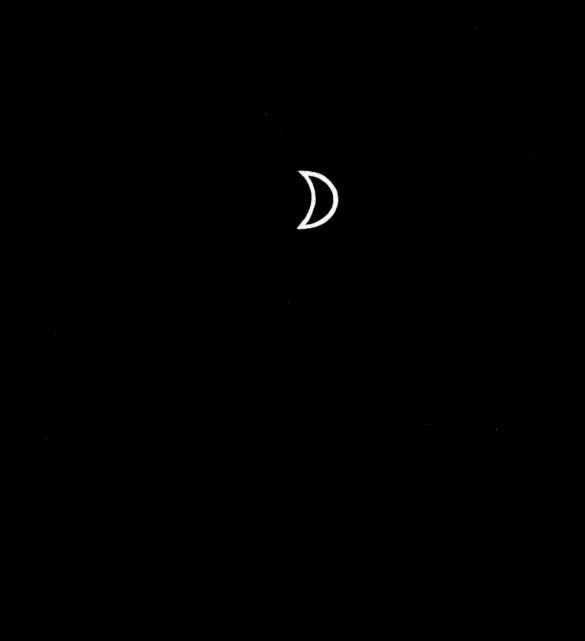

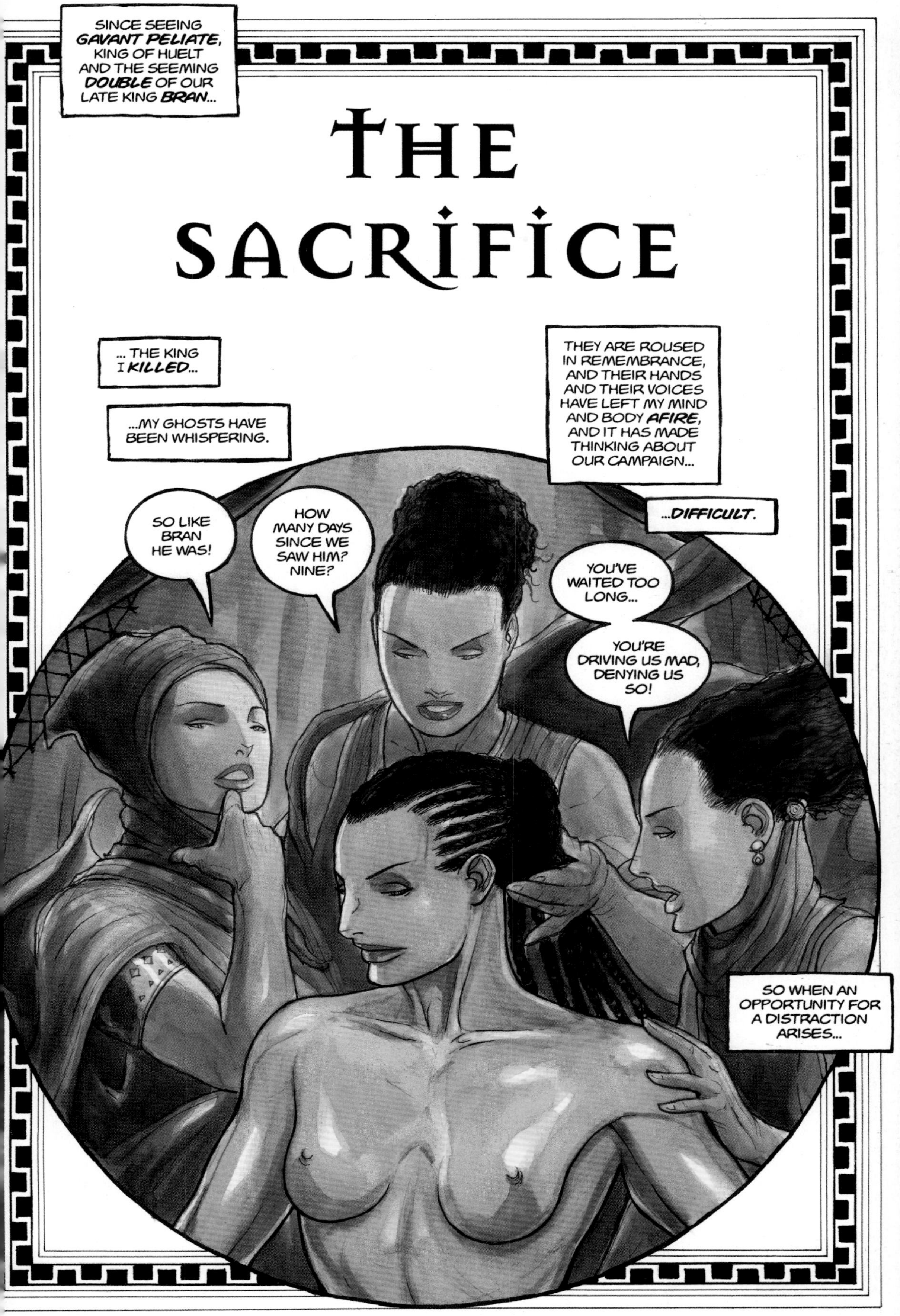
SINCE SEEING GAVANT PELIATE, KING OF HUELT AND THE SEEMING DOUBLE OF OUR LATE KING BRAN...
THE SACRIFICE
... THE KING I KILLED...
...MY GHOSTS HAVE BEEN WHISPERING.
THEY ARE ROUSED IN REMEMBRANCE, AND THEIR HANDS AND THEIR VOICES HAVE LEFT MY MIND AND BODY AFIRE, AND IT HAS MADE THINKING ABOUT OUR CAMPAIGN...
...DIFFICULT.
SO LIKE BRAN HE WAS!
HOW MANY DAYS SINCE WE SAW HIM? NINE?
YOU'VE WAITED TOO LONG...
YOU'RE DRIVING US MAD, DENYING US SO!
SO WHEN AN OPPORTUNITY FOR A DISTRACTION ARISES...

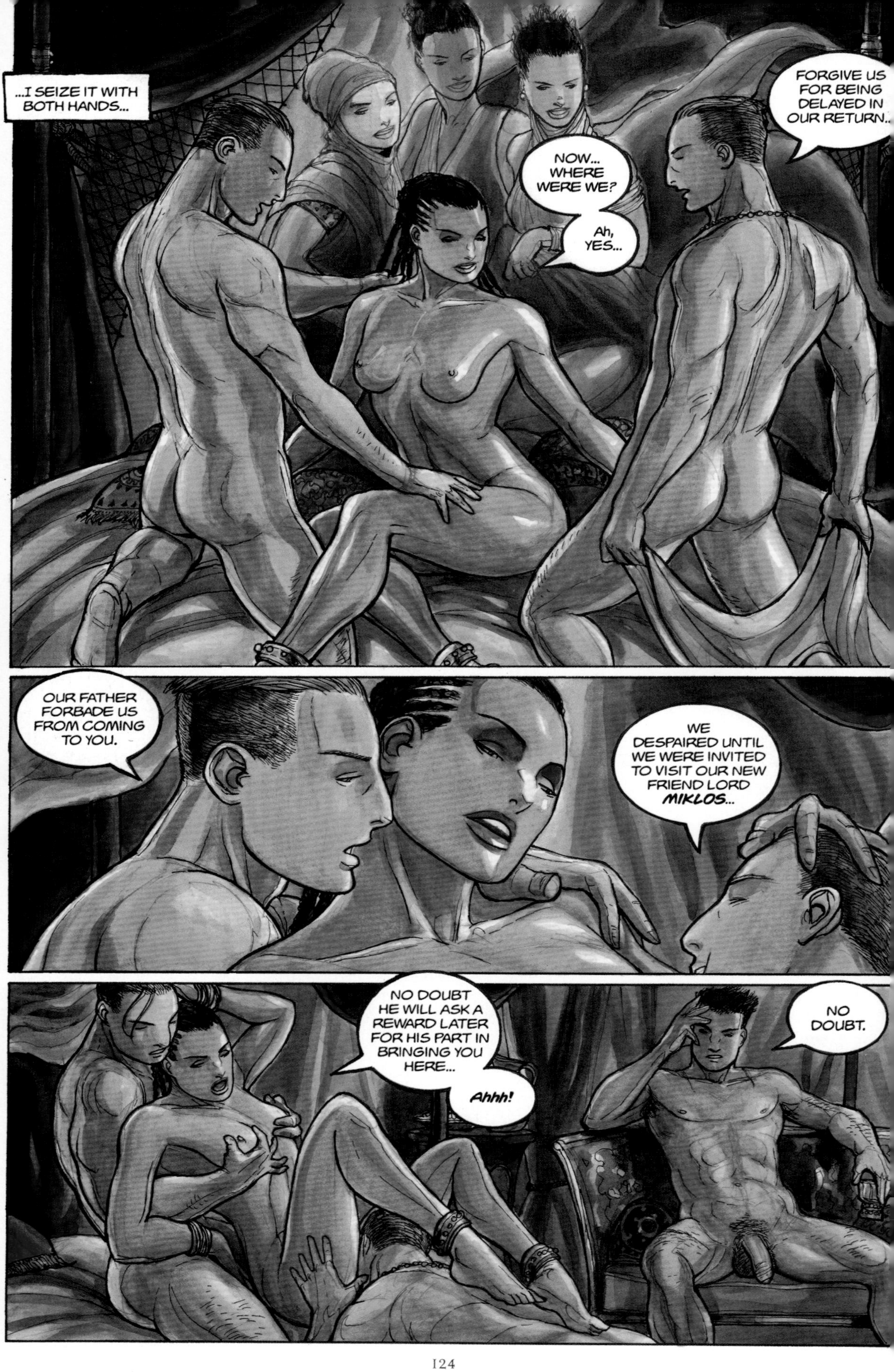
...I SEIZE IT WITH BOTH HANDS...
NOW... WHERE WERE WE?
Ah, YES...
FORGIVE US FOR BEING DELAYED IN OUR RETURN...
OUR FATHER FORBADE US FROM COMING TO YOU.
WE DESPAIRED UNTIL WE WERE INVITED TO VISIT OUR NEW FRIEND LORD MIKLOS...
NO DOUBT HE WILL ASK A REWARD LATER FOR HIS PART IN BRINGING YOU HERE...
Ahhh!
NO DOUBT.

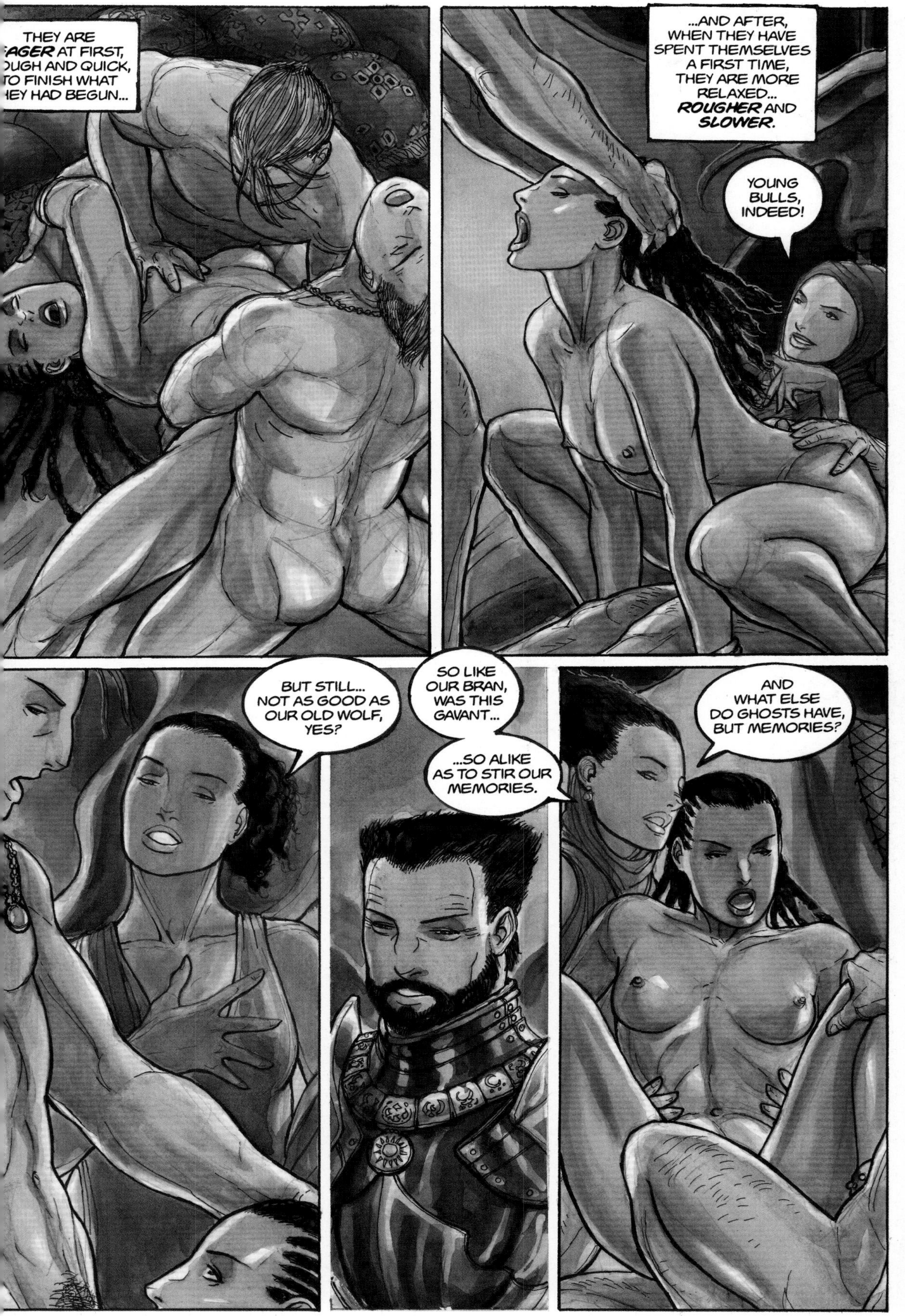
THEY ARE EAGER AT FIRST, OUGH AND QUICK, TO FINISH WHAT HEY HAD BEGUN...
...AND AFTER, WHEN THEY HAVE SPENT THEMSELVES A FIRST TIME, THEY ARE MORE RELAXED... ROUGHER AND SLOWER.
YOUNG BULLS, INDEED!
BUT STILL... NOT AS GOOD AS OUR OLD WOLF, YES?
SO LIKE OUR BRAN, WAS THIS GAVANT...
...SO ALIKE AS TO STIR OUR MEMORIES.
AND WHAT ELSE DO GHOSTS HAVE, BUT MEMORIES?

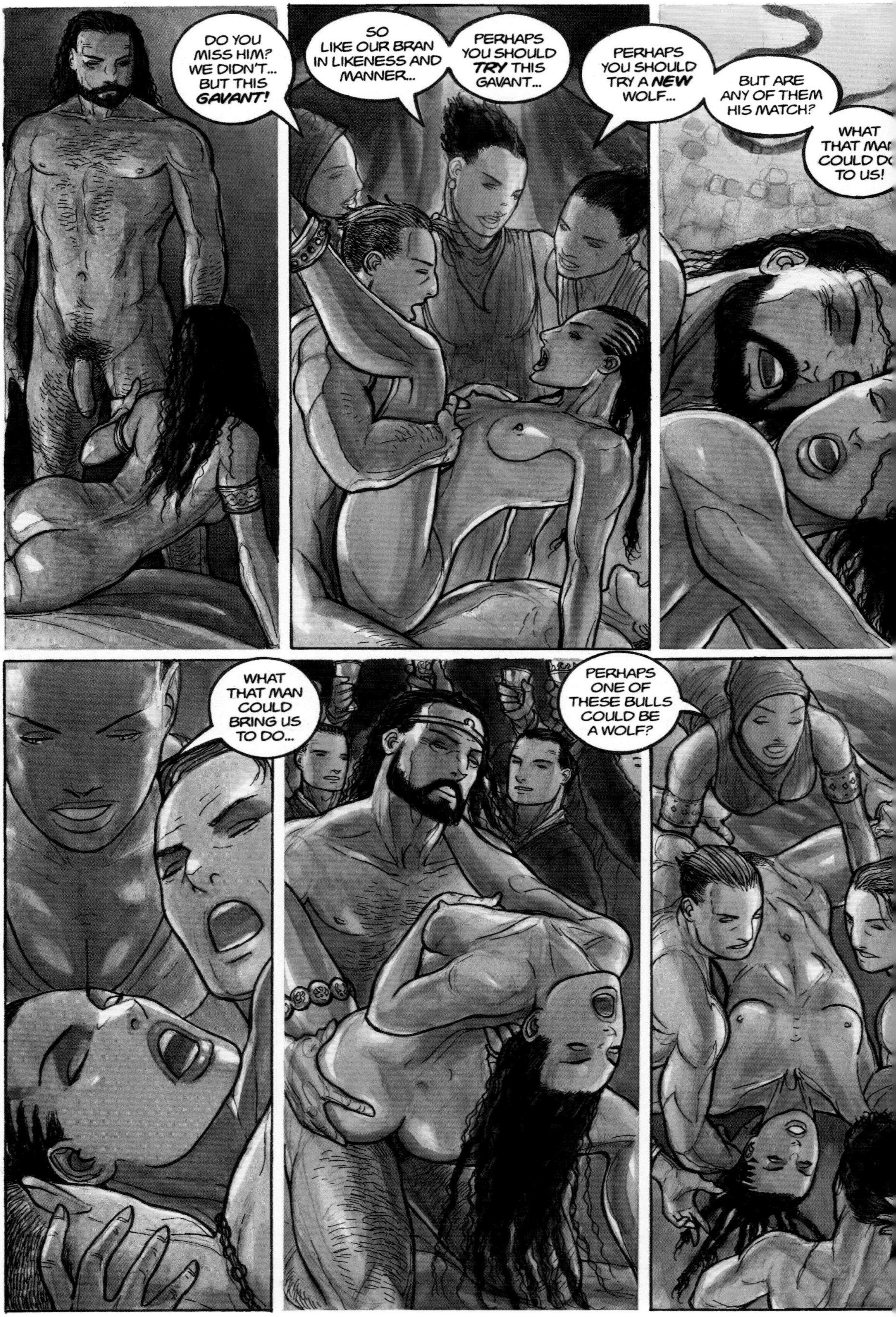
DO YOU MISS HIM? WE DIDN'T... BUT THIS GAVANT!
SO LIKE OUR BRAN IN LIKENESS AND MANNER...
PERHAPS YOU SHOULD TRY THIS GAVANT...
PERHAPS YOU SHOULD TRY A NEW WOLF...
BUT ARE ANY OF THEM HIS MATCH?
WHAT THAT MA COULD D TO US!
WHAT THAT MAN COULD BRING US TO DO...
PERHAPS ONE OF THESE BULLS COULD BE A WOLF?

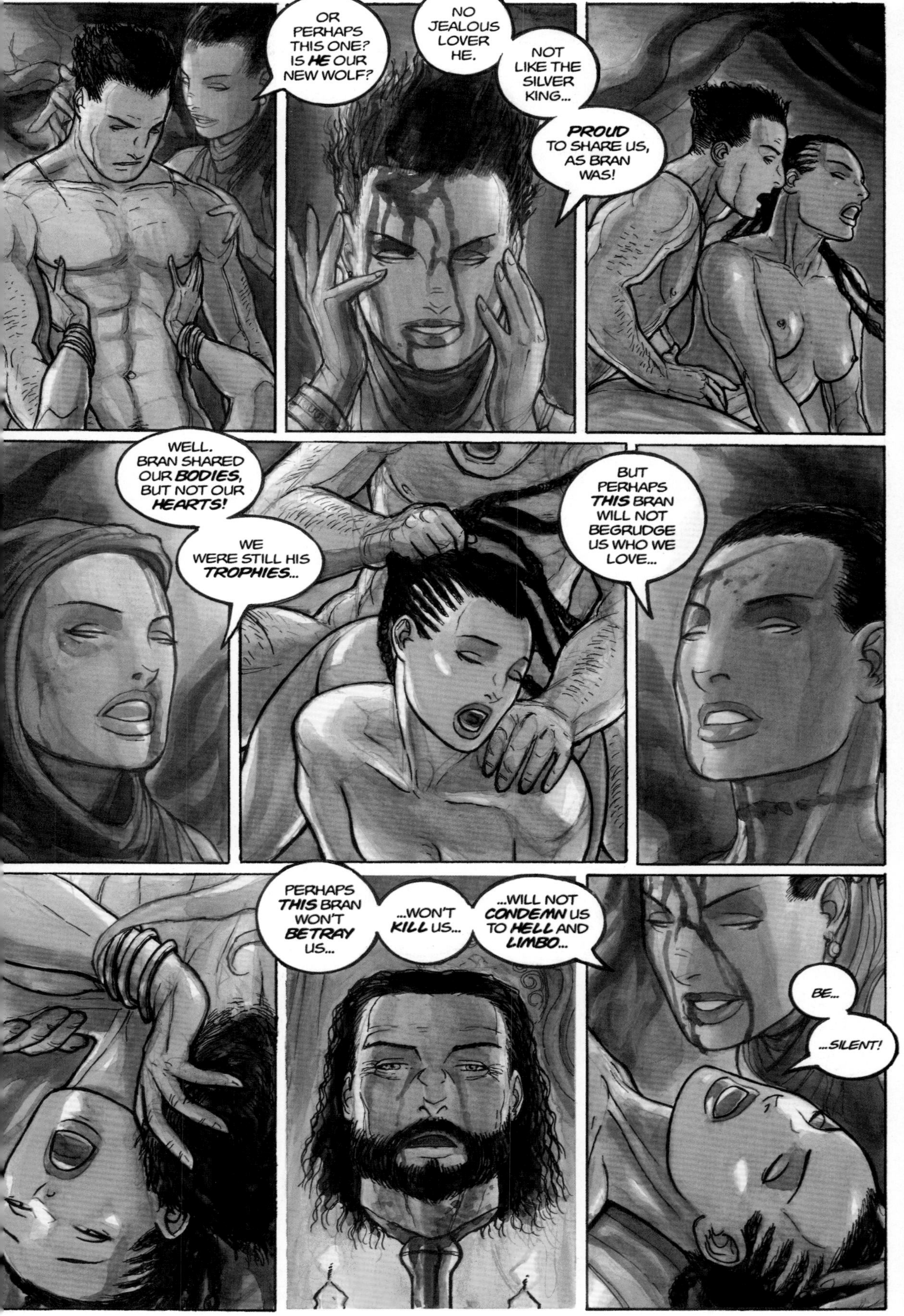
OR PERHAPS THIS ONE? IS HE OUR NEW WOLF?
NO JEALOUS LOVER HE.
NOT LIKE THE SILVER KING...
PROUD TO SHARE US, AS BRAN WAS!
WELL. BRAN SHARED OUR BODIES, BUT NOT OUR HEARTS!
WE WERE STILL HIS TROPHIES...
BUT PERHAPS THIS BRAN WILL NOT BEGRUDGE US WHO WE LOVE...
PERHAPS THIS BRAN WON'T BETRAY US...
...WON'T KILL US...
...WILL NOT CONDEMN US TO HELL AND LIMBO...
BE...
...SILENT!

Unhh! DIEVA!

THAT'S IT!

YOUR GRACE...

QUEEN MYRINA IS HERE...

THANK YOU, SAVA...

LORD MIKLOS! SEE OUR GUESTS TO THEIR CAMP...

YOU'RE BRUISED! SHALL I SUMMON THE PHYSICIANS?

NO. THE PHYSICIANS ARE NOT FOR THE WOUNDS OF DIEVA'S WAR...

BETTER TO SUMMON HER PRIESTESSES!

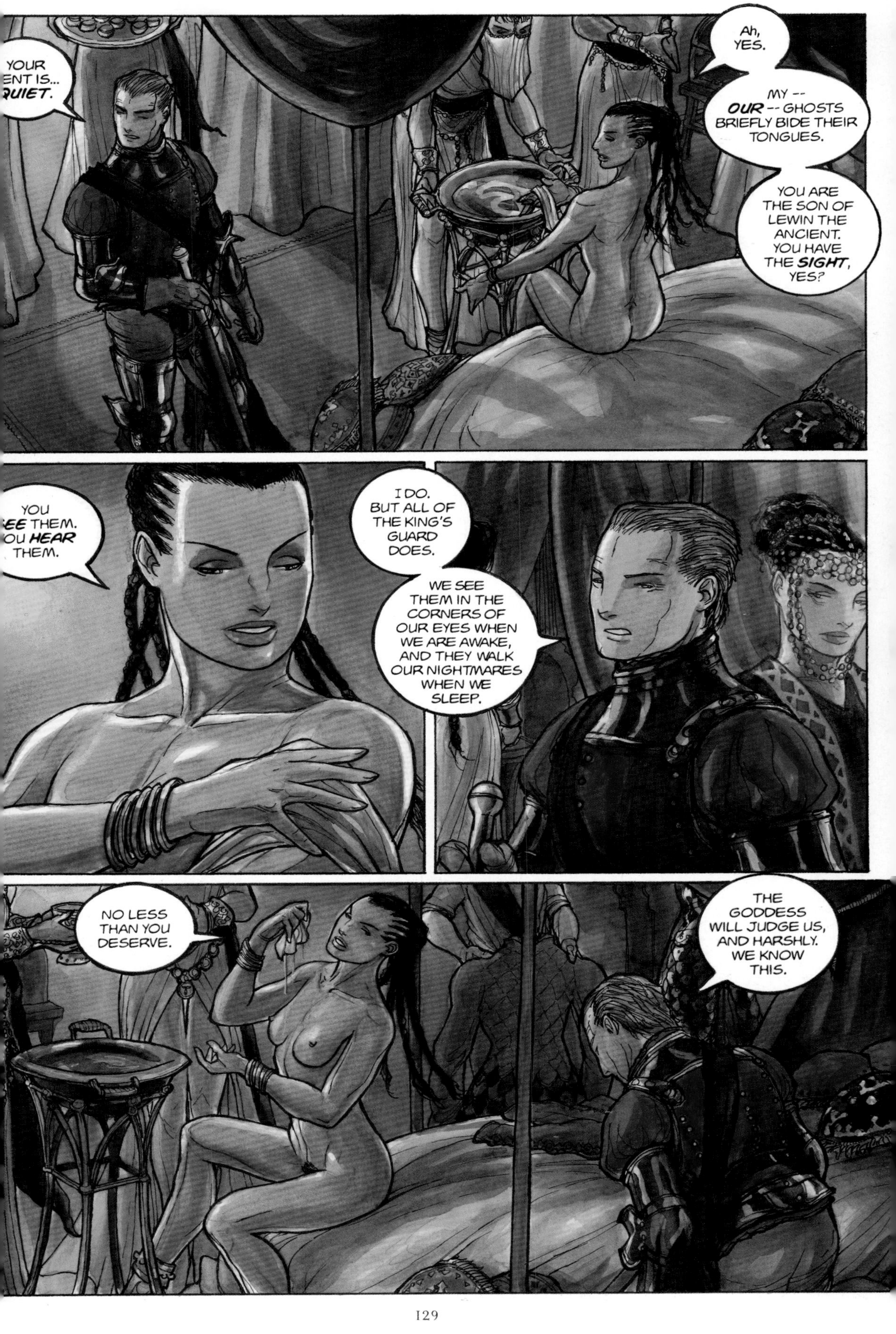
YOUR
ENT IS...
QUIET.
Ah, YES.
MY -- OUR -- GHOSTS BRIEFLY BIDE THEIR TONGUES.
YOU ARE THE SON OF LEWIN THE ANCIENT. YOU HAVE THE SIGHT, YES?
YOU
SEE THEM.
OU HEAR
THEM.
I DO. BUT ALL OF THE KING'S GUARD DOES.
WE SEE THEM IN THE CORNERS OF OUR EYES WHEN WE ARE AWAKE, AND THEY WALK OUR NIGHTMARES WHEN WE SLEEP.
NO LESS THAN YOU DESERVE.
THE GODDESS WILL JUDGE US, AND HARSHLY. WE KNOW THIS.

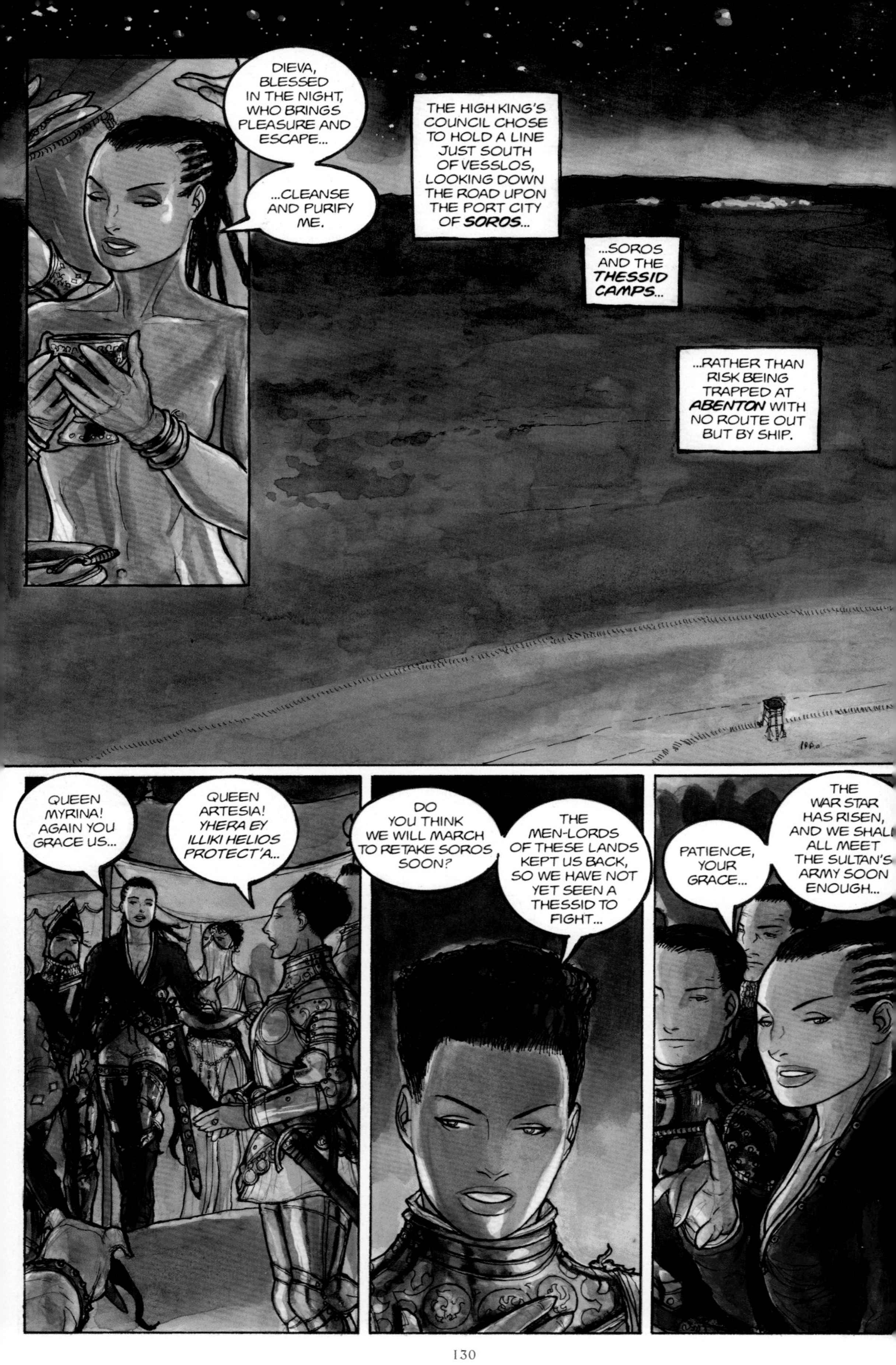
DIEVA, BLESSED IN THE NIGHT, WHO BRINGS PLEASURE AND ESCAPE...
...CLEANSE AND PURIFY ME.
THE HIGH KING'S COUNCIL CHOSE TO HOLD A LINE JUST SOUTH OF VESSLOS, LOOKING DOWN THE ROAD UPON THE PORT CITY OF SOROS...
...SOROS AND THE THESSID CAMPS...
...RATHER THAN RISK BEING TRAPPED AT ABENTON WITH NO ROUTE OUT BUT BY SHIP.
QUEEN MYRINA! AGAIN YOU GRACE US...
QUEEN ARTESIA! YHERA EY ILLIKI HELIOS PROTECT'A...
DO YOU THINK WE WILL MARCH TO RETAKE SOROS SOON?
THE MEN-LORDS OF THESE LANDS KEPT US BACK, SO WE HAVE NOT YET SEEN A THESSID TO FIGHT...
PATIENCE, YOUR GRACE...
THE WAR STAR HAS RISEN, AND WE SHALL ALL MEET THE SULTAN'S ARMY SOON ENOUGH...

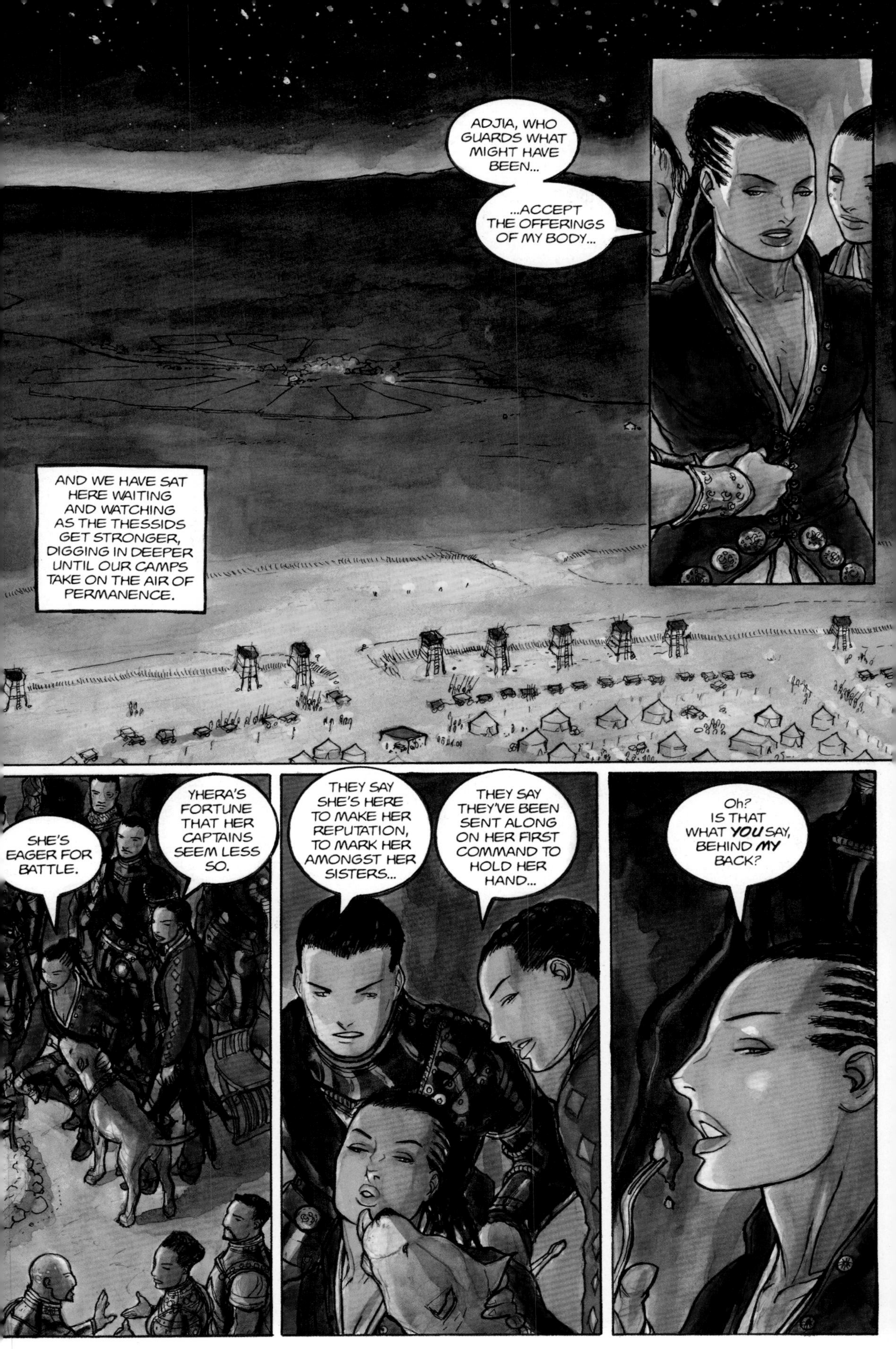
ADJIA, WHO GUARDS WHAT MIGHT HAVE BEEN...
...ACCEPT THE OFFERINGS OF MY BODY...
AND WE HAVE SAT HERE WAITING AND WATCHING AS THE THESSIDS GET STRONGER, DIGGING IN DEEPER UNTIL OUR CAMPS TAKE ON THE AIR OF PERMANENCE.
SHE'S EAGER FOR BATTLE.
YHERA'S FORTUNE THAT HER CAPTAINS SEEM LESS SO.
THEY SAY SHE'S HERE TO MAKE HER REPUTATION, TO MARK HER AMONGST HER SISTERS...
THEY SAY THEY'VE BEEN SENT ALONG ON HER FIRST COMMAND TO HOLD HER HAND...
Oh? IS THAT WHAT ***YOU*** SAY, BEHIND ***MY*** BACK?

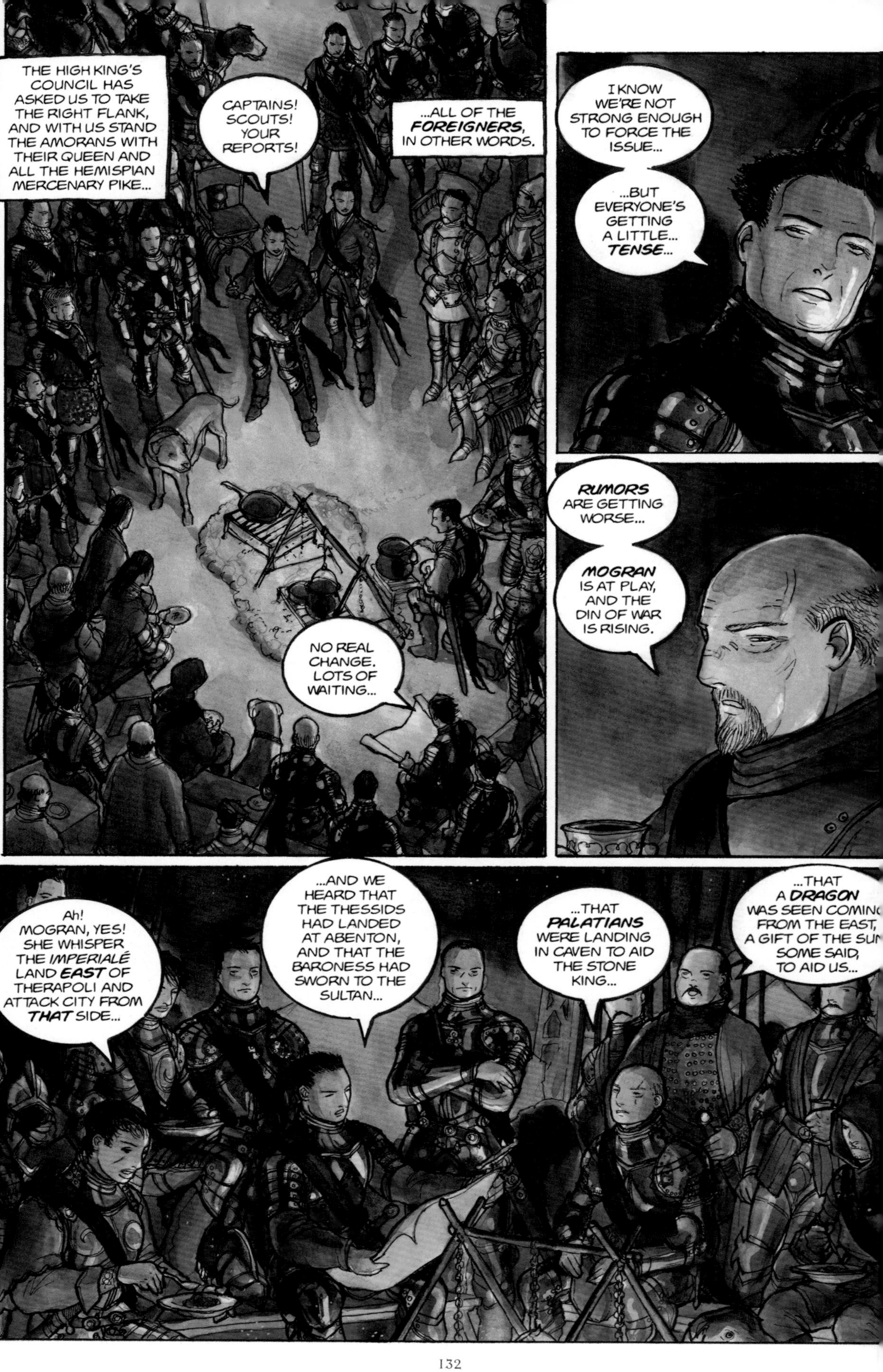
THE HIGH KING'S COUNCIL HAS ASKED US TO TAKE THE RIGHT FLANK, AND WITH US STAND THE AMORANS WITH THEIR QUEEN AND ALL THE HEMISPIAN MERCENARY PIKE...
CAPTAINS! SCOUTS! YOUR REPORTS!
...ALL OF THE FOREIGNERS, IN OTHER WORDS.
I KNOW WE'RE NOT STRONG ENOUGH TO FORCE THE ISSUE...
...BUT EVERYONE'S GETTING A LITTLE... TENSE...
RUMORS ARE GETTING WORSE...
MOGRAN IS AT PLAY, AND THE DIN OF WAR IS RISING.
NO REAL CHANGE. LOTS OF WAITING...
Ah! MOGRAN, YES! SHE WHISPER THE IMPERIALÉ LAND EAST OF THERAPOLI AND ATTACK CITY FROM THAT SIDE...
...AND WE HEARD THAT THE THESSIDS HAD LANDED AT ABENTON, AND THAT THE BARONESS HAD SWORN TO THE SULTAN...
...THAT PALATIANS WERE LANDING IN CAVEN TO AID THE STONE KING...
...THAT A DRAGON WAS SEEN COMING FROM THE EAST, A GIFT OF THE SUN SOME SAID, TO AID US...

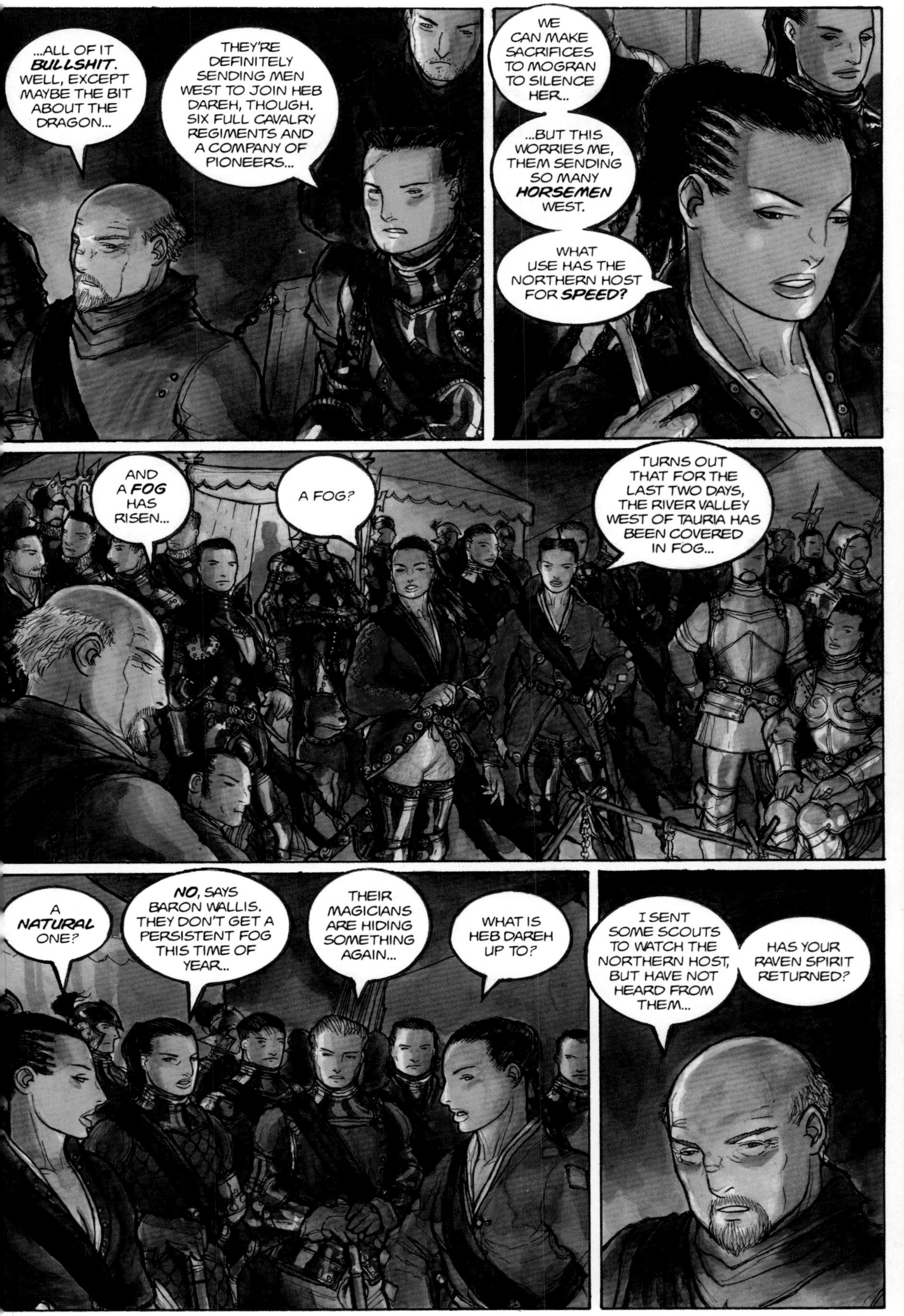
...ALL OF IT **BULLSHIT**. WELL, EXCEPT MAYBE THE BIT ABOUT THE DRAGON...
THEY'RE DEFINITELY SENDING MEN WEST TO JOIN HEB DAREH, THOUGH. SIX FULL CAVALRY REGIMENTS AND A COMPANY OF PIONEERS...
WE CAN MAKE SACRIFICES TO MOGRAN TO SILENCE HER...
...BUT THIS WORRIES ME, THEM SENDING SO MANY **HORSEMEN** WEST.
WHAT USE HAS THE NORTHERN HOST FOR **SPEED?**
AND A **FOG** HAS RISEN...
A FOG?
TURNS OUT THAT FOR THE LAST TWO DAYS, THE RIVER VALLEY WEST OF TAURIA HAS BEEN COVERED IN FOG...
A **NATURAL** ONE?
NO, SAYS BARON WALLIS. THEY DON'T GET A PERSISTENT FOG THIS TIME OF YEAR...
THEIR MAGICIANS ARE HIDING SOMETHING AGAIN...
WHAT IS HEB DAREH UP TO?
I SENT SOME SCOUTS TO WATCH THE NORTHERN HOST, BUT HAVE NOT HEARD FROM THEM...
HAS YOUR RAVEN SPIRIT RETURNED?

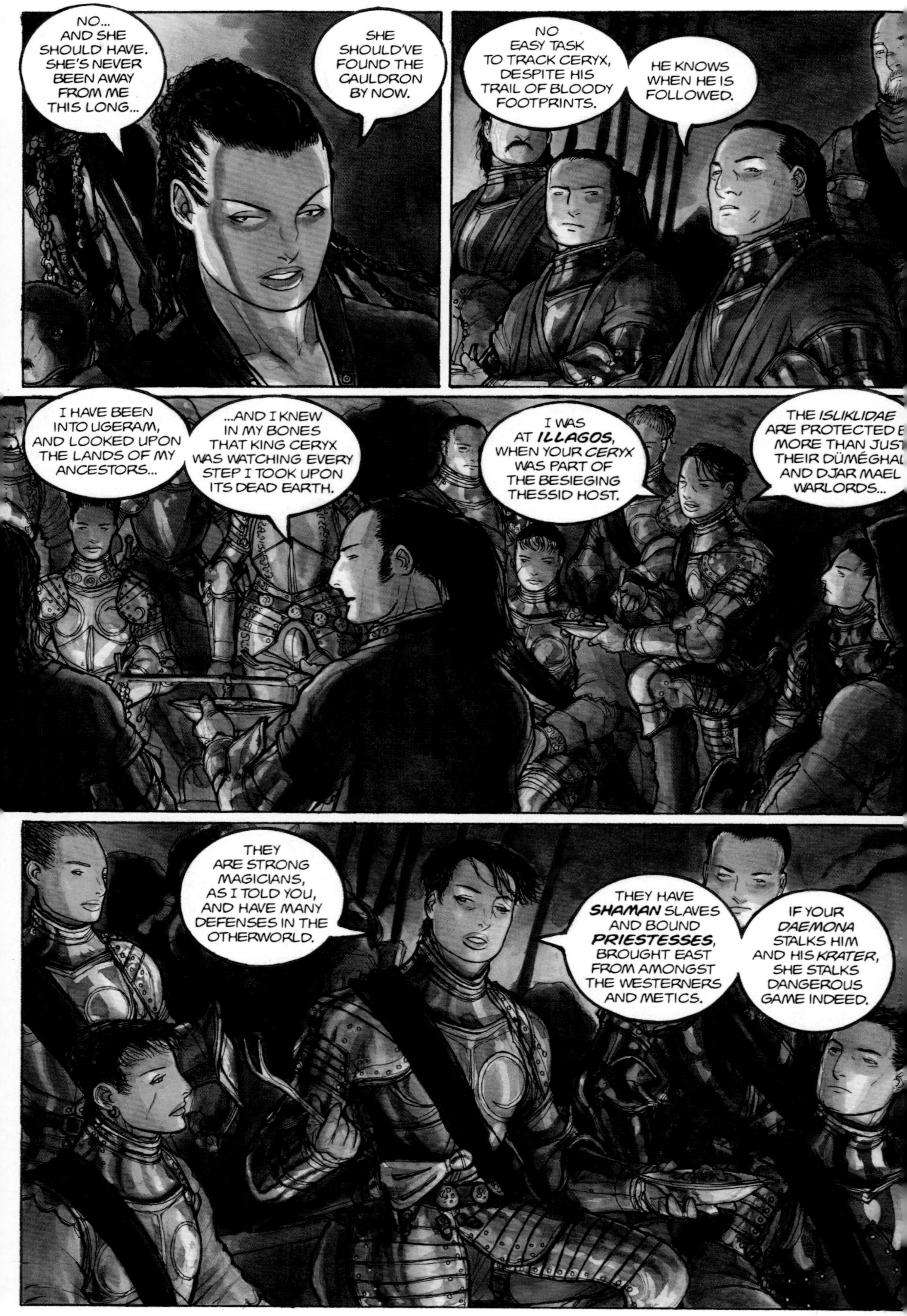
NO... AND SHE SHOULD HAVE. SHE'S NEVER BEEN AWAY FROM ME THIS LONG...
SHE SHOULD'VE FOUND THE CAULDRON BY NOW.
NO EASY TASK TO TRACK CERYX, DESPITE HIS TRAIL OF BLOODY FOOTPRINTS.
HE KNOWS WHEN HE IS FOLLOWED.
I HAVE BEEN INTO UGERAM, AND LOOKED UPON THE LANDS OF MY ANCESTORS...
...AND I KNEW IN MY BONES THAT KING CERYX WAS WATCHING EVERY STEP I TOOK UPON ITS DEAD EARTH.
I WAS AT ***ILLAGOS***, WHEN YOUR *CERYX* WAS PART OF THE BESIEGING THESSID HOST.
THE *ISLIKLIDAE* ARE PROTECTED B MORE THAN JUST THEIR DÜMÉGHAL AND DJAR MAEL WARLORDS...
THEY ARE STRONG MAGICIANS, AS I TOLD YOU, AND HAVE MANY DEFENSES IN THE OTHERWORLD.
THEY HAVE ***SHAMAN*** SLAVES AND BOUND ***PRIESTESSES***, BROUGHT EAST FROM AMONGST THE WESTERNERS AND METICS.
IF YOUR *DAEMONA* STALKS HIM AND HIS *KRATER*, SHE STALKS DANGEROUS GAME INDEED.

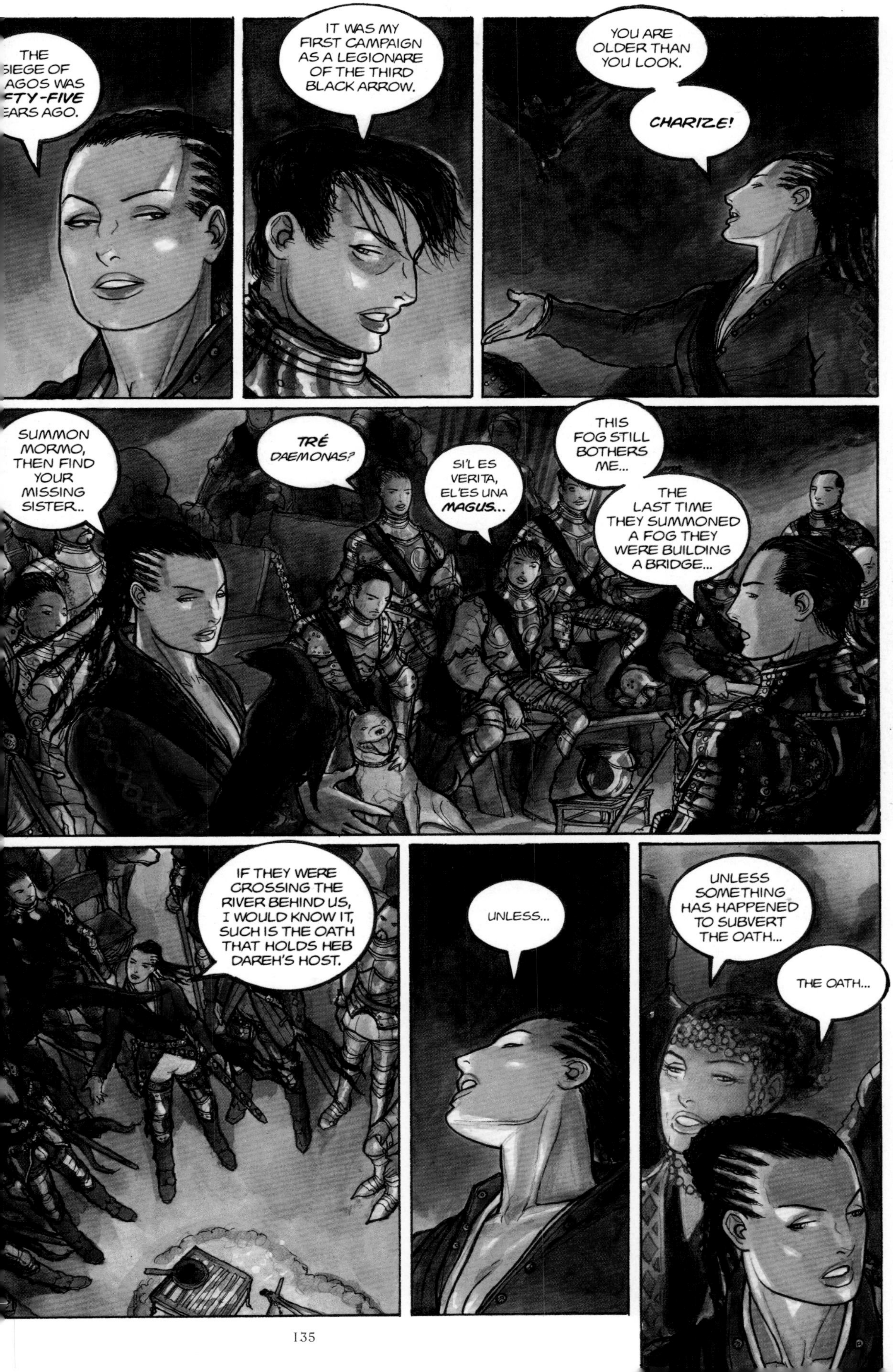
THE SIEGE OF AGOS WAS FTY-FIVE EARS AGO.
IT WAS MY FIRST CAMPAIGN AS A LEGIONARE OF THE THIRD BLACK ARROW.
YOU ARE OLDER THAN YOU LOOK.
CHARIZE!
SUMMON MORMO, THEN FIND YOUR MISSING SISTER...
TRÉ DAEMONAS?
SI'L ES VERITA, EL'ES UNA MAGUS...
THIS FOG STILL BOTHERS ME...
THE LAST TIME THEY SUMMONED A FOG THEY WERE BUILDING A BRIDGE...
IF THEY WERE CROSSING THE RIVER BEHIND US, I WOULD KNOW IT, SUCH IS THE OATH THAT HOLDS HEB DAREH'S HOST.
UNLESS...
UNLESS SOMETHING HAS HAPPENED TO SUBVERT THE OATH...
THE OATH...

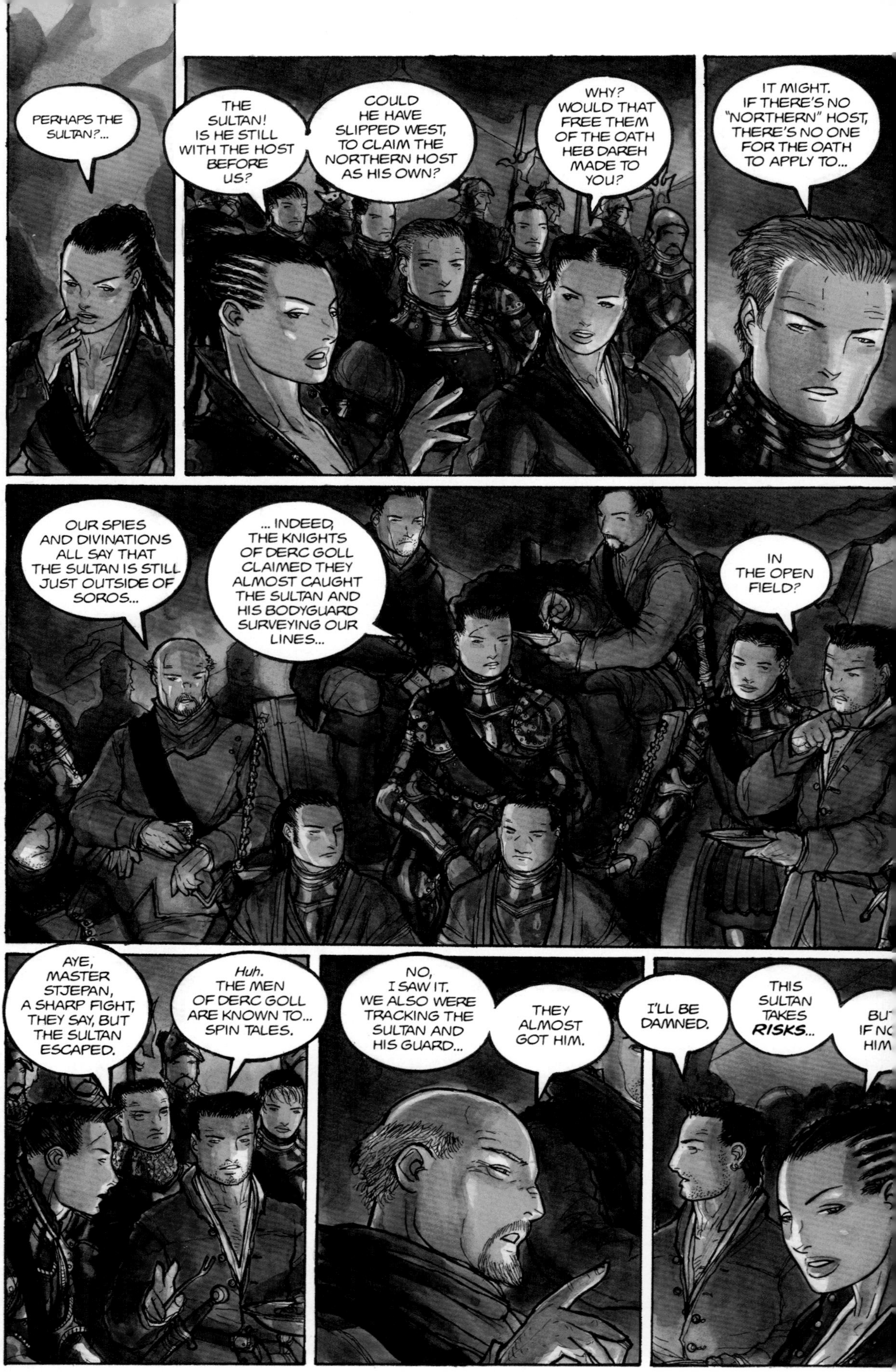
PERHAPS THE SULTAN?...
THE SULTAN! IS HE STILL WITH THE HOST BEFORE US?
COULD HE HAVE SLIPPED WEST, TO CLAIM THE NORTHERN HOST AS HIS OWN?
WHY? WOULD THAT FREE THEM OF THE OATH HEB DAREH MADE TO YOU?
IT MIGHT. IF THERE'S NO "NORTHERN" HOST, THERE'S NO ONE FOR THE OATH TO APPLY TO...
OUR SPIES AND DIVINATIONS ALL SAY THAT THE SULTAN IS STILL JUST OUTSIDE OF SOROS...
... INDEED, THE KNIGHTS OF DERC GOLL CLAIMED THEY ALMOST CAUGHT THE SULTAN AND HIS BODYGUARD SURVEYING OUR LINES...
IN THE OPEN FIELD?
AYE, MASTER STJEPAN, A SHARP FIGHT, THEY SAY, BUT THE SULTAN ESCAPED.
Huh. THE MEN OF DERC GOLL ARE KNOWN TO... SPIN TALES.
NO, I SAW IT. WE ALSO WERE TRACKING THE SULTAN AND HIS GUARD...
THEY ALMOST GOT HIM.
I'LL BE DAMNED.
THIS SULTAN TAKES ***RISKS***...

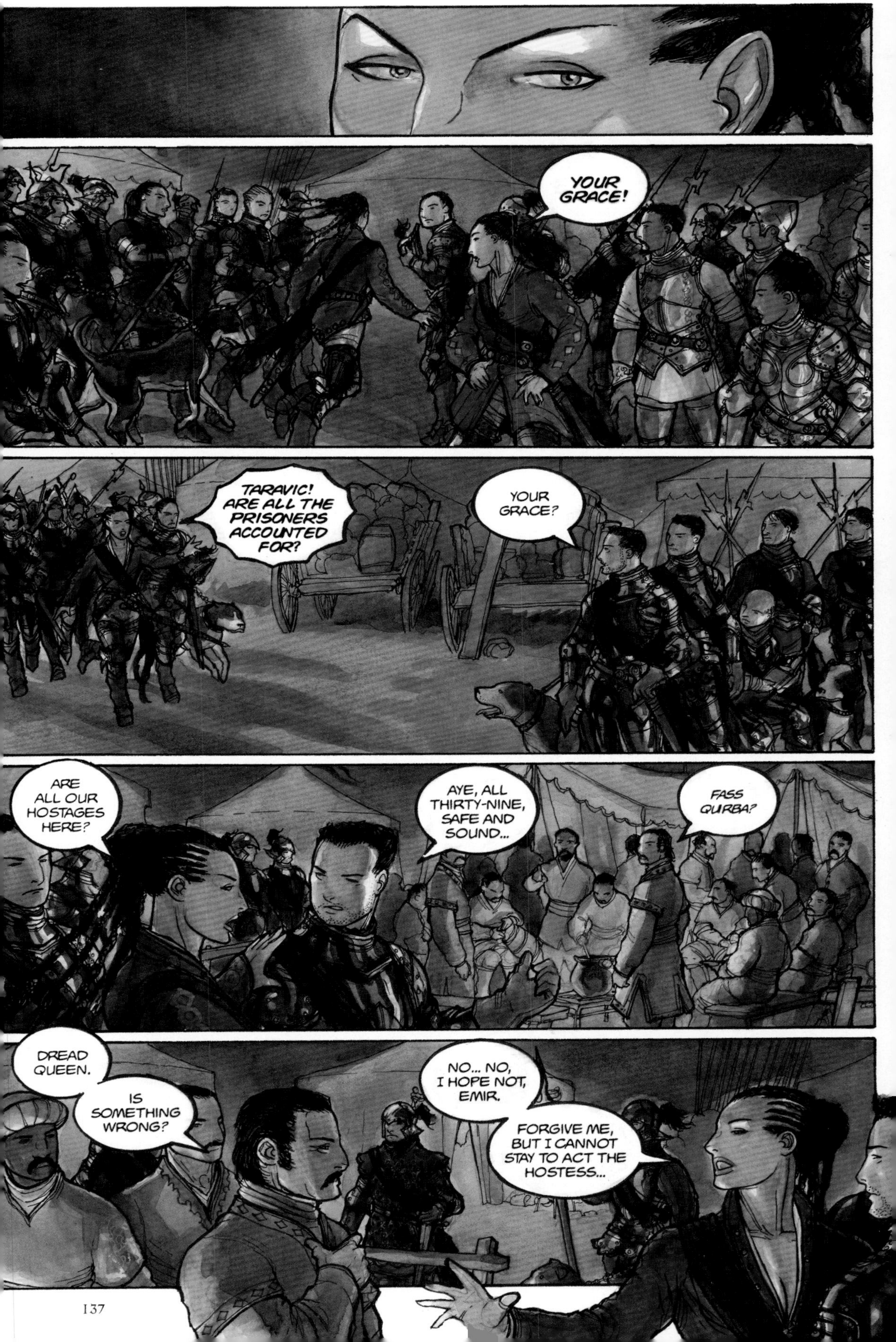
YOUR GRACE!
TARAVIC! ARE ALL THE PRISONERS ACCOUNTED FOR?
YOUR GRACE?
ARE ALL OUR HOSTAGES HERE?
AYE, ALL THIRTY-NINE, SAFE AND SOUND...
FASS QURBA?
DREAD QUEEN.
IS SOMETHING WRONG?
NO... NO, I HOPE NOT, EMIR.
FORGIVE ME, BUT I CANNOT STAY TO ACT THE HOSTESS...

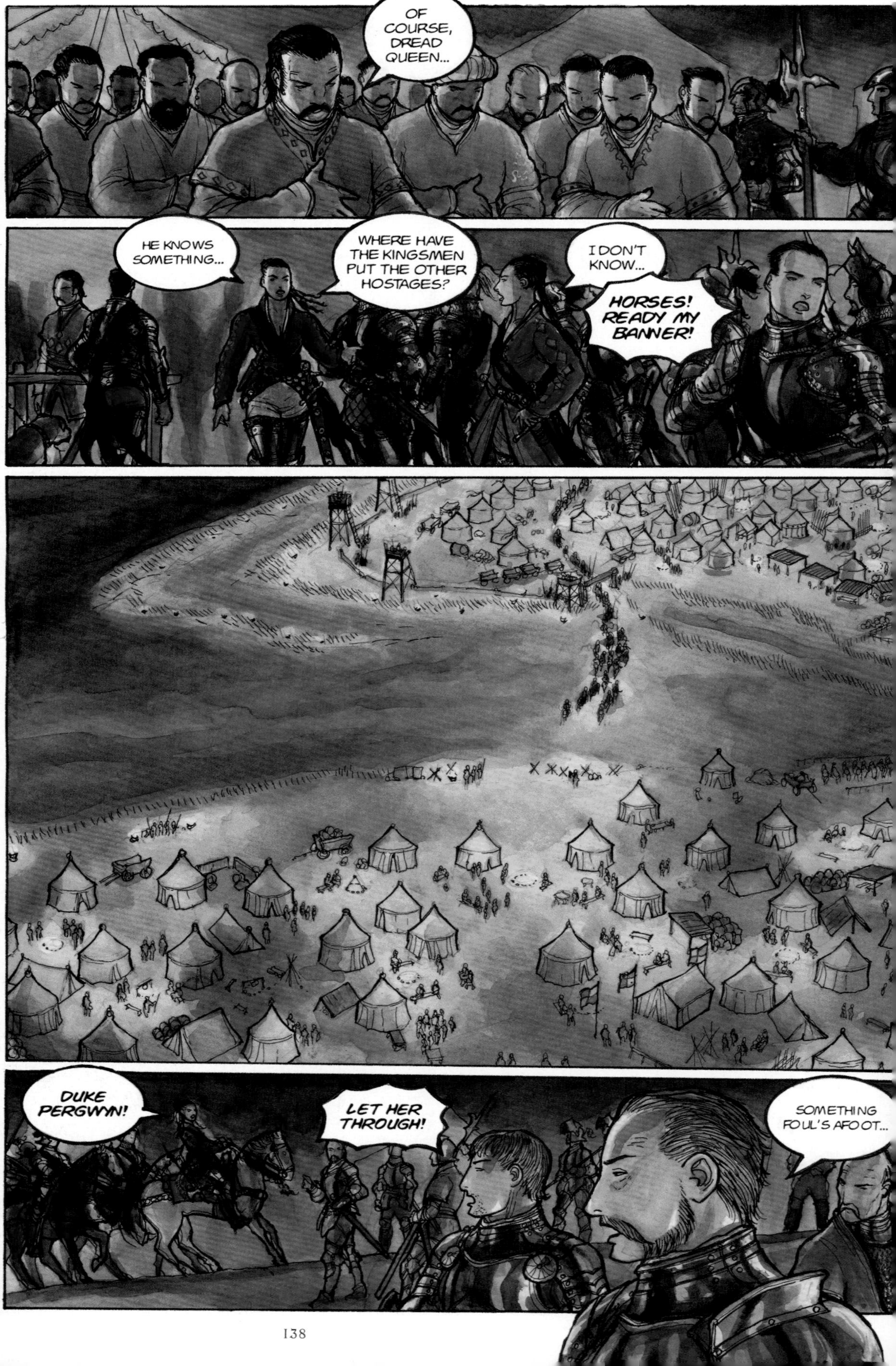
OF COURSE, DREAD QUEEN...
HE KNOWS SOMETHING...
WHERE HAVE THE KINGSMEN PUT THE OTHER HOSTAGES?
I DON'T KNOW...
HORSES! READY MY BANNER!
DUKE PERGWYN!
LET HER THROUGH!
SOMETHING FOUL'S AFOOT...

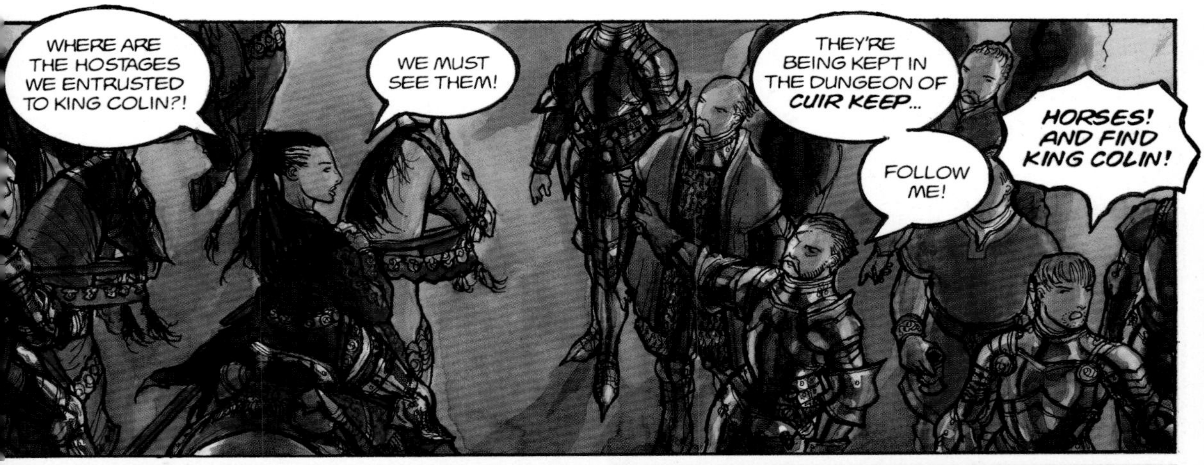
WHERE ARE THE HOSTAGES WE ENTRUSTED TO KING COLIN?!
WE MUST SEE THEM!
THEY'RE BEING KEPT IN THE DUNGEON OF CUIR KEEP...
FOLLOW ME!
HORSES! AND FIND KING COLIN!

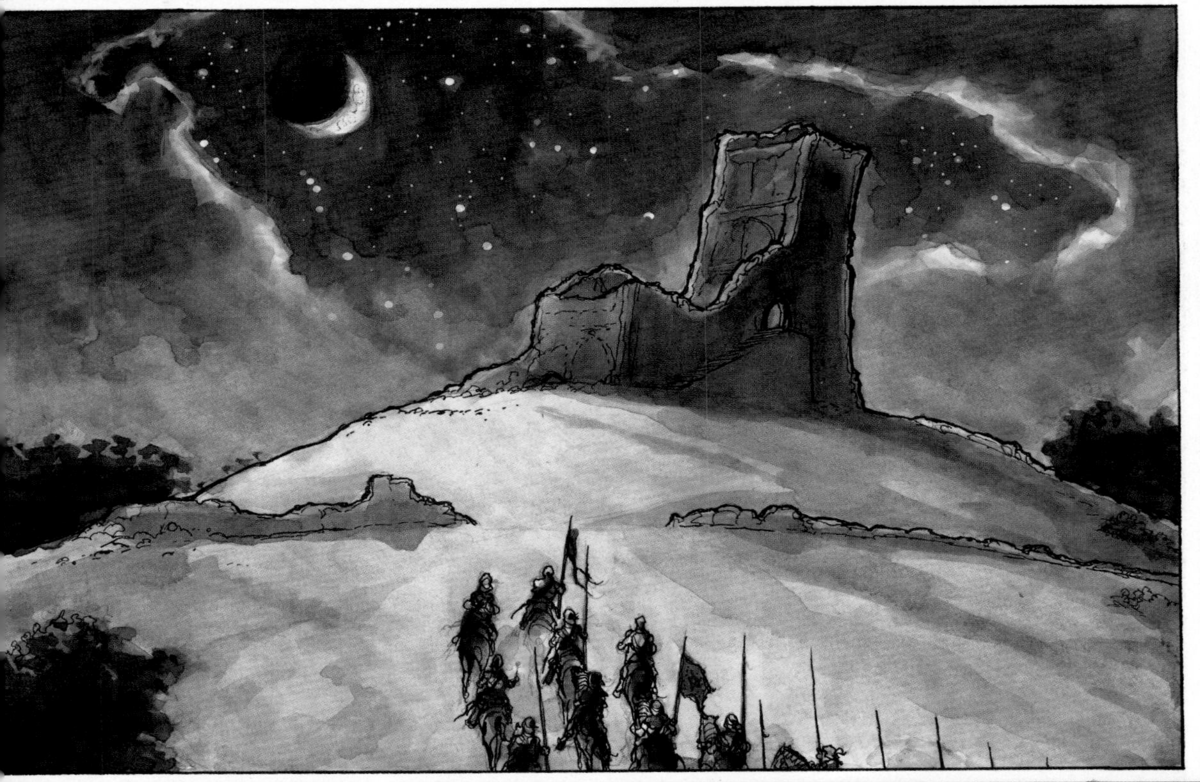

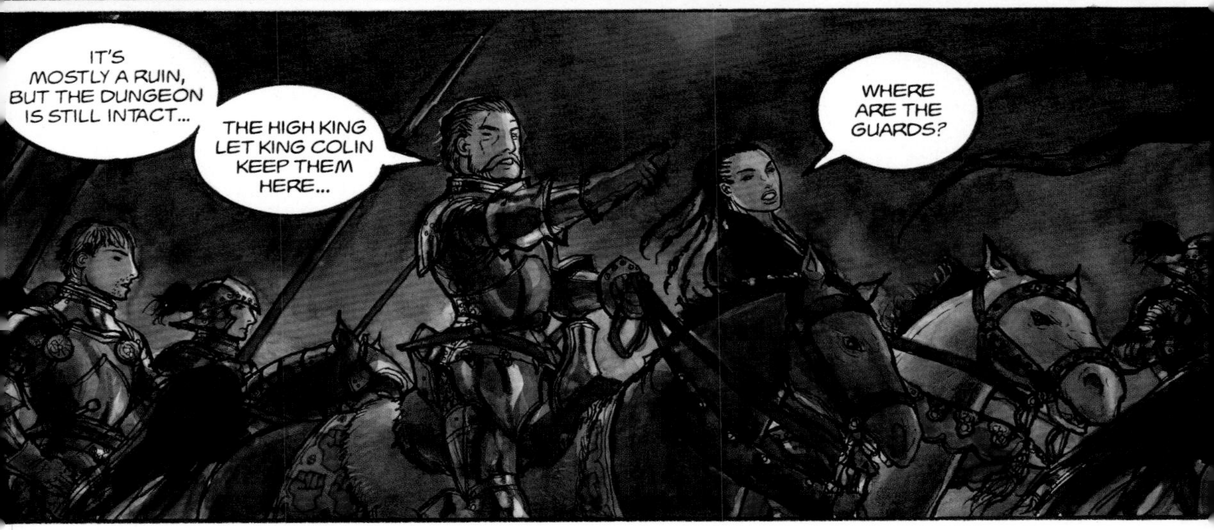
IT'S MOSTLY A RUIN, BUT THE DUNGEON IS STILL INTACT...
THE HIGH KING LET KING COLIN KEEP THEM HERE...
WHERE ARE THE GUARDS?

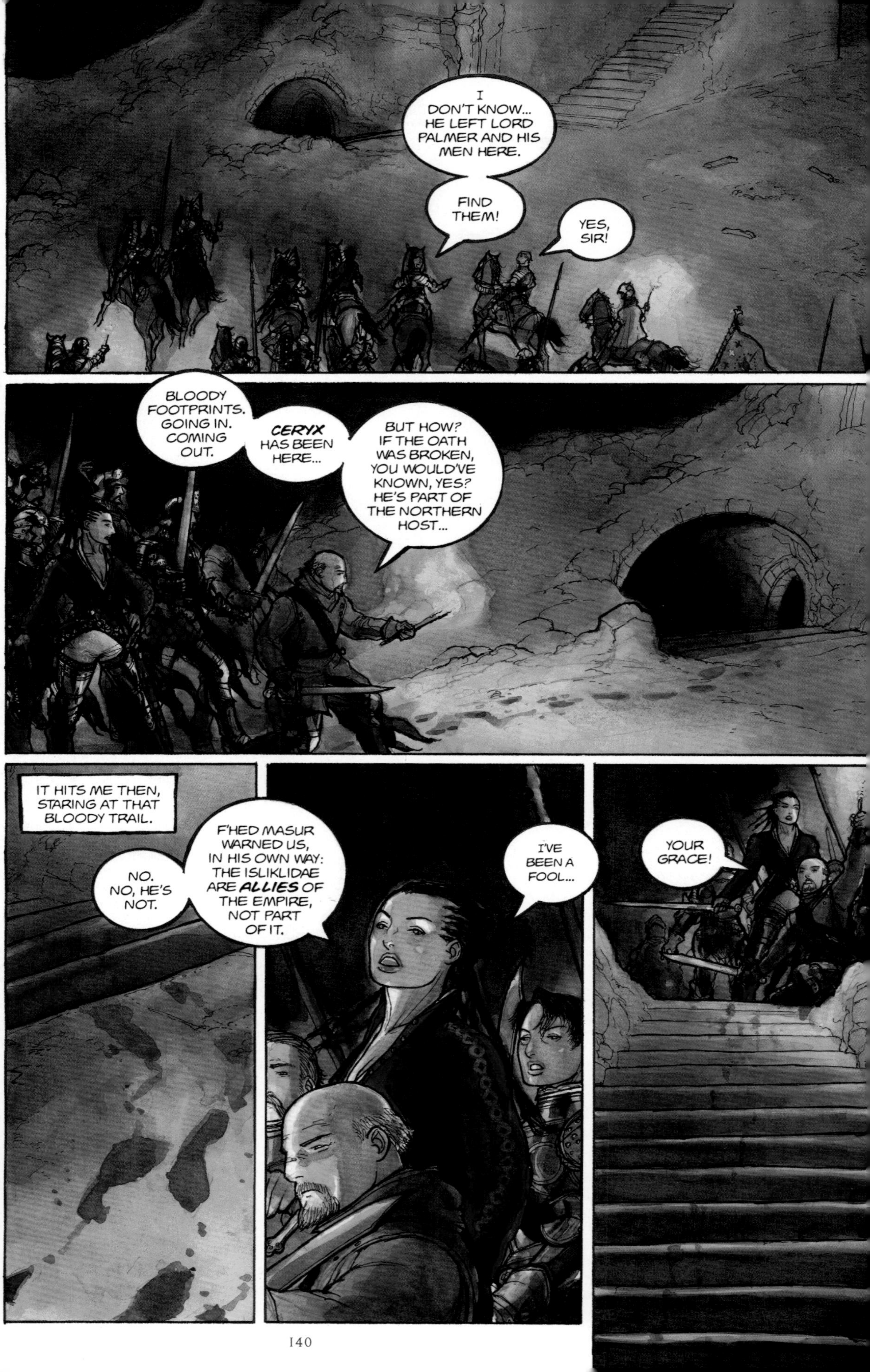
I DON'T KNOW... HE LEFT LORD PALMER AND HIS MEN HERE.
FIND THEM!
YES, SIR!
BLOODY FOOTPRINTS. GOING IN. COMING OUT.
CERYX HAS BEEN HERE...
BUT HOW? IF THE OATH WAS BROKEN, YOU WOULD'VE KNOWN, YES? HE'S PART OF THE NORTHERN HOST...
IT HITS ME THEN, STARING AT THAT BLOODY TRAIL.
NO. NO, HE'S NOT.
F'HED MASUR WARNED US, IN HIS OWN WAY: THE ISLIKLIDAE ARE ALLIES OF THE EMPIRE, NOT PART OF IT.
I'VE BEEN A FOOL...
YOUR GRACE!

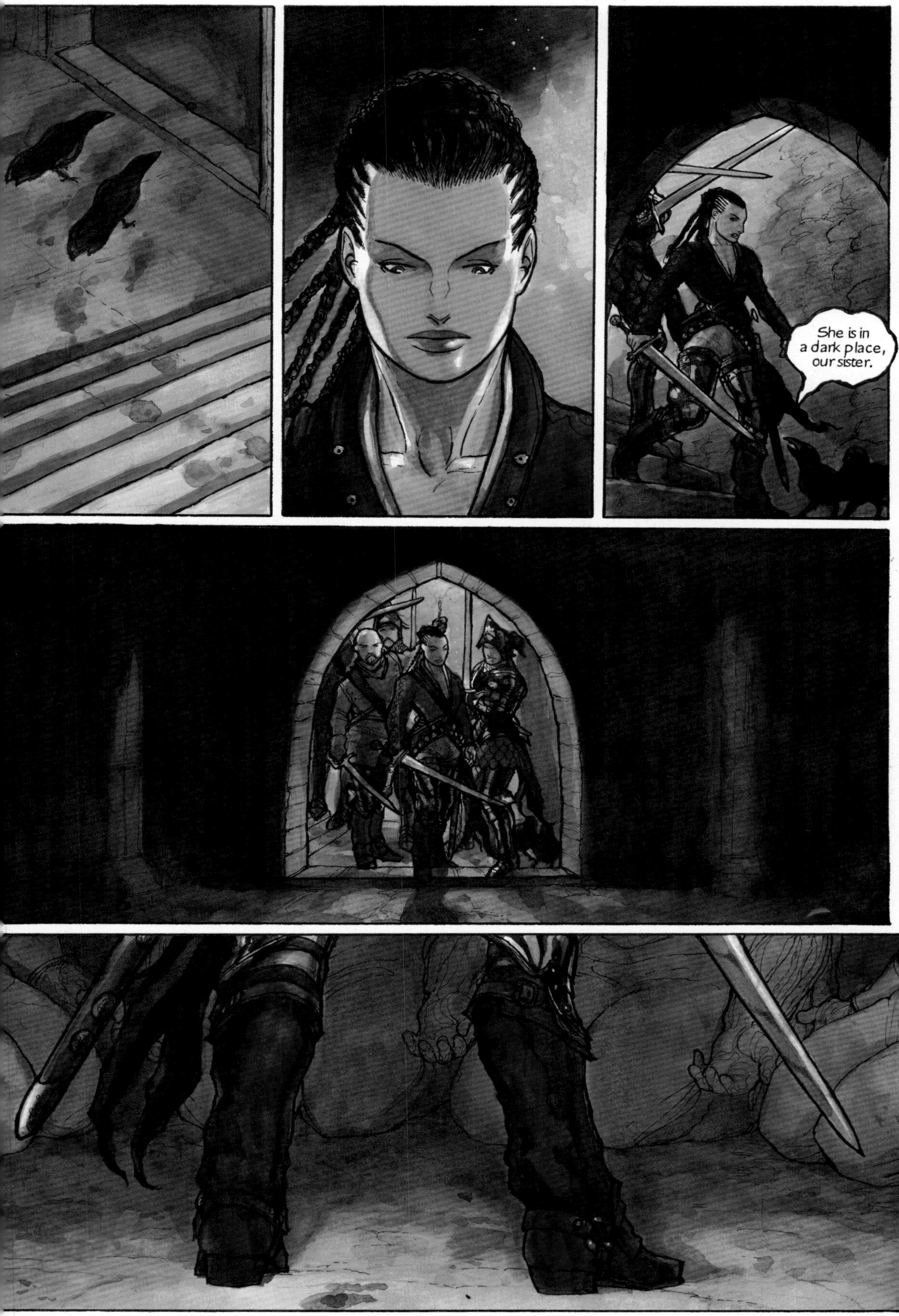
She is in a dark place, our sister.

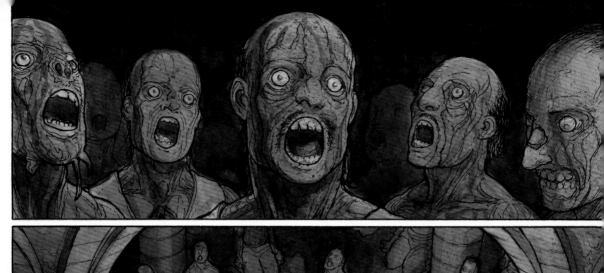

I FIGHT THE BILE RISING IN MY THROAT.

WHAT...

...WHAT HAPPENED TO THEM?

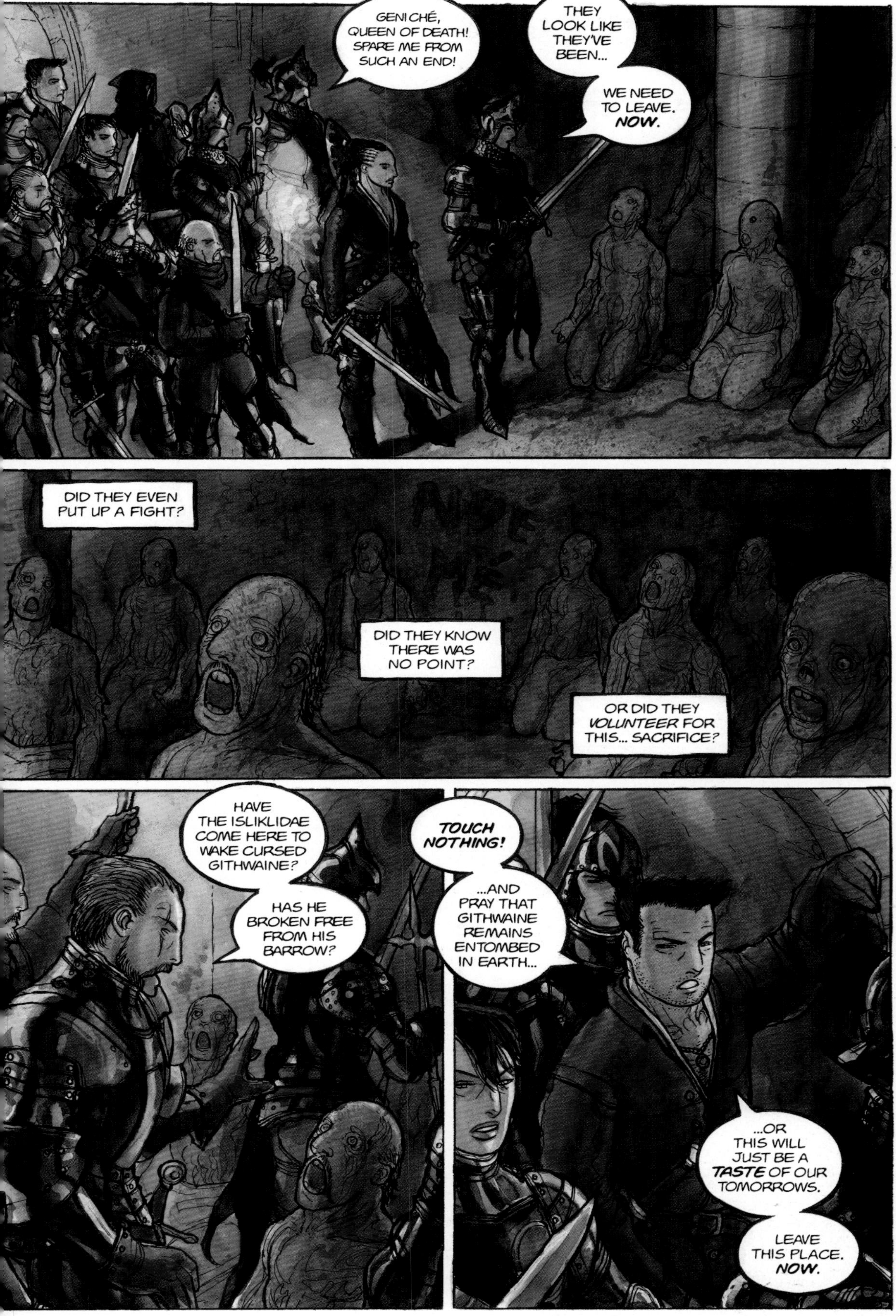
GENICHÉ, QUEEN OF DEATH! SPARE ME FROM SUCH AN END!
THEY LOOK LIKE THEY'VE BEEN...
WE NEED TO LEAVE. NOW.
DID THEY EVEN PUT UP A FIGHT?
DID THEY KNOW THERE WAS NO POINT?
OR DID THEY VOLUNTEER FOR THIS... SACRIFICE?
HAVE THE ISLIKLIDAE COME HERE TO WAKE CURSED GITHWAINE?
HAS HE BROKEN FREE FROM HIS BARROW?
TOUCH NOTHING!
...AND PRAY THAT GITHWAINE REMAINS ENTOMBED IN EARTH...
...OR THIS WILL JUST BE A TASTE OF OUR TOMORROWS.
LEAVE THIS PLACE. NOW.

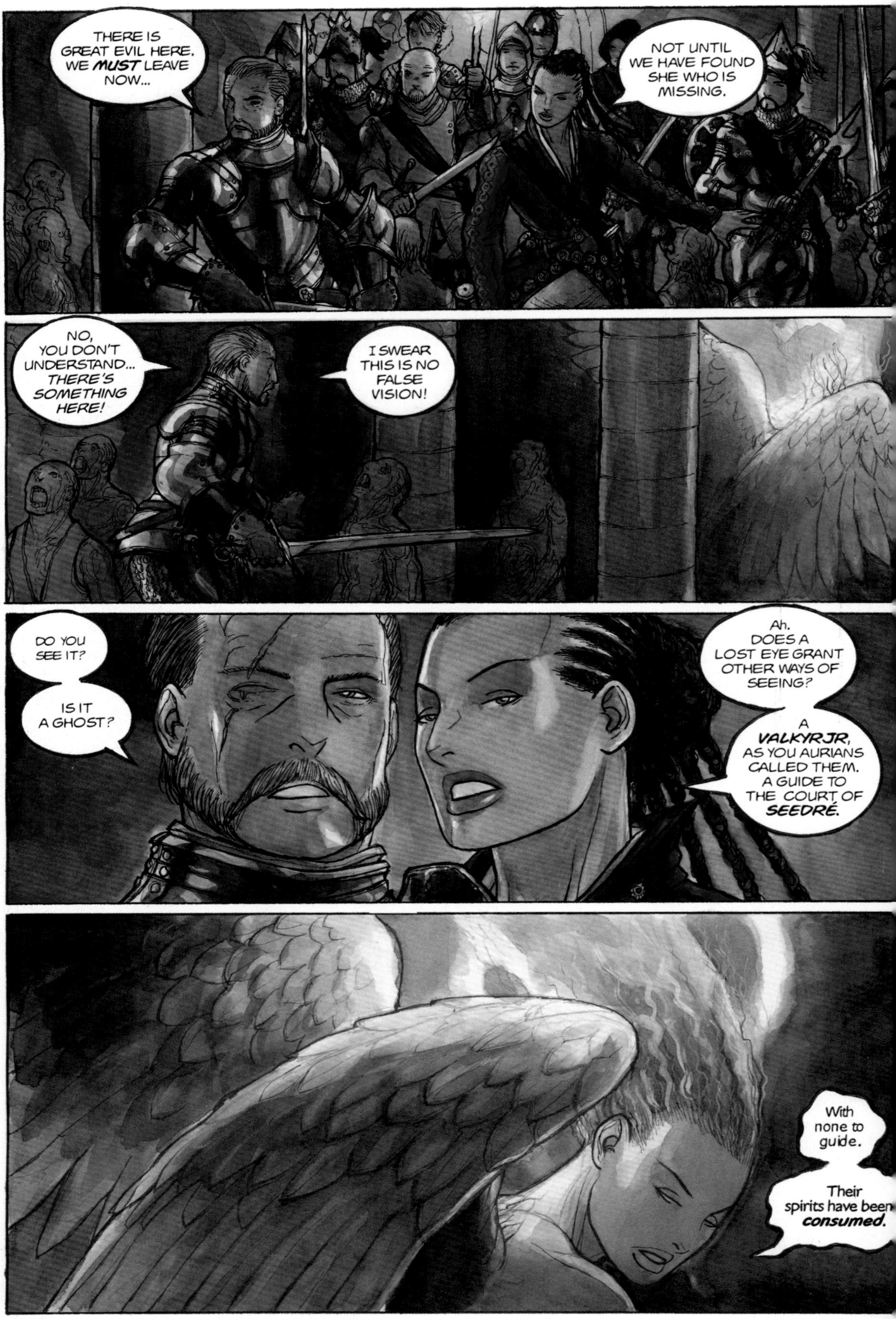
THERE IS GREAT EVIL HERE. WE MUST LEAVE NOW...
NOT UNTIL WE HAVE FOUND SHE WHO IS MISSING.
NO, YOU DON'T UNDERSTAND... THERE'S SOMETHING HERE!
I SWEAR THIS IS NO FALSE VISION!
DO YOU SEE IT?
IS IT A GHOST?
Ah. DOES A LOST EYE GRANT OTHER WAYS OF SEEING?
A VALKYRJR, AS YOU AURIANS CALLED THEM. A GUIDE TO THE COURT OF SEEDRÉ.
With none to guide.
Their spirits have been consumed.

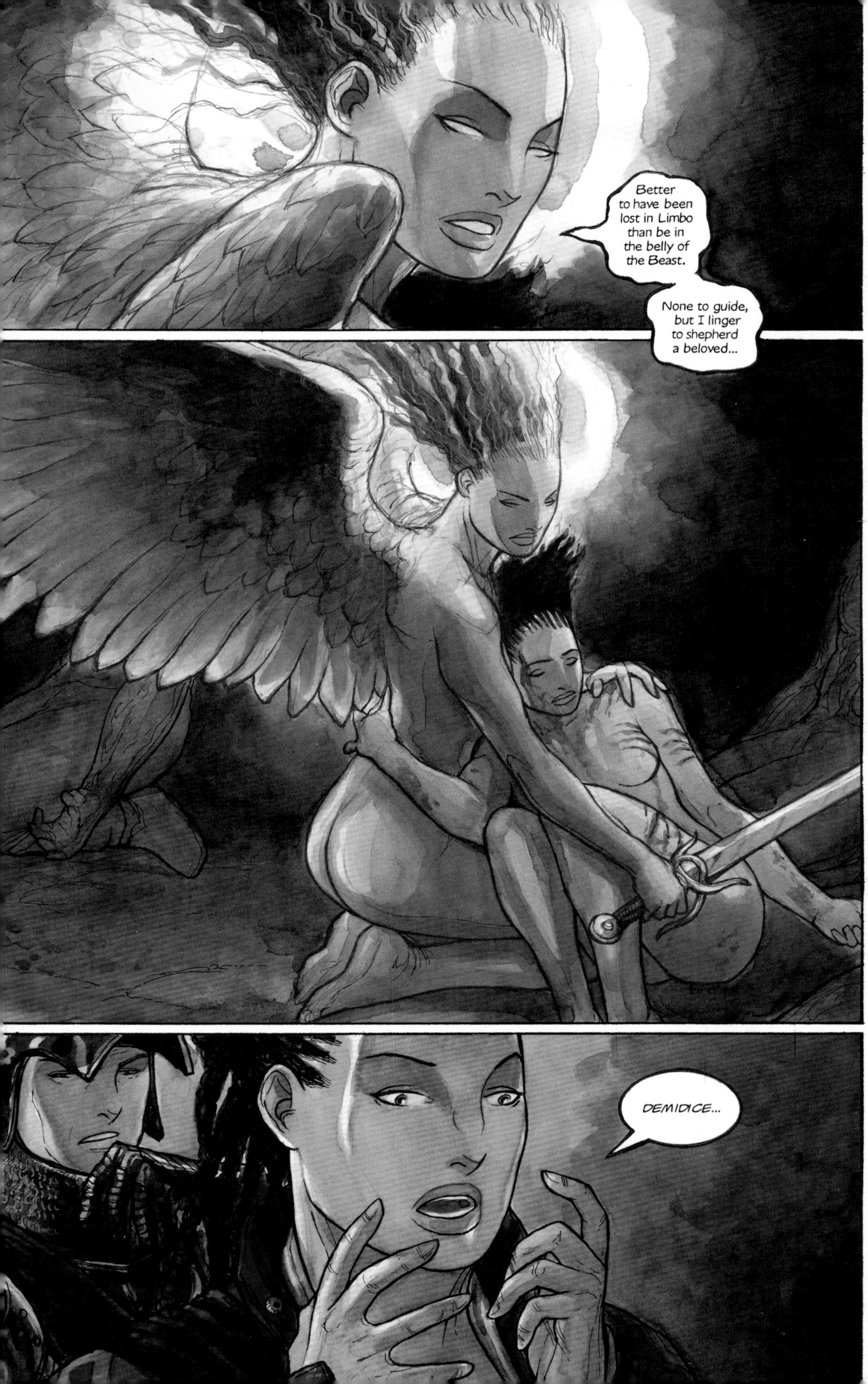

Better to have been lost in Limbo than be in the belly of the Beast.
None to guide, but I linger to shepherd a beloved...
DEMIDICE...

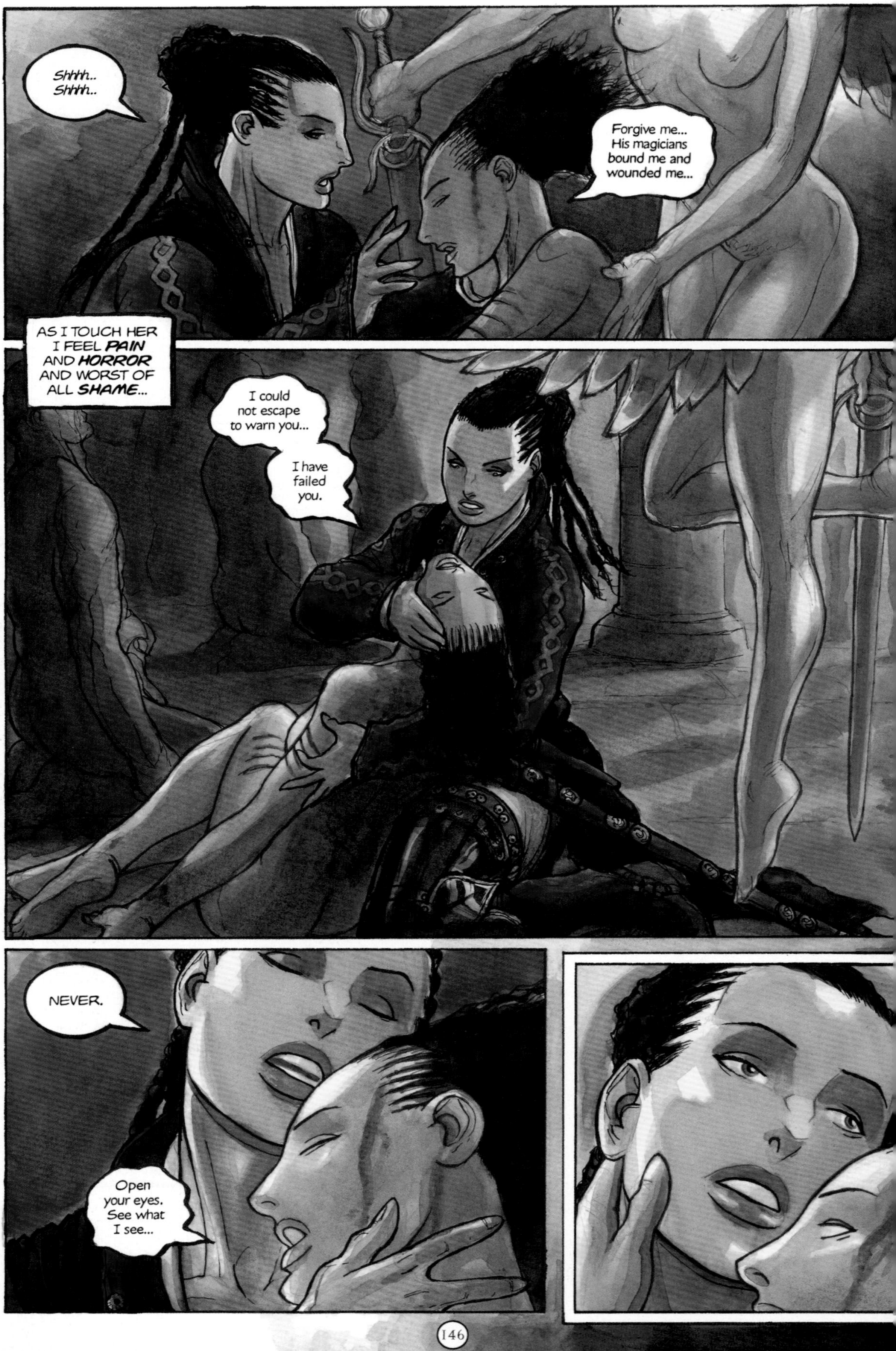
Shhhh..
Shhhh..
Forgive me... His magicians bound me and wounded me...
AS I TOUCH HER I FEEL PAIN AND HORROR AND WORST OF ALL SHAME...
I could not escape to warn you...
I have failed you.
NEVER.
Open your eyes. See what I see...

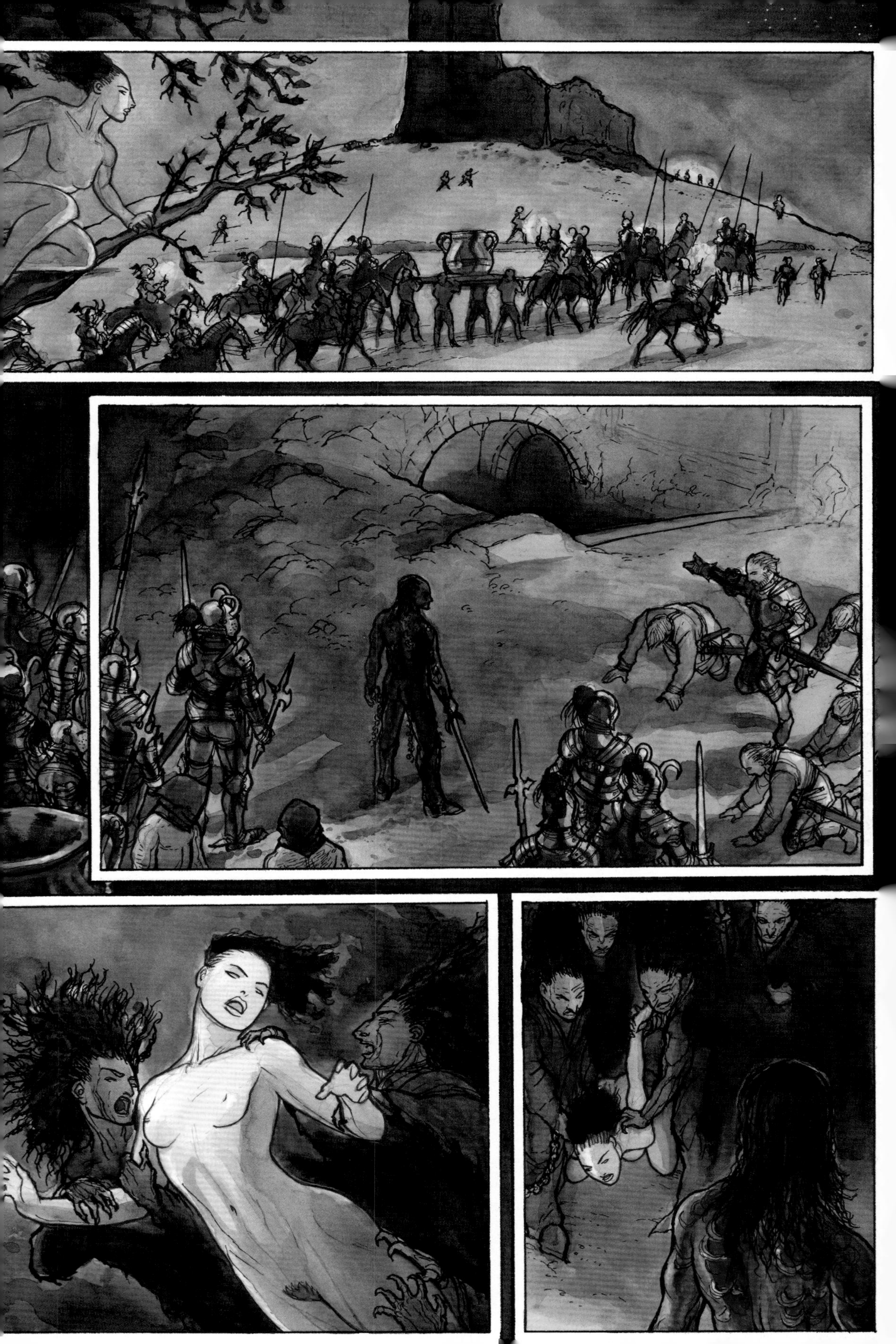

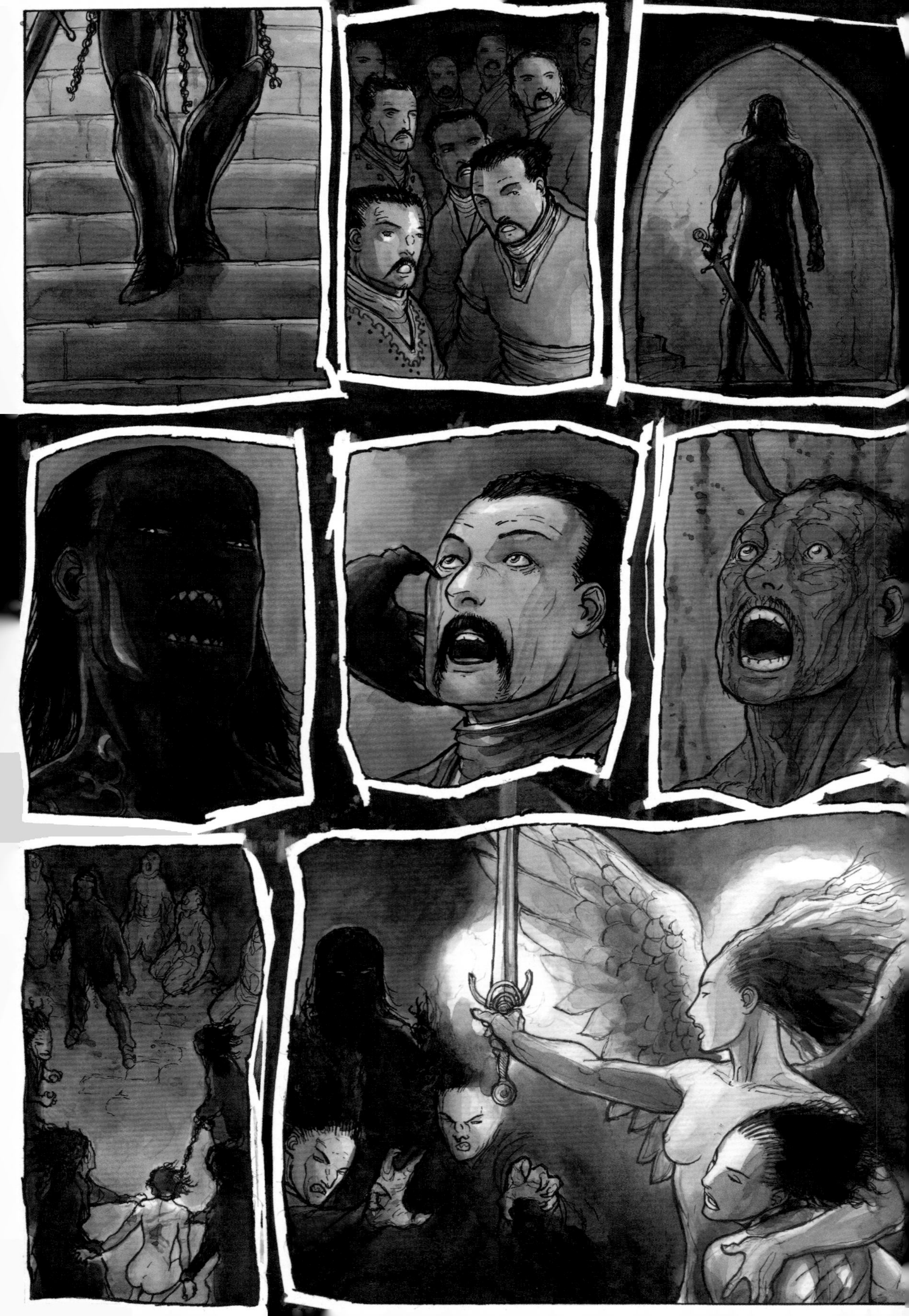

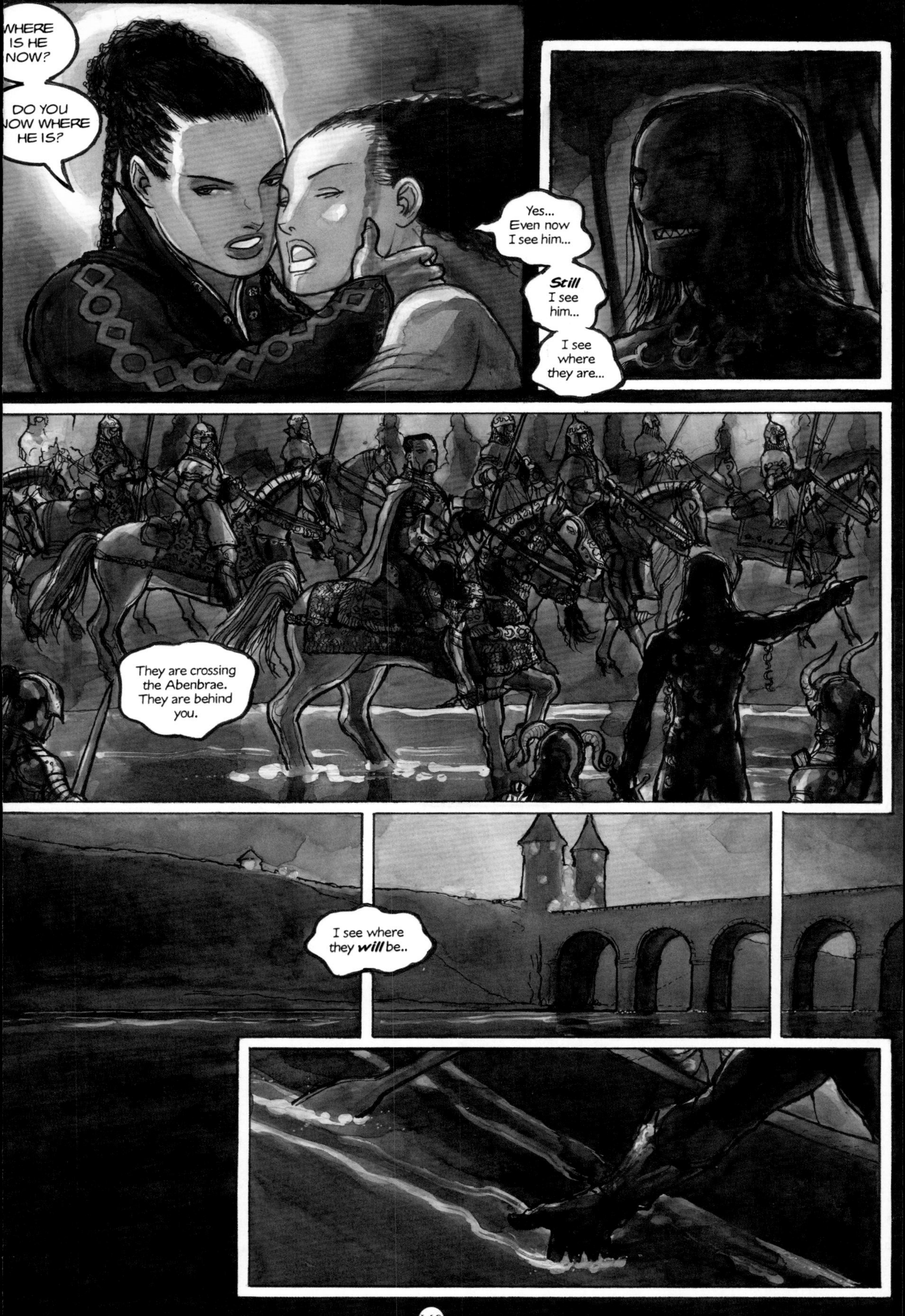
WHERE IS HE NOW?
DO YOU NOW WHERE HE IS?
Yes... Even now I see him...
Still I see him...
I see where they are...
They are crossing the Abenbrae. They are behind you.
I see where they will be..

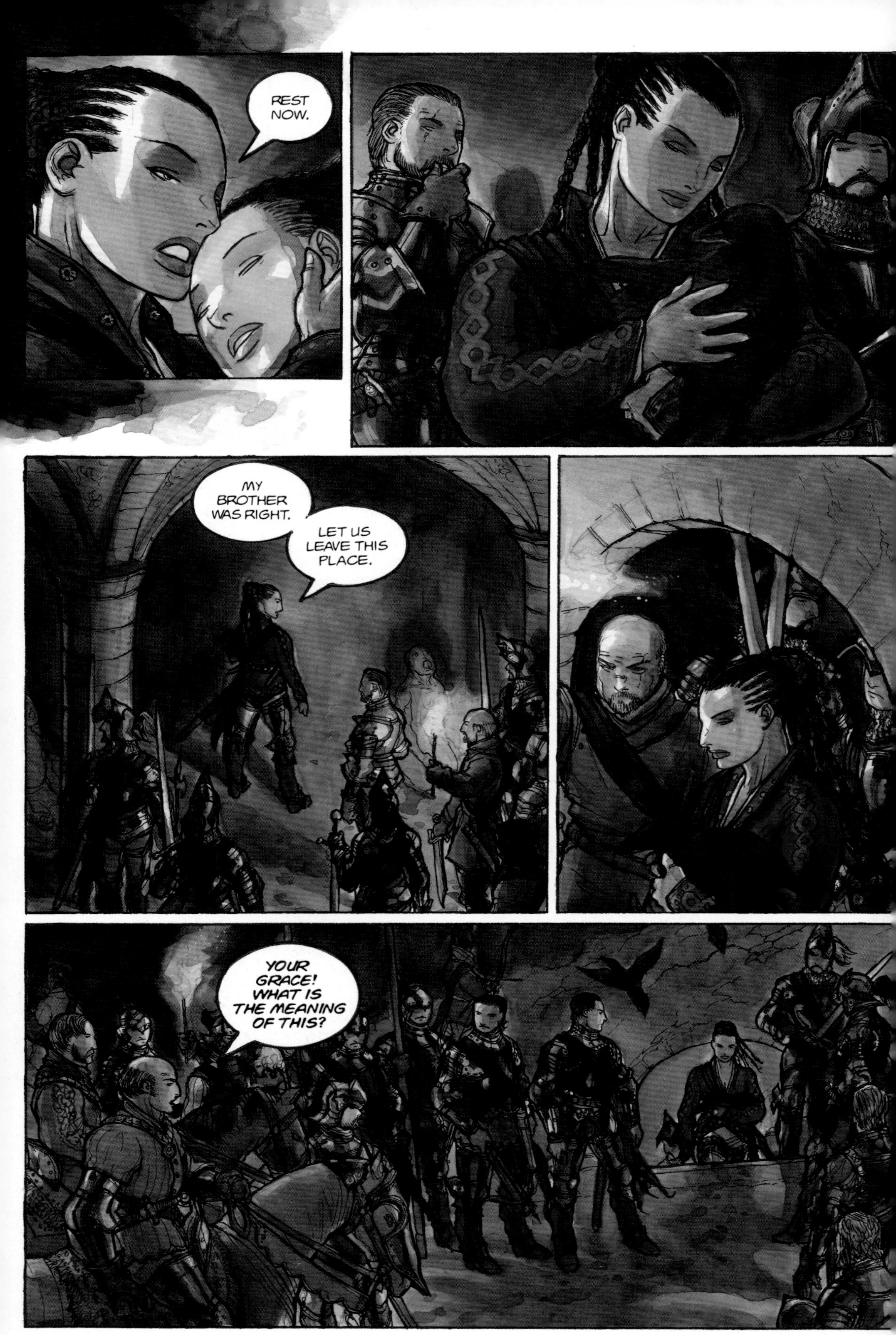
REST NOW.
MY BROTHER WAS RIGHT.
LET US LEAVE THIS PLACE.
YOUR GRACE! WHAT IS THE MEANING OF THIS?

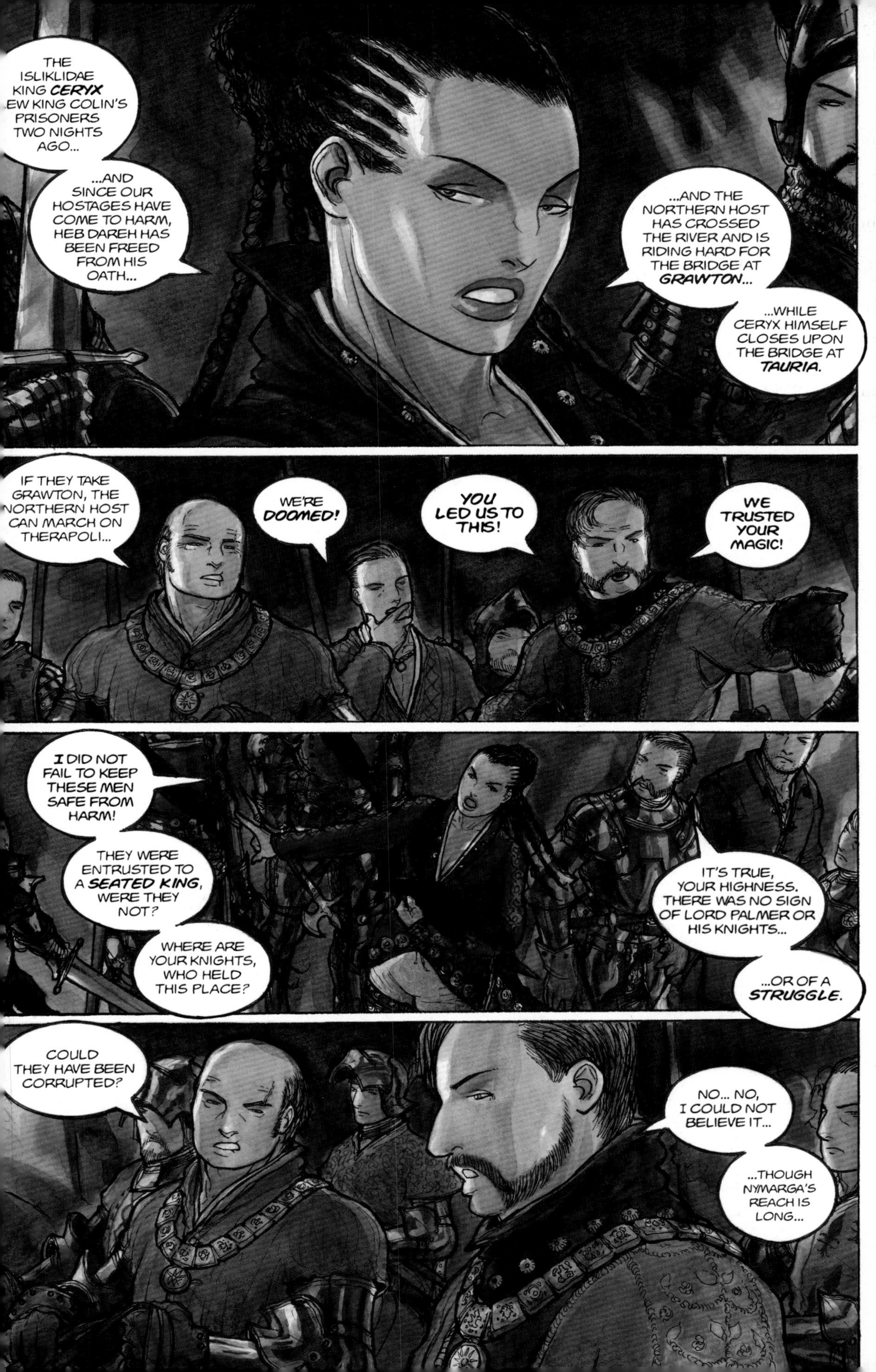

THE ISLIKLIDAE KING CERYX ...EW KING COLIN'S PRISONERS TWO NIGHTS AGO...
...AND SINCE OUR HOSTAGES HAVE COME TO HARM, HEB DAREH HAS BEEN FREED FROM HIS OATH...
...AND THE NORTHERN HOST HAS CROSSED THE RIVER AND IS RIDING HARD FOR THE BRIDGE AT GRAWTON...
...WHILE CERYX HIMSELF CLOSES UPON THE BRIDGE AT TAURIA.
IF THEY TAKE GRAWTON, THE NORTHERN HOST CAN MARCH ON THERAPOLI...
WE'RE DOOMED!
YOU LED US TO THIS!
WE TRUSTED YOUR MAGIC!
I DID NOT FAIL TO KEEP THESE MEN SAFE FROM HARM!
THEY WERE ENTRUSTED TO A SEATED KING, WERE THEY NOT?
WHERE ARE YOUR KNIGHTS, WHO HELD THIS PLACE?
IT'S TRUE, YOUR HIGHNESS. THERE WAS NO SIGN OF LORD PALMER OR HIS KNIGHTS...
...OR OF A STRUGGLE.
COULD THEY HAVE BEEN CORRUPTED?
NO... NO, I COULD NOT BELIEVE IT...
...THOUGH NYMARGA'S REACH IS LONG...

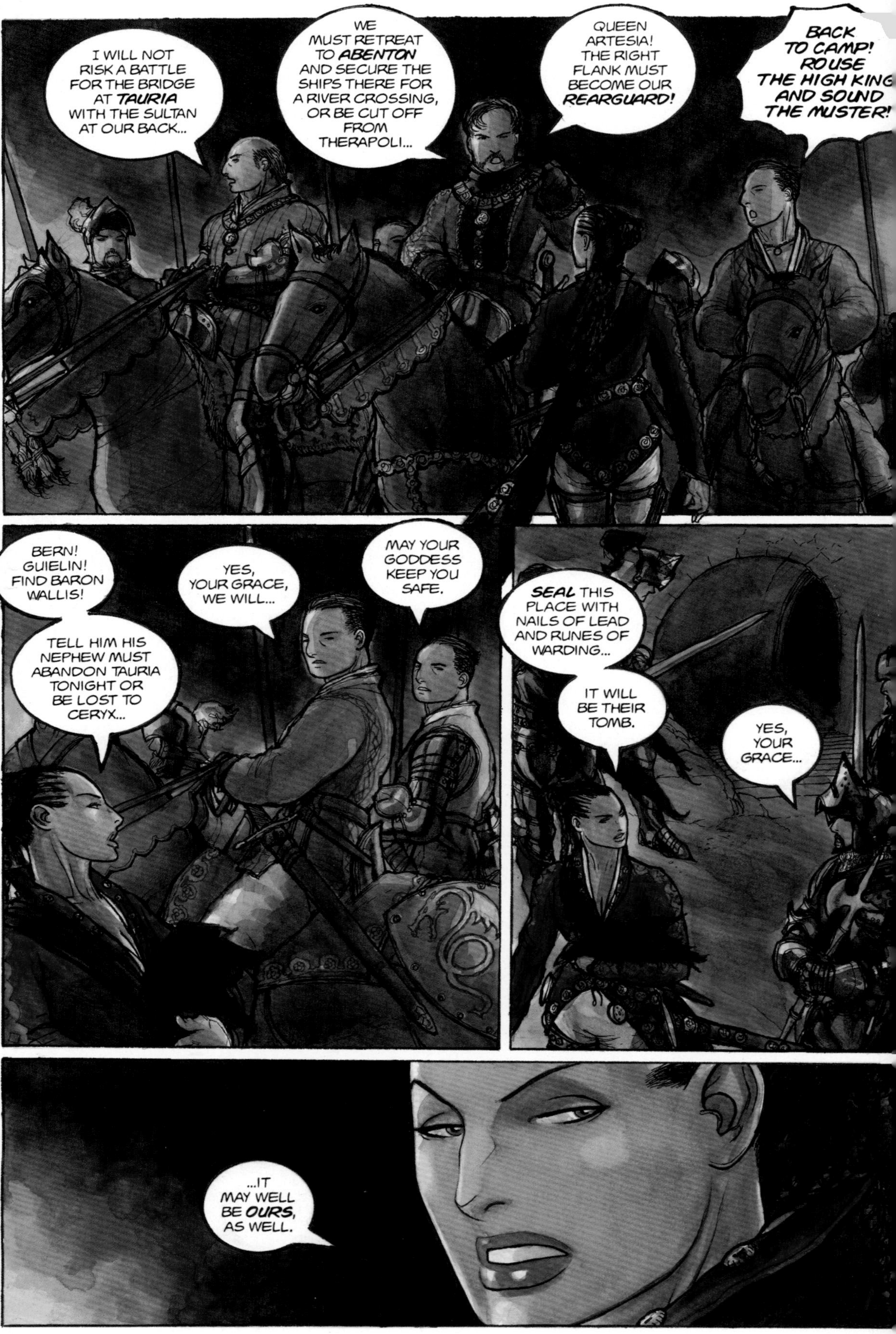

I WILL NOT RISK A BATTLE FOR THE BRIDGE AT TAURIA WITH THE SULTAN AT OUR BACK...
WE MUST RETREAT TO ABENTON AND SECURE THE SHIPS THERE FOR A RIVER CROSSING, OR BE CUT OFF FROM THERAPOLI...
QUEEN ARTESIA! THE RIGHT FLANK MUST BECOME OUR REARGUARD!
BACK TO CAMP! ROUSE THE HIGH KING AND SOUND THE MUSTER!
BERN! GUIELIN! FIND BARON WALLIS!
TELL HIM HIS NEPHEW MUST ABANDON TAURIA TONIGHT OR BE LOST TO CERYX...
YES, YOUR GRACE, WE WILL...
MAY YOUR GODDESS KEEP YOU SAFE.
SEAL THIS PLACE WITH NAILS OF LEAD AND RUNES OF WARDING...
IT WILL BE THEIR TOMB.
YES, YOUR GRACE...
...IT MAY WELL BE OURS, AS WELL.

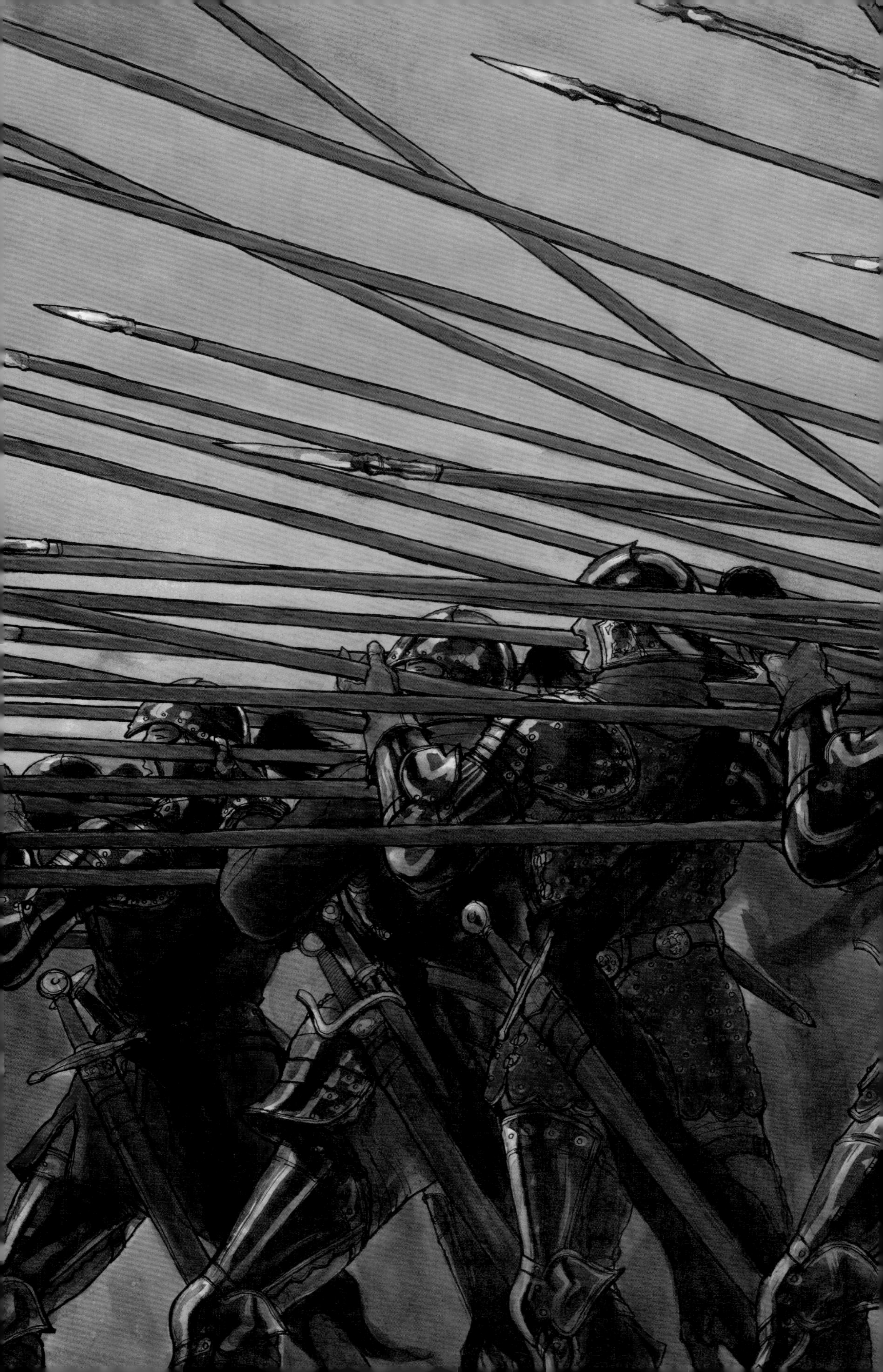

Chapter Five

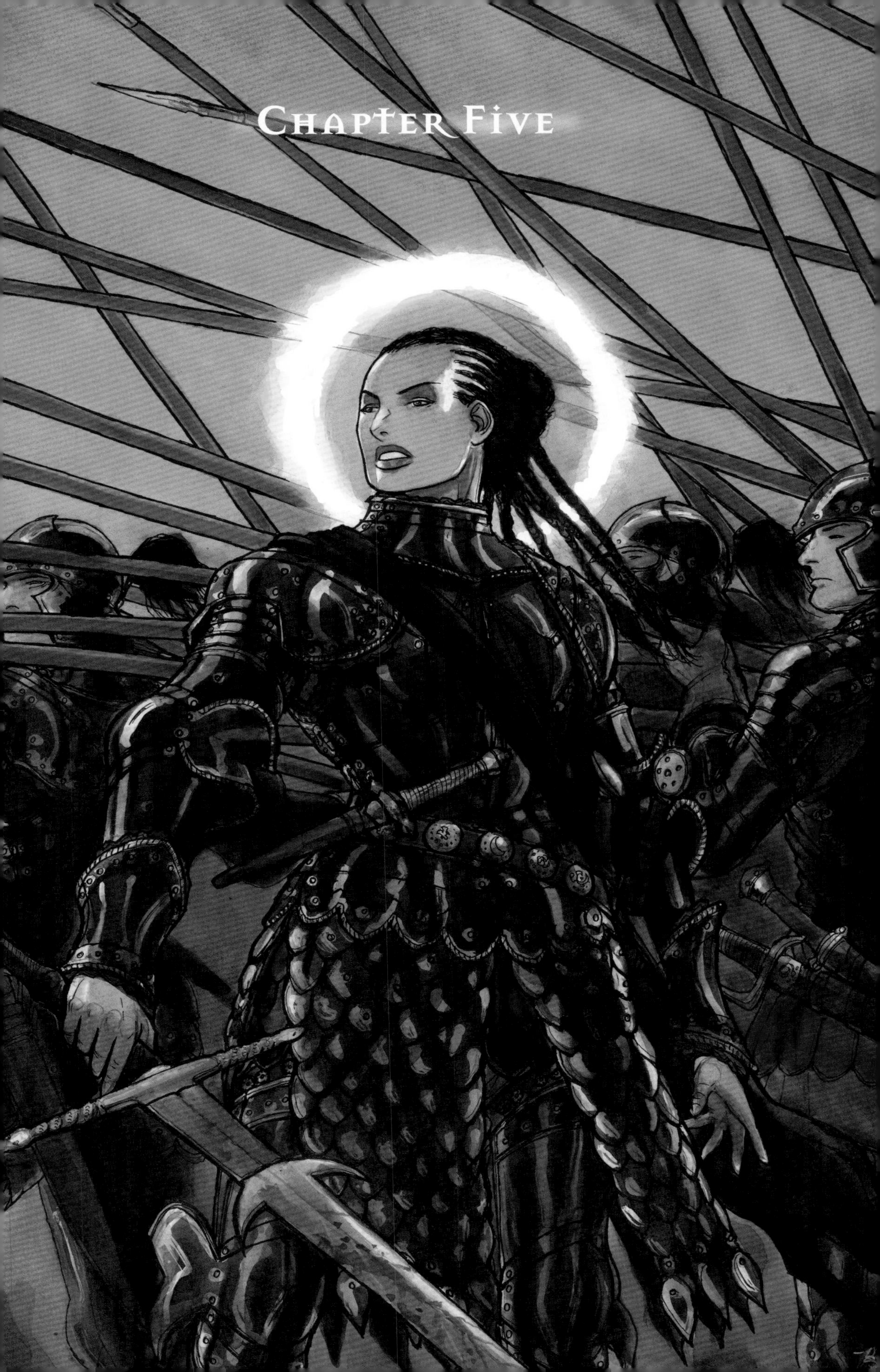

THE RETREAT

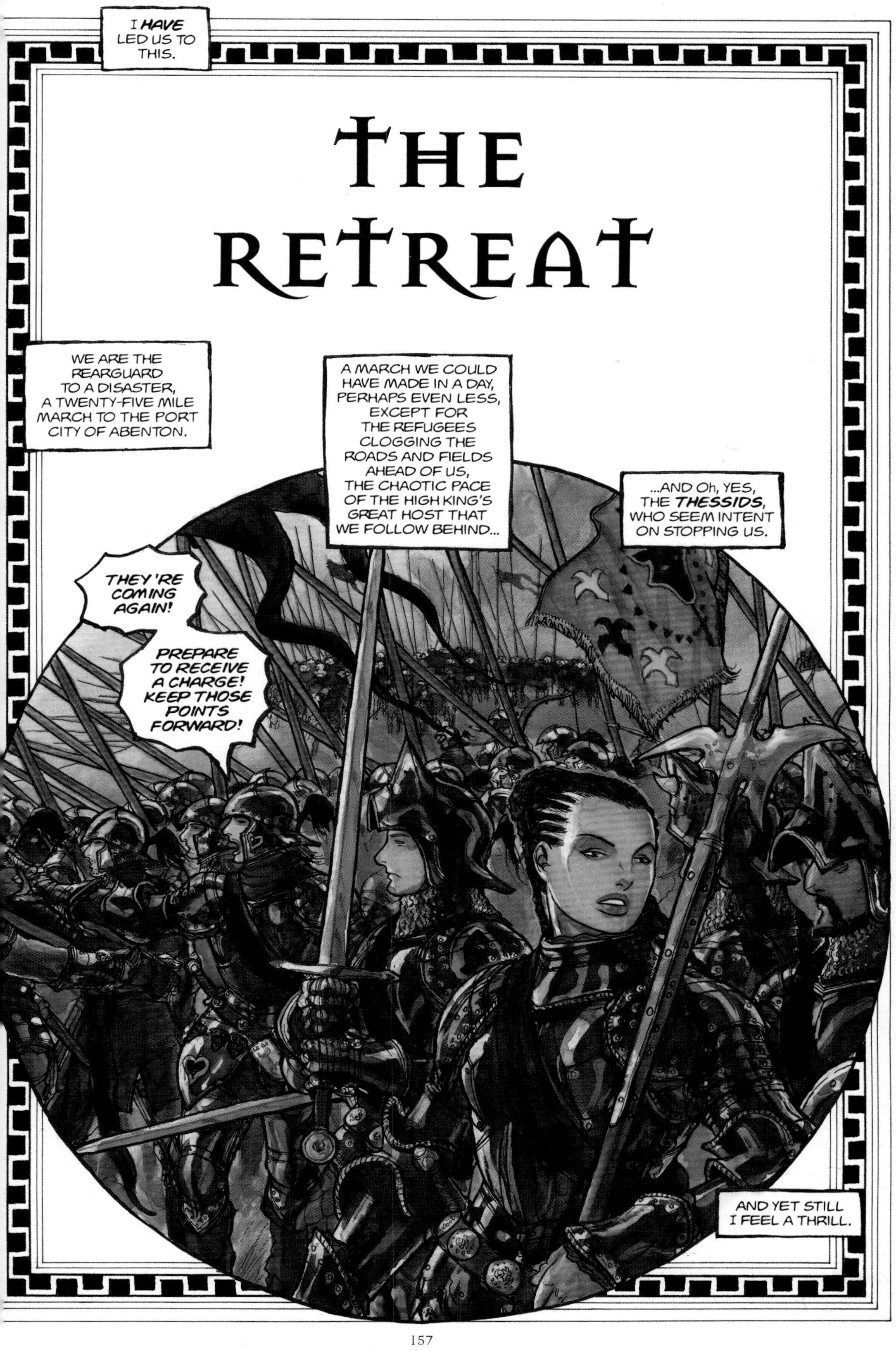

I HAVE LED US TO THIS.
WE ARE THE REARGUARD TO A DISASTER, A TWENTY-FIVE MILE MARCH TO THE PORT CITY OF ABENTON.
A MARCH WE COULD HAVE MADE IN A DAY, PERHAPS EVEN LESS, EXCEPT FOR THE REFUGEES CLOGGING THE ROADS AND FIELDS AHEAD OF US, THE CHAOTIC PACE OF THE HIGH KING'S GREAT HOST THAT WE FOLLOW BEHIND...
...AND Oh, YES, THE THESSIDS, WHO SEEM INTENT ON STOPPING US.
THEY'RE COMING AGAIN!
PREPARE TO RECEIVE A CHARGE! KEEP THOSE POINTS FORWARD!
AND YET STILL I FEEL A THRILL.

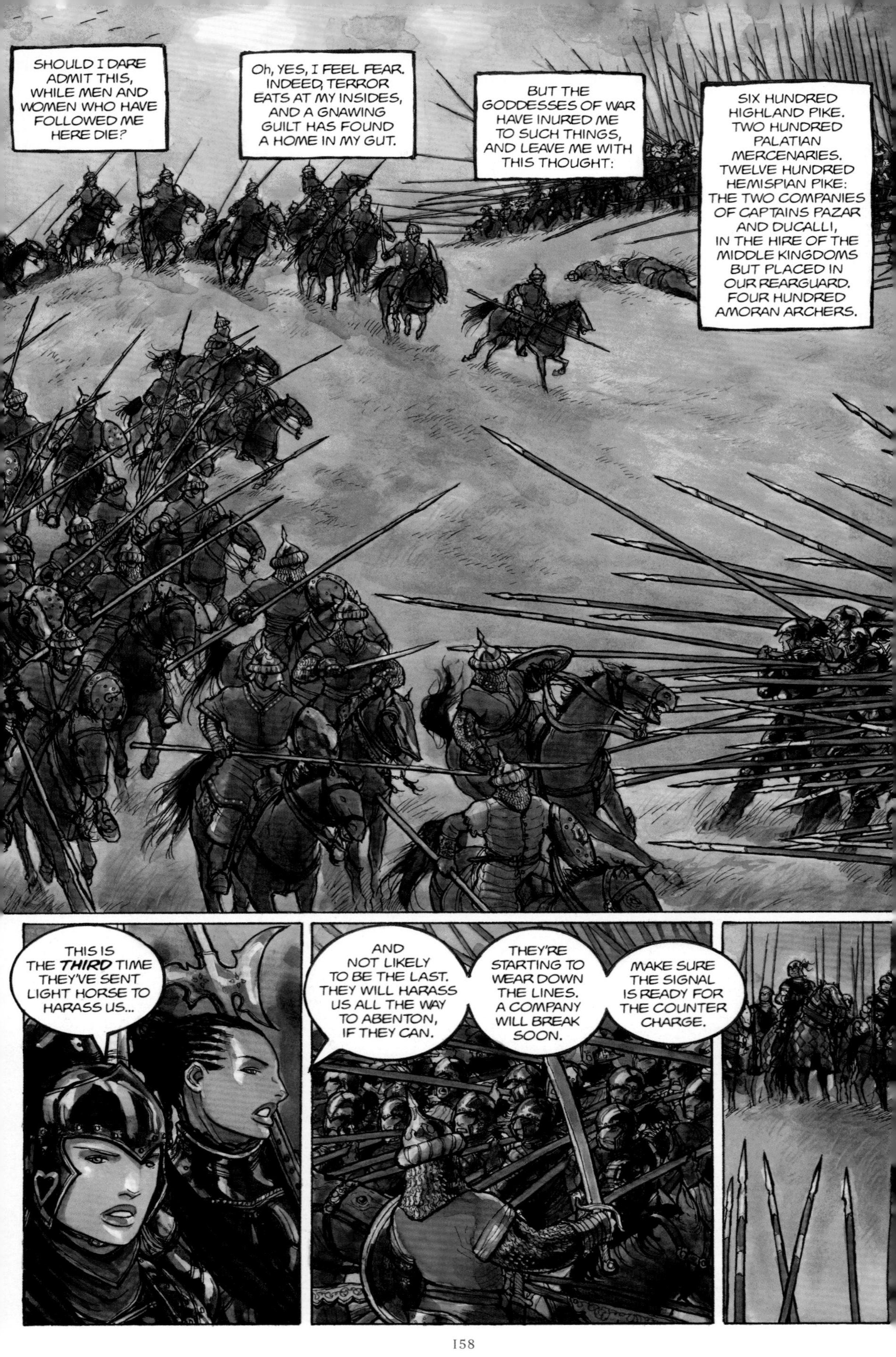

SHOULD I DARE ADMIT THIS, WHILE MEN AND WOMEN WHO HAVE FOLLOWED ME HERE DIE?
Oh, YES, I FEEL FEAR. INDEED, TERROR EATS AT MY INSIDES, AND A GNAWING GUILT HAS FOUND A HOME IN MY GUT.
BUT THE GODDESSES OF WAR HAVE INURED ME TO SUCH THINGS, AND LEAVE ME WITH THIS THOUGHT:
SIX HUNDRED HIGHLAND PIKE. TWO HUNDRED PALATIAN MERCENARIES. TWELVE HUNDRED HEMISPIAN PIKE: THE TWO COMPANIES OF CAPTAINS PAZAR AND DUCALLI, IN THE HIRE OF THE MIDDLE KINGDOMS BUT PLACED IN OUR REARGUARD. FOUR HUNDRED AMORAN ARCHERS.
THIS IS THE ***THIRD*** TIME THEY'VE SENT LIGHT HORSE TO HARASS US...
AND NOT LIKELY TO BE THE LAST. THEY WILL HARASS US ALL THE WAY TO ABENTON, IF THEY CAN.
THEY'RE STARTING TO WEAR DOWN THE LINES. A COMPANY WILL BREAK SOON.
MAKE SURE THE SIGNAL IS READY FOR THE COUNTER CHARGE.

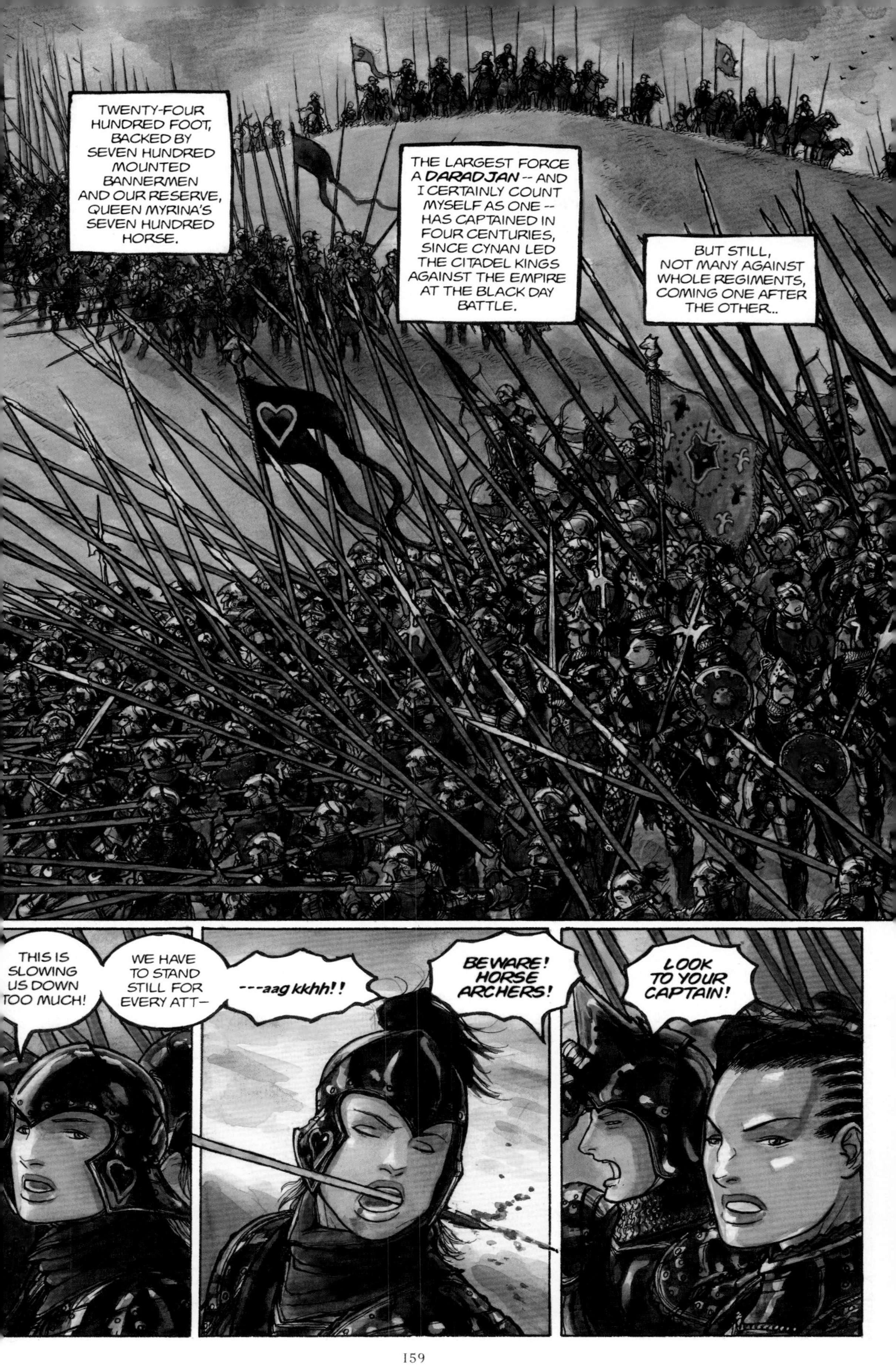
TWENTY-FOUR HUNDRED FOOT, BACKED BY SEVEN HUNDRED MOUNTED BANNERMEN AND OUR RESERVE, QUEEN MYRINA'S SEVEN HUNDRED HORSE.
THE LARGEST FORCE A DARADJAN -- AND I CERTAINLY COUNT MYSELF AS ONE -- HAS CAPTAINED IN FOUR CENTURIES, SINCE CYNAN LED THE CITADEL KINGS AGAINST THE EMPIRE AT THE BLACK DAY BATTLE.
BUT STILL, NOT MANY AGAINST WHOLE REGIMENTS, COMING ONE AFTER THE OTHER..
THIS IS SLOWING US DOWN TOO MUCH!
WE HAVE TO STAND STILL FOR EVERY ATT—
---aag kkhh!!
BEWARE! HORSE ARCHERS!
LOOK TO YOUR CAPTAIN!

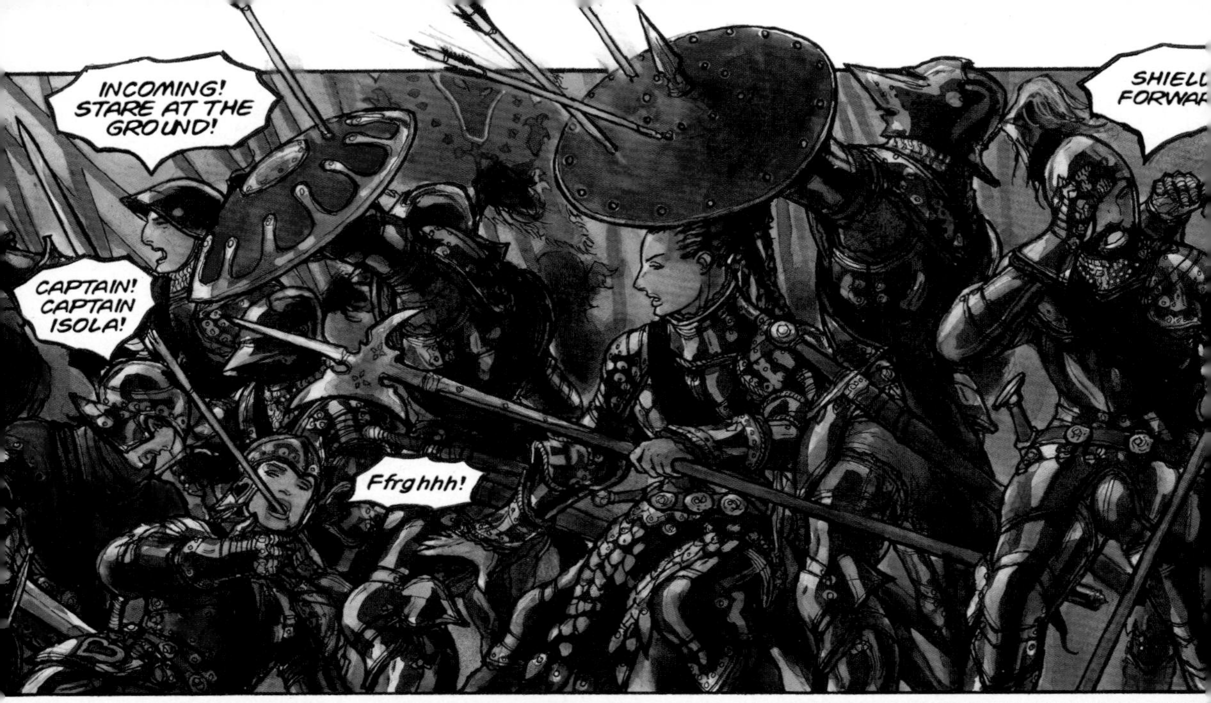
INCOMING! STARE AT THE GROUND!
SHIELD FORWAR
CAPTAIN! CAPTAIN ISOLA!
Ffrghhh!

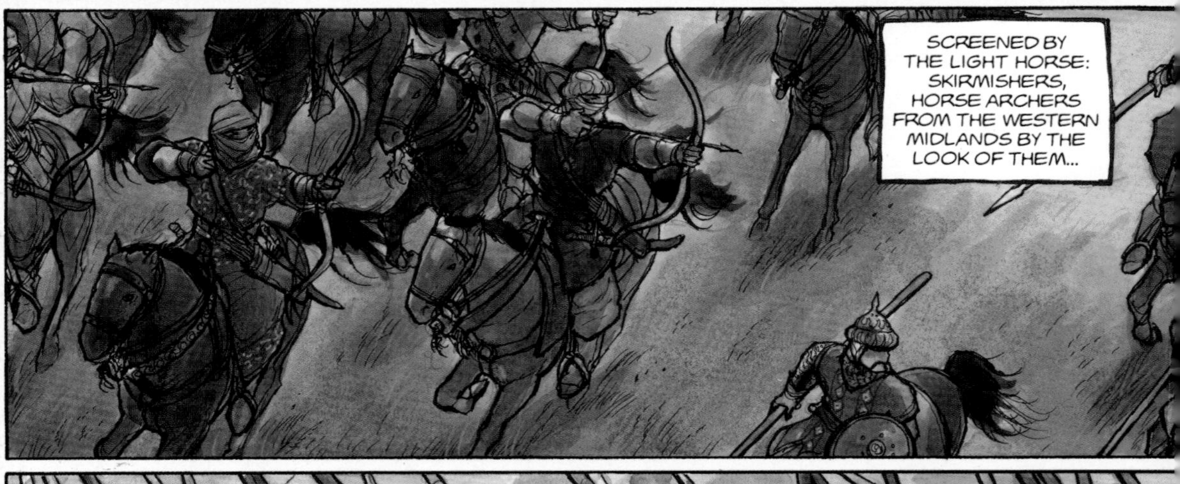
SCREENED BY THE LIGHT HORSE: SKIRMISHERS, HORSE ARCHERS FROM THE WESTERN MIDLANDS BY THE LOOK OF THEM...

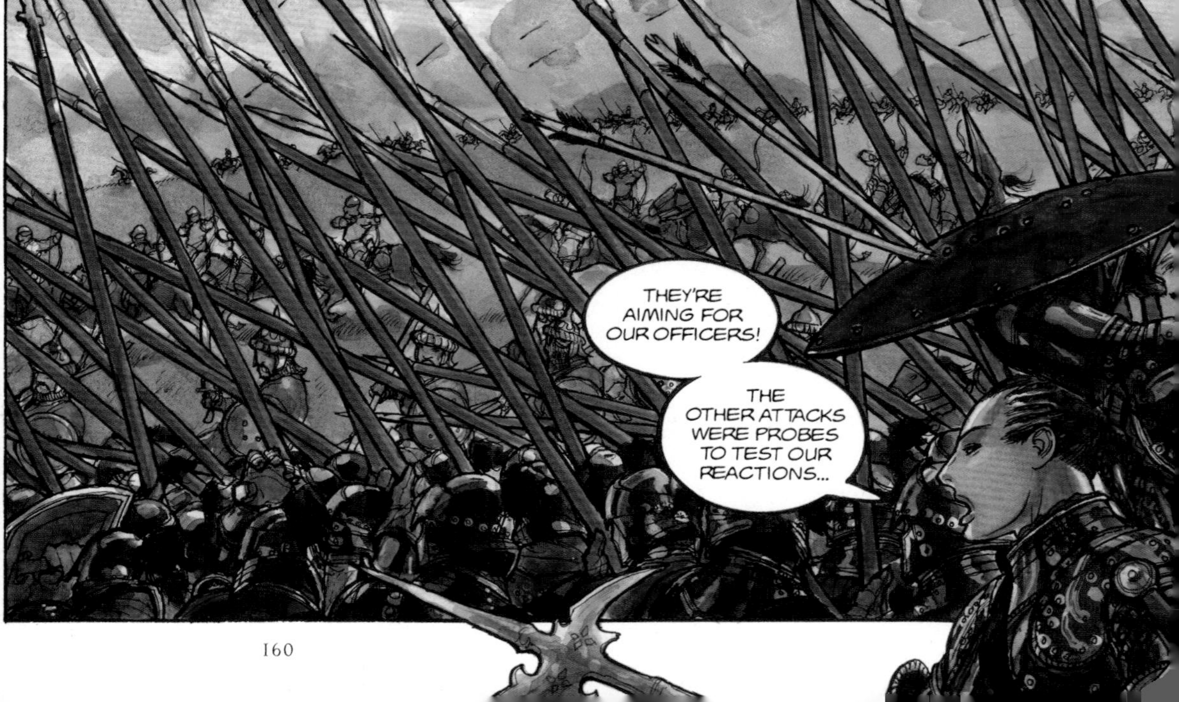
THEY'RE AIMING FOR OUR OFFICERS!
THE OTHER ATTACKS WERE PROBES TO TEST OUR REACTIONS...

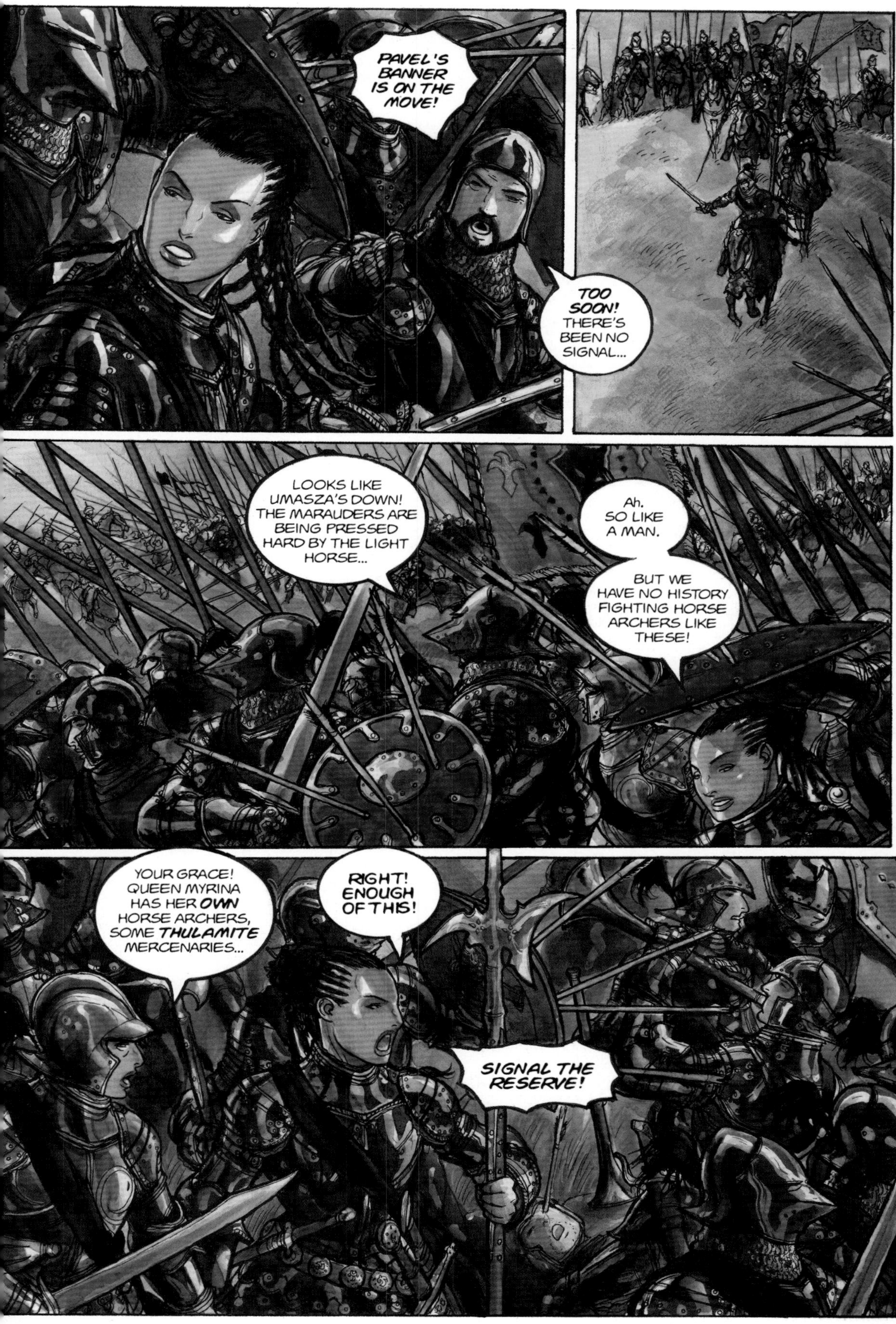
PAVEL'S BANNER IS ON THE MOVE!
TOO SOON! THERE'S BEEN NO SIGNAL...
LOOKS LIKE UMASZA'S DOWN! THE MARAUDERS ARE BEING PRESSED HARD BY THE LIGHT HORSE...
Ah. SO LIKE A MAN.
BUT WE HAVE NO HISTORY FIGHTING HORSE ARCHERS LIKE THESE!
YOUR GRACE! QUEEN MYRINA HAS HER OWN HORSE ARCHERS, SOME THULAMITE MERCENARIES...
RIGHT! ENOUGH OF THIS!
SIGNAL THE RESERVE!

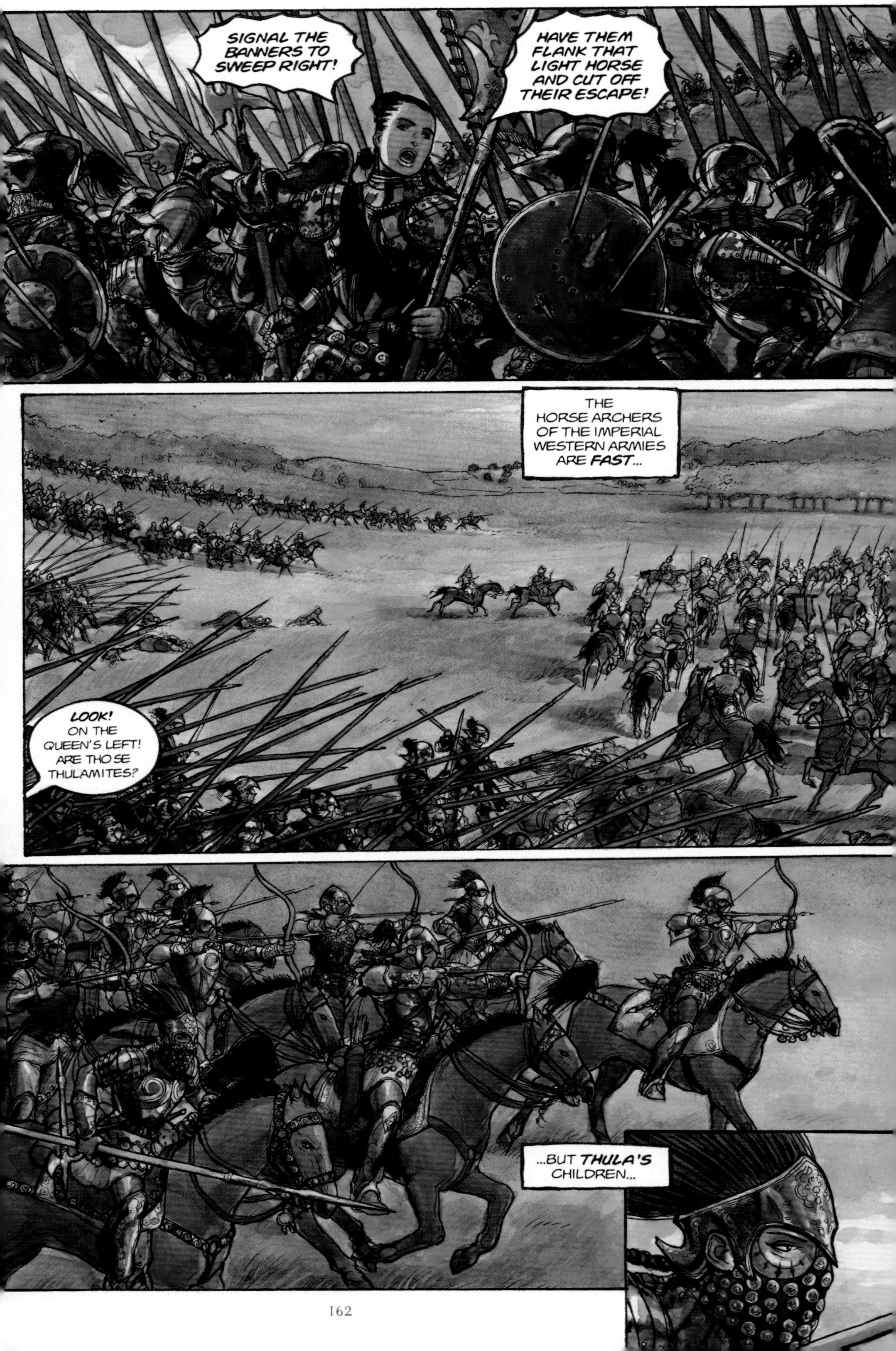
SIGNAL THE BANNERS TO SWEEP RIGHT!
HAVE THEM FLANK THAT LIGHT HORSE AND CUT OFF THEIR ESCAPE!
THE HORSE ARCHERS OF THE IMPERIAL WESTERN ARMIES ARE FAST...
LOOK! ON THE QUEEN'S LEFT! ARE THOSE THULAMITES?
...BUT THULA'S CHILDREN...

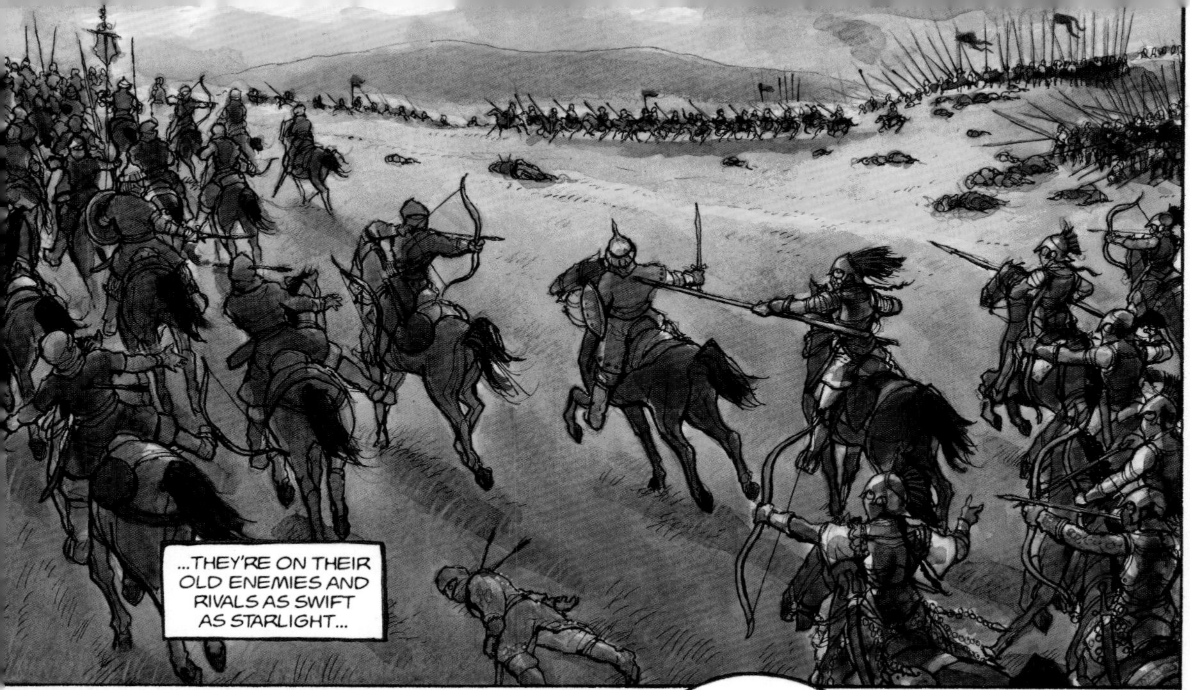
...THEY'RE ON THEIR OLD ENEMIES AND RIVALS AS SWIFT AS STARLIGHT...

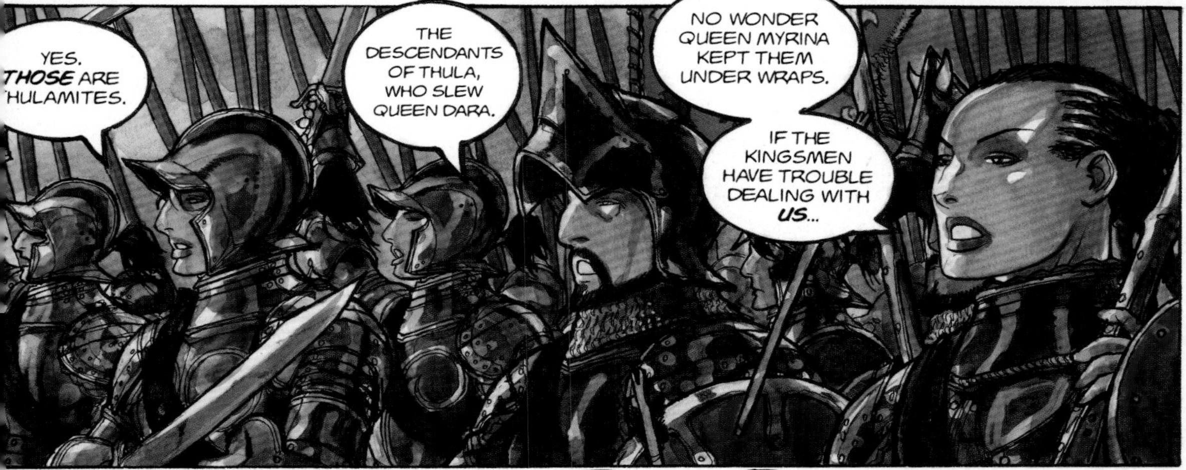
YES. THOSE ARE HULAMITES.
THE DESCENDANTS OF THULA, WHO SLEW QUEEN DARA.
NO WONDER QUEEN MYRINA KEPT THEM UNDER WRAPS.
IF THE KINGSMEN HAVE TROUBLE DEALING WITH US...

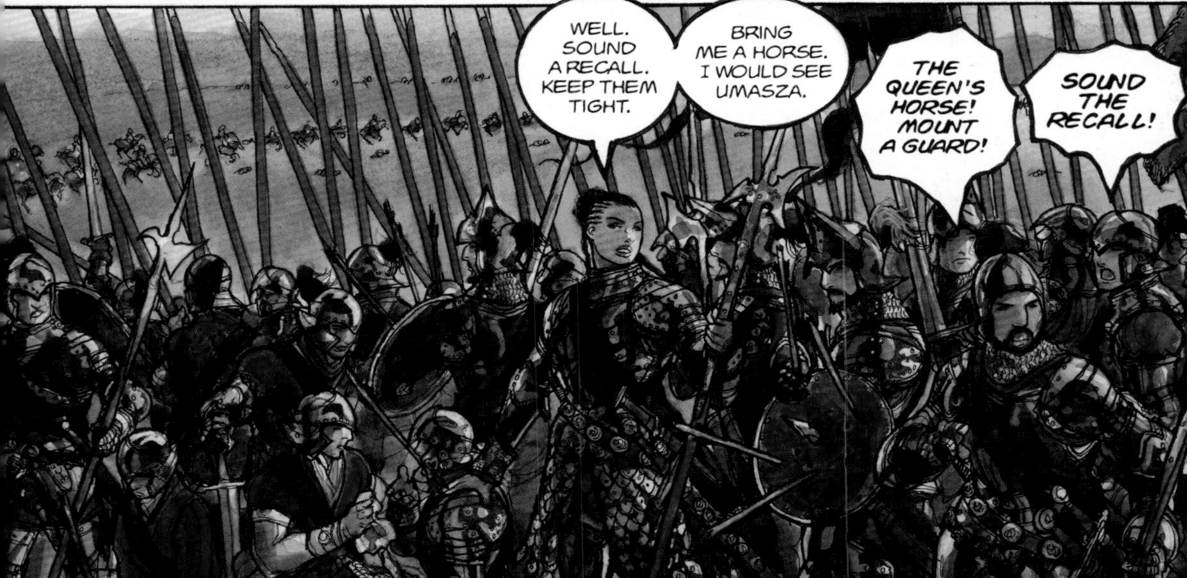
WELL. SOUND A RECALL. KEEP THEM TIGHT.
BRING ME A HORSE. I WOULD SEE UMASZA.
THE QUEEN'S HORSE! MOUNT A GUARD!
SOUND THE RECALL!

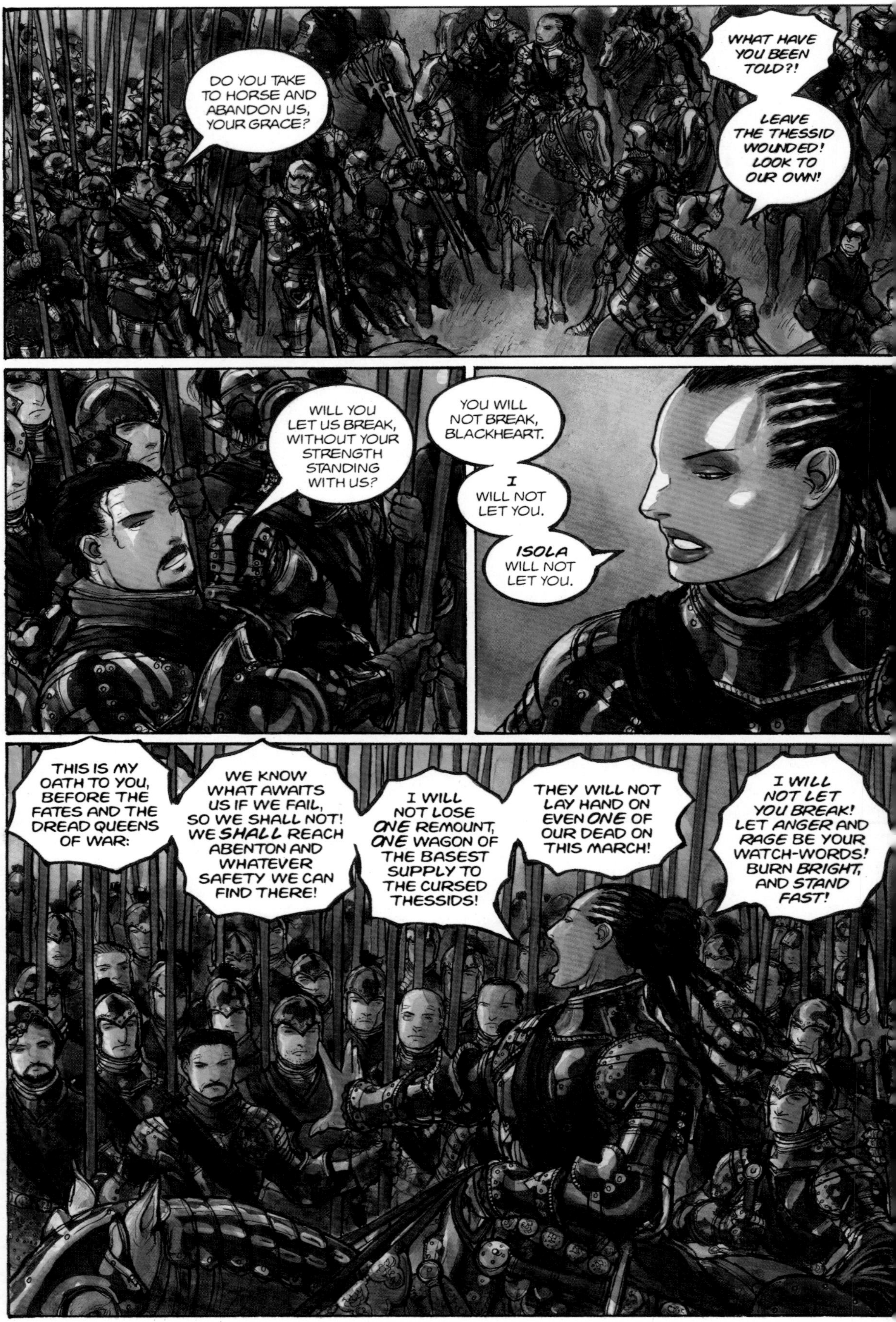
DO YOU TAKE TO HORSE AND ABANDON US, YOUR GRACE?
WHAT HAVE YOU BEEN TOLD?!
LEAVE THE THESSID WOUNDED! LOOK TO OUR OWN!
WILL YOU LET US BREAK, WITHOUT YOUR STRENGTH STANDING WITH US?
YOU WILL NOT BREAK, BLACKHEART.
I WILL NOT LET YOU.
ISOLA WILL NOT LET YOU.
THIS IS MY OATH TO YOU, BEFORE THE FATES AND THE DREAD QUEENS OF WAR:
WE KNOW WHAT AWAITS US IF WE FAIL, SO WE SHALL NOT! WE SHALL REACH ABENTON AND WHATEVER SAFETY WE CAN FIND THERE!
I WILL NOT LOSE ONE REMOUNT, ONE WAGON OF THE BASEST SUPPLY TO THE CURSED THESSIDS!
THEY WILL NOT LAY HAND ON EVEN ONE OF OUR DEAD ON THIS MARCH!
I WILL NOT LET YOU BREAK! LET ANGER AND RAGE BE YOUR WATCH-WORDS! BURN BRIGHT, AND STAND FAST!

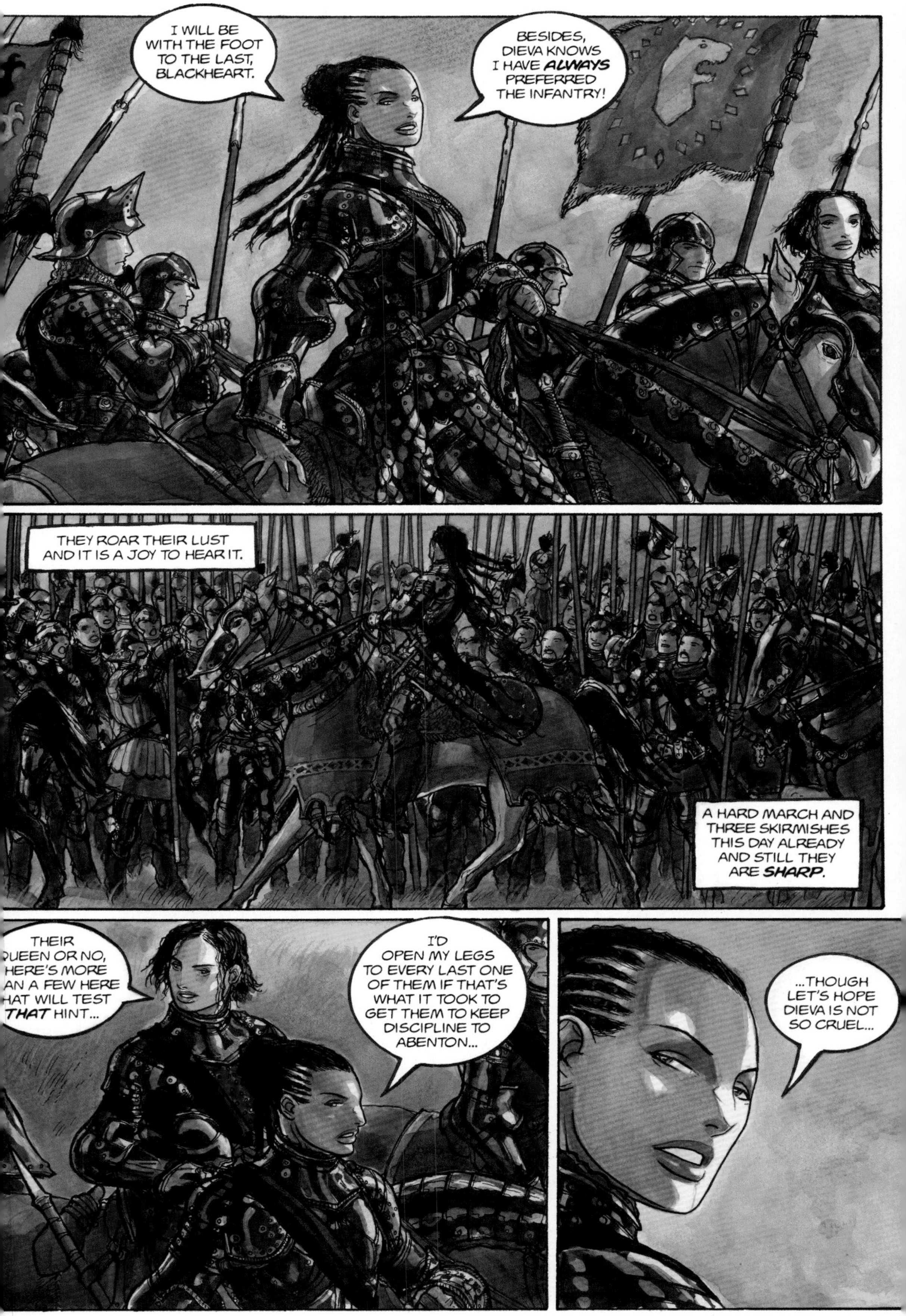
I WILL BE WITH THE FOOT TO THE LAST, BLACKHEART.
BESIDES, DIEVA KNOWS I HAVE ALWAYS PREFERRED THE INFANTRY!
THEY ROAR THEIR LUST AND IT IS A JOY TO HEAR IT.
A HARD MARCH AND THREE SKIRMISHES THIS DAY ALREADY AND STILL THEY ARE SHARP.
THEIR QUEEN OR NO, HERE'S MORE AN A FEW HERE HAT WILL TEST THAT HINT...
I'D OPEN MY LEGS TO EVERY LAST ONE OF THEM IF THAT'S WHAT IT TOOK TO GET THEM TO KEEP DISCIPLINE TO ABENTON...
...THOUGH LET'S HOPE DIEVA IS NOT SO CRUEL...

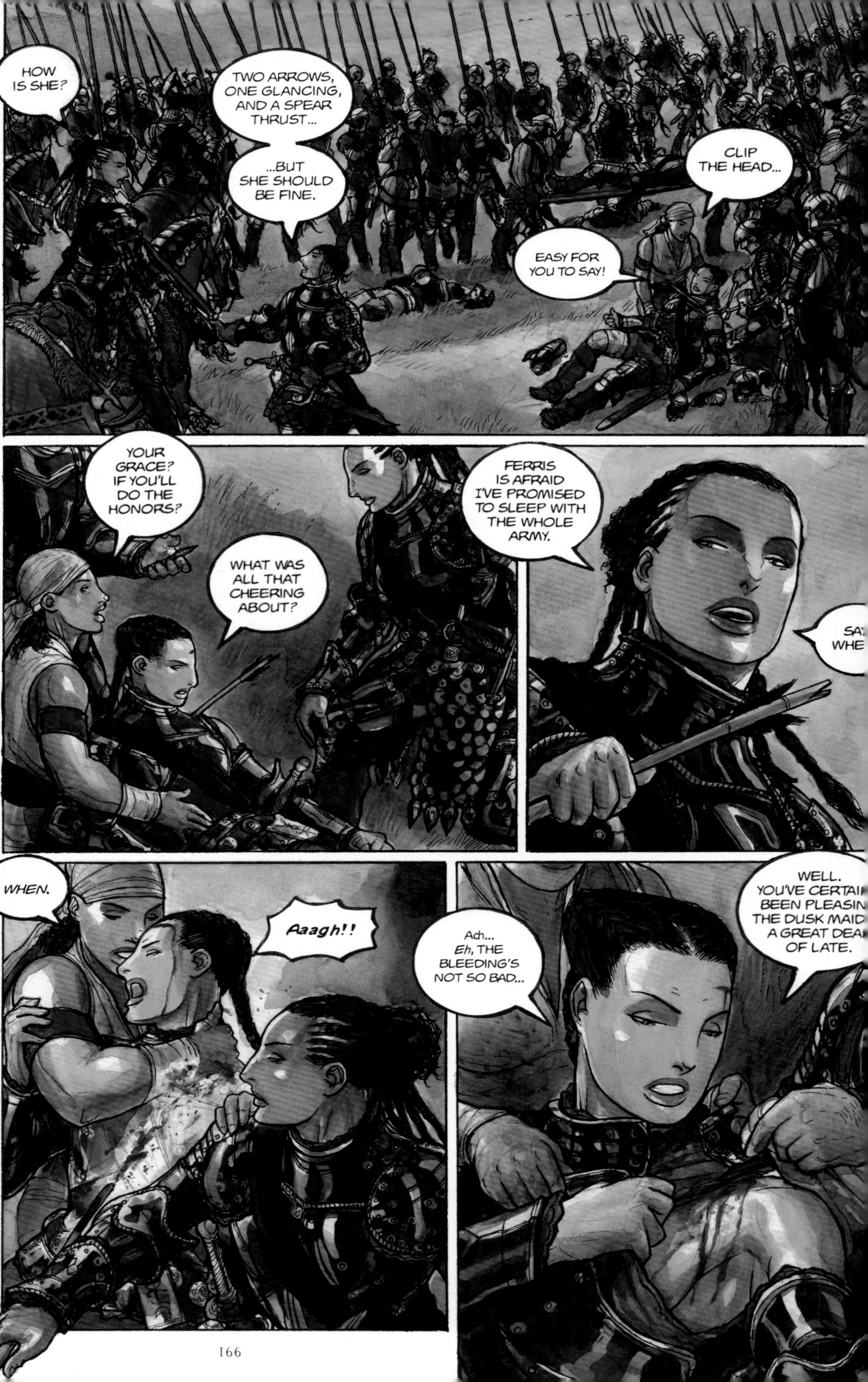
HOW IS SHE?
TWO ARROWS, ONE GLANCING, AND A SPEAR THRUST...
...BUT SHE SHOULD BE FINE.
CLIP THE HEAD...
EASY FOR YOU TO SAY!
YOUR GRACE? IF YOU'LL DO THE HONORS?
WHAT WAS ALL THAT CHEERING ABOUT?
FERRIS IS AFRAID I'VE PROMISED TO SLEEP WITH THE WHOLE ARMY.
WHEN.
Aaagh!!
Ach... Eh, THE BLEEDING'S NOT SO BAD...

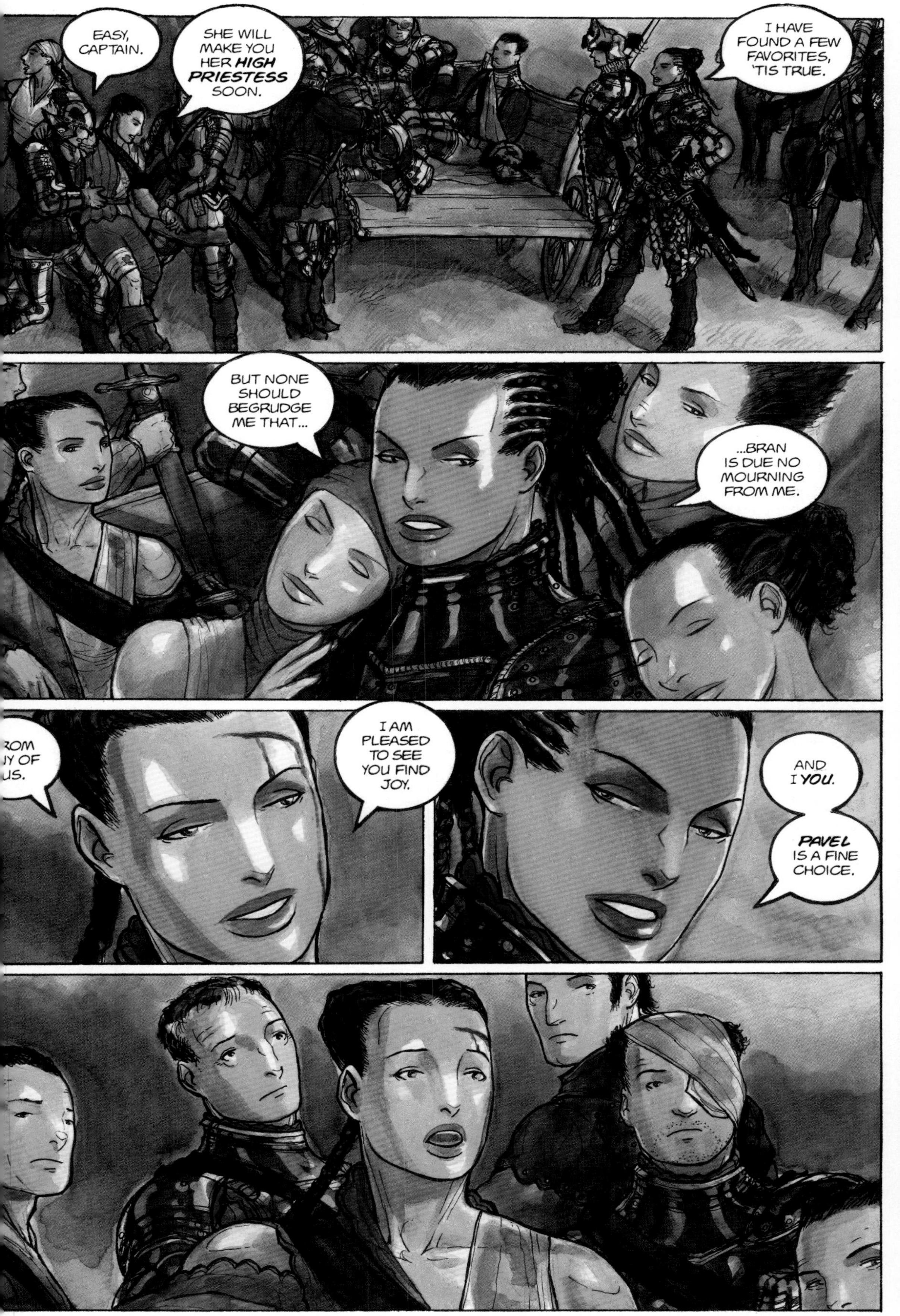
EASY, CAPTAIN.
SHE WILL MAKE YOU HER HIGH PRIESTESS SOON.
I HAVE FOUND A FEW FAVORITES, 'TIS TRUE.
BUT NONE SHOULD BEGRUDGE ME THAT...
...BRAN IS DUE NO MOURNING FROM ME.
ROM
NY OF
US.
I AM PLEASED TO SEE YOU FIND JOY.
AND I YOU.
PAVEL IS A FINE CHOICE.

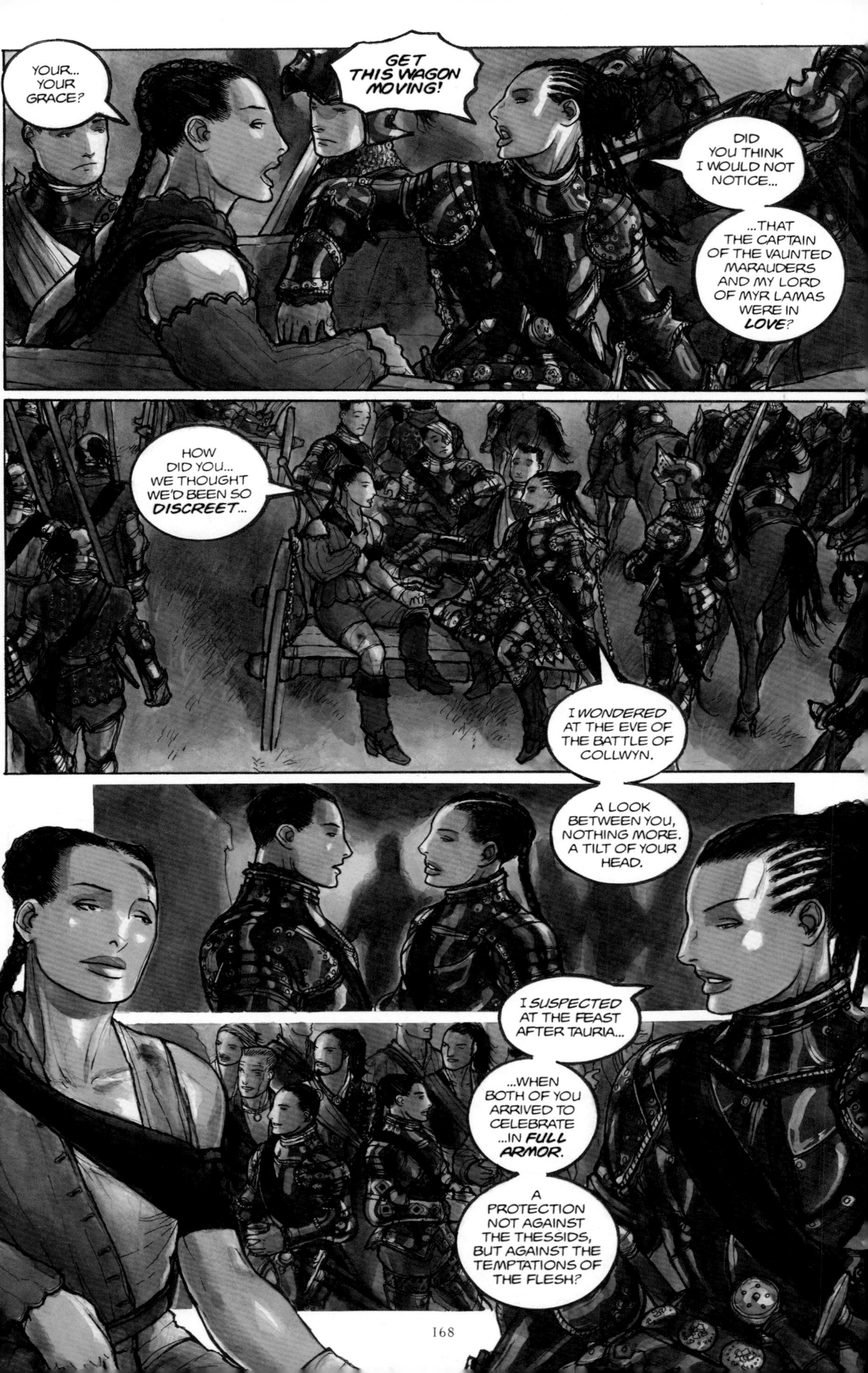
YOUR... YOUR GRACE?
GET THIS WAGON MOVING!
DID YOU THINK I WOULD NOT NOTICE...
...THAT THE CAPTAIN OF THE VAUNTED MARAUDERS AND MY LORD OF MYR LAMAS WERE IN LOVE?
HOW DID YOU... WE THOUGHT WE'D BEEN SO DISCREET...
I WONDERED AT THE EVE OF THE BATTLE OF COLLWYN.
A LOOK BETWEEN YOU, NOTHING MORE. A TILT OF YOUR HEAD.
I SUSPECTED AT THE FEAST AFTER TAURIA...
...WHEN BOTH OF YOU ARRIVED TO CELEBRATE ...IN FULL ARMOR.
A PROTECTION NOT AGAINST THE THESSIDS, BUT AGAINST THE TEMPTATIONS OF THE FLESH?

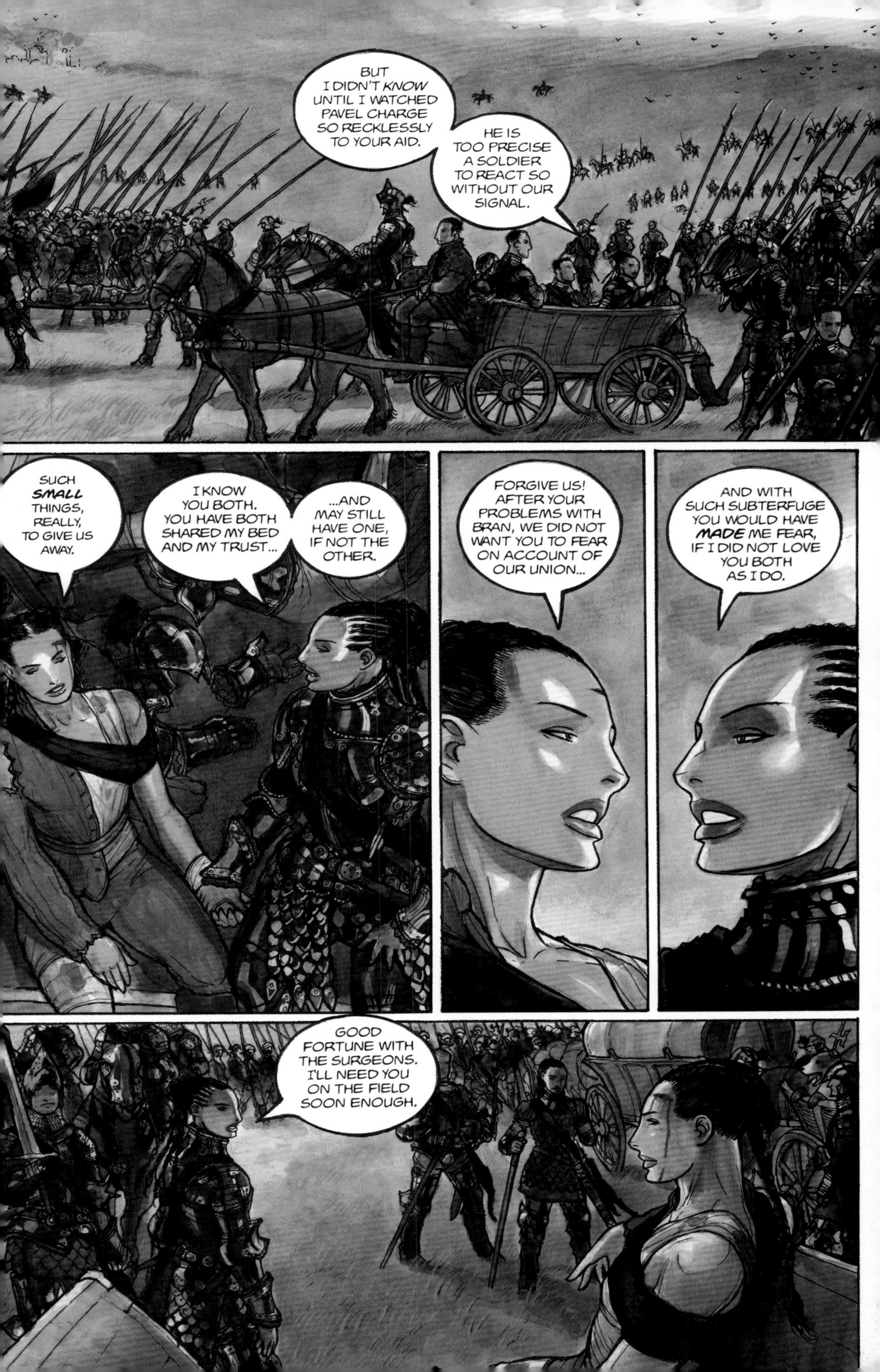
BUT I DIDN'T KNOW UNTIL I WATCHED PAVEL CHARGE SO RECKLESSLY TO YOUR AID.
HE IS TOO PRECISE A SOLDIER TO REACT SO WITHOUT OUR SIGNAL.
SUCH SMALL THINGS, REALLY, TO GIVE US AWAY.
I KNOW YOU BOTH. YOU HAVE BOTH SHARED MY BED AND MY TRUST...
...AND MAY STILL HAVE ONE, IF NOT THE OTHER.
FORGIVE US! AFTER YOUR PROBLEMS WITH BRAN, WE DID NOT WANT YOU TO FEAR ON ACCOUNT OF OUR UNION...
AND WITH SUCH SUBTERFUGE YOU WOULD HAVE MADE ME FEAR, IF I DID NOT LOVE YOU BOTH AS I DO.
GOOD FORTUNE WITH THE SURGEONS. I'LL NEED YOU ON THE FIELD SOON ENOUGH.

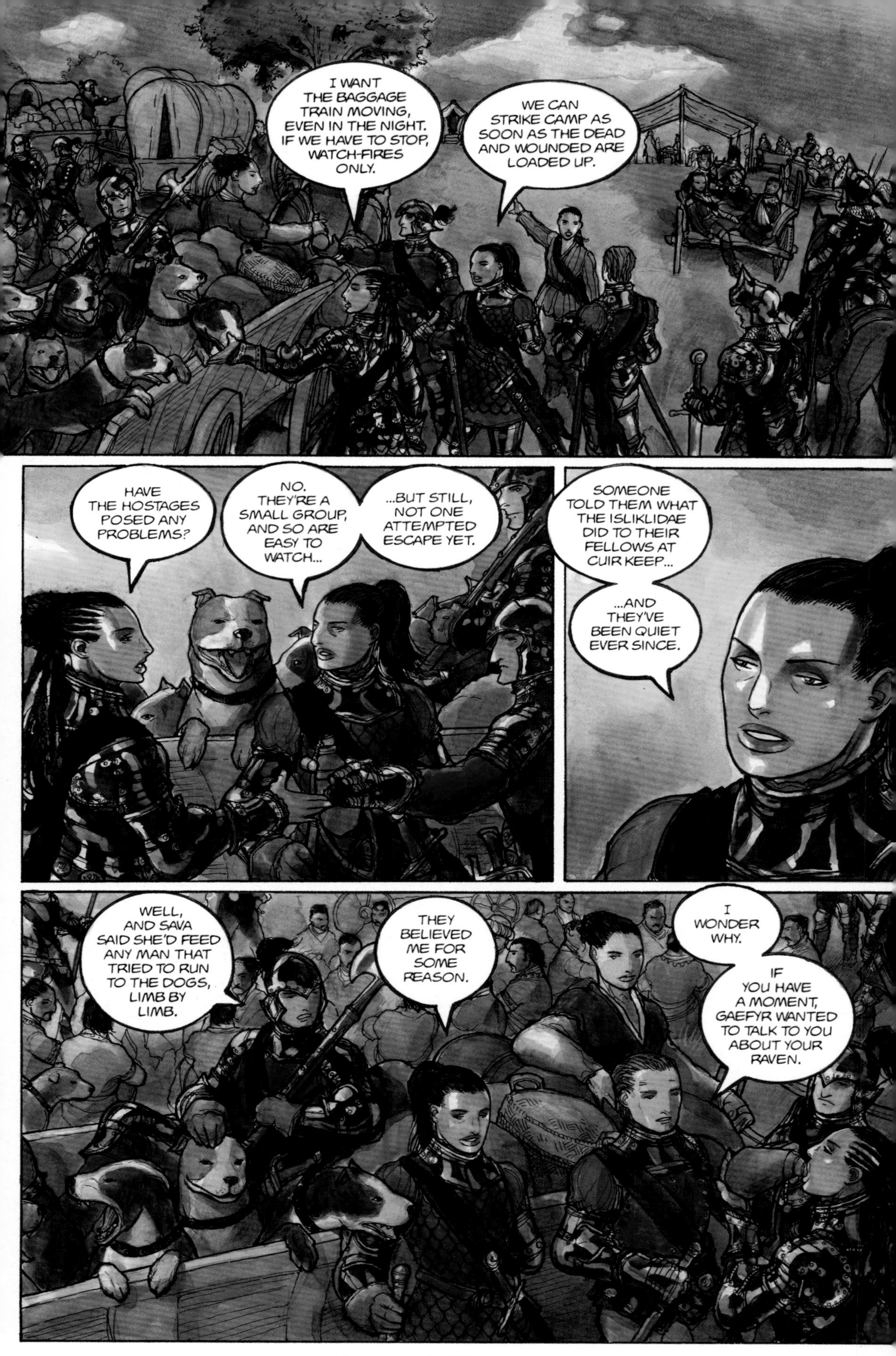
I WANT THE BAGGAGE TRAIN MOVING, EVEN IN THE NIGHT. IF WE HAVE TO STOP, WATCH-FIRES ONLY.
WE CAN STRIKE CAMP AS SOON AS THE DEAD AND WOUNDED ARE LOADED UP.
HAVE THE HOSTAGES POSED ANY PROBLEMS?
NO. THEY'RE A SMALL GROUP, AND SO ARE EASY TO WATCH...
...BUT STILL, NOT ONE ATTEMPTED ESCAPE YET.
SOMEONE TOLD THEM WHAT THE ISLIKLIDAE DID TO THEIR FELLOWS AT CUIR KEEP...
...AND THEY'VE BEEN QUIET EVER SINCE.
WELL, AND SAVA SAID SHE'D FEED ANY MAN THAT TRIED TO RUN TO THE DOGS, LIMB BY LIMB.
THEY BELIEVED ME FOR SOME REASON.
I WONDER WHY.
IF YOU HAVE A MOMENT, GAEFYR WANTED TO TALK TO YOU ABOUT YOUR RAVEN.

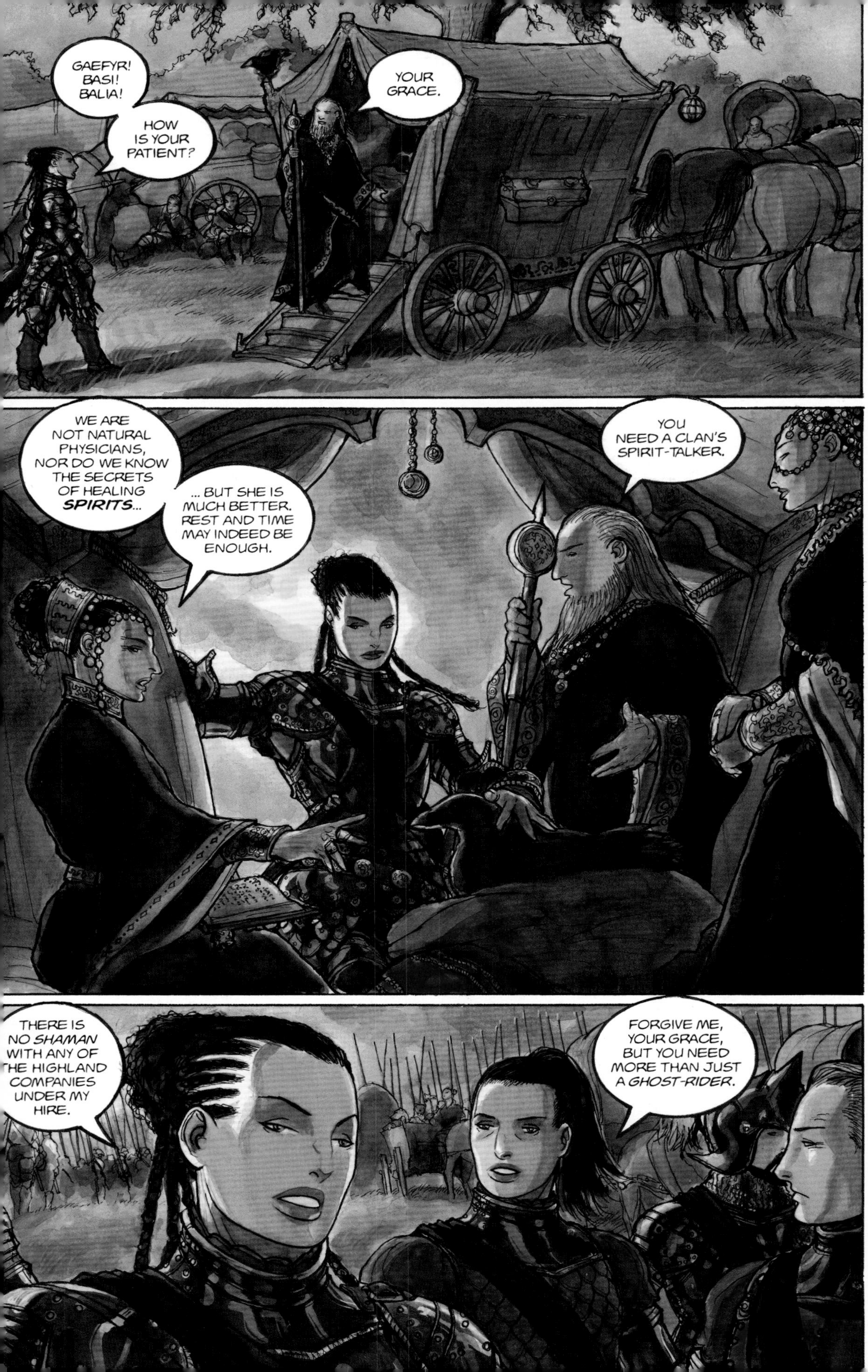
GAEFYR! BASI! BALIA!
HOW IS YOUR PATIENT?
YOUR GRACE.
WE ARE NOT NATURAL PHYSICIANS, NOR DO WE KNOW THE SECRETS OF HEALING **SPIRITS**...
... BUT SHE IS MUCH BETTER. REST AND TIME MAY INDEED BE ENOUGH.
YOU NEED A CLAN'S SPIRIT-TALKER.
THERE IS NO *SHAMAN* WITH ANY OF THE HIGHLAND COMPANIES UNDER MY HIRE.
FORGIVE ME, YOUR GRACE, BUT YOU NEED MORE THAN JUST A *GHOST-RIDER*.

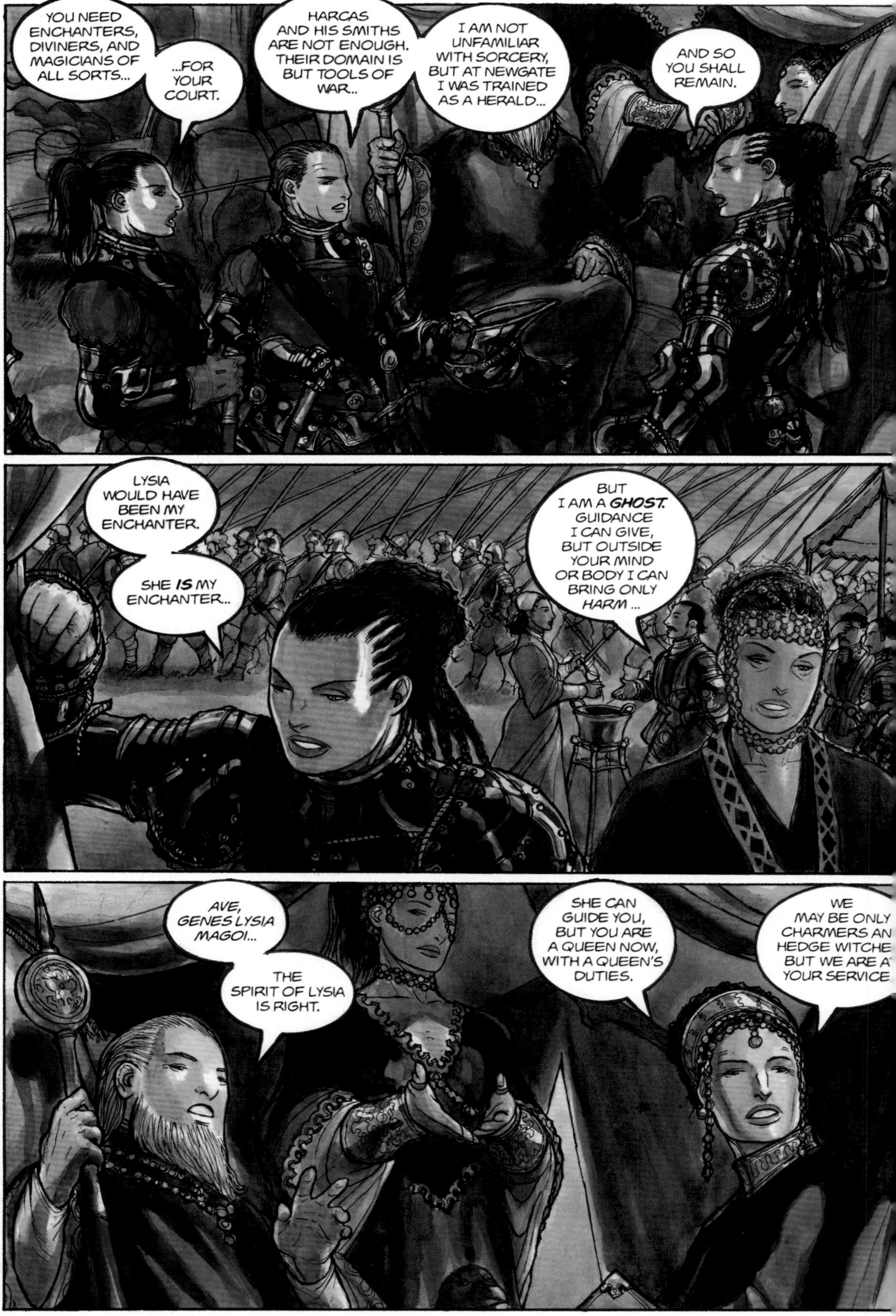
YOU NEED ENCHANTERS, DIVINERS, AND MAGICIANS OF ALL SORTS...
...FOR YOUR COURT.
HARCAS AND HIS SMITHS ARE NOT ENOUGH. THEIR DOMAIN IS BUT TOOLS OF WAR...
I AM NOT UNFAMILIAR WITH SORCERY, BUT AT NEWGATE I WAS TRAINED AS A HERALD...
AND SO YOU SHALL REMAIN.
LYSIA WOULD HAVE BEEN MY ENCHANTER.
SHE *IS* MY ENCHANTER...
BUT I AM A ***GHOST.*** GUIDANCE I CAN GIVE, BUT OUTSIDE YOUR MIND OR BODY I CAN BRING ONLY *HARM* ...
AVE, GENES LYSIA MAGOI...
THE SPIRIT OF LYSIA IS RIGHT.
SHE CAN GUIDE YOU, BUT YOU ARE A QUEEN NOW, WITH A QUEEN'S DUTIES.
WE MAY BE ONLY CHARMERS AN HEDGE WITCHE BUT WE ARE A YOUR SERVICE

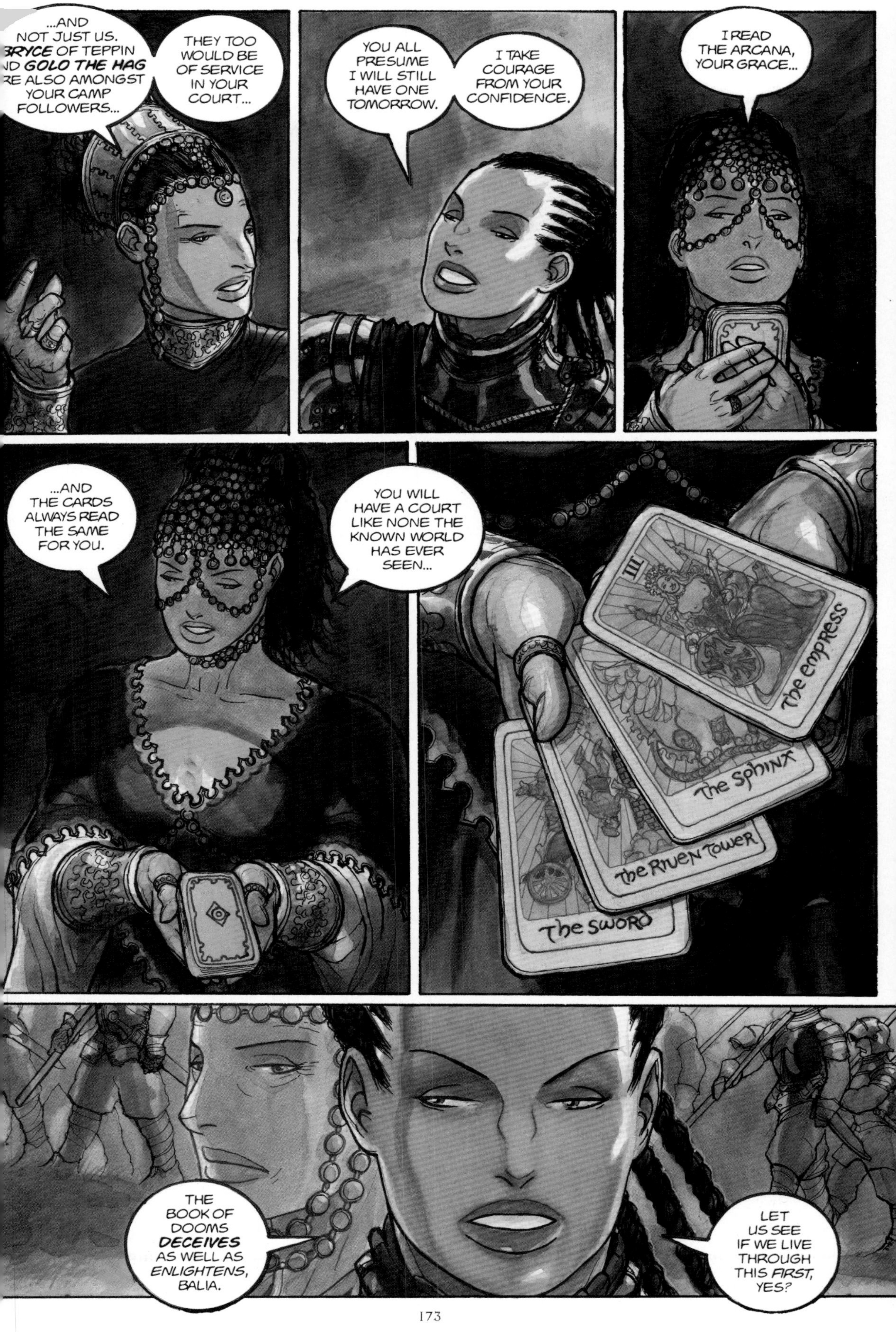
...AND NOT JUST US. BRYCE OF TEPPIN ND GOLO THE HAG RE ALSO AMONGST YOUR CAMP FOLLOWERS...
THEY TOO WOULD BE OF SERVICE IN YOUR COURT...
YOU ALL PRESUME I WILL STILL HAVE ONE TOMORROW.
I TAKE COURAGE FROM YOUR CONFIDENCE.
I READ THE ARCANA, YOUR GRACE...
...AND THE CARDS ALWAYS READ THE SAME FOR YOU.
YOU WILL HAVE A COURT LIKE NONE THE KNOWN WORLD HAS EVER SEEN...
III
The empress
The Sphinx
The Riven Tower
The sword
THE BOOK OF DOOMS DECEIVES AS WELL AS ENLIGHTENS, BALIA.
LET US SEE IF WE LIVE THROUGH THIS FIRST, YES?

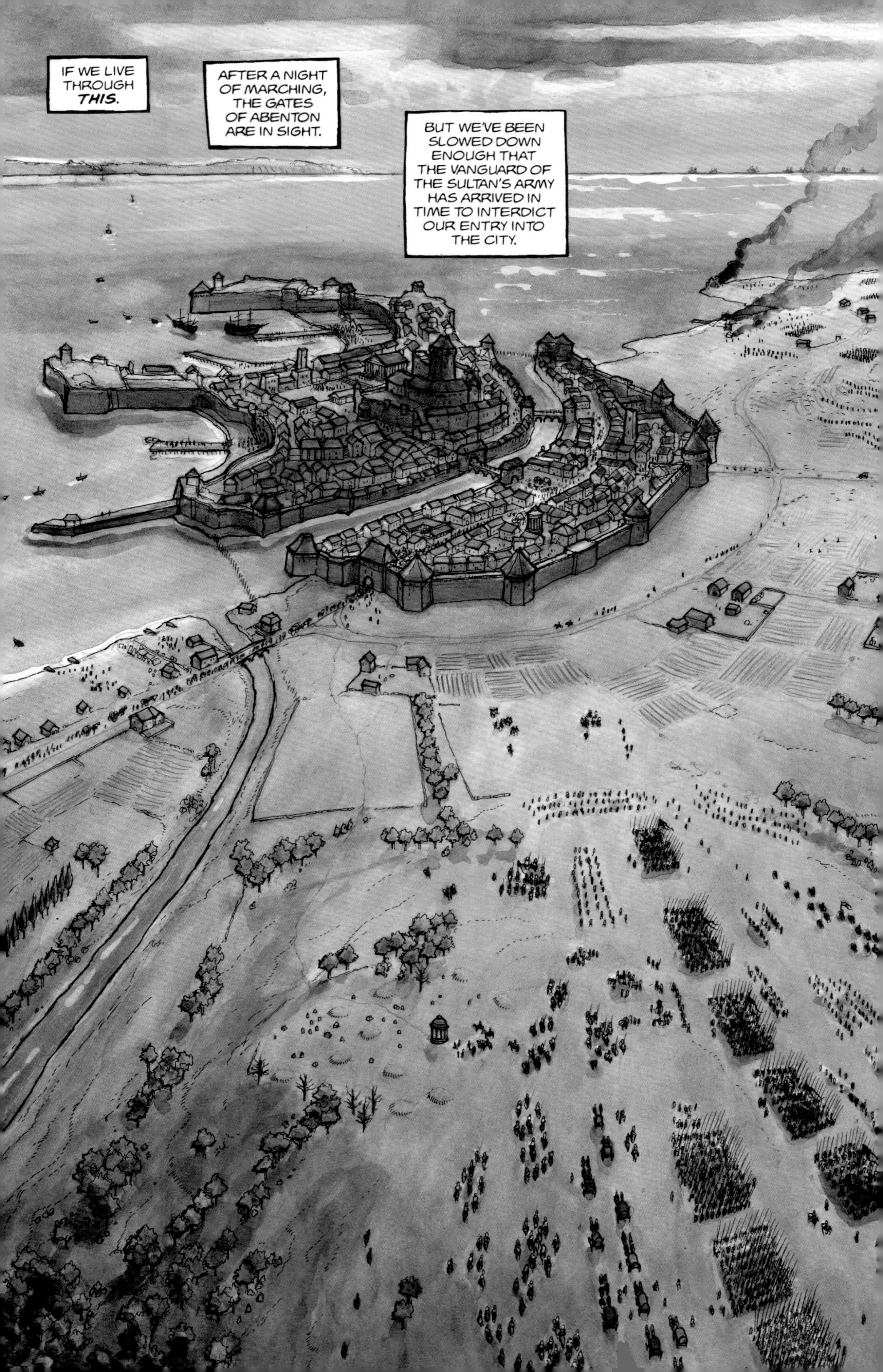
IF WE LIVE THROUGH THIS.
AFTER A NIGHT OF MARCHING, THE GATES OF ABENTON ARE IN SIGHT.
BUT WE'VE BEEN SLOWED DOWN ENOUGH THAT THE VANGUARD OF THE SULTAN'S ARMY HAS ARRIVED IN TIME TO INTERDICT OUR ENTRY INTO THE CITY.

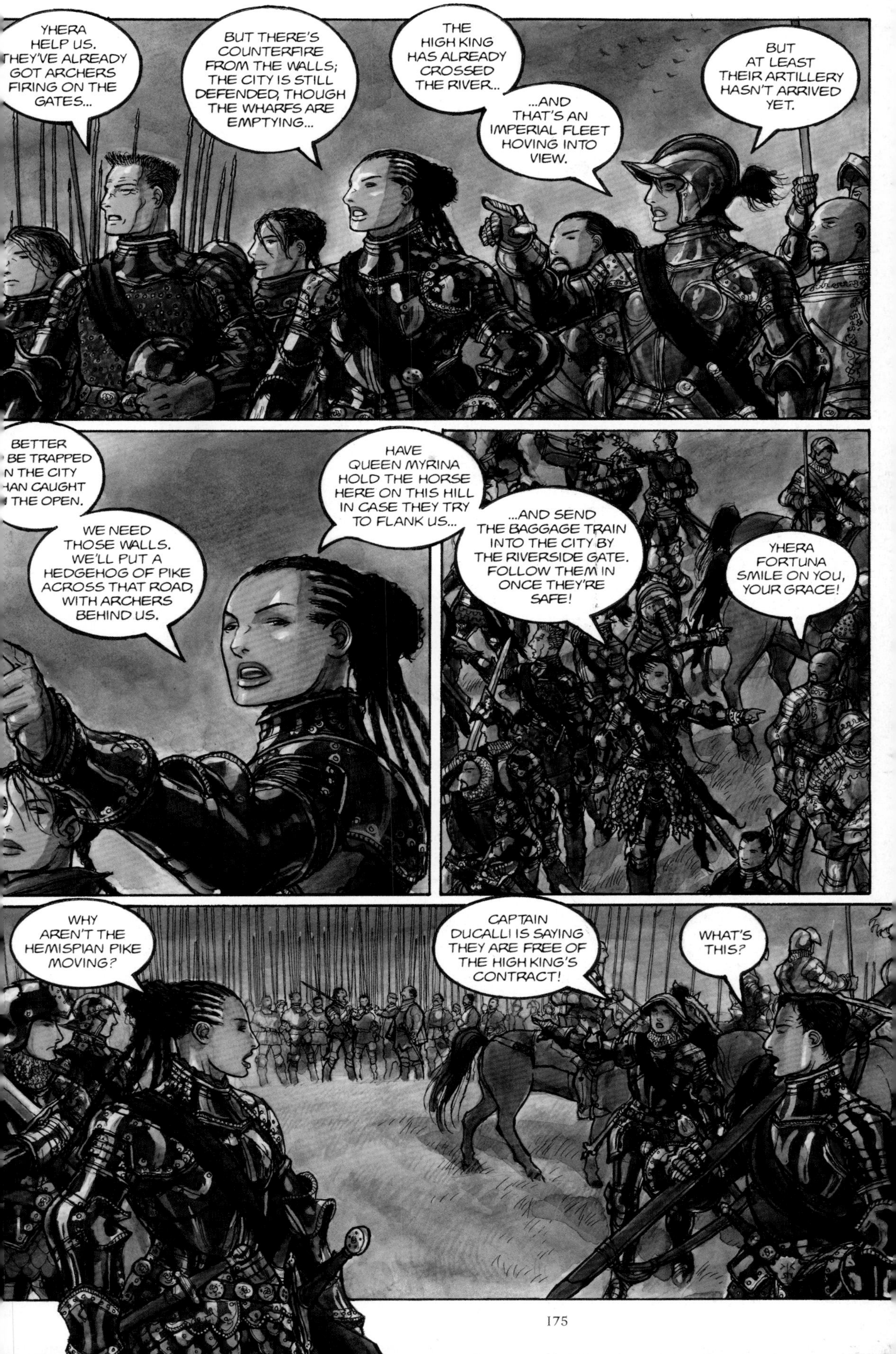
YHERA HELP US. THEY'VE ALREADY GOT ARCHERS FIRING ON THE GATES...
BUT THERE'S COUNTERFIRE FROM THE WALLS; THE CITY IS STILL DEFENDED, THOUGH THE WHARFS ARE EMPTYING...
THE HIGH KING HAS ALREADY CROSSED THE RIVER...
...AND THAT'S AN IMPERIAL FLEET HOVING INTO VIEW.
BUT AT LEAST THEIR ARTILLERY HASN'T ARRIVED YET.
BETTER BE TRAPPED IN THE CITY THAN CAUGHT THE OPEN.
WE NEED THOSE WALLS. WE'LL PUT A HEDGEHOG OF PIKE ACROSS THAT ROAD, WITH ARCHERS BEHIND US.
HAVE QUEEN MYRINA HOLD THE HORSE HERE ON THIS HILL IN CASE THEY TRY TO FLANK US...
...AND SEND THE BAGGAGE TRAIN INTO THE CITY BY THE RIVERSIDE GATE. FOLLOW THEM IN ONCE THEY'RE SAFE!
YHERA FORTUNA SMILE ON YOU, YOUR GRACE!
WHY AREN'T THE HEMISPIAN PIKE MOVING?
CAPTAIN DUCALLI IS SAYING THEY ARE FREE OF THE HIGH KING'S CONTRACT!
WHAT'S THIS?

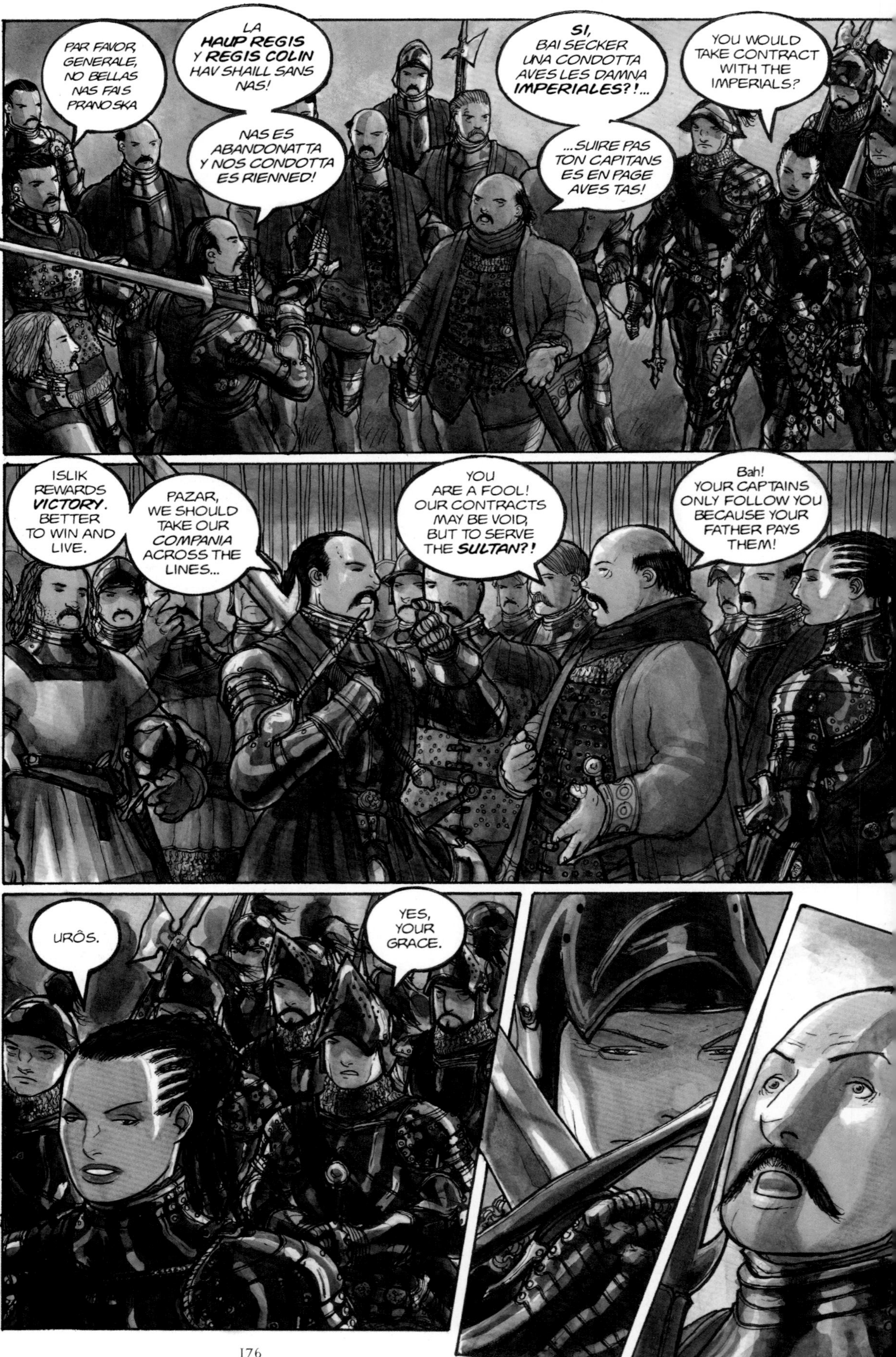
PAR FAVOR, GENERALE, NO BELLAS NAS FAIS PRANOSKA
LA **HAUP REGIS** Y **REGIS COLIN** HAV SHAILL SANS NAS!
NAS ES ABANDONATTA Y NOS CONDOTTA ES RIENNED!
SI, BAI SECKER UNA CONDOTTA AVES LES DAMNA **IMPERIALES?!...**
...SUIRE PAS TON CAPITANS ES EN PAGE AVES TAS!
YOU WOULD TAKE CONTRACT WITH THE IMPERIALS?
ISLIK REWARDS **VICTORY**. BETTER TO WIN AND LIVE.
PAZAR, WE SHOULD TAKE OUR *COMPANIA* ACROSS THE LINES...
YOU ARE A FOOL! OUR CONTRACTS MAY BE VOID, BUT TO SERVE THE **SULTAN?!**
Bah! YOUR CAPTAINS ONLY FOLLOW YOU BECAUSE YOUR FATHER PAYS THEM!
URÔS.
YES, YOUR GRACE.

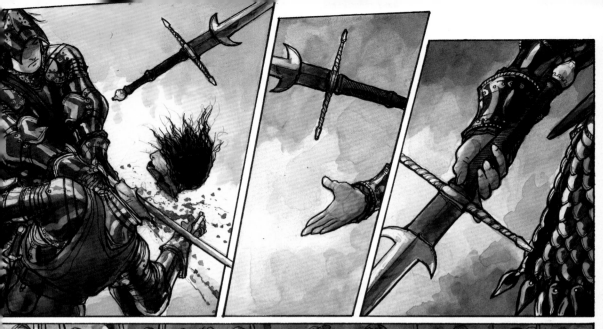

ISLIK REWARDS VICTORY? WELL, SO DO I.

IF YOU NO LONGER SERVE THE MIDDLE KINGS, I OFFER A YEAR'S *CONDOTTA* UNDER MY BANNER.

I'LL EVEN OFFER A BONUS, A DUCAT FOR EACH MEMBER OF THIS HOST THAT YOU GET SAFELY INTO ABENTON...

...BUT WE WILL NOT LET YOU CROSS THE LINES.

DONE. DONE. DONE. DONE. DONE.

OVER THREE THOUSAND DUCATS FOR ONE BATTLE...

DONE.

THEN FOLLOW ME.

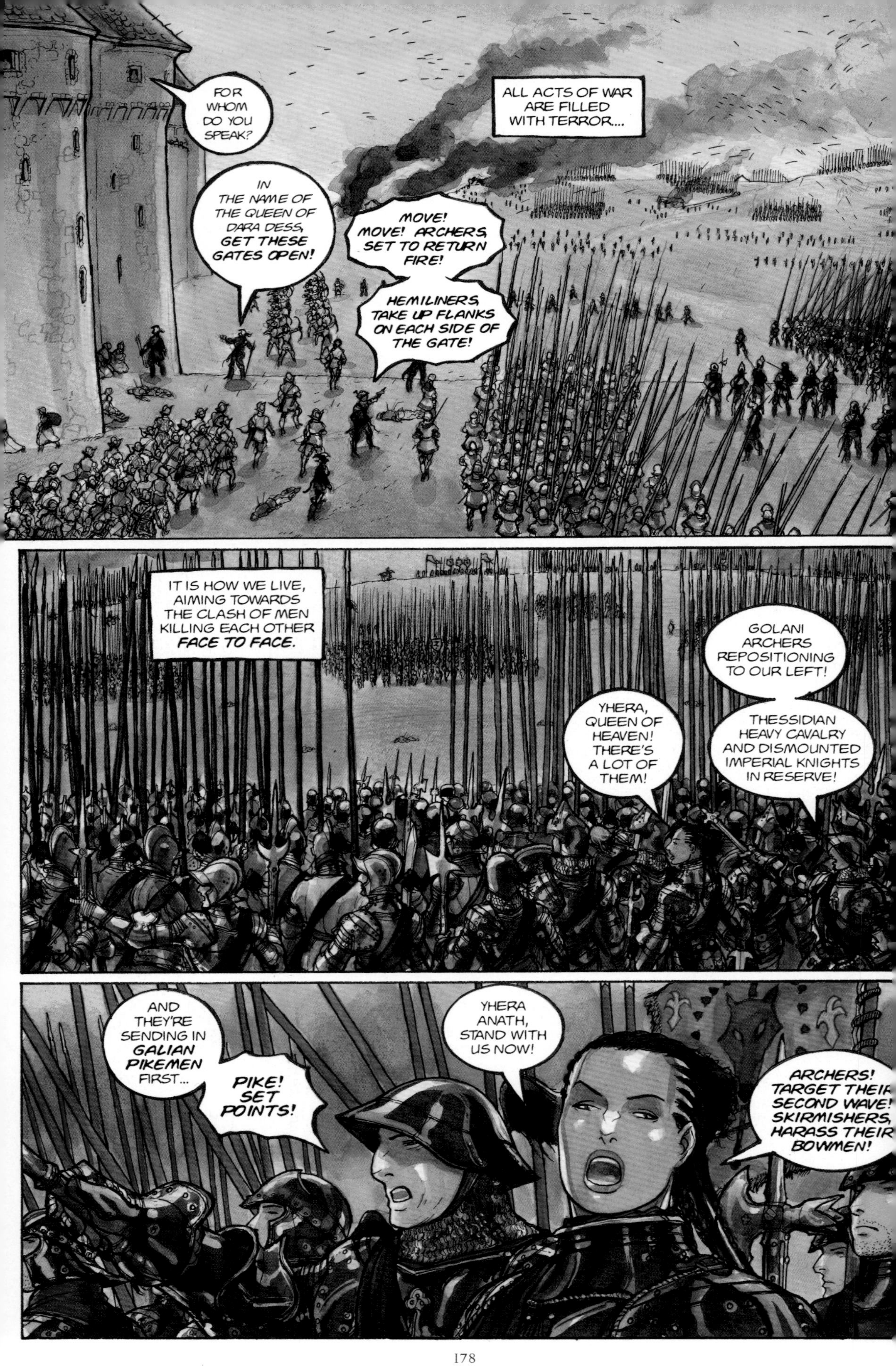
FOR WHOM DO YOU SPEAK?
ALL ACTS OF WAR ARE FILLED WITH TERROR....
IN THE NAME OF THE QUEEN OF DARA DESS, GET THESE GATES OPEN!
MOVE! MOVE! ARCHERS, SET TO RETURN FIRE!
HEMILINERS, TAKE UP FLANKS ON EACH SIDE OF THE GATE!
IT IS HOW WE LIVE, AIMING TOWARDS THE CLASH OF MEN KILLING EACH OTHER FACE TO FACE.
GOLANI ARCHERS REPOSITIONING TO OUR LEFT!
YHERA, QUEEN OF HEAVEN! THERE'S A LOT OF THEM!
THESSIDIAN HEAVY CAVALRY AND DISMOUNTED IMPERIAL KNIGHTS IN RESERVE!
AND THEY'RE SENDING IN GALIAN PIKEMEN FIRST...
PIKE! SET POINTS!
YHERA ANATH, STAND WITH US NOW!
ARCHERS! TARGET THEIR SECOND WAVE! SKIRMISHERS, HARASS THEIR BOWMEN!

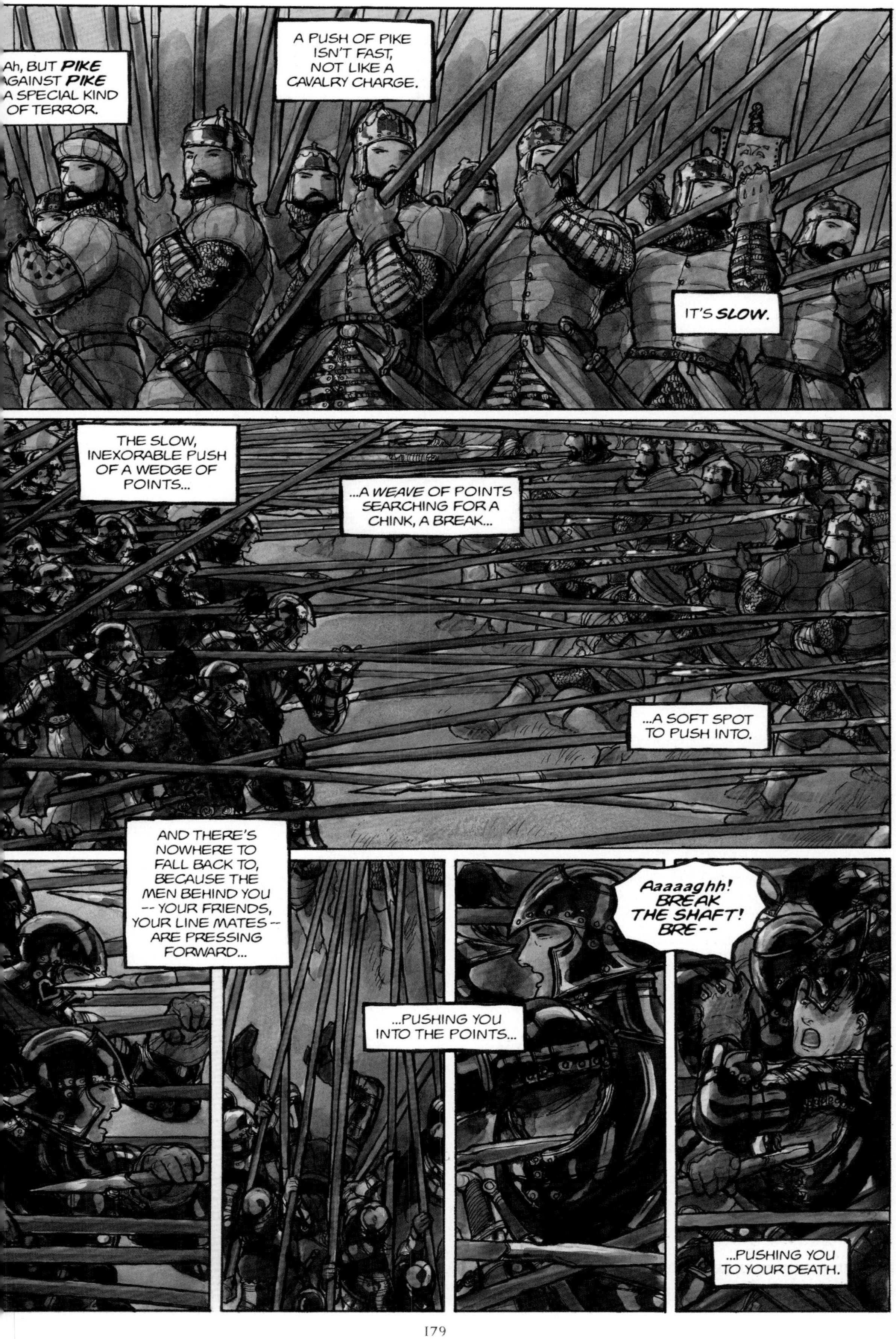
Ah, BUT PIKE AGAINST PIKE A SPECIAL KIND OF TERROR.
A PUSH OF PIKE ISN'T FAST, NOT LIKE A CAVALRY CHARGE.
IT'S SLOW.
THE SLOW, INEXORABLE PUSH OF A WEDGE OF POINTS...
...A WEAVE OF POINTS SEARCHING FOR A CHINK, A BREAK...
...A SOFT SPOT TO PUSH INTO.
AND THERE'S NOWHERE TO FALL BACK TO, BECAUSE THE MEN BEHIND YOU -- YOUR FRIENDS, YOUR LINE MATES -- ARE PRESSING FORWARD...
...PUSHING YOU INTO THE POINTS...
Aaaaaghh! BREAK THE SHAFT! BRE--
...PUSHING YOU TO YOUR DEATH.

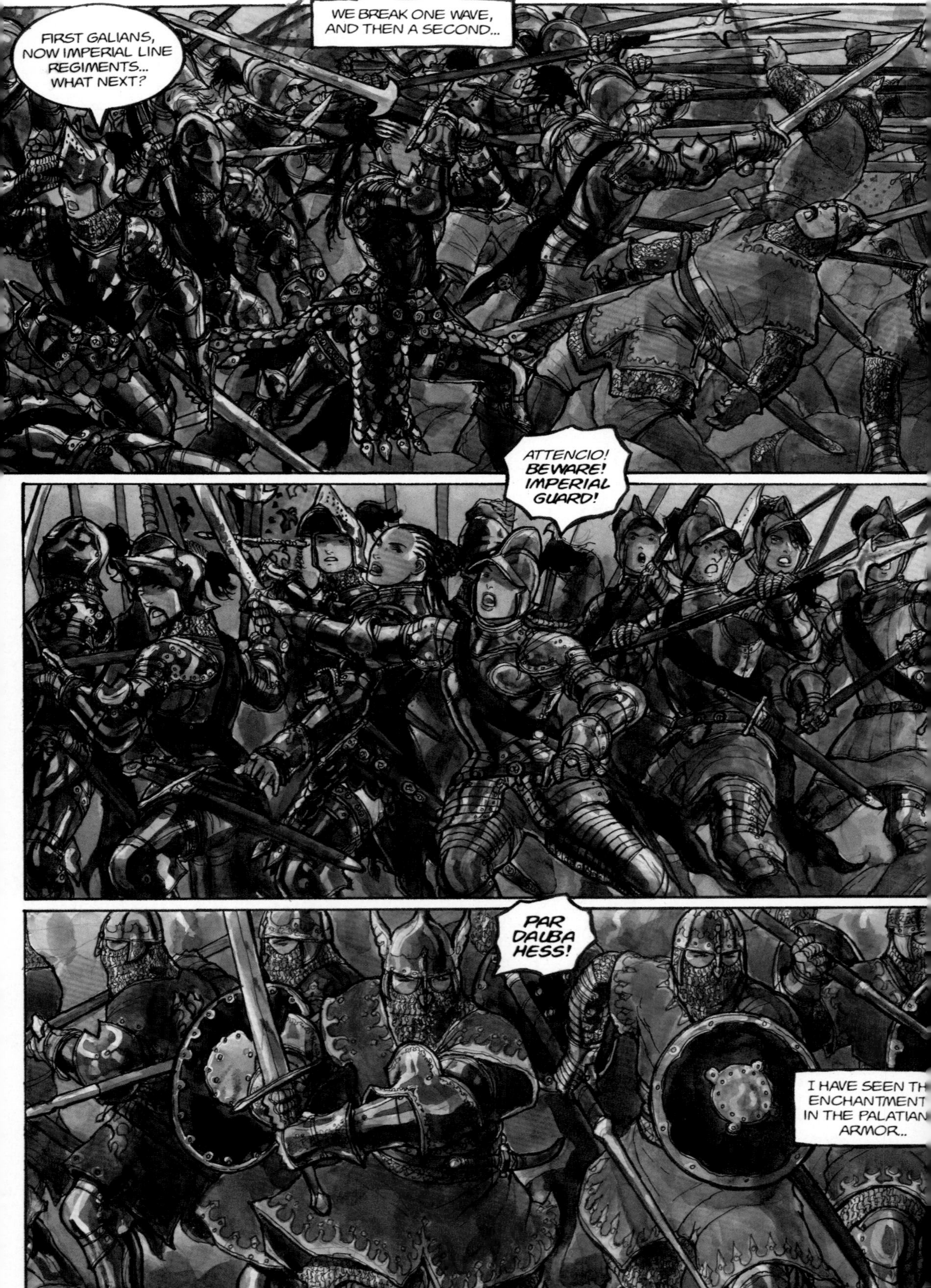

WE BREAK ONE WAVE, AND THEN A SECOND...
FIRST GALIANS, NOW IMPERIAL LINE REGIMENTS... WHAT NEXT?
ATTENCIO! BEWARE! IMPERIAL GUARD!
PAR DALBA HESS!
I HAVE SEEN TH ENCHANTMENT IN THE PALATIAN ARMOR...

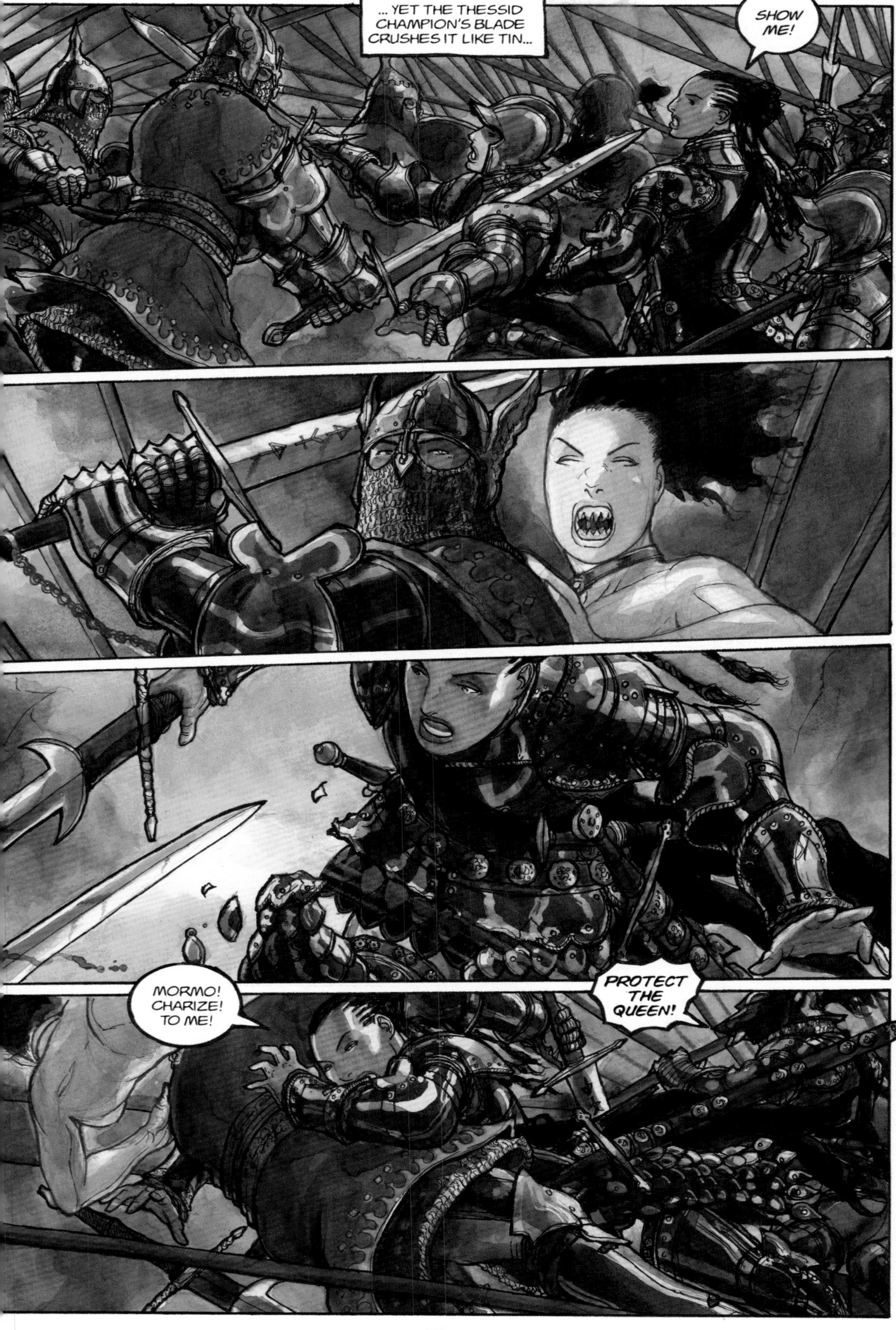
... YET THE THESSID CHAMPION'S BLADE CRUSHES IT LIKE TIN...
SHOW ME!
MORMO! CHARIZE! TO ME!
PROTECT THE QUEEN!

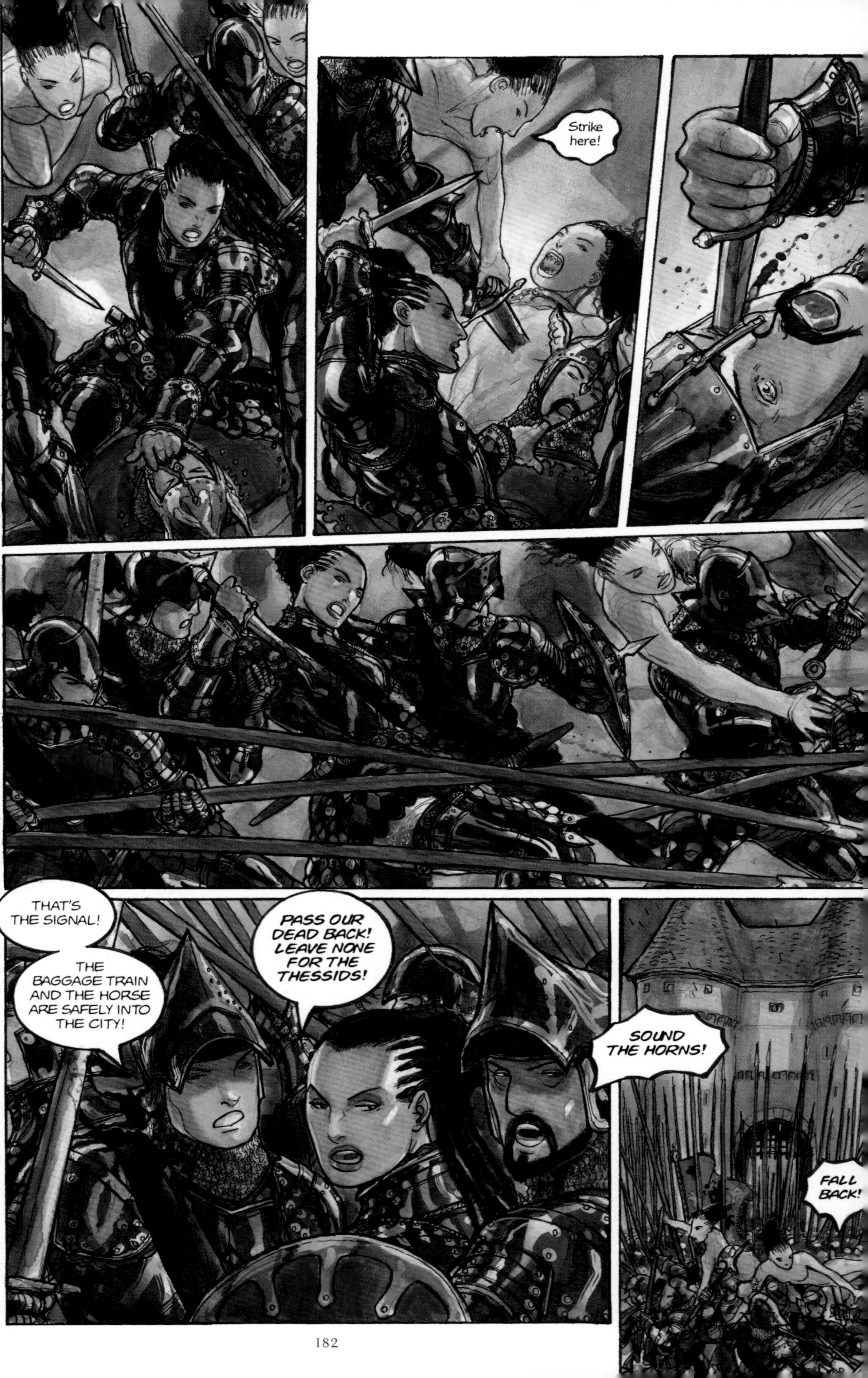
Strike here!
THAT'S THE SIGNAL!
THE BAGGAGE TRAIN AND THE HORSE ARE SAFELY INTO THE CITY!
PASS OUR DEAD BACK! LEAVE NONE FOR THE THESSIDS!
SOUND THE HORNS!
FALL BACK!

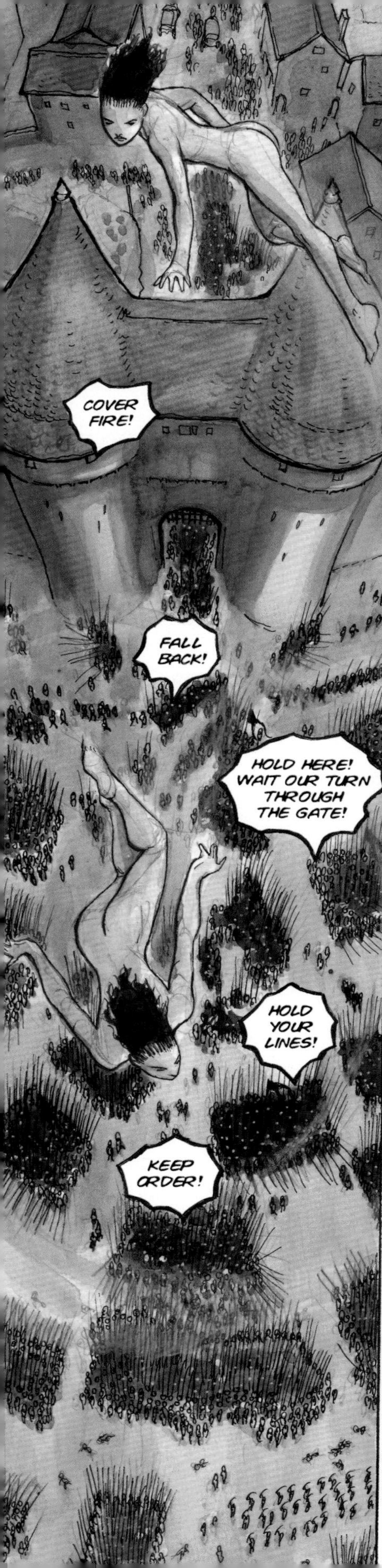
COVER FIRE!
FALL BACK!
HOLD HERE! WAIT OUR TURN THROUGH THE GATE!
HOLD YOUR LINES!
KEEP ORDER!

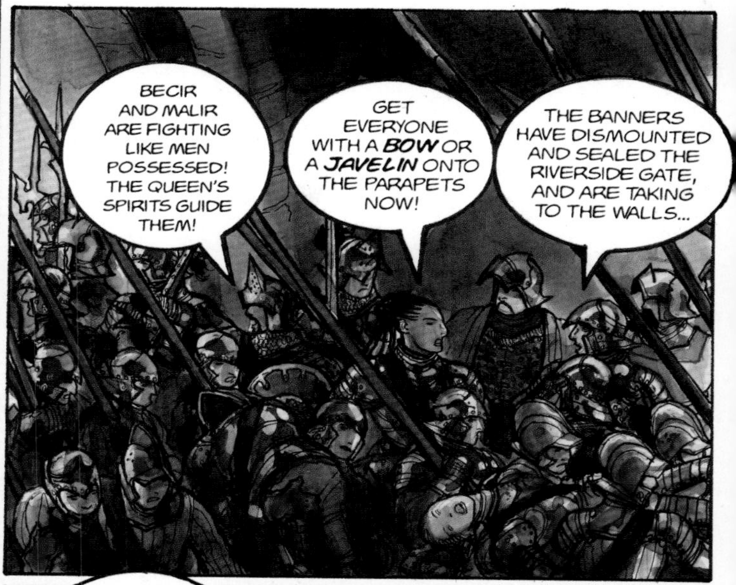
BECIR AND MALIR ARE FIGHTING LIKE MEN POSSESSED! THE QUEEN'S SPIRITS GUIDE THEM!
GET EVERYONE WITH A **BOW** OR A **JAVELIN** ONTO THE PARAPETS NOW!
THE BANNERS HAVE DISMOUNTED AND SEALED THE RIVERSIDE GATE, AND ARE TAKING TO THE WALLS...

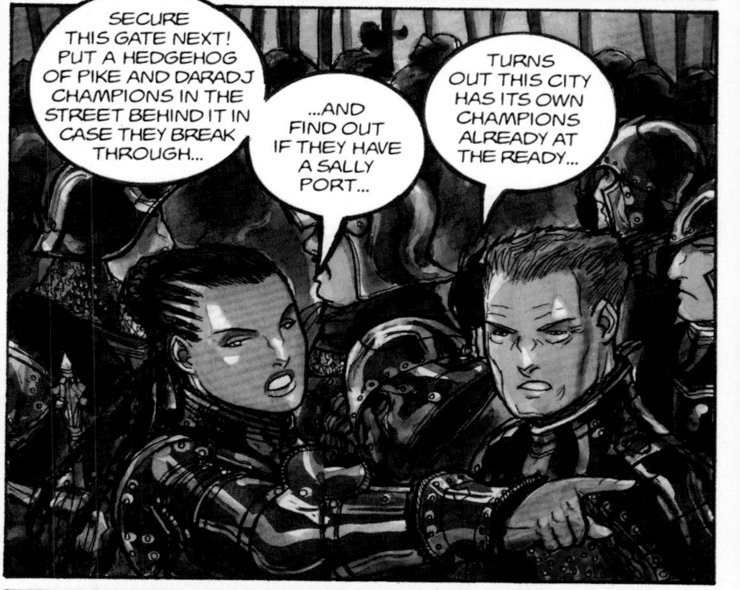
SECURE THIS GATE NEXT! PUT A HEDGEHOG OF PIKE AND DARADJ CHAMPIONS IN THE STREET BEHIND IT IN CASE THEY BREAK THROUGH...
...AND FIND OUT IF THEY HAVE A SALLY PORT...
TURNS OUT THIS CITY HAS ITS OWN CHAMPIONS ALREADY AT THE READY...

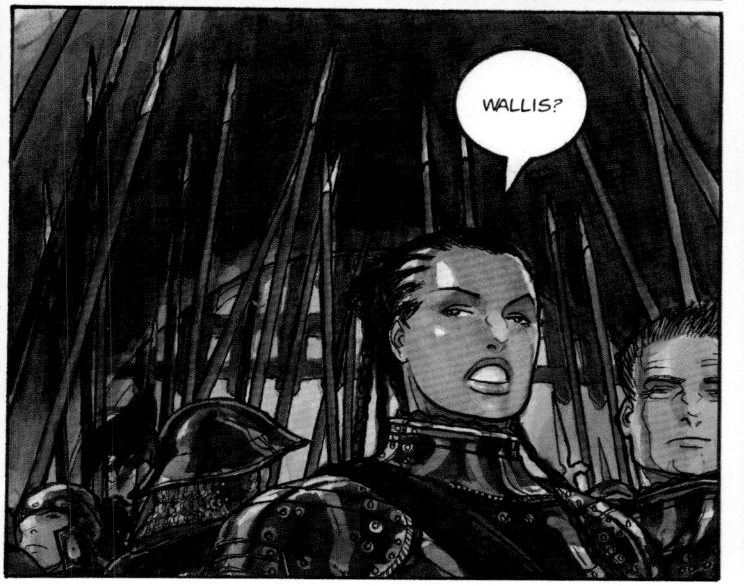
WALLIS?

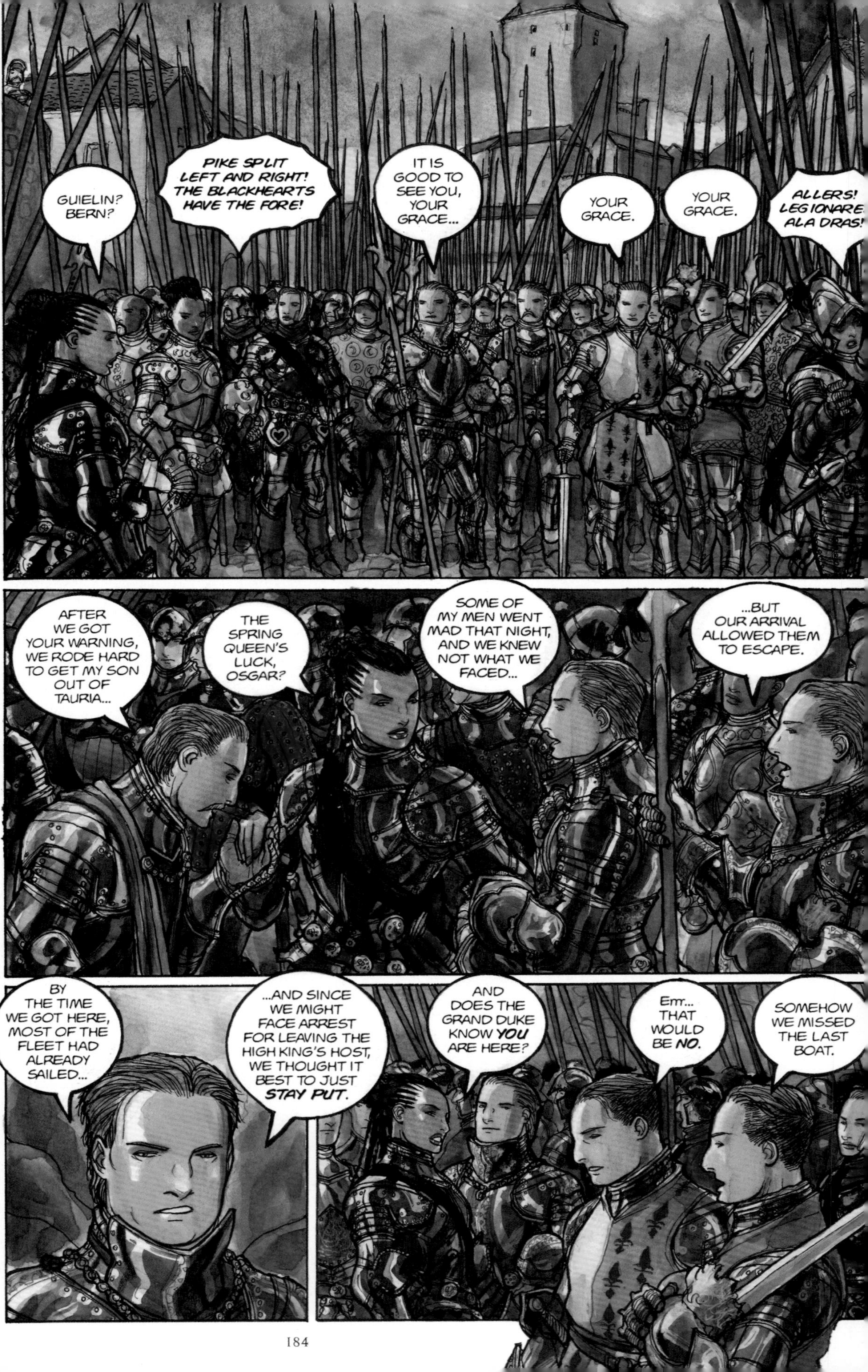
GUIELIN? BERN?
PIKE SPLIT LEFT AND RIGHT! THE BLACKHEARTS HAVE THE FORE!
IT IS GOOD TO SEE YOU, YOUR GRACE...
YOUR GRACE.
YOUR GRACE.
ALLERS! LEGIONARE ALA DRAS!
AFTER WE GOT YOUR WARNING, WE RODE HARD TO GET MY SON OUT OF TAURIA...
THE SPRING QUEEN'S LUCK, OSGAR?
SOME OF MY MEN WENT MAD THAT NIGHT, AND WE KNEW NOT WHAT WE FACED...
...BUT OUR ARRIVAL ALLOWED THEM TO ESCAPE.
BY THE TIME WE GOT HERE, MOST OF THE FLEET HAD ALREADY SAILED...
...AND SINCE WE MIGHT FACE ARREST FOR LEAVING THE HIGH KING'S HOST, WE THOUGHT IT BEST TO JUST STAY PUT.
AND DOES THE GRAND DUKE KNOW YOU ARE HERE?
Errr... THAT WOULD BE NO.
SOMEHOW WE MISSED THE LAST BOAT.

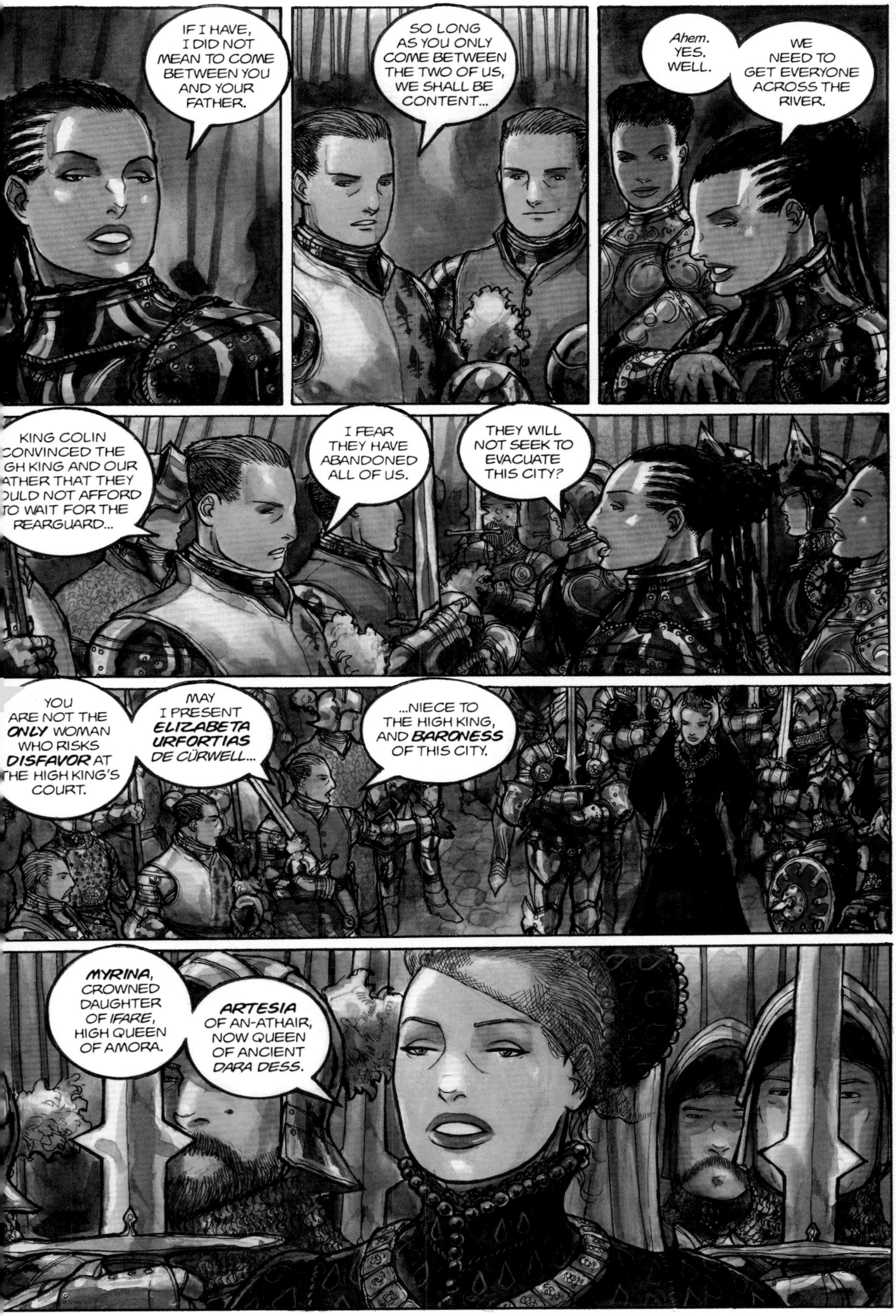

IF I HAVE, I DID NOT MEAN TO COME BETWEEN YOU AND YOUR FATHER.
SO LONG AS YOU ONLY COME BETWEEN THE TWO OF US, WE SHALL BE CONTENT...
Ahem. YES. WELL.
WE NEED TO GET EVERYONE ACROSS THE RIVER.
KING COLIN CONVINCED THE GH KING AND OUR ATHER THAT THEY OULD NOT AFFORD TO WAIT FOR THE REARGUARD...
I FEAR THEY HAVE ABANDONED ALL OF US.
THEY WILL NOT SEEK TO EVACUATE THIS CITY?
YOU ARE NOT THE ***ONLY*** WOMAN WHO RISKS ***DISFAVOR*** AT THE HIGH KING'S COURT.
MAY I PRESENT ***ELIZABETA URFORTIAS*** *DE CÜRWELL*...
...NIECE TO THE HIGH KING, AND ***BARONESS*** OF THIS CITY.
MYRINA, CROWNED DAUGHTER OF *IFARE*, HIGH QUEEN OF AMORA.
ARTESIA OF AN-ATHAIR, NOW QUEEN OF ANCIENT *DARA DESS*.

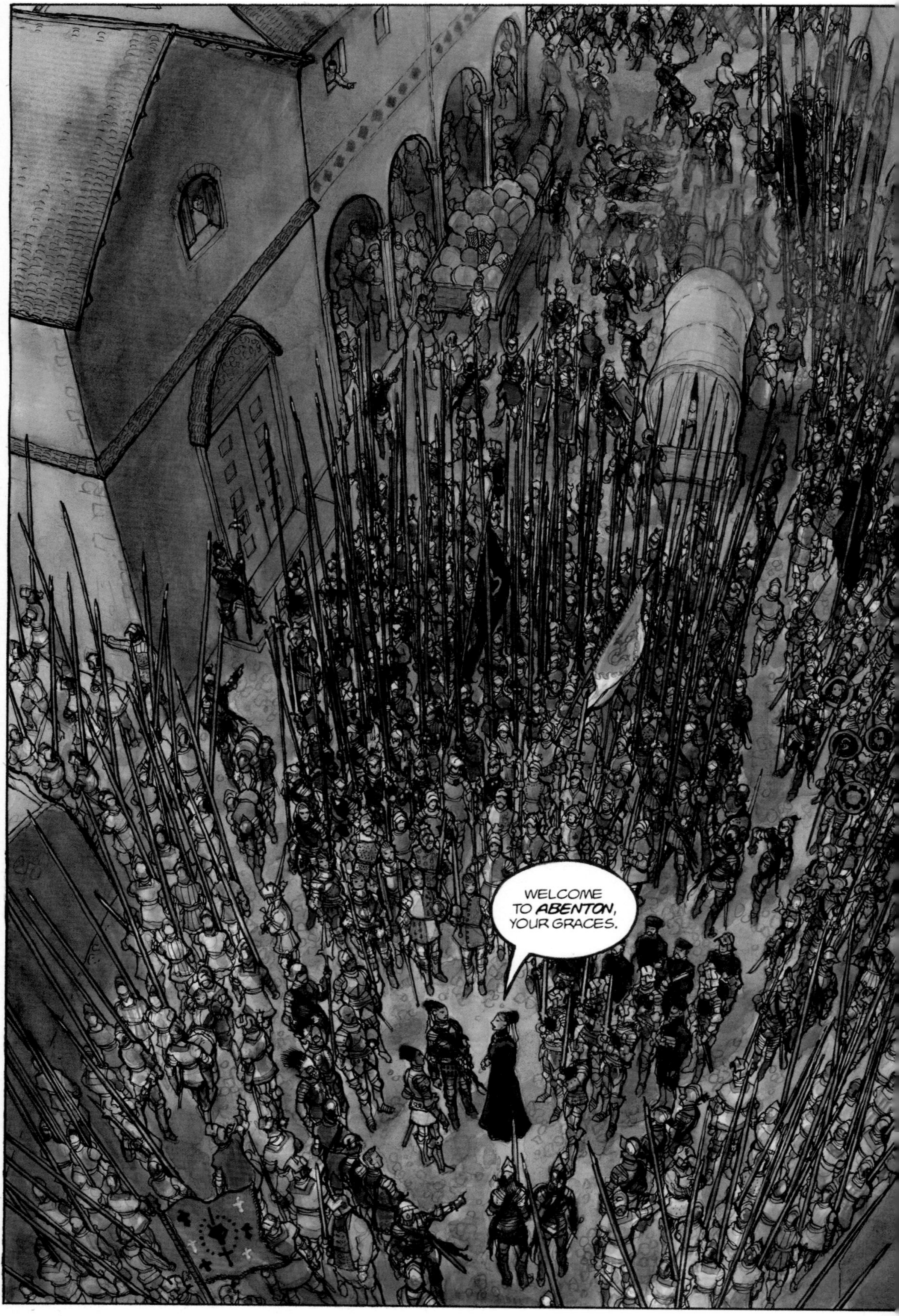
WELCOME TO ABENTON, YOUR GRACES.

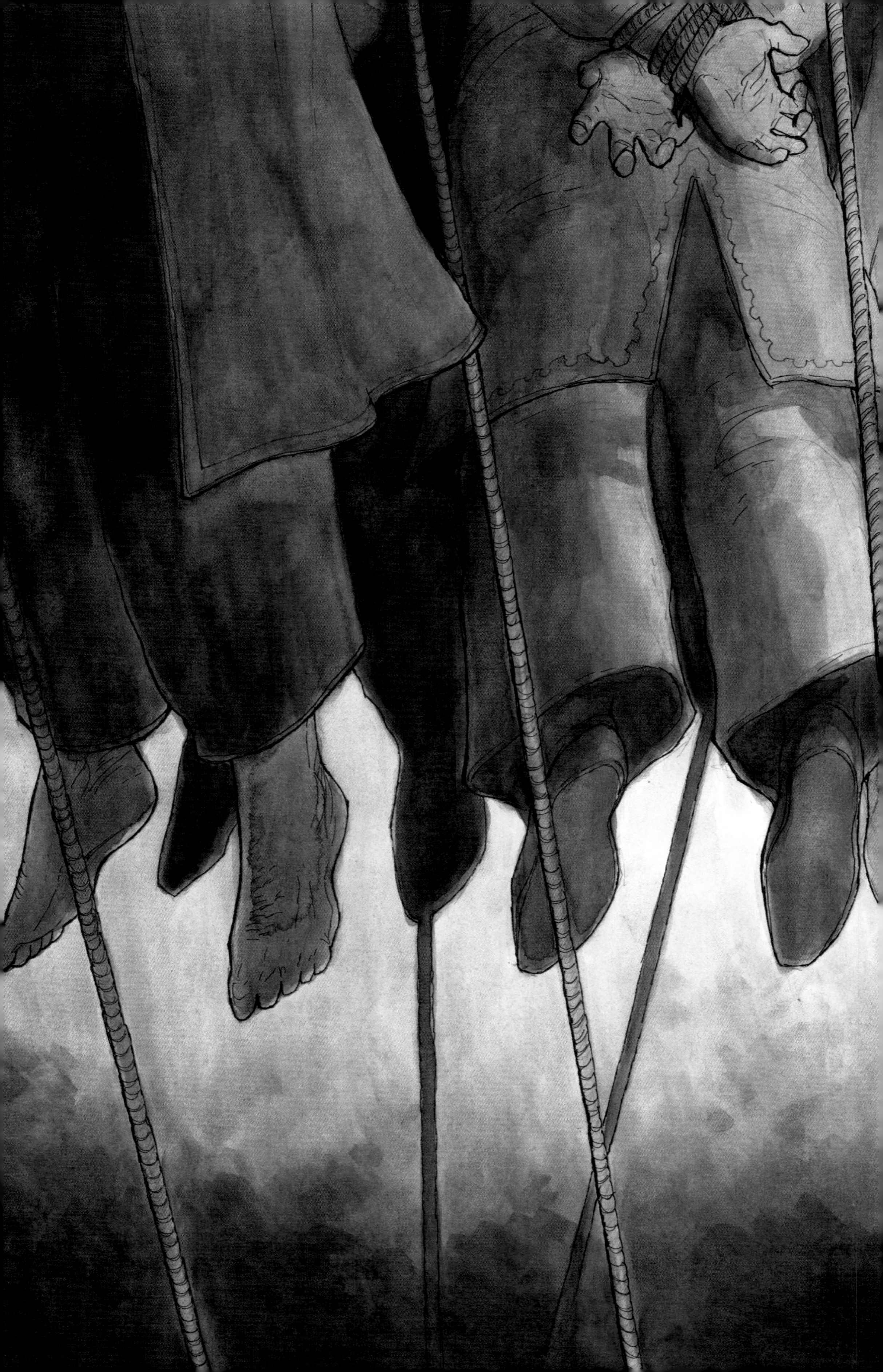

Chapter Six

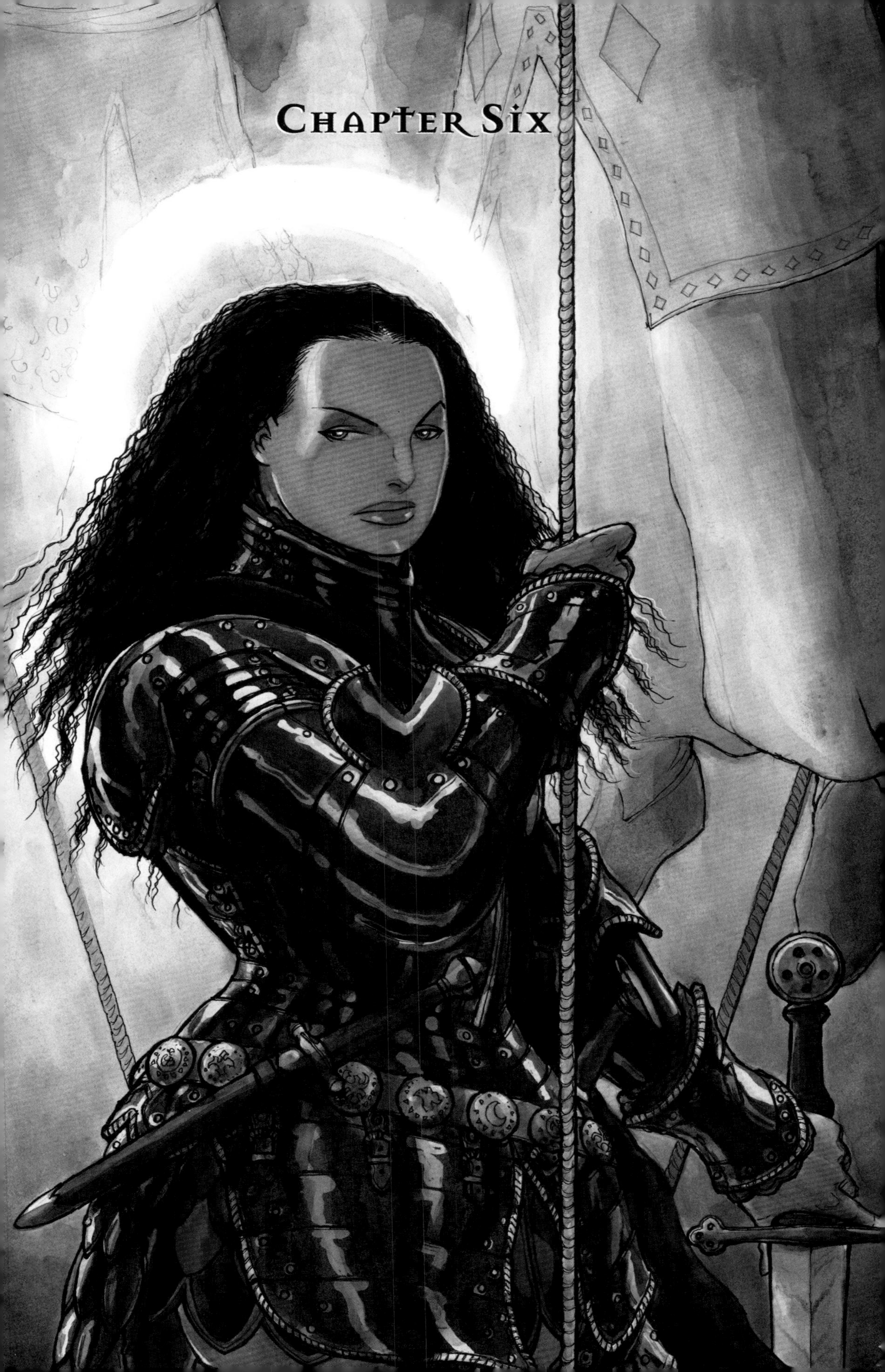

THE STAND

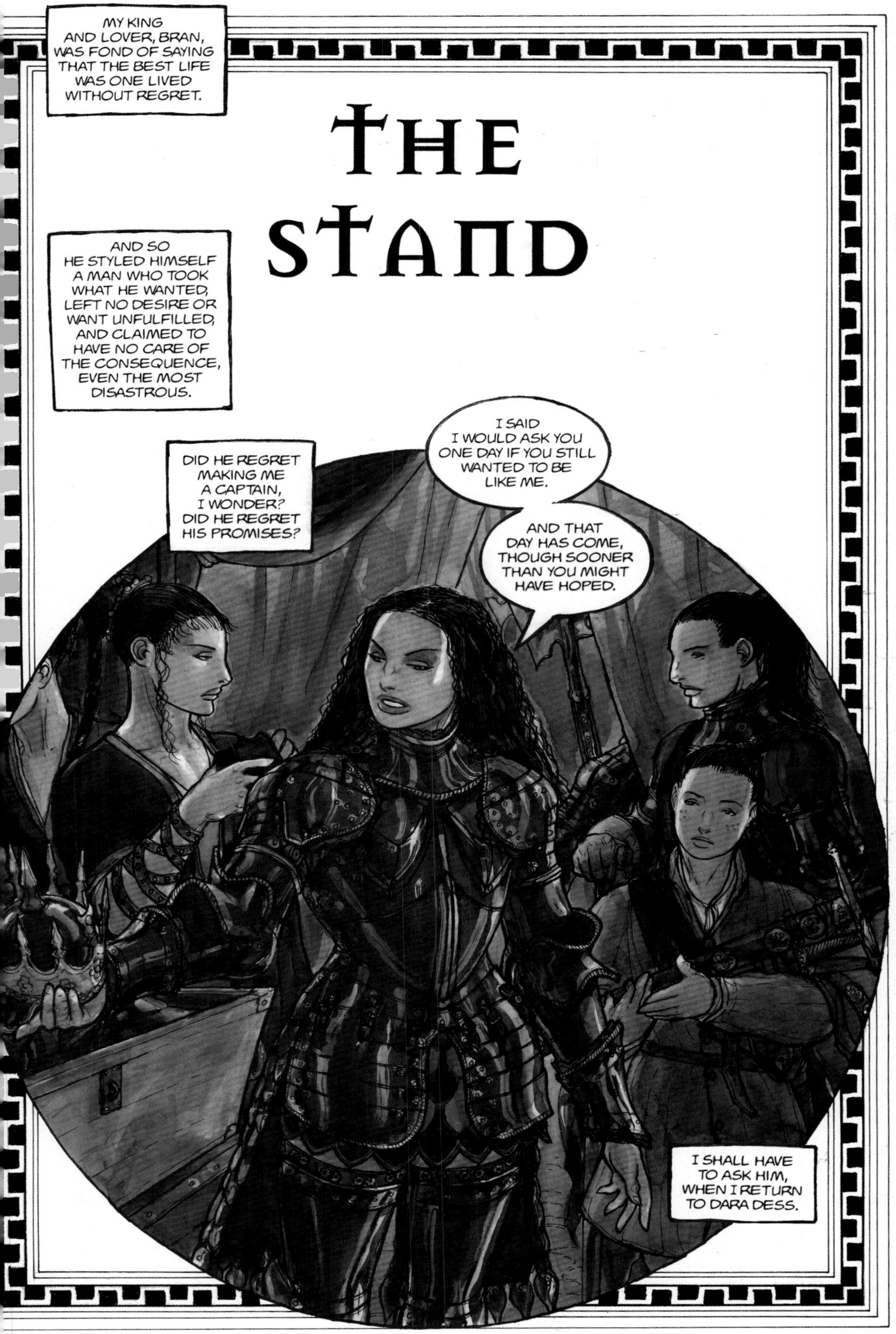
MY KING AND LOVER, BRAN, WAS FOND OF SAYING THAT THE BEST LIFE WAS ONE LIVED WITHOUT REGRET.
AND SO HE STYLED HIMSELF A MAN WHO TOOK WHAT HE WANTED, LEFT NO DESIRE OR WANT UNFULFILLED, AND CLAIMED TO HAVE NO CARE OF THE CONSEQUENCE, EVEN THE MOST DISASTROUS.
DID HE REGRET MAKING ME A CAPTAIN, I WONDER? DID HE REGRET HIS PROMISES?
I SAID I WOULD ASK YOU ONE DAY IF YOU STILL WANTED TO BE LIKE ME.
AND THAT DAY HAS COME, THOUGH SOONER THAN YOU MIGHT HAVE HOPED.
I SHALL HAVE TO ASK HIM, WHEN I RETURN TO DARA DESS.

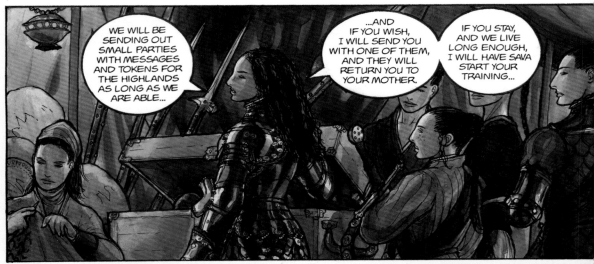

WE WILL BE SENDING OUT SMALL PARTIES WITH MESSAGES AND TOKENS FOR THE HIGHLANDS AS LONG AS WE ARE ABLE...

...AND IF YOU WISH, I WILL SEND YOU WITH ONE OF THEM, AND THEY WILL RETURN YOU TO YOUR MOTHER.

IF YOU STAY, AND WE LIVE LONG ENOUGH, I WILL HAVE SAVA START YOUR TRAINING...

...BUT YOU SHOULD KNOW IN A SIEGE WE WILL ALL FACE A SLOW DEATH MUCH WORSE THAN A FAST ONE.

I'M SCARED.

SO AM I.

SAVA...

SAVA ALREADY STARTED MY TRAINING.

DID SHE NOW?

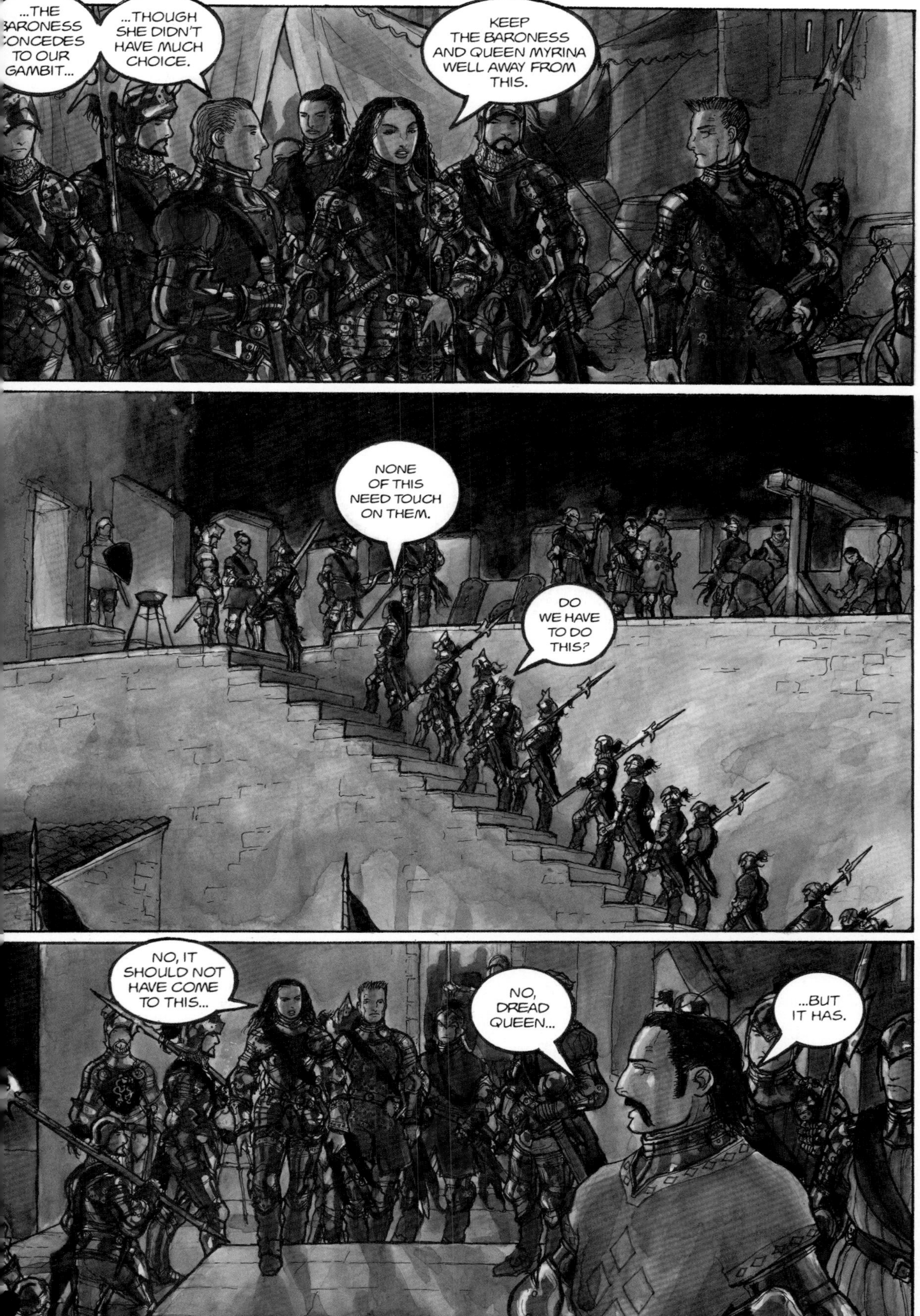
...THE BARONESS CONCEDES TO OUR GAMBIT...
...THOUGH SHE DIDN'T HAVE MUCH CHOICE.
KEEP THE BARONESS AND QUEEN MYRINA WELL AWAY FROM THIS.
NONE OF THIS NEED TOUCH ON THEM.
DO WE HAVE TO DO THIS?
NO, IT SHOULD NOT HAVE COME TO THIS...
NO, DREAD QUEEN...
...BUT IT HAS.

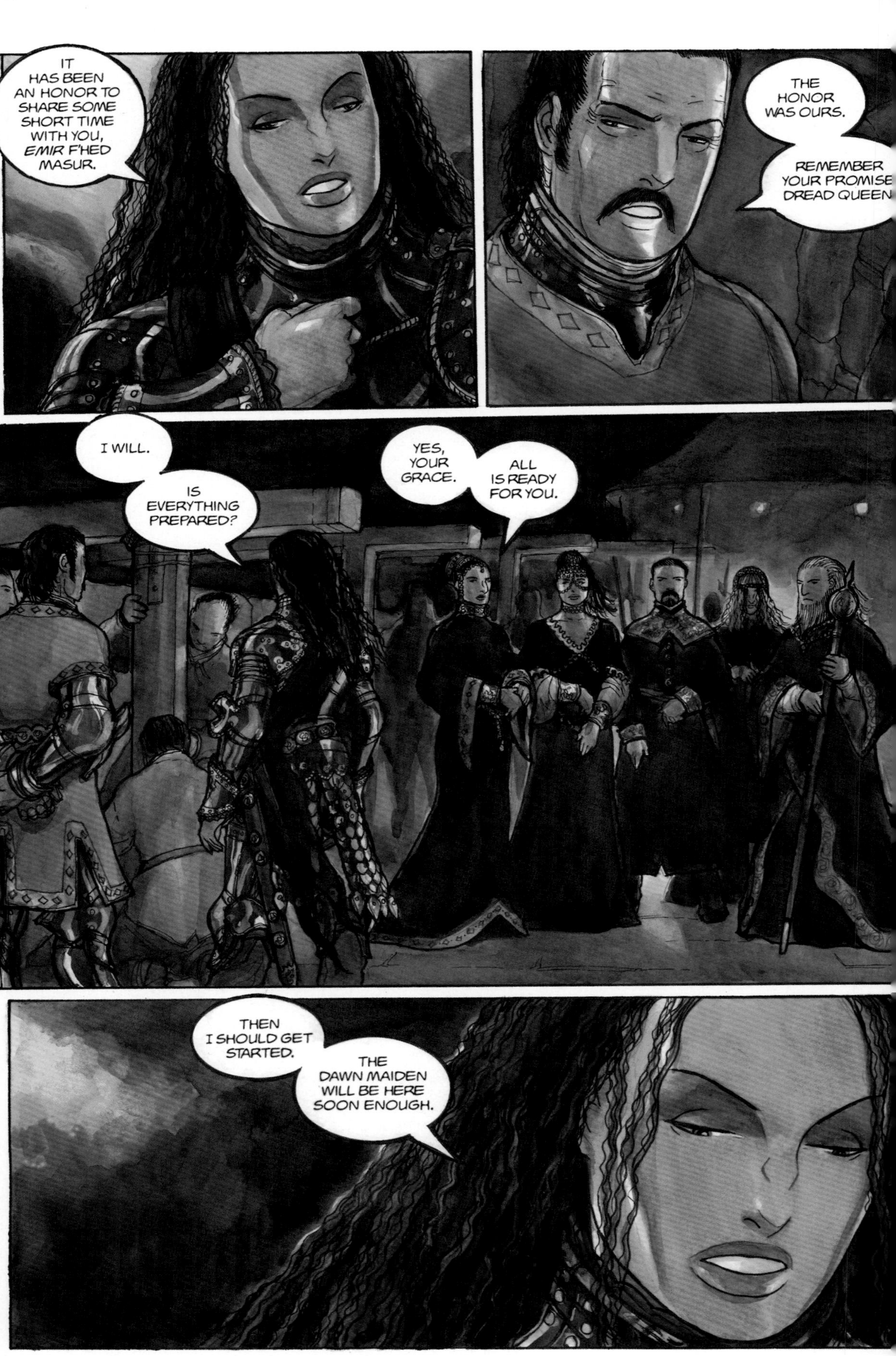
IT HAS BEEN AN HONOR TO SHARE SOME SHORT TIME WITH YOU, *EMIR F'HED MASUR.*
THE HONOR WAS OURS.
REMEMBER YOUR PROMISE DREAD QUEEN
I WILL.
IS EVERYTHING PREPARED?
YES, YOUR GRACE.
ALL IS READY FOR YOU.
THEN I SHOULD GET STARTED.
THE DAWN MAIDEN WILL BE HERE SOON ENOUGH.

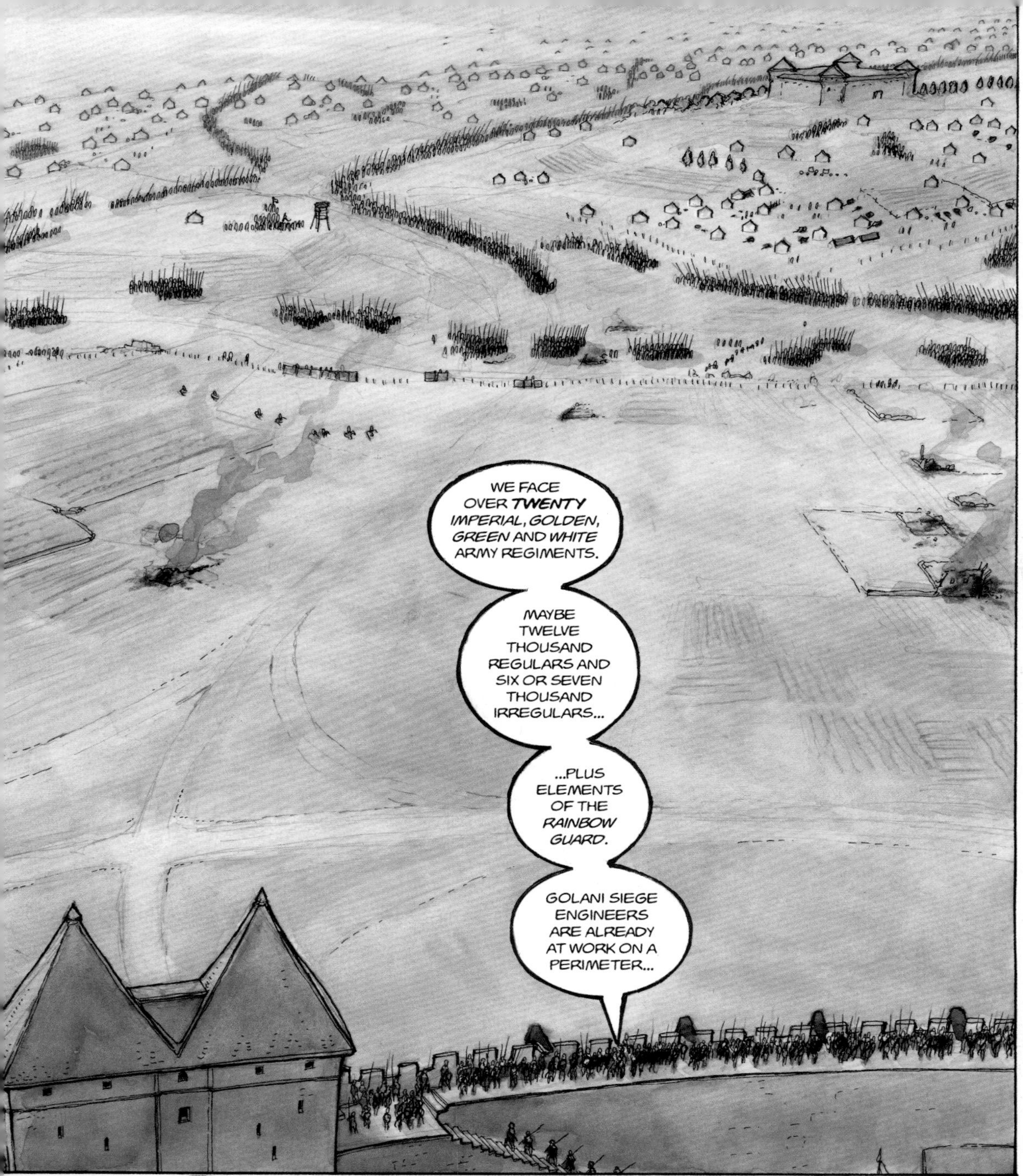
WE FACE OVER TWENTY IMPERIAL, GOLDEN, GREEN AND WHITE ARMY REGIMENTS.
MAYBE TWELVE THOUSAND REGULARS AND SIX OR SEVEN THOUSAND IRREGULARS...
...PLUS ELEMENTS OF THE RAINBOW GUARD.
GOLANI SIEGE ENGINEERS ARE ALREADY AT WORK ON A PERIMETER...

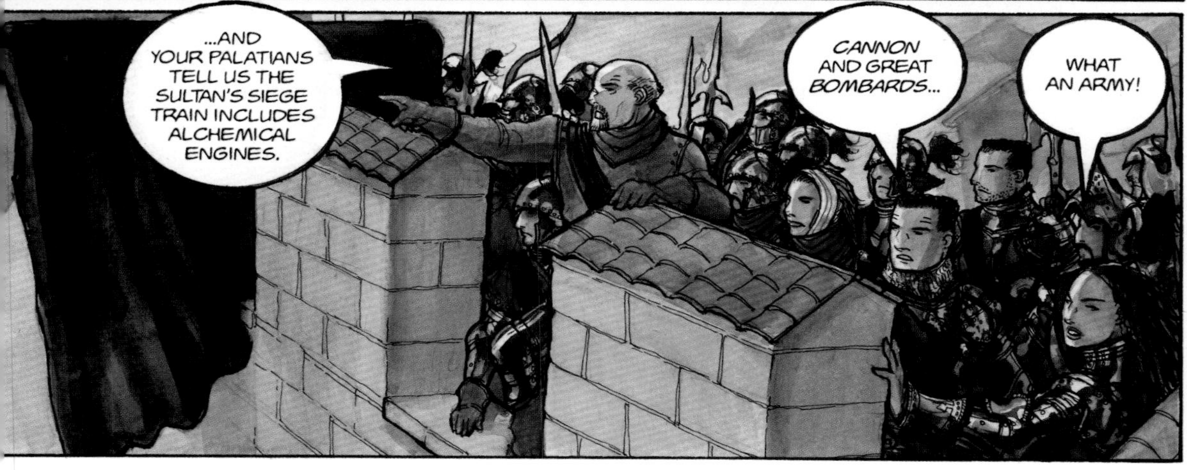
...AND YOUR PALATIANS TELL US THE SULTAN'S SIEGE TRAIN INCLUDES ALCHEMICAL ENGINES.
CANNON AND GREAT BOMBARDS...
WHAT AN ARMY!

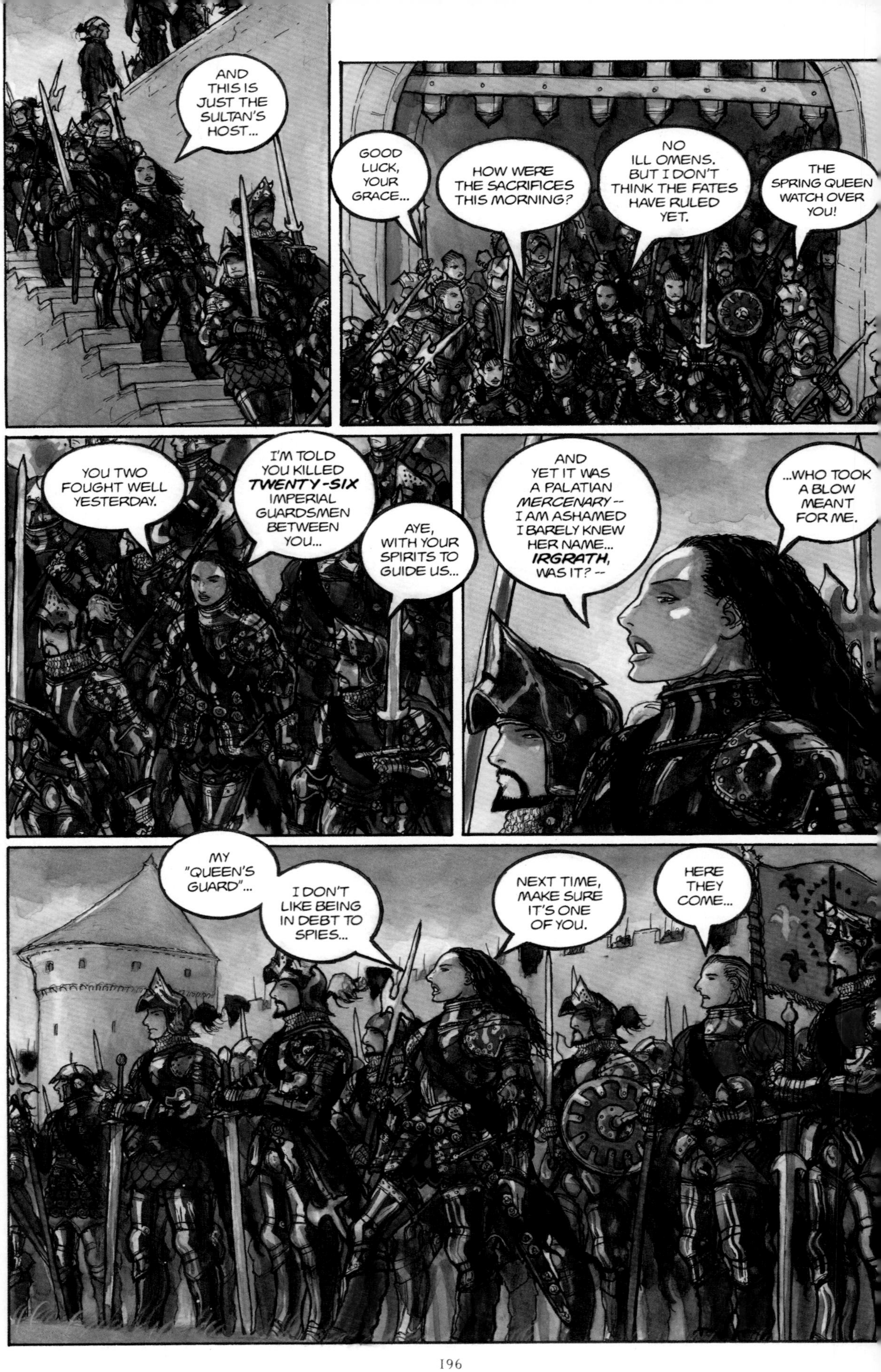
AND THIS IS JUST THE SULTAN'S HOST...
GOOD LUCK, YOUR GRACE...
HOW WERE THE SACRIFICES THIS MORNING?
NO ILL OMENS. BUT I DON'T THINK THE FATES HAVE RULED YET.
THE SPRING QUEEN WATCH OVER YOU!
YOU TWO FOUGHT WELL YESTERDAY.
I'M TOLD YOU KILLED **TWENTY-SIX** IMPERIAL GUARDSMEN BETWEEN YOU...
AYE, WITH YOUR SPIRITS TO GUIDE US...
AND YET IT WAS A PALATIAN *MERCENARY* -- I AM ASHAMED I BARELY KNEW HER NAME... ***IRGRATH***, WAS IT? --
...WHO TOOK A BLOW MEANT FOR ME.
MY "QUEEN'S GUARD"...
I DON'T LIKE BEING IN DEBT TO SPIES...
NEXT TIME, MAKE SURE IT'S ONE OF YOU.
HERE THEY COME...

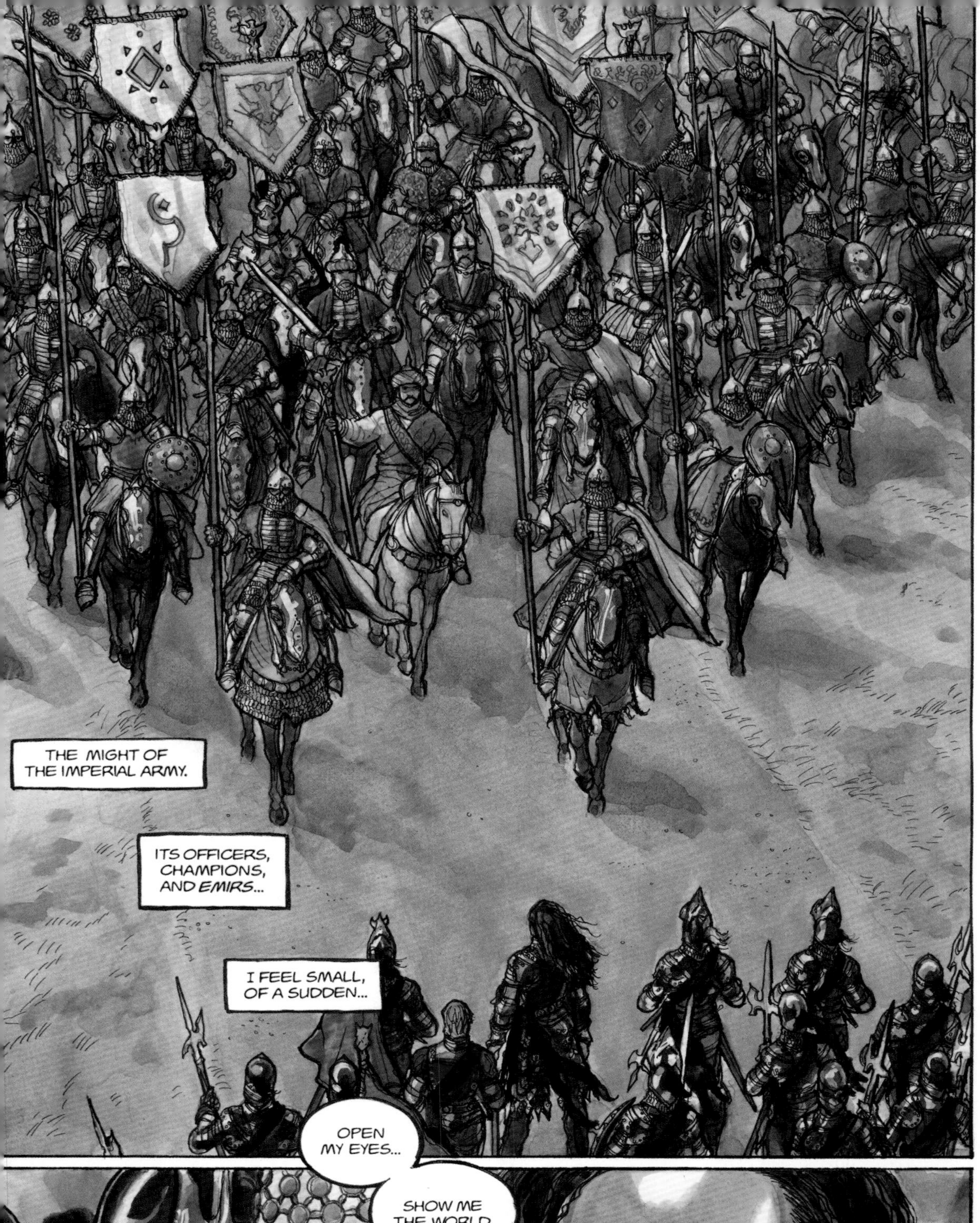
THE MIGHT OF
THE IMPERIAL ARMY.
ITS OFFICERS,
CHAMPIONS,
AND EMIRS...
I FEEL SMALL,
OF A SUDDEN...

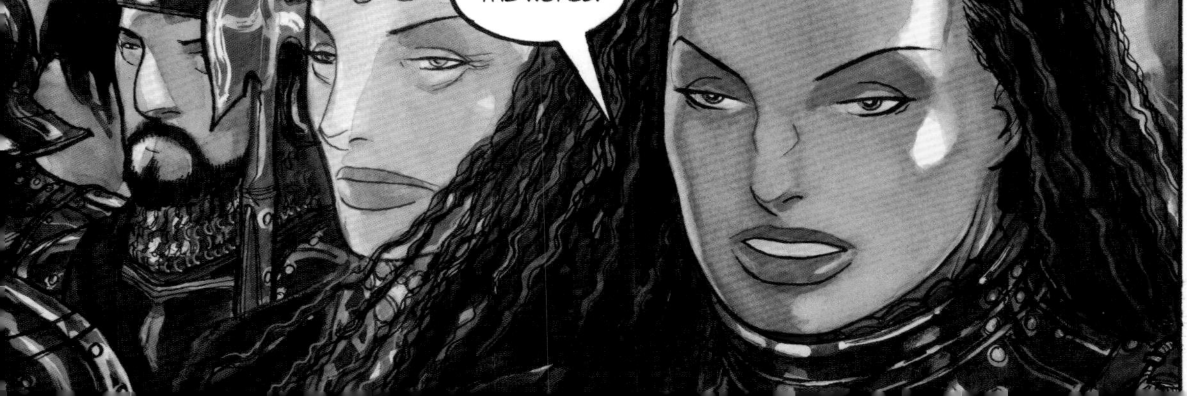
OPEN
MY EYES...
SHOW ME
THE WORLD.

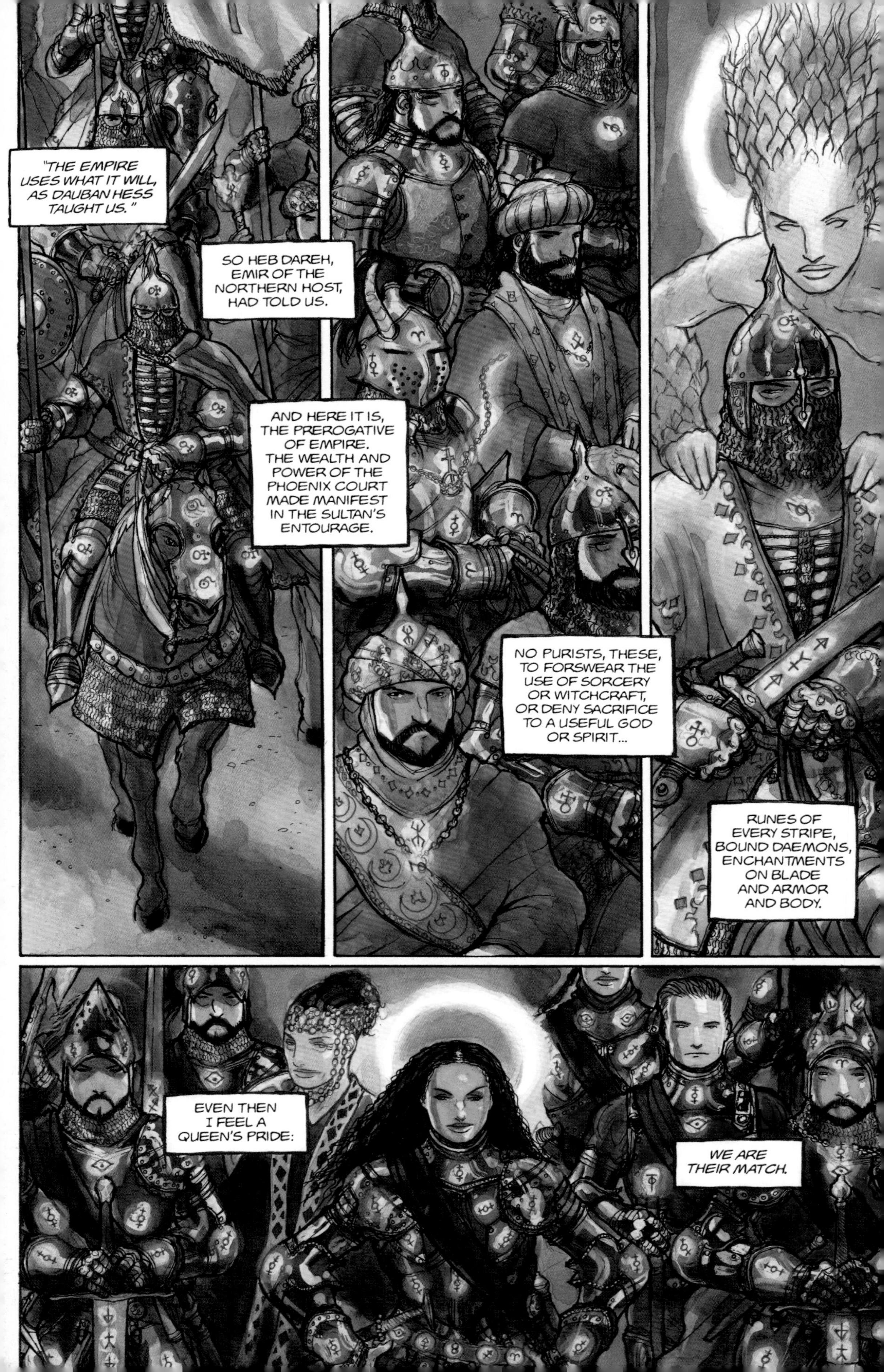
"THE EMPIRE USES WHAT IT WILL, AS DAUBAN HESS TAUGHT US."
SO HEB DAREH, EMIR OF THE NORTHERN HOST, HAD TOLD US.
AND HERE IT IS, THE PREROGATIVE OF EMPIRE. THE WEALTH AND POWER OF THE PHOENIX COURT MADE MANIFEST IN THE SULTAN'S ENTOURAGE.
NO PURISTS, THESE, TO FORSWEAR THE USE OF SORCERY OR WITCHCRAFT, OR DENY SACRIFICE TO A USEFUL GOD OR SPIRIT...
RUNES OF EVERY STRIPE, BOUND DAEMONS, ENCHANTMENTS ON BLADE AND ARMOR AND BODY.
EVEN THEN I FEEL A QUEEN'S PRIDE:
WE ARE THEIR MATCH.

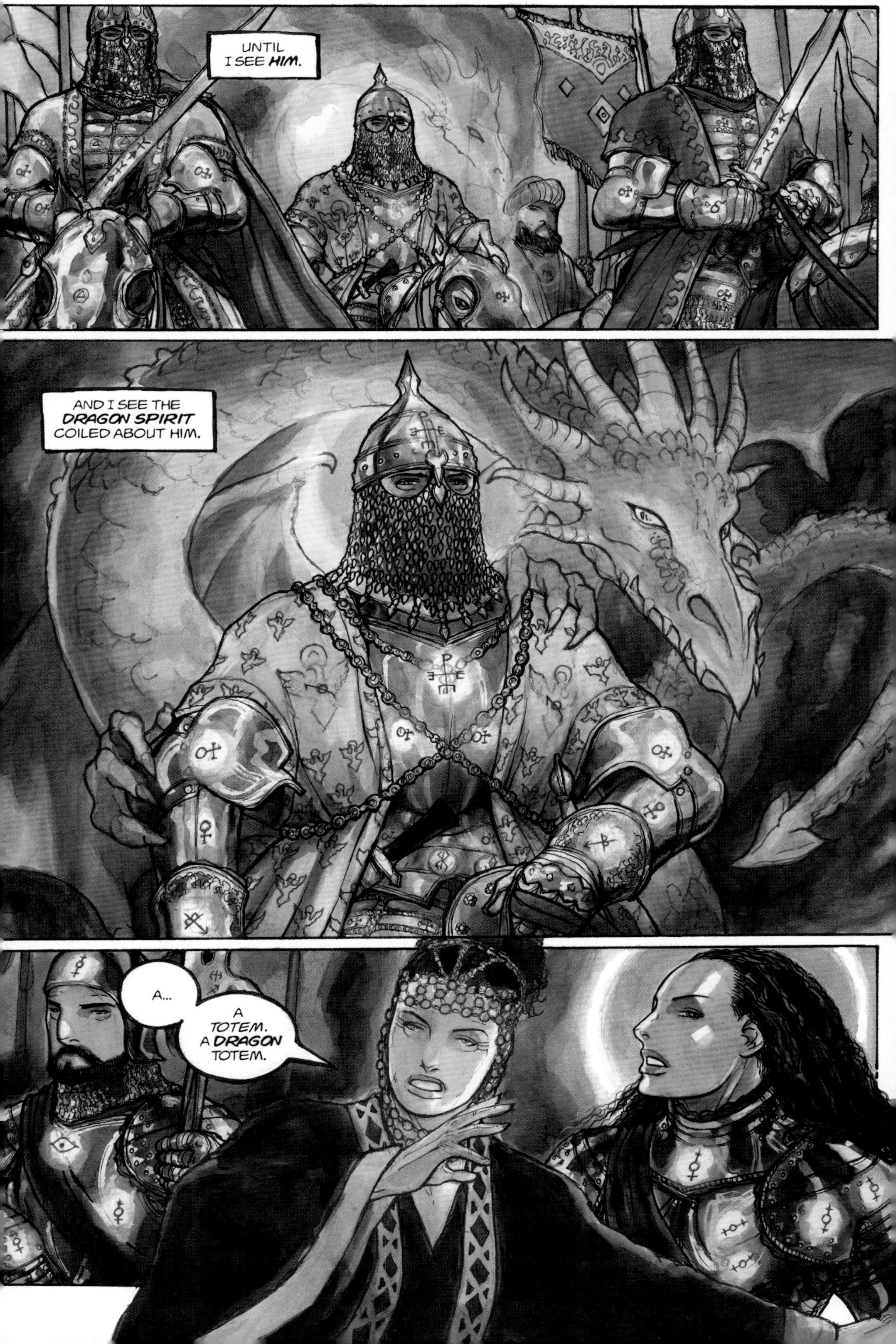
UNTIL I SEE ***HIM***.
AND I SEE THE ***DRAGON SPIRIT*** COILED ABOUT HIM.
A...
A *TOTEM*. A ***DRAGON*** TOTEM.

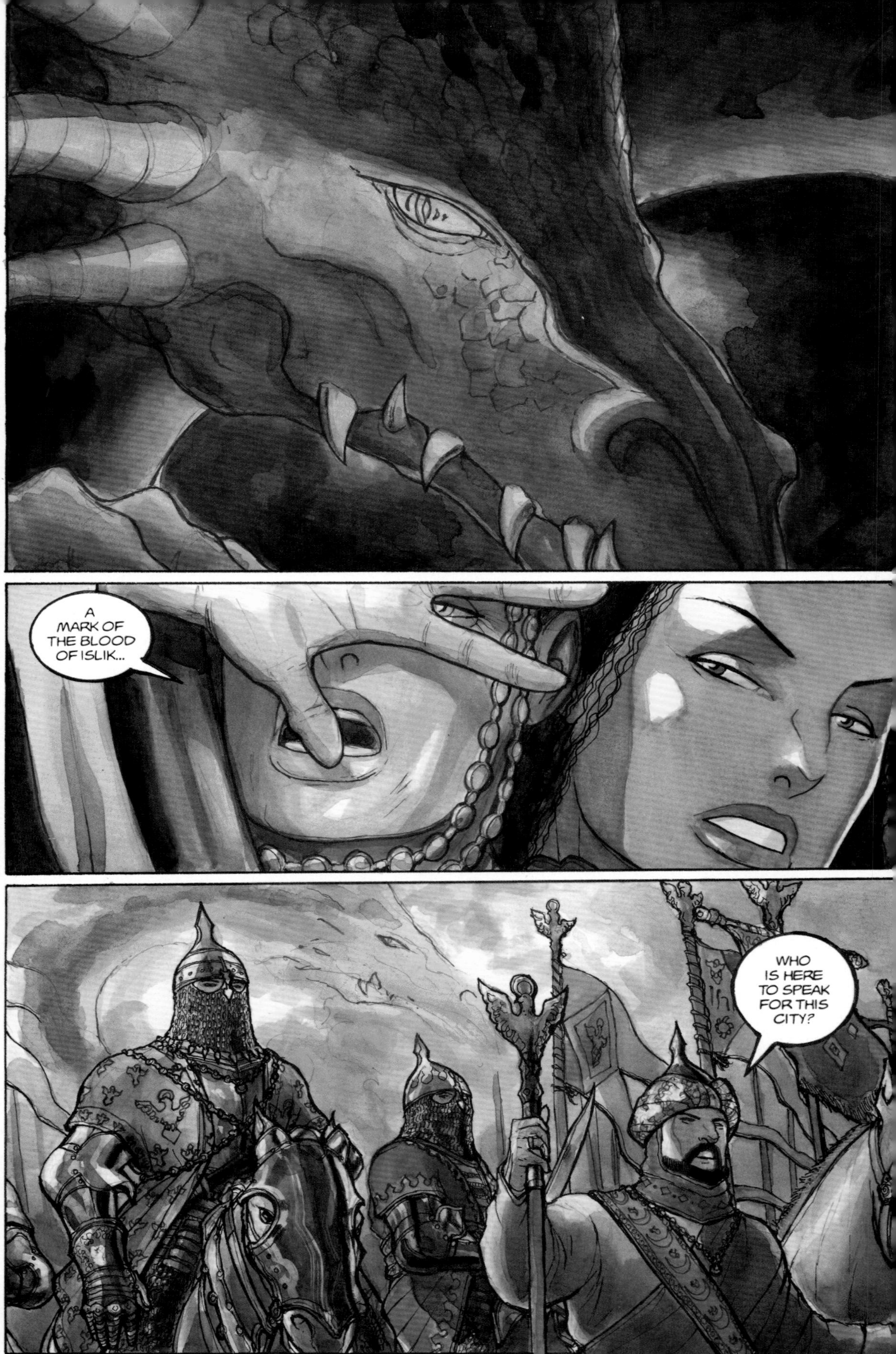
A MARK OF THE BLOOD OF ISLIK...
WHO IS HERE TO SPEAK FOR THIS CITY?

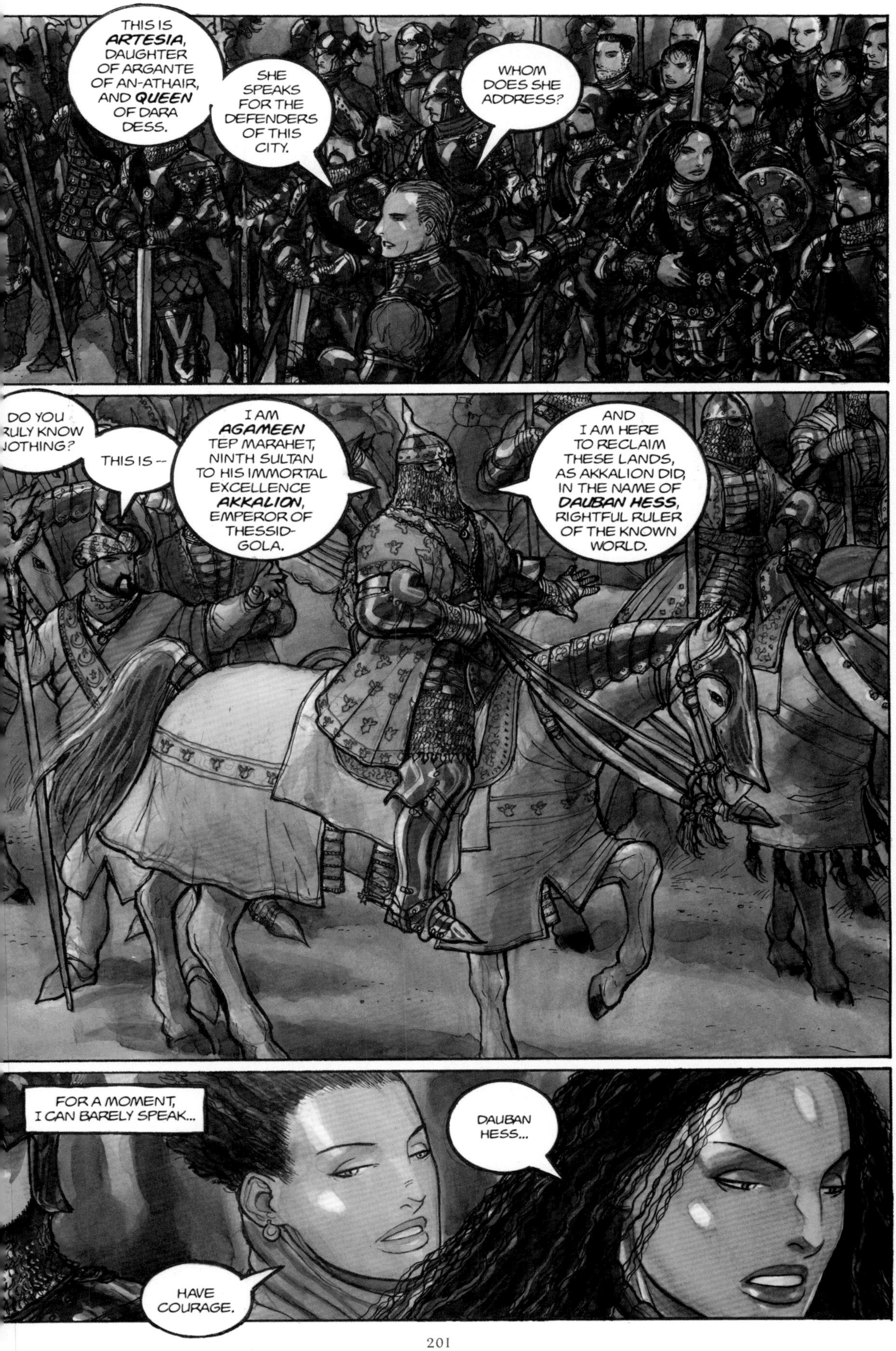

THIS IS ARTESIA, DAUGHTER OF ARGANTE OF AN-ATHAIR, AND QUEEN OF DARA DESS.
SHE SPEAKS FOR THE DEFENDERS OF THIS CITY.
WHOM DOES SHE ADDRESS?
DO YOU TRULY KNOW NOTHING?
THIS IS --
I AM AGAMEEN TEP MARAHET, NINTH SULTAN TO HIS IMMORTAL EXCELLENCE AKKALION, EMPEROR OF THESSID-GOLA.
AND I AM HERE TO RECLAIM THESE LANDS, AS AKKALION DID, IN THE NAME OF DAUBAN HESS, RIGHTFUL RULER OF THE KNOWN WORLD.
FOR A MOMENT, I CAN BARELY SPEAK...
DAUBAN HESS...
HAVE COURAGE.

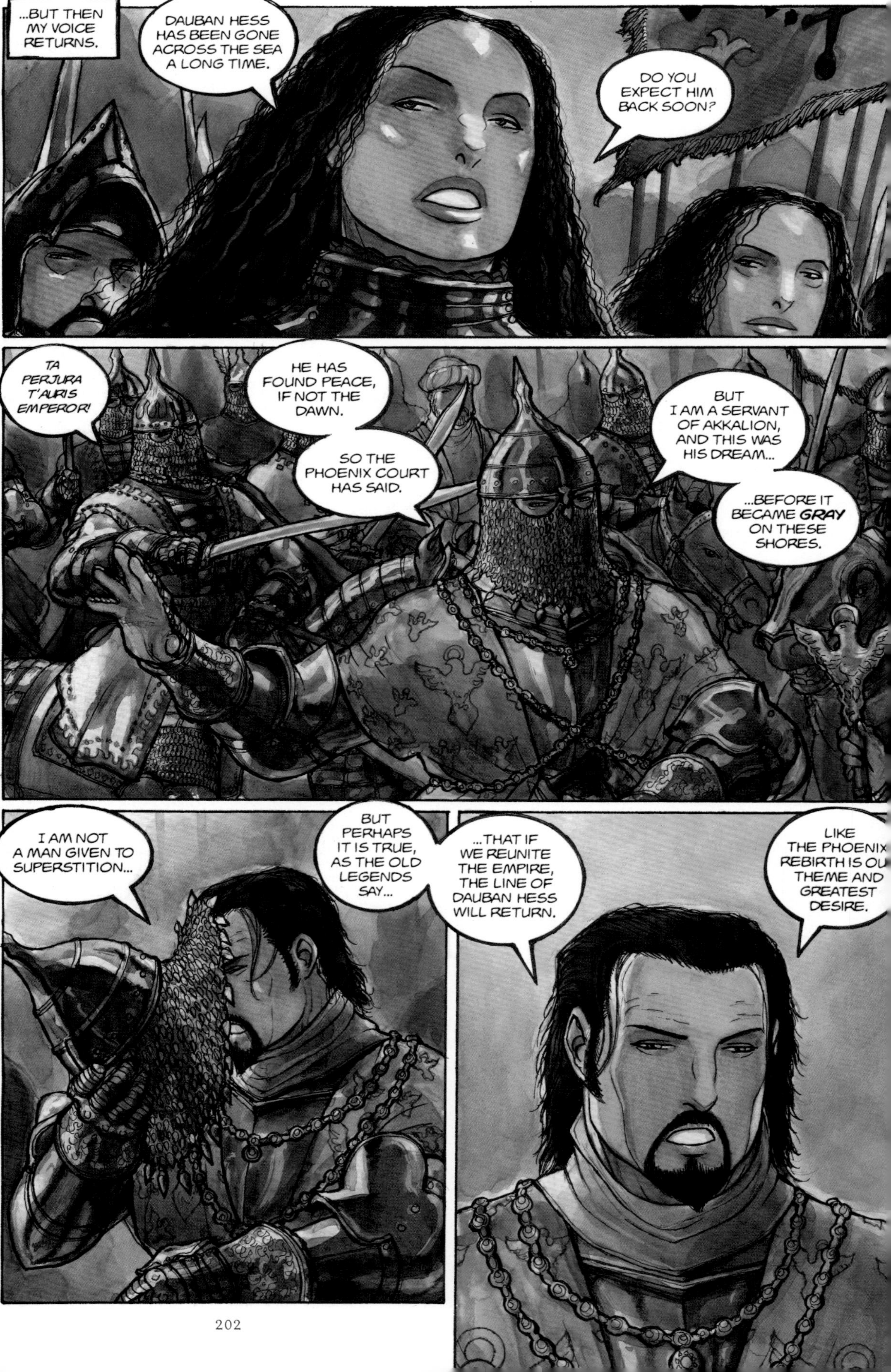
...BUT THEN MY VOICE RETURNS.
DAUBAN HESS HAS BEEN GONE ACROSS THE SEA A LONG TIME.
DO YOU EXPECT HIM BACK SOON?
TA PERJURA T'AURIS EMPEROR!
HE HAS FOUND PEACE, IF NOT THE DAWN.
SO THE PHOENIX COURT HAS SAID.
BUT I AM A SERVANT OF AKKALION, AND THIS WAS HIS DREAM...
...BEFORE IT BECAME GRAY ON THESE SHORES.
I AM NOT A MAN GIVEN TO SUPERSTITION...
BUT PERHAPS IT IS TRUE, AS THE OLD LEGENDS SAY...
...THAT IF WE REUNITE THE EMPIRE, THE LINE OF DAUBAN HESS WILL RETURN.
LIKE THE PHOENIX REBIRTH IS OU THEME AND GREATEST DESIRE.

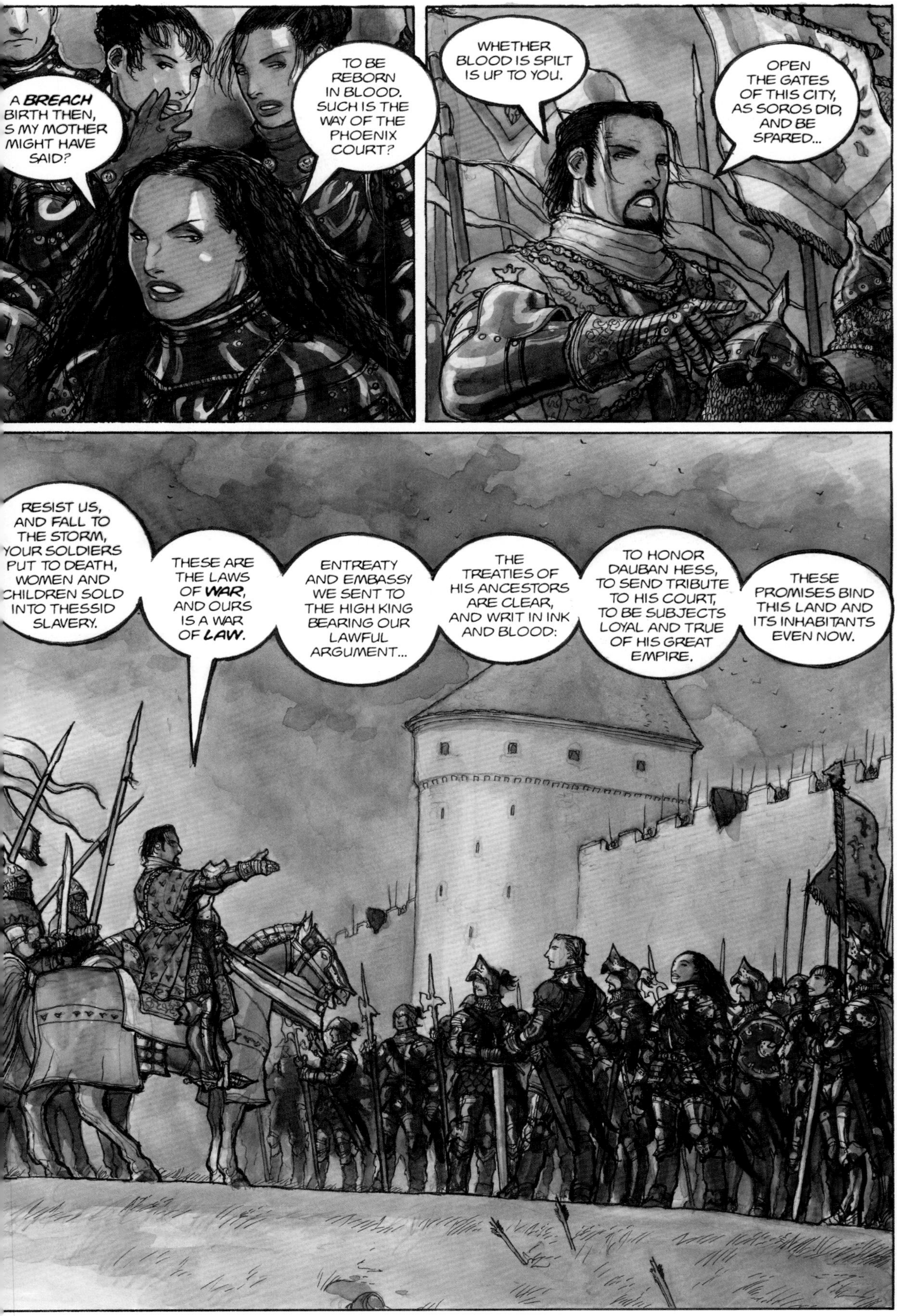
A BREACH BIRTH THEN, S MY MOTHER MIGHT HAVE SAID?
TO BE REBORN IN BLOOD. SUCH IS THE WAY OF THE PHOENIX COURT?
WHETHER BLOOD IS SPILT IS UP TO YOU.
OPEN THE GATES OF THIS CITY, AS SOROS DID, AND BE SPARED...
RESIST US, AND FALL TO THE STORM, YOUR SOLDIERS PUT TO DEATH, WOMEN AND CHILDREN SOLD INTO THESSID SLAVERY.
THESE ARE THE LAWS OF WAR, AND OURS IS A WAR OF LAW.
ENTREATY AND EMBASSY WE SENT TO THE HIGH KING BEARING OUR LAWFUL ARGUMENT...
THE TREATIES OF HIS ANCESTORS ARE CLEAR, AND WRIT IN INK AND BLOOD:
TO HONOR DAUBAN HESS, TO SEND TRIBUTE TO HIS COURT, TO BE SUBJECTS LOYAL AND TRUE OF HIS GREAT EMPIRE.
THESE PROMISES BIND THIS LAND AND ITS INHABITANTS EVEN NOW.

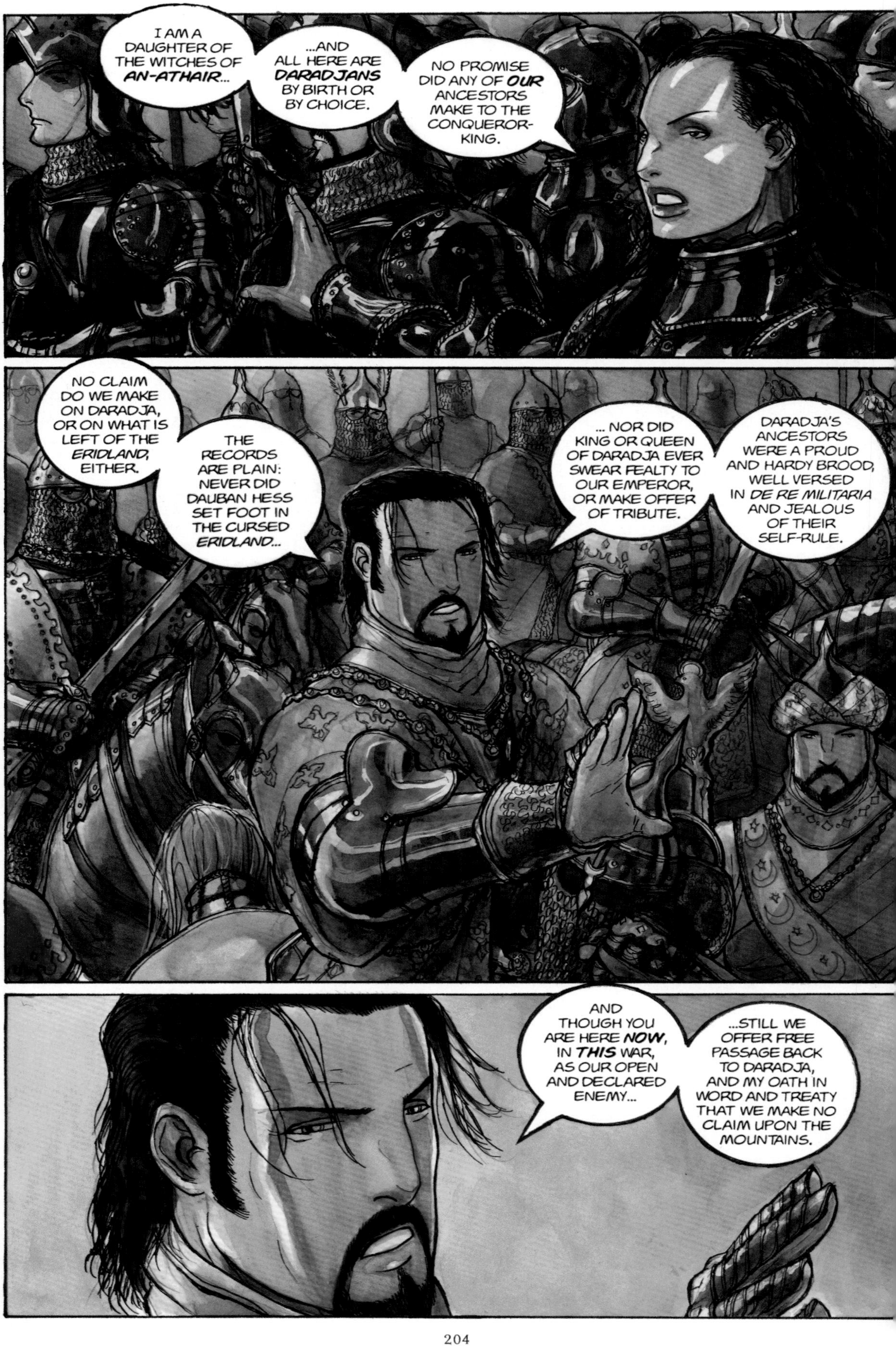
I AM A DAUGHTER OF THE WITCHES OF AN-ATHAIR...
...AND ALL HERE ARE DARADJANS BY BIRTH OR BY CHOICE.
NO PROMISE DID ANY OF OUR ANCESTORS MAKE TO THE CONQUEROR-KING.
NO CLAIM DO WE MAKE ON DARADJA, OR ON WHAT IS LEFT OF THE ERIDLAND, EITHER.
THE RECORDS ARE PLAIN: NEVER DID DAUBAN HESS SET FOOT IN THE CURSED ERIDLAND...
... NOR DID KING OR QUEEN OF DARADJA EVER SWEAR FEALTY TO OUR EMPEROR, OR MAKE OFFER OF TRIBUTE.
DARADJA'S ANCESTORS WERE A PROUD AND HARDY BROOD, WELL VERSED IN DE RE MILITARIA AND JEALOUS OF THEIR SELF-RULE.
AND THOUGH YOU ARE HERE NOW, IN THIS WAR, AS OUR OPEN AND DECLARED ENEMY...
...STILL WE OFFER FREE PASSAGE BACK TO DARADJA, AND MY OATH IN WORD AND TREATY THAT WE MAKE NO CLAIM UPON THE MOUNTAINS.

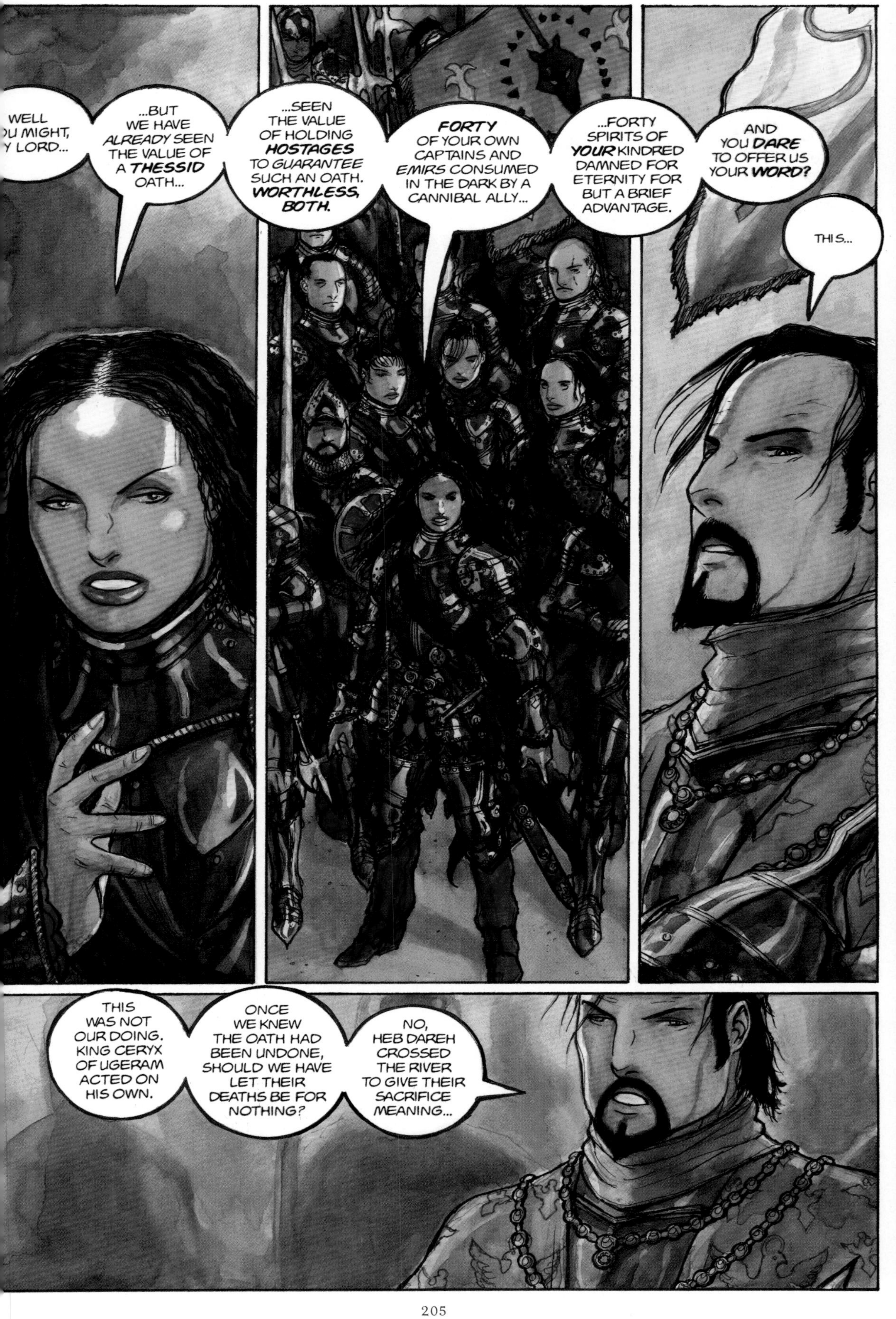
WELL ...OU MIGHT, ...Y LORD...
...BUT WE HAVE ALREADY SEEN THE VALUE OF A THESSID OATH...
...SEEN THE VALUE OF HOLDING HOSTAGES TO GUARANTEE SUCH AN OATH. WORTHLESS, BOTH.
FORTY OF YOUR OWN CAPTAINS AND EMIRS CONSUMED IN THE DARK BY A CANNIBAL ALLY...
...FORTY SPIRITS OF YOUR KINDRED DAMNED FOR ETERNITY FOR BUT A BRIEF ADVANTAGE.
AND YOU DARE TO OFFER US YOUR WORD?
THIS...
THIS WAS NOT OUR DOING. KING CERYX OF UGERAM ACTED ON HIS OWN.
ONCE WE KNEW THE OATH HAD BEEN UNDONE, SHOULD WE HAVE LET THEIR DEATHS BE FOR NOTHING?
NO, HEB DAREH CROSSED THE RIVER TO GIVE THEIR SACRIFICE MEANING...

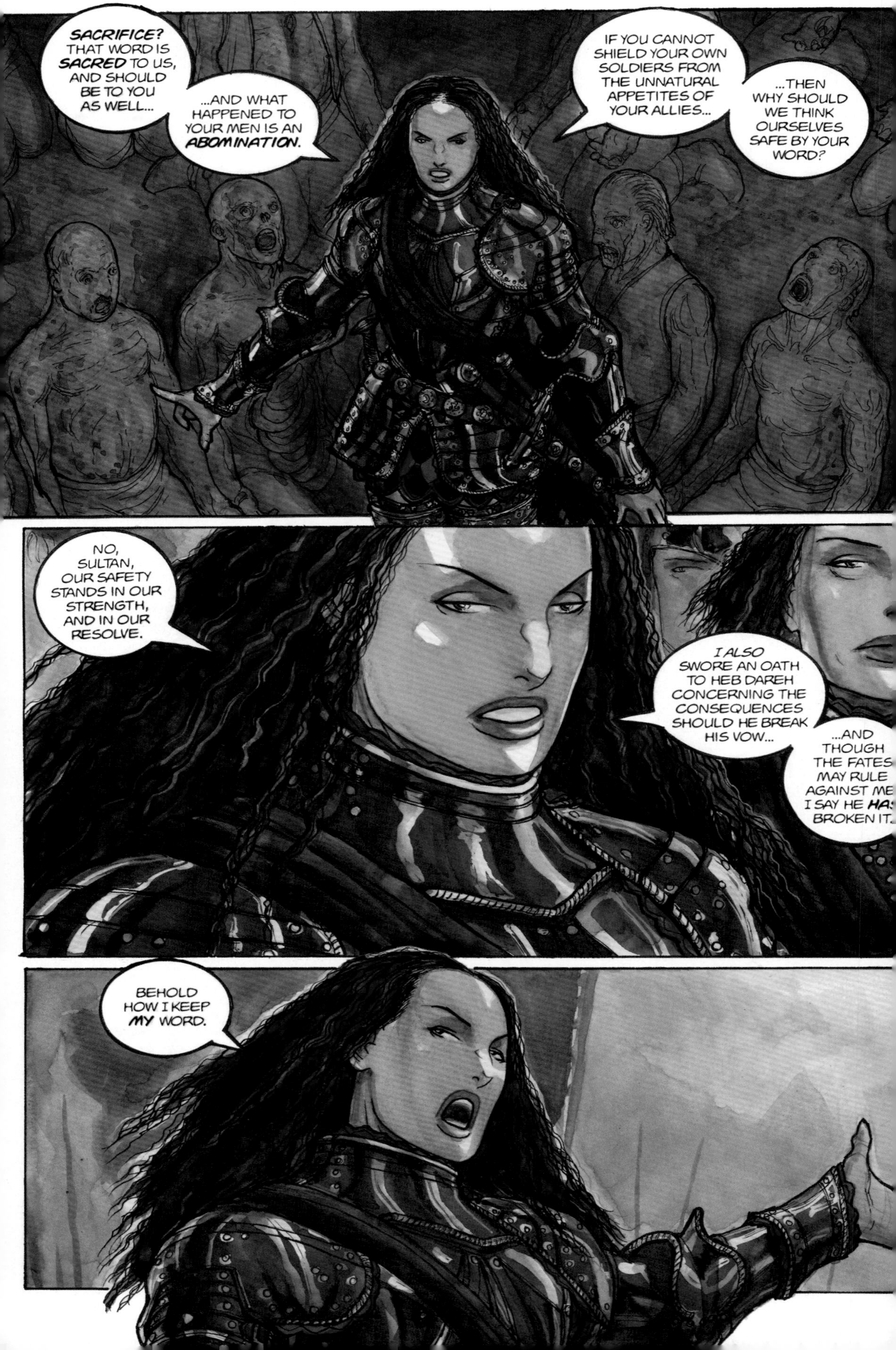
SACRIFICE? THAT WORD IS SACRED TO US, AND SHOULD BE TO YOU AS WELL...
...AND WHAT HAPPENED TO YOUR MEN IS AN ABOMINATION.
IF YOU CANNOT SHIELD YOUR OWN SOLDIERS FROM THE UNNATURAL APPETITES OF YOUR ALLIES...
...THEN WHY SHOULD WE THINK OURSELVES SAFE BY YOUR WORD?
NO, SULTAN, OUR SAFETY STANDS IN OUR STRENGTH, AND IN OUR RESOLVE.
I ALSO SWORE AN OATH TO HEB DAREH CONCERNING THE CONSEQUENCES SHOULD HE BREAK HIS VOW...
...AND THOUGH THE FATES MAY RULE AGAINST ME I SAY HE HAS BROKEN IT.
BEHOLD HOW I KEEP MY WORD.

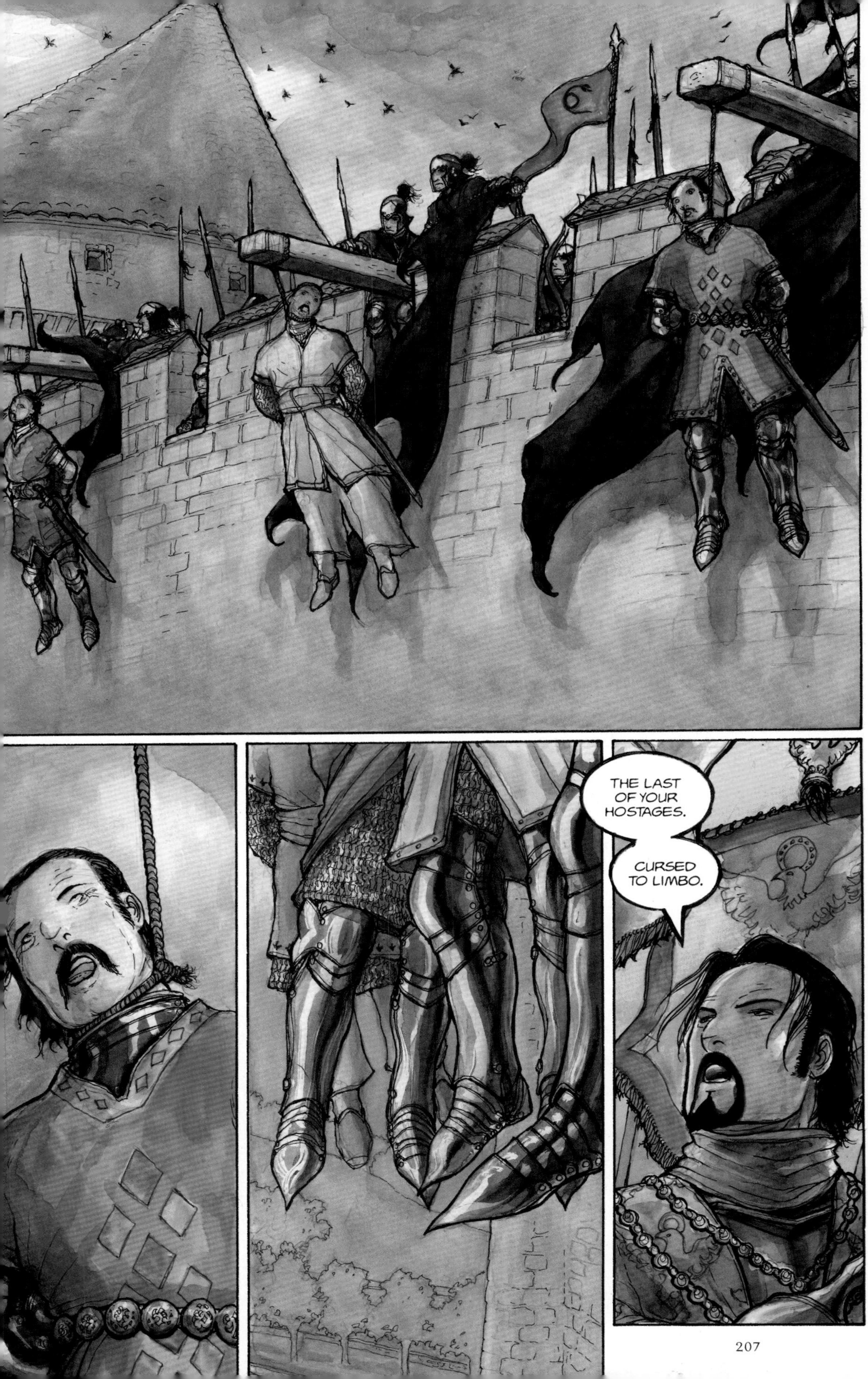
THE LAST OF YOUR HOSTAGES.
CURSED TO LIMBO.

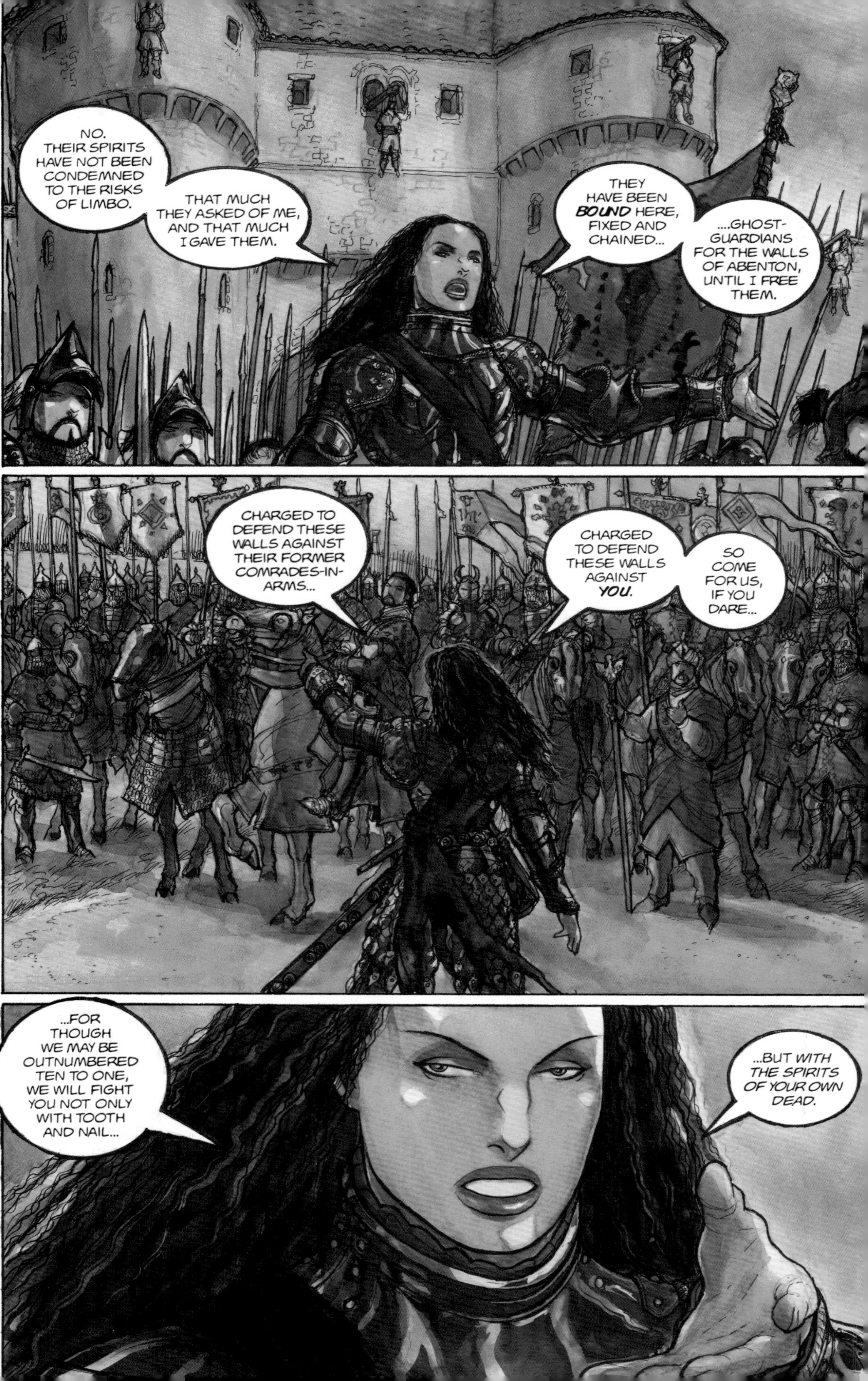
NO. THEIR SPIRITS HAVE NOT BEEN CONDEMNED TO THE RISKS OF LIMBO.
THAT MUCH THEY ASKED OF ME, AND THAT MUCH I GAVE THEM.
THEY HAVE BEEN BOUND HERE, FIXED AND CHAINED...
....GHOST-GUARDIANS FOR THE WALLS OF ABENTON, UNTIL I FREE THEM.
CHARGED TO DEFEND THESE WALLS AGAINST THEIR FORMER COMRADES-IN-ARMS...
CHARGED TO DEFEND THESE WALLS AGAINST YOU.
SO COME FOR US, IF YOU DARE...
...FOR THOUGH WE MAY BE OUTNUMBERED TEN TO ONE, WE WILL FIGHT YOU NOT ONLY WITH TOOTH AND NAIL...
...BUT WITH THE SPIRITS OF YOUR OWN DEAD.

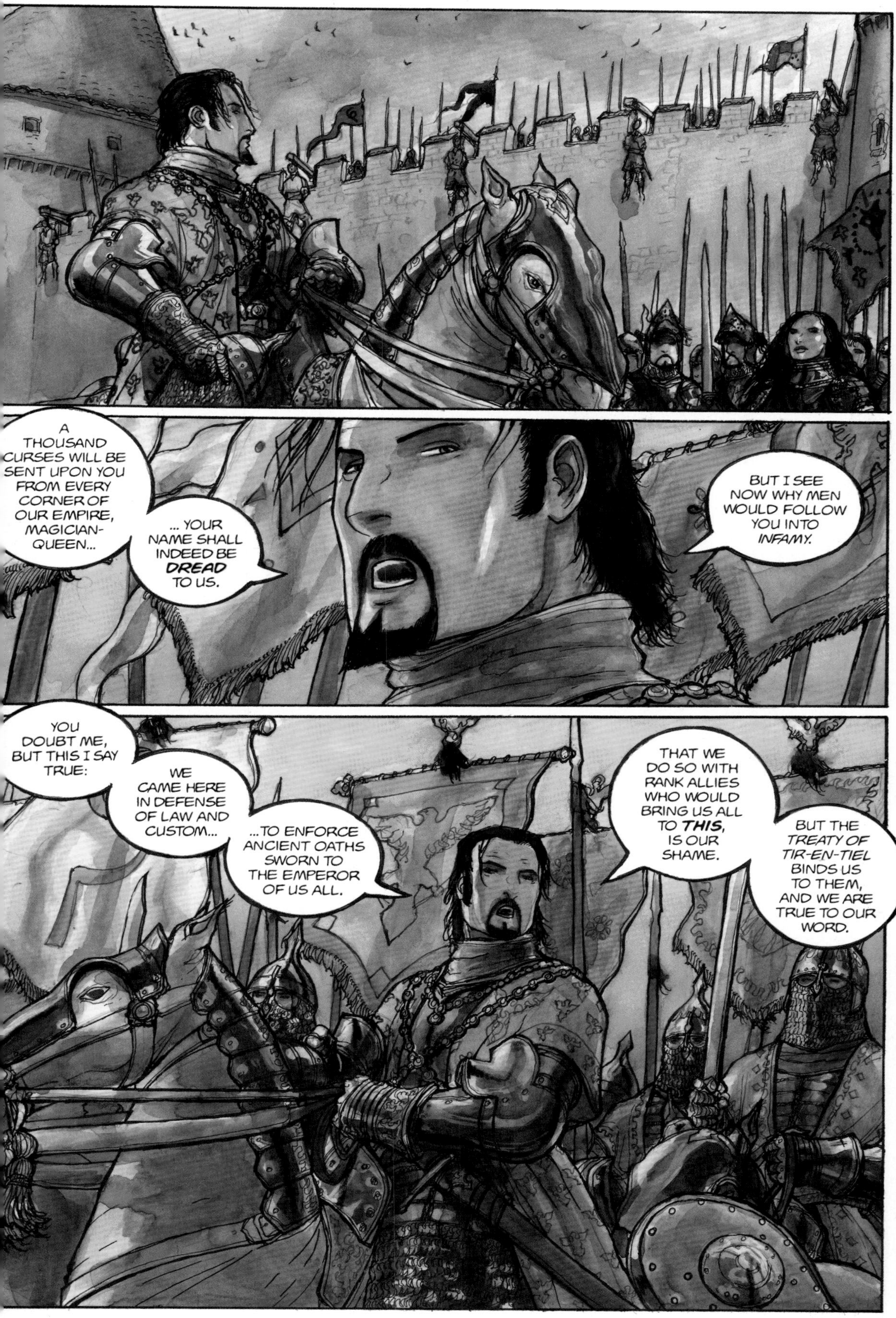
A THOUSAND CURSES WILL BE SENT UPON YOU FROM EVERY CORNER OF OUR EMPIRE, MAGICIAN-QUEEN...
... YOUR NAME SHALL INDEED BE *DREAD* TO US.
BUT I SEE NOW WHY MEN WOULD FOLLOW YOU INTO *INFAMY*.
YOU DOUBT ME, BUT THIS I SAY TRUE:
WE CAME HERE IN DEFENSE OF LAW AND CUSTOM...
...TO ENFORCE ANCIENT OATHS SWORN TO THE EMPEROR OF US ALL.
THAT WE DO SO WITH RANK ALLIES WHO WOULD BRING US ALL TO ***THIS***, IS OUR SHAME.
BUT THE *TREATY OF TIR-EN-TIEL* BINDS US TO THEM, AND WE ARE TRUE TO OUR WORD.

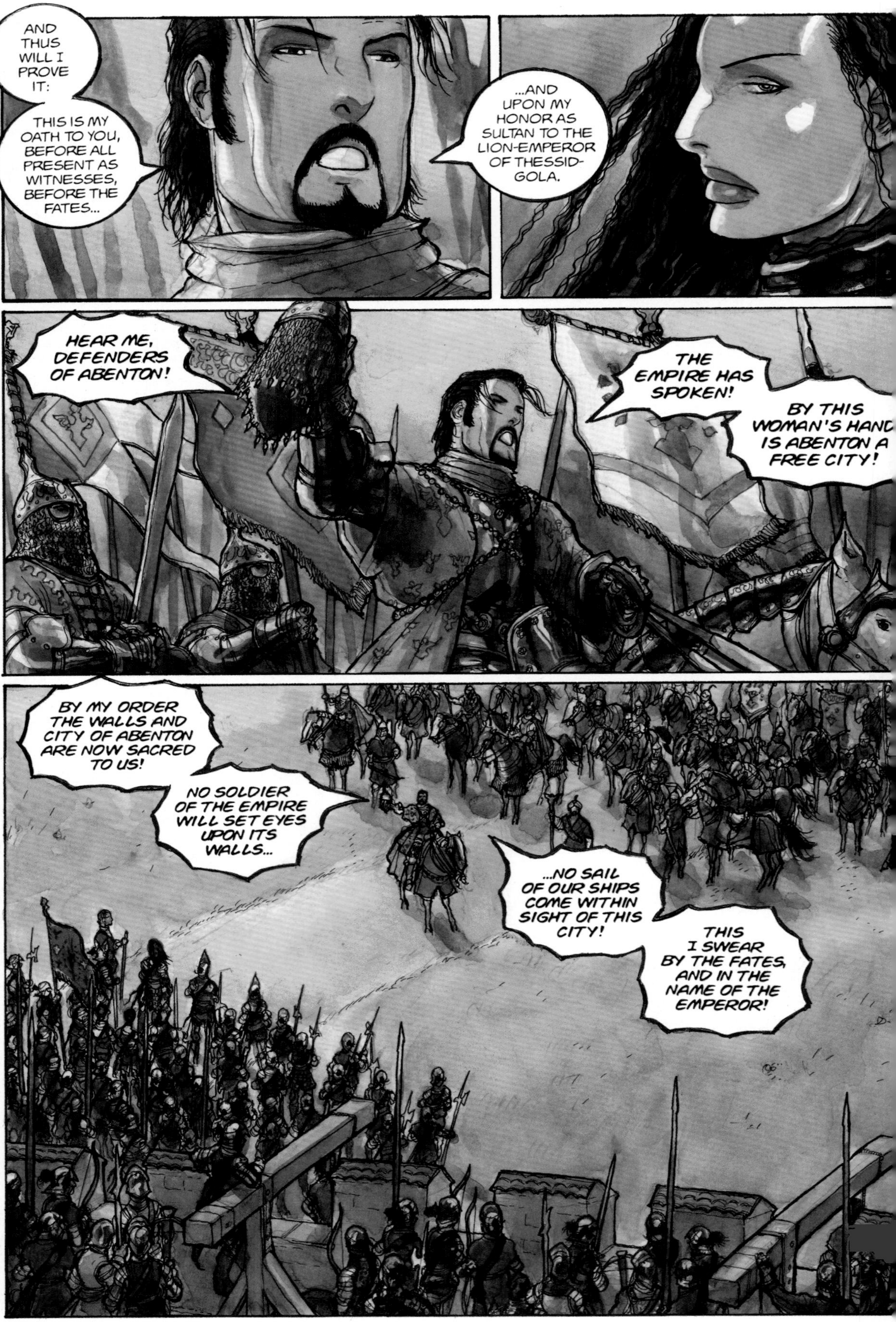
AND THUS WILL I PROVE IT:
THIS IS MY OATH TO YOU, BEFORE ALL PRESENT AS WITNESSES, BEFORE THE FATES...
...AND UPON MY HONOR AS SULTAN TO THE LION-EMPEROR OF THESSID-GOLA.
HEAR ME, DEFENDERS OF ABENTON!
THE EMPIRE HAS SPOKEN!
BY THIS WOMAN'S HAND IS ABENTON A FREE CITY!
BY MY ORDER THE WALLS AND CITY OF ABENTON ARE NOW SACRED TO US!
NO SOLDIER OF THE EMPIRE WILL SET EYES UPON ITS WALLS...
...NO SAIL OF OUR SHIPS COME WITHIN SIGHT OF THIS CITY!
THIS I SWEAR BY THE FATES, AND IN THE NAME OF THE EMPEROR!

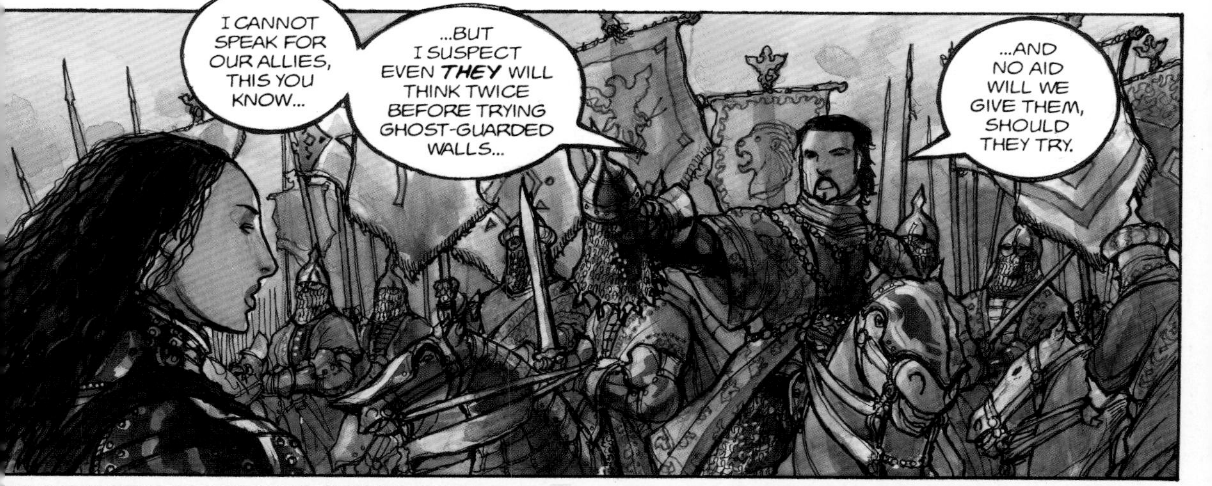
I CANNOT SPEAK FOR OUR ALLIES, THIS YOU KNOW...
...BUT I SUSPECT EVEN **THEY** WILL THINK TWICE BEFORE TRYING GHOST-GUARDED WALLS...
...AND NO AID WILL WE GIVE THEM, SHOULD THEY TRY.

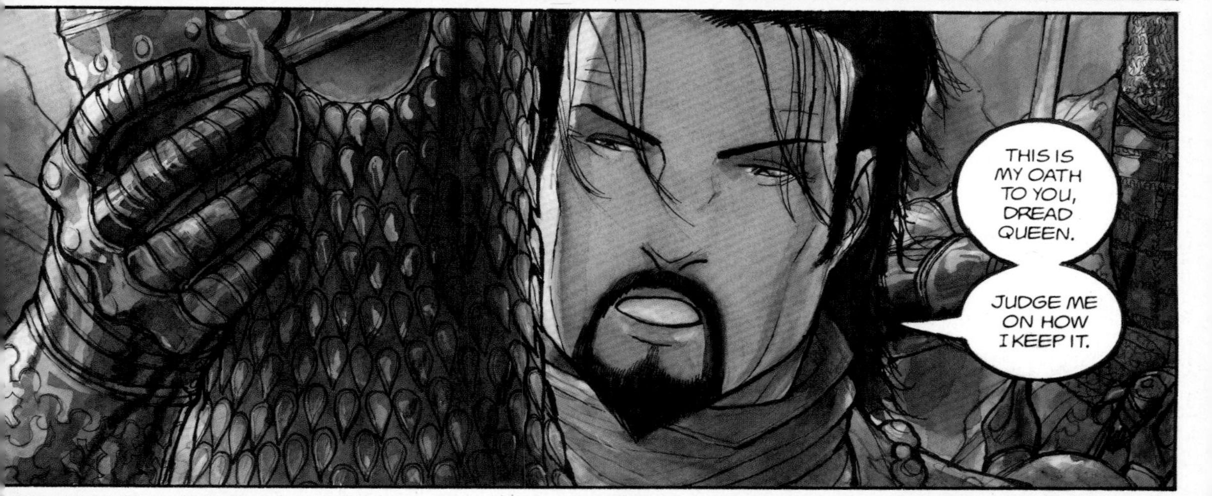
THIS IS MY OATH TO YOU, DREAD QUEEN.
JUDGE ME ON HOW I KEEP IT.

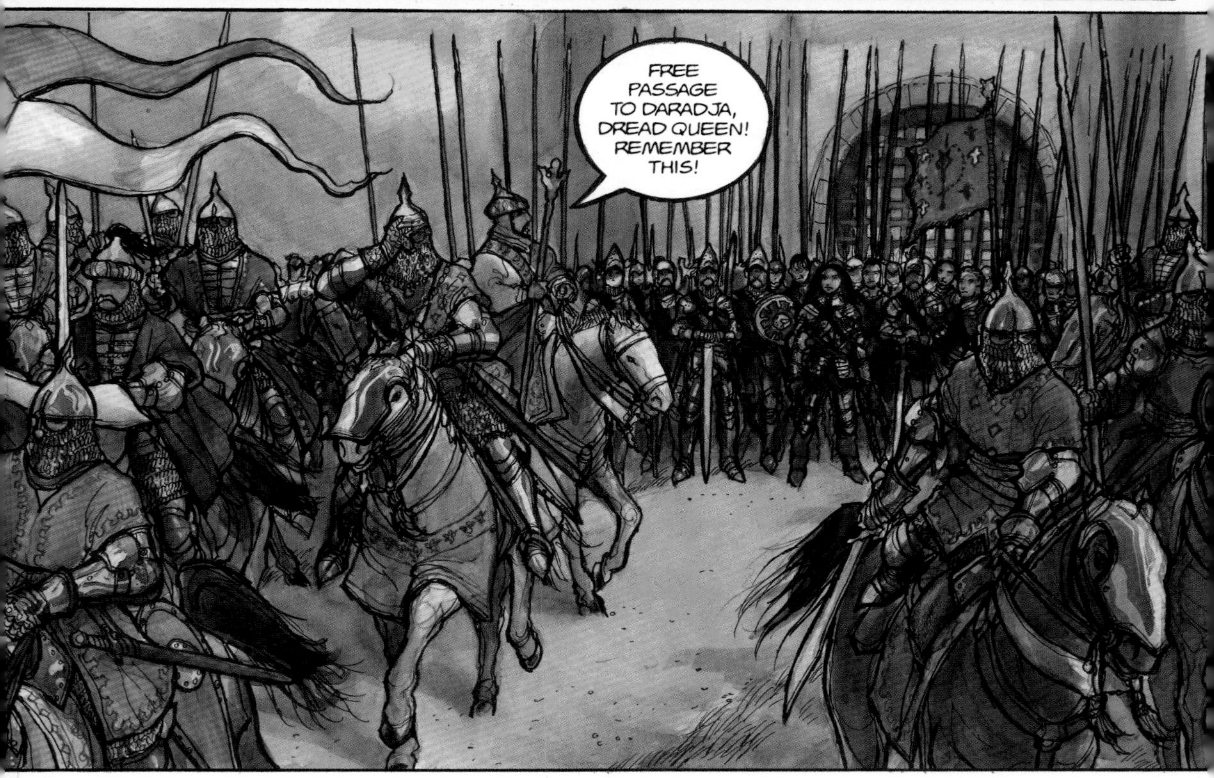
FREE PASSAGE TO DARADJA, DREAD QUEEN! REMEMBER THIS!

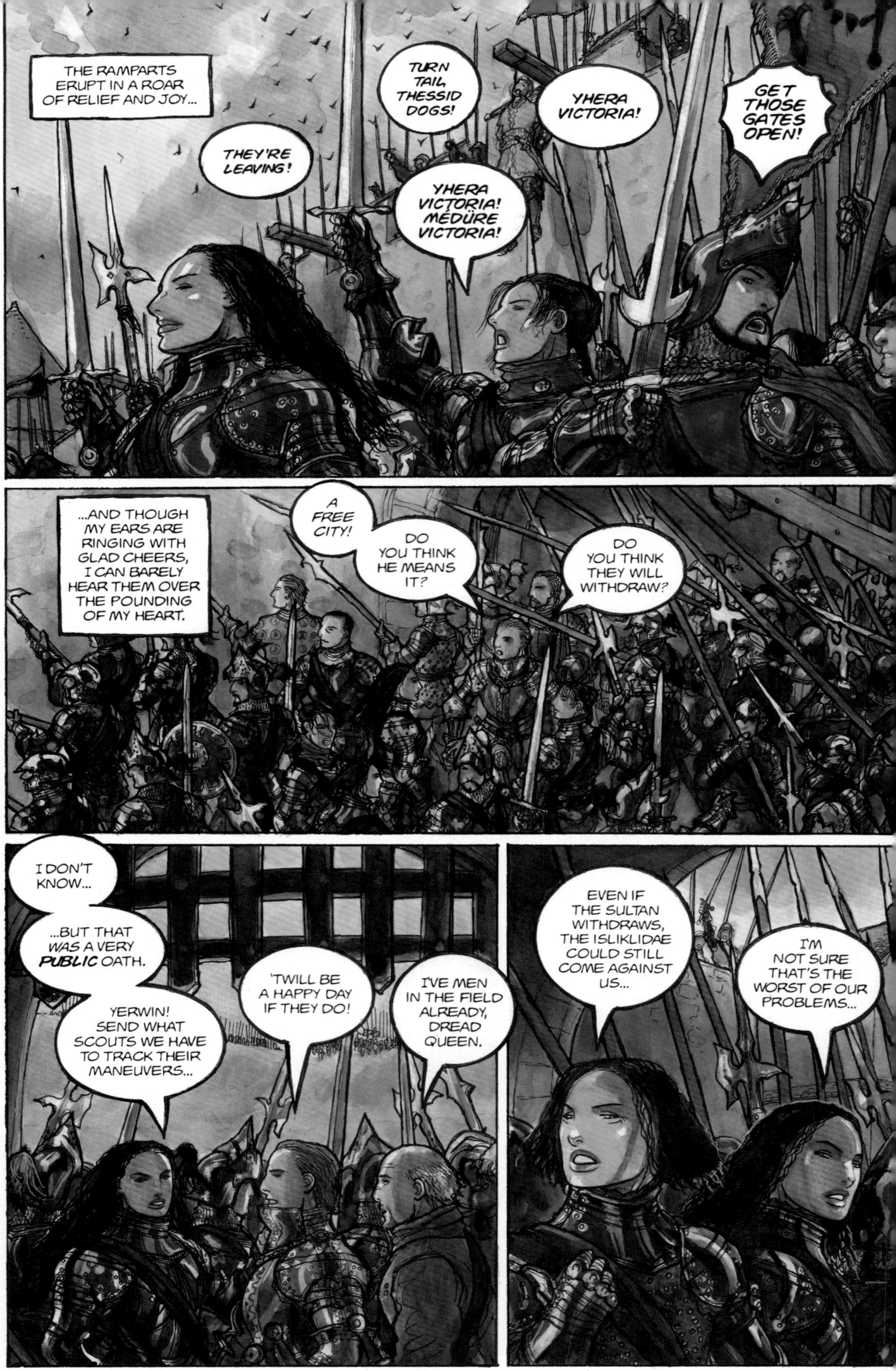

THE RAMPARTS ERUPT IN A ROAR OF RELIEF AND JOY...
THEY'RE LEAVING!
TURN TAIL, THESSID DOGS!
YHERA VICTORIA! MÉDÜRE VICTORIA!
YHERA VICTORIA!
GET THOSE GATES OPEN!
...AND THOUGH MY EARS ARE RINGING WITH GLAD CHEERS, I CAN BARELY HEAR THEM OVER THE POUNDING OF MY HEART.
A FREE CITY!
DO YOU THINK HE MEANS IT?
DO YOU THINK THEY WILL WITHDRAW?
I DON'T KNOW...
...BUT THAT WAS A VERY PUBLIC OATH.
YERWIN! SEND WHAT SCOUTS WE HAVE TO TRACK THEIR MANEUVERS...
'TWILL BE A HAPPY DAY IF THEY DO!
I'VE MEN IN THE FIELD ALREADY, DREAD QUEEN.
EVEN IF THE SULTAN WITHDRAWS, THE ISLIKLIDAE COULD STILL COME AGAINST US...
I'M NOT SURE THAT'S THE WORST OF OUR PROBLEMS...

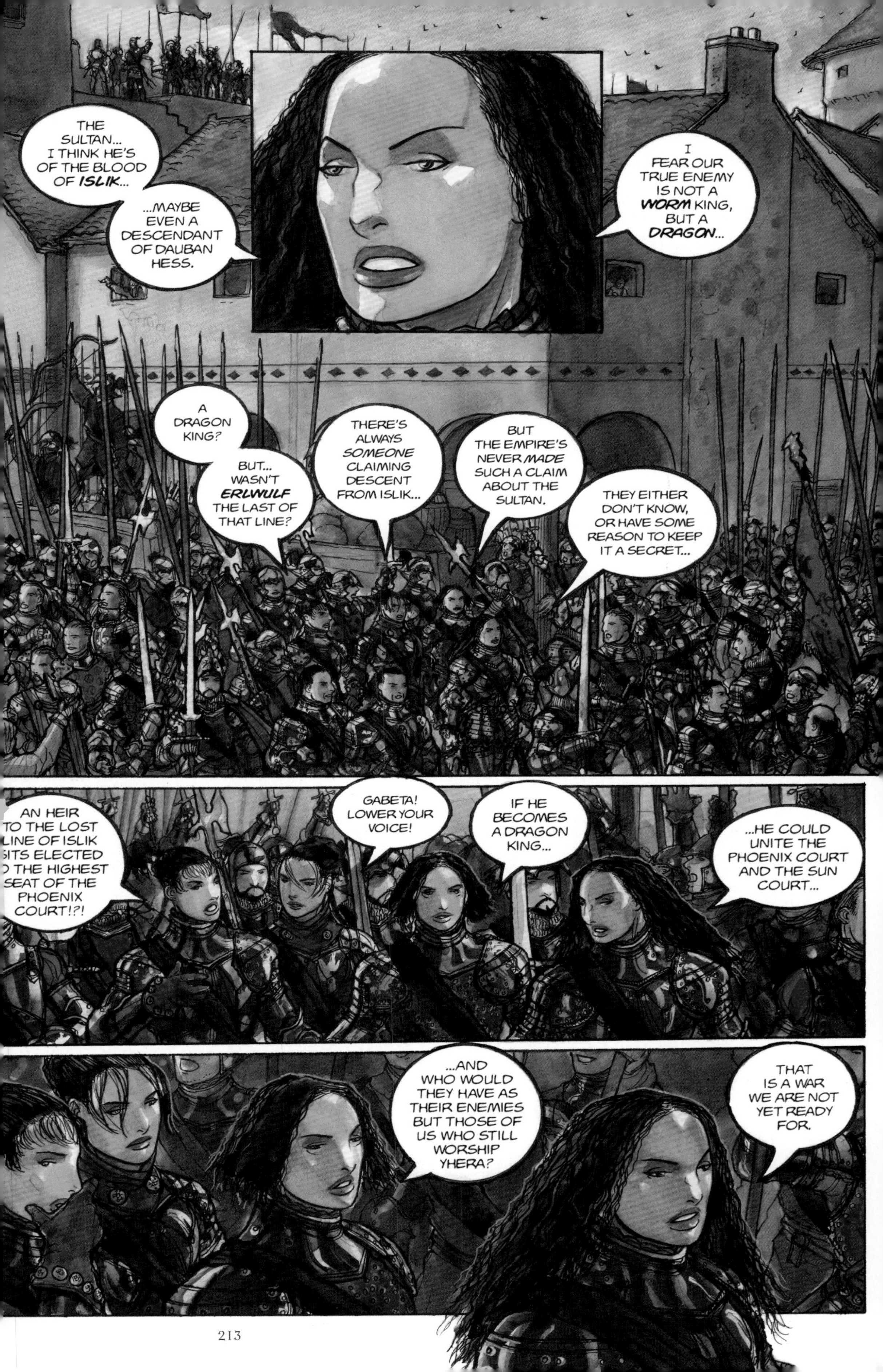
THE SULTAN... I THINK HE'S OF THE BLOOD OF ISLIK...
...MAYBE EVEN A DESCENDANT OF DAUBAN HESS.
I FEAR OUR TRUE ENEMY IS NOT A WORM KING, BUT A DRAGON...
A DRAGON KING?
BUT... WASN'T ERLWULF THE LAST OF THAT LINE?
THERE'S ALWAYS SOMEONE CLAIMING DESCENT FROM ISLIK...
BUT THE EMPIRE'S NEVER MADE SUCH A CLAIM ABOUT THE SULTAN.
THEY EITHER DON'T KNOW, OR HAVE SOME REASON TO KEEP IT A SECRET...
AN HEIR TO THE LOST LINE OF ISLIK SITS ELECTED TO THE HIGHEST SEAT OF THE PHOENIX COURT!?!
GABETA! LOWER YOUR VOICE!
IF HE BECOMES A DRAGON KING...
...HE COULD UNITE THE PHOENIX COURT AND THE SUN COURT...
...AND WHO WOULD THEY HAVE AS THEIR ENEMIES BUT THOSE OF US WHO STILL WORSHIP YHERA?
THAT IS A WAR WE ARE NOT YET READY FOR.

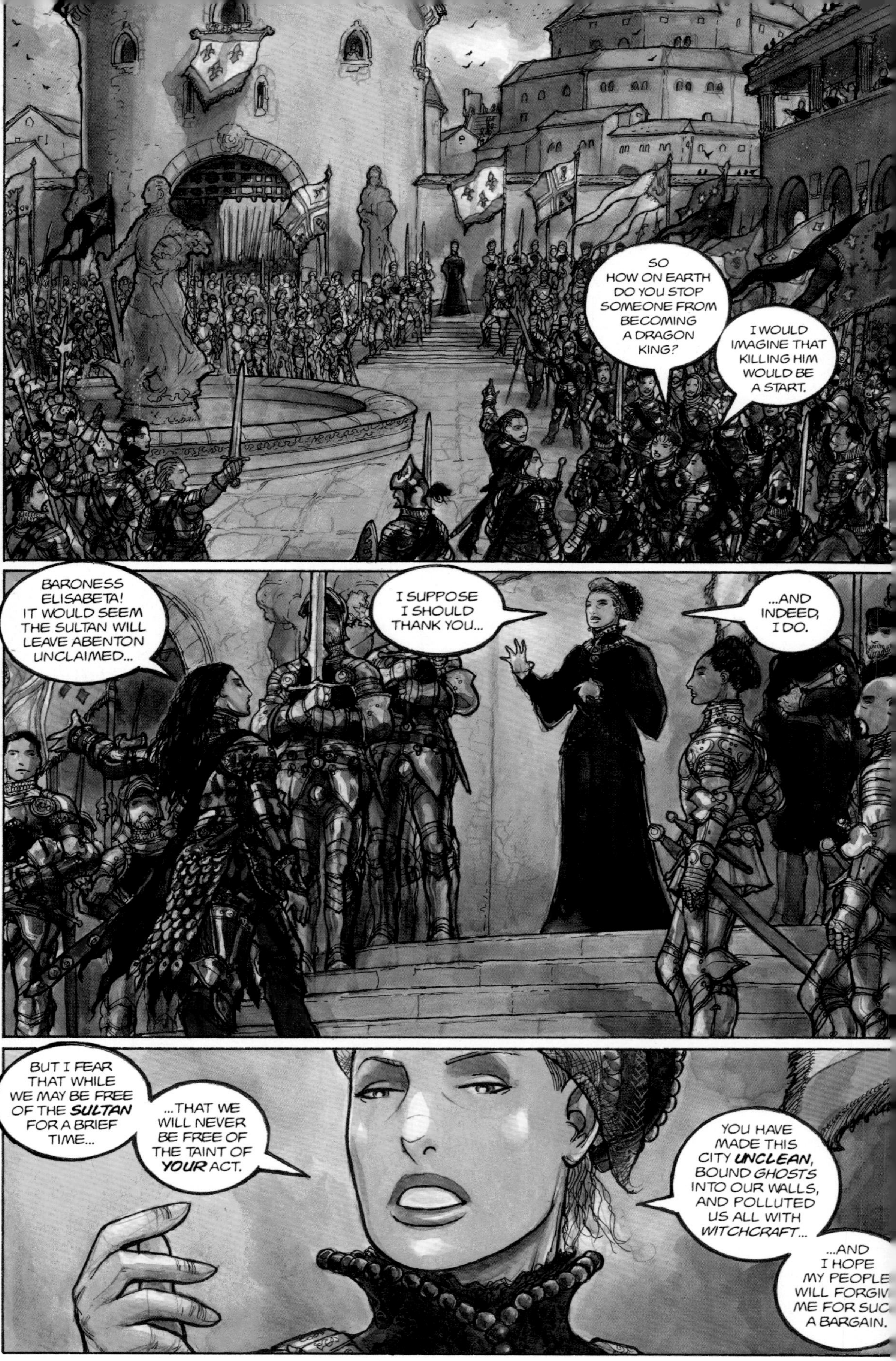
SO HOW ON EARTH DO YOU STOP SOMEONE FROM BECOMING A DRAGON KING?
I WOULD IMAGINE THAT KILLING HIM WOULD BE A START.
BARONESS ELISABETA! IT WOULD SEEM THE SULTAN WILL LEAVE ABENTON UNCLAIMED...
I SUPPOSE I SHOULD THANK YOU...
...AND INDEED, I DO.
BUT I FEAR THAT WHILE WE MAY BE FREE OF THE SULTAN FOR A BRIEF TIME...
...THAT WE WILL NEVER BE FREE OF THE TAINT OF YOUR ACT.
YOU HAVE MADE THIS CITY UNCLEAN, BOUND GHOSTS INTO OUR WALLS, AND POLLUTED US ALL WITH WITCHCRAFT...
...AND I HOPE MY PEOPLE WILL FORGIV ME FOR SUC A BARGAIN.

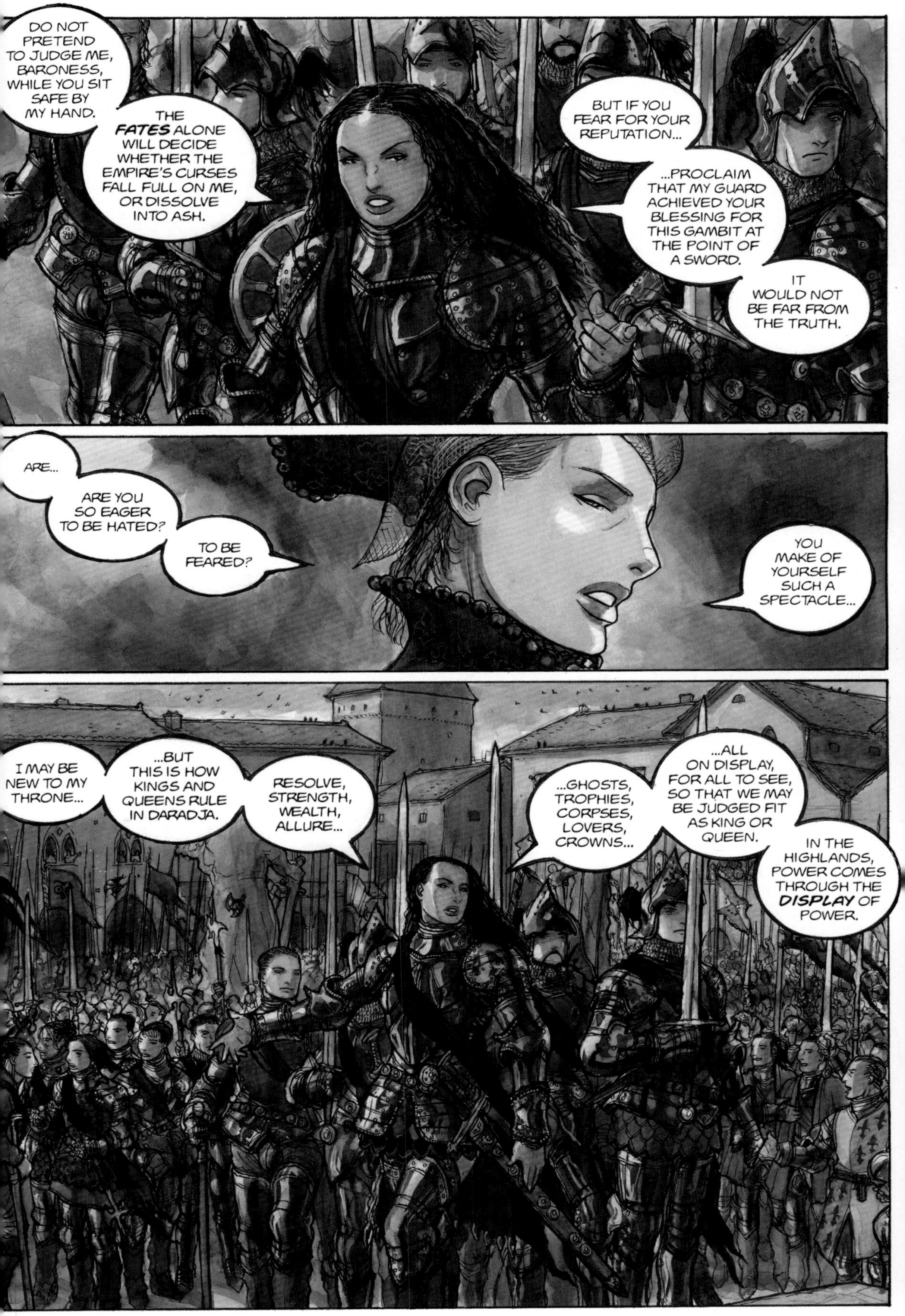
DO NOT PRETEND TO JUDGE ME, BARONESS, WHILE YOU SIT SAFE BY MY HAND.
THE *FATES* ALONE WILL DECIDE WHETHER THE EMPIRE'S CURSES FALL FULL ON ME, OR DISSOLVE INTO ASH.
BUT IF YOU FEAR FOR YOUR REPUTATION...
...PROCLAIM THAT MY GUARD ACHIEVED YOUR BLESSING FOR THIS GAMBIT AT THE POINT OF A SWORD.
IT WOULD NOT BE FAR FROM THE TRUTH.
ARE...
ARE YOU SO EAGER TO BE HATED?
TO BE FEARED?
YOU MAKE OF YOURSELF SUCH A SPECTACLE...
I MAY BE NEW TO MY THRONE...
...BUT THIS IS HOW KINGS AND QUEENS RULE IN DARADJA.
RESOLVE, STRENGTH, WEALTH, ALLURE...
...GHOSTS, TROPHIES, CORPSES, LOVERS, CROWNS...
...ALL ON DISPLAY, FOR ALL TO SEE, SO THAT WE MAY BE JUDGED FIT AS KING OR QUEEN.
IN THE HIGHLANDS, POWER COMES THROUGH THE *DISPLAY* OF POWER.

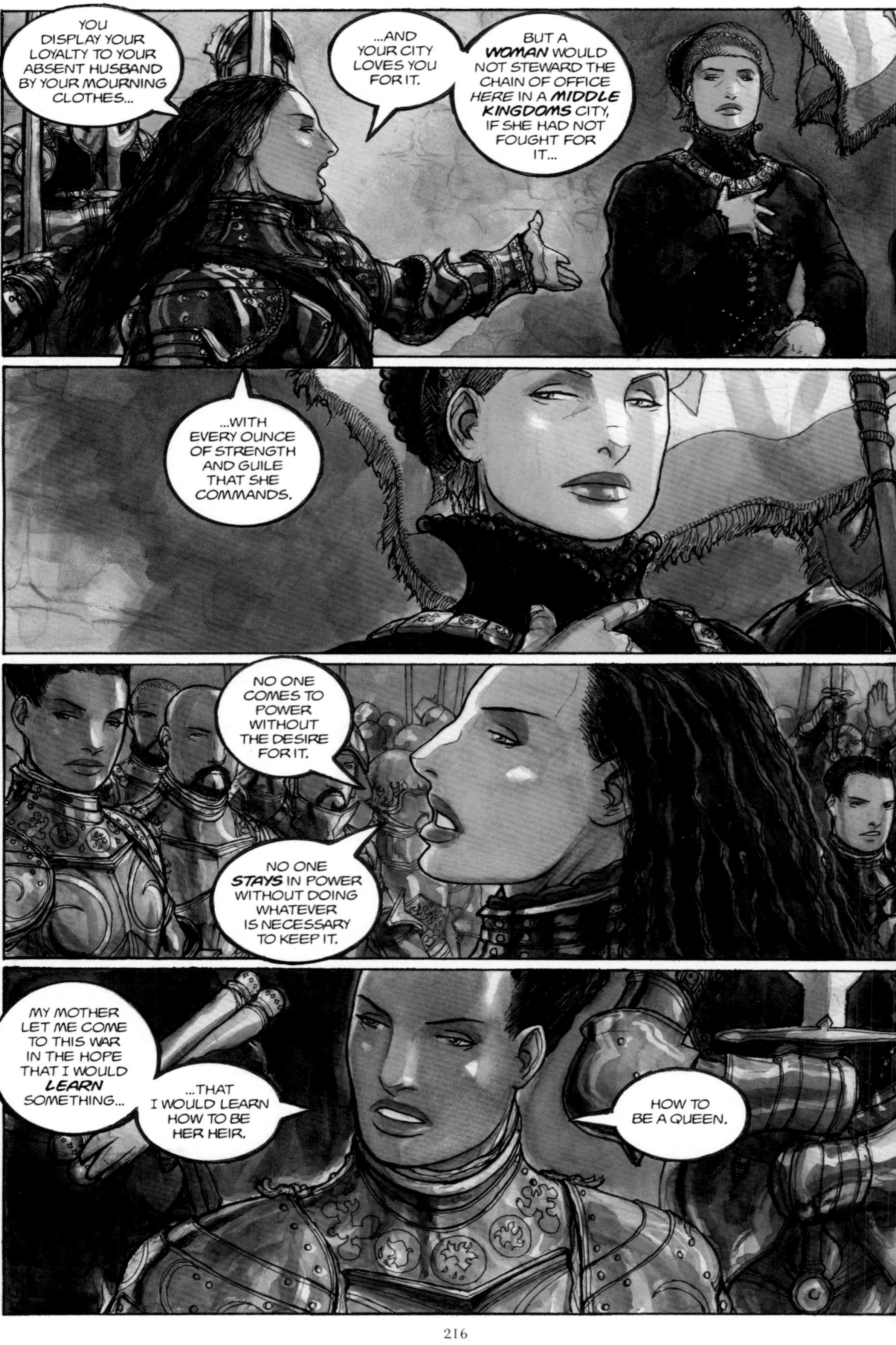
YOU DISPLAY YOUR LOYALTY TO YOUR ABSENT HUSBAND BY YOUR MOURNING CLOTHES...
...AND YOUR CITY LOVES YOU FOR IT.
BUT A WOMAN WOULD NOT STEWARD THE CHAIN OF OFFICE HERE IN A MIDDLE KINGDOMS CITY, IF SHE HAD NOT FOUGHT FOR IT...
...WITH EVERY OUNCE OF STRENGTH AND GUILE THAT SHE COMMANDS.
NO ONE COMES TO POWER WITHOUT THE DESIRE FOR IT.
NO ONE STAYS IN POWER WITHOUT DOING WHATEVER IS NECESSARY TO KEEP IT.
MY MOTHER LET ME COME TO THIS WAR IN THE HOPE THAT I WOULD LEARN SOMETHING...
...THAT I WOULD LEARN HOW TO BE HER HEIR.
HOW TO BE A QUEEN.

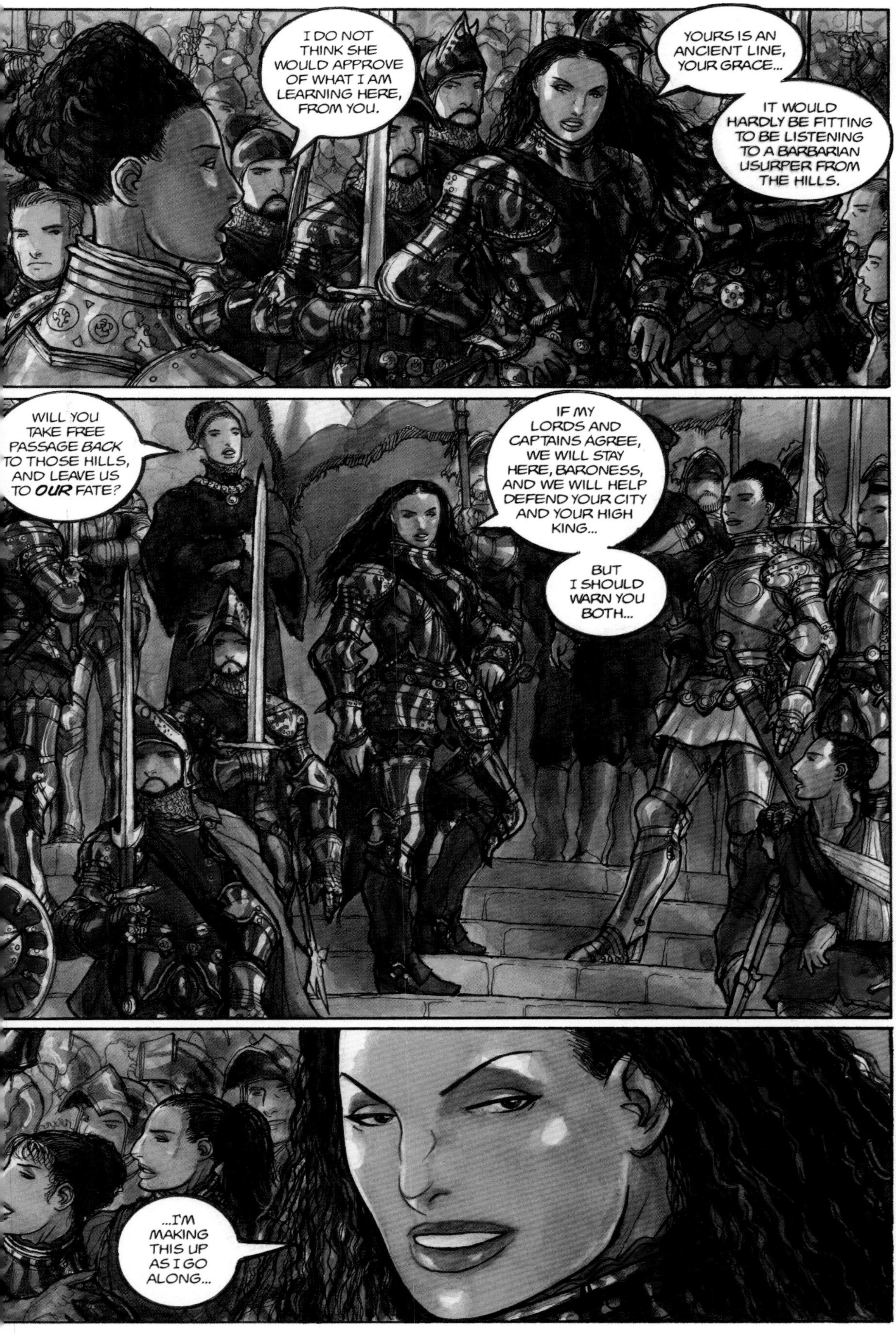
I DO NOT THINK SHE WOULD APPROVE OF WHAT I AM LEARNING HERE, FROM YOU.
YOURS IS AN ANCIENT LINE, YOUR GRACE...
IT WOULD HARDLY BE FITTING TO BE LISTENING TO A BARBARIAN USURPER FROM THE HILLS.
WILL YOU TAKE FREE PASSAGE BACK TO THOSE HILLS, AND LEAVE US TO OUR FATE?
IF MY LORDS AND CAPTAINS AGREE, WE WILL STAY HERE, BARONESS, AND WE WILL HELP DEFEND YOUR CITY AND YOUR HIGH KING...
BUT I SHOULD WARN YOU BOTH...
...I'M MAKING THIS UP AS I GO ALONG...

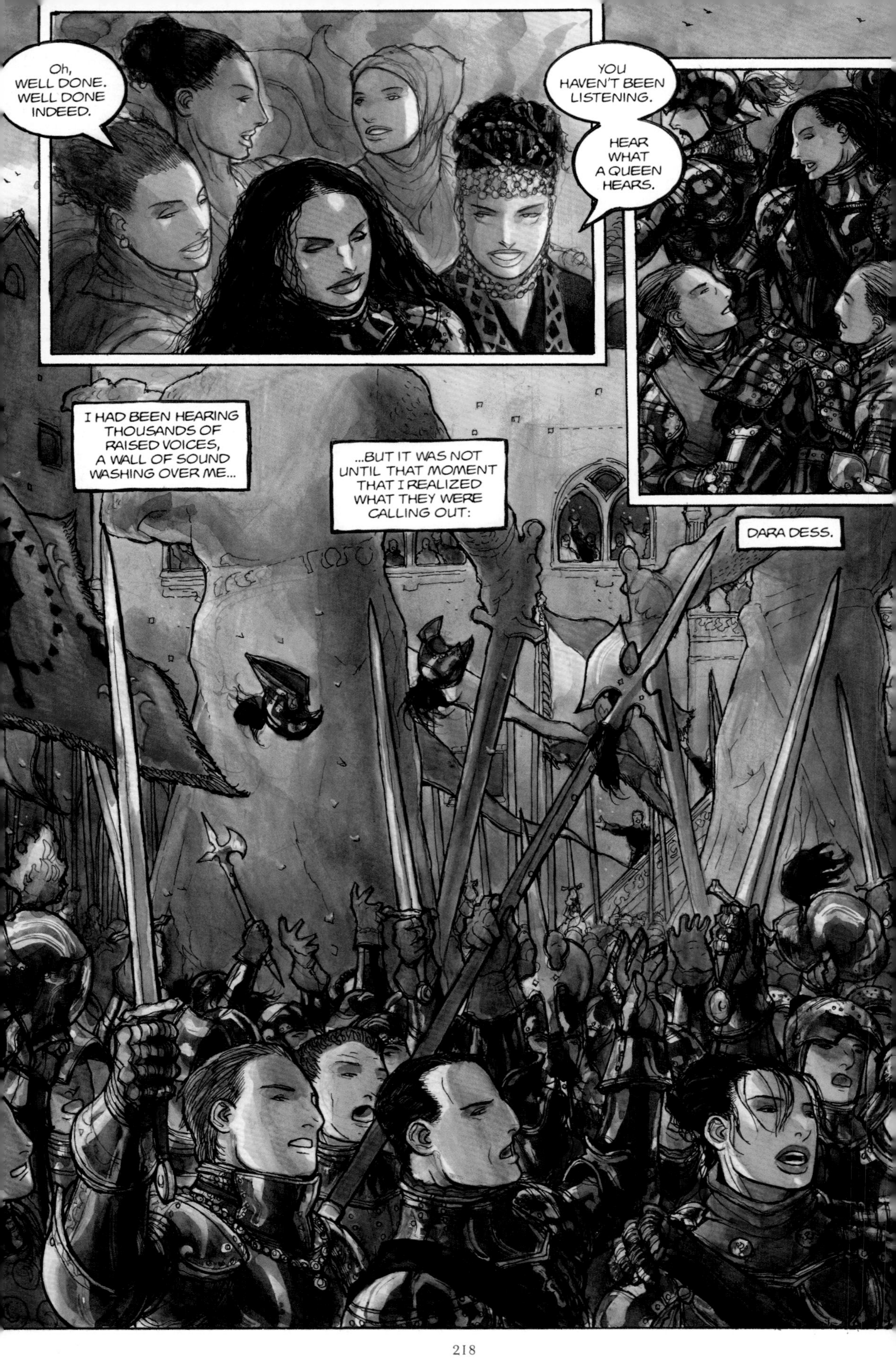
Oh, WELL DONE. WELL DONE INDEED.
YOU HAVEN'T BEEN LISTENING.
HEAR WHAT A QUEEN HEARS.
I HAD BEEN HEARING THOUSANDS OF RAISED VOICES, A WALL OF SOUND WASHING OVER ME...
...BUT IT WAS NOT UNTIL THAT MOMENT THAT I REALIZED WHAT THEY WERE CALLING OUT:
DARA DESS.

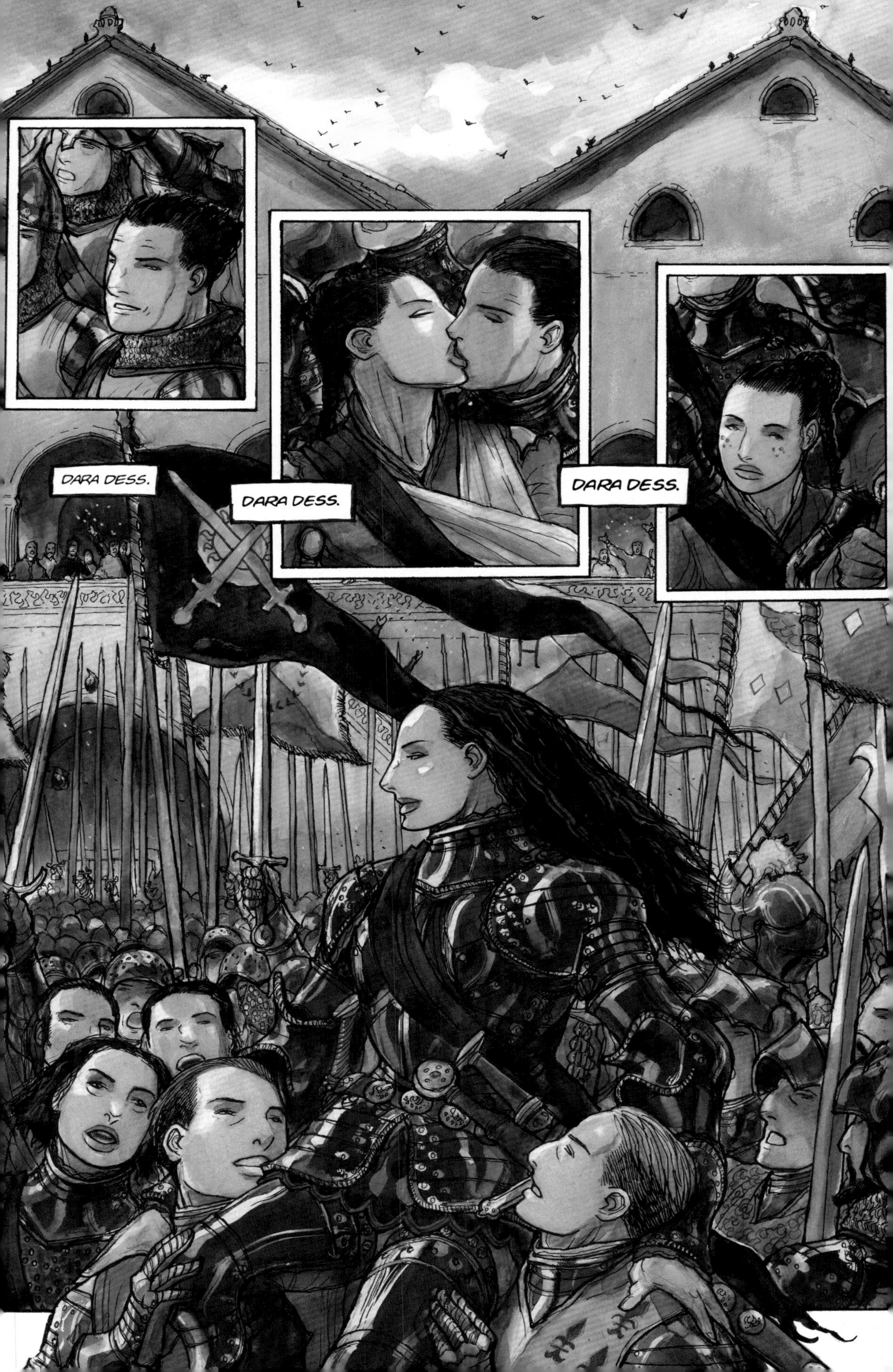
DARA DESS.
DARA DESS.
DARA DESS.

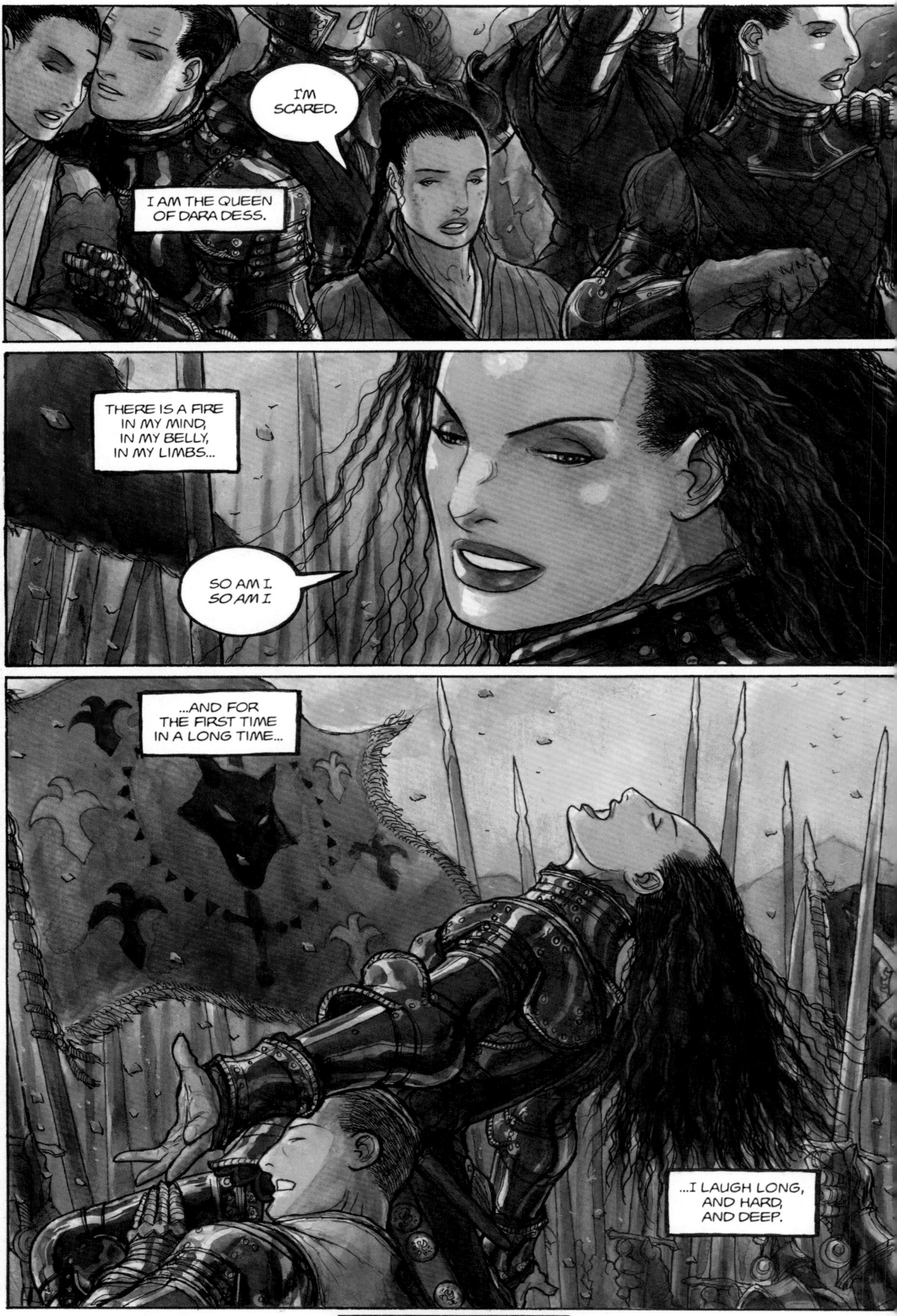
I'M SCARED.
I AM THE QUEEN OF DARA DESS.
THERE IS A FIRE IN MY MIND, IN MY BELLY, IN MY LIMBS...
SO AM I. SO AM I.
...AND FOR THE FIRST TIME IN A LONG TIME...
...I LAUGH LONG, AND HARD, AND DEEP.

To be Continued

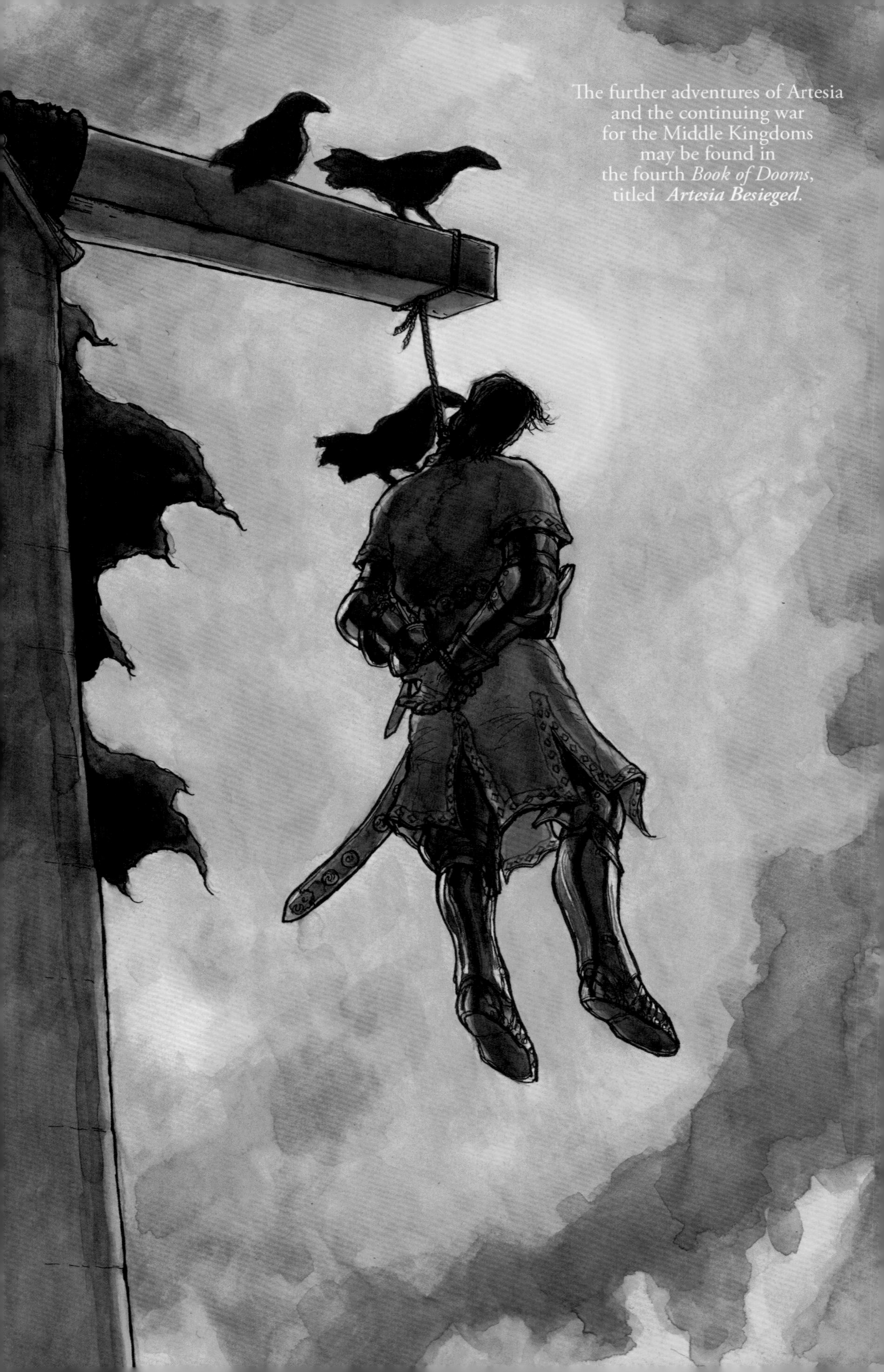

The further adventures of Artesia
and the continuing war
for the Middle Kingdoms
may be found in
the fourth *Book of Dooms*,
titled *Artesia Besieged*.

A BRIEF GLOSSARY
of DEITIES, PLACES, PEOPLE, *and* EVENTS

ACHRE – rebellious daughter of *Brage*, who refused to become an *Oracle Queen*. Instead she wounded her father, bound a great Dragon, and became ancestress of the Palatians (see *Palatia*).

ADJIA LUNA – the Moon Huntress, one of the three goddesses of the Moon. She is the goddess of birth, growth, maturity, maternity, the hunt, dreams, and death. Sometimes called *Adjiana*.

AGALL – demigod son of *Agdah Cosmopeiia*; the First Hero, famous for his considerable temper, strength and courage. The Sacker of Cities, he fought alongside *Geteema's* children at the destruction of *Ürüne Düré*. One of the *Four Kings in Exile*, slain in the *Far West* but redeemed by *Islik*.

AGDAH COSMOPEIIA – the Year God and God of the Shining Sky, the god of the year-cycle. Slain by *Geteema* in defense of *Düréa*, but later restored by *Yhera* to the Heavens. Also called *Agdah Helios* (the Cosmos Sun) and *Ammon Agdah* (the Household Protector and the Keeper of Animals).

AGE OF LEGENDS, the – the second age of Known World history, beginning with *Islik's* ascension and ending with the *Catastrophe* some 498 years later.

AKKALION – the Lion Emperor of *Thessid-Gola*, first to claim the throne of *Dauban Hess* since the wars of the *Worm Kings*. He embarked on a series of conquests to restore the Empire to its former glory until he was overcome by the *Gray Dream* the night before the *Black Day Battle*. He has sat on the throne ever since, his mind trapped in the Gray Dream.

AMAYMON – the Whisperer, the Prince of Intrigue and Secret Power, god of secret knowledge, bribery, corruption, and assassins. He counseled *Irré* to overthrow *Illiki Helios* and *Ishraha* to begin his rebellion against *Islik*, thus beginning the *War in Heaven*.

AMI - the Morning Star, the Dawn Maiden, twin sister of *Dieva*, and the goddess of love, fertility, and romance.

AMORA – anciently a *Düréan* colony favored by *Illiki Helios*; once part of the *Thessid-Golan Empire*, Amora is now independent with the help of *Palatia*, and has annexed nearby *Meretia* as a buffer state with the Empire.

AN-ATHAIR – a castle and small city in the *Erid Wold*, once the center of a realm ruled by the *Spring Queens*.

ANGOWRIE – one of the *Middle Kingdoms*, originally the hold of one of the *Watchtower Kings*. The current King, Euwen Jaraslas, is a traitor who swore an oath of fealty to the *Sultan*.

ARCHAIA – the daughter of *Achre*, student of *Ariahavé*, and the founder of the city of *Palatia* and builder of its Seven Gates. She bore three daughters, who founded the three most ancient Houses of Palatia. She sailed to war against *Geteema's* children, and was slain defending *Düréa*.

ARIAHAVÉ – the Civilizer, *Yhera's* brightest and most rebellious daughter. Protectress of cities and citadels and their citizens and defenders; patroness of civilization, its heroes, and the arts of society -- agriculture, poetry, spinning, pottery, music, and mining. Also Yhera's general and the chief war goddess of the Palatians (see *Palatia*).

AUDRA – the Voyager, legendary Queen of *Palatia* at the beginning of the *Bronze Age* largely responsible for that city's rise to current power. Last of the Black Arrow Queens and first of the Copper Queens.

AURIA – a principality of the *Middle Kingdoms*, and ancient name for the lands settled by the Aurians, seagoing pillagers descended of *Heth*.

AWAIN – the current High King of *Therapoli* and the *Middle Kingdoms*; a descendant of *Fortias the Brave*.

BLACK DAY BATTLE, the – battle on the shores of *Dania* between the allied forces of the *Middle Kingdoms*, the *Watchtower Kings*, and *Daradja* against the invading *Thessid-Golan Empire* when *Irré* rose in the sky and *Akkalion* was absent due to the *Gray Dream*; the Empire was routed.

BLACK HUNTER, the – a son of *Geniché* and leader of the Wild Hunt. He leads a host of ghosts, spirits, and demons across the Known World hunting the unwary and unprotected.

BOOK OF DOOMS, the – book of 22 plates created by *Brage* for the *Oracle Queens* of *Khael*. Based upon the Celestial Book of *Yhera*. Briefly lost, but recovered by *Audra*.

BRAGE – the first smith, the creator of the arts of metal-working, the fire-god of hearth, kiln, and foundry, creator of rune-systems and artifacts of great power. Brage eloped with a *Düréan* Queen to the Isle of *Khael*, and their daughters became the *Oracle Queens*. Also called *Abrage* and *Braphagos*.

BRONZE AGE, the – the third age of Known World history, dating from the *Catastrophe* to *Akkalion* taking the throne of the *Thessid-Golan Empire* some 528 years later.

CATASTROPHE, the – volcanic destruction of Millene, capital of the *Thessid-Golan Empire*, at the end of the *Age of Legends*; caused by a curse from the *Oracle Queens* on the *Worm Kings*.

CELESTIAL COURT, the – divine court of King *Surep* during the *Golden Age*. During the *War in Heaven* the Court was ruled by *Nymarga*, until he was deposed by the return of *Jala*. The Court faded in power during the *Age of Legends*, was held by the *Isliklids* for a dark time, and ended after the vanishing of its last hero-savior, *Dauban Hess*.

CERAM – the Thunderer, a son of *Thula* and *Illiki Helios*; ancestor-god of the nomads of the *Midlands*. Ceram hunted the *Four Kings in Exile*.

COROMAT – a son of *Geteema*, once King of *Vanimoria* but banished for withdrawing from his mother's war on *Düréa*; he became one of the *Four Kings in Exile* and went mad for many years before reconciling with his people and resuming his throne. Deposed and slain by *Nymarga*.

DAEDEKAMANI – a son of *Yhera*; the first magician, creator of the magical arts and the first magical runes; an avid wanderer, a patron of travelers, and sometimes a guide to the dead.

DALL and PULMA – twin daughters of *Thula* and chief amongst her children. They bound horses, fought by Thula's side in defense of *Düréa*, and appear in the Heavens as the Twins constellation.

DANIA – lands of the Danians, now part of the *Middle Kingdoms*. Once comprised of Uthed Dania and Dania proper, until Uthed Dania was lost in the war against *Githwaine* (see *Lost Uthedmael*) and Dania split into Dain Dania and Erid Dania. Also the name of the peninsula jutting into the *Silver Scale Sea* where these lands are found.

DARA – first legendary barbarian Queen of *Daradja*, and builder of *Dara Dess*; known for her wisdom and beauty, she was slain by *Thula*.

DARA DESS – the oldest of the four ancient citadels of *Daradja* (Dara Dess, Heth Moll, An-Athark, and Finleth).

DARADJA – name for the highlands of the *Middle Kingdoms* that means "Realm Of *Dara*" in *Old Éduinan*.

DAUBAN HESS – the Golden Emperor, the Conqueror King, greatest of the *Dragon Kings* and reputed to be a son of *Islik*. He defeated *Nymarga* and drove the *Isliklids* out of the *Celestial Court*, and came to rule the whole of the Known World. He set sail to find the *Dawn Isles* and was never seen again.

DAWN ISLES, the – fabulous islands at the edge of the world, where every morning *Ami* throws open the Gates of the Dawn to let in the Sun.

DÉSKÉDRÉ – swath of coastal cities just north of the *Middle Kingdoms*, known for their wicked licentiousness.

DIEVA – the Evening Star, the Dusk Maiden, twin sister of *Ami*, and the goddess of sex and physical pleasures.

DJAR MAEL – land of the Maelites, a people related to the Daradjans and Danians, now thralls of the *Isliklids*.

DJARA LUNA – the Moon goddess of Death and Darkness, the queen of ghosts and dark magic, the giver of lunacy and nightmares, the keeper and revealer of secrets and treasures. Also called *Urgale* or *Morgale*.

DRAGON KINGS, the – ancient Kings with great might and powers of dominion. *Islik* was the first, *Dauban Hess* was the greatest; descent from either indicated Dragon King blood and great latent power, but they were wiped out in wars against the *Worm Kings*.

DÜMÉGHAL – warlords and warriors of the *Isliklids*, recruited from their subjects in the *Far West* and bound to their service by foul magics.

DÜRÉA – ancient queendom of the *Golden Age* and crucible of civilization. Lost to the armies of *Geteema* and sunk beneath the *Silver Scale Sea* at the end of the Golden Age. (See *Ürüne Düré*).

ÉDUINS – the Dain, Harath, Bora, Djar, and Tel mountain ranges in the *Midlands*; the backbone of the Danian peninsula into the *Silver Scale Sea*.

EMIR –an officer of high rank in the *Thessid-Golan Empire*.

ERID WOLD, the – a great wood in *Dania*, once home of the *Spring Queens*, now haunted by ghosts and spirits and a refuge of witches fleeing the persecution of the *Sun Court*.

ERLWULF – last of the known *Dragon Kings*, slain by *Githwaine*.

FAR WEST, the – common name for any lands west of the *Midlands*.

FORTIAS THE BRAVE – hero-knight of *Auria*; slew *Githwaine* and built the Great Wall that stands between the *Middle Kingdoms* and *Lost Uthedmael*.

FOUR KINGS IN EXILE, the – four kings banished from their domains during the War in Heaven. *Islik, Agall, Coromat,* and *Jala* fought many battles, resisted the temptations of the Queen of *Daradja*, were pursued by *Ceram* across the *Midlands*, and broke up their fellowship in the *Far West* after the death of Agall at the hands of an enemy called the Blooded (see *Isliklids*).

GENICHÉ – Queen of the Underworld and once Queen of the Earth, the giver of life, and, with her sister *Geteema*, the

mother of all within *Yhera's* creation. She ruled the Earth as a Paradise until she created the Underworld and spoke the First Law, declaring that all born of her Earth must follow her into Death.

GETEEMA – sister to *Geniché* and *Yhera*; monstrous Queen of the Dark Earth, the Dragon Mother, the Mother of the Giants. Out of jealousy she sent many of her children to destroy *Ürüne Düré*, and she herself consumed the body of *Agdah Cosmopeiia*, after which Yhera chained her in the Underworld.

GITHWAINE – last of the *Worm Kings*, who hid amongst the warlords of *Djar Mael*. He killed *Erlwulf* before being slain by *Fortias the Brave*.

GOLA, the – lands of the southern *Silver Scale Sea* and home to some of the oldest cities in the Known World.

GOLDEN AGE, the – first age of Known World history after *Geniché* left the Earth for the Underworld. Begins with the founding of *Düréa* and lasts just over 1000 years, until the fall of *Ürüne Düré* and the *War in Heaven*.

GORGONAE, the – the Triple War Goddess, daughters of *Djara*. Chained in the Underworld, only *Yhera* Anath or her general, *Ariahavé*, may free them.

GRAY DREAM, the – dream that befell *Akkalion* before the *Black Day Battle*, now the subject of intense speculation amongst mystery cults throughout the *Thessid-Golan Empire*, the *Hemapoline League,* and *Palatia*.

HALÉ – the Goddess of Slaughter, goddess of (mindless) rage and berserker fury. One of the *Gorgonae*.

HATHAZ-GHÚL – Old *Éduinan* name for things that should be dead but cling to life by feeding on the bodies of the living and recently deceased. Often said to come from *Lost Uthedmael*.

HATHHALLA – the Devouring Fire of the Sun, the lion-headed goddess of battle and vengeance, goddess of the Sun's righteous strength.

HEMAPOLINE LEAGUE, the – a patchwork of city-states and kingdoms in *Hemispia* and *Illia* dedicated almost exclusively to trade. Stronghold of the followers of the *Sun Court*.

HEMISPIA – great peninsula east of the *Silver Scale Sea* now ruled by the *Hemapoline League*. Anciently the lands of the first *Dragon Kings*.

HETH – the Sea Bull, the Sea King, god of surface waves, and ancestor-god of the Aurians (see *Auria*).

ILLIA – isle just north of *Hemispia* favored by the Sun gods; birthplace of *Islik* and home to the *Sun Court*.

ILLIKI HELIOS – the Sun-Bull, a son of *Agdah Cosmopeiia* and *Ami*; the

Spring Sun, bestower of progeny and protector of crops. Cast into the Underworld by *Irré*, restored by *Yhera*.

IRON AGE, the – the fourth and current age of Known World history, beginning with *Akkalion's* assumption of the Imperial throne 446 years ago and leading to the current date: 1472 in the standard Imperial Avellan calendar, 2616 in the old *Düréan* calendar, or 2432 in the Celestial calendar.

IRRÉ – the Black Sun, bringer of unbearable heat and drought; the Bow Bearer, god of plague and fire; the Black Goat, god of war, struggle, disaster, disorder, the desert and the wilderness; the Last Defender, last guardian of the gates of *Düréa*. He overthrew *Illiki Helios*, starting the *War in Heaven*.

ISHRAHA – the Rebel Angel, a son of *Ligrid* and a general to *Islik* when he was King of *Illia*. At the start of the *War in Heaven* Ishraha led a rebellion against Islik and usurped his throne, but Islik returned from exile and imprisoned Ishraha in the Underworld.

ISLIK – the Divine King, demigod son of *Illiki Helios*; first of the *Dragon Kings* of *Illia* and founder of the *Sun Court*. During the *War in Heaven* Islik lost his throne to *Ishraha*. He wandered for 21 years as one of the *Four Kings in Exile*, returned to reclaim his throne, and after imprisoning Ishraha in the Underworld he ascended to the Heavens. His worshippers do not sacrifice to the old gods and believe that after death, they go to the Heavens to Islik's Palace rather than to *Geniché's* Underworld; they are divided into two rival schisms, the *Sun Court* and the *Phoenix Court*.

ISLIKLIDS, the – strange and evil Kings from the *Far West* who recently conquered the lands of *Djar Mael*, some 200 years ago. They claim descent from *Islik*, and are served by the *Düméghal* and Maelite warlords. Also called *Isliklidae, Islikids,* and the *Pretenderai*.

JALA – the Good Prince, son of *Surep*. One of the *Four Kings in Exile*, he returned to *Samarappa* to confront *Nymarga*, regain his father's throne, and restore the *Celestial Court*.

KHAEL – isle just east of *Palatia* where the *Oracle Queens* live. Sacked by the *Worm Kings* at the end of the *Age of Legends*, but restored by *Audra*.

LIGRID – the Temptress, the Queen of Perversity, the breaker of taboos and the corruptor of flesh and spirit; a rival, tutor, or mask of *Dieva*.

LOST UTHEDMAEL – name accorded to Maelite and Danian lands loyal to *Githwaine* after they were cursed by the *Sun Court* (see *Djar Mael* and *Dania*). A haunted wasteland.

MAECE –vanished realm of the Maelite Kings who stood against *Githwaine* (see *Djar Mael*). Their strength was wasted in wars against the *Isliklids*, and they remain only as the *Watchtower Kings*.

MÉDÜRE – the Cunning One, goddess of warlike skill and heroic valor. One of the *Gorgonae*.

MERETIA – small realm next to the *Gola*, once part of the *Thessid-Golan Empire* and now annexed by *Amora*.

MIDLANDS, the – common name for the lands to the west of the *Silver Scale Sea*. Once the Paradise of *Geniché*, now inhospitable desert and mountain.

MIDDLE KINGDOMS, the – Aurian and Danian kingdoms on the Danian peninsula in the *Silver Scale Sea* (see *Auria, Dania*), all aligned with the *Sun Court* and ruled by the High King of *Therapoli*. Sometimes referred to simply as *the Kingdoms*; their inhabitants are usually called *Kingsmen*.

MOGRAN – the Riot Goddess, goddess of terror, confusion, and dissension. One of the *Gorgonae*.

NYMARGA – the Magician, called by some the first and greatest evil. He slew King *Surep* to usurp the throne of *Samarappa* and held it until *Jala*'s return. He slunk off to *Vanimoria*, killed *Coromat*, conquered Thessidia, and ruled as the Worldly Tyrant until *Dauban Hess* destroyed him.

OLD ÉDUINAN – ancient tongue of *Dania, Daradja*, and the Maelites (see *Djar Mael*), akin to that of *Düréa*.

ORACLE QUEENS, the – descendants of *Brage* with uncanny oracular visions, and rulers of the Isle of *Khael*.

OSIDRED – a son of *Geniché* who was the first to follow his mother to the Underworld and became the Judge of the Dead. Also called *Seedré*.

PALATIA – city-state of the northern *Silver Scale Seas*, founded by *Achre* and *Archaia*. A minor city in the *Golden Age*, but now the center of a vast and expanding empire, rivaled only by the *Hemapoline League* and *Thessid-Golan Empire*, each of which it has defeated in recent wars. Now ruled by the *Usurper*.

PHOENIX COURT, the – Imperial Court of the *Thessid-Golan Empire* and its worshippers of *Islik*. The Phoenix Court advocates kingship based on appointment or election rather than inheritance, and so chooses or elects the officers of the Court and the emirates of the Empire. Briefly but disastrously corrupted by the *Worm Kings*.

SAMARAPPA – fabled and sensuous land of spices in the *Far West*.

SEATED KING – a King recognized by and part of the *Sun Court*. The

position was created once it was obvious there would be no more *Dragon Kings*.

SILVER SCALE SEA – inland sea framed by *Hemispia* and *Illia* in the east, the *Gola* in the south, the coast of the *Midlands* to the west, and the territories of *Palatia* in the north.

SPRING QUEENS, the – priestesses of the Green Temple of *An-Athair* during the *Age of Legends*, who married the kings of nearby realms and created a wondrous and magical land.

SULTAN – title given an *Emir* elected by the *Phoenix Court* to speak in the name of *Akkalion*. The ninth and current Sultan is Agameen tep Marahet.

SUN COURT, the – the highest religious authority in eastern lands devoted to *Islik*. Located on *Illia*, the Sun Court champions the tradition of hereditary kingship passed from father to son. Sun Court lands include the *Hemapoline League, Amora* and *Meretia,* and the *Middle Kingdoms*.

SUREP – son of *Yhera* and *Agdah Cosmopeiia*; a legendary and divine ruler of *Samarappa* during the *Golden Age*, slain by *Nymarga*.

THERAPOLI – capital of the *Middle Kingdoms*, built during the *Golden Age*.

THESSID-GOLAN EMPIRE, the – vast empire first created by *Dauban Hess*, then dismembered after his disappearance, first during civil wars between the *Sun Court* and rebel generals, and then by the wars of the *Worm Kings*. At its height only *Palatia* and *Khael* lay outside the Empire, and even they sent tribute. *Akkalion* began to rebuild the Empire until he lapsed into the *Gray Dream*; his efforts have been continued recently by the new *Sultan*. Includes *Vanimoria*, Thessidia, Grand Sekeret, Galia, and many minor emirates in the *Gola* and the west.

THULA – a daughter of *Geniché*; the Forked Tongue, the Mother of Heroes, the Fire Queen who stole the secrets of magic and civilization for her children and charges, the *Thulamites*. She killed *Dara* in one of her many raids, and dueled *Achre* with both weapons and dance to a standoff. Thula sailed to defend *Ürüne Düré* against *Geteema*'s children, though she had herself weakened its defenses. Mother of *Ceram* and *Dall and Pulma*.

THULAMITES – barbarian raiders of the *Midlands* who dwell in great stone citadels. Now allied to *Palatia*.

URGRAYNE – a daughter of *Djara Luna*, called the Witch-Queen of the Harath *Éduins* and a mysterious meddler active everywhere since the days of *Düréa*. Some in *Daradja* are said to follow her devious instructions and are

called members of the Witch's Host.

ÜRÜNE DÜRÉ – a great isle in the *Silver Scale Sea*, where *Ariahavé* led her favorites in the *Golden Age* to teach the arts of civilization and found the realm of *Düréa*, now long lost beneath the sea. Usually translated from the Düréan as "Mountain of Thrones."

USURPER, the – soubriquet for Urech Aiths, the current Duke of *Palatia*, who took the Ducal Throne in a coup.

VANI – eagle- or vulture-headed son of *Geteema*; the Mountain King who brings the Spring thaw, and ancestor of the Vanimorians (see *Vanimoria*).

VANIMORIA – mountainous part of the *Midlands*, but during the *Golden Age* the earthly realm of *Geteema*, and so spared some of the desolation that marked the rest of *Geniché*'s Paradise. Its proud, martial barbarians are a key part of the *Thessid-Golan Empire*.

WATCHTOWER KINGS, the – descendants of Maelite and Danian warlords who fought against *Githwaine* and were granted holds to keep watch over *Lost Uthedmael* by *Fortias the Brave*. Their domain was called *Maece*.

WORM KINGS, the – generals of the *Thessid-Golan Empire* who became twisted by dark magics after *Dauban Hess* disappeared. To retain their appointed thrones, they embraced foul rituals that extended their lives but corrupted and decayed their bodies. The *Oracle Queens* cursed them in revenge for the sack of *Khael*, and after the *Catastrophe* the last *Dragon Kings* hunted them to extinction.

WAR IN HEAVEN, the – 21-year war at the end of the *Golden Age*. After the sinking of *Ürüne Düré* while *Yhera* wandered in grief, *Irré* accused *Illiki Helios* of abandoning *Düréa* and cast him down. On Earth, *Ishraha* usurped the Dragon Throne of *Illia* from *Islik* in a parallel rebellion. At the war's end, Yhera returned from the Underworld and restored Agdah and Illiki to the Heavens, and Islik returned to claim both the Dragon and Sun Thrones.

YHERA – Queen of Heaven, Goddess of Night, Queen of the Waters, one of the goddesses of the Moon, and often worshipped as the Creatrix, the divine origin of all that is. She is the Great Goddess of language, sovereignty, love, dominion, wealth, wisdom, fertility, war, and protection. She is also known as *Yhera Tredea, Yhera Luna, Yhera Negra, Yhera Cosmopeiia, Yhera Chthonia, Yhera Genetra, Yhera Parage, Yhera Fortuna, Yhera Hegemone, Yhera Daradja, Dread Yhera, Yhera Anath,* and *Yhera Invictus*, amongst other epithets.

THE WAR IN HEAVEN
AS TOLD IN THE HIGHLANDS OF DARADJA

After the death of Agdah Cosmopeiia at the hands of Geteema, his son Illiki the Bull left the embattled walls of Ürüne Düré and rode the Moon Path into the Heavens. There he assumed the Sun Throne and was hailed as Illiki Helios, the Sun Bull, the new god of the Sun, and he took over the solar duties of Agdah Cosmopeiia, seeing that golden Helios followed its route along the Sun Path each day. But Yhera, the Queen of Heaven, did not greet Illiki as the new Sun, so gripped by mourning was she for the loss of Agdah; for nine years Yhera grieved, even as Ürüne Düré fell to Geteema's jealous children. Yhera grieved until Hathhalla came to her and woke the anger in her, and guided her to where Geteema hid in her Garden, mourning her own losses. Yhera and Geteema fought and the world roiled with their battle, until Yhera drove her sister into the Underworld and imprisoned her there. But Yhera too experienced death of a sort, and she wandered lost in the Underworld clothed in ashes, seeking the spirit of her lover, Agdah.

THE CLAIM OF IRRÉ

While she searched the Underworld for 27 years, the War in Heaven began, for not all accepted the new order. Irré the Black Goat, the Locust of the Wilderness, had been the last consort of Yhera to stand on the walls of Ürüne Düré, and the exiled Düréans now held him as the Last Defender, who had brandished his courage at the howling hordes of Geteema's children. And Irré looked about the Heavens and did not like what he saw. Agdah had been consumed, but death to a god, even at the hands of another god, is not a final state, and he should have returned; but Irré instead saw Illiki on the Sun Throne.

Irré came to the Heavens wrapped in a mantle of dark fire and smoke, and came to the Court of Heaven and stood before the Sun Throne itself, and there he accused Illiki of abandoning the defense of Düréa. Illiki freely admitted doing so: the Sun Throne had been vacant, and needed to be filled, and so he had taken the seat of Helios. And then Irré used these words from Illiki's own mouth to condemn him further, saying that Illiki had seized the Sun Throne improperly and was a Usurper, as it was Yhera's right to appoint the next Sun God, and that Illiki's haste to claim power had sealed the death of Agdah Helios, his own father, by preventing his return.

Illiki at first laughed, thinking Irré was quite mad to come and accuse him of such things in his own Court, but then he realized that very few were laughing with him. Irré had done his work well, as had Amaymon, and many of the Court had already had their hearts poisoned against Illiki. Fear and anger gripped Illiki then, and he cried out for his guards to arm themselves, and he flung himself off the Sun Throne at Irré and they battled in the Court of Heaven.

For a year and a day they fought, and around them battled the Celestial orders; on Illiki's side fought many of the angels of light and the celestial spirits of fire and air, but many of them also fought on Irré's side, as did many of the Star Dragons and the spirits of storm and thunder, even nightmares and angels of death who came up from the Underworld. And finally Irré prevailed, and sent Illiki the Bull crashing down from the firmaments of Heaven into the pit of the Underworld, where he was imprisoned. Irré took the Sun Throne then, and it was a Black Sun that rose the next day, and for the next 22 years. But the spirits and angels that had sided with Illiki refused to accept Irré on the Sun Throne, and so the War in Heaven continued unabated, as angel killed angel and Star hunted Star across the turbulent Heavens.

A WAR ON EARTH

On Earth the reign of Islik in Illia grew troubled; his father had been cast out of Heaven, and now a Usurper rose each morning in his place. In anger Islik renounced Irré as a murderer, and renounced the gods for allowing Illiki's ouster, and he ordered that sacrifice be withheld from the gods until they restored his father to the Sun Throne and the Cosmos to its rightful order. Yhera had been silent for some years, and

many of the priests and priestesses had already begun to doubt her return, so most accepted his law. But some did not, and they began to speak out against the King on Earth. Amongst his Court was a general named Ishraha, a prideful half-angel born of the blood of Ligrid, who had come down from the Heavens to serve in Islik's army. Ishraha was displeased with Islik's renunciation of the gods and he wished to side with those that wanted to keep to the old ways, and Amaymon knew this and began to whisper to Ishraha. *Had not Islik sat idly by while his own father was thrown down from Heaven?* asked Amaymon. And as Ishraha thought on this he realized that if Islik had not aided his father it was because he **could not** have aided his father; that despite his power, Islik did not have the strength or the knowledge to travel any of the Paths to Heaven.

And so Ishraha came to suspect that the real cause of Islik's anger at the gods was Islik's own weakness, his own inability to aid his father in his time of need, and Ishraha found delight in this, and a great hate for Islik and his weakness was born in him. He conspired with others in the Court of Illia and with other spirits of the Celestial Realms, and he overthrew Islik, and cast him into exile. Ishraha reinstated sacrifices and offerings to all the gods, beginning with Irré.

Islik wandered for 21 years in the wilderness, and during this time the War in Heaven came often to the Known World, as the angels and spirits seeking to depose Irré also turned to war against Ishraha on the Throne of the World, and men and angels fought side by side and against each other under the visage of the Black Sun.

THE RETURN OF THE QUEEN

Yhera's wanderings came to an end in the Court of her sister Geniché, who initiated her into the mysteries of death and loss and showed her the path back to the Heavens. But Yhera could not leave without Agdah, and naked and unveiled she bowed down before her sister and pleaded for Agdah's release. Geniché relented, and revealed the secret of where Agdah was imprisoned, and guided by a small but bright light Yhera quested deep into the Underworld to find him in the belly of Geteema, and they battled once again until Yhera had Geteema pinned within the Earth. Yhera held her sister's gaping maw open and reached in and plucked Agdah out, and to her surprise she found Illiki had been swallowed too, and so she freed both of her consorts, and left Geteema chained and bound in deepest darkness.

Yhera returned to the Heavens with Agdah and Illiki to find the Celestial World aflame with war, and Irré upon the Sun Throne. As Yhera gazed upon the angels of Heaven their fighting stopped. Irré rose and greeted his Queen and his King, but at first he would not step down from the Sun Throne, for neither Agdah nor Illiki had returned from the Underworld by their own power. Yhera saw the hatred that had grown in the Heavens during Irré's reign, and did not want to confirm him as the Sun, and she despaired until there was a clangor of trumpets, and Islik ascended to the Heavens.

For Islik, too, had been recently in the Underworld, where he had journeyed to free his companion Agall from the clutches of Death, and he had returned in triumph to reclaim his Throne on Earth from Ishraha. He had finally seen the Way to Heaven, and after setting his earthly kingdom in order he had ascended the Sun Path, and stood to claim the Sun Throne of his fathers. Yhera welcomed him and Irré acquiesced before his brightness, and Islik became a King in Heaven, as he was a King on Earth. Agdah became Cosmopeiia again, the Cosmos King, and Illiki became the Sun Bull again, and Irré too still laid a claim to the Sun Throne on some days, but none was truly the Sun King anymore; instead, they shared that title in turn.

Irré returned to the dark parts of the Earth from whence he came, but many of the angels and celestial spirits that had fought with him did not much like the new King in Heaven, and they followed Irré into darkness and fire, and became the orders of the dark angels of the Underworld, the *Rahabi*: the Dhuréleal and the Golodriel, the Bharab Dzerek and the Sharab Deceal, the Gamezhiel and the Ghazharab. And many of the Rahabi remained armed for war, and still fight the War in Heaven when they think Yhera is not looking.

HE TEN VICTORIES OF ISLIK
HILE IN EXILE FROM HIS EARTHLY THRONE

e main text of the Divine King's cult is the *Islikinaem* – called *Timit Ashvail Islik* by the Phoenix Court – which is composed of the ed *The Ten Victories of Islik* and then the appended *King Cycles*, the s of Hemispian Dragon Kings and their Deeds that followed in the turies immediately after Islik's ascension. According to the *kinaem*, these are the Ten Victories of Islik:

S FIRST: OVER THE LIONS OF TELESIA

er being exiled from Illia, Islik journeyed south into Hemispia, to ancient kingdom of Telesia and its capital of Agrapios. He sought and allies against the Rebel and Usurper Ishraha, and petitioned g Buradis of Telesia to withhold tribute from Ishraha and sacrifice m the gods until he was restored to his throne and his father to his. instead the lion-headed sons of King Buradis, each of whom had strength of a dozen men, challenged his fitness as King and sought mprison him as a prize for Ishraha, to whom they had sworn giance. Islik defeated them in ceremonial combat, and realizing that had few allies amongst the traitor Kings of the south, he left mispia with their lion heads on the prow of his ship.

S SECOND: OVER THE SIRENS OF THE SILVER SCALE SEA

k crossed over the Silver Scale Sea with his friend and companion, ll of the Black Sail, once King of Galia, who renounced sacrifice became the second of the Four Kings in Exile, and a handful of sals who were loyal to him as the True King of Illia. The sirens of Silver Scale Sea called to them with their enchanted songs, and ll and the others on board their ship were overcome and would have ed their ship into danger, but Islik heard the songs of the sea-spirits was not moved. He saved his companions from being lost forever he mists of the Sea.

S THIRD: OVER THE CRUELTY OF THE DANIAN KING

k and Agall landed in Dania, where they were taken prisoner by the riors of the Danian King, Myrad, lord of Therapoli. They were risoned in his dungeons, from which none had ever escaped, and rein met two other Kings who were in Exile, Jala the Good, Prince listant Samarappa, and Coromat, once King of Vanimoria. Islik vinced them to renounce sacrifice, and they joined him as blood thers. Islik solved the puzzles of King Myrad's dungeons, and led other Kings in Exile to their freedom.

S FOURTH: OVER THE LURES OF THE DARADJ QUEEN

Four Kings in Exile crossed over the mountains into the Highlands Daradja, and there they were enchanted by the charms of the Daradj een, Arathea. They lingered in her Court for many moons, and one one they were seduced by her lies and honeyed words – first Jala, n Agall, and then Coromat – until she attempted to compromise k. He alone amongst his companions saw through her disguise and glamours to the ugliness within her, and he exposed her to his ow Kings, freeing them from the spells she had cast upon them.

S FIFTH: OVER THE HUNT OF CERAM

Kings in Exile fled Daradja and its Spider Queen into the ghtness of the Sun's Anvil. There they found the camps of a fifth g in Exile, Ceram the Storm King, the Thunderer. Ceram invited m to share his fire, and they sought to convince him to renounce rifice and join their wandering life, but in the morning Ceram ealed his base nature and set them as the sacrificial prey to his hunt. ram hunted them across the Sun's Anvil and into the Sea of Sands, they despaired of his pursuit, but Islik found Ceram's Gate into the in Éduins, and there the Four Kings hid among his trophies in the e of Bones until Ceram had thundered into the distance.

S SIXTH: OVER THE DANGERS OF THE SEA OF SANDS

Four Kings in Exile went back out into the Sea of Sands after ram departed, having failed in his hunt, and headed West, hoping to to reach lands close to Jala's former home in Samarappa. But the Sea of Sands is a vast and trackless waste, full of curses and traps, and they were brought close to the brink of death. But Islik would not let the ill will of the Dead Earth overcome him, and he found great wells of strength within himself, and these he shared with his companions. He persevered and led them out of the Sea of Sands when it seemed as though they would at last perish.

HIS SEVENTH: OVER THE WESTERN WARLOCK-KINGS

When the Four Kings in Exile came out of the trackless wastes, they were set upon by the evil Warlock-Kings of the desert peoples of the West, the Rajiks and the Khaghals, who barred them from crossing the Ferras Nash, the Mountains of Iron, into the valleys of Lake Hazrat. Each of the Four Kings in Exile attempted to cross the mountain passes, but only Islik was able to pierce through the strange magics of the Warlock-Kings and lead the others through. When they saw their magics had been overcome by his purity, the Warlock-Kings of the Rajiks and the Khaghals slunk into the mountains, and the Four Kings in Exile came to rule the Lands of the Lake, outlawing sacrifice and taking wives amongst the Rajiks and Khaghals.

HIS EIGHTH: OVER THE TREACHERY OF THE BLOODED

Their peaceful reign lasted for 19 years, until some amongst their Rajik and Khaghal subjects rebelled and made sacrifice once more to the gods. The rebels, called the Blooded, strove against the Kings in Exile with sword and magic and argument. Jala was convinced by trickery to join with the Blooded, and he fell into sacrilege and fled back to his homeland, abandoning the other Kings in Exile; Coromat killed many of their attackers, but was driven insane by their magics, and fled into the wastes; great Agall lost his legendary strength and was slain by the enemy. Islik alone stood to the very end against the Blooded, and though they had ended the Four Kings in Exile, he was able to drive them from the battlefield and stand there alone, protecting the body of his friend and stalwart companion, Agall.

HIS NINTH: OVER DEATH

Standing over the body of his boon companion Agall, Islik swore an oath to not be conquered by Death, and he swore that he would save those that had been loyal to him from the cold embrace of the Underworld. Islik followed the spirit of Agall into the Underworld, pausing once he was past its Gates to curse the Blooded so they could not follow him, and in the depths of Hell he came to grips with the Queen of the Dead, and there he learned her secrets and his mind became illuminated by forbidden knowledge. While in the Underworld he saw two great Leviathans fighting, and in the belly of one he spied the spirit of his father, and he freed his father's spirit while the dark Leviathans were in combat. He found and freed Agall from the clutches of the Queen of the Dead, and brought his spirit back to the Known World.

HIS TENTH: OVER ISHRAHA THE USURPER

Having returned with the secrets of the Underworld and the spirit of Agall in his keeping, Islik returned to Illia in disguise, and came before Ishraha upon his usurped throne. Ishraha and his traitorous courtiers did not recognize him, until he threw off his disguise and burned them with the fury of his righteousness and the illumination of his spirit. Despite his hurts Ishraha assailed Islik with sword and claw, but Islik was infused with the power of Death and the strength of the spirit of Agall, and he tore Ishraha's wings from his body and hurled him into the Underworld. Those at the Court that had supported the Rebel Angel fled, but Islik and those that had remained loyal to him while he was in exile hunted many of them down.

These are the Ten Great Victories of Islik, which he performed while in exile to prove his worth to reclaim the Throne of Illia and the title of King of the Earth, and his divinity, so that he could enter the Heavens as the true heir to the Sun Throne of his father and claim the title of the King of Heaven, as only a true and pure hero marked by the divine can return whole from the Underworld.

THE GOLDEN REALM OF AN-ATHAIR

AFTER THE FALL OF ÜRÜNE DÜRÉ

The Known World was a tumultuous place after the fall of Ürüne Düré, and for many, it seemed as though the desperate and hard times that wracked the world after Geniché left the earth and imposed the First Law had returned. In a few spots civilization and wonder remained, and one of those places was in Daradja, where Queen Lanys, descended of lamented Dara, ruled over Daradjans, Danians, and Düréan exiles. Word of her beauty and the strengths of her realm reached the ears of the wandering Four Kings in Exile, and they visited to vie for her hand and win her aid in regaining their thrones. She saw greatness in each of them and she desired those qualities for her own realm as well, but she also saw in them jealousy and possessiveness; they were Kings, after all, and each wanted to claim her for himself. So she secretly took each of them as a consort without telling the others, and bore them each a daughter, before the Kings in Exile discovered her ploy and continued on their way.

Eventually Yhera returned from the Underworld and commanded Irré to relent his place, and Islik assumed the mantle of the Sun King, and the world rejoiced, though sorrow and despair and hardship lingered. Lanys' daughters grew in power and might, but in the end the jealousy Lanys had seen in their fathers was their undoing, and Goatis, daughter of Agall, grew jealous of her sister Damara, daughter of Islik, and murdered her in a drunken rage. The bright future Lanys had sought for Daradja disintegrated in a civil war from which the land never fully recovered.

Many Daradjans sought refuge amongst their neighbors from the bloody wars that wracked the Highlands. The Danians, who had paid tribute to Daradja since Dara's time, no longer did so after the death of Damara, and they did not wish to allow exiles in their lands, fearing they might be drawn into the wars of the mountain citadels; all of the Kings and Queens of the Danians turned the refugees away. But the Athairis, the Danians who lived in the great Erid Wold, invited those fleeing the mountain wars to settle in the spirit-filled woods of their domain.

THE SPRING QUEENS OF AN-ATHAIR

This proved to their advantage, for amongst the refugees were Düréan priestesses descended from those who had held the Great Garden Temple of Geniché in Ürüne Düré, where the Queen of the Underworld had still been the Queen of the Earth, and they knew secrets of the natural world long since lost. They showed the Athairis how to reawaken the Earth abandoned by Geniché, where to find power in it, where to draw strength. And they showed the Athairis how they could make the land resemble the lost Paradise of Geniché once again, at least to some small degree. The Athairis built a wondrous temple out of living tree and carved rock, a Green Temple that nourished, refreshed, and healed all who entered it, and the High Priestesses of the Temple came to be called the Spring Queens. The Erid Wold grew green and lush, a bounty for those that lived there, and the land and the people lived in balance and in harmony, and the sheen of Paradise lay upon them both.

The neighboring Kings and Queens of the Danians marveled at the beauty and wealth of An-Athair; some made tribute, and became part of what came to be called the Golden Realm. Others, however, sought to take the wealth of the Athairis by force, but here again Daradja's plight was An-Athair's fortune, for amongst the exiled Daradjans and Düréans were many veterans of the mountain wars and the descendants of those who had fought at Ürüne Düré. They knew war well, and they taught their secrets to the Athairis. But the Athairi knights of the Golden Realm fought not only with secret war knowledge but also with magical vigor to protect the Queens of the Green Temple.

The exploits of the knights of the Golden Realm became the stuff of Danian legend. Just as legendary, if not more so, were the feasts and celebrations in their honor and at the Green Temple, where the fertility of the land was ensured by the ritual union of the Spring Queens of An-Athair with local heroes who wore golden Sun Masks to invoke Islik, the returned Sun King. Women came from far and wide to serve as Spring Queens, and heroes, knights, and woodsmen came too to do their duty and bless the land, and with every union the land grew greener and the Golden Realm grew brighter.

THE COMING OF THE SEA BULLS

A shadow soon fell on An-Athair: the sails of the Sea Bulls, the Aurians, the descendants of Heth the Sea King. Raiders and pillagers from the far north, they had been fought off, if barely, by the Veiled Queens of Palatia, and had found safe landing on the unpopulated eastern coast of Dania, which they called the Gift of Heth. Soon they came through the pass of Édain, and they conquered portions of the Danian lands and subjected their peoples, until they came to the borders of An-Athair. They marveled at the plenty of the Plain of Horns, and sought to make it their own, but the knights of the Golden Realm rode from the Erid Wold to disrupt their hunts and war parties, and the Aurians retreated to the east. Some amongst the Aurians became enchanted with the knights of the Golden Realm, and sent emissaries to the Green Temple, and lay with the Spring Queens and were granted domain over lands in the east.

However, most of the Aurians were not enchanted, but were still instilled with the fury and rage of their ancestor and god, Heth, who embodied the hurricane and the tidal wave. Their magicians sought ways to fight the knights of the Golden Realm, and one day a Horned Man visited one of them, and told him how to make an axe and enchant a stone that could cut down an Erid Wold tree and prevent it from growing again. The Horned Man explained that the trees were the source of the knight's power, and once they were cut down the knights would be made weak and vulnerable.

So the Aurians brought axe and fire to the Erid Wold, and began at the river Abenbrae. They burned and cut down the trees of the wood, and on the each stump they placed an enchanted stone, and as the Horned Man had promised the trees did not grow back. The knights of the Golden Realm fought valiantly, but once the Aurians knew the trick, their fate was sealed; they became weaker and weaker as the forest disappeared, and one by one the knights of the Golden Realm fell.

THE SACK OF THE GREEN TEMPLE

The Erid Wold being destroyed acre by acre, the knights of the Golden Realm falling; the fate of the Green Temple became fixed, though it took years of pillage to bring about the end. Eventually the Aurians weakened the knights' defenses enough to strike directly at the Green Temple, and the trees and stones of the Green Temple were pulled down and ruined, and the Spring Queens were raped and then drowned in the Eridbrae, and the paradise that had been An-Athair faded in an instant.

The Aurians' moment of triumph was short-lived, however, for the body of the last Spring Queen floated down the Eridbrae to the sea, and there she was found by Heth; and Heth the Sea King had been a lover of Geniché's, and he knew that the Earth and the Sea were one, and that Yhera was Queen of both. Heth has always been fickle and arbitrary, and though he too destroyed without pity it enraged him that his children had done so dark a deed. So he turned his back on them and withdrew his blessings, so that when the Aurian lords put to sea to continue on their pillaging, the waves crushed their boats and water spirits dragged them drowning into the depths.

The end of the Golden Realm left a rent Dania and the dispirited, land-locked Aurians open to the arrival of Dauban Hess, who came and subjected the land with ease, bringing with him the teachings of the Sun Court, which were embraced by the Aurians in particular, as they had lost their patron and ancestor. The Erid Wold in time recovered, but is a place of dark memories and vengeful spirits; Aurian lords of the east destroyed a vast part of the forest, and the trees never returned, and that land became the Plain of Stones. To this day, Aurians are considered cursed at sea, and rarely leave the land.

GITHWAINE The Last Worm King

By the end of the Age of Legends, the **Worm Kings** had been [rou]ted from their seats of power in the Phoenix Court, first by the [cur]se of the Catastrophe called upon them by the dying **Oracle Queen** [En]Khael, which engulfed their capital in Millene in volcanic ash and [fire]; and then, during the Winter Century that followed, by the hunts [of] the **Dragon Kings**, the scions of Islik who took Hathhalla as their [gu]iding light and sought to destroy at all costs those Worm Kings that [ha]d survived the Catastrophe.

For a time, at least one known Worm King in the East managed to [fin]d safety unseen by the questing Dragon Kings: **Githwaine**, son of [Du]rast, lord of the Uthed Danian citadel of Na Caila, and once a [ge]neral to **Dauban Hess**. Records of the time are poor but most [be]lieve him to have been but 26 when Dauban Hess made him Lord-[G]eneral of Tir-en-tiel in Vanimoria, a position of great honor as it [in]cluded guarding the sacred fields where Dauban Hess had defeated [N]ymarga the Tyrant. **Hurias** of Truse, the last great Danian scholar [to] study Githwaine, showed conclusively that with the title had also [co]me guardianship of the secrets of Nymarga's final resting place, his [cur]sed and salted tomb.

Proximity to such evil has its costs, and despite the trust of Dauban [H]ess, Githwaine grew close to many of Nymarga's old magicians as [th]ey returned to advise the Lord-Generals of the Phoenix Court. In [th]e tumultuous years after Dauban Hess' disappearance, Githwaine [sp]ent increasing time at the Golden Court in Millene playing games [of] intrigue, and is widely thought to have secretly become a Whisperer [de]voted to Amaymon. His name is recorded as amongst the first lords [of] the Phoenix Court to embrace the foul rituals that transformed [th]em into the undead things that would so plague the Age of Legends. [Bu]t he was believed to be away in Tir-en-tiel when the Catastrophe [de]stroyed Millene, and he hid in shadows while his fellows perished in [th]e Dragon Kings' hunts.

GITHWAINE RETURNS TO UTHED DANIA

In i627 Githwaine's now-distant relations in Na Caila – who [pr]obably did not know he was even still alive, as he had been gone [fr]om there almost four hundred years, and there were none there who [ha]d known him in life – were all killed by poison, accident, disease, or [ag]e. This appears to have marked Githwaine's return to Uthed Dania, [ha]ving escaped the detection of the Dragon Kings and their allies as [th]ey swept through Thessidia and Vanimoria on their way West. But [rat]her than reclaim it, Githwaine let Na Caila stand vacant, a cursed [an]d blackened ruin that brought death to any that tried to inhabit it, [an]d instead he used magic and fell powers to masquerade as a young [l]ordling of the nearby citadel of Arath. He used that keep's position [gu]arding the approach to Bora Gara to make contact with the [ba]rbarian Djar Maelite lords there and cultivate them as his allies, and [he] used them as proxies to begin raids and trouble along Uthed [Da]nia's mountainous borders.

The last Dragon King of Uthed Dania, **Heraud**, had perished in [Se]keret hunting Worm Kings, but had left behind a Council of Kings [fr]om amongst his Danian and Mael subjects, and Githwaine began by [wh]isper and intrigue to grow a secret network at their Court in Sanas [Ti]l. In secret he began to introduce the worship of corruption [am]ongst those that followed him, and human sacrifices and [un]speakable rites were performed in hidden catacombs and temples. [Th]e cults of Amaymon and Ligrid gained new converts in the Uthed [co]urts, and some say the modern cult of Nymarga, the cult of [N]ymarga after his death (as opposed to the cult of the living Nymarga [or] the Worldly Tyrant ruling Thessidia), was begun by Githwaine in [Ut]hed Dania, where he taught secret ways of contacting Nymarga's fell [sp]irit gleaned from his guardianship of Nymarga's tomb. The Uthed [Co]uncil of Kings was greatly weakened by the Djar Mael raiders on [th]eir borders and the insidious corruption that beggared the Court, [bu]t none knew the cause of their troubles.

A LIGHT CAST UPON POISONED SHADOW

Erlwulf, Dragon King of Dania, of the blood of Islik the Divine King and the last known of his kind, returned to his realm in i648 as the last of those that had journeyed West to finish off the Worm Kings. He and his entourage thought to find a peaceful end, having completed their task of destroying their Worm King enemies, but instead he discovered to his horror the telltale signs of a Worm King's presence amongst his neighbors. He raised an army of Danian, Aurian, and Daradjan knights, and sent word to the Sun Court seeking whatever help they could provide. The Winter Century had marked a growing isolationism in the lands of the Silver Scale Sea, but small bands of heroes from the cities of Hemispia and even Sekeret and Thessidia responded to Erlwulf's call. With the nominal aid of the Uthed Council of Kings, Erlwulf began searching through Uthed Dania for the source of the corruption he sensed, but the allies of Githwaine fought a war of stealth and cunning against him, never warring openly but only through disguise and ambush and poison. This was a cruel war, with none knowing who was friend or foe, and Githwaine and his allies preyed upon the noblemen and common folk of the country alike, visiting foul and grievous dooms upon those that aided Erlwulf in his search.

True Dragon Kings could see into the hearts of men, past guile and disguise and sometimes even enchantment, and Erlwulf sensed the corruption in the heart of the Council of Kings, and so never trusted them fully, instead making his chief bases the Erid Maelite citadel of Warwark in the south and the Daradjan citadel of Heth Moll in the north. It was while returning to Heth Moll through the Vale of Barrows in i657 with his closest aides that Erlwulf was fatally ambushed by Githwaine himself at the head of a force of Djar Maelite warlords and Daradj brigands. Through nine years of their war, Githwaine had heretofore avoided direct confrontation with Erlwulf, but he chose to strike when hard campaigning had finally exhausted the Dragon King and his entourage. From their heights the knights of Heth Moll saw the attack, and sent a strong relief party, but they arrived too late to do aught but save the body of Erlwulf from the clutches of their dark enemy. The body of the last Dragon King was brought to Heth Moll, and he was interred there as a bulwark against the evils of the Vale of Barrows.

The danger and strength of the Worm Kings had been their powers of corruption and sorcery and poison, as they struck with honeyed words and spells of black magic and a touch that brought disease and decay; their physical battles with the Dragon Kings had always been fought with mortal proxies unless cornered in their hidden lairs, for the powers of Islik's blood in the melee were unrivaled. But the knights of Heth Moll and the few that survived of Erlwulf's entourage reported that Githwaine had sought out Erlwulf on the field of battle and slain him in direct combat undisguised, armed, and face-to-face, and this turn shocked and worried many.

GHAVAURER, DAYBRINGER, AND *GLADRINGER*

Divinations were performed, and though a veil of shadows lay about Githwaine a secret was gleaned: the Worm King had armed himself with an enchanted sword, the fell and infamous blade called *Ghavaurer,* made by Nymarga himself to have special powers against the blood and the worshippers of Islik. Nymarga had wielded it against Dauban Hess in their battle at Tir-en-Tiel, and when tested against Dauban Hess' famed *Daybringer*, the great heirloom of the Sun Court forged of sun-metal by Daedekamani, *Ghavaurer* had been found to be lacking. Though perhaps the weakness had been in the hand that wielded it, for now Githwaine held it, plundered from Nymarga's tomb when he had been its guardian, and he used it to end the known line of Islik.

The death of Erlwulf was a disaster for the forces arrayed against Githwaine, but even in their disarray he chose to remain in the shadows, a phantom preying upon the weaknesses of men. New generals took up Erlwulf's banner and rallied those that did not shirk from the search, and though their numbers were greatly reduced by fear and corruption and battle, those that continued the fight against Githwaine did so with almost fanatical zeal. Chief amongst those who hunted the Last Worm were **Gavir**, the Warlock Lord of Heth Moll; **Daurus Tull**, Knight-Captain of the Company of Sails; **Yifyr Surehand**, King of Dania; and their greatest champion, the Aurian hero-knight **Fortias** of Édain.

In i666, after more than a decade of this continued shadow war, the lords of the Middle Kingdoms called for a great council in Sanas Sill, and there all the Kings and nobles of Uthed Dania gathered. The magisters of the University of Therapoli and the priests of the Sun Court had prepared a secret ritual at the behest of Fortias, and when the Uthed Court had gathered they performed it suddenly, and Githwaine's disguise was lifted, and he was revealed in all his horror. But his foes had underestimated the depths of corruption in Sanas Sill and did not realize they were outnumbered there, and once Githwaine was revealed, his followers in the Court drew arms against his enemies and a great slaughter ensued from which few escaped.

Fortias was one of those that did, and he rallied the last of the uncorrupted Uthed and Mael lords and with knights of Dania, Auria, and Daradja at his side he led them in the sack of Sanas Sill, but Githwaine too escaped. The Worm King took as his seat the citadel at Liss Dyved, and ruled there openly and without disguise, and nine years of dark and haunted war followed as Uthed Dania was contested. The atrocities of the war now reached worse depths than anything that had come before. The cults of Amaymon, Ligrid, and Nymarga revealed themselves openly, and human sacrifice and foul rites were practiced in the light of day, and the constraints of law, tradition, and culture melted away into anarchy, debasement, and desecration. Citadels and cities were besieged and razed, with each side scorching the earth to deny their enemies the slightest advantage. Githwaine would raise his slain soldiers as *Hathaz-Ghúl* to fight his enemies even in death, and he called up wights and ghosts from the Vale of Barrows to stalk them in the night.

Against *Ghavaurer* and the unnatural foot soldiers of Githwaine's army Fortias sought a counter, but *Daybringer* had been lost with Dauban Hess, and for a time Fortias despaired of finding its equal. But **Gobelin**, the great Daradj smith of the Bodmall clan, made for him *Gladringer,* a sword forged in the ruins of the Green Temple and quenched in the pools of the Spring Queen's blood that could still be found there, along with harnesses of bronze armor enchanted against the unquiet dead. With that the tides turned, and fire and sword were brought to all those that aided Githwaine in Uthed Dania, until Fortias sacked Liss Dyved and hunted Githwaine to his death, piercing his magics and illusions and finally his corrupted body with *Gladringer's* enchanted blade.

But a full and final victory eluded Fortias even then, for loyal Djar Mael lords spirited away Githwaine's body even as the knights of Heth Moll had recovered Erlwulf's, and it is said they buried it in secret and protected it with grave glyphs, bound ghosts, and warriors who accepted the curse of undeath to guard the body of their master. Some believe it was interred beneath Holl Ari, as an icon against the body of Erlwulf at Heth Moll; others that it was returned to his birthplace at Na Caila; others that it was taken deep into Djar Mael to the citadel at Ardeal; and still others believe that he was buried in an unmarked barrow in the Vale, its location amongst hundreds of other anonymous barrows now lost even to the Djar Maelites. The Sun Court pronounced a great curse upon Uthed Dania to scour it of the Worm King's taint, and Uthed Dania became a vast and ashen wasteland, ever afterwards called *Lost Uthedmael*.

The cursed *Ghavaurer* was never found and is believed buried with Githwaine's body. Four centuries later *Gladringer* was lost in the Black Day Battle when it fell from the hand of High King **Darwain Urfortias**, ever afterwards called the Fumbler, the one sour note to the resounding victory of the Middle Kingdoms over the Thessid-Golan Empire. None know who took it from the field, or where it is today.

THE WARS OF THE THRONE THIE[

THE ISLIKLIDS APPEAR

Soon after the Peace of Tir-en-tiel, when the Empire of Thessid-Gola made secret pact with the Isliklidae and warded off an invasion of the Imperial lowlands, the Isliklidae crossed the Red Wastes with their Düméghal army and appeared in the southern reaches of the Dain Éduins. They struck hard and fast against the wily and dangerous mountain kings of the Djar Maelites, and by i1214 they had conquered and pacified those most unruly people and proclaime[three Kingdoms of their own: Ugeram, Boradja, and Morica. Thoug[separated from the Middle Kingdoms by Lost Uthedmael, the arriva[of the Isliklidae and their heretical claims of descent from Islik himse[did not go unnoticed by their eastern neighbors. No great love existed between the Middle Kingdoms and the subjected Djar Maelites, but the Watchtower Kings of Maece roused themselves int[a crusade to rid the mountains of the new arrivals. For over thirty years the armies and heroes of Maece and Dania crossed the horrors of Lost Uthedmael and the Vale of Barrows to reach the western mountains, only to be defeated time and again by the Düméghal and[Djar Mael warlords commanded by the Isliklidae. In i1239 the last o[the Kings of Maece, **Gwyrfyr Brightstar**, and his chief warlords reached the furthest into the Isliklid realms of any of their kin, but were massacred attempting to besiege the plateau tower-gate of Cir At'tor. No heir to the throne of Maece survived, and the High King, **Fergus**, appointed no other, signaling an end to the realm of Maece and their wars against the Isliklidae.

A THRONE DISAPPEARS

The throne of the Kings of Maece, like the thrones of the other sovereign kings of the Middle Kingdoms, had been built in imitation of the Dragon Throne of Therapoli, itself based on the original Dragon Throne of Illia made by Brage himself and lost in the Catastrophe. Dauban Hess had ordered a version of the Dragon Throne made for each of his Kings and Generals before he left to fin[the Dawn, and the Dragon Throne in Therapoli was one of the few remaining copies. Great power resided in it and in whoever rightfull[took its seat, and some of that power was conferred into the thrones that were modeled after it and given to the petty kings and nobles of the Middle Kingdoms. Not as much, for sure, but enough for the thrones to be considered relics of great power and authority. With n[King left in Maece, the throne of Maece was ordered returned from Angora to Therapoli in i1240, but on the West King's Road on the way to Truse it vanished from the procession in the middle of the night.

A great hue and cry was raised, and a search of the Plain of Stones begun, but no sign of the throne or who had taken it could be found[Talk of witchcraft and treachery began – how else could a throne of power disappear from within an armed camp? – but the priests of the Divine King could find no proof of either in their divinations. The disappearance of the throne was a considerable loss, but seemed destined to become a minor mystery of legend, retold over tankards o[ale and wine – until the throne of Dain Dania disappeared as well.

SUSPICIONS ARISE

The throne of Dain Dania disappeared from the very throne room in the Dain King's castle at Aprenna one night; it simply vanished by morning, though the King's Guard watched over the hall. Once agai[a great search was conducted, but no trace of the throne or who had taken it could be found. With two thrones now missing, suspicions began to arise in earnest, both about who could be taking the thrones and why. Soon the courts of the Middle Kingdoms abounded with rumor and innuendo and speculation. The King of Erid Dania, neighbor to Dain Dania and who had last seen charge of the throne

Maece as it made its way to Truse, was quickly suspected, as were the
[wit]ches and warlocks said to reside in the haunts of the Erid Wold.
[So]me suggested brigands from the Highlands, or cultists of Nymarga
[see]king some secret power in the thrones, or a secret cult of Ishraha the
[Rebel] seeking to undermine the Seated Kings, or the new threat from
[the] west, the Isliklidae, sending their hidden hands forth to rob those
[who] had so recently warred against them. Others dismissed it as
[co]incidence, or even suggested that the Dain King had hidden his own
[thr]one to divert suspicion from his involvement in the theft of the
[thr]one of Maece, which he had long coveted. An emissary of the High
[Kin]g was sent to the Danias to question the Dain and Erid Kings, and
[wh]ile the emissary was in royal Westmark in conference with the Erid
[Kin]g **Dyvryn**, the Ivory Throne of Dainphalia disappeared.
[ ] This caused great consternation in Therapoli, for up to that point
[the] problem was to some extent assumed to be a Danian problem; but
[now] whoever was taking the thrones had reached past the capital to
[ta]ck the Ivory Throne, though a minor one, from the hall of Urphalia
[whi]le the Phalian Duke hunted in the Marek Mole. There was no
[lon]ger any question in the courts of the land but that some intelligent
[des]ign was at work, an evil intent at play. A year of searching yielded
[few] clues, however, and in i1241 the minor thrones of Huelt and Édain
[dis]appeared, though the hall guards swore they saw nothing, even
[un]der torture before they were executed.

[TH]E WARS BEGIN

[ ] The next year, the throne of Auria in the city of Loria disappeared;
[but] this time, the guards caught someone in the castle who wasn't
[sup]posed to be there: an Umati merchant. The merchant forswore any
[kno]wledge of the disappearance of the throne, but died in the custody
[of t]he guards before the Divine King's priests could question him.
[On]ce **Theodric** of Auria and King **Cawal** of Umat exchanged heated
[bar]bs, and soon Aurian knights were raiding across the Dyer Moors,
[tho]ugh King Cawal swore oaths before the Sun Court's emissaries that
[he] had no part in the taking of the thrones and the High King Fergus
[ord]ered an end to the attacks. Within a year full-fledged war broke out
[bet]ween Umat and the lords of Auria and Dainphalia, both pressing for
[the] return of their thrones, and soon the Dain King **Chidric** had
[mo]ved against the Erid King Dyvryn, laying siege to Westmark. The
[Hig]h King's marshals took the field to stop the minor wars lest they
[spr]ead like contagion, but the fear and mystery that gripped the land
[pro]ved too strong.
[ ] Once started, the wars did not seem to end; nor did the theft of the
[thr]ones. The throne of Erid Dania disappeared from the royal hall of
[We]stmark in i1246, though the Dain King accused Dyvryn of simply
[ta]king it off into the Erid Wold. Umat lost its war with Dainphalia
[and] Auria by i1247, and Lysias was sacked and the Silver Throne carted
[off] to Loria as booty; it disappeared from the throne room in Loria the
[nex]t year, prompting King Cawal to renew hostilities with an army of
[me]rcenary knights from the pirate holds of the Barren Coast. The
[leg]endary throne of Umis in Caven disappeared in i1248 as well, and
[the] chairs of the magisters of the University of Truse disappeared the
[sa]me year, though some weren't sure if it wasn't just a student prank,
[and] scholars from the University of Therapoli started turning up dead
[at a]n alarming rate. The throne of the Watchtower King of Warwark
[disa]ppeared in i1249, though it was not enchanted like the thrones of
[the] Seated and minor Kings, and on it went until a general paranoia
[had] become the standard way of life for the entire Middle Kingdoms,
[and] not a chair was considered safe anywhere.
[T]he region exploded in flame in i1250, when the heavily guarded
[Dr]agon Throne in Therapoli disappeared. The High King Fergus
[ord]ered the city turned upside down; foreigners, vagrants, and
[cri]minals were put to the sword wholesale, but no trace of the Dragon
[Th]rone was found. Soon search parties spread out from the capital,
[and] knightly hosts hunted through city street, sleepy village, and
[wo]oded copse alike, questioning everyone from the highest noble to
[the] lowliest peasant. Witch burnings, already on the rise, began in

earnest; over a thousand were burned in An-Athair alone over the next
decade. Every rumor of the secret worship of Nymarga, Amaymon,
Ligrid, and Ishraha was taken as truth, and hundreds put to death by
emissaries of the Sun Court. Renewed fighting broke out between
Umat and the other Kingdoms, between the Danias and the High
King's host, between minor noblemen and their neighbors, and
between the Middle Kingdoms and the Highlands, as search parties
sought access to the Highlands citadels and the brigand camps of the
mountains. Accusations were leveled against the Empire of Thessid-
Gola, the Queens of Palatia, and even the merchants of the League,
though no evidence of foreign involvement was ever offered.

In i1253 attention shifted to Umis; alone amongst the Seated and
minor Kings of the Middle Kingdoms, he had retained his original
king's throne, because it was carved from the very rock of his hall in
Caven More in what was called the Daradjan style; the throne in
Caven, stolen years before, was not the true seat of his power, as Caven
More was the true King's hold in Umis. The Umisi were well known as
a strange and barbaric people who held themselves aloof and separate
from the rest of the Middle Kingdoms, and the High King formally
accused the Stone King **Golgosyn** of orchestrating the throne thefts,
though he presented no proof, and he led a great host against him. But
this was Fergus' undoing, for though his army sacked Caven, the wild
territory of the Umis Mole proved beyond their control, and each
campaign to take Caven More or the other hill towers proved
disastrous. The High King Fergus was killed besieging Hardagh in
i1266 on his sixth campaign in Umis; his oldest son and heir **Fairal** was
killed attempting Rhodia from the sea only six months later, and his
second son **Fergrain** was slain by Gologsyn himself in hillside ambush.

THE WARS END AND NEW KINGDOMS APPEAR

Fergus' third son, **Forwain**, called the Wise, became High King next
and sealed off the borders of Umis, but made no further attempt on its
interior. Instead he began the painstaking task of bringing the various
wars and general mayhem in the Middle Kingdoms to a halt. Thirty
years, it took him, before the last armed conflicts and purges of the
Wars of the Throne Thief came to an end in exhaustion and futility.

With the blessing of the Sun Court he elevated the Watchtower
King of Angora, who had distinguished himself in service to the High
King, to become Seated King of Angowrie, and elevated the minor
kings of Umat, Umis, Huelt and Dainphalia to be Seated Kings as well.
The Sun Court pardoned King Golgosyn of Umis for his part in the
deaths of three High Kings, as he swore his innocence in the throne
thefts before the Sun Court's emissaries, and so was held to be acting in
defense of his rightful Kingship. A general amnesty was issued for
crimes, war deaths, and murders during the Wars of the Throne Thief
by both the High King and the Sun Court, and a reward posted for the
thrones' return, but the stolen thrones were never recovered.

Several theories have persisted to this day as to the identity of the
Throne Thief. The first and most prevalent continues to be King
Golgosyn of Umis, despite the Sun Court's vindication of his defense;
the relative isolation of the Kings of Umis only emboldens the talk that
the halls of Caven More hold a secret room with a circle of stolen
thrones. The second popular theory blames witch powers in the Erid
Wold, who reportedly buried the stolen thrones in a magical pattern to
increase the enchanted powers of the wood. The third popular theory
blames the Isliklids, who have come to be seen as bogeymen in the eyes
of the Middle Kingdoms, though like theories of the Erid witches this
seems more to result from popular prejudice than any suggestive
evidence. A fourth theory now increasingly popular is that the thrones
were stolen by agents of the High King Fergus himself, seeking to
diminish the powers of his subject Kings, and that the theft of the
Dragon Throne was orchestrated to justify the invasion of Umis and the
destruction of the Stone Throne in Caven More, the last great throne
outside his possession. Proponents of this theory claim that the thrones
are held in the catacombs beneath the High King's Hall in Therapoli.
The reward for the return of the stolen thrones stands to this day.

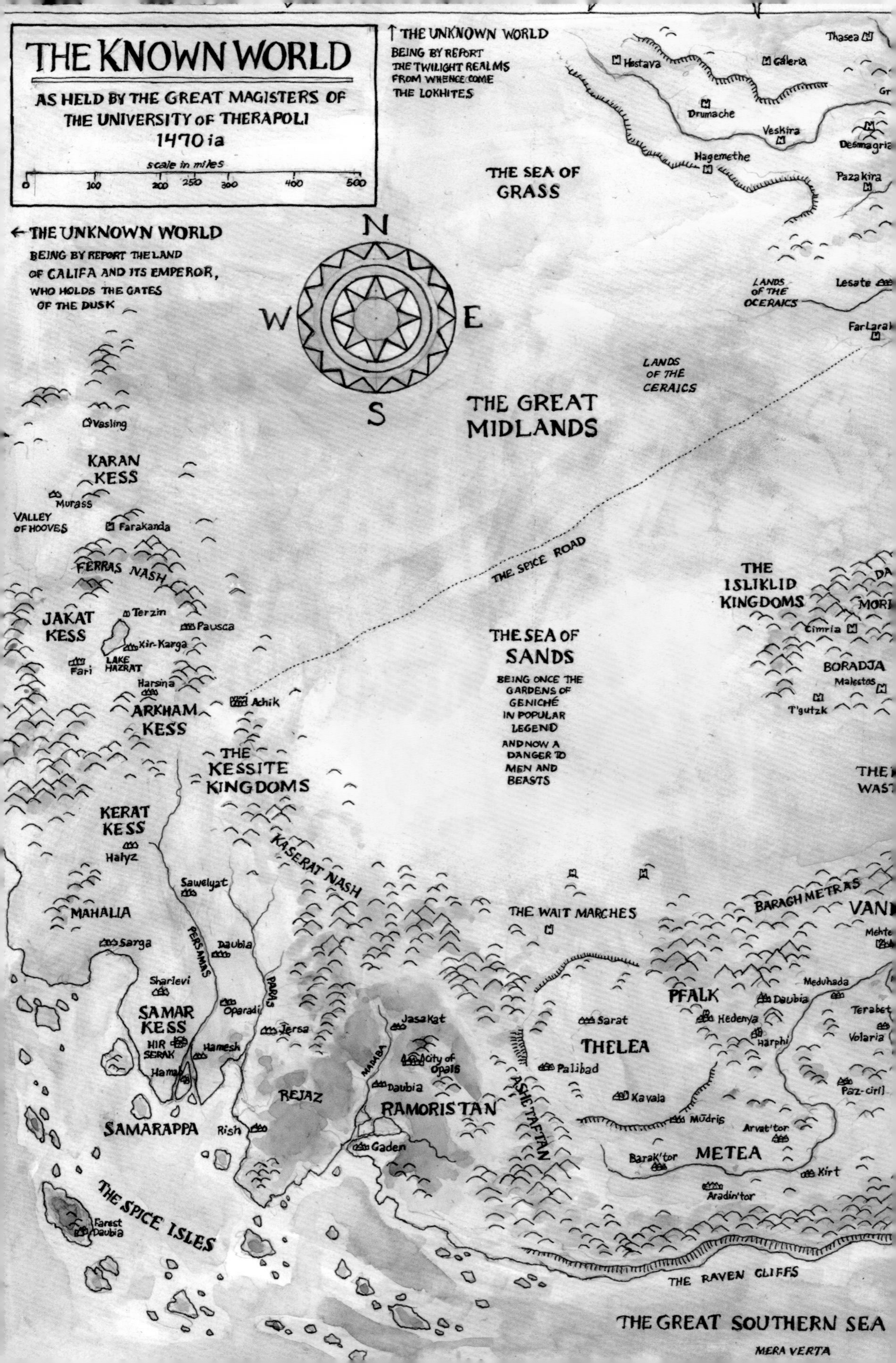

THE KNOWN WORLD
AS HELD BY THE GREAT MAGISTERS OF THE UNIVERSITY OF THERAPOLI
1470 ia
scale in miles
0 100 200 250 300 400 500
↑ THE UNKNOWN WORLD
BEING BY REPORT THE TWILIGHT REALMS FROM WHENCE COME THE LOKHITES
← THE UNKNOWN WORLD
BEING BY REPORT THE LAND OF CALIFA AND ITS EMPEROR, WHO HOLDS THE GATES OF THE DUSK
N
W
E
S
Thasea
Hestava
Galeria
Drumache
Veskira
Hagemethe
Pazakira
THE SEA OF GRASS
LANDS OF THE OCERAICS
Lesate
LANDS OF THE CERAICS
THE GREAT MIDLANDS
Vasling
KARAN KESS
Murass
VALLEY OF HOOVES
Farakanda
FERRAS NASH
THE SPICE ROAD
THE ISLIKLID KINGDOMS
JAKAT KESS
Terzin
Pausca
Kir-Karga
Fari
LAKE HAZRAT
THE SEA OF SANDS
BEING ONCE THE GARDENS OF GENICHÉ IN POPULAR LEGEND
AND NOW A DANGER TO MEN AND BEASTS
Cimria
BORADJA
Malestos
T'gutzk
Harsina
Achik
ARKHAM KESS
THE KESSITE KINGDOMS
KERAT KESS
Halyz
KASERAT NASH
Sawelyat
MAHALIA
THE WAIT MARCHES
BARAGH METRAS
Sarga
PERSAMAS
Daubia
Sharlevi
PARAS
SAMAR KESS
Oparadi
PFALK
Meduhada
Daubia
Terabet
Hedenya
Volaria
Harphi
Jasakat
Jersa
Sarat
HIR SERAK
Hamesh
Hamar
City of Opals
THELEA
Palibad
MADABA
Daubia
ASHE TAFTAN
REJAZ
Paz-ciril
Kavala
RAMORISTAN
SAMARAPPA
Rish
Mudris
Arvat'tor
Gaden
METEA
Barak'tor
Kirt
Aradin'tor
THE SPICE ISLES
Forest Daubia
THE RAVEN CLIFFS
THE GREAT SOUTHERN SEA
MERA VERTA

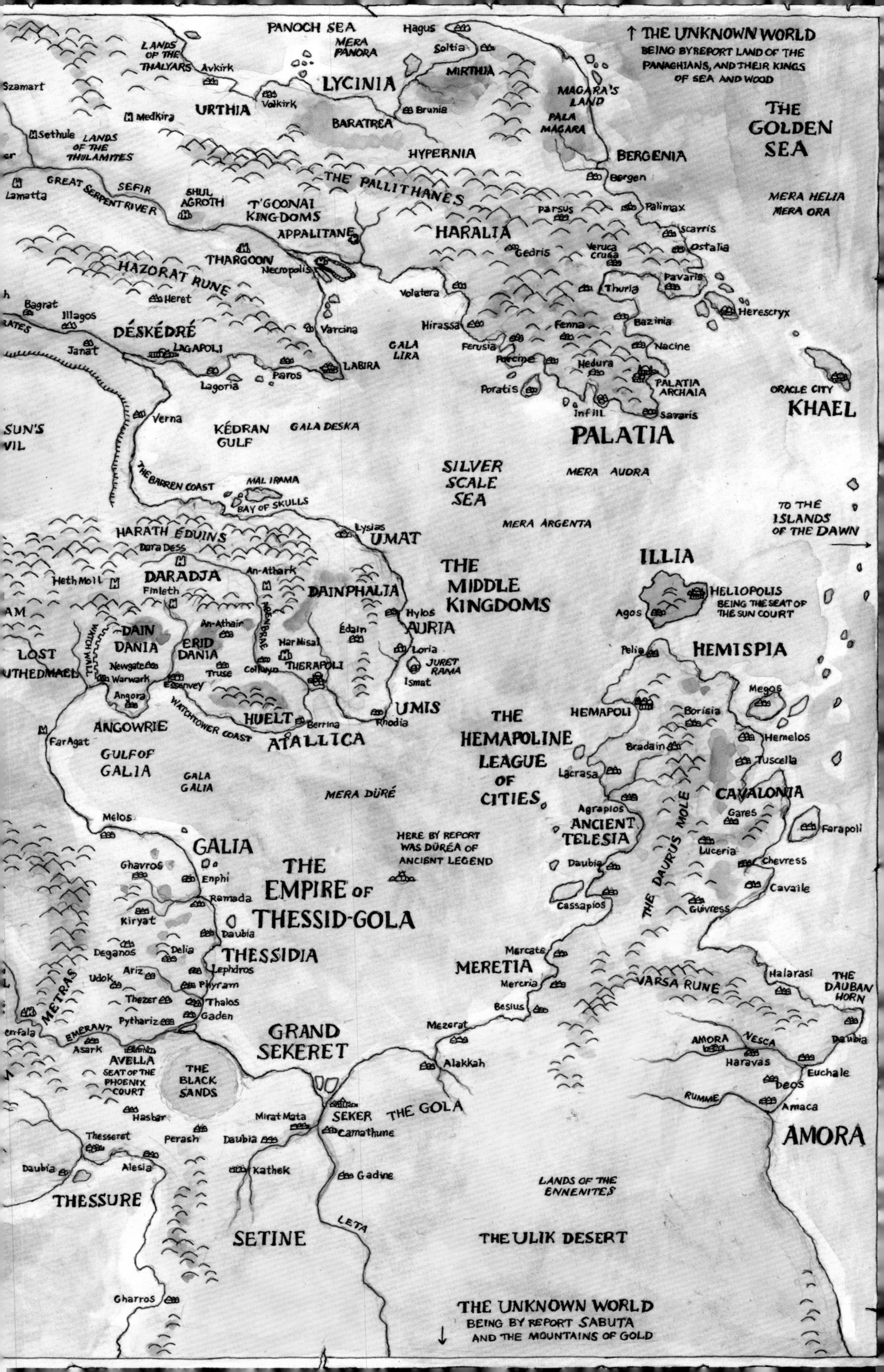
PANOCH SEA
Hagus
MERA PANORA
Soltia
THE UNKNOWN WORLD
BEING BY REPORT LAND OF THE PANACHIANS, AND THEIR KINGS OF SEA AND WOOD
LANDS OF THE THALYARS
Avkirk
Szamart
LYCINIA
MIRTHIA
MAGARA'S LAND
Voikirk
URTHIA
Brunia
THE GOLDEN SEA
Medkira
BARATREA
PALA MAGARA
Sethule
LANDS OF THE THULAMITES
HYPERNIA
BERGENIA
Bergen
THE PALLITHANES
Lamatta
GREAT SERPENT RIVER
SEFIR
SHUL AGROTH
T'GOONAI KINGDOMS
Parsus
Palimax
MERA HELIA
MERA ORA
APPALITANE
HARALIA
Scarris
Ostalia
THARGOON
Gedris
Veruca Crusa
Necropolis
HAZORAT RUNE
Pavaris
Thuria
Volatera
Heret
Bagrat
Herescryx
Illagos
Bazinia
Hirassa
DÉSKÉDRÉ
Varcina
Fenna
Janat
LAGAPOLI
GALA LIRA
Ferusia
Nacine
Porcine
LABIRA
Hedura
Paros
PALATIA ARCHAIA
Lagoria
Poratis
ORACLE CITY
KHAEL
Infill
Savaris
Verna
SUN'S
VIL
KÉDRAN GULF
GALA DESKA
PALATIA
SILVER SCALE SEA
MERA AUDRA
THE BARREN COAST
MAL IRAMA
BAY OF SKULLS
TO THE ISLANDS OF THE DAWN
MERA ARGENTA
Lysias
UMAT
HARATH ÉDUINS
Dara Dess
ILLIA
THE MIDDLE KINGDOMS
An-Athark
Heth Moll
DARADJA
DAINPHALIA
HELIOPOLIS
BEING THE SEAT OF THE SUN COURT
Finleth
Agos
Hylos
AURIA
An-Athair
DAIN DANIA
ERID DANIA
WATCH WALL
Édain
LOST
Har Misal
Loria
JURET RAMA
Pelia
HEMISPIA
UTHEDMAEL
Newgate
THERAPOLI
Warwark
Truse
Collwyn
Ismat
Essenvey
Angora
Megos
UMIS
HUELT
Berrina
Rhodia
THE HEMAPOLINE LEAGUE OF CITIES
HEMAPOLI
Borisia
ANGOWRIE
WATCHTOWER COAST
FarAgat
ATALLICA
Hemelos
Bradain
GULF OF GALIA
Tuscella
GALA GALIA
Lacrasa
MERA DÜRÉ
CAVALONIA
Agrapios
Gares
Melos
ANCIENT TELESIA
Farapoli
HERE BY REPORT WAS DÜREA OF ANCIENT LEGEND
GALIA
Luceria
Ghavros
THE DAURUS MOLE
Chevress
Daubia
THE EMPIRE OF THESSID-GOLA
Enphi
Cavaile
Ramada
Cassapios
Kiryat
Guivress
Daubia
Deganos
Delia
Mercate
THESSIDIA
MERETIA
Lephdros
Ariz
Udok
Halarasi
Mercria
THE DAUBAN HORN
Phyram
VARSA RUNE
Thezer
METRAS
Thalos
Besius
Pythariz
Gaden
Mezerat
GRAND SEKERET
EMERANT
AMORA
NESCA
Daubia
Asark
AVELLA
SEAT OF THE PHOENIX COURT
Haravas
Alakkah
Euchale
THE BLACK SANDS
Deos
RUMME
Amaca
Hasbar
Mirat Mata
SEKER
THE GOLA
Thesseret
Perash
Daubia
Camathune
AMORA
Daubia
Alesia
Kathek
Gadine
LANDS OF THE ENNENITES
THESSURE
LETA
SETINE
THE ULIK DESERT
Gharros
THE UNKNOWN WORLD
BEING BY REPORT SABUTA AND THE MOUNTAINS OF GOLD

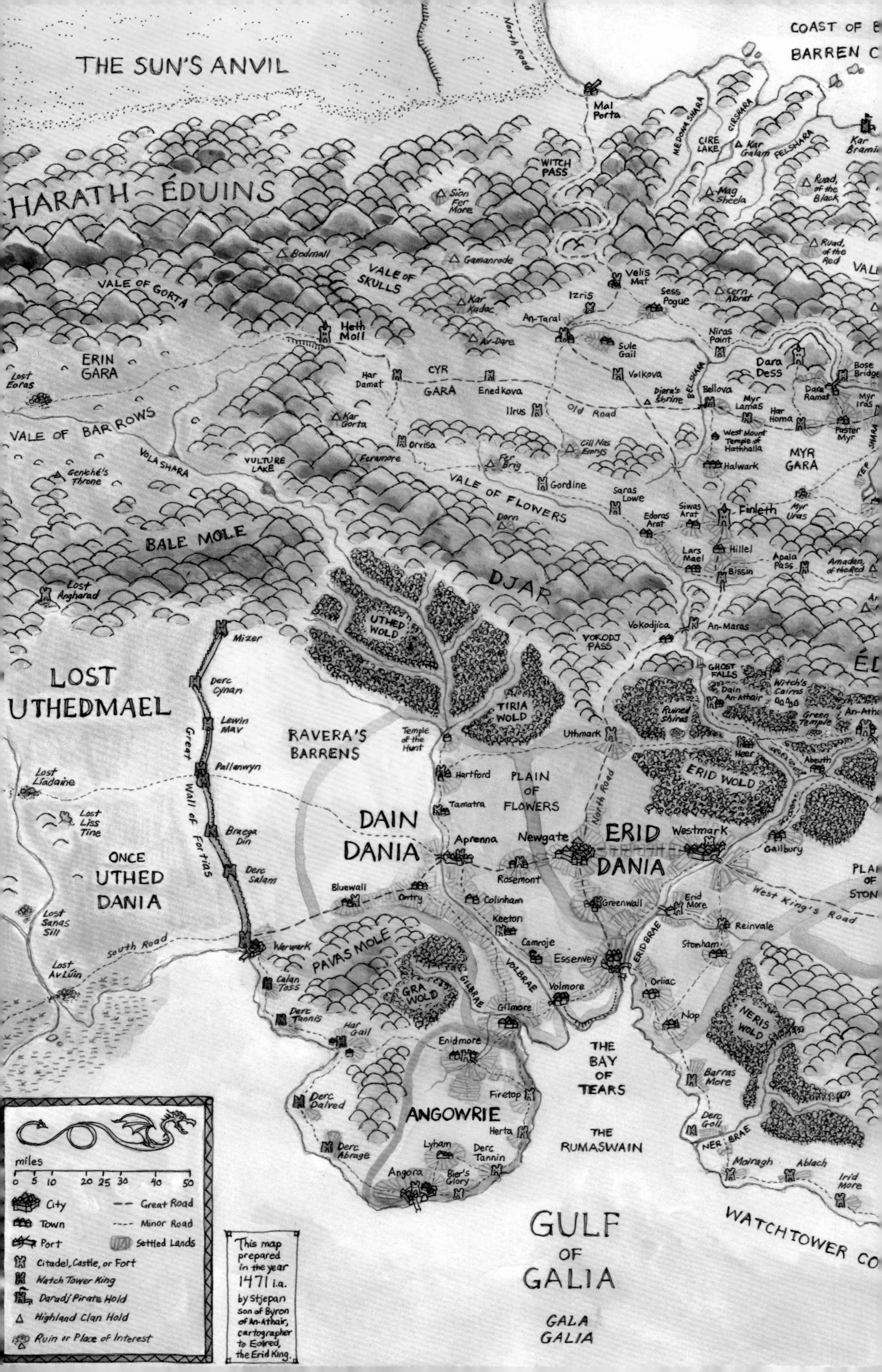
THE SUN'S ANVIL
North Road
COAST OF B
BARREN C
Mal Porta
HARATH-ÉDUINS
WITCH PASS
Sion Fer More
MEDONASHARA
CIRE LAKE
CIRSHARA
Kar Galam
FELSHARA
Kar Bramin
Mag Sheela
Ruad, of the Black
Ruad, of the Red
Bodmall
Gamanrode
VALE OF SKULLS
VALE OF GORTA
Velis Mat
Izris
Sess Pogue
Cern Abrat
Kar Kadac
An-Taral
Heth Moll
Ar-Dare
Sule Gail
Niras Point
ERIN GARA
Lost Eoras
Har Damat
CYR GARA
Enedkova
Volkova
Dara Dess
Bose Bridge
Djara's Shrine
BELSHARA
Bellova
Dara Ramat
Myr Iras
Ilrus
Old Road
Myr Lamas
Har Homa
VALE OF BARROWS
Kar Gorta
Paster Myr
West Mount Temple of Hathhalla
Orvisa
Cill Nas Emrys
VOLASHARA
VULTURE LAKE
Feramore
Fer Brig
MYR GARA
Halwark
Genkhé's Throne
VALE OF FLOWERS
Gordine
Saras Lowe
Edoras Arat
Siwas Arat
Finleth
Myr Uras
Dorn
BALE MOLE
Lars Mael
Hillel
Apala Pass
Amadan, of the Red
Bissin
DJAR
Lost Angharad
UTHED WOLD
Mizer
VOKODJ PASS
Vokodjica
An-Maras
LOST UTHEDMAEL
Derc Cynan
GHOST FALLS
Dain An-Athair
Witch's Cairns
Lewin MAV
TIRIA WOLD
Ruined Shiras
Green Temple
An-Atha
Great Wall of Fortias
RAVERA'S BARRENS
Temple of the Hunt
Uthmark
Heer
Abeuth
Lost Liadaine
Pallenwyn
Hartford
PLAIN OF FLOWERS
ERID WOLD
Lost Liss Tine
Tamatra
North Road
DAIN DANIA
Newgate
ERID DANIA
Westmark
Braega Din
Aprenna
Gallbury
ONCE UTHED DANIA
Derc Salam
Rosemont
PLAI OF STON
Bluewall
Ontry
Colinham
West King's Road
Greenwall
Lost Sanas Sill
Keeton
Erid More
Reinvale
Camroje
Stonham
South Road
Warwark
Essenvey
PAVAS MOLE
ERID BRAE
Lost Av Lúin
Calan Toss
GRA WOLD
GILBRAE
VOLBRAE
Volmore
Orliac
Derc Tannis
Gilmore
Nop
NERIS WOLD
Har Gail
Enidmore
THE BAY OF TEARS
Barras More
Firetop
Derc Dalred
ANGOWRIE
Derc Goll
Herta
THE RUMASWAIN
Derc Abrage
Lyham
Derc Tannin
NER BRAE
Mairagh
Ablach
Irid More
Angora
Bier's Glory
miles
0 5 10 20 25 30 40 50
City
Town
Port
Citadel, Castle, or Fort
Watch Tower King
Daradj Pirate Hold
Highland Clan Hold
Ruin or Place of Interest
Great Road
Minor Road
Settled Lands
This map prepared in the year 1471 i.a. by Stjepan son of Byron of An-Athair, cartographer to Eoired, the Erid King.
GULF OF GALIA
WATCHTOWER CO
GALA GALIA

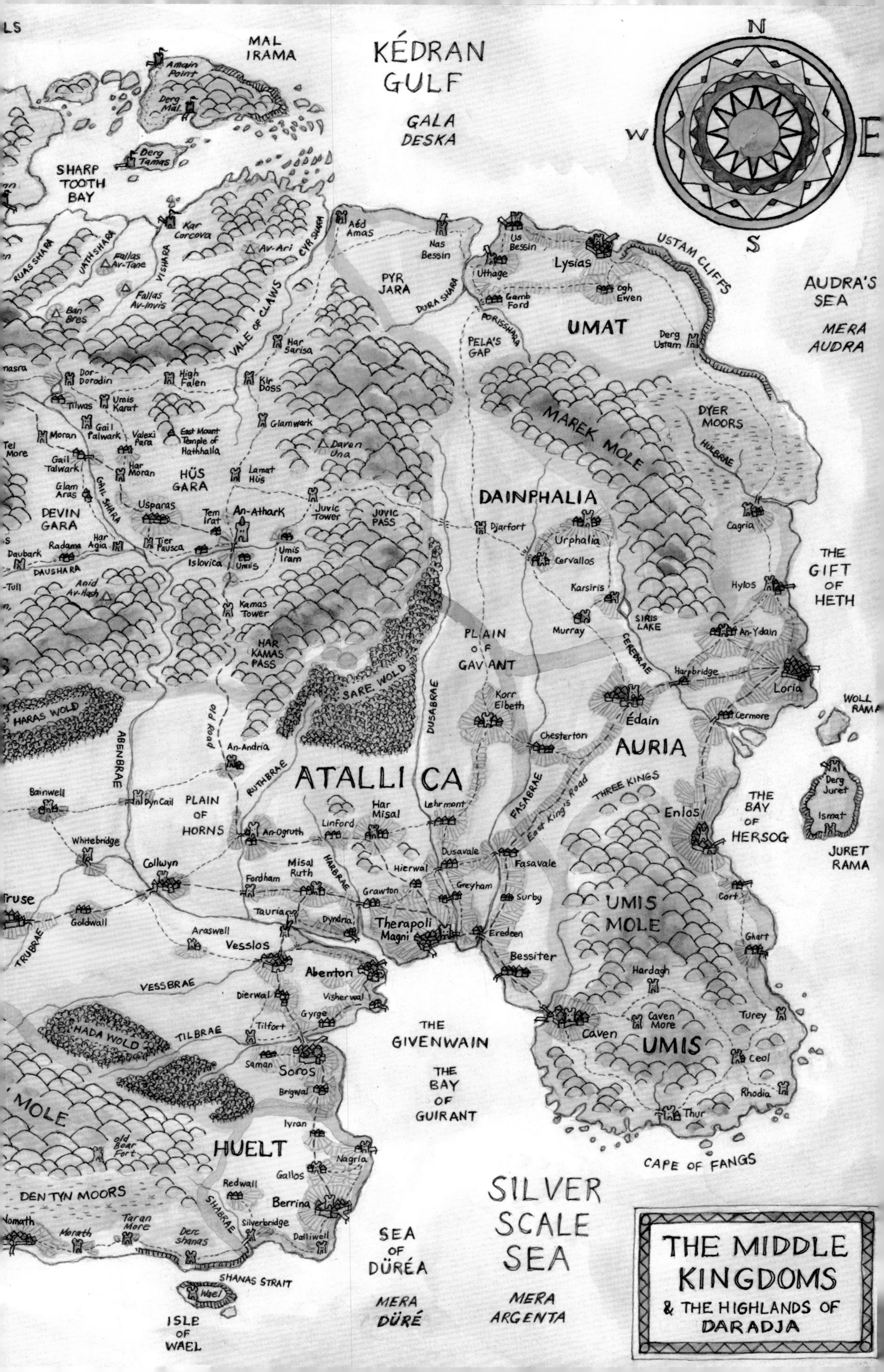
THE MIDDLE KINGDOMS
& THE HIGHLANDS OF DARADJA
KÉDRAN GULF
GALA DESKA
MAL IRAMA
Amain Point
Derg Mal
Derg Tamas
SHARP TOOTH BAY
Kar Corcova
Av-Ari
Fallas Av-Tane
Fallas Av-Invis
Ban Bres
RUASSHARA
UATHSHARA
VISHARA
CYRSHARA
VALE OF CLAWS
Aéd Amas
Nas Bessin
PYR JARA
DURA SHARA
Us Bessin
Uthage
Lysias
Gamb Ford
ogh Ewen
USTAM CLIFFS
AUDRA'S SEA
MERA AUDRA
UMAT
Derg Ustam
PORISSHARA
PELA'S GAP
Har Sarisa
Dor-Dorodin
High Falen
Kir Doss
Tilwas
Umis Karat
Glamwark
Moran
Gail Falwark
Valexi Para
East Mount Temple of Hathhalla
Daren Una
MAREK MOLE
DYER MOORS
HULBRAE
Tel More
Gail Talwark
Har Moran
HÜS GARA
Lamat Hüs
Glam Aras
GAIL SHARA
DEVIN GARA
Usparas
Tem Irat
An-Athark
Juvic Tower
JUVIC PASS
DAINPHALIA
Djarfort
Urphalia
Cervallos
Cagria
Radama
Har Agia
Tier Pausca
Islovica
Umis
Umis Iram
Daubark
DAUSHARA
Anid Av-Hash
Kamas Tower
Karsiris
THE GIFT OF HETH
Hylos
SIRIS LAKE
Murray
An-Ydain
HAR KAMAS PASS
PLAIN OF GAVANT
CEREBRAE
Harpbridge
Loria
SARE WOLD
DUSABRAE
Korr Elbeth
Édain
Cermore
WOLL RAMA
HARAS WOLD
Old Road
ABENBRAE
An-Andria
Chesterton
AURIA
ATALLICA
RUTHBRAE
FASABRAE
East King's Road
THREE KINGS
Derg Juret
Ismat
Bainwell
Dyn Cail
PLAIN OF HORNS
Har Misal
Lehrmont
Linford
An-Ogruth
Enlos
THE BAY OF HERSOG
JURET RAMA
Whitebridge
Misal Ruth
HARBRAE
Hierwal
Dusavale
Fasavale
Collwyn
Fordham
Grawton
Greyham
Surby
Cort
Goldwall
Tauria
Dyndria
Therapoli Magni
Eredeen
UMIS MOLE
TRUBRAE
Araswell
Vesslos
Bessiter
Ghart
Abenton
VESSBRAE
Dierwal
Visherwal
Hardagh
Gyrge
Tilfort
Caven
Caven More
Turey
HADA WOLD
TILBRAE
THE GIVENWAIN
UMIS
Saman
Soros
Ceol
Brigwal
THE BAY OF GUIRANT
Rhodia
MOLE
Thur
Iyran
old Boar Fort
HUELT
Nagria
CAPE OF FANGS
Gallos
Redwall
DEN TYN MOORS
Berrina
SILVER SCALE SEA
SHABRAE
Silverbridge
Taran More
Morath
Derc Shanas
Dalliwell
SEA OF DÜRÉA
Wael
SHANAS STRAIT
ISLE OF WAEL
MERA DÜRÉ
MERA ARGENTA

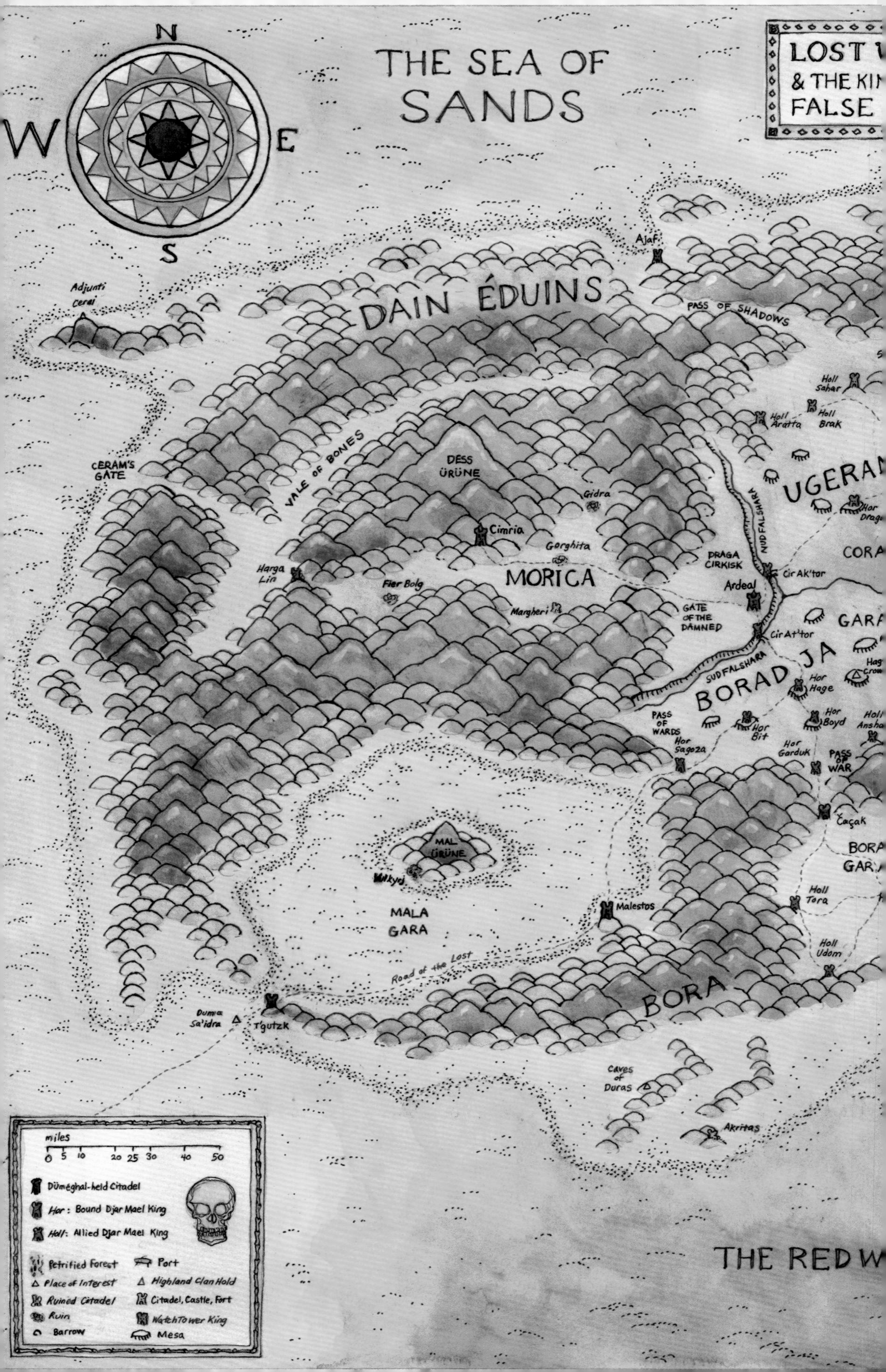

N
W
E
S
THE SEA OF SANDS
LOST
& THE KI
FALSE
Ajaf
Adjunti Cerai
DAIN ÉDUINS
PASS OF SHADOWS
Holl Sahar
Holl Aratta
Holl Brak
CERAM'S GATE
VALE OF BONES
DESS ÜRÜNE
Gidra
NUDFALSHARA
UGERA
Hor Drag
Cimria
Gorghita
DRAGA CIRKISK
CORA
Harga Lin
MORICA
Cir Ak'tor
Fier Bolg
Ardeal
Margheri
GATE OF THE DAMNED
Cir At'tor
GAR
SUDFALSHARA
BORADJA
Hag Crow
Hor Hage
PASS OF WARDS
Hor Sagoza
Hor Bit
Hor Boyd
Holl Ansha
Hor Garduk
PASS OF WAR
Çaçak
MAL ÜRÜNE
BORA
GAR
Milkyej
Holl Tora
MALA GARA
Malestos
Holl Udom
Road of the Lost
BORA
Duma Sa'idra
Tgutzk
Caves of Duras
Akritas
miles
0 5 10 20 25 30 40 50
Dümeghal-held Citadel
Hor: Bound Djar Mael King
Holl: Allied Djar Mael King
Petrified Forest
Port
Place of Interest
Highland Clan Hold
Ruined Citadel
Citadel, Castle, Fort
Ruin
WatchTower King
Barrow
Mesa
THE RED W

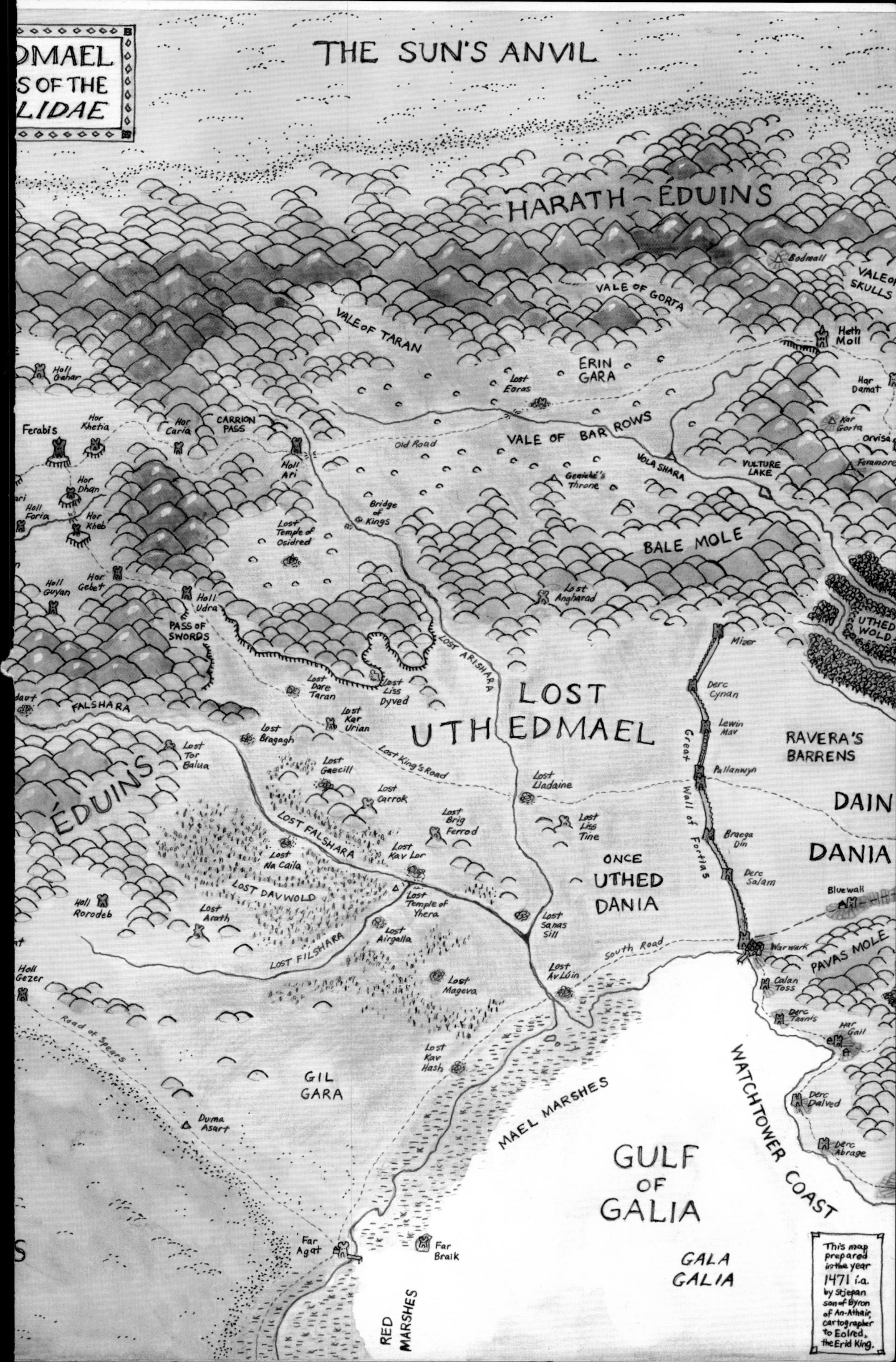

DMAEL
S OF THE
LIDAE
THE SUN'S ANVIL
HARATH-EDUINS
Bodmall
VALE OF
SKULLS
VALE OF GORTA
VALE OF TARAN
Heth Moll
Holl Gahar
ERIN GARA
Lost Eoras
Har Damat
Ferabis
Hor Khetia
Hor Caria
CARRION PASS
Holl Ari
Old Road
VALE OF BARROWS
Kar Gorta
Orvisa
Hor Dhan
Holl Foria
Hor Kheb
Geniché's Throne
VOLA SHARA
VULTURE LAKE
Feramore
Bridge of Kings
Lost Temple of Osidred
BALE MOLE
Holl Guyan
Hor Gebet
Holl Udra
PASS OF SWORDS
Lost Angharad
Mizer
UTHED WOLD
LOST ARISHARA
Lost Dare Taran
Lost Liss Dyved
FALSHARA
LOST UTHEDMAEL
Derc Cynan
Lost Kar Urian
Lost Bragagh
Lewin Mav
RAVERA'S BARRENS
Lost Tor Balua
Lost King's Road
Lost Gaecill
Great Wall of Fortias
Pallanwyn
ÉDUINS
Lost Lladaine
DAIN
Lost Carrok
Lost Brig Ferrod
Lost Liss Tine
LOST FALSHARA
Braega Din
DANIA
Lost Na Caila
Lost Kav Lor
ONCE UTHED DANIA
Derc Salam
LOST DAVWOLD
Bluewall
Holl Rorodeb
Lost Arath
Lost Temple of Yhera
Lost Sanas Sill
Lost Airgalla
Warwark
PAVAS MOLE
LOST FILSHARA
South Road
Holl Gezer
Lost Mageva
Lost Av Lóin
Calan Toss
Derc Tannis
Har Gail
Road of Spears
Lost Kav Hash
GIL GARA
WATCHTOWER COAST
MAEL MARSHES
Derc Dalved
Duma Asart
Derc Abrage
GULF OF GALIA
Far Agat
Far Braik
GALA GALIA
RED MARSHES
This map prepared in the year 1471 i.a. by Stjepan son of Byron of An-Athair, cartographer to Eolred, the Erid King.

ACKNOWLEDGMENTS

I wish to express my thanks to the folks at Sirius Enterainment who first gave *Artesia* a home:
Robb Horan (and Brenda and now Isabel), Larry Salamone, my former editor Mark Bellis,
and the ever-resourceful Keith Davidsen.
My thanks as well to Mark McNabb of McNabb Studios
for his invaluable prepress and design work on the first two *Artesia* series;
to Lisa Webster (and Tim) and Wendy Wellington for their help on www.ArtesiaOnline.com;
to Michael, Bob, and Paul (and family) at PrintSolutions in Englewood;
to Cindy, Jessica, Kristin, and everyone at Brenner Printing;
to Filip Sablik, Mark Herr, Patricia Moore, Andrew Smith, and the other fine folks at Diamond Comics;
to Wayne Markley and everyone at FM International;
to Mark Thompson, Matthew High, and everyone at Cold Cut Comics;
and to Brian Petkash and Liz Fulda at Sphinx Group.
Thanks also to Dawn Murin and Robert Raper at Wizards of the Coast;
Jim Pinto at Alderac Entertainment Group (AEG);
and Becky Jollensten, Rich Thomas, and Mike Chaney at
White Wolf Publishing and its Swords & Sorcery studios.

For their occasional encouragement, comments,
criticisms, conversation, and continual example, my thanks to
John Kovalic, Joe Linsner, Eva Hopkins, Voltaire, Jill Thompson, Brian Azzarello,
Mark Crilley, Jason Alexander, Mike Norton, Sherard Jackson, Michael Kaluta,
Kevin Tinsley, Tony Caputo, Dave Napoliello, Thomas Harlan, Arvid Nelson,
Alec Peters, Chris Gossett, Alex Smits, Joe Koch, Dave Elliot,
Kensuke Obayashi, Chris Moeller, and Ray Lago. amongst others.

As always, my thanks to my brother John, Lillian, Hide, Michael & Naomi (and Noah and Eli),
John & Heather (and Colombine), Aki & Tammy (and Gordo), Patti, Liz, Alice,
Ray & Lucy (and Winston), Vera, Al & Kaoru, David N., David C.,
Marc & Lisa (and Scott and Patrick), Mikey & Meg, Dennis & Kelly, my father,
and Joe Scott, who got the ball rolling on this world, and Chris and Aimee (and Spencer and now Chloe),
whom I *still* hold, much to their continued seeming bemusement,
as my Ideal Readers.

A Select Bibliography of books that have influenced the writing of *Artesia Afire* and the content of the Known World:

-- Roberto Calasso, *The Marriage of Cadmus and Harmony*, Alfred A. Knopf, 1993.
-- Yves Bonnofoy (compiler) and Wendy Doniger (translator), *Mythologies,* University of Chicago Press, 1991.
-- Marcel Detienne and Jean-Pierre Vernant (translated by Paula Wissing), *The Cuisine of Sacrifice Among
   the Greeks,* University of Chicago Press, 1989.
-- Christopher A. Faraone, *Talismans & Trojan Horses: Guardian Statues in Ancient Greek Myth and Ritual,*
   Oxford University Press, 1992.
-- Christopher A. Faraone and Dirk Obbink, editors, *Magika Hiera: Ancient Greek Magic & Religion,* Oxford
   Universtiy Press, 1991.
-- Jennifer Larson, *Greek Heroine Cults,* University of Wisconsin Press, 1995.
-- Neil Forsyth, *The Old Enemy: Satan & The Combat Myth,* Princeton University Press, 1987.
-- Carlo Ginzburg, *Ecstasies: Deciphering the Witches' Sabbath,* Pantheon Books, 1991.
-- Barbara Ehrenreich, *Blood Rites: Origins and History of the Passions of War,* Metropolitan Books 1997.
-- Bruce Lincoln, *Death, War, and Sacrifice: Studies in Ideology and Practice,* University of Chicago Press, 1991.
-- Antonia Fraser, *Boadicea's Chariot: The Warrior Queens,* Weidenfeld and Nicholson, 1988.
-- John Keegan, *The Face of Battle,* Viking Press, 1976.
-- Victor Davis Hanson, *The Western Way of War: Infantry Battle in Classical Greece,* Hodder & Stoughton, 1989.
-- Donald W. Engels, *Alexander the Great and the Logistics of the Macedonian Army,* University of California
   Press, 1978.
-- Malcolm Vale, *War and Chivalry: Warfare and Aristocracy in England, France, and Burgundy at the End of
   the Middle Ages,* University of Georgia Press, 1981.
-- J. R. Hale, *War and Society in Renaissance Europe, 1450-1620,* Johns Hopkins University Press, 1985.
-- Sydney Anglo, *The Martial Arts of Renaissance Europe,* Yale University Press, 2000.
-- Mary Gentle, *The Book of Ash* (four volumes), Avon, 1999.
-- George R.R. Martin, *A Song of Ice and Fire* (three volumes so far), Bantam Spectra, 1996 - present.
-- Jacqueline Carey, *Kushiel's Legacy: Kushiel's Dart, Kushiel's Chosen, Kushiel's Avatar,* TOR, 2001-2003.